Writings of Leon Trotsky
Supplement 1934-40

Writings of Leon Trotsky is a collection, in twelve volumes, plus a two-part supplement, of pamphlets, articles, letters, and interviews written during Trotsky's third and final exile (1929–40). They include many articles translated into English for the first time. They do not include the books and pamphlets from this period that are permanently in print, nor most of the unpublished material in the Trotsky Archives at Harvard University Library.

WRITINGS OF LEON TROTSKY

SUPPLEMENT (1934-40)

PATHFINDER
New York London Montreal Sydney

Edited by George Breitman

Copyright © 1979 by Pathfinder Press
All rights reserved

ISBN 978-0-87348-565-4
Library of Congress Catalog Card Number 73-80226
Manufactured in the United States of America

First edition, 1979
Tenth printing, 2025

Pathfinder
pathfinderpress.com
Email: pathfinder@pathfinderpress.com

Contents

France (1934–35)

An offer to 'Le Peuple' *(January 9, 1934)*	15
The IS reply to the British majority *(January 23, 1934)*	16
Differences with the British minority *(January 23, 1934)*	19
The Jewish question has been internationalized *(January 28, 1934)*	21
Questions about Holland *(January 29, 1934)*	23
On the workers' militia *(February 1934)*	24
Things are on the move *(February 12, 1934)*	26
Against centrism at the youth conference *(February 15, 1934)*	27
Rakovsky's statement of submission *(February 21, 1934)*	36
Ultraleft tactics in fighting the fascists *(March 2, 1934)*	38
After the Austrian defeat *(March 13, 1934)*	41
Reproaching the Dutch section *(March 17, 1934)*	44
Field's expulsion *(March 18, 1934)*	46
A concert for Herriot *(March 1934)*	47
The youth conference's unsatisfactory resolution *(March 19, 1934)*	48
The proposal to fuse the CLA and the AWP *(March 20, 1934)*	52
The errors of our youth delegates *(March 29, 1934)*	54
Continuing the struggle through unifications *(April 10, 1934)*	58
My interrogation by the police *(Mid-April 1934)*	60
Why I am being expelled from France *(April 18, 1934)*	63
Suggestions for a French program of action *(Spring 1934)*	66

Proposals for the next ICL plenum *(June 15, 1934)*	72
Our response to the French CP's new turn *(June 16, 1934)*	74
Concentrate inside the Socialist Party *(June 1934)*	76
The state of the League and its tasks *(June 29, 1934)*	78
The Catalan conflict and the tasks of the proletariat *(Summer 1934)*	88
Alternatives for the Young Socialists *(July 12, 1934)*	92
Cross the Rubicon *(July 16, 1934)*	96
The Stalinists and organic unity *(July 19, 1934)*	98
Supplementary arguments and suggestions for articles *(July 21, 1934)*	101
Tasks of the ICL *(July 21, 1934)*	103
Clouds in the Far East *(Published August 1934)*	110
Soviets in America? *(August 17, 1934)*	115
The 'Belgian' tradition in discussion *(September 22, 1934)*	129
The present situation in the labor movement and the tasks of the Bolshevik-Leninists *(October 1934)*	133
Cannon's mission in Europe *(November 3, 1934)*	140
How to answer the London-Amsterdam Bureau *(November 1934)*	141
No compromise on the Russian question *(November 11, 1934)*	143
We should join the Belgian Young Socialists *(November 19, 1934)*	144
Suggestions for the GBL *(November 20, 1934)*	146
Remarks on the Kirov assassination *(December 10, 1934)*	149
On the draft political statutes *(December 1934)*	154
A few remarks on 'Revolution' *(December 1934)*	157
Once more on our turn *(December 15, 1934)*	160
Notes on the GBL's internal problems *(Late 1934 or early 1935)*	167
Remarks on our general orientation *(Late 1934 or early 1935)*	170
The state and the USSR *(Late 1934 or early 1935)*	172

Against desistance for the Radicals *(Late 1934 or early 1935)*	174
Answers to questions by Louise Bryant *(Late 1934 or early 1935)*	175
A proposal to co-opt Dubois into the plenum *(January 31, 1935)*	178
Disturbing signs *(January 31, 1935)*	180
After the Belgian conference *(March 24, 1935)*	182
On the Teachers' Federation *(March 24, 1935)*	184
Notes on the SAP and the London-Amsterdam Bureau *(Mid-April 1935)*	185
News about the family *(April 25, 1935)*	192
Laval and the French CP *(May 1935)*	193
Toward the new youth international *(Spring 1935)*	195
Why are we Bolshevik-Leninists? *(Spring 1935)*	197
Three telegrams to Norway *(June 7–12, 1935)*	201
Underground work in Nazi Germany *(June 1935)*	202

Norway (1935–36)

Please pay attention to the youth question *(June 21, 1935)*	219
Chen Tu-hsiu and the General Council *(August 10, 1935)*	221
For a bloc against Oehler *(August 13, 1935)*	225
The Cannon-Shachtman group should make concessions *(September 4, 1935)*	227
The policy of the Abern-Weber group *(September 4, 1935)*	231
Nothing in common with the decadent Comintern *(September 18, 1935)*	234
An appeal to A.J. Muste *(September 24–25, 1935)*	236
The open letter and the ILP *(Autumn 1935)*	245
Foreword, Mitt Liv *(October 1, 1935)*	246
For or against? *(October 16, 1935)*	251
Youth secretary nominations *(October 21, 1935)*	252
Support of the Dutch fight against SAPism *(November 5, 1935)*	253

Conversations with Earle Birney *(November 1935)*	254
Greetings to 'Robitnichi Vysti' *(November 26, 1935)*	262
Letters about Anton Ciliga *(December 1935–January 1936)*	263
The Lenin-Trotsky papers *(December 28, 1935)*	271
Results of the Open Letter *(January 18, 1936)*	273
Schmidt's trip to England *(January 19, 1936)*	275
Educating against centrism *(January 24, 1936)*	277
The heyday of the People's Front *(January 24, 1936)*	278
Two statements on Hearst *(January 28, 1936)*	280
A conversation with Maurice Spector *(February 1936)*	281
How to avert a split *(February 8, 1936)*	291
Remarks for an English comrade *(April 8, 1936)*	294
The center must stay in Europe *(April 8, 1936)*	295
Orient to the Spanish youth *(April 14, 1936)*	297
Eleven letters to Victor Serge *(April–August 1936)*	299
Our kind of optimism *(April 27, 1936)*	334
Walter Held's thesis on the evolution of the Comintern *(May 26 and June 18, 1936)*	336
Let's end this nonsense *(May 28, 1936)*	338
'State capitalism' data sought *(June 7, 1936)*	339
The international conference and the Dutch section *(June 16, 1936)*	340
Congratulations on a good publishing job *(June 18, 1936)*	343
The London Bureau and the Fourth International *(July 1936)*	344
Deep differences with the Dutch comrades *(July 7, 1936)*	350
How the conference was and wasn't prepared *(July 17, 1936)*	352
Molinier's expulsion *(July 1936)*	360
When the conference selects the leadership *(July 24, 1936)*	363
Advice for the conference *(July 25, 1936)*	365
GPU and Gestapo *(August 27, 1936)*	366
A possible hunger strike *(End of August 1936)*	369

Our friends should not wait *(End of August 1936)*	370
Translator troubles, publisher problems *(September 10, 1936)*	371
Still imprisoned *(October 4, 1936)*	374
Still gagged *(October 12, 1936)*	375
The trip to Copenhagen *(October 12, 1936)*	376
Reading Ibsen again *(October 1936)*	384
Pyatakov and the trial in Novosibirsk *(November 26, 1936)*	386
Posthumus and the archives *(December 2, 1936)*	389

Mexico (1937–40)

Answers to a Mexican press service *(January 23, 1937)*	393
Two crooked lawyers *(February 1, 1937)*	395
Postponing the Swiss trial *(February 19, 1937)*	396
Answers to the 'Chicago Daily News' *(March 3, 1937)*	398
A correction and requests *(March 26, 1937)*	400
Stalin's latest threat *(March 29, 1937)*	401
Opinions and information *(May 12, 1937)*	403
Obstacles in Britain *(May 21, 1937)*	405
No reason to complain *(August 10, 1937)*	406
Literary theft *(August 21, 1937)*	407
A pamphlet on Spain *(September 17, 1937)*	408
The international conference must be postponed *(September 25, 1937)*	410
The U.S. recession and a new political orientation *(October 2, 1937)*	412
An article on Kronstadt *(November 14, 1937)*	416
Suggestions for a pamphlet on Kronstadt *(November 19, 1937)*	417
An article on the Soviet state *(November 30, 1937)*	419
Sale of the archives *(December 21, 1937)*	420
Kronstadt and the commission's function *(January 17, 1938)*	422
Thomas's letter and Dewey's speech *(January 26, 1938)*	423
Eastman and 'The Young Lenin' *(February 3, 1938)*	425

Explanation of a complaint *(February 5, 1938)*	426
Why I can't pay now *(February 7, 1938)*	428
Jules Romains on Lenin *(February 7, 1938)*	429
Marx's living thoughts *(February 10, 1938)*	430
Leon Sedov's papers *(February 28, 1938)*	432
Questions about Sedov's death *(March 1, 1938)*	433
Krestinsky's repudiation *(March 2, 1938)*	435
The third Moscow trial *(March 4, 1938)*	437
Answers to Mrs. Celarie *(March 6, 1938)*	439
Roosevelt and a visa *(March 30, 1938)*	442
Carlo Tresca is a target *(March 31, 1938)*	443
Finishing the transitional program *(April 5, 1938)*	444
A Russian encyclopedia *(April 26, 1938)*	445
Political personality and the milieu *(May 10, 1938)*	446
Muenzenberg's expulsion *(June 5, 1938)*	449
Molinier and the international conference *(June 9, 1938)*	450
An introduction worthy of Rosa Luxemburg *(June 14, 1938)*	452
Fusion with the Lovestoneites? *(July 29, 1938)*	453
Answers to Gladys Lloyd Robinson *(August 18, 1938)*	457
Isaacs's book about China *(October 23, 1938)*	460
Latin American problems: A transcript *(November 4, 1938)*	461
Lombardo Toledano's lies *(November 8, 1938)*	477
Can the 'Daily News' be sued? *(November 11, 1938)*	479
A conversation with William R. Mathews *(Published December 13, 1938)*	482
Investigate the U.S. fascists *(December 12, 1938)*	492
The French question *(December 13, 1938)*	493
Letters about Sieva Volkov *(September 1938–April 1939)*	494
No doubts about Rudolf Klement's fate *(November 1938–August 1939)*	504
A GPU stool pigeon in Paris *(January 1, 1939)*	506
The Hearst press changes its mind *(January 6, 1939)*	508
The plight of our refugee comrades *(January 9, 1939)*	509

What the youth do to our principles *(January 9, 1939)*   510
Letters to the POI Central Committee
  (February–July 1939)   512
A trap in Palestine *(February 14, 1939)*   518
Money-raising appeals *(February 20, 1939)*   519
Utilize the opportunities in the Communist Party
  (March 8, 1939)   520
James's trip to Mexico *(March 29, 1939)*   522
Diego Rivera's defection *(March–April 1939)*   524
Where Munis should go *(May 1, 1939)*   527
Pan-American Committee personnel *(May 1, 1939)*   528
Victor Serge's crisis *(May 6, 1939)*   529
Another anonymous letter *(May 10, 1939)*   530
Problems of the 'Socialist Appeal' *(May 27, 1939)*   532
A visa for Elsa Reiss *(June 5, 1939)*   534
A party census *(June 23, 1939)*   535
For the Ukrainian pamphlet *(September 1939)*   536
A disagreeable incident *(September 7, 1939)*   537
The first article in the Russian discussion
  (September 28, 1939)   538
Accepting the invitation of the Dies Committee
  (October 12, 1939)   539
Outline of a magazine article *(November 15, 1939)*   541
A false report *(December 26, 1939)*   543
Dialectics and the answer to Burnham
  (January 9, 1940)   544
Farrell Dobbs's arrival *(January 16, 1940)*   545
A discussion with Carleton Smith
  (Published February 2, 1940)   546
Factionalism and the IEC *(February–April 1940)*   547
Rivera's wild denunciation *(April 6, 1940)*   553
A serious work on Russian revolutionary history
  (May 2, 1940)   555
To Colonel Sanchez Salazar *(May 31, 1940)*   558
A letter to 'El Nacional' *(June 6, 1940)*   561
The GPU and the Comintern *(July 17, 1940)*   562
A bed and a plate waiting *(July 17, 1940)*   563

Unfinished writings and fragments
- Petty-bourgeois democrats and moralizers *(1938 and 1939)* ... 565
- Fragments from the first seven months of the war *(1940)* ... 574
- Fragments on the USSR *(1940)* ... 583
- Preface to a book on war and peace *(March–April 1940)* ... 590
- Last words *(August 20, 1940)* ... 597

Notes and acknowledgments ... 599
Works of Leon Trotsky published by Pathfinder ... 696
Index (1929–40) ... 697

France (1934–35)

An offer to 'Le Peuple'[1]

January 9, 1934

To the editors of *Le Peuple:*

The December 16, 1933, issue of your paper mentioned my opinions on the perspectives which are opening up before the Belgian Labor Party, and on the positions that the other proletarian political groupings should take toward it.

In his speech to your party congress, de Man mentioned my opinion of the "labor plan," with a reference to my appeal to back this plan (*Le Peuple*, December 23, 1933). In neither case are my real words quoted, and it is not stated when or where I uttered or wrote them. It is clear that the two quotations are false, if for no other reason than that at the time de Man gave his speech I had not yet had any occasion to say a single word about the labor plan.

If the editors feel that my opinion may be of interest to the Belgian workers who read *Le Peuple*—and the fact that someone quoted me on two occasions gives me some right to think this is the case—I am ready to express in the columns of *Le Peuple* my views regarding the labor plan and the political and economic problems connected with it. I think I would be able to do so adequately within the framework of two or three articles. Since such a critique can be of interest to your readers only if it is expressed with complete frankness, the proposal presupposes that you are ready to grant me *complete freedom of expression*.

Since we belong to two irreconcilable currents of political thought, you are not, of course, in any way bound to give any space to my articles. But neither was the Soviet government, of which I was then part, bound to give Vandervelde, on Soviet territory, in Moscow, the right to defend the terrorists who had carried out attacks against the representatives of Soviet power.[2] Nevertheless we granted him that right on the basis that it was politically advisable. Perhaps you too will find it advisable, in place of quoting me incorrectly, to give me the chance to express myself in my own words before your audience.

L. *Trotsky*

The IS reply to the British majority[3]
January 23, 1934

The majority of the British section has expressed the desire to have its policy statement distributed to all sections. Since this statement contains a number of serious mistakes, we consider it necessary to provide the following critical remarks along with it.

The National Committee elaborates mainly on the theme that discipline in an organization should be based on subordination of the minority to the majority. This idea, stated generally in this way, is as indisputable as it is empty. Discipline does not fall from the sky. It has to be cultivated. Real discipline is possible only with an authoritative leadership which proves its ability, through several major phases of development, to evaluate situations and draw the necessary practical conclusions. The British section is one of the very newest. It does not yet have forty members. Its work amounts mostly to individual propaganda. Under these conditions, there can be no question of a strong, authoritative leadership having been built; that is still a very long way off.

In putting ahead of everything the question of formal discipline, which in itself is very important, the National Committee forgets that discipline is not confined to national limits. The International Secretariat, which represents all of our sections—now numbering several thousand members—has expressed itself *unanimously* in favor of the British section entering the ILP. The IS, supported by all of the sections on this question, could have approached it right from the start on the level of formal discipline. Why did it not do this? Because, having assessed the limited political experience of the British section in advance, it wanted to avoid anything that could provoke a sharp dispute and place the British section outside of our organization. On the contrary, the IS wanted to give the British section the chance to make a transition, with as little shock as possible, from a period simply of study groups and propaganda to one of much broader political activity. Unfortunately, the National Committee did not understand the British situation, displayed a sectarian conservatism, and forced a split over the issue. Political responsibility for the split lies squarely on the majority, which has disdained the unanimous recommendations of our international organization. To this we must add that the conduct of the National Committee makes it more difficult now for the minority—which stands in solidarity with the majority of our International—to carry out its tasks.

Particularly surprising and unpleasant is the tone in which the National Committee refers to the other sections and our international organization as a whole. Everywhere they see an alleged failure to understand the principles of Bolshevism, which is the cause of factional conflicts, etc., while, in contrast to that, the National Committee of the British section is the only one that carries out a correct organizational policy.

A failure to grasp the proportions of political reality, which is characteristic of every conservative group, poses an extreme threat to the further development of the majority. To avoid a faction fight by causing a split is a very simple technique, but it has nothing at all in common with Bolshevism or Marxism, instead it is a product of the caricature of Bolshevism created by the epigones. It was with just such methods that the Comintern has destroyed itself and all of its sections. The British Communist Party was always the weakest section of the Comintern, and our British comrades have had no other experience than that of the British Communist Party. They should therefore pay more attention than ever to the voice of the other sections, which are working in a wider arena and have acquired far more substantial experience.

In any event, the split is a fact. And the split means there will be no organizational connection at all between the two groups. There can be no question of the National Committee's controlling the work of the minority, since control would make such work impossible. From now on both groups will have equal rights and be independent of each other in their affiliation with the International Left Opposition. The fate of each group will become clear in the course of its subsequent activity. The International Secretariat will carefully follow the work of each group in order to prepare, if that should prove possible, their reunification at another political stage. ∎

Differences with the British minority[4]

January 23, 1934

Emergency Committee
Minority British Section

Dear Comrades:
　Re your letter of January 7:
　I am entirely in agreement with the proposal of the IS which you subject to criticism in your letter of January 5.
　We all agreed that after its entry into the ILP the British section as such should cease its independent organizational existence. But you split. It is not a question now of a section but of its part. The existence of an organization of Bolshevik-Leninists can by no means hinder you as long as you declare openly that you split off from this organization, do not submit to its discipline, and in general are not connected with it. Such a statement, which corresponds fully to the actual situation, must show more clearly to every member of the ILP the honesty of your intentions.
　You write that your future relations to the majority of the section are not clear to you. From the letter of the Sec-

retariat it is absolutely clear that *no organizational relations* are presumed.

Until this date you have as yet not entered the ILP and apparently made no effort in this direction. This shows that you lose time out of purely fictitious considerations. Can you demand of the IS that it break with the majority of the section when you have not at all proved in practice that you can really enter the ILP and develop useful activity there? And if the ILP should for any reason whatsoever not admit you? Then it would be necessary to reunite with the majority of the section. It is absolutely wrong, therefore, to demand a break with that group which remains outside of the ILP.

Your criticism of the draft of the declaration proposed by the IS seems to me not just. First of all, the IS, of course, did not intend at all to bind you in every word. Instead of starting correspondence and losing time you should have introduced certain changes in the declaration. But also your criticism of points "b" and "f" does not seem to me correct. You affirm that you also have other differences with the majority, outside of the attitude to the ILP. Possibly. But other differences were by no means causing a split. Only the question of the ILP lent to these disagreements an extreme sharpness. For the ILP itself this disagreement is of the greatest importance. Finally, the IS would not object, of course, if you had added: "and also differences on certain other questions." Needless to start a correspondence on such details.

Even less weighty are your objections to point "f." You take no responsibility for the majority. It is wrong to assert in advance that it is incapable of learning by experience. If not all will learn, then perhaps a part will, etc.

The split can be justified only by your actual success within the ILP. Otherwise the split will prove a grave error, the responsibility for which will rest on you. You must clearly realize this. At this moment you should forget the existence of the majority of the section, enter the ILP and develop energetic activity. Then all the difficulties will be solved by themselves.

With best wishes for your successful work.

Fraternally yours,
L. *Trotsky*

Minority British Section

Dear Comrade:

I received from Comrade Weber of the American League an outline of lectures on the question of the state. Even a cursory reading convinced me that this is a serious work basing itself on a rich Marxian bibliography. I am forwarding this outline to you and hope that it will be useful in your propagandistic work.

Fraternally yours,
L. *Trotsky*

The Jewish question has been internationalized[5]

January 28, 1934

Dear Comrade Kling:

I was very pleased to learn from your letter that you have in the past year become an active worker in the American

League and a member of *Unzer Kamf*'s editorial board.

One of the most active representatives of our Polish Jewish organization[6] is now in Paris. I met with him once. We spoke at length about the situation in Poland, as well as the work among Jewish workers, and, in particular, I passed on to him your idea about a certain degree of centralization of propaganda among the Jewish workers. I am speaking of *propaganda* because it is impossible, of course, to centralize the active political work in the different countries. The Warsaw comrade promised to think over this question and to introduce your suggestion to the Executive Committee. You will, of course, be notified of further developments regarding this matter.

As regards the Jewish question as a whole, it now, more than any other question whatsoever, cannot be resolved by means of "reform." The Jewish question has become at this time, as never before, a component part of the world proletarian revolution.

Regarding Birobidzhan,[7] its fate is tied up with the whole future destiny of the Soviet Union. In any case, we are dealing here not with a resolution of the Jewish question as a whole, but only with an attempt at resolving it for a certain section of the Jews living in the USSR. The Jewish question, as a result of the whole historical fate of Judaism, has been internationalized. It cannot be settled by means of "socialism in one country." Under present conditions of the vilest and basest anti-Semitic persecution and pogroms, the Jewish workers can and must derive revolutionary pride from the consciousness that the fate of the Jewish people can only be resolved by a complete and final victory of the proletariat.

With communist greetings. ■

Questions about Holland[8]

January 29, 1934

Dear Comrade Held:

Where do things stand with the youth conference? Was the commission of four in Amsterdam, which had been picked in Paris to prepare the youth conference, created, or did the Dutch conflict bury that with all the other things? That would be a crime.

Please insist on learning about Maria Reese and her eventual residence in Holland. It seems that she is also waiting in vain, but not with indifference, to collect payments for her articles.

Are there any new events that should be reported in the development of the NAS question?

Has the remainder of de Kadt's article been published? If so, I would really like to have it, because I promised Sneevliet I would answer de Kadt.

Are the theses "War and the Fourth International" being discussed in one form or another? If not, you yourself should take the thing in hand and send us the opinions, and eventually the proposals, of the Dutch. In a short while you will receive an addition to these theses about the USSR. ∎

On the workers' militia[9]

February 1934

The workers' militia is the strongest weapon in the class struggle. The class struggle attains its most conscious expression in the party. The role of the party, as well as the role of the workers' militia, increases in proportion with the deepening of the class struggle.

Those who enter the militia are the most militant, the most revolutionary, and the most dedicated elements of the proletariat and, above all, of the party itself. This is why the revolutionary party cannot confer power of attorney for the fighting units on some other organization that uses different methods and pursues different aims.

It is true that at present the task of the workers' militia has a defensive, not offensive, character owing to the danger of fascism, which threatens not only the revolutionary parties but also the reformist ones. But this does not change anything. The workers' militia is not a mere technical organization "outside the realm of politics." On the contrary, both the revolutionary party and the reformist party are well aware that the workers' militia is the keenest weapon of political struggle. And political struggle between revolutionary and reformist organizations at times reaches the point of civil war. This is why both the revolutionary party and the reformist party view merging the ranks of their supporters in one common militia as neither desirable nor possible.

The reformists will say to their own workers: "We are in agreement on a joint defense with the Communists against the fascists, but we cannot permit the Communists to get us involved in some adventure or other; we will decide ourselves when and with whom we will fight."

The Communists will say (should say): "We are ready, if need arises, to defend the editorial offices of *Populaire* or the CGT headquarters, arms in hand and alongside the reformists; but for us this is only a stage in the struggle for power. We want to gradually teach our supporters how to maneuver and how to struggle, how to fight and how to retreat, how to defend and how to attack. This is why we can neither merge our supporters with the reformists into one indistinct mass nor place our supporters under reformist command for an undetermined length of time."

The more extensive and the more successful the movement for developing a workers' militia becomes, the faster and more sharply will come the arguments cited above. If so far they have yet to be heard, it is only because the movement itself is still in infancy. We are duty bound, however, to anticipate the period ahead so that our supporters will not be caught off guard.

There are certain circles of workers who, while fed up with parties and politics, are aware of the fascist danger: former Communists, anarcho-syndicalists, or simply young militant workers, down to whom the old generation's disappointment in the parties has filtered. Elements of this type, which are particularly numerous in Paris, are inclined to respond to the slogan for a "common militia." All sorts of illusions are bound up in this slogan (getting rid of parties, splits, discussions, etc.). Our young comrades in the Leninist Youth have made an attempt to launch a movement for arming workers under the slogan of a "common militia." In other words, they want to make use of the illusions of a certain section of workers in order to prod them along a progressive path. Such an experiment can be undertaken only on the condition that:

1. *La Verite* explains that the slogan for a common militia is in no way an ultimatum aimed at socialists, reformists, Stalinists, etc. We will organize a common militia with those who sympathize with this slogan; we are ready to

come to practical agreements with organizations that create their own militias.

2. Inside the common militia, if one is actually formed, the members of the League will create a nucleus of their organization that will act under the absolute and sole direction of the League's Executive Committee. ∎

Things are on the move[10]
February 12, 1934

Dear Comrade Glotzer:

I am very glad that you have come to Europe at this particular time, a time which is for you, as for us, of great interest. You will be able to report in New York that in the most conservative country in Europe, France, things, including the League, are on the move. In a little while, of course, as soon as things have quieted down a bit, you will give the League a report on the work and the successes of the American League.

It goes without saying that the most important thing is your participation in the youth conference. I am sure that your presence will be of great value. If you meet the youth representative of the Weisbord organization in Holland, treat this comrade—if I may take the liberty to give you a piece of advice—in a friendly and objective fashion and make clear to him the senselessness of Weisbord's positions.

Don't you think that by applying pressure from all sides Weisbord could be compelled:

1. to publish a theoretical organ together with the League;
2. to stop all public attacks against the League;
3. to agree to a division of labor with the League?

I have not received any answer from the American comrades on this proposal or, better put, this suggestion.

Of course we will see each other and have an extensive discussion about all pending questions. For the moment, a couple of practical matters:

1. Have you seen Comrade Maria Reese? It is absolutely necessary that you visit her and discuss practical details of her trip to America.

2. You probably have heard that Maslow and Ruth Fischer are about to join us (this is *not to be made public!*). Since they are both concerned with Anglo-Saxon affairs, I consider it very desirable for you to visit them to bring them information about America. You can arrange this through Comrade Schwarz [Sedov]. I will write to these comrades about you.

Until we see each other,
Your Old Man

Against centrism at the youth conference[11]

February 15, 1934

Dear Friend:

I have just read the discussion theses of the SJV of Holland. The impression is very sad. Were it a document of the young people themselves, insufficient theoretical and political maturity could be assumed, and the document could be regarded from a purely pedagogical point of view. Unfortunately, it gives the impression of being written by an inveterate centrist (two-and-a-half times over) who covers himself here and there with general, abstract, and radical sounding formulas. I cannot subject the document to a complete critique, because every sentence calls for criticism. I will pick out only the most important centrist and obfuscatory examples.

1. "Immediate national and international disarmament" (page 2). This pacifist-Kautskyist[12] slogan has nothing to do with Marxism.

2. "The shortcomings of the democratic republic and the grave mistakes of the Communist parties and the Social Democracy" (page 2) are stated to be the cause for fascism. Not the *class character* of the capitalist republic, but its *shortcomings!* Not the reformist-imperialist leadership of the Social Democracy, and not the bureaucratic-centrist orientation of the Comintern, but their "mistakes." But real Marxists also make mistakes. The sequence is also interesting: first the Communist parties and only then the Social Democracy.

3. The characterization of the Second International (pages 4 and 5) is partly insufficient and partly false. The Social Democracy is only characterized as a reformist party, where reformism is defined as "insufficient" from the standpoint of the social revolution. It is not mentioned that the workers' aristocracy and its bureaucracy have integrated themselves into the capitalist state and—what is even more important—that the decay of capitalism has completely cut the ground out from under reforms. This in fact was what precipitated the decline of the Second International.

4. Even worse is the characterization of the official Communists (pages 5 to 8). Not a word about their political

orientation, about the direction of their political line, i.e., *bureaucratic centrism*, which, driven by incredible contradictions, is developing along the sharpest zigzag course. Obviously there is no mention whatever of the social basis of bureaucratic centrism. Everything is explained in typically Brandlerite and Lovestoneite manner by saying that the line is dictated from Moscow and that all things cannot be rightly assessed from Moscow: hence the "mistakes." But why these "mistakes" in all countries have the same character and why two opposition currents against these "mistakes" developed, the Right and the Left, which are also *international* in character—this question does not exist for the author of the theses.

The only indication of a political explanation consists of the mention that the Comintern is guided by the "interests" of the Soviet Union. Thus it is conceded—in agreement with Brandler—that the Comintern correctly understands and defends the interests of the Soviet Union.

What is said about the bad Comintern regime is idealist and Menshevik. The regime is regarded as a thing by itself, not as the expression of the conflict between the political orientation (bureaucratic centrism) and the historical interests of the proletariat, including the interests of the Soviet Union.

5. The chapter about the united front policy could have been written by Balabanova,[13] Paul Louis, etc. The united front is supported with the argument that "despite many tactical differences" unity is necessary in practical matters. As if the Marxists were differentiated from the reformists and the Stalinists by "tactical differences." It should read: despite irreconcilable principled differences in program and strategy, the united front in many *tactical* questions is forced upon the working class by the class struggle.

What follows is even worse. The "moral" decay of the proletariat is explained in a philistine-sentimental manner by "the split [of the Second International] and the ensuing fraternal strife." As if, on the contrary, the split had not pulled the political vanguard out of the desperation of social imperialism.

The united front is further defended with arguments about the "highest feelings" and similar stuff. It seems like a dissertation of the pre-Marxian True Socialists.

"The Communists don't recognize the principle of loyalty and fidelity" (page 8). Thus it is proven that the Communists do not support the united front for itself, but pursue egoistic aims of enlarging their own influence. The question could not be posed in a more ridiculous way. As if it were not the right and the duty of every party to try to attract the workers to itself by means of the united front. As if it were not the bounden duty of the revolutionary party, in the course of the united front, to unmask and compromise the treacherous scoundrels of the Social Democracy and the miserable centrist charlatans. One can only do the Stalinists a service by accusing them, as Wels, Leon Blum,[14] Tranmael, and other traitors do, of trying to "intrigue their way into other organizations."

This is the voice of the frightened centrist, not the Marxist. We accuse the Stalinists of having proved themselves incapable, with their fundamentally false political line, of splitting the Social Democracy, compromising its leaders and drawing the masses towards themselves.

All the additional drivel (pages 9 and 10) about the "honorable" and "loyal" united front is idealist and Menshevik. Nothing is said about the content of the politics, only the abstract form of the united front is praised. This derives no additional weight from being covered with ethical rigmarole.

Too much talk about abstract morals is always a bad sign: class morals can only develop out of correct revolutionary class politics. They are not an independent higher entity which, in the sense of the Kantians, holds sway above social reality.

6. The chapter "attitude towards the Soviet Union" (pages 10 to 13) is extremely sloppy, purely descriptive, and abounds with small and large mistakes. Thus, for example, the paragraph starts by contrasting the October Revolution as a social transformation with "the bourgeois revolutions, which only aim at a political transformation." A dead wrong liberal-conservative view! The real bourgeois revolutions were also social: they transformed feudal property relations into bourgeois ones, while the October Revolution has turned bourgeois economic relations into socialist ones.

The real contradictions in the Soviet economy, which have long been pointed out in detail by the Left Opposition, appear in this document in a totally distracting and confused manner. Now and then the author refers to the "fiasco" of the Soviet economy, which is totally wrong.

The whole chapter amounts to a plaintive accusation against the Soviet Union because it did not support the economic boycott of Germany. As if larger and more important things should not be mentioned. The OSP tried to initiate the boycott movement in a very superficial and false way, obviously suffered a fiasco in this area, and now wants to cover itself by a totally superficial and even false critique of Soviet policy.

7. About *colonial policy* (page 13), the theses assert that the oppressed peoples "have no other way to liberation but a relentless fight, including passive resistance and insurrection." Despite the best intentions, centrism appears most blatantly in this sentence. "Relentless struggle" does not include passive resistance but rather excludes it. It goes without saying that we also defend passive resistance against the imperialist troops. But at the same time we denounce before the colonial masses the treacherous aspects

of Gandhism, whose mission is to retard the fight of the revolutionary masses and to exploit it in the interest of the "national" bourgeoisie.

8. The chapter about the youth organization is very thin—even though it deals with a youth conference! But in principled matters, too, the chapter is wrong in many points. As the social basis for the organization the "working, unemployed, and student youth" are cited. Again purely descriptive, not social. For us it is a question of the proletarian youth and those elements among the students that lean towards the proletariat. Working, unemployed, and student youth are for a Marxist in no way equal links in the social chain.

According to the theses, in the area of culture, the youth organization fights "against capitalist-bourgeois 'education' and for a proletarian culture." Abstract, rhetorical, idealistic, and vacuous! At the moment bourgeois culture includes the invaluable wealth of the positive sciences. The aim of the working class is to appropriate this treasure. In the "area of culture" this can happen only in a highly inadequate way. Only through the proletarian revolution will the proletariat gain access to these treasures of bourgeois culture in order to build up on this basis—with the removal of all falsifications—a new socialist culture. What "proletarian culture" in this connection should really mean is not clear, especially since it is abstractly counterposed to bourgeois culture as a whole.

That youth should carry out its "historic task" "mainly (!) by propagating the united front" is wrong to the point of despair. The united front is only a tactical concomitant of the revolutionary struggle. Youth "mainly" has to prepare itself for the most bitter struggles—defensive struggles against fascism and offensive struggles against capitalism.

Further (still page 14) it is said that the revolutionary

socialist youth should work together with the OSP. Does this apply to the international youth? . . . since the theses are submitted to an international conference as the basis of discussion. Why is only the OSP mentioned, i.e., just the party that up till now has had no time to take a clear programmatic and strategic position?

9. The conditions for membership in the new International (pages 16, 17) are totally insufficient, and partly wrong. The Paris Declaration of Four stands in its precision far above the confused six points of the document under criticism. The first two paragraphs in this general version are very ordinary and universally accepted—including by Wels and Manuilsky. The third paragraph demands the rejection of reformism and Stalinism. Reformism is for Marxists a very concrete notion. What the theses mean by Stalinism is unfortunately incomprehensible. The fourth paragraph about the "honorable" united front is completely vague and, after what is said above, even dangerous because it is directed against "fraternal strife" and against split and thus in no way is able to explain the founding of a new International. The fifth point speaks for the proletarian revolution and the dictatorship of the proletariat. Nothing about the acquisition of power and nothing about workers' soviets as the historically determined form for organizing the working class for the conquest and exercise of power. Point six talks about the "defense of a truly proletarian state." What does that mean? It is a very concrete question whether we acknowledge the duty to defend the USSR as it is, isn't it? This life-and-death question is avoided by talking about *a truly revolutionary state.*

This criticism is intended for our comrades (Internationalist-Communists), to make the task of public criticism easier for them. In my opinion, our delegates should present the critique in a quiet, propagandistic, pedagogic manner, of course without making the slightest concessions in principle.

It is very good that the OSP (de Kadt?) had the imprudence to submit these confused and contradictory theses. The whole conference should be dedicated to the critique of these theses and to counterposing sentence for sentence. For this counterposition is recommended:

a. the eleven points of the Left Opposition;
b. the Declaration of Four;
c. the theses against war;
d. the theses about the USSR (two pamphlets);
e. the documents newly developed for the conference.

Our delegates should pick the best formulations out of the above-mentioned literature of the ICL and counterpose them to the formulations of the theses for discussion. This work should be done now, in advance, so that our delegation can prove ready at every moment.

The old philistines will bait their young people against us because they will feel insulted by our criticism. Our friends must be very polite and friendly in their answers to the young people: we are only carrying out the right of mutual criticism so pompously spoken of in the theses (e.g., page 16).

The only positive thing about these theses is that they distinctly declare themselves for a new International and thus sharply counterpose themselves to the reformists as well as the Stalinists. We must use that against the NAP, against the leaders of the ILP, etc. There are no concessions to be made on this point. If the people from the OSP abandon the new International in order to bring about their "honorable, loyal united front" with Tranmael and Fenner Brockway, then we must vote against the theses and make a strong protest statement: not to say openly to the workers now that salvation lies in the creation of a new International means to betray the workers.

If we can put through improvements in all major questions, we can vote for the theses with an explanation in which we mention the weak points and the shortcomings in a general way.

In any case our delegates must reserve their final decision for after the meeting of the international commission of the Internationalist-Communist youth.

The question of the NAP will (must) play a big role in the discussion together with the question of the London, now Amsterdam Bureau. Our delegates must be very well armed on this question. Somebody should specialize. Included are some documents which refer to the NAP. Comrade Glotzer promises to return these documents after the conference.

P.S. It is best to counterpose the declaration of principles of the four organizations to the six conditions of membership in the new International. If the SAP and the OSP object to this, they will only compromise themselves badly. But it would be best to win them in advance for it.

P.P.S. In the whole document the word "centrism" is not mentioned a single time. This is very characteristic and must be especially emphasized. Consistent reformism does not dare to come forward openly these days. Wels, Hilferding, Blum, de Man admit the bankruptcy of reformism, at least in words. All hide behind a pseudorevolutionary, i.e., centrist attitude, or at least terminology. Centrism now dominates almost the whole field of the workers' movement. Centrism is what we have to fight against now. Why do the theses not mention the existence and the danger of centrism? Because they themselves are within the framework of centrism. ■

Rakovsky's statement of submission[15]

February 21, 1934

Dear Comrades:

The dispatch concerning Rakovsky's statement will undoubtedly create a big impression. We must counter its negative effects with an immediate statement of our own. And as always, the best course is to say what is.

Rakovsky has in no way "capitulated" in the same sense that Zinoviev, Kamenev, and their colleagues did. He has not renounced a single word of the ideas he fought for alongside us. He has not "confessed" any of the so-called "errors" committed by the Left Opposition. Under the conditions prevailing in the USSR, with which we are all familiar, this basic feature of Rakovsky's statement has an exceptional eloquence. It only accentuates the fact that there is nothing in Rakovsky's past that he wishes to disown or recant, with respect to either theory or politics.

Rakovsky declares that he is ending his struggle and submitting to discipline. That is the only content of his statement. To appreciate this statement at its true value—and naturally we condemn it—we must understand fully the situation in which Rakovsky found himself. In fact he had ceased active struggle three or four years earlier. He could neither communicate with his friends, nor write articles, nor receive literature of the Left Opposition and information on the international workers' movement in general. In this absolute isolation he remained without any perspective.

All the same, Rakovsky's statement, while far from being an ideological or political capitulation, is an act not only to be regretted but to be condemned. This example will no doubt be widely used by the Stalinist bureaucracy to lure many youths imprisoned and isolated like Rakovsky, onto the road to capitulation, and perhaps not in Rakovsky's way, but in Zinoviev's.

We have many times repeated that the restoration of a Communist Party in the USSR can take place only through international channels. The case of Rakovsky confirms this in a negative but striking way. The Bolshevik-Leninists in the USSR learn from *Pravda* only the barest outlines of international life: Hitler's victory, the threat of war, and now the crushing of the Austrian proletariat. They have no opportunity to orient themselves on the real causes of these events, or to discern the different groupings in the workers' movement.

To rebuild a powerful internationalist-communist movement in the USSR, the struggle for the Fourth International must take shape and become a powerful factor that the Stalinist bureaucracy will not be able to conceal from the eyes of the Soviet workers, including the Bolshevik-Leninists. We record the purely formal statement of the old fighter who has demonstrated his unshakable devotion to the revolutionary cause throughout his whole life; we record it with sorrow and we proceed to the next point on the agenda, that is, redoubled efforts to build new parties of the new International. ■

Ultraleft tactics in fighting the fascists[16]

March 2, 1934

Dear Friends:

Since I am in Switzerland, I cannot follow the events in France at close hand. But let me say that before emigrating here, I accumulated a certain amount of experience in these matters in Germany. And the Menilmontant affair fills me with the direst foreboding. If things proceed along this line, catastrophe is inevitable.

What is the objective, not just for the moment but for the entire coming period? It is to get the workers to take up the struggle against the fascists before these elements have become the dominant force in the state, to get the workers used to not being afraid of the fascists, to teach them how to deal blows to the fascists, to convince them that they are stronger in numbers, in audacity, and in other ways.

In this period it is very important to distinguish between the fascists and the state. The state is not yet ready to subordinate itself to the fascists; it wants to "arbitrate." We know what this means from the sociological point of view. However, this is not a matter of sociology but of giving blows and taking them. Politically it is part of the nature of a pre-Bonapartist, "arbiter" state that the police hesitate, hold back, and on the whole are far from identifying with the fascist gangs. Our strategic task is to increase these hesitations and apprehensions on the part of the "arbiter," its army and its police. How? By showing that we are stronger than the fascists, that is, by giving them a good beating in full view of this arbiter without, as long as we are not absolutely forced to, directly taking on the state itself. That is the whole point.

In the case of Menilmontant, as far as I can tell from here, the operation was handled in the diametrically opposite way. *L'Humanite* reports that there were no more than sixty fascists in a thoroughly working class neighborhood! The tactical, or if you will, "technical," task was quite simple—grab every fascist or every isolated group of fascists by their collars, acquaint them with the pavement a few times, strip them of their fascist insignia and documents, and without carrying things any further, leave them with their fright and a few good black and blue marks.

The "arbiter" defended freedom of assembly (for the moment the state is also defending workers' meetings from the fascists). This being the case, it was totally idiotic to want to provoke an armed conflict with the police. But this is precisely what they did. *L'Humanite* is exultant—they erected a barricade! But what for? The fascists weren't on the other side of the barricade, and it was the fascists they came to fight. Was this an armed insurrection perhaps? To establish the dictatorship of the proletariat in Menilmontant? This makes no sense. As Marx said, "One does not play at insurrection." That means, "One does not play with barricades." Even when there is an insurrection, you don't erect barricades just any where, any time. (You can learn something from Blanqui on this score—see the documents published in *La Critique Sociale*.)[17]

They succeeded in (a) letting the gilded youth[18] return home in fine shape; (b) provoking the police and getting a worker killed; (c) giving the fascists an important argument—the Communists are starting to build barricades.

The idiot bureaucrats will say: "So, you want us to forget about building barricades out of fear of the fascists and love of the police?" It is a betrayal to reject building barricades when the political situation demands it and when you are strong enough to erect them and defend them. But it is a disgusting provocation to build sham barricades for a little fascist meeting, to blow things up out of all political proportions, and to disorient the proletariat.

The task is to *involve* the workers in increasing numbers in the fight against fascism. The Menilmontant adventure can only isolate a small, militant minority. After such an experience, a hundred, a thousand workers who would have been ready to teach the young bourgeois bullies a few lessons will say, "No, thanks, I don't want to get my head broken for nothing." The upshot of the whole undertaking was just the opposite of what was intended. And not to mince words, it wouldn't surprise me very much if it came out after a while that the ones who shouted loudest for the barricades were fascist agents planted in the ranks of the Stalinists, fascists who wanted to get their friends off the hook by provoking a confrontation with the police. If this was the case, they succeeded well.

What should the most active and perceptive elements have done on the spot? They should have improvised a small general staff, including a Socialist and a Stalinist if possible. (At the same time it should have been explained to the workers that the neighborhood general staff should have functioned on a permanent basis on the eve of the demonstration.) This improvised general staff, with a map of the district spread out in front of them, should have worked out the simplest plan in the world—divide up one or two hundred demonstrators into groups of three to five, with a leader for each group, and let them do their work. And after the battle the leaders should get together and draw the balance sheet and the necessary lessons for the future. This second meeting could provide a good core for a permanent general staff, a good underpinning for a permanent workers' militia in the district. Naturally, there would have to be leaflets explaining the need for a permanent general staff.

For the perceptive, revolutionary elements, the balance sheet offers the following lessons:

a. You have to have your own general staff for such occasions.
b. You have to anticipate the possibilities and eventualities in such conflicts.
c. You have to establish a few general plans (several variants).
d. You have to have a map of the district.
e. You have to have the proper leaflets for the situation.

This is all I can say for the moment. I am almost sure that these suggestions are completely in accord with your own ideas. So much the better. ■

After the Austrian defeat[19]
March 13, 1934

Comrade Reese's pamphlet speaks more from direct political and personal experience than from general theoretical-historical considerations—and this is its strong point. In it, every thinking worker will live through the great events in Germany and taste the political consequences they entailed. This is necessary even for the German workers, but this pamphlet will be especially useful for the workers of those countries where fascism is just preparing to transform state power into a murderous bludgeon for use against the proletariat. It will be possible to put a stop to the activities of the fascists only when the vanguard of the international proletariat has lived through, thought through, and thoroughly understood the causes of the terrible defeat of the German proletariat.

Comrade Reese's pamphlet is an indictment of both apparatuses that played a role in the sabotage of the proletarian revolution: the German sections of the Second and the Third Internationals. Although their motivations and methods were indeed different, the results they brought about were equally fatal. The proletarian party proves its mettle in a revolutionary situation the way an army does in a war. The mere fact that the contradictions of bourgeois democracy had grown to the point that they could no longer be resolved by democratic methods spelled political death for the Social Democratic Party. The fact that the Communist Party faced this unprecedented deepening of contradictions helpless, confused and without a plan is irrefutable proof that its previous theoretical and political positions and education were inadequate and false.

The behavior of the Austrian Social Democracy after the German experience proved that even the "left" parties of the Second International are completely ossified, bogged down, and incapable of learning the revolutionary lessons of the terrible experience of the German proletariat. The courageous struggles of the Austrian workers only prove that the proletariat can be bold and ready to struggle even under the most unfavorable conditions and with the worst leadership. The fact that a few Social Democratic leaders took part in the battles is at best only testimony to their personal valor. But the working class demands political insight and revolutionary courage from its leadership. Personal virtues— and moreover those that are induced by the pressure of events—cannot substitute for a lack of these qualities. Even the narrow-minded petty bourgeois is at times capable of doing his talking with a gun if he is threatened with being deprived of his comforts and forced out of his usual mode of existence. What is necessary, however, is systematic revolutionary education of the vanguard and winning the trust of the majority of the proletariat in the practical intelligence and daring of the proletarian general staff. Without this precondition, victory is completely impossible. For years, the Austrian Social Democracy threatened to answer with force, *when* their democratic rights were impinged upon. It turned revolutionary action into a legalistic-literary threat that it did not take seriously itself. Only a leadership that recognizes in advance that the revolution is unavoidable, that makes this the fundamental principle guiding its actions, and draws all the practical conclusions flowing from this can measure up to the situation at the critical hour. Thus despite the heroic actions of the Austrian proletariat and to a certain extent because of these actions—the bankruptcy of the Second International in Austria is no less plain and certain than was the case in Germany.

Let us turn our attention to the example of little Norway. There too we find a Social Democratic Party "powerful" in numbers only. This party, led by Tranmael, although thus far prevented by adverse circumstances from officially affiliating with the Second International, is steering the exact same course as the Austro-Marxists, making its "victorious advance" and as a result striving with all its might to clear the way for Norwegian fascism.

But the situation is no better in the Third International. People who only read the confirmation of the so-called prognosis of the Comintern leadership in the German and Austrian events represent nothing but bureaucratic stupidity in its purest form. If they have learned nothing from the German Communist Party's passive, demoralizing failure to act and the Austrian Communist Party's complete abstention in the fateful hour, what in the world could possibly teach them anything? Meanwhile we observe that once again the theory of "social fascism" is in full bloom in the French, English, and every other section of the ill-starred Comintern. The Communist bureaucrats stuff their mouths with slogans like "October Revolution," "Soviets everywhere," etc. But they don't understand the first letter in the alphabet of the proletarian revolution. Soviets develop out of the organizational forms of the united front of the working class in struggle. From defensive actions, street demonstrations, large strikes, etc., arises the organizational unification of the worker-masses, which forces even the conservative organizations to join in, even if only with the intention of destroying the organization in the long run (the Mensheviks in 1917, the German and Austrian Social Democrats in 1918–19). The Stalinist parties, which foreswear, sabotage, and destroy all forms of the united front, block the road to the formation of soviets in practice. And the sage wisdom of "social fascism" was and is the theoretical crowning of this sabotage of the revolution.

One can draw no other lesson from events than the conclusion that a new revolutionary selection is necessary. The proletarian vanguard must be gathered under a new banner, i.e., new parties and a new International must be formed. Maria Reese's pamphlet ends with this call. And therein lies its political merit. ∎

Reproaching the Dutch section[20]

March 17, 1934

Dear Friend:

1. Enclosed I send you a strong article against de Kadt in the form of a letter addressed to you, thus stressing our

solidarity on the questions of principle. I hope that this article will be useful.

2. I strongly regret that your party is so stubborn on the NAS question (last summer you seemed to me more flexible on this matter). In any case, let us handle this question in such a way that the centrists (OSP and SAP) cannot profit from it. That of course implies as much goodwill on your side as on ours.

3. The extradition of the four German comrades is a really unprecedented case. What have the RSP and the NAS done about this? And you personally as a deputy?

4. The conduct of the RSP toward the International Secretariat is not altogether comprehensible. The IS is now developing important activity. But it does not have the full support of the sections, even the richest. Involved are not large sums of money but regular monthly contributions. And the whole burden of this should not be placed on the French and the Russian *Biulleten*.

At present this relates to a burning question: in Greece Witte is trying to rally his section against us, but he has encountered energetic opposition in the Political Bureau and especially in the ranks. The fraction of the leadership which sides with us asks that someone from the IS go to Athens for the coming party congress. I consider this absolutely necessary, because the fate of an important workers' organization is at stake. But for this some thousands of francs are needed. We count here firmly on a contribution from the RSP. But this should be made immediately, because there is no time to lose.

It would be very good if Vereecken could go to Greece. But I do not know if he is now thinking about undertaking this trip.

This time I am counting on an *immediate* response.

P.S. Could you tell me what *Het Fundament* represents? I have received an invitation from its editors to write an article. This does not seem to me to be very appropriate. ■

Field's expulsion[21]

March 18, 1934

[*Trotsky can in no way declare himself in agreement with Field's point of view. Furthermore he is not in a position to form an independent opinion.*]

... The [Communist] League is, however, the nucleus of the new party and thereby of the new International. To me it seems completely unforgivable to break with one's own organization at the first practical test. Your explanations for this are unfortunately full of contradictions. In discussing the NC's reorganization of the [League's hotel union] fraction, you say there are no political reasons for the artificial differences of opinion. But then you maintain that the League is sectarian, sterile, incapable of mass action, and even dead. If in your opinion the League is dead, the break with the corpse is understandable. This means however that you are breaking with our movement. But since the League does not regard itself as dead—and I believe rightly so—it cannot allow its members to freelance. Rather it wishes to exercise control over its members. If it had not desired this, it would not be worthy of existence.

In the Social Democratic parties, it was and still is the rule that when gifted members of the party with the party's help win important posts in the municipality, the parliament, or the ministry, they immediately become tired of party discipline and declare that the official leadership of the party is incompetent in order to carry out their own political line—always in order to "save" the party, of course.

I don't know whether the League entered into practical agreements with the Lovestoneites and the Stalinists. In

Here I will emphasize only a few points where our delegation revealed itself as unreliably conciliatory.

1. Beginning with the title, we read "Conference of Revolutionary Socialist Youth Organizations." But we are Communist and not Socialist. Why wasn't our name included in the title "... Socialist and Communist Youth Organizations"? Did our delegates ask for this? Or did they merely overlook this "petty detail"? Politics, at least in the preparatory stages, consists of such details.

2. The question of centrism is completely ignored. Only once, in paragraph VII (page 4), do we find centrism named between reformism and Stalinism. Thus, the word is used only for a legalistic alibi. There is not one word to the effect that not only the various independent organizations but also those of the Second International reflect centrism in all its colors, and that hence the construction of the Fourth International depends upon liberating the working class youth from centrist confusion. One of the letters to Glotzer was devoted to this all-important question, and, as I have been informed, the IS found this letter to be correct. Yet there is not a hint of this idea to be found in the document. The "sharp," "irreconcilable" criticism of Stalinism and reformism actually serves only as a cover for the toleration of centrism. And our delegation fell into this error as well.

I don't find the final version of the text concerning the Fourth International. The original version is slippery. For "transcending the Second and Third Internationals" with the goal of "creating proletarian unity" sounds not only like Tranmael, but also like Louis Sellier,[25] who, moreover, figures in the debates of the [French parliamentary] commission of inquiry as a candidate for a semifascist government. "Transcending" both Internationals is Tranmael's fraudulent formulation: "I don't want a Fourth International, there are too many already." This formulation is classical Menshevism. Year after year, especially during the imperialist war, Lenin led a struggle against the philosophy of "transcending" [the Second International] put forward by the revisionists, opportunists, chauvinists, etc., etc. In Lenin's writings the word is always set in quotes as a symbolic word, representing an entire program. Everything Walcher's people write is unwitting plagiarism from Martov.

4. It is true that after the departure of Finn Moe,[26] the SAP graciously accepted the new international formulation, but only in connection with transcending. We cannot agree to this under any circumstances. It is not simply a question of a new International; the Two-and-a-half International would be a new International, too, as would a unification of the Second and Third. For us there is something quite different at issue—the Fourth International that must be built in irreconcilable struggle against the two existing Internationals and against centrist tendencies in general. To make the slightest concession on this is a betrayal and a crime. Walcher is not fighting about terminology. He needs an elastic formulation for smuggling in his centrist goods, and this is the very thing we cannot allow.

A suggestion: We can sign this document (with qualification, i.e., with a special official statement) only if

1. the title is changed;
2. "transcending the Second and Third Internationals" is removed and/or replaced by liberating the workers from the Second and Third Internationals through irreconcilable struggle against all opportunist and centrist currents; and
3. the goal set is the creation of the Fourth (and not the new) International.

These three points must be put forward as an absolute ultimatum and we cannot give an inch. An open break would be a thousand times better than a conscious deception at the heart of the youth International.

We must also demand, not as an ultimatum but as very important, that a sentence be added where the role of the Austrian Social Democracy is discussed, to the effect that the Norwegian Labor Party is following in the footsteps of Austro-Marxism and preparing a similar catastrophe for the Norwegian proletariat.

If the three points above are accepted by the SAP, we will sign the document. But we will make a written declaration in which we make the point that neither the youth nor ourselves take the slightest responsibility for the destructive London-Amsterdam Bureau, which now serves as nothing more than a figleaf for Tranmael, whose politics are simply a new edition of Austro-Marxism, etc.

P.S. If our young delegates feel that they are being "repudiated," that is only partially true. The IS is there not just to approve of its delegates, but also to repudiate them. With many of our comrades one notices the following: they understand very well how to explain and ridicule the psychology and methods of the centrist bigshots, but not how to combat them on the practical plane.

On the organizational question: As far as the three-member secretariat is concerned, we must for the moment wait for the official position of the Swedish youth before committing ourselves. A single comrade in Sweden, where we have no organization, is not sufficient surety for the consistency of our political line in the future secretariat. At least a principled basis must be laid through clarification: a) the correction of the document; b) the position of the Swedes. ∎

The proposal to fuse the CLA and the AWP[27]

March 20, 1934

The attempt at unification is extremely interesting and symptomatic. It shows that the case of the SAP and the OSP was not and is not accidental but rather part of the course of the further development of the revolutionary workers' movement. It was, is, and will be necessary to go through such attempts and experiments in all countries, in most countries several times.

The American Workers Party hardly stands on a higher political level than the SAP. The dangers that immediate unification entails are clear. But the American comrades have not closed their eyes to this either, as can be seen from Comrade Swabeck's letters. They correctly understand that they are dealing with a centrist party that is moving toward the left. Comrade Solow, a friend of the League, writes me that Muste is the member of the AWP leadership most capable of developing (moreover he is a former minister). The arguments in favor of unification presented by Comrade Swabeck on behalf of the leadership are substantial. Our comrades are more numerous, better educated theoretically, and have no illusions about the difficulties they will face in working together with the AWP. It is very difficult to reach a decision from here without knowing all the elements of the situation, including the personal ones. But then this is not the question. Our American friends must make the decision themselves. It is enough for us to express our confidence in them in this matter. At most, the following points might be projected as desirable:

a. A discussion period of at least two months' duration in which our comrades speak at the meetings of the AWP and the Muste people speak at our meetings. Also joint discussion evenings.

b. Conferences of both organizations with mutual representation to precede formal unification so that we can get a good clear picture of the groupings within the AWP.

c. A good editorial committee for the theoretical organ so that educational work will be carried out in a true Marxist spirit.

d. The establishment of a solid, regularly published internal bulletin where all pending questions are clarified.

e. Appropriate forms must be found for joint education of the youth.

f. It is desirable that the joint platform approve the Declaration of Four.

These are, more or less, the points that, in my opinion, can be projected as desirable from here. What will the international relations of the united party be like? Either it can join the International Secretariat directly or, if for the time being the AWP is not particularly inclined toward this, the united party can directly join the so-called Bloc of Four, which will thus become the Bloc of Five and open up new possibilities for us even in the event of further passive sabotage on the part of the SAP and the OSP. The united party could join the IS and the Bloc of Four at the same time. ■

The errors of our youth delegates[28]

March 29, 1934

Dear Comrade Held:

1. My understanding of the first, rather delayed and inexact information about the results of the youth conference is that you and Brandt were assigned to do the final editing of the call [for the new youth International], and, as always in such instances, it was to be hoped that, if the proper pressure were applied, the editing would make an unfortunate document less harmful. But, since this seems to be impossible, our international organization has no other choice, I think, than to publicly characterize at least the most harmful aspects of the document.

2. Maintaining an "elastic" position with respect to youth with possibilities for development does not at all mean remaining silent about their fundamental mistakes. The error was that our delegation completely disregarded the instructions they were given. This is not to mention that we had a right to expect some independent initiative in the way of Marxist implacability from our comrades, who are far better trained in theoretical matters than the other delegates.

3. I am astounded that you fail to recognize the obvious error in the very title of the resolution. Why shouldn't we be mentioned by name just like the Socialist organizations? I cannot understand this at all. Did we at least ask for this? Did they refuse? For what reason? Did you simply accept the refusal and their reasons without comment? An organization's name is also its banner. One does not surrender the banner in such a frivolous manner.

Instead of simply admitting the insufficiency of our delegation's actions on this point, you invoke the fact that we have accepted the Dutch RSP into our ranks. This is pure sophism, and not very clever sophism at that! Did we change the name of our international organization for the sake of the RSP? Did we accept their program? Did we make any principled concessions? Quite the contrary. On the international level the RSP belongs to the *Communist* League. Where then is the analogy? No one is demanding that the OSP and the SAP be forced to call themselves "Communist." We only ask that they not rebaptize us as "Socialists." Is this, perhaps, not our right?

Not long ago, I wrote that a centrist treats a Marxist the way a petty bourgeois treats a proletarian, i.e., with contempt. But woe to the proletarian who does not know how to maintain his class dignity in negotiations with a petty bourgeois!

You defend the historically notorious formula of "transcending" [the Second and Third Internationals] by saying that it can also be interpreted in a "good" way. But a political manifesto is not supposed to be an equivocal, oracular pronouncement; it is supposed to enlighten, not deceive the workers. It is better to have no manifesto than an ambiguous one. In any case, you were obligated to counterpose in writing your own clear formulation to the ambiguous one in order then to communicate it to the working class as the authentic expression of our views.

4. You repeatedly remark that one cannot require the OSP and the SAP to characterize themselves as centrist. To this I say:

(a) We were dealing with the youth, and from them one can expect or hope for an "elastic" relationship with their own party.

(b) In politics what is required is foremost to express one's own point of view and not to hasten to represent the point of view of one's opponent.

You were obligated to suggest amendments about centrism, the NAP, the Amsterdam Bureau, and bring them to a vote. If the others reject these amendments with an ultimatum, you at least have the advantage of clarity: You can make these amendments public and thereby document your position. Whether we would have signed the resolution after all is a separate question. The final decision on this was from the outset reserved for the International Secretariat.

5. Your arguments about the general situation in Holland are just as incorrect. You say that the unification [of the RSP and the OSP] was necessary and would have opened up broad perspectives. But you consider the RSP's line on the trade unions to be disastrous and this was one of the decisive points for the unification. You accuse the center [IS] of not having forced the RSP to alter its trade union line. On the one hand, you consider it impossible to introduce a Marxist amendment to a resolution, i.e., to make a simple change in the text, and on the other hand you think that it is possible, using some mysterious means, to bring a forty-year-old organization [the NAS] to its knees with a single blow. Our position on the trade union question is completely clear—even to the RSP. This is proven by the fact that the RSP officially declares that it wishes to change the line of the International Communist League on the trade union question. With all of our sections, even the smallest ones, we have learned by experience that one cannot change much through formal decisions alone, that educational work and particularly independent experience is necessary and that the creation of real homogeneity in thinking can be achieved only through protracted crises (see, e.g., Greece).

If you consider the NAS line to be disastrous, how do you imagine it to be possible for the RSP to assimilate the OSP through unification? You make reference to Lenin, who carried along even non-Bolshevik elements in the party. But in Holland we have no strong Bolshevik Party, and the Dutch leadership is tied down by the NAS, which cannot be corrected by a few impatient letters.

What do you suggest *post festum?* An ultimatum to the RSP and an unavoidable break? That would be completely insane since we have here a friendly organization that is capable of development. Or should we support the OSP, which in a purely formal way is correct on the trade union question (fundamentally it cannot be correct since it is opportunistic) against the RSP? A break with the RSP would be the consequence.

I developed this entire perspective for you last summer. I tried to impress upon you that support for our line had to be developed through tireless detail work, especially in the OSP. Unfortunately there is not a great deal you can say about this educational work among the young members. You make reference to the fact that the NAS question created a lot of problems for you in your educational work with the OSP youth. (But when you talk about the fusion question, you almost exclude the NAS question altogether.) Of course, it is difficult to do Marxist propaganda work when the leadership of the organization is not Marxist. But that was the task at hand, and I don't believe that the NAS question could have been so disruptive in *this* work. A systematic series of classes on the history of the Left Opposition together with the history of the Third International could have surely educated a youth group in a solid Marxist spirit, and that would have been the only correct course of action.

6. I heard from comrades that there is a plan to send you to Sweden as a representative of the Left Opposition. That is a very important mission. In my opinion, however, this time there must be a clear and exact understanding of what is actually to be accomplished. I see this as educational work among the youth. If, after six months, you have ten young people around you who are familiar with our views and methods in all the most important questions and are able

to apply them to the Swedish situation more or less on their own, that would be a great accomplishment. But if you are going to Sweden with the idea that you can open up broad perspectives at a single blow by working at the top and through personal combinations, you will be disillusioned once again and transform your disillusionment into reproaches against the center. In other words, to be quite frank, in order to put the good qualities you possess to work for our common cause, you must radically reorient yourself in the work. It would be very important for you, like every other official representative of the center, to send in a short but detailed monthly report on your work. Then we can stand by you with advice and practical help.

I hope that you will not take offense at my frankness, which is meant not to endanger but to strengthen friendly relations.[29] ■

Continuing the struggle through unifications[30]

April 10, 1934

Dear Comrade Glotzer:

I read your letter of March 26 to Shachtman with great interest. What you communicate about our experience with the centrists in Europe is completely correct and the American comrades must carefully follow and consider this experience. I would, however, like to call attention to the following point: regarding the SAP. We (and I personally) insisted on immediate unification. But the SAP, after a short period of vacillation, opposed this. In the case of the OSP, the course of development proceeded in the opposite direction: the OSP insisted on immediate unification and the RSP opposed this. These two examples show that while completely maintaining our principled relationship to centrism, the practical road toward approaching (and at the same time combating) centrist tendencies can turn out to be very different. If we feel that we are theoretically and practically (also numerically) strong enough, we can accept a centrist organization and then continue the education of its best elements within a unified organization. There is no general formula for these things.

There must be revolutionary elements in the AWP that are pushing toward us; otherwise it would be incomprehensible that the leadership has gone so far. This situation must be exploited. If we declare that we are ready for unification and the right wing then balks, or completely blocks it, we will have a very favorable point of departure vis-a-vis the left wing.

This is not to suggest a "recipe" for America: I am too far away and too little informed for this. I only wish to draw your attention to the fact that principled intransigence must be supplemented with organizational flexibility. We must not merely understand centrism theoretically and criticize it, not just put it to the test politically, we must also maneuver with it organizationally. Under certain conditions, unification is the best maneuver. We should not superstitiously regard unification as the end of the process (the fight against centrism). Unification can, at times, only create better conditions for continuing the struggle against centrism. Of course, the methods of struggle must be adapted to the framework of the unified party. Please share the contents of this letter with Shachtman and other comrades when you have the opportunity.

And now on the youth conference. There you were not nearly critical and exacting enough. I have already written a good deal about this to the IS and Comrade Held. I am enclosing copies.

How do things stand with the antiwar theses? As far as I know they have been translated into English by Sara.[31] They should be reproduced and sent to all sections for discussion. First of all, the National Committee should take a position on them. The question is highly important. The theses are now being discussed in the European sections. We need to hear from you on this in the near future, before the theses are passed in final form by the IS.

Yours,
L. Trotsky

My interrogation by the police[32]

Mid-April 1934

1. The inspectors visited me officially only in order to interrogate me as a "witness" in the business about the motorcycle, which supposedly had not been settled.

2. It was during the interrogation about the motorcycle that the district attorney from Melun told me that I had only received a residence visa for Corsica and my presence at Barbizon was irregular. I protested most categorically against this arbitrary charge, which, moreover, had nothing to do with the matter in question—the motorcycle.

By the way, it should be mentioned that it was in my letters to Mr. Parijanine, a French writer and translator of my books, that I wrote about the possibility of residence in Corsica. As far as I know, Parijanine showed this letter to Mr. Guernut, who had at that time intervened in favor of a visa. But the responsible authorities have never mentioned Corsica as a place assigned for my residence in France. The French consul general in Istanbul presented me a visa with no restrictions. The official of the Surete Generale who received me in Marseilles had me sign a paper that accorded me residence in France on the same terms as any other foreigner, at my own risk and with no restrictions.

I have never been to Corsica. I spent several months in Charente-Inferieure. I moved to Seine-et-Marne, all the while keeping the proper authorities informed. All assertions to the contrary are inventions without the slightest basis in fact.

3. The press relates the substance of my interrogation as a witness in a totally fanciful and malevolent fashion. But what astonishes me the most is that this supposed account contains statements I made (more or less accurate) and facts the inspectors observed. Without getting into the question of whether observations made by inspectors who have entered the house for the purpose of examining a witness can be divulged through the press, I will limit myself to the affirmation that I had nothing to hide. Thus the press talks about two revolvers that were on my table. This is correct. When I saw the police enter our house, I not only left my revolver where it was but I put my wife's revolver on the table, as these were the only objects that the police could have been interested in.

4. There is talk in the press about the Fourth International. This topic was not brought up at all by the inspectors who honored me with their visit. No one mentioned any of the Internationals, neither the ones that are dying nor the one

that is being born. If anyone had raised a question about this, I would undoubtedly have given him some pamphlets or articles on the Fourth International that I have published in various languages.

I have been quoted as saying: "I am an old conspirator." But this has been distorted. After repeating insistences about the "irregularities" committed by my co-worker [Klement] in connection with the business about the motorcycle, I commented that it is impossible to foresee everything and that personally I was not interested in this question. I added that as an "old conspirator," if I had had anything to hide from the French authorities, I would have perhaps paid more attention—even to the question of the motorcycle.

5. A great deal has been written about the "strange" existence of the inhabitants of the villa in Barbizon. This is correct. We don't spend our time there vacationing in the countryside or relaxing. We work very hard. Usually neither the piano nor the radio is to be heard, but rather the typewriter.

I am busy with a book about Lenin, which is supposed to be ready for publication in various countries, including France, by January 1, 1935. I need extensive documentation. My son and my co-workers bring me voluminous materials, sometimes dozens of thick volumes or copies, according to my instructions.

I should add that every day I receive letters and documents from every corner of the globe, sent spontaneously by people whom, for the most part, I do not know. Usually they concern questions on the world economic and political situation, the phenomenon of fascism, the workers' movement, etc. Unfortunately, because I am absorbed by my book, not only am I unable to reply, but I cannot even read a tenth of the documents and letters received.

It is clear that I had no interest in divulging my place of residence, thereby bringing about some complication or other that might impede my regular work. The need to guard my anonymity means that I cannot receive my voluminous correspondence at my Barbizon address. My co-workers bring it to me from Paris two or three times a week. And this was how my correspondence happened to be found on my co-worker when he was seized because the headlight on his motorcycle was out.

As for secret printing presses and other such nonsense that the least intelligent part of the press talks about, there is no point in discussing this. ■

Why I am being expelled from France[33]

April 18, 1934

The press gives an explanation from an unofficial source for the government's decree depriving me of the right to stay in France. This explanation is false, as is the statement that the press attributes to the minister of the interior.

1. It is correct that in letters addressed to private persons who were interested in my visa I had openly declared my firm intention to abstain from any political activity, not to appear on a public platform, take part in public demonstrations, write pamphlets, or be a member of a combat organization. Anyone who says I have broken the word I gave in this statement, which was made on my own initiative and never demanded by anyone, is telling a falsehood.

2. As for the French authorities, nobody has imposed

special restrictions on me. On the contrary, on my arrival in France I signed a statement announcing that I had been admitted to French territory on the same conditions as any other foreigner. I know of no law that forbids a foreigner to express his opinions in the form of books or articles. Nobody indicated to me that my writings published during my stay in France would overstep the bounds of legality.

3. The press quotes the Communist League and its paper, *La Verite*. They forgot to add that the League and *La Verite* have existed for almost five years. In about twenty other countries there are organizations and periodicals that are similar, that is, they adhere to the ideas that I also defend in my writings. The League existed before my arrival in France; it published my articles and my pamphlets, many of which concerned the political situation in France. It is only since my entry into France that I have abstained from making pronouncements in the press on questions of French politics. The articles that appeared in *La Verite* during the nine months of my stay in France were all translated by the editors, on their own initiative, from Russian or German, and dealt with foreign questions.

Such is the situation in fact; the unofficial motive for my expulsion does not stand up. The real reasons are quite different; there are two.

The collapse of French Radicalism is the first and most immediate reason. It was a Radical government in the honeymoon of power that gave me authorization [to stay in France]. There was no reason to hope that the right of asylum for a foreign revolutionary would be respected after the complete collapse of the Radicals in the face of the wave of reaction. There are other rights that are threatened, rights that more immediately affect the toiling masses of the French people themselves.

The second reason is the idea of the Fourth International. It is no accident that almost the whole bourgeois press has imputed to me an incoherent statement on the Fourth International at the time of my meeting with the inspectors from Melun. In reality, I had no opportunity to make pronouncements before the public prosecutor and the examining inspector on burning questions of the international revolutionary movement. But it is true—I have no reason to hide it; on the contrary, I have every interest in proclaiming it loudly—that I am a staunch advocate of the creation of the Fourth International on the foundation of Marx and Lenin. It is also correct that the Communist League of France, like twenty or so other organizations, is working in the same spirit.

The semiofficial report emphasizes the weakness of the League and even affirms that the circulation of *La Verite* is less than five hundred copies. Because of my retired life, I was not able to participate in the life of the League and its press. I am absolutely certain that the stated figure would have to be multiplied by twenty or thirty in order to approach the real figure. That is not much; I see no need to hide or mask the relative weakness of the groupings of the Fourth International; revolutionary politics in the long run has nothing in common with bluff. But the very fact that—despite this semiofficially exaggerated weakness and the lack of credible accusations that I can be charged with—the government has found it necessary to take exceptional measures against me shows that the idea of the Fourth International has already become a force to be reckoned with.

And justly so! What the working masses in Germany and in Austria lacked during their decisive struggles was a clear and correct line, a strong and flexible leadership, the true banner of the world revolution. The Third International, after the Second, has thoroughly compromised itself. In the service of the conservative Stalinist bureaucracy, it strives to hide, with extravagant and contradictory lies and slanders, the bankruptcy of its ideas and methods. Only the Fourth

International can regroup nationally as well as internationally the revolutionary cadres to bar the road to fascism and to guide the proletariat to the conquest of power and the socialist transformation of society.

The little episode of my expulsion falls within this political framework. I am pursued as a partisan of the Fourth International, that is, of the ideas of Marx and Lenin: this is the truth that cannot be obscured or distorted by all of the dishonest or malicious commentaries. ∎

Suggestions for a French program of action[34]

Spring 1934

The national conference [of the Communist League] should not be a gathering for receiving reports, analyzing past experience and general perspectives, but rather a body for action and combat.

It should work out a program of action made up of essential points for directing all of our propaganda, agitation, and action.

Since this document is not ready, the national conference can concern itself with general discussion on the slogans to be introduced into the program of action and with instructing the Executive Committee (perhaps with the assistance of the IS) to come up with a definitive version within ten days at most. The EC can form a somewhat larger commission by bringing in some comrades from outside of the EC to work out the program of action.

Here are some suggestions for the program itself:

The question of the "economy," "the balanced budget": This is a question of reducing wages, pensions, unemployment compensation, etc., and it is now the most burning issue. We are on the defensive here, but we must conduct the fight in a concrete and vigorous fashion.

The ruling classes complain that they cannot afford new taxes. They heap taxes on the peasants and the urban petty bourgeoisie and they want to starve the lower-ranking government employees, the disabled veterans, etc. The question is posed in this form: "Are the ruling classes going to become as poor as poor Chiappe?"[35] The ruling classes have a very good idea of the incomes, wages, and pensions of the little people they starve and crush. But the people have no idea of all the wealth and income of the ruling classes. They conceal these by invoking "business secrets," "professional secrets," etc. All of these are nothing but the secrets of the employers used to promote their exploitation. Down with the secrets of the rich! Open the books! Before consenting to, or better, before refusing new sacrifices, we want to see what the real national income is and how it is divided.

The Stavisky affair[36] showed us, in concentrated form, a tiny part of the "national economy" and its secrets. We want to know about all the Stavisky-type machinations of the ruling classes. After "unprecedented efforts," they lay before us a few of Stavisky's check stubs. The working class wants to see the bourgeoisie's whole checkbook with its own eyes. That is the essence of workers' and peasants' control. The workers should have the opportunity to familiarize themselves in depth with all the affairs of their industry. With the help of honest bank employees, the peasants should have a complete financial accounting from the banks that force them into debt and ruin them.

Whatever the plan for the reform of the country's economic life might be, the first condition is absolute clarity about the wealth of the nation and its division. The veterans, whom they are once again trying to influence with patriotic slogans, have the same interests as the workers and peasants in knowing everything about the machinery of the society which has led to crisis, confusion, and unprecedented corruption. Our slogan is: Workers' and peasants' (including veterans') control of the banks, commerce and industry.

The bourgeoisie will never consent to this willingly. If its secrets are divulged, there will be nothing left for it to do but commit suicide, like Stavisky. That is why it is financing fascist gangs. From now on, the question of the division of the national income will be settled with arms. That is the policy of the exploiters at bay.

The exploited must defend themselves. To defend even their meager wages and pensions, they have to organize and arm themselves against the gangs of reactionary capitalism.

For months, *L'Humanite* has been calling for disarming and dissolving the fascist gangs. What democratic illusions! We have just seen the parliamentary commission of inquiry apply *L'Humanite*'s slogan on "disarming." They are beginning, it is true, with the fascists, since they are the only ones armed. By doing this, they are creating a democratic cover for not allowing the proletariat to have the means to defend itself.

Our slogan is not the disarming of finance capital's gangs by finance capital's police, but rather a workers' and peasants' militia, that is, the arming of the exploited people.

They want to frighten us with the specter of civil war. If the real people arm themselves, the exploiters won't be able to launch a civil war. On the other hand, if the people are unarmed, they can be made to bow by successive bloodlettings.

Our slogan is: For a workers' and peasants' militia! Arm the people!

With the workers' and peasants' control and the militia we are still at the level of defense. We don't want to allow society to be plunged into barbarism and decomposition. But that is not enough. It is necessary to lead society out of the impasse it finds itself in, and for that it is necessary to reorganize the national economy from top to bottom by adapting it to the interests of the working people and sacrificing the privileges of the usurers and Staviskys at the top.

To reorganize the economy, a government of the working people, a workers' and peasants' government, is necessary. There is a lot of talk about strong government, and this is not an accident. The exploiters have bogged society down in the mud to such an extent that ferocious energy and real revolutionary efforts will be required to extricate it. The Jacobins gave us a fine example 140 years ago. It was the poor, the little people, the exploited, who established the government of the Mountain,[37] the strongest government France has ever known. And it was that government which saved France under the most tragic conditions. In addition, the October Revolution has given us a more recent example of what the working people can do when they take their destiny into their own hands. The first condition for establishing a strong government is for the workers to break all their political ties with the bourgeoisie. The bloc of the working class should extend a fraternal hand to the peasants and the urban petty bourgeoisie so that together they can vigorously oppose the bloc of the exploiters, which is called "the government of national reconciliation," "the national union," etc.

The government issuing directly from the working people should liberate the small peasants from the debts that are crushing them, to assure them a place in the planned economy worthy of a civilized people.

The bourgeoisie, the real expropriators of the land and of little people in general, frighten the farmers with the specter of violent expropriation by the proletariat. That is a lie! The example of Soviet Russia, an example moreover that is distorted by the bourgeois press, is not the rule. France has some great advantages: (a) its population is far more cultured than the population of czarist Russia; (b) the French proletariat can expect support from the USSR; (c) it will be able to avoid not a few of the mistakes the Russian proletariat made when it began transforming capitalist society.

What crushes the peasant, the artisan, the small businessman, is competition and taxes. By expropriating the wealth of the exploiters for the benefit of the people, the government can considerably ease the burden of taxes that falls on the peasants and the urban petty bourgeoisie. By eliminating competition through a planned economy, the workers' and peasants' government will be able to grant the small producers (peasants, artisans, businessmen) full liberty to dispose of their property and at the same time assure them of state orders at a price that will considerably raise their standard of living.

The nationalization of the banks, the large landed property holdings, the key industries, the railroads, does not mean the total bureaucratization of economic life. The state economy can create the necessary balance with the peasant and petty bourgeois economy, to aid it, raise it up, and give it free choice to transform itself. The proletariat can enter into an agreement with the peasants whereby the final transformation of agriculture will take place only with the consent of the peasants themselves. These honorable contracts between two classes can be realized and at the same time guaranteed by a workers' and peasants' government.

This is the perspective we see for workers' and peasants' control. In order to take the banks, transport, and key industries firmly in hand, the working people should begin by extending their union organizations—factory committees, bank committees, railroad committees—throughout the whole capitalist system. Workers' and peasants' control, in its first stages a defensive measure against crushing taxes and wage cuts, becomes quite naturally the preparatory stage for a planned, i.e., socialist, economy.

P.S. These are only hastily written suggestions which make no claim beyond serving as a point of departure for the discussion. The agrarian question has to be formulated in precise terms. It is necessary to try to give an overall picture of the large estates and to indicate how the land will be divided up (state farms, distribution to sharecroppers, agricultural workers' production cooperatives with state credits, etc.) It would also be well to give an overall picture of peasants' indebtedness and indicate the terms for liberating the small peasants' holdings from the mortgages that are crushing them.

For the working class, it would perhaps be well to begin by stipulating that a planned economy would allow an immediate transition to a seven-hour day, and for mining and hazardous industries to a six-hour day, and the establishment of a comprehensive system of real social insurance.

Before launching the program of action, it would be well to submit it for analysis to the members and sympathizers of the League, impressing upon them the necessity for a concerted campaign. The manifesto containing the program of action should be concise and should be widely distributed in the form of a leaflet. A special issue of *La Verite* (possibly even with an enlarged format) and a special issue of *Octobre Rouge*[38] should be devoted to this campaign. Every comrade should participate with full understanding of the great task the League is undertaking.

P.P.S. The essential thing is that everything be done "quickly and decisively": no more than ten days for working out the final text. The eleventh and twelfth days for preparatory meetings and speeches throughout France. During this time the manifesto should be at the printer's. Within two weeks, the manifesto should more or less have "covered" France. It should be presented everywhere through speeches by adult and youth members.

Those are my thoughts on the subject. ∎

Proposals for the next ICL plenum[39]

June 15, 1934

Dear Friend:

Thank you for your letter, which I found very instructive. I received it today when leaving my administration, which intends to discharge me. No matter. . . . As to the question of the [French] League, I speak of it in my criticism of the action program. I am sending you a copy. This is the most convenient form of explanation, because it requires everyone to use exact formulations and that eliminates misunderstandings and unnecessary discussions.

I am very uneasy about the situation in the League. Not from the standpoint of principled differences, but from the standpoint of its way of functioning. But it would be a big mistake to make the plenum an arena for bitter discussions concerning the League. Through discussion one can clarify ideas but not change characters and habits. Of course I am not opposed to discussion, but it must be kept to a few very precise points and be open to all the delegates. That means, in my opinion, that it is absolutely necessary to get rid of the misunderstandings in the French commission, *before the plenum*, to find common formulations for questions where there are no fundamental differences, and to counterpose exact formulations for points of difference. That is the only procedure that can avoid poisoning the atmosphere of the plenum.

As far as I know, they want to pose the question of an international conference. I have observed that the comrades and sections that give the least aid to our international organization are the most demanding in regard to an international conference. The question must fit the political reality. A conference means a few dozen delegates. How will the expenses be covered? And above all, where will the conference be held, to avoid harmful consequences as in Holland? If the Labour Party takes power in England, or in Norway, the situation can become politically more favorable for a conference. But in any case the financial question will remain. To speak of a conference today or even to try to set the date for it would just be bureaucratic lightmindedness. In illegal organizations—and that is what we are, internationally—organizational democracy is necessarily limited. The plenum, as fully attended as is possible, must take the place of a conference until there is a change in the political conditions. Those who disagree should present a practical alternative.

As for the Secretariat, I have already communicated my view—my conviction, even—to Geneva: Dubois[40] must be formally placed on the Secretariat. The plenum could agree to the following resolution:

"To strengthen the Secretariat, especially its work in the Anglo-Saxon countries, the plenum decides to include Comrade Dubois [on the Secretariat], with decisive vote."

That is a thousand times better than creating a transitional system that is subject to misinterpretation, will create a distorted situation, and will end up in a crisis. As a full member

Comrade Dubois will vote on each question and assume his responsibilities. Experience will show—I hope and desire it with my whole heart—that that is the only correct way.

I am writing nothing to you on the Greek question; I have not yet had time to read the documents, nor the documents on the Polish question. I will write to you about that next time.

I draw your attention to the draft directive on the militia. I think this document is very important, because it dots all the i's. I am sending you some notes concerning this directive.

Fraternally yours,
Crux [Leon Trotsky]

P.S. As to your article, I am returning it attached. My agreement with the substance and my disagreement with the slogan of a socialist government are explained in the other writings. ■

Our response to the French CP's new turn[41]

June 16, 1934

A new abrupt turn by the Stalinists in the policy of the united front seems to be an accomplished fact. There can be no question of a new theoretical orientation. The immediate cause of the turn is their panic before the disintegration of the CP of France. An eventual coming together of Saint-Denis[42] and the Communist League, this is what frightens the Stalinists and with good reason.

They reply to the danger by a maneuver, which in its external features corresponds to the confused but intense desires of the working masses.

Some hundreds, perhaps some thousands, of class-conscious workers will have verified the adventurism and lack of principles of the Stalinists and the correctness of our policy. But scores and hundreds of thousands will only grasp the main fact that the CP is for common action.

Not to appreciate the importance of this fact would be a serious mistake. Saint-Denis can this day lose the ground from under its feet, given the fact that its whole program reduces itself to unity in action.

We shall have to observe a skillful plot of two bureaucracies whose "unity of action" will consist of mutual assurances of each other's privileges, by means of common struggle against the real necessities of revolutionary class action.

That is why the center of gravity must be shifted from the abstract formula of the united front to the real content of the struggle. This is the tendency of the two documents: the article of Comrade Feroci (I omit the question of the socialist government, which has been dealt with by me elsewhere) and the directives concerning the militia. This poses the question of the struggle very practically.

If the [French] program of action is already drawn up, above all if the practical tasks of the struggle are made evident, this program can and must become the important instrument for thwarting the plot of the two bureaucracies. But this instrument cannot work by itself. It is necessary to have bases, connections, channels of influence. In the event of the creation of a mutual benefit society by Cachin[43] and Blum, the Committees of Vigilance[44] will be swept away at one stroke, and this will be precisely the first aim of the mutual benefit society. In order not to be ousted from the movement, the League must be present not only outside the mutual benefit society but also and above all within its very cadres.

Practically, today this means within the Socialist Party. Now what is the League's activity within the bosom of the Socialist Party? It appears that it is at a minimum, which can mean that the policy carried out in that respect was false. Assiduous and systematic work inside, the creation of a fraction of sympathizers, a reasonable adaptation to the milieu, regrouping, education seem to have been replaced by some articles in *La Verite* and by rather vague talk about joint actions.

There is no other path if we are not to remain isolated. The most correct ideas, if one does not know how to apply them, adapt them, and make them enter people's minds, must remain false and sterile. It is necessary to have a new orientation toward the Socialist Party. It is necessary to penetrate it, to give it ten times the forces that has been done till now. This is the only possibility for gaining influence in the CP and even in Saint-Denis. ■

Concentrate inside the Socialist Party[45]

June 1934

Dear Comrade:

The enclosed letter was written several days ago on the boat during the crossing from Marseilles to Algeria. At that time, the agreement between the Stalinists and Blum appeared to have been concluded. But I have just now received the latest issues of *L'Humanite* and *Le Populaire,* which inform me that the negotiations have been broken off. Nevertheless, I consider it necessary to send you this letter, for the various episodic relations between the Stalinist and reformist leaders *do not change* the fundamental line put forward in my letter. Even Blum and Cachin refer to a "breakdown" of negotiations in the sense of a *temporary* interruption: they feel the pressure from below and they are afraid of the masses. In any case, the united front between the local organizations will advance under the pressure of events, and the League cannot and must not stand aside. The break-off of the talks gives the League a certain *respite* to prepare its tactical turn. But this respite should be measured in weeks, not months. The rhythm of events is now extraordinarily accelerated in comparison with the preceding period: we must not forget that, in any case. How to make use of this respite? *Concentrate our main forces inside the Socialist Party,* and establish therein a firm nucleus and a fraction of sympathizers. *In the event of a new favorable opportunity this fraction can address itself to the League with an open appeal: to enter the Socialist Party for a common struggle on behalf of a revolutionary Marxist policy.*

So, I repeat, the episodic breakdown in negotiations does not at all change the essence of this line, which is developed in the enclosed letter (needless to say, this letter is in no way meant for publication).

I do not have your new address at hand, and I am forced to send this letter from Marseilles, where our boat has just arrived again, by the intermediary of one of our friends.

I hope to receive your reply quickly, as time is pressing.

Yours,
Crux [Leon Trotsky]

P.S. I am also sending you a small article for *La Verite.* ■

The state of the League and its tasks[46]
A contribution to the discussion
June 29, 1934

1. The year 1934 has been marked by a daily aggravation of the world economic crisis. Instead of forming a horizontal line, the graph for the first six months shows a decline (not very pronounced but nevertheless a decline) toward the lowest point of the crisis. The sharpness of interimperialist contradictions forecasts the imminence of a world conflagration.

As for France, all the statistics show that the French economy is becoming increasingly affected. Through its policy of "collective security" and its speedup in arms production, French imperialism is openly making its preparations for the coming war. The increasingly acute character of the economic crisis in France and the corresponding struggle of the social layers to find a way out of this situation—each at the expense of the other—determine the tempo and ferocity of the struggle and the principal features of the present deep political crisis in France. *This crisis no longer shares any of the aspects of the previous crises since 1920.* The period of solutions through parliamentary debate is finished. The February days—the violent offensive of the reactionary vanguard and the furious and oft-repeated response of the proletarian vanguard—have opened up the arena of decisive revolutionary struggles in this crisis.

There can be no question of prolonged stability for the present transitory Bonapartist government, which is only the first form of Bonapartism to follow the February events.

A return to the "coalition" type of government could come about only as the result of an intensification of mass pressure, which would either pass beyond this form of government or recede as the result of a reactionary victory won, as always, on the extraparliamentary field. Passage to another form of Bonapartist government will have to be based on violent repression of the proletariat.

The reactionary forces, even though they advanced their position through their February offensive, have not yet succeeded in making themselves masters of the decisive layers of the nation. Their rise seems in fact to have been checked among the poor peasantry, the petty bourgeoisie, and the working masses—social layers for which the "government of national reconciliation" has done nothing but impose heavy taxes. The vast propaganda offensive of the reactionary vanguard is notable more for its extent than for its results. The furious replies of the organized working masses found an echo among the intermediary social strata, providing a point of support for the "left" in its convulsive attempts at resistance under the fierce attack of the right during the period of reconciliation (Cudenet, the measures taken by Doumergue,[47] the threats of Daladier).

The working masses, hard hit by the government of reconciliation, have not been able to resist effectively on the economic field because of the state of their organizations. But on the political plane their ferment is clear. The battle tends to extend its scope at a rapid pace. We have entered a period of intense prerevolutionary struggle in which regroupments decisive for a whole period will take place among the masses.

The reaction of the organized masses and those layers of society influenced by them reflects a deep-seated mood among the working masses. A determination to unify their efforts has become manifest in the character of their street demonstrations as well as in the debates in their trade unions.

The latest CGT conventions, involving categories of workers considered to be conservative—postal employees, government employees, railroad workers—have expressed a growth in the desire for united action. The bureaucratic leaderships have been forced to take this into account: the 180-degree turn of the SFIO in 1934 as compared to its positions of 1933; the speeches of Jouhaux;[48] the radical turn of the Communist Party following grave threats of split and disintegration (Saint-Denis, the withdrawal of the boatmen and naval dock workers from the CGTU). The lesson of Germany has hit home, although belatedly. *The bureaucracies are seeking a foothold among the masses, the masses are seeking a solution in action.* This convergence of the maneuvers made by the apparatuses will have *the effect of pushing forward the masses who are already seething.* The political consciousness of important sections of militants will rapidly become transformed in the course of action, the conservative resistance of the bureaucracies will be weakened by action, and so will their defensive arsenal. History is opening up its book; little attention will be paid to the catechisms of the bureaucracies.

All this creates an entirely new situation for our vanguard, one which demands a serious examination of our tasks.

2. Our situation. The very fact of our existence on an international scale, our political homogeneity, the training of our cadres, such as they are, constitutes a factor which may become decisive for the revolutionary movement. Politically our ideas are victorious at the present moment. But the disproportion between the potential strength of our politics and our influence as an organization reappears with even greater force. This disproportion is in large part a product of the situation which created us. Our struggle was and remains "against the stream," but this is a stream that exploits all possibilities of claiming credit for the October conquests. While holding our ground, we have progressed little by little

in the midst of a terrible upheaval.

Our League has made important progress in extending its political influence; however in the field of organizational consolidation—when measured by the favorable possibilities created for it by our new orientation and by the development of the political situation—the League has been marking time for more than a year. The League has rooted our ideas in every part of France and its colonies. There are no workers' districts where we do not have a "receptive audience." But a receptive audience—that does not mean "groups" working systematically, according to a plan and with a coherent centralized direction, growing little by little through systematic recruitment. Outside the Parisian district even an *attempt* at this has hardly been made. The leading cadres of our organization are weak, new people have not yet come to us, a new process of selection is now taking place. But our ability to improve the old cadres remains limited because of the lack of a mass base favorable to their development.

The League has not become a revolutionary pole of attraction, a force to be reckoned with. The desire to gain a place in the present struggle in France has been the driving force behind all our activity during the whole past period. This was a step forward, but our organic weakness arose as an obstacle at each stage, as did our social composition. The united front with the SFIO (alliance committee, Pere-Lachaise[49]) appeared on these occasions and others as another caricature of the united front, making us an appendage of Amsterdam, a united front in which the SFIO pulled us out of their sleeves whenever it suited their interests. The attempt to win over the Saint-Denis militants resembled a patient and luckless courtship more than a political struggle. *La Verite* remains too caught up in the wake of other formations to tend to its own affairs. (I limit myself to assertions here, but I am ready in each case to amplify, if necessary.)

In the revolutionary struggles that are beginning, our

frail cruiser will throw itself into battle—but in the wake of large political formations, which are starting to put their ranks in battle order through the united front. The maneuver itself absorbs the entire attention of the crew, whose eyes are fixed anxiously on the horizon, and the tougher the struggle becomes the more the respective general staffs will be able to isolate our frail ship, even to sink it. *That is the real danger in the present situation:* we seem to be coming to these struggles *from the outside;* we have no corresponding organized forces in the mass organizations, particularly in the trade unions; our permanent ties with the working class are almost nil.

Nowhere in the CGTU is there a solid fraction; only twelve members at the most hold responsible posts in it.

There is no fraction in the CGT.

There is no nationally coordinated fraction in the SFIO although we have members active in it.

In general, there are no fractions at all in the mass organizations; along with this goes an underestimation of this work and the necessary attention to be given to isolated militants active in the mass organizations and to their observations. (All this on a national scale, in the case of the adult organization.)

Our direct agitation among the masses is in its initial probing stage; each militant feeling his way in this work realizes that we have not yet hit on the proper "tone." Often our agitation remains superficial because our social composition cuts us off from the workers of the locality after a meeting is finished. How many courageous efforts have been made! Aren't the participants astonished at the feeble response to these efforts? In the sum total causes of this disproportion, the mistakes, even the most serious ones, can be considered only a small factor. It is possible to coordinate our efforts better, to establish serious rules in our organizational relationships, to modify the character of the paper, to change this or that aspect, *but all this would continue within the limits of our original handicap.* To be sure, certain mistakes can be avoided, efforts can be made, improvements can be achieved—but at what pace and in what proportion to this sea that rises up and engulfs us?

What sort of reception will our little organization get when all eyes are fixed on the struggle, on the upheavals and the blocs of the old established organizations? What chance will it have now that the lever of the united front has been wrested from its hands? The broad layers of the population will not judge us by the back issues of our ever-so-valiant *Verite.* Who can dare assert that in this new situation we can become the decisive pole of attraction for these struggles *without a radical change of tactics?* Hurled from outside the battle, the slogan of a new party resembles a medication more than a decisive weapon. It runs the risk of attracting more intellectuals than fighters. The [German] Spartacus League was crushed because it had insufficient ties with the masses. What are we compared to Spartacus?

3. *The problem of the new party is more urgently posed than ever before.* In this whole period of struggles of a revolutionary character, in which all the problems of revolutionary strategy and of the conquest of power (organs of power, etc.) have to be solved, the vanguard party is the indispensable weapon for the victory of the proletariat. The bureaucratic zigzags of the Stalinist party have nothing in common with the tactics of such a vanguard party. Release the brake of "socialism in one country" today and who can tell what will happen tomorrow? The totally independent character of the proletarian party has nothing in common with the Stalinist formation, which is held in chains by the conservative interests of the Soviet bureaucracy.

The method by which cadres decide on a proposed course of action, through Marxist analysis, *has nothing in common with the CP's forced acceptance of the latest turn.* Revolutionary workers tied down to a miserable centrist bureaucracy by their attachment to the Russian Revolution—this is not the party of the revolution. *That party has yet to be created. Not one whit of our ten years of criticism, of our explanation of the defeats that have been suffered, or of their meaning and the conclusions that they imply needs to be softened or rejected.* Turns and zigzags of the centrist apparatus may contain elements that are progressive or regressive, depending on the case at hand; but the Comintern is no longer the guide of the proletariat. Today, just as yesterday, in the face of the rising tide of revolution and the threat of world war, the first point in our program remains: *build the revolutionary party, construct the Fourth International!*

Nor is there anything to retract in our analysis of the Second International and of the SFIO's role in the relationship of classes. What is of interest to us in the differences between this reformist party and the centrist Stalinist party is:

a. The fact that the bankruptcy of the Comintern, instead of putting an end to the Social Democracy, has permitted it to grow and regroup among sections of workers who—under the impact of events in Germany, Austria, and France—are becoming oriented toward revolution and will not hesitate to enter into battle against their own bureaucracy.

b. The fact that the [SFIO's] internal regime, in spite of the bureaucracy's power, has not yet straitjacketed the rank and file and permits a certain freedom of movement among sections of the workers.

In the Stalinist party the rank and file is dependent on the bureaucracy; but in the SFIO, up to now, the ranks have been relatively independent of the bureaucracy. This form of internal regime was the original form of the democratic party in the democratic state and will suffer the consequences of the state crisis; the present form is favorable for the rank and file in this period of regroupment, so the bureaucracy may be in for a fight.

As revolutionary parties, the SFIO and the CP are equally bankrupt. But in this period of upheavals and readjustments it is our task to adjust our tactics according to both our knowledge of the environment and our opportunities for creating the new revolutionary party. We must therefore observe that the internal political life of the Stalinist party is nil and that the possibility of developing a tendency in its midst must be excluded (the apparatus has just undertaken a 180-degree turn in the orientation of the work of the party members and Monmousseau[50] is surprised that no one is surprised). The Socialist Party, on the other hand, has preserved throughout this whole period a relatively intense life, all proportions considered. In this respect, the present period is comparable to that which preceded the [1920] Tours congress.

All these elements are important facts to be considered in connection with the problem of the "new party."

4. What is the solution? Shall we continue along the path we have followed—though improving our methods? My answer to that is already given in section 2. No matter what path we choose, *it will be necessary to rearm our organization in all of its internal life, in all of its organizational procedures. That is an urgent task*. It means tempering our arms anew, but it does not mean making the same use of them as before. It is apparent that with the present state of our forces and maintaining our present positions we would not be able to grow with sufficient rapidity to become a decisive pole of attraction. On the contrary, we would be kept out of the center of the struggles, to the detriment of their outcome. To reserve the greater part of our forces for fractional work within a mass organization would be to acknowledge the scanty returns we have received from our independent work. But given our numerical weakness, it would also mean not putting adequate forces in any one area. For example, the militants of our League, scattered here and

there in the SFIO, would see their effectiveness decreased by the clandestine character of the entry. This fractional work in the SFIO, which has been neglected for more than a year, cannot suffice now even if it is improved.

It is necessary to take a decisive step, to bring ourselves closer to a group of workers that is evolving toward revolutionary ideas, to become its catalyst, thereby increasing our opportunities.

Without renouncing any of our positions and without dissolving ourselves, it is necessary to carry the fight into the very midst of a group that is in the process of evolving. We have outlined our special difficulties and weaknesses above, *but we must not underestimate the value of our propagandist nuclei and their abilities.* It is enough to put them in the right place in order to transform their slow advances into decisive leaps forward.

Where? Access to the Communist Party is cut off to us because of its internal regime. And a capitulation is totally out of the question.

There remains the SFIO. Its internal situation permits the possibility of our entering it under our own banner. The environment suits the aims we have set for ourselves. What is necessary now is to act in such a manner that our declaration will not in any way strengthen the leading bourgeois wing, *but rather will support the progressive proletarian wing;* that its text and its distribution will allow us to hold our heads high in case of acceptance as well as in case of dilatory maneuvers or rejection. There is no question of dissolving ourselves. *We enter as the Bolshevik-Leninist faction, our organizational ties remain the same, our press continues to exist just as do* Bataille Socialiste *and others.*[51]

There are two things necessary for the success of this step, that can, within a short period of time, completely transform the whole political constellation in the labor movement: organizational cohesion (through the steadfastness of each member) and promptness of implementation. To drag out such decisions means to lose the opportune moment for their implementation, that is, to put ourselves at a disadvantage.

Further on we shall examine some suggestions concerning the means of implementation. The organization must take an inventory of its forces and understand that in the present situation the means of increasing them tenfold lie not in sticking to routine but in making a courageous effort to win to revolutionary ideas the thousands of workers whom the degeneration of the Comintern prevented from taking the path of Bolshevism.

Before proposing implementation I must emphasize that this whole orientation is directly dependent upon the political characterization of the present crisis and of the relationship of forces in the proletarian movement.

It would be useful to draw the membership's attention to the necessity that our debates on this question maintain the character of a serious discussion carried on before the whole labor movement. Any empty polemicizing could seriously hamper our ability to achieve the aims we have set for ourselves.

How are we to begin the orientation?

a. Put this orientation on the agenda of the leading bodies—(1) Political Bureau, (2) Central Committee, (3) regional committees—and draft a resolution on it.

b. Immediately publish an internal bulletin containing the resolution drafted probably by the Central Committee, send it out to the groups, assign a Central Committee reporter to each of them, and distribute the bulletin in time to have an adequate discussion.

c. Assign a comrade for "preparation" in the press (discussion article presenting the orientation) to convince our circle of sympathizers.

d. Assign a comrade to meet with Georget and Danno for the purpose of probing into the possibilities of one of the [SFIO] left-wing factions (Just's or another) issuing an appeal on our behalf.[52]

e. Prepare a draft declaration to the SFIO, to be presented by a delegation. Publicize the text and the reply.

f. Prepare a special number of *La Verite* with the text of the declaration to the SFIO and of the program of action that is to serve as the basis of our propaganda.

g. Don't neglect the "youth" aspect of the problem. On point a, it is necessary to convince our national youth committee at the same time as the Central Committee and to seriously consider with them the "youth" aspect of the problem—perhaps the appeal (d.) can be issued by the [Seine] Federation of Young Socialists. In any case, this attitude may denote a slowing down (for the immediate period) of the drive toward a split in the Young Socialists.[53]

h. Call a Central Committee meeting for the purpose of submitting our declaration to the National Committee of the SFIO on July 15. ■

The Catalan conflict and the tasks of the proletariat[54]

Summer 1934

1. Evaluation of the Catalan conflict and the possibilities flowing from it must take as its point of departure the fact that Catalonia unquestionably represents today the strongest position of the defense forces led against the Spanish reac-

tion and against the fascist danger.⁵⁵ Should this position be lost, the reaction would gain a decisive victory and for a long time to come. With a correct policy the proletarian vanguard would utilize the strong defensive position as the starting point for a new offensive of the Spanish revolution. Such should be our perspective.

2. This development is not possible unless the Catalan proletariat succeeds in taking the leadership of the defensive struggle against the reactionary central government at Madrid. But this is not possible if the Catalan proletariat promises to support this struggle only in the event that it is initiated [by other forces]. [The policy of the proletariat must not be dependent on] either the intransigence of the Madrid government or the regressiveness of the Catalan petty bourgeoisie (Maurin's policy of tail-ending [behind the petty bourgeoisie] is pursued by our comrades in the Catalan Workers Alliance).⁵⁶ [It can be successful] only if it places itself at the head of the defense movement, if it outlines the perspectives, raises bolder slogans, and begins leading the struggle not only in words but in action.

3. A victorious resistance is conceivable if it not only mobilizes all the mass forces (all the prerequisites now exist) but pushes forward toward the offensive. That is why it is of decisive importance that the proletarian vanguard should explain from now on to the masses of workers and peasants in the rest of Spain that the victory or defeat of the Catalan resistance will also decide their victory or defeat. The mobilization of these allies throughout Spain must be completed now and not at the moment when a reactionary offensive by Madrid shall have become a fact (this is the position of our comrades and of the majority of the Workers Alliance).

4. Catalonia can remain the axis of the Spanish revolution. Winning the leadership in Catalonia must be the basis of our policy in Spain. The policy of our comrades makes this completely impossible. This policy must be changed speedily

if we do not want a decisive situation to end, because of us, in a new defeat of the Spanish revolution which would be decisive for a long time to come. It should not be concealed that the policy of our comrades in this question has strongly injured the prestige not only of our own organization and of the Workers Alliance but of the proletariat itself and cannot be repaired except by a radical turn based on a real understanding of the facts. The position of our comrades and of those in the Workers Alliance cannot be understood by the nonproletarian working masses except in the following way: "The proletariat agrees through the voice of its organizations to participate if others begin [the struggle]; but in return it demands from the petty-bourgeois Esquerra its own price (the terms imposed by the Workers Alliance),[57] ignoring completely the particular interests of the peasantry and the petty-bourgeois masses, and will seek as soon as the possibility offers itself to lead the struggle in the direction of its own class aims—the dictatorship of the proletariat." Instead of appearing as the leader of all the oppressed strata of the nation, as the leader of the national liberation movement, the proletariat here appears only as a partner of the other classes; indeed a very selfish partner, to whom it is necessary to give or to promise [concessions] because and for as long a time as it shall be needed. The Catalan petty bourgeoisie, the big bourgeoisie, and the reaction, basing itself on the bankruptcy of this petty bourgeoisie, could ask for nothing better than to have the proletariat in such a position.

5. Our comrades must base their turn above all on this: They must agitate (through their own organizations and through the Workers Alliance) for the proclamation of the independent republic of Catalonia and must demand, in order to guarantee it, the immediate arming of the whole people. They should not wait for the government to arm them but begin immediately to form workers' militias which then should not only demand better equipment from the gov-

ernment but must obtain it by disarming the reactionaries and the fascists. The proletariat must prove to the Catalan masses that it has a sincere interest in the defense of Catalan independence. Here will lie the decisive path toward the conquest of the leadership in the struggle of all the strata, prepared for the defense of the city and the country. The arming of the people must become the center of our agitation in coming weeks around the slogans of: No stoppage of wages: the government and the employers must bear the cost of equipment and supplies. The existing military forces must be enrolled as instructors in the formation of the militia. The officers shall be elected by the members of the militia. The base of the militia is the factory. The workers in large industries, the railroads, etc., and all the public utilities shall automatically become part of the militia. Most of the people shall be asked to join up. Every regiment elects its committee which for its part sends a representative to the central committee of all the divisions of the Catalan militia. The central committee (i.e., the central soviet) functions as the political state, but first and foremost as the controlling body and later as the central authority for supplying and equipping the forces. In achieving this task, it will have to become [transformed] from a body alongside of the government into, properly speaking, the government itself. This is the form and concrete development of soviets in the present situation in Catalonia.

6. Because the extreme divisions among the Catalan proletariat do not allow it to exercise its hegemony in Catalonia, it cannot alone and by itself proclaim the independence of Catalonia. But it can and it must appeal for independence with all its strength and demand it of the petty-bourgeois Esquerra government. It must make up for its tardiness by the immediate holding of new elections. "We need a government which represents and leads the real will to struggle of the popular masses." The regimental committees of the

militia must become the principal means for the preparation and realization of these elections. In other words, to the extent that the two phases of the problem—the proclamation of independence and the arming of the people—can be separated from each other, it is the latter by means of which it is necessary to achieve the former.

7. The proletariat must not only place in the foreground the democratic demands (freedom of the press, a state which is not costly, levelling of the salaries of functionaries, a democratic economy, more indirect taxes, graduated direct taxation of the propertied classes to finance the resistance, etc.)—[raising these] not only for itself along with its own class demands—[but it also must] put them forward with all the specific demands of the peasants and of the petty-bourgeois masses.

Information is lacking on the details of the agrarian question, but above all the proletariat should on its own initiative arm the masses with these slogans as demands to be fought for. But it must not pose these demands as conditions for its readiness to participate in the struggle.[58] ∎

Alternatives for the Young Socialists[59]

July 12, 1934

Dear Comrade Craipeau:

Since my last letter to you I have presented my view in a letter addressed to the leadership, but I feel the need to supplement what I wrote to you. The foremost question is the JS. The perspective you set out is a very tempting one, but I am afraid that it may be somewhat too optimistic and that you may be making the same kind of error in judgment as your failure to recognize the necessity to carry out a bold turn.

You say: "We have 150 members, the JS in Paris 950. They are in a struggle against their leadership. All they need to give them a new leadership is us. We will have 1,000 Bolshevik-Leninists." Are you sure of that? The youth are gravitating toward our ideas. A portion, I imagine, have decided to follow us to the end. But the majority, faced with the necessity to make a definitive and irrevocable choice between us and the SFIO will decide against us so as not to be separated from the mass of workers. And at that moment you will lose all access to the Young Socialists.

Don't forget the strength of the apparatus. It follows closely what is happening among the youth and it has in hand an instrument of imposing strength, the united front with the Stalinists. Paul Faure[60] will tell the youth, if he has not already done so: "You must choose between the small group of Leninists, who simply proclaim the idea of the united front, and the real united front represented by the SFIO and the CP."

Keep in mind the experience with the members of the PUP. That was a small rehearsal of what will happen again with the Socialists. We were likewise almost on the eve of a fusion. But there was the pressure of the apparatus, which counterposed proletarian unity (of the SFIO, the CP, and the PUP) to the small sect of the Leninists, and as a result your whole perspective collapsed. It is correct that the PUP's youth group also collapsed; but the JS, with its present ideology, may well collapse too in contact with the Stalinists, and without any gain for the revolution.

In any case, you will have perhaps about fifty of this

thousand, more or less. And it is precisely that fifty, ready to follow us, which is inclined to oppose our entry into the SP. But the 900 would be very happy if you were not to force them right now to choose between correct ideas that they do not understand sufficiently and the "united front," with its base among the masses. If you enter the JS you will create for yourselves the possibility not only of winning the thousand persons in Paris, but of spreading your influence throughout the whole of France. Unless that happens, the bureaucracy will bring about an *abortion*.

Naturally the fifty (I take this number hypothetically) who are loyal to us are very precious to us, but since they have already understood our basic ideas they will be quite capable of understanding as well the necessity of a broad roundabout action in support of those same ideas while the others, the 900, are still to be won.

What is the meaning of the almost general aversion to the proposal of the comrades of Bes.? That hatred of reformism, social patriotism, and the Second International is deeply rooted in our own ranks, despite the loathing that the Stalinists' policy so rightly inspires in us. But without that unyielding hostility toward reformism, the Bes. proposal would in no way be possible, because what is involved is a maneuver (in the good, not the bad, sense of the word) that is completely unique, dictated by exceptional circumstances and involving many risks for the organization that undertakes it. But passive hostility to reformism is not enough. One must know how to strike blows against it and circumstances permit such blows to be struck only from within, by both saving the bulk of the party from decomposition and winning it to the revolution.

The course of events—don't forget this, I beg of you—does not leave us very much time, perhaps only a few months more. The situation can be saved only through a sharp and vigorous reorientation of the proletarian vanguard. If that perspective is achieved, we will be borne aloft by the radicalization of the Socialist workers, and within a few months we will reap the fruit of the work of the previous years. If on the contrary the French proletariat is doomed to catastrophe (which I choose not to believe), the total decomposition of its two great parties is inevitable, but the most courageous nucleus of the SFIO will remain with us in illegality if we enter its ranks today.

We must know how to identify our immediate tasks not from the standpoint of some ready-made formulas or of traditional and essentially justified sentiments, but from the standpoint of the whole situation, which is unprecedented and which imposes corresponding decisions on us.

Here are my conclusions. We have launched the action program. It summarizes a long propagandist period. We must now know how to draw the balance sheet of the results of this important action; but not a vague balance sheet, not to speak of a fictitious one, as has been done often enough, but a serious and conscientious balance sheet that talks in facts and figures. One month, beginning with the opening of the discussion, should generally suffice for that.

During this same time, that is, the two or three weeks that remain, you should evaluate more objectively your relations with the JS and the dynamics of those relations, and from these two experiences you must draw the necessary conclusion. Above all, do not lose time; there is not much left.

With best greetings,
Vidal [Leon Trotsky]

P.S. I would like to add some further thoughts to these conclusions, on the slogan for a new party, on the one hand, and on organic unity (fusion between the SFIO and the CP),[61] on the other. To be understood by the masses we should pose the question in the following way: "We are not opponents of organic unity either, but on condition that it is preceded by a clarification on both sides. The Bolsheviks, in analogous situations, had a recognized formula: first demarcation, then unification." In this framework our entry into the SFIO would be aimed at accelerating the preliminary demarcation in order to prepare the unification of the proletarian vanguard.

I ask you to share the contents of this letter with the comrades of the leadership who express the desire to be acquainted with it. ■

Cross the Rubicon[62]

July 16, 1934

Dear Friend:

Following our last conversation, I would like to clarify several points in writing and to add some supplementary arguments.

Some people say: first we were a faction of the Third International; then we were an independent organization (the Fourth International); after that we had connections with the centrists (of the Second and the Two-and-a-Half Internationals); and now we are being urged to rejoin the Second International. Presenting the facts in this fashion does indeed paint a bizarre picture. But using the same method (or using no method at all) one could state: Lenin belonged to the Second International; he broke with it at Zimmerwald and at Kienthal; he formed an alliance with elements of the Two-and-a-Half and even of the Second Internationals. On the eve of the February revolution he was already calling for a split with them, although at the same time he was disturbed with the slow pace of development of the Third International. After the October Revolution he advised the British Communists to enter the Labour Party, etc. . . . These "contradictions" are only different ways of applying the same ideas in different circumstances.

I believe that the consistency and continuity of our program are unquestionable. Events have vindicated us time and again and continue to do so. If our program obliges us to maneuver energetically in a constantly changing environment, among unparalleled difficulties, that is not our fault. We do not choose the conditions under which we must function any more than we choose our own parents.

The debates as well as the most recent decisions of the Socialist National Committee meeting reveal how intense the mass pressure for unity is. The turn will either include us or hurl us into oblivion. However, there are two ways in which it could include us: either bound hand and foot like captives or as a group that knows how to manage its affairs consciously and skillfully in the swirl of events. Woe to us if we are too late! It would give us a tremendous advantage if we could declare our adherence today, the day after the National Committee meeting. That is not possible. But six weeks! Six weeks are worth more than six years would be in another period! It is necessary to make an immediate decision—the situation is absolutely clear and urgent.

It is necessary to cross the Rubicon in order to conquer an empire! ■

The Stalinists and organic unity[63]

July 19, 1934

Dear Comrades:

After the National Committee meeting of the SFIO, the situation and, at the same time, the course to follow have become so clear and so obvious that you have to deliberately close your eyes not to see them.

The representatives of the CAP [Permanent Administrative Committee of the SFIO] and the Central Committee [of the CP] have already had a preliminary discussion on the possibility of organic unity. Thorez[64] has declared that he too considers unity in action as a stage leading toward organic unity. This conversation was stenographically recorded. Severac[65] gave the stenographic report to the National Committee to read. (We must at all costs get a copy of the text.)

This fact gives us an idea of the extent of the historic *retreat* carried out especially on the level of the party. Let's consider it carefully. The necessity of breaking with the Social Democratic parties was already proclaimed in 1914. This break was effected in France in 1921. The years of party purges followed, and today, in 1934, the heads of the Communist Party proclaim openly that their goal is organic unity with the Social Democratic party. What a formidable retreat!

We are not the ones who either wanted it or created it. It is a fact presented by the situation, especially by the influence of the Stalinist bureaucracy. But it is also a fact that those who try to reject or underestimate this basic fact will inevitably break their necks. But the retreat has not run its full course. It is not enough that the CP leadership sees itself compelled—no matter what its ulterior motives—to broach the perspective of organic unity with the Social Democracy, after thirteen years of independent existence and twenty-nine years after proclaiming that it was impossible to work together in the same party with the Social Democrats.

Things could be better, and things could also be worse. We Marxists are obliged to recognize that for the moment fusion of the two parties would constitute an *advance*, not with respect to Lenin's slogans of 1914, nor with respect to the congress at Tours, but with respect to the present situation, such as it is. The fusion of the two parties would mean the opportunity to begin again. Therein lies everything. The workers' movement has been thrust into a historic impasse. It is the consciousness of the impasse that has pushed the Stalinists into "capitulationist" schemes, and it is the existence of this impasse that makes a progressive fact out of this "capitulation." The fusion of the two parties would unavoidably open the path to discussion, analysis, study, the struggle of factions on a grand scale, and at the same time to the crystallization of a new revolutionary party, a section of the Fourth International.

The historic retreat—I repeat for emphasis—consists not only of the fact that the Stalinist bureaucracy is forced to adapt to the exigencies of the working class by fraternization with the Social Democrats, but also of the fact that this fraternization—which is trite, sentimental, without content—represents a tremendous step forward compared to the absolute impasse of yesterday. To see this in its proper light, we have to understand the extraordinary dialectic inherent in the development of everything that has occurred during the last twenty years in the French workers' movement. Without this, we are condemned to become slaves of our own subjectivism or of proud but empty formulas. Faced with the situation I have briefly characterized above, anyone who says "I never will belong to the Social Democracy! Capitulation! Treason! etc.," is nothing but a sentimental wretch who perhaps knows some greenhouse Marxist formulas, but who is frightened by living trees, and especially by a forest.

If objective analysis tells us—and let anyone try to deny it!—that the fusion of the two parties, such as they are, would constitute at this time a big step forward, how can anyone claim for the League the right to remain isolated, standing apart from this great new perspective?

I do not mean to say that the fusion of the two parties is assured in advance. No, there are too many factors involved for us to be able to mathematically predict the result. The Stalinist bureaucracy, which is today in a panic, may later become cocksure again and try to provoke an abortive split in the SFIO. Doriot[66] may rejoin the latter, new sections may go from the CP to the SP, etc., but all these possible episodes change nothing in our characterization of the current situation in the workers' movement and its urgent requirements.

If the fusion doesn't take place, if the Stalinists try to disrupt the SP with their customary methods (zigzags, demagogy, even individual bribery), only *our* ideas and *our* methods can inoculate the new revolutionaries of the SP with the power to resist complete disintegration. The ILP would be a different thing today if our British section had entered it a year ago to defend within it the policy we had developed in a series of articles and letters. It is also the answer to the possible objection: "Well, let's wait till unity has been established between the two big parties, and then we will present ourselves with our calling card." That would mean that instead of anticipating, acting, and preparing, we would be waiting around for the moment when we would be practically wiped out by the actions of others.

Comrades, our responsibility before the French proletariat and before international Marxism is enormous. We must look reality in the face, and shake off the prejudices of a small closed circle.

There is no other course but this is a sure one.

V. [Leon Trotsky]

Supplementary arguments and suggestions for articles[67]

July 21, 1934

If the Communist Party were to open its doors to our comrades today, would the irreconcilable comrades agree to enter? Yes or no? It would do them too great an injustice to presume that they would refuse to join. From this it follows that some of our comrades see a fundamental difference between the Communist Party and the Socialist Party. They disregard our analysis, which has demonstrated that we are faced with two kinds of centrism: one evolving to the left and another stagnating or even orienting toward the right.

It is precisely at the present moment that events are furnishing a striking confirmation of this analysis. Abandoning criticism altogether, the Stalinist leadership declares that its objective is organic unity. By that in itself they prove that there is no *fundamental* difference between the CP and the SP. The comrades who are prepared to join the CP but threaten to split if we should join the SP reveal not only that they are still prisoners of their own past and of traditional terminology, but also that they do not recognize the real evolution of the two parties and their current condition.

All members of the League would be prepared to join with the Saint-Denis organization in principle. On the other hand, those comrades who have dealt with that organization are unanimous in recognizing the extremely low level of ideological development of its membership. Doriot shows by his actions that he is no closer to Marxism than Marceau Pivert or even Zyromsky.[68] Only the Saint-Denis organization is much more conservative and even more permeated with paralyzing prejudices than, for example, the Socialist Party in the Paris area. What arguments can be made for the platonic defense of defrocked Stalinists like Doriot, on the one hand, and on the other this aversion to a Socialist organization that is rapidly developing in a revolutionary direction?

Some comrades are threatening us with a split. What will they do then? It is still not possible to enter the CP without repudiating our program, and the correctness of that program is at present clearer than ever. But by refusing to enter the SP *in principle,* the irreconcilables, the intransigents, will have to repudiate their principles in order in the last analysis to fuse with the Socialists all the same. Where is the logic of that?

Each new day brings fresh confirmation that the politics of the so-called united front, with its fanfare, its publicity, and its hollowness, serves no purpose except to conceal from the working class the real dangers, the real tasks at hand, and the real means for accomplishing them. It is more necessary than ever to pose the concrete questions of the struggle and its tactics.

It is necessary to ask the Socialists and Stalinists whether they continue to hope that Doumergue, Sarraut and Tardieu[69] will disarm the fascists and disperse their gangs. Yes or no? And if they do not cling to that idiotic hope, what do they plan to use against the fascists, who are certain to make speedy progress over the summer? The question of the workers' militia must be posed in the sharpest, most aggressive, most precise way. It is necessary to put out leaflets with plans for organizing the workers' militia. It is necessary to publish H.'s article on the July 8 demonstration in *La Verite* and to initiate an important new column in the paper to deal with these questions. At the same time, in every issue, it is necessary to make use of short excerpts from our program of action as political slogans.

Every section [of the International] must be kept fully informed about all the discussions that are taking place in the French League. The comrades who say that entry into the SP is part of an international policy that signals the liquidation of our international organization are badly mistaken. Joining the SP—like the ILP in Britain—is determined by a particular national situation. It is not a principle but an opportunity. However, if we let it pass, we take the risk of making our principles meaningless for years and years to come. There is not and could not be any mechanical precept that would oblige all the national sections to enter the SP. It would be completely absurd to want to impose that kind of "policy." Nevertheless, more or less analogous situations could develop in other countries, and all the sections must have the opportunity to follow step by step the evolution of the discussion in the French League. ■

Tasks of the ICL[70]

July 21, 1934

1. The Bloc of Four fell apart because of the rightward development of its centrist participants, who pulled back from the independent propaganda of the Fourth International under pressure of the fascist attack and the pressure of the new centrist "mass currents" because they lacked a broad perspective and failed to understand the teachings of Marx and Lenin, creating the genial theory of unprincipled

combinations and propaganda through silence.

The Bloc of Four as such was an indispensable step on the way to the Fourth International, a step that must and will be repeated on a higher level. Nevertheless, we should not close our eyes to the fact that following the demise of the Bloc of Four, the ICL is at the moment the only organization that openly and consistently raises the question of the new, communist, Fourth International. This fact imposes new and important tasks on our organization and imparts increased significance to it and to its development.

2. Aside from this fact, when considering our new tasks we should recognize and take into account in full measure the turn that the Comintern has completed in France and is initiating in other countries (Switzerland, Czechoslovakia). Our basic attitude toward the Comintern on the one hand and the new International on the other cannot be altered in the least by this. Our evaluation of Stalinism as bureaucratic centrism enabled us to predict just such a turn without being surprised by it. Even though the turn will hardly make the Comintern capable of helping the revolutionary cause to victory in any country—and even though its opportunistic character will have a disorienting effect in the long run—it is clear that this turn puts the objective development of the class struggle in various countries on a new plane and largely alters and to a certain extent improves the Comintern's relationship to the masses. An insufficient or incorrect reaction to this turn could lead to a considerable weakening of our organization.

Not the least significant aspect of the Stalinists' turn toward the united front, insofar as it takes mass pressure into account, is that it is a vindication and a confirmation of the political line of our organization, especially the line we have pursued for the last five years. This is a line that has not only allowed us to significantly strengthen and develop existing sections (such as the American, French, Belgian, and German sections) but that has also allowed us to win important new sections throughout the world (in Holland, Poland, Chile, etc.). Overlooking these successes would be just as fatal as would be holding the illusion that we could continue moving forward in the old manner, living off of accumulated capital.

3. It is apparent that the Stalinists' opportunist turn can go far beyond the united front in certain countries, especially in France. In the most recent negotiations between the heads of the French CP and SP the question of a *unified party* was openly and positively considered by both sides! The reasons for this are clear: the turn of the Comintern is at least as much an expression of Russian foreign policy as it is a result of mass pressure. Litvinov's foreign policy no longer has any revolutionary perspective. Its only goal is to prevent wars by forming alliances. In pursuit of this goal it is making an effort to keep regimes of the Doumergue type at the helm in France. The united front is supposed to create a left bloc to balance off the right bloc. In order to demonstrate to the French bourgeoisie (and more recently to the British bourgeoisie, which is approaching this bloc) how serious they are about this turn, the Soviet bureaucracy through Thorez, Cachin, etc., not only makes the united front conform to the wishes of the SFIO, but even steers toward the liquidation of the French CP, subordinating the revolutionary element in a unified party to the discipline of Leon Blum.

Regardless of whether the bureaucracy will carry this through to the end, or whether the continual regrouping of the powers will create a new situation, the importance of our independent role, our role in the revolution, is immensely increased. Of course, the broad masses will at first be caught up in the unity delirium; but on the other hand, the best communist elements in France and even more so in other countries will be drawn into our ranks, assuming that we know how to correctly respond to the situation. It appears as if the moment is drawing near when the theoretical liquidation of Marxism-Leninism by the Stalinists, which we have perceived and fought against since 1923, is going to break through visibly in practice, thereby opening up new opportunities for us.

4. The future destiny of our organization, like the development of the Fourth International, will depend above all on the existence of an international cadre that understands how to answer the questions of revolution and counterrevolution—especially in their fascist and Bonapartist guises—and that understands the question of the war threat and of how to implement our slogans and put them into practice. On an international plane, the answer to these questions can only flow from a politically and organizationally independent component. Even while making the most strenuous efforts to find allies, this component can never give up its independence, its efforts to select and educate its own cadre, and its thorough ideological work.

5. The first goal we proposed on the way to the revolution was the united front against fascism. The Stalinist turn is an important step in this direction. It is necessary to expose the indecisiveness of the bureaucracy and its inability to take further steps, drawing the connection between what has been achieved and what is still lacking, and making the sharpest attacks on the bureaucracy's opportunist conceptions. What is necessary is to transform the united front in meetings into the united front in action and to demand the transformation of the united front of two parties into the united front of all workers' organizations. It is necessary to prepare the transformation of the united front of organizations into a soviet movement.

6. Entering the united front ourselves is not in the least utopian. Good possibilities for this already exist in the ranks. And even where we are at present excluded, sympathy for us and for the demand for our inclusion will grow because

we will be the only ones in a position to provide the united front with concrete content and concrete goals.

The question of practical proposals and practical slogans assumes the greatest importance in this context (demands for a militia, arming, concrete local and factory demands). Working out such measures will eliminate from our ranks the last remnants of a purely speculative and literary way of looking at things. This will at the same time be the best way to win the trust of the working masses and break the influence of the bureaucrats in the united front.

7. Insofar as the united front is actually realized and not sabotaged (which would lead to an important process of differentiation in the reformist parties) it cannot remain in the form the bureaucrats strive for—the united front in meetings, one that misleads the working class and lulls it to sleep. Either it will broaden out to include us and break through the bureaucratic framework (a process that will bring about the formation of left wings in *both* parties, which we must influence) or what is probably more likely in many countries—one of the two bureaucracies will be driven to break with the expanding united front for the sake of self-preservation, a development that will immediately place on the agenda the question of a split in the parties concerned. Systematic work on our part will make us a pole of attraction for the left wings of both parties and create the basis for a new communist party.

The possible formation of united parties confronts us with an entirely new situation. A momentary decline in mass response would be accompanied by our winning the best revolutionary elements. Clearly, further development would make our organization appear publicly as the only communist organization and would allow us to fill the role of the Communist parties at a disproportionately rapid pace, counterposing the demands and preparation for revolutionary action to hollow, opportunistic unity verbiage.

8. Any successful work we do must be based on a complete break with our past methods of work, the methods of the faction. The ideological work of the faction was for the most part critical in nature. The ideological work of the nucleus of the new party and the new International must center around positive, constructive, direction-giving work that does not in the least shy away from concretization. The previous activity was consciously limited to propaganda, since the faction consciously submitted itself to the discipline of the party in action. In its work the nucleus of the new party and the new International must on the contrary attempt to go beyond the bounds of propaganda at every opportunity and to prove the seriousness and value of our revolutionary determination through independent action or through participation in action. In this, we must take as our starting point the fact that the only way to convince broad masses of the correctness of our ideas is in action. This is the central point in our new orientation. There are no organizational measures that can get around this step and make it superfluous.

9. Alongside independent propaganda and active work all means must be employed—always in keeping with the concrete situation—to link up with the masses, push them forward, and consolidate new revolutionary cadres from their ranks.

Above all this includes:

a. Systematic fraction work in the trade unions under the slogan of trade union unity. The opportunity to reach and influence the worker masses is better here than in any party. In many countries trade union unity is almost of greater practical significance than the united front between the parties. The immediate economic effects of the reactionary development and the deep differentiation in the trade unions provide the best jumping-off point for our work.

b. Systematic fraction work in all workers' parties and organizations, not just by forming fractions out of the sympathizers already present there, but also possibly by sending in really solid elements.

    c. Very special attention to promoting work among the youth in existing youth organizations as well as by building and broadening new youth organizations.

    d. Forming alliances and blocs with organizations striving for a new communist party and International. These must be based on a clear principled basis and concrete formulation of goals.

    e. Fusion with such organizations on the basis of a clear communist program.

    f. Under very exceptional circumstances, the entry of an entire section into a centrist organization can prove useful in increasing our influence and accelerating the construction of the Fourth International (the ILP in England). Calling these entry tactics a panacea [as some comrades have done] amounts to a declaration of bankruptcy for the political line followed up till now, means the liquidation of the independent organizations, is both a cause and effect of complete demoralization, and must be categorically rejected. [According to these comrades] even the proposed entry of the French League into the SFIO with the object of extending our influence must lead not only to de facto liquidation of our influence and de facto capitulation in France but also to the *discrediting and disorientation of the entire ICL at the very moment when it is involved in expansion and has the greatest perspectives and tasks ahead of it*. A thorough testing of this question, *which is a life-and-death question for the entire ICL*, and an immediate and vigorous rejection of this view are absolutely necessary so that the ICL does not lose a second in utilizing the immense new opportunities *rather than falling to pieces*.

    A correct understanding of the newly created situation and a carrying out of the measures noted above, combined with the revitalization of the revolutionary forces in numerous countries, will make possible significant progress on the road to the Fourth International as well as effective preparation for the decisive confrontation between the bourgeoisie and the proletariat. ∎

Clouds in the Far East[71]

Published August 1934

At first sight one becomes astonished by the insignificance of those military forces which were concentrated in the Far East during the months of extreme tension in Soviet-Japanese relations. On February 3 the Japanese minister of war, Hayashi,[72] declared that his government had only 50,000 soldiers in Manchuria while the Soviets had concentrated 100,000 men and 300 planes on their nearest border. Bluecher,[73] the commander in chief of the Far Eastern army, refuted Hayashi, stating that the Japanese had actually concentrated in Manchuria 130,000 men, more than one-third of their regular army, plus 115,000 Manchukuo soldiers—all told, 245,000 men and 500 planes. At the same time, Bluecher added reassuringly that the Soviet armed forces were not inferior to the Japanese. On the scale of a major war, we are dealing here, one may say, with partisan detachments.

The concentration of masses of millions, an unbroken and deep front and a positional war are excluded by the properties of the Far Eastern arena (immense and sparsely populated areas, extremely broken terrain, poor means of communication, remoteness from the key bases). In the Russo-Japanese war of 1904–05, 320,000 soldiers participated on the Russian side, and toward the end, i.e., when the czarist army was completely routed—500,000. The Japanese hardly numbered as many. The czarist army lacked not transport, not numbers, but ability. Since that time, the technology of war has changed beyond recognition. But the basic properties of the theater of war in the Far East have remained the same. To Japan, Manchuria is an intermediate base, separated from the key bases by sea. The Japanese fleet rules on sea, but not under sea nor in the air. Sea transport is bound up with dangers. The Chinese population of Manchuria is hostile to the Japanese. Like the Soviets, Japan will be unable to concentrate masses of millions on the Far Eastern front. The most modern technology must, of necessity, be correlated with the tactical methods of the past. The strategy of Napoleon, and even of Hannibal, remains to a large measure in force for the Trans-Baikal and the Maritime Provinces. Large-scale cavalry raids will introduce decisive changes into the map of war. The Japanese railroads in Manchuria will be subjected to greater dangers than the Soviet line running along the Amur. In the operations of isolated detachments, in cavalry raids at the enemy's rear, colossal work will entail upon modern technology in the form of aviation as the means of scouting, of maintaining connections of transport, and of bombing. Insofar as the war in the Amur and Maritime Provinces will bear, in general, a mobile and maneuvering character, its outcome will depend to a decisive degree upon the ability of isolated detachments to operate independently; upon the initiative of the lowest ranking officers; and upon the resourcefulness of every soldier who is left to act on his own. In all these respects, the Soviet army, in my opinion, will prove superior to the Japanese, at least by as much as the Japanese army proved superior to the czarist in 1904–05.

As the events of last year have demonstrated, Tokyo

cannot make up her mind to begin right now. And in the meantime, with every additional year, the interrelation of forces will not change in favor of Japan. The development of the Kuznietsk military-industrial base has already freed the Far Eastern front from the necessity of depending upon the European rear. The radical reconstruction of the carrying capacity of the Moscow-Khabarovsk railway, by double-tracking the line, was set by the Soviet government as one of the principal tasks for 1934. Conjointly work was begun on the railroad from Lake Baikal to the lower Amur regions, 1,400 kilometers long. The new main line will tap the richest coal regions of Bureya and the mines of Khingan. The Bureya region—which is only 500 kilometers away from Khabarovsk, i.e., one-tenth the distance to the Kuznietsk region—will be transformed by the program of industrial construction into an independent industrial military-technological base for the Far East. The correlation of the gigantic undertakings in transportation and industry with the substantial economic privileges extended to the population of the Far East must lead to a rapid settlement of the territory—and this will cut the ground from under the Siberian plans of Japanese imperialism.

Nevertheless Japan's internal situation makes war almost inevitable, just as thirty years ago there was no forestalling czarism from it, despite all the voices of warning. There is no paradox in the statement that after the war has broken out in the Far East, it will be either very short, almost instantaneous, or very, very long. Japan's goal—the seizure of the Far East, and if possible of a considerable section of the Trans-Baikal territory—requires of itself very long periods of time. The war could end quickly only provided the Soviet Union will be able to shatter at the very outset the Japanese offensive, decisively and for a long time to come. For the solution of this defensive task, aviation provides the Soviets with a weapon of inestimable power.

One need not be a devotee of "integral" aerial warfare, i.e., believe in the transference of the decisive military operations to the air, in order to realize that, under certain conditions, aviation is unquestionably capable of solving the war problem by radically paralyzing the offensive operations of the enemy. Such is precisely the case in the Far East. In his complaint about the concentration of Soviet air forces in the Maritime Provinces, Hayashi divulged the easily understood alarm of Japan's ruling circles, whose political centers, whose military-industrial combines and whose most important war bases are exposed to the blows of the Red air fleets. With the Maritime Provinces as a base, it is possible to spread the greatest havoc among the vital centers of the island empire by means of long-range planes. Even should one concede what is hardly likely, that Japan will be able to muster an equal or superior air force, the danger to the islands will only be lessened but not eliminated. There is no creating an impassable aerial barrier; breaches will be only too frequent, and every breach is pregnant with great consequence. In this duel, the decisive importance will be borne not by the material, technological preponderance which unquestionably lies on the side of Soviet aviation, and which can only increase in the immediate future, but by the relative geographic position of the two sides.

While almost all the Japanese centers are exposed to attack from the air, the Japanese air forces cannot retaliate with blows anywhere nearly equivalent; not only Moscow but also the Kuznietsk base (6,000–7,000 kilometers away!) cannot be reached without a landing. At the same time, neither in the Maritime Provinces nor in Eastern Siberia are there centers so vital that their destruction could exert a decisive or even a telling influence on the course of the war. The advantages of position multiplied by a more powerful technology will give the Red Army a preponderance which is difficult to express in terms of a precise coefficient, but which may prove of decisive importance.

Should the Soviet aviation, however, prove unprepared for the solution of the grandiose task of the third dimension, the center of gravity would revert to the two-dimensional plane, where the laws of the Far Eastern theater would enter into full force; and the principal law reads: slowness. The time has obviously elapsed for the sudden seizure of the Maritime Provinces. Vladivostok today represents a strongly fortified position which may become the Verdun of the Pacific Coast. The attempt to capture a fortress can be made only by land, and would require say a dozen divisions—two and a half to three times more than are required for the defense. Even in the event of complete success this operation would consume months, and thereby leave at the disposal of the Red Army an invaluable supplementary period of time. The westward movement of the Japanese would require colossal preparatory labor: intermediate bases must be fortified; railways and roads must be built. Japan's very successes in this line would create increasing difficulties for her; because the Red Army would retreat to its own bases while the Japanese would become dispersed within inhospitable territories, having behind their backs enslaved Manchuria, crushed Korea and hostile China. A protracted war would open up the possibility of forming, in the deep rear of the Japanese, a Chinese army with the aid of Soviet technology and Soviet instructors.

But here we already enter into the sphere of world relations, in the true sense of the word, with all the possibilities, dangers and unknown quantities latent in them. Many of the considerations and estimates which were stated above would, of course, be eliminated should the war last a number of years and force the Soviets to place twenty million men under arms. In such a case, the weakest link after transport, or together with transport, would probably prove to be the Soviet rural economy, the fundamental problems of which are still far from solution. However, it is precisely in the perspective of a major war that it is absolutely impermissible to take the question of the USSR in an isolated form, i.e., without direct connection with the entire world situation. What will be the groupings of countries in the East and the West? Will the military coalition of Japan and Germany be realized? Would the USSR find allies, and precisely whom? What will happen to the freedom of the seas? What will be the subsistence level and, in general, the economic position of Japan? Will Germany find itself within a new blockading ring? What will be the relative stability of the regimes of the warring countries? The number of such questions could be multiplied indefinitely. All of them will flow inevitably from the conditions of a world war; but no one can answer them a priori. The answer will be found during the actual course of the mutual destruction of peoples, and this answer may turn out to be a merciless sentence upon our entire civilization. ∎

Soviets in America?[74]

August 17, 1934

"Don't you think our NRA[75] is laying the groundwork for your kind of soviets?"

Coming from Cooper, the question struck Troshin as strange. The ship was rolling hard, and Troshin was not at all in his best spirits. The almost imperceptible irony in

Cooper's voice annoyed him a little, and he replied with some irritation, "When you decide to go in for soviets, I advise you to work out your own standards for them; ours won't suit you."

They were both engineers, and there was a bond between them, if not of friendship then of amicable relations that went back to the time during the war when Troshin, a true-born Muscovite, worked in factories in Chicago as an emigrant. Cooper, of pure Yankee stock, was already in his fourth year of Soviet service.[76] Now both were en route to America as members of a trade commission. Each respected the other's knowledge, experience, and talent, but each also saw the other's faults. To Cooper, Troshin appeared to be a technological dreamer and a bit of a dilettante; to Troshin, Cooper seemed a hidebound empiricist. They argued often but never ventured into the sphere of politics, partly out of tact, partly out of caution. During the first three days of their ocean voyage their conversations flowed along the customary channels. When they were not trading shipboard impressions, they discussed the orders they would soon be placing in America. Cooper for the hundred-and-first time accused Troshin of a barbaric passion for "gigantism," while Troshin retorted in the same vein that the wings of the American technological mind had been neatly clipped by the crisis. Only on the fourth day, after he finished reading a book on the NRA that he had taken along for the trip, did Cooper ask the unexpected question about soviets in America. Perhaps the nearness of his native shores loosened his tongue.

"American soviets," Troshin continued a little more amiably, "will differ from the Russian soviets as much as the United States of Roosevelt differs from the Russia of Nicholas II. Of course, that's if you will grant me the assumption that soviets will someday spring up in America."

"Suppose we make such a fantastic assumption. How do you envisage the rise of soviets among us? What would they look like? And how are we Yankees—me, for example—going to be comfortable on this Procrustean bed?"

"Soviet America can only come into being the way America became independent and democratic—through revolution. Quite a lot of crockery will get broken in the process; that's the American temperament. I think, Cooper, that you yourself would participate in the fight very energetically, although I'm not quite sure on which side."

"Is that unbelievably presumptuous remark supposed to mean that you think I have no principles?"

"Oh, why put it so harshly—you naturally consider yourself a staunch individualist. But the enormous energy you put into your work in Soviet industry—I won't say anything about your talent—was that of a sportsman, not a specialist. (I won't rub it in by calling you an enthusiast.) Who can tell what tricks your temperament and your empiricism will play when great events break? One thing is certain: you'll be smashing dishes along with the rest.

"But the overhead costs of your revolution will be totally insignificant compared with ours, at least in percentages if not in absolute terms. You look surprised? After all, my friend, civil wars aren't fought by the top 5 or 10 percent who control 90 percent of the national wealth; there aren't enough of them, and besides, they love their comfort too much. The counterrevolution can only raise its army from the lower middle class. But your farmers and your small shopkeepers in the cities would support the revolution too if it could show them the way out of their problems. The present crisis has brought terrible devastation to all the intermediate layers. It has dealt a crushing blow to farming, which was already in trouble for a decade before. You can hardly expect serious political resistance to the revolution on the part of these classes who, unfortunately, have nothing to lose. Of course that's assuming that the new regime would adopt a sensible and farsighted economic policy toward them.

"Once the soviet government was firmly in possession of the commanding heights of the economy—the banks, the basic branches of industry, transport—it would give the farmers and the small manufacturers and traders plenty of time to think things over and come to a decision. The rest would depend on the successes of the nationalized industry. And here, Cooper, I expect real miracles from you. 'Technocracy'[77] can become a reality only under a soviet regime, when the barriers of private property are removed. The most daring proposals of the Hoover commision[78] for standardization and rationalization will seem childish compared with the new possibilities. National industry would be organized on the model of the assembly-line system; that is, planning would be extended from the individual factory level to the economy as a whole.

"You could cut production costs in half or even to a fifth of what they are now. There would be a big and rapid increase in the purchasing power of the farmer's dollar. That would be enough for a start. But the soviets would also create their own model agricultural enterprises on a gigantic scale, as schools of voluntary collectivization. Your farmers are excellent calculators, if not statisticians. In time they would see how the accounts balance out: whether to remain as an isolated link or to join the public chain.

"At the same time, the soviets would make plenty of room in their industrial plan for all the viable medium-sized and small businesses. The government, the local soviets, and the cooperatives would make sure they got a guaranteed quota of orders, the credit they needed, and raw materials. Gradually, and without any compulsion, they would be drawn into the orbit of the socialized economy.

"In the United States it will be possible to fully apply those educational methods for influencing the middle classes that proved to be beyond the reach of the soviets of our backward country with its semipauperized and illiterate peasant majority. I don't have to explain the benefits that would flow from that: your development will be smoother, the overhead costs of social conflict would be reduced, and the tempo of cultural growth increased."

"Aren't you forgetting how religious we Anglo-Saxons are? That's the most important bulwark of social conservatism."

"Look, Cooper, you can't talk about doing anything on the basis of mutually contradictory assumptions. If we are going to talk about what American soviets would be like, you have to start from the assumption that the pressure of the social crisis will prove to be more powerful than all the psychological brakes. This has been demonstrated more than once in history. Some of the brakes will be burned out quickly; others will be reshaped to fit new circumstances. Don't forget that the Gospels themselves contain some pretty explosive maxims."

"And what would you do, I'd like to know, with the big shots of our capitalist world?"

"I would trust to your inventiveness, Cooper. It may well be that you would give those who refuse to make their peace with the new system a picturesque island somewhere, with lifelong pension payments, and let them live there as they wished."

"You're awfully generous, Troshin!"

"It's my weakness, Cooper."

"But you don't seem to take into account the possibility of military intervention. That could certainly lead to a big increase in the 'overhead costs' of a soviet revolution.

"Or do you imagine, maybe, my optimistic friend, that Japan, Great Britain, and the other capitalist countries would sit quietly by and accept a soviet overturn in America?"

"What else could they do, Cooper? The United States is the most powerful fortress of capitalism. Once you grant, at least in theory, such a deepening of the social crisis as would be needed for the establishment of soviets in the United States, then you have to grant that similar processes would be taking place in other countries as well. In all probability semifeudal Japan would drop out of the ranks of world capitalism even before the establishment of soviets in America. The same prognosis has to be extended to Great Britain—but in any case the idea of sending His British Majesty's fleet against a soviet America would be crazy. As for the idea of landing an expeditionary force on the southern half of the continent? It would be a hopeless undertaking and would never become more than a second-rate military escapade.

"Within a few months, or maybe even weeks, after you established a soviet regime—think about this, Cooper—the governments of Central and South America would be pulled into your federation like iron filings to a magnet. The same with Canada. The movements of the masses in these countries would be so irresistible they would accomplish this great unifying process in short order and with insignificant sacrifices. I'm ready to bet that the first anniversary of the inception of the first American soviet would find your hemisphere transformed into the Soviet United States of North, Central, and South America. Then you'd see the realization of the Monroe Doctrine,[79] although not the way it was foreseen by its author. You'd have to move your capital to Panama."

"Is that so? But you haven't answered my question about Roosevelt. Is he laying the groundwork for soviets, or not?"

"You're more perceptive than to ask a question like that, Cooper. The NRA is aimed at overcoming difficulties. It's supposed to strengthen the foundations of the capitalist system, not destroy them. Your Blue Eagle isn't going to give birth to soviets. On the contrary, it will be the difficulties the bird is too weak to overcome which will do that. Even the most 'leftist' of the professors in your Brain Trust[80] aren't revolutionists; they're only frightened conservatives. Your president abhors 'systems' and 'generalities.' But a soviet government is the greatest of all possible systems, a gigantic generality in action."

"Pretty good. So far you've managed to happily transform the whole character of the New World from Alaska to Cape Horn; you've guaranteed our international security, and changed the location of our capital.

"Before I thank you for this labor of Hercules, I would like to know what will happen to me, engineer Cooper.

"I just happen to be accustomed to roast beef, a cigar, and my own car. When you get done with all this am I going to end up on famine rations, having to wear mismatched shoes that don't fit, read monotonous stereotyped propaganda in the one newspaper that will be left, elect hand-picked candidates in soviets chosen at the top, rubber-stamp decisions made without my participation, keep my real thoughts to myself, and sing praises every day to the Leader fate has sent me, from fear of being arrested and shipped off somewhere? If that's what you have in mind, I'm telling you now you can have my ticket to paradise. I'll take my chances on one of those islands in the Pacific you've been so kind as to set aside for the dying race of individualists."

"Don't be in such a rush to take refuge on an island, Cooper. You'd die of boredom there. How could you end up on famine rations when you eat the way you do today *despite* the fact that your system has been compelled to artificially restrict the area under cultivation and the scope of production? For almost two decades now, we in Russia have had to build the basic branches of industry almost from scratch. In your America the problem is just the opposite. The powerful technological resources already exist, but they stand paralyzed by the crisis and clamor to be put to use.

"Our continuing successes in laying the foundations of a planned economy have been made at the expense of the day-to-day consumption of the masses. Your problem, on the contrary, is to plan the revival of an already existing economy, and this must take the rapid growth of consumption by the people as the point of departure from the very beginning. Nowhere else has the study of the internal market been carried so far as in the United States. This has been done by your banks, trusts, individual businessmen, merchants, traveling salesmen, and farmers. A soviet government would begin by doing away with trade secrets; it would combine and generalize the capitalist methods of calculation, transforming them into methods of overall economic accounting and planning.

"On the other hand, your sophisticated and critical consumers wouldn't tolerate any sign of indifference toward their needs. A flexible system for serving the needs of the population would be guaranteed by a combination of democratically controlled cooperatives, a network of state stores, and private trade outlets. Don't worry about your roast beef, Cooper. You'll get it whenever you want."

"After I get three different bureaucrats to approve my requisition?"

"No, you'll use hard cash. The dollar, you see, will be the basic regulator of this soviet economy. It's a big mistake to see the use of money as incompatible with a planned economy. 'Managed money'—if your radical professors will forgive me—is an academic fiction. Arbitrary changes of currency value inevitably lead to the disruption of internal coordination in all branches of the economy. This kind of dislocation, being molecular in character, deforms the most profound, the innermost processes in production and distribution."

"But in the Soviet Union—!"

"Unfortunately with us a bitter necessity has been converted into an official virtue. The lack of a stable gold ruble is an important cause of the many troubles and weaknesses of our economy. Without a stable currency, how can you even think of really regulating wages, the prices of basic necessities, and quality control? An unstable ruble in a planned economy is like having different-sized molds for the same part in assembly-line production.

"Of course, after the socialist regime becomes experienced enough to keep the economy in balance through administrative technique alone, money will lose its meaning as an economic regulator. Then money will become simply coupons, like bus or theater tickets. As social wealth grows the need for these coupons will also disappear. You won't have to control individual consumption when there is more than enough of everything for everybody. America will certainly reach that level before any other country does.

"But you can't get to the stage of a moneyless economy without first assuring the dynamic equilibrium and harmonious growth of all social functions. That's a big job and it can't be done solely through administrative pressure and radio pep talks. In its initial stages—that is, for a certain number of years—the planned economy needs a stable currency even more than liberal capitalism did. Trying to regulate the economy by meddling with the currency is like trying to lift both feet off the ground at the same time—"

"Troshin, are you making insinuations about our monetary policy?"

"I'm not making any insinuations. I'm only saying that soviet America will have a big enough gold reserve to ensure a stable dollar. What a priceless asset, Cooper. You know that our economy has been growing at 20 to 30 percent a year. But you also know about the weak side of this unprecedented growth rate: The real economic growth does not correspond to the figures given for gains in production and technology. One reason for that disproportion is the subjective administrative manipulation of our monetary system. You'll be spared that evil. The American soviet dollar will be running on all eight cylinders. Your growth rate will greatly surpass ours, not only in technical output but in real economic advances. What the result would be is obvious: living standards of your population, and therefore their cultural level too, would leap ahead at a very rapid rate."

"Troshin, if you're trying to entice me by the joyful prospect of owning three or four pairs of standardized pants, all either too big or too small, and a compulsory set of the complete works of William Z. Foster—"[81]

"Cooper, you can't take your eyes off the unhappy plight of our mass consumer. Do you expect me to deny it? I've already told you the reasons for the scarcity and poor quality of our consumer goods: the inheritance of poverty from the old regime, the low cultural level of the peasantry, the need to create the means of production at the expense of current consumption, chronic monetary inflation, and last but not least, bureaucratism."

"Monstrous bureaucratism, you mean, Troshin."

"Yes, monstrous bureaucratism, Cooper. But you are not obliged to repeat it. Among us, the scarcity of basic necessities produces a struggle of each against all for an extra pound of bread or yard of cloth. The bureaucracy steps forward in the guise of peacemaker and all-powerful arbiter. But you are immeasurably wealthier and could assure the country all the necessities without much difficulty. The needs, tastes, and habits of your people would never permit a bureaucracy to gain uncontrolled power of decision over the national income. The task of organizing a socialized economy for the best satisfaction of human needs would stir your entire population to its depths, and give rise within it to the formation of new tendencies and parties, intensely struggling with one another—"

"You're a poor Bolshevik, Troshin. You talk about struggles between parties under the soviet regime. The nearness of capitalist shores is having a harmful effect on you. You're degenerating before my very eyes. Which are you for—democracy or dictatorship?"

"I'm for soviet democracy, Cooper. Soviets are a very flexible form of government. That is one of their advantages. But precisely because of that, soviets can't achieve miracles; they only reflect the pressure of the social milieu they exist in. The bureaucratization of our soviets, as a result of the political monopoly of a single party, which was moreover reduced to a bureaucratic apparatus, was itself the result of the exceptional difficulties of socialist pioneering in a poor and backward country. The bureaucratization of the regime further reacts disastrously on our economy, our literature, our art, our entire culture. As I see the American soviets, they will be full-blooded and vigorous. Dictatorship? Of course, defenders of the capitalist regime will find no place for themselves inside the soviets. I confess that I can't imagine Henry Ford[82] as the president of the Detroit soviet. But a wide-ranging struggle between various interests, programs, and groupings is not only possible but inevitable on the basis of a soviet regime. One-year, five-year, ten-year economic plans; national education systems; the construction of great transport lines; the transformation of the farms; the problem of sharing the highest technological and cultural achievements with South America; the problem of probing outer space; eugenics—all of these tasks will give rise to competing doctrines and schools of thought, electoral struggles in the soviets, and passionate debate in the newspapers and at public meetings."

"This smacks of freedom of the press, Troshin. Watch out!"

"Cooper, do you really think that the monopolization of the press in the USSR by the top ranks of the bureaucracy is the norm for a workers' state? No. Regardless of what historical conditions may have produced it, it is only a temporary deformity."

"But even in the United States, if you put all the printing plants, all the paper mills, and all the means of distribution in the hands of the state, that would automatically place the whole press in the hands of the government. Do you suppose the government wouldn't use it to promote the dogma of its own infallibility?"

"The nationalization of the mass media would be a purely negative measure. The only reason for it is to prevent private capital from deciding what can be printed: progressive or reactionary, 'wet' or 'dry,'[83] puritanical or pornographic. Your soviets will have to find a new solution for the question of how to apportion the socialized printing facilities and what to use them for. One starting point could be proportional representation on the basis of votes received in the soviet elections. The right of each group of citizens to use the printing equipment would depend on their numerical strength. You could use the same principle for allocating the use of meeting halls, radio time, and so on. This way the management and editorial policy of publications would be decided by groups of people with similar ideas, not by individual bank accounts.

"You may object that under such a system every new ideological tendency or new philosophical or aesthetic school that doesn't yet have a large following will be denied access to the press. There is some point to this argument. But it only implies that under any regime a new idea has to prove its right to existence. In any case, under a soviet regime this would be easier than it is now. A rich soviet America would be able to set aside vast funds for research, inventions, discoveries, and experiments in all spheres of human creativeness, both material and spiritual. You won't neglect your bold architects and sculptors, your unconventional poets and audacious philosophers.

"In fact, I'll admit, Cooper, that I think the Yankees of the coming epoch are going to have something new to say in those very areas where until recently they have been the pupils of Europe. The four years I spent in your country, mainly in the factories, weren't wasted, if only because they helped me understand what a change your technology has produced in the fate of the human race. I have nothing but scorn for that phony superior tone used in certain circles in Europe when they talk about 'Americanism,' especially since the present crisis began. I'll even go so far as to say that in a certain sense it was Americanism that marked the final dividing line between medievalism and the modern history of humanity.

"But your conquest of nature has been pursued so violently and passionately that you haven't taken the time either to modernize your theoretical methods or to create your own art forms. You grew and became rich according to the laws of the simple syllogism. Your old puritanism has fermented in a giant vat of material successes, to produce a religion of practical rationalism. Because of this you have remained hostile to Hegel, Marx, and even Darwin. Are you surprised, Cooper? Yet, the burning of Darwin's works by the Baptist preachers of Tennessee[84] is only a crude reflection of the aversion of the majority of Americans for the doctrine of evolution. I don't mean only religious prejudices, but also your general mental makeup. Yankee atheists are imbued with rationalism no less than Quakers. Your rationalism doesn't even have in it the merciless consistency of the Cartesians or Jacobins. It is restricted and weakened by your empiricism and moralism. But this means that your philosophic method is just that much more antiquated and out of keeping with your technology and historical possibilities.

"Today you are really coming face to face for the first time with the kind of social contradictions that develop unobserved, behind people's backs. You conquered nature by means of instruments your genius has created; but your own instruments have driven you to your knees. Contrary to all expectation, your unheard-of wealth has given birth to intolerable misfortunes. This is teaching you the truth that Aristotle's syllogism doesn't apply to the laws of social development. You have finally entered the school of the dialectic, and you can't go back to the methodology of the seventeenth and eighteenth centuries. Don't be sorry about it, Cooper. There should be some fine fruit out of the grafting of the dialectic onto the sturdy trunk of practical American thought. I'm looking forward to seeing it. In the next decades you are bound to make great contributions in the sphere of generalized thought, poetry, and the arts. They will be on the level of your technology—which still has a long way to go to realize the potential it already contains.

"While the romantic numskulls of Nazi Germany are dreaming of restoring the race of the Teutoburg forest in all its pristine purity, or, rather, its filth, you Americans, after taking possession of your economy and your culture, will extend the application of genuine scientific methods to the sphere of the reproduction of human beings as well. Within a century, out of your melting pot of races there will come a new human being, the first really worthy of the name."

"Are you seriously betting on that, Troshin?"

"I'm betting on even more than that: I'll bet you that in the third year of soviet rule you will no longer chew gum. Verily I say unto you, even Andrew Jackson[85] can enter the kingdom of heaven, if his heart but desire it. And he can't help desiring it."

"You're very generous with our future, Troshin. But I hope you're not arrogant enough to think you've convinced me. The poet in you has been ruined by the good engineer. You got rid of the danger of soviet bureaucratism much too easily—with words. But there's the dinner bell. Tomorrow I'll tear you apart. Your famous dialectic will be plucked like a chicken." ■

The 'Belgian' tradition in discussion[86]

September 22, 1934

To the Belgian Section of the International Communist League
Copy to the International Secretariat

Dear Comrades:
　I have just received a copy of the letter addressed to the IS by Comrade Vereecken on September 14, a letter whose tone and contents I can only greatly regret.
　1. Comrade V. finds that the French youth have misinterpreted his September 3 statement. Instead of contenting himself with giving us the authentic interpretation, Comrade V. talks about "patent falsifications" and "shameful exploitation." This is unjust. The September 3 statement leaves itself open to being misinterpreted. Three or four times I myself brought to Comrade V.'s attention the objectionable nature of the phrase "on the political basis that this turn will apply only to France. . . ." Comrade V. thought it well to preserve this formulation, which is at the very least unfortunate, and if the French youth have misunderstood what he meant, he himself is at least partly responsible. In any case, an incident like this—a member of the plenum body launching such grave accusations against the youth of one of our sections—should not have occurred.
　I for my part have always emphasized the restrained tone the Belgian comrades use in discussing questions of principle and politics. I saw in it the external manifestation of a revolutionary sense of responsibility. I regret to say that in this particular instance Comrade V. departs from the "Belgian"

tradition, which is the proletarian norm. Let us hope that a single occurrence does not determine the rule.

2. While I cannot venture an opinion on the details of the negotiations about the convening of the plenum, I must say, however, that Comrade V.'s presentation did not seem in any way to demonstrate the existence of maneuvers, manipulations, etc. Only one thing is clear, that there was uncertainty about whether to yield to Comrade V. and immediately call a plenum, which however did not promise any positive results, or, given the situation, to postpone the plenum. Comrade V. unexpectedly concluded this part of his presentation with the sentence: "Calling a plenum where the votes would have been divided, moreover, would not in any way have changed the will of the majority of the IS." In other words, calling a plenum would not have yielded any positive results. This indicates that the vacillations and the discussions about calling a plenum are to be explained by reasons that are inherent in the situation itself and not by maneuvers and intrigues. Once again, it is unfortunate that in writing this letter Comrade V. allowed himself to be carried away by feelings that could only have been of an ephemeral nature.

3. Comrade V. supports "the Dutch delegate's reproach directed toward Comrade Vidal for sending his proposal to the French section instead of sending it to the responsible members of the international leadership." I regret that I cannot accept this reproach, which seems to me more like a pure misunderstanding. Ever since the expulsion of the Neos[87] in France, I had theoretically considered the possibility of the League's affiliating to the SFIO; but there was more involved than the united front. It seemed to me that the time was ripe.

But it was simply a question of my own opinion concerning the French situation. How could I have gone over the heads of the French section to place a proposal concerning that section before the international leadership? Not only would this have appeared disloyal to the French leadership, but it was absolutely necessary for me to be sure that my own evaluation was correct, to test it against the ideas and the criticism of the best informed and most interested comrades. Just imagine if I made an important proposal concerning the Belgian section directly to the international leadership without consulting the Belgian leadership.

I wrote my first letter to the Central Committee of the French League to indicate the urgency of the question. After that I had personal conversations, which took some time. I did not give any publicity to my letter before attempting to explain my views and, if possible, come to an understanding with the French leadership. Agreement was not reached, but the discussions convinced me that entry into the SFIO was absolutely necessary. It was then that I decided to formally introduce the question at the international as well as the national level. It must be added that there were material difficulties—with discussions, correspondence, etc.

In conclusion, I can only add that if tomorrow I had some proposal or even a suggestion concerning the relations between the RSP and the OSP, or the question of the NAS, I would address myself first of all to the leadership of the RSP, which is the most competent to judge and the most closely affected party, before deciding to formally place the question before the international organization.

4. It is true that I emphasized with Comrade V. the necessity of an "organizational truce"—not just in the interests of the French section, but above all in the interests of the Belgian section.

"After having discharged your responsibility," I told Comrade V., "give the French comrades a chance to go through the experience, under your international supervision." In his September 3 statement, Comrade V. agreed to authorize the

League to put into effect the decision of its last national conference on its own responsibility. This prescription, issued by Comrade V. after ample explanations to various comrades of the League, is very important, above all because of its preciseness. Comrade V. speaks about the French section, about the League, which is involved in a certain course of action, and he is absolutely astounded by the proposal to recognize the "two French groups"[88] as two sections of the ICL.

If you count the combined votes of the adult group and the youth, the relationship between the majority and the minority stands at two-thirds to one-third. The majority put the decision of the national conference into effect, being authorized to do this by the IS, including the consultative votes of Sneevliet and Vereecken. The minority totally disagreed and not by chance: its ideas were purely negative, conservative, routinist. Still worse, Pierre Naville saw fit to repudiate the national conference of the League through the medium of the bourgeois press, speaking in the name of a nonexistent central committee.

During my conversation with Comrade V., I emphasized that any attempt to put the minority on the same footing with the majority would mean not an "organizational truce" but a fight to the finish with the danger of carrying the conflict over into other sections. I told Comrades Sn. and V. that if the minority displayed the slightest vitality and at the same time honestly desired to remain within the framework of our international organization, we might consider allowing it to belong to the ICL as a sympathizing group. Pierre Naville's attitude greatly diminished this possibility, which the plenum should rule on. But what is out of the question is to sanction the lack of discipline and responsibility of a heterogeneous minority without perspective, by according it the right to sabotage the work and the experience of our French section. On this basis there can be no "organizational truce."

Vidal [Leon Trotsky]

The present situation in the labor movement and the tasks of the Bolshevik-Leninists[89]

From a propagandist group to mass work
October 1934

1. The last ten years have been characterized by the growing decay and ossification of the Communist International, which in the first five years of its existence had assembled under its banner the most revolutionary elements of the proletariat. The larger part of the present cadres of the International Communist League comes from the ranks of the Comintern. The majority in the groups and sections of the ICL had been expelled at various periods by the bureaucracy as a preventive measure, in order to avoid the possibility of introducing into the Communist Party a struggle for Leninist principles. Constituting themselves the "Left Opposition," the Bolshevik-Leninists set as their first task the regeneration of the Comintern. In the course of a decade they have struggled indefatigably against the centrist backsliding and adventurist zigzags of the Stalinist bureaucracy. There has been no major question, no major event, to which the Bolshevik-Leninists have not responded, either as an international organization or through the various sections. There has been no major question on which the analysis and prognosis of the Bolshevik-Leninists have not been confirmed by events. But the conservative power of the bureaucratic apparatus has prevailed. The events in Germany connected with the victory of fascism have made the internal degeneration of the Comintern apparent, and

have once and for all buried the hopes of regeneration insofar as the revolutionary vanguard is concerned.

2. Abandoning its role as a "faction of the Comintern," the Bolshevik-Leninists, on the basis of the old program enriched by new experience, have set up an independent organization, whose task is the struggle for *new parties and a new international, the Fourth International*. The new orientation of the ICL—which was strengthened at the outset by the adherence of the Dutch Revolutionary Socialist Party—made it necessary to examine anew the entire field of the international labor movement, to take stock of modifications which had taken place, to accurately estimate new groupings, and to find in each country the most favorable point at which to apply the Marxist lever.

3. The degeneration and compromises of the Comintern inevitably lead to the absolute or at least the relative bolstering of the Social Democratic parties. The preservation of these parties and, still more, their growth by the attraction of fresh elements have led and will lead inevitably in their turn to the formation of internal groupings, the sharpening of factional struggles and splits. Nothing more strikingly illustrates the total loss of the Comintern's attractive power than the fact that in recent years left-centrist groupings, including those which broke with the Social Democracy or were expelled by it, did not enter the ranks of the Comintern but endeavored and still endeavor to lead an independent existence (ILP, OSP, SAP, AWP, etc.). In a number of countries the Social Democratic parties have undergone a certain evolution. After long years of adaptation by the Austrian Social Democracy to bourgeois governments, its proletarian wing entered into armed conflict with the bourgeoisie. The Spanish party, only yesterday collaborating in a bourgeois government and launching continuous repressions against so-called revolutionary excesses, today finds itself constrained to call the masses to armed insurrection for the

defense of democratic liberties.[90] On the other hand, the Belgian Labor Party puts the knife to its still quite moderate left wing. The Dutch Social Democracy is revising its program in a reactionary spirit. All these trends develop under the influence of the same factors: the crisis of capitalism and of the democratic state, counterreforms in the place of reforms, the growing misery of the masses, the threatening danger of war in various countries. These basic factors have varying reflections and brings about multiple and even contradictory tendencies, groupings, and reciprocal relations.

4. Internal policy has lost every trace of stability and is now characterized by sudden maneuvers, finding a striking expression in the fact that Socialists who yesterday were the cabinet ministers of the bourgeoisie are today arrested by the police of the bourgeoisie. The objective situation of the Social Democracy within the bourgeois state undergoes, in a brief span of time, a turn of 180 degrees. As for consciousness, this changes much less rapidly and in a manner not only not uniform but even heterogeneous in the various groups: in certain levels of the apparatus towards corporative Bonapartism ("Neo-Socialists," some Hollanders and others), on the other flank toward revolution. The consciousness of the Social Democracy lags so much behind its own objective situation in the bourgeois state that it finds itself plunged into armed insurrection without having had time to abandon its democratic and reformist prejudices.

5. In these conditions there could be nothing more dangerous or unfortunate than time-worn formulas. To satisfy oneself with abstractions—"reformism," "Second International"—is to ignore or blur the difference between a Social Democracy which constitutes the power of the bourgeoisie and a Social Democracy which participates in a revolution against the bourgeoisie. Between these two extreme poles there are numerous transitional stages which must be carefully studied, measurements being taken of the extent of the swing and

the rhythm of the development, in order always to apply the lever with the greatest effectiveness for the formation of genuinely revolutionary proletarian parties.

6. We repeat again: if the Comintern had not been crushed by the Soviet bureaucracy, but had continued and developed the policies of the first four congresses, it would long ago have guaranteed the victory of the revolution in a whole series of European and Asiatic countries. On the other hand, if the degenerate apparatus of the Comintern, leaning on the authority of the USSR, did not stand in the way of the vanguard of the world proletariat, the ICL could have become, in the course of the past decade, the independent pivot of the revolutionary party. In either case the proletariat would have experienced victories rather than defeats and capitulations. In practical politics, however, we must make our point of departure not from imaginary but from real conditions, those in which the world labor movement finds itself today and whose basic traits we have characterized above.

The ICL is the only international organization which has a correct general conception of the world situation and of the tasks facing the world proletariat. It does not, however, possess sufficiently important forces to become a center of attraction for the masses who, under the Damocles sword of fascism and war, fear to cut themselves off from the big organizations. The ICL cannot act as an independent party of the proletariat, it is only the instrument *for the creation of independent parties*. This instrument must be employed in accordance with the situation in each country.

7. Psychology, ideas, and customs usually lag behind the developments of objective relations in society and in the class; even in the revolutionary organizations the dead lay their hands upon the living. The preparatory period of propaganda has given us the cadres without which we could not make one step forward, but the same period has, as a heritage, permitted the expression within the organization of extremely abstract

concepts of the construction of a new party and a new International. In their chemically pure form these conceptions are expressed in the most complete manner by the dead sect of Bordigists, who hope that the proletarian vanguard will convince itself, by means of a hardly readable literature, of the correctness of their position and sooner or later will correctly gather around their sect. Often these sectarians add that revolutionary events inevitably push the working class towards us. This passive expectancy, under a cover of idealistic messianism, has nothing in common with Marxism. Revolutionary events always and inevitably pass over the heads of every sect. By means of propagandistic literature, if it is good, one can educate the first cadres, but one cannot rally the proletarian vanguard which lives neither in a circle nor in a schoolroom but in a class society, in a factory, in the organizations of the masses, a vanguard to whom one must know how to speak in the language of its experiences. The best prepared propagandist cadres must inevitably disintegrate if they do not find contact with the daily struggle of the masses. The expectation of the Bordigists that revolutionary events will of themselves push the masses to them as a reward for their "correct" ideas represents the crudest of illusions. During revolutionary events the masses do not inquire for the address of this or that sect, but leap over it. To grow more rapidly during the period of flux, during the preparatory period, one must know how to find points of contact in the consciousness of wide circles of workers. It is necessary to establish proper relations with the mass organizations. It is necessary to find the correct point of departure corresponding to the concrete conditions of the proletarian vanguard in the person of its various groupings. And for this it is necessary to see oneself not as a makeshift for the new party, but only as an instrument for its creation. In other words, while preserving in its totality an intransigence on principle, it is necessary to free oneself radically from sectarian hangovers which subsist as a heritage from a purely propagandist period.

8. Those of our comrades who have manifested sectarian tendencies to the highest degree allege that the centrists of the SAP and the OSP always accused us of sectarianism, and that consequently we are now recognizing the justice of their charges, as well as the injustice of our criticism of the NAP, Paul Louis, etc. With such arguments these comrades once again illustrate how easily sectarianism consorts with opportunism. The leaders of the SAP and of the OSP accused us of sectarianism not because of what was weak in us, but just because of our strong points: tenaciousness of theory, hostility to all programmatic confusion and to unprincipled conciliationism and sterile combinations. Opportunism accuses and always will accuse Marxists of "sectarianism," of "talmudism," of "a tendency to split hairs." It is necessary to reply with the severest condemnation of the apologetic position taken by some comrades toward the leaders of the SAP and their clear tendency to revise our criticism of the centrist leadership in general. To free ourselves from the sectarian hangovers of the propagandist period does not mean to us the renunciation of Marxist criteria, but on the contrary to learn to carry them over into a wider field, that is to say, to wed them with the struggle of ever larger sections of the working class.

9. It is only in the light of the above considerations that one can correctly estimate the radical turn taken by our French section, which, after ample discussion, has entered the SFIO on the basis of the decision of its national conference. The opposition to this turn was dictated by considerations of two sorts. One sort, like those of Bauer and his supporters, saw in this entry an abandonment of Leninism, "a capitulation before reformism," and "a going over to the position of the Second International." Others fear, a fear altogether natural in itself, that our French section could not develop its position within the SFIO, that it would be forced to furl

its banner and thus would compromise the ICL. Comrade Naville and his group took an eclectic position in this question, running back and forth from one of these arguments to the other. The purely passive "intransigence" of Comrades Naville and Lhuillier[91] was but the complement of their opportunist policy in the preceding period, when they prevented systematic work within the SFIO, substituting for it with adaptation from the outside to the policy of the leadership. Finally, Comrade Bauer, under the influence of the fact that he was rebuffed, began to cover his basically purely sectarian Bordigist position with the purely empirical argument that the entrance of the League into the SFIO was "inopportune." The last declaration of Bauer, Lehmann, and others (September 20, 1934) is a mechanical amalgam of sectarianism and opportunism covered here and there with a fig leaf of "concrete realistic" considerations.

10. As for the natural and entirely legitimate fears of other sections that the turn of our French section might tie it hand and foot, the answer to these fears, incomplete and not definitive but nevertheless extremely important, has already been given by the facts. The plenum notes that the position openly taken by the Bolshevik-Leninist Group within the SFIO (Program of Action, three numbers of *Verite*, pamphlets on the militia, youth work) have nothing in common with capitulation but represent the application of the principles and methods of the ICL in its new orientation and under new conditions. In particular the plenum notes the indisputable progress of *Verite* as compared with the preceding period. This alone settles the question as to whether the entrance was "opportune" or "inopportune." The theoretical discussion on the character of the SFIO, its regime, etc., has received an empirical verification. The objective situation and the internal condition of the SFIO at the present stage are such as to give the Bolshevik-Leninists a serious possibility of participating in the internal life of the party and of push-

ing propaganda for their ideas on the basis of a real struggle of a sizeable party of the proletarian vanguard.

In view of the fact that the discussion on the French turn has led to sharp factional struggle between those favoring and those opposing entry, in the course of which errors were made on both sides, the plenum, while condemning the fact that the Naville faction in its factional activity took external steps damaging to the political life of our organizations, reminds the League of the necessity of a healthy political and organic life, and invites all members of the minority who value their connection with the ICL to immediately join the Bolshevik-Leninist Group of the SFIO on the basis of a common discipline. Consequently, every member of the minority who permits himself insinuations against our French section with the object of compromising it in the eyes of Socialist workers, by this very act places himself outside the ranks of the ICL. The plenum orders the IS to regularly furnish materials to all sections illustrating the work of the French section in the new situation, in order that the ICL as a whole may utilize the experiences thus acquired. ■

Cannon's mission in Europe[92]

November 3, 1934

Dear Comrade Cannon:

I regret that I cannot write you in English. I await with the greatest impatience your report on the important mission the IS gave you. I strongly hope that you have succeeded in settling the matter. The results would justify your trip to Europe two or three times over.

I will expect a letter from you in New York about the fusion with the AWP and other questions on the agenda.

I hope that you will take with you the manuscript of the *Verite* pamphlet, with which I am in full agreement. Its publication in America could be useful in my opinion.

Fraternally yours,

How to answer the London-Amsterdam Bureau[93]

November 1934

Dear Friends:

I do not believe that it would be proper to participate in the London-Amsterdam Bureau conference. They are at an impasse because of their heterogeneity. They can do nothing but repeat once again the hollow phrases of their previous resolutions. The vacuousness of their conference must inevitably become apparent now. But if we participate in their conference, they would all rise up as one against us in order to unmask our "sectarianism" and to teach us some lessons in political realism, etc., and this diversion would give an appearance of content to their conference: they would all become very self-satisfied and more conservative than ever.

I propose to respond somewhat as follows:

"Dear Comrades:

"You set forth two tasks for your conference at the end of November: (1) to assure the homogeneity of the positions of the various independent organizations regarding the movement toward proletarian unity; (2) to give each other mutual support for the purpose of participating in the united front.

"As far as we are concerned, we believe that it is absolutely impossible to assure a homogeneous position in the absence of a common foundation of principles, or, more precisely, in the absence of any principled foundation at all. The essential characteristic of your international grouping is its avoiding discussion of questions upon which the struggle and destiny of the proletariat depend. Your conferences are occupied, as a rule, with generalizations whose object is to obscure the absence of revolutionary principles and methods. Thus, despite the participation of a party as important as the NAP in your ranks, you have never settled your position—"homogeneous" or otherwise—on the disastrous politics of the leadership of that party, and that question is a hundred times more important than a homogeneous attitude toward the unity movement. To be frank, you replace revolutionary politics with the politics of summit diplomacy. In the past, all of our attempts to provoke a straightforward response from you or from the various organizations composing your bureau on fundamental principles have failed (our declaration at the time of your [1933] conference in Paris, the Declaration of Four in favor of the Fourth International, our theses on war, our offer to elaborate jointly a program for the Fourth International, that is, the fundamental principles which must guide the struggle of the proletarian vanguard in our epoch). *Never have you declared your position on fundamentals; you always hide behind procedural formalities to avoid doing so;* the agenda you propose is a continuation of the same policy.

"At such a time as you decide to place discussion of the Declaration of Four on the agenda of your conference—or discussion of our theses on war, or discussion of other similar documents, and above all the Norwegian question: namely, what the correct proletarian policy ought to be in Norway in order to save that country, and with it Scandinavia and indirectly all of Europe, from fascism—at that time you will be able to count on our active participation in your work. With Bolshevik-Leninist greetings, etc." ■

No compromise on the Russian question[94]

November 11, 1934

We have been informed by various sources that there is a tendency among our friends in Paris to deny the proletarian nature of the USSR, to demand that there be complete democracy in the USSR, including the legalization of the Mensheviks, etc. Please convey our position on this matter to the Central Committee officially: we regard this tendency *as treason* which must be fought implacably. One does not change one's attitude toward a question of such dimensions lightly; we have official resolutions which state clearly that denying the proletarian character of the USSR is incompatible with membership in the Bolshevik-Leninists. We have an official pamphlet on this decisive question. If there are comrades who have doubts about the correctness of our official doctrine, they are obligated to present counterresolutions for discussion, that is, for formal revision of the most important principles of our international politics. An openly conducted international discussion, even the possibility of a split, would be ten times better than the slightest equivocation.

The Mensheviks are the representatives of bourgeois restoration and we are for the defense of the workers' state by every means possible. Anyone who had proposed that we not support the British miners' strike of 1926 or the recent large-scale strikes in the United States with all available means on the ground that the leaders of the strikes were for the most part scoundrels, would have been a traitor to the British and American workers. Exactly the same thing applies to the USSR!

I repeat: no compromise on this question! Lay all the cards on the table! It is necessary to eradicate the bohemian influence which is poisoning certain elements in our organization and which drives them to change their position on fundamental questions as the spirit moves them. No, no compromise and no equivocation on this question! ■

We should join the Belgian Young Socialists[95]

November 19, 1934

Dear Comrades:

I have just read two documents: the undelivered speech by W. Dauge[96] (to the POB convention) and the JGS report for the 1934 national convention. Reading them was a revelation and a great moral satisfaction for me. I warmly congratulate Comrade Dauge both for his speech and for his contributions to the JGS report. There are a few secondary questions in the above-mentioned documents with which I cannot associate myself. We have no need, for example, to create a "mystique" around the [de Man] plan. The working class has no need at all of a "mystique" but rather of full awareness and a strong will. We can freely cede all mystique to de Man as his indisputable property. In this case, however, I am sure it's only a matter of an unfortunate choice of words. I by no means suspect Comrade Dauge of being an idealist or a mystic. More important is a nuance of idealization of the plan and its author. The report goes right up to the point of defending de Man's deliberately ambiguous and politically pernicious formulation on "national solidarity." I also find that we use the terms "fascism," "fascist," etc., too loosely, without distinguishing between fascism and Bonapartism. This distinction is extremely important in the current situation in Belgium. Having made those reservations, I state all the more willingly that the speech is excellent and that the spirit permeating the JGS report is revolutionary, encouraging, and refreshing.

De Man's plan is an equivocation. But the JGS poses the problem of the plan in a truly revolutionary way. The Bolshevik-Leninists must take up the most active and decisive participation in the JGS's campaign for the plan without sharing the illusions certain comrades, even JGS leaders, have about the plan. But criticism of the plan will be progressive only to the extent that our comrades base themselves on the campaign for the plan; that is, for the conquest of power as the only way of carrying out the plan by transforming it.

The fact that we cannot only join the JGS but can give speeches like Dauge's shows that our friends should immediately join the JGS. I must admit, dear comrades, that after reading the two above-mentioned documents, I simply cannot understand how Marxists, Bolsheviks, can hesitate for one minute on the question of entry. This shows a high degree of political petrification. Doctrinaire intransigence is an essential trait of Bolshevism, but it makes up only 10 percent of its historic content; the other 90 percent is applying principles to the real movement; it's participating in the mass organizations, above all the youth, who ask only for our support. Beyond that, allow me to advise our young Bolshevik-Leninist comrades to join the JGS not only to enlighten and educate them, but also to enlighten and educate themselves. The JGS report and above all the contributions of Godefroid[97] and Dauge show me that our friends have a lot to learn in this excellent milieu. Too much time has been lost. There is not a minute more to lose. ■

Suggestions for the GBL[98]

November 20, 1934

Dear Frangin:

This time I want to speak of a number of things—in my own name and that of several friends here and at B. ["Besancon"], from whom I have just received a very interesting letter. To take them in order:

1. The question of the [CGT's labor] plan increases in importance and, in passing, I think you should put this question in your trade union opposition platform; but above all the paper must take a position: the comrades in B. think we

must devote a special number of the paper to this question, continuing and developing the series "Whither France?" but on the plan. If you are in agreement, you should create a special commission on this question, perhaps the same as for the previous text, and enter into collaboration with the B. group, which wants to propose a text on this question. They request, in case of your consent, some necessary documents (among others, Varga's[99] pamphlet on the de Man plan, the SP's documents on planning, the CGT's *Peuple*, etc.). The elaboration of a text will naturally take ten or twelve days.

2. It seems to me in general that *La V[erite]* cannot and should not imitate the big papers, using the same type of headlines, etc. It loses its effectiveness if the text is spread out. The most homogeneous numbers (like that devoted to the militia) are the best. This, generally, should be the orientation. Of course, this is not a pedantic rule, but a general tendency. If you plan a series of special numbers, you should get other comrades to collaborate who are outside your leadership and outside Paris. Preparation will then be better and more methodical.

3. Don't you think that after a certain "stabilization" on the new basis, *La V.* can send out a questionnaire along the following lines to sympathizing individuals and groups?

a. Have you noticed a change in the line of *La V.* since entry into the SP?

b. Don't you find that the possibilities for struggle for a revolutionary Marxist policy in the SFIO have increased through this experience?

c. What prevents you from joining the SFIO to strengthen the left wing?

d. What advice have you for improving the content or form of our paper, etc.?

4. I think a special number should be devoted to the CP, composed of quotations with sober comments. The policy of the Comintern and its French section, at least since the German catastrophe, should be reviewed. Oskar Fischer wrote such a

pamphlet on Germany, translated by you. Such a work should be done for France, using the files of *L'Humanite, Cahiers du Bolchevisme*, etc., and contrasting them with quotations from *La V.* Don't forget that you are addressing a new audience that does not know your past. Don't forget that you have to vaccinate the revolutionary socialists against Stalinism. Above all, don't forget that the CP, in its new phase, is the most serious barrier to a mass revolutionary policy. Readers must be shown their zigzags of the last two years at least so as to discredit their present line. A number like this could have a great repercussion inside the CP. Two or three young comrades could prepare it. The editors need only write a lead article criticizing the Stalinist zigzags and the miserable regime that prevents revolutionary education of the youth above all.

5. Given the unfavorable social composition of the Young Socialists, a supplementary rule should perhaps be established: each member of our tendency who does not win two young workers within a certain time should be excluded from our tendency. It seems to us that the young comrades do not give decisive enough importance to this question. We also think that an environment of young workers would have a salutary effect on our own youth, without which a dangerous development can be expected; it is always dangerous when young students talk in the name of the proletariat without daily contact with the young workers and without learning many things about them before setting themselves up as educators.

6. The threat to Blum and *Le Populaire*'s reaction seem to us extremely important from the point of view of [our agitation for] the militia. It should be used to this end.

7. Are our comrades concerning themselves with Saint-Denis? It is possible a good harvest can be reaped there. In any case the Saint-Denis workers' pulse should be felt.

8. A friend writes me that Treint has given talks on the USSR at Socialist meetings that are along the line of Laurat's[100] view. In this case we must sharply demarcate ourselves

from Treint. Nothing helps push revolutionary workers toward the Stalinists more than an equivocal attitude toward the USSR on our part. This is why the Stalinists, always and everywhere, call us enemies of the USSR. Each equivocal statement on this question, even in private conversation, is a political crime, which weakens our future. Beware!

9. It seems nothing can be expected from Just, for whom socialism is not a question of immediate revolutionary struggle but "the noblest expression of human solidarity." You don't say! He occupies himself with making designs for the future socialist administration instead of occupying himself with the struggle against the capitalist state. The last number of *Bataille Socialiste*, despite its insufficiency, gives a more favorable impression. The article by H. and R. Modiano[101] on the plan was written with intelligence and understanding. Unfortunately the authors imply the best intentions to Jouhaux because Jouhaux supports bourgeois democracy. Instead of denouncing Jouhaux they caress him, although a bit gingerly.

Fraternally,
B. [Leon Trotsky]

Remarks on the Kirov assassination[102]

December 10, 1934

Although a week has passed since Kirov's assassination, it is impossible at the present moment to arrive at a correct assessment of this event because of lack of information. Let us try, however, to review the matter in a general way. Since 1927, when a GPU leader was killed in White Russia and a bomb was thrown at the GPU headquarters in Moscow, there have been no terrorist acts in the USSR. The terrorist acts of 1927, which, moreover, had the nature of a final convulsion, like those which had preceded them (Volodarsky, Uritsky, Vorovsky,[103] and others), had been organized and executed by White Guards (or previously by Social Revolutionaries), in any case, by representatives of the classes and parties of old Russia.

In our opinion what clearly distinguishes the assassination of Kirov is that it does not compose a new link in the chain of terrorist acts—which, moreover, had become weak and disjointed—of the first ten years of the revolution, but that it constitutes a phenomenon *which is entirely new and of directly Soviet origin.*

Nikolaev, the assassin, is a man whose life was molded entirely under Soviet conditions (he was only thirteen when the October Revolution broke out), and he certainly did not act at the instigation of a foreign country or any political organization. We have no definite information and we do not know whether Nikolaev was a member of the Communist Party. We think that the latter is not at all excluded. In any case, he was a Soviet employee, working in the central departments (the very fact that he was able to gain admittance to the Smolny, which is rather well guarded, can be interpreted as a sign that he knew his way around).

What motivated the assassin? Many hypotheses have been presented in the press.

1. Nikolaev may have been connected with the same organization that killed King Alexander.[104] We will pass over that one.

2. The Nazi and the White Guard press speak of a provocation on the part of the GPU: the GPU may have killed Kirov in order to show that it is indispensable and to augment its power.

In this connection mention is made of the rivalry between the GPU and the party apparatus. That such rivalry exists is incontestable. But to think that it has reached such dimensions that the GPU assassinates leaders of the party—the least one can say is that this exaggeration is altogether out of proportion with the state of affairs. Today the rivalry of the GPU manifests itself over the questions of the GPU statutes, the limits of its jurisdiction, and the composition of its leadership (for example, the underhanded and very prolonged struggle which took place over the replacement of Menzhinsky by Yagoda).[105]

3. In *Le Populaire* Leon Blum champions the theory of personal revenge, which enables him to dodge the political question more easily. We hold this hypothesis to be almost out of the question, especially the idea that Nikolaev might have wanted revenge for having been fired from his job. It is much too easy to find work in Russia for the loss of a job to become a tragedy and for an individual to choose a terrorist act and certain death.

Other plausible hypotheses: a lunatic, a fanatic.

The fact that it took a whole day to force him to give his name—and more than a week has passed without any confessions being published—does not give the impression that Nikolaev is a lunatic. Moreover, this hypothesis has been raised nowhere.

We are entirely inclined to think that it is the case of a *political assassination*. In striking at Kirov, one of the leaders of the Communist Party and one of the most eminent members of Stalin's inner circle, Nikolaev must have intended by this act, to strike a blow at the party in power, its policies, and its leaders.

That we are not dealing with a chance terrorist act seems to be confirmed by the fact that enormous importance has been attached to it in the USSR. The [Central] Executive Committee of the Soviets not only adopted a special decree mandating rapid and merciless trial procedures against terrorist groups, but a *change* is also being prepared along the same lines in *the criminal codes of the USSR*. This is a sign that the assassination causes the greatest anxiety among the Soviet leadership, and that they consider it not the act of a lunatic or personal revenge but something much deeper and far graver, against which they have to take measures for the future. The sixty-six who were shot and the mass arrests confirm the same thing.

Are we dealing with a man who has been disappointed by the revolution or with a conscious Thermidorean? Whatever the answer, it does not at all change the fact that Nikolaev's blow is in reality aimed against Soviet Russia, against the working class in power. Needless to repeat here that our position cannot be any other than that of the most absolute, clear and vehement condemnation of this assassination, which, like the whole terrorist method in general, can serve but one goal: *to clear the road for Bonapartism and fascism in the USSR*.

We cannot here pass in silence over the fact that the Stalinist regime at times drives honest people into the blind alley of despair; among them, unfortunately, there may still grow up other Nikolaevs. If there are still potential and active anti-Soviet elements in the USSR—because the classes are far from being liquidated and the Soviet Union, contrary to the pretenses of the Stalinist doctrine, cannot "make an abstraction" of world relations—then Stalinism helps the growth of these counterrevolutionary cadres by driving into their ranks discouraged or misguided elements who might have been saved but are unable to find the correct road in the darkness of the internal regime. The Stalinist policies and the regime that stifles the slightest stirrings of political life inside the party bear no small share of the responsibility for the fact that counterrevolutionary tendencies manifest themselves at times even among elements that are not hostile to the regime.

It is enough to recall that in 1932, the period of the most acute crisis in the USSR, there was much talk of various groups with terrorist aims, particularly among the youth. When arrested, some youths told of having heard everywhere, within the family circle, in the factory or in the school, words of hatred against Stalin; they saw him as the cause of the state of affairs in the USSR; and they thought that by eliminating this cause, they would effect a change in this state of affairs. The personalization of the regime in the USSR, where the party does not exist, where only the leaders count, can only work in favor of terrorist tendencies. Up to now, fortunately for the USSR and for the working class movement, these terrorist tendencies did not crystallize into action.

It would be a monstrous mistake to attempt to identify the discontent of the Soviet masses with the act of Nikolaev. The Soviet worker is discontented, but he is deeply attached to the regime, and he seeks a solution inside the Soviet framework through the road of reform. In his eyes, Nikolaev is only a class enemy.

But the very existence of these terrorist tendencies and the shot fired by Nikolaev reflect—although in an exceptional and extremely distorted way—the profound political crisis which the Russian Revolution is passing through.

As to the sixty-six who were shot: Apparently they have nothing to do with the Nikolaev affair itself. They were arrested prior to and entirely independently of Kirov's assassination. Their execution aims at spreading terror among new and potential Nikolaevs. Parallel measures were taken during Lenin's lifetime too; but then everything was done in broad daylight: everyone knew *who* was shot and *why*. The list of the executed does not contain any biographical material or anything else which would allow one to draw any conclusions whatever.

Contained in the list is a name rare in Russia: Eismont. There was an Eismont[106] who was an old member of the party, a people's commissar. He was arrested in 1932, accused of conspiring against Stalin. However, there is nothing that permits us to say that it is the same Eismont. If it is he, an entirely different evaluation would be necessary.

We must be on guard. If Nikolaev acted on his own, and in any case has had no connection with any political organization whatever, we may count on all sorts of possible surprises. In order to draw a greater political profit from this event, that is to say, in order to enable him to deal a counterblow, Stalin may seek to link up Nikolaev even with . . . the ICL. This is not very probable but it is not excluded. There is nothing extraordinary in such a supposition. With his continual amalgams and his Wrangel officer,[107] Stalin has already shown what he is capable of in an internal struggle.

As the contents of this letter indicate, it is confidential, and only certain opinions expressed in it should be utilized. The axis of an article on this question from our point of view should be the absolute condemnation of the assassin and the defense of the USSR against its class enemies, both external and internal. We again specify that we have as yet no information that permits us to pass definitive judgment, and that subsequent information may again render necessary a radical change in the appraisal of the event. ∎

On the draft political statutes[108]

December 1934

I will confine myself to the most important remarks on this document. Point 4, "Against support for parliamentary democracy." In this general and absolute form, it is false, especially in the present situation in France. We are in favor of maintaining parliamentary democracy when it is being attacked by fascism or Bonapartism. It is precisely on this basis that the united front has become possible and even the entry of the League into the SFIO. At the same time, we are for overthrowing parliamentary democracy with soviet democracy. These *two* sides of our policy must be formulated separately.

Point 5. Defense of democracy and defense of the USSR are put on the same plane. These two questions must be divided by linking the defense of the USSR to point 7a (which should itself be divided into two or three points).

The same point 5 takes a stand in favor of the transformation of the imperialist war into a civil war, but it says nothing about revolutionary activity to prevent the war from breaking out. At the present time, when we are in the midst of a political and social crisis, when the struggle against fascism can only grow sharper and sharper, we can and must foresee the possibility of launching large-scale revolutionary movements against war. It is that task which we must emphasize above all others.

Point 6 speaks of the "disintegration" of the bourgeois army. This formulation should perhaps be avoided for legal reasons. It would be sufficient to say: "in order to win over its best elements to the cause of the proletariat."

Point 7a. It is quite characteristic that the point which speaks of the revolutionary defense of the USSR carries the letter "a." This suggests that in the original text the question of the defense of the USSR was not mentioned at all. I dwell on this "peculiarity" because it reveals a state of mind which I find disastrous. If the young Leninists want to discredit themselves and perish, they need only adopt an equivocal position on the defense of the USSR, by putting this question on the same level as the defense of democracy; that is, by equating capitalist property relations with nationalized property relations, by equating the most perfect bourgeois state (where does one exist, by the way?) with the most deformed workers' state.

My conclusions: the point dealing with the revolutionary defense of the USSR must be placed among the first points of the statutes and completely separated from the question of the "right to criticize the Soviet bureaucracy." Moreover, the latter formulation is not very clear; it is not apparent whether we are demanding these rights for the Soviet workers or for ourselves. It seems that in the eleven points of the preconference of the International Left Opposition (February 1933) the same idea is formulated more correctly.

Point 9 speaks of a new youth organization, of a new party. This is too abstract and does not explain why we have entered the JS. A campaign for a united youth organization is now under way. We need to state that this campaign will prove fruitful only on the basis of the revolutionary principles set out in our political statutes. We propose these statutes as a charter for the united youth organization.

The greatest defect of the statutes is that they do not deal with the real situation of the JS, to which you belong, and of the Seine Alliance in particular. Your weakness is your totally unfavorable social composition. You have hardly any young workers, and that is the question which should be at the center of your political statutes, which are written not for the universe and for all time, but for your small group, which is inside the Seine Alliance in 1934. The conclusion must state: that principles set out in our statutes can really be applied only if our organization is anchored in the working class itself. Otherwise it will have only an ephemeral, inconsequential existence. That is why our supreme task—the task of the entire organization and of each individual member—is to recruit young workers. Our real successes will be measured not by how much we repeat the same superrevolutionary formulas, but by how much we can radically change the social composition of our organization.

The statutes say nothing on the question of the united front. This is a serious omission. We must indicate that the united front must pursue concrete tasks of the mass struggle while maintaining the right of each organization to criticize, within the framework of discipline in action.

You speak again of the "autonomy" of the youth. This is a formulation which has been compromised, because it has been identified with the tendency to split from the party. At the present time, this is not our tendency, but that of the right-wingers who really would like to have us outside the party! Speaking of autonomy in the statutes provides the best possible service to Levy and the others. We should speak of the youth's right to freedom of discussion and freedom of criticism in the framework of discipline in action. This is completely adequate and has the advantage of not inciting the adult workers to oppose us.

Vidal [Leon Trotsky]

A few remarks on 'Revolution'[109]

December 1934

1. *Revolution* must be a workers' newspaper or it must not be at all. A workers' newspaper is not a newspaper written *for* workers. Nor is it necessarily a newspaper written *by* workers. But it must reflect the life of the working class and give timely answers to the questions raised among young

workers by events, both large and small.

2. It is necessary to write clearly; to do this it is necessary to understand well both the question being dealt with and the goal of the presentation. Never write merely for the sake of writing, in order to create a lead story, or to fill up a given column.

3. Before writing an article on a specific question, it is necessary to speak with some young workers about the topic and to listen closely to their questions, suggestions, objections, etc. After the article is written, it must be submitted to the young workers' criticism.

4. Do not copy the big papers either in the layout of the columns or in the treatment of the subject or in the tone of presentation. When an important question for the working class and especially for the youth arises, it is possible and necessary to sweep aside the regular columns and devote the entire issue to that question (for example, unemployment among the youth, an important strike in which youth are taking part, etc.) from different angles: an accurate presentation of the facts, eyewitness reports, a theoretical article on the same theme, analogous episodes from international experience, etc. Such an issue of the paper is like an artillery shell that blasts open its own path.

5. Never adopt the tone of a teacher of little children. Always speak to the readers as your equals, but speak honestly, after study and preparation, without covering up for your deficiencies with empty phrases.

6. Never give articles the character of commentaries on events which it is assumed that the reader knows all about. Each article must contain its own solid framework, composed of precise facts and dates. Commentaries must be sober, flowing from the presentation of the facts themselves. This is the only way to avoid sterile and demeaning didacticism.

7. Do not be afraid to repeat the most elementary things, always refreshing them with new facts.

8. Follow carefully the entire French press—bourgeois and working class, political and trade union, Parisian and local; clip out all facts, even insignificant ones, which relate to the life of working class youth; place the clippings in file folders; consult the files each time an article has to be produced on this or that question.

9. Create immediately a revolutionary reporters' roster. Assign each reporter a district of the city or a special function (the workers and bourgeois justice, unemployment, soup kitchens, foreign workers, the barracks, etc.). The reporters must also be agitators and recruiters. They must be in constant contact with the milieu they are covering.

10. Once, twice, or four times a month, depending on the frequency of publication, all the writers, reporters, and some young workers should meet to exchange impressions, compile suggestions, and discuss the articles being prepared.

11. The news columns of the press contain heaps of facts which are highly significant for understanding society in general and the life of young workers in particular. Every day brings news of the suicides of young people who have lost all hope, of the murder of children by desperate parents, etc. A whole page can often be filled by carefully matching up these news items and adding short vigorous comments.

12. Signed articles are not very appropriate for the working class press in general and the young workers' press in particular. The reader should become accustomed to seeing in the newspaper a collective personality, that is, the organization.[110]

13. The question of socialist society as an alternative to capitalist society must be highlighted by this or that feature in each issue and on every possible occasion. It is necessary to find in the writings of the great socialists, starting with the Utopians, penetrating formulations, each a few lines long. Two or three of these should be published on every page.

14. It is absolutely intolerable to use allusions which can

be understood only by young "bureaucrats," slangy insiders' expressions, and abbreviations which are absolutely incomprehensible for the average young worker.

15. The newspaper can only become a workers' newspaper provided that all the forces of the organization are directed toward the workers' districts, the industrial districts, etc. The newspaper which does not recruit workers to the organization does not deserve to exist.

16. Finally, the nature of our epoch must be reflected well by the paper. The essential feature of this epoch is that it raises the most profound questions about society and demands the most radical answers. The prerevolutionary epoch we live in needs only a real combat party to transform it into a revolutionary epoch. The newspaper must be combative and courageous, and aim high.

A Group of Readers [Leon Trotsky]

Once more on our turn[111]

December 15, 1934

To the International Secretariat
For all Sections

Dear Comrades:

As of this writing I still do not know the decision of the Belgian national conference. But I must state with the greatest regret that there is a faction in the Belgian section that does not wish to learn from events because it is satisfied with abstract formulas that demand little and allow nothing. Isn't the experience of the French section clear enough?

The Belgian "intransigents" supported the Naville group in France as the most intransigent tendency. The experiment has been tried and only the deliberately blind can avoid drawing the necessary lessons. Naville represented conservatism, a wait-and-hope attitude, and a closed-circle discussion-group mentality—Souvarinism. He systematically refrains from criticizing the politics of the SFIO in order to be able to "act" under its protection. We have denounced this antirevolutionary attitude many times. But to no avail. At the moment of the turn, Naville tried to cover his conservatism with intransigent formulations. He called the entry "capitulation" because basically he was frightened by the prospect of a ferocious battle against a powerful apparatus. It is much easier to defend "intransigent" principles in a sealed jar. . . . Our analysis of Naville was made in a very factional period. But since then, I repeat, the experiment has been tried. Since then Naville has entered the Socialist Party. But he abandoned the banner of the organization, the program. He does not wish to be more than the left wing of the SP. He has already presented motions in common with the left wing, confused opportunist motions, full of the verbiage of so-called left centrism. The Belgian "intransigents" have been well punished. "Tell me who your friends and international allies are, and I'll tell you who you are."

The most intransigent opponent of the entry, even more so than Naville, was Bauer. Comrade Give's most important arguments seem to be drawn from Bauer's arsenal. What is Bauer's attitude, then, toward entry? He demands that our German section join the SAP, and while awaiting this development he has become a contributor to the SAP paper—against us. Is a more clear and complete bankruptcy imaginable? The SFIO is a mass organization, not a homogeneous propaganda group. The state of this organization is such that the possibility is open to us to enter it as a homogeneous propaganda group. They say to us: "That will never be possible." Well, the experiment has been tried. On the plane of principle our French section has remained what it was. But on the political plane, it has graduated from a preparatory course to a more advanced course.

The SAP is not a mass organization. It is itself a propaganda group. This being the case, fusion is impermissible in the absence of a common program and method. Our attempt a year ago to find this common ground failed: the leaders of the SAP did not want to accept our principles. In a series of documents Bauer dealt with them as incorrigible centrists, or more simply, people without principles. It is possible that the leaders of the SAP have evolved in a favorable direction. If this is the case, we should renew our attempt to come to an understanding with them on a programmatic basis. But to condemn the entry of our French section into a mass organization and at the same time demand the dissolution of our German section into a small propaganda group, which Bauer himself characterized as centrist just a short time ago—isn't this an abominable mockery of the ABCs of Marxism?

Once again I ask Comrade Give and those who support him how they explain the fact that the "intransigents" in France have turned out to be opportunists and adventurers while the "capitulators" continue to support our principles with redoubled energy, principles which for the first time now directly or indirectly influence the internal life of the Socialist Party, as well as that of the Communist Party, and even of the trade unions (see, for instance, the documents of the departmental union of Isere). Comrade Give will tell us that these two instances of Naville and Bauer are questions of personality, etc. But we do not allow anyone to hide behind this individualist, idealist, and anti-Marxist explanation. We have all the more right to make a point of this since we predicted the evolution of the Navilles and Bauers after deciphering the real meaning of their "intransigence." And we say: "Comrade Give bears full responsibility for his allies in France whom he supported as the truly revolutionary tendency."

We've tried the experiment, Comrade Give. We have had enough generalities. Explain to us your bad luck in France if you please. In the eyes of the International you bear part of the responsibility for Naville-Bauer.

The "disastrous" picture Comrade Give paints of the International (see the Belgian national committee minutes for November 25) is completely tendentious or else it reveals a total lack of comprehension about what is really going on. "In Poland a three-way split," "a split in Greece," etc. Comrade Give is only echoing Naville and Bauer, who, of course, for their part, see only the reverse side of the turn. Give doesn't mention that the French comrades have won the 6,000-member Federation of the Seine to our program of action and that our youth are in the leadership of the Seine Alliance with its 1,450 members. We do not wish to exaggerate the revolutionary weight of this success. There is more to do than we have succeeded in doing in the three-and-a-half months that have passed since our entry. But really one would have to be deaf and blind to fail to grasp the radical change in the activity of our French section and the enormous possibilities that have opened before it. There are comrades who hold up the incident with Leon Blum as proof of our French comrades' dependence.[112] Arguments of this sort are proof of their own total political bankruptcy. If we want to win over the Socialist workers, we must present our ideas in language they can understand. They can understand our arguments against Blum, but they cannot accept ridicule, especially now, at a time when the Stalinists are fraternizing with Blum and Company. The psychological transgression against the mood of the Socialist workers that was committed by the editors of

La Verite was far more serious than the juridical transgression against the statutes of the SFIO. But precisely because *La Verite* now breathes the same air as the workers, it has forthrightly corrected its error and as a result it has been able to increase its prestige in the eyes of the best elements of the Socialist Party. To seize upon this incident of a purely technical nature in order to accredit the tattered remnants of the arguments raised by the "intransigents" before our entry—what further certification of bankruptcy is necessary?

Other comrades of the same Bordigist and Hennautist tendency will object: "You told us that Doumergue would yield to the fascists, and look, it's Flandin[113] who has replaced him. The whole perspective of the entrists has proven false. We do have time to grow independently . . ." It is fatal to let an incorrect position deform your whole perspective and all your criteria. Never did we say that Doumergue would *personally* hand over power to the fascists; we spoke of French Bonapartism, of which Doumergue was the first (but not the last) representative.

In Germany, Bruening, the first representative of semi-parliamentary Bonapartism, yielded to von Papen, the direct extraparliamentary agent of Hindenburg, but von Papen had to yield to Schleicher, who was more "social" and more parliamentary than he was. One can never predict personal combinations and concrete developments. It is enough to predict the general tendency. For us, Flandin represents a feebler version of the Doumergue regime. If French Bonapartism had only a few weeks to live, this change in the regime would be of no avail. It is precisely because the Bonapartist regime in France still has a certain lease on life that the change can yield important and even decisive results.

There is much talk of diminishing of the economic crisis. If this actually comes about (let us accept the hypothesis), then the showdown will be postponed for one, two, or even three years. If that were the case, would we establish ourselves on the basis of the new conjuncture in order to take advantage of the workers' economic struggles and to prepare their mobilization as a revolutionary force? But even an important conjunctural change (and we are still a long way from that) would not change our general line of development or our orientation. After a very short time, a new crisis far more terrible than the present one would break out and the whole political process would assume a much quicker tempo than at present. Thanks to the turn executed while there is still time, we still have the chance to enter the decisive battle—that is, the armed conflict between the proletariat and fascism—not as a small sect that looks on and criticizes, but as the prime mover of the revolutionary vanguard.

Instead of rejoicing over the fact that our French section was able to draw the lessons of the German events, etc., in time, Comrades Bauer and the others wax indignant: "We've been deceived: we entered the SFIO and fascism hasn't arrived yet." It is true that thanks to the efforts of Comrade Give and others, Naville and Bauer were able to weaken the French section for a certain time. By entering, our youth lost more than a few comrades, even workers. But thanks to the effectiveness of the turn, we are now winning back the elements who left us for a certain time, while the intransigents, the instigators of the split, have lost everything: program, prestige, principles.

It is absurd to say that the international situation is disastrous. In what way? In Holland, the OSP, after expelling de Kadt from its ranks, has evolved in a Marxist direction and thanks to the turn in France has decided to fuse with our section, the RSP. In America the AWP (Muste's party), long courted by the Lovestoneites and the Stalinists, decided to fuse with our section. Those are two remarkable successes. The unified party in America will have great opportunities on the socialist left. We can predict that the unified party in Holland will create new breaches in the Social Democratic Party and among the Stalinists. The Polish section is one of the newest sections. It is going through its period of infantile disorders. The split in the Greek section has nothing to do with the French turn. The faction hostile to our international organization is led by Witte, whom Vereecken tore to pieces fifteen months ago for having a total lack of principles and conducting intrigues dictated by vulgar motives. Now it turns out that the Witte faction is "intransigent" and severely condemns entry into the SFIO. Comrade Give should be more prudent and not invoke the Greek events. Allies like Witte are really too compromising.

Much more disturbing is the passivity of our Spanish section (with a few honorable exceptions) during the [recent] great revolutionary events. We have always criticized the leaders of the Spanish section for being imbued with a purely propagandistic spirit and a wait-and-see attitude. Every comrade can and should reread the international discussions with the Spanish leadership. And here is the significant point: the Spanish comrades have openly declared their hostility to the French turn. This is another confirmation that "intransigence" on this question is nothing but a mask for purely propagandistic and journalistic passivity. As far as we are concerned, we will continue to repeat: the greatest error that has been committed by any of our sections is the error of the Spanish section in not joining the Socialist Party when the preparation for armed struggle was beginning.

Where did the majority of the Belgian section go wrong on the question of entry into the SFIO? We pointed it out at the time: instead of analyzing the real condition of the workers' movement in each country, Vereecken manipulated absolute abstract notions—*reformism, Second International,* etc., . . ."reformism cannot tolerate this . . ." "reformism cannot accept that. . . ." Recent events in Spain have greatly contributed to discrediting this Bordigist, anti-Marxist, metaphysical method. The leadership of the POB wanted to expel the *Action Socialiste* group. The trade union leaders called for the same thing. But changes in the situation forced the bureaucracy to tolerate *Action Socialiste* and pushed de

Man into flirting with the JGS, whose revolutionary character, given inevitable ups and downs, is constantly on the increase. We can see that history makes use of more colors than just red and yellow. It possesses transitional shades, and the art of politics consists in discerning them in order to influence their change by the appropriate means. To lose even one more day because of Bordigist scruples is a crime. Entry into the Young Socialist Guards in order to defend Leninist ideas with patience, energy, and tact—this is the only road for the construction of a revolutionary party.

Every great turn occasioned by a change in the objective situation has a profound impact on the organization, whose mood reflects the previous period. In such cases, individual defections or even partial splits of sections are inevitable. But a turn executed in time is a hundred times more important than the loss of a few comrades who wish at all costs to mark time. The best of these splitters will repent the errors they have committed and return to our organization so that we will eventually be able to reinforce it by linking it to the mass movements.

My best revolutionary and antisectarian greetings,
X [Leon Trotsky]

Notes on the GBL's internal problems[114]

Late 1934 or early 1935

These comments may lag behind events, but I will make them just the same. Comrade Gerard [Rosenthal], as I see in the minutes, tries to justify collaboration with *Lutte de classes*, which was created as a competitor of the GBL.[115] Working with it would mean becoming uninvolved with one's own organization. But without dedication to one's own organization nothing important can be done in the working class movement.

I consider the (rather belated) publication of *Lutte de classes* a mistake on the part of Comrade Naville. But I hope that the mistake will be remedied by a merger [of the two groups]. Abstractly, a conference could be dispensed with, but the Naville group, bound by its past (and above all by its mistakes), insists on a conference. Why not comply? Why not show the Naville group and the Socialist milieu around us our willingness to collaborate in good faith, our freedom from considerations of false pride, etc.?

The leadership's reorganization of itself[116] is an experiment. An experiment is judged by its results. What deserves praise in this experiment is the goodwill of the majority in applying reasonable suggestions from the minority. The censure of resignations[117] is excellent. Let us hope there will be no need to repeat it.

As for the Central Committee's new organization of its work, I have only one point to make, and that concerns the relation of the Political Bureau to everyday administrative work. Comrade Gerard is right in pointing out that the omnipotent secretariat is a Stalinist innovation. But in Lenin's time, in addition to the Political Bureau, which met once a week (except in special cases), there was another bureau of five comrades operating continuously and issuing directives for day-to-day work. There was a rule that one negative vote in this other bureau was enough for the question to be referred to the first bureau. I mention this for information. I do not draw any conclusions for our organization. We are much too weak. Our task is to find a line that will save us from two pitfalls: concentrating the leadership in the hands of a very small number of comrades, and dispersing it among independent bodies. Only experience can point to the most suitable form of organization.

As for the personal composition [of the Political Bureau], I have no comments to make. In the minutes I find this sentence from Comrade Meche[118]: "I will work harder than ever despite not being chosen for the Political Bureau." There's a truly revolutionary remark.

I return to the question of the merger conference. I read the objection of Comrade Frank, who asserts that nothing can come of the conference. Why nothing, since it can bring about the merger? The conference could be organized in a thoroughly modest way to avoid expense and waste of time. Naville himself suggests a small-scale meeting. Why oppose that suggestion?

I find that, absorbed as you are by your day-to-day work, you still are not addressing international questions which could soon take on great importance.

Legally speaking, we have "lost" our American section and we are "losing" our Dutch section; at the same time, we could do with a more solid base to work for the Fourth International.

The question of the London-Amsterdam Bureau should not be neglected. Their conference in February (???) has to be considered. To take part in such a conference would be an unforgivable blunder. It seems that the NAP has let them down. Only the SAP, OSP, and ILP are left. But the SAP and OSP previously signed the Declaration of Four, only to betray it the following day. If they are willing to reaffirm this declaration, we would be quite happy to give the matter another try. But to go to this conference without prior assurances would be a criminal mistake. It would be tantamount to entering a conference with Rimbert, Lhuillier, Lasterade,[119] etc., without prior understandings, giving them an opportunity to sit in judgment on us, defame us, etc.

It is important to stress the activity of the SAP members

in the SFIO. I have reason to believe that this activity may be quite harmful. They declare themselves in agreement with us "in principle" only to denigrate and compromise us as much as possible. That kind of company is always dangerous (which is why, in particular, I insist on the need to settle the question with the Naville group: either we join forces, or we contend openly). And since the SAP influences the left formations, especially M. Pivert, an article in *Verite* should be devoted to this party.

In the latest issue of *Verite* a comrade poses the question of organic unity. I do not think it would be useful to return to that question in all its breadth. It would only confuse matters. All we need to do is consider the current situation: everyone has now emerged from that period of confusion when the byword organic unity meant everything and nothing. Now we are facing the problem of a program for the united front, as we did for organic unity. That is enough for us to say: we are committed to follow this through to its conclusion. The letter in question should be answered, I think, along those lines. ■

Remarks on our general orientation[120]

Late 1934 or early 1935

No one among us doubts the correctness of our general orientation. The only question is whether the tempo of events confirms this orientation. To this we reply:

a. Political forecasts can never pretend to fix in advance the *tempo* of events.

b. Our assessment was not only a *forecast* but above all a *warning:* workers, events *can* develop very rapidly, we must prepare. We are dealing not with astronomy but with revolutionary action.

c. Nothing has happened yet to indicate that the tempo of events has moderated for an entire period. The lull can be fleeting, we do not yet know what this winter will bring.

The immediate perspective could change seriously only on one condition—that the economic conjuncture improves. All classes orient themselves for the moment toward that perspective. If the next months show an increase in economic activity on a world scale, that would affect the political situation in France very materially, even if France lags behind economically, which is almost inevitable. Improvement of the conjuncture would not change our general orientation but it would change the pace and the stages, which is very important for practical work. Improvement of the conjuncture would create a favorable basis for immediate demands and would thus unloose a wave of strikes, reinforce the trade unions, etc. For us that would mean an additional period for education, for preparation on the basis of the everyday activity of the masses.

If the crisis is continued or aggravated, disappointment will take more acute forms among all the classes, even in the very near future. Flandin's corporatism does not change very much. He himself may be swept away by a new "explosion" like that of February 6. Under such conditions, fascist reaction, like the revolution, will have a new and powerful impulsion.

It seems to me that today, like yesterday, we must stress this last possibility and draw all the political consequences.

At the same time we must keep our hand on the pulse of the country's economy in order to recognize changes in time. A comrade should be specially assigned to study the economic conjuncture in connection with the activity of the capitalists and the strike movements.

In any case, it must be foreseen that any new "prosperity" will be very unstable and, giving rise to great hopes, will be followed by a new crisis, perhaps more acute than the present one, and that this new crisis will have enormous and almost immediate political consequences. It should be well understood that this epoch, with its social instability and economic changes, brings profound political repercussions, which, despite their instability, are proof of the tension of class relations. ■

The state and the USSR[121]

Late 1934 or early 1935

On the question of the *state*, as on all important questions, there are three points of view: that of capital, that of the proletariat, and that of the petty bourgeoisie.

Capital understands its state well, despite the diverse forms in which it presents itself. Capital is never defeatist [toward its state] merely because it does not like the government. The bourgeoisie becomes defeatist when it is expropriated, that is, when it ceases to be a bourgeoisie.

The proletariat has a less well-developed class consciousness, but it clearly discerns, through its vanguard, its position in the bourgeois state. The Soviet proletariat, despite its hate of the bureaucracy, regards the state as its own. The sympathies of the working masses for the USSR, in spite of the crisis in the Soviet bureaucracy, prove the same thing.

The situation is different in regard to the petty bourgeoisie, especially the intellectuals. They have no state of their own. They continually swing back and forth. They base their evaluation of the state on secondary symptoms, fleeting impressions, etc.

Thus the German Social Democratic bureaucracy, fiercely patriotic under the Hohenzollerns[122] and more so under "democracy," has become defeatist since the advent of Hitler.

The fundamental character of the German state has changed for neither the German bourgeoisie nor the conscious proletariat; the bourgeoisie remains patriotic as it was under "democracy" and the proletariat remains defeatist as it was under "democracy," but the petty-bourgeois intellectuals have made a 180-degree turn. Why? Because the *form* of the state has changed, and the intellectuals live precisely on the state "form" (press, education, parliament, etc.).

It seems to me that from these fundamental considerations important lessons must be drawn for our evaluation of the USSR. The oscillations on this question have the origin indicated above: they spring from the superficial viewpoint of the petty-bourgeois intellectuals. This does not mean that the comrades in question are "petty bourgeois." They may be excellent proletarian revolutionaries, but the best revolutionaries commit mistakes, and Marxism obliges us to seek the social origins of these mistakes: here it is a matter of petty-bourgeois intellectual influence over a proletarian revolutionary. ∎

Against desistance for the Radicals[123]

Late 1934 or early 1935

I find the position of the comrades who propose to desist in favor of the Radicals absolutely false and even incomprehensible—conditionally or unconditionally does not matter. The argument—that the Radicals must be unmasked by allowing them to make their experiment—is absolutely abstract and unhistorical. The political crisis in France arises precisely from the fact that Radicalism has made an experiment that coincides more or less with that of the Third Republic. If the middle classes do not break with Radicalism rapidly, it is not because they have any great illusions in its political possibilities, but because they do not see any upsurge. Fascism, which wishes to (and may) succeed Radicalism, is far from supporting it or taking the least responsibility for its actions or words. On the contrary, at the present stage fascism is more implacable toward Radicalism and the Freemasons than toward the workers' organizations.

The fascist policy is absolutely correct. An upsurge must present itself to the middle classes as a force absolutely distinct from Radicalism and irreconcilably opposed to it. The same road is indicated for the proletariat. Every hesitation on this question will be fatal.

Analogies from Kerensky and Kornilov are really badly chosen. It was not a matter of elections when Kerensky was in the same government as Kornilov, but of an armed struggle against Kerensky by Kornilov. The Bolsheviks were of course ready to fight Kornilov side by side with Kerensky's detachments. But without the least political responsibility for his [Kerensky's] party. As for those Radicals who are ready to fight against the fascists or to help the workers to arm, we are naturally ready to accept their aid—and this is the only acceptable form of united front with the handful of Radicals that really want to fight. But this has nothing in common with desistance at the time of the parliamentary or municipal elections—or else our pledge to oppose "national unity" means absolutely nothing. ∎

Answers to questions by Louise Bryant[124]

Late 1934 or early 1935

Is it true that while in France you have been occupied with building the Fourth International?

My answer depends on how the word "building" is interpreted. By virtue of all the conditions of my existence in France, I could not be and have not been engaged in any "building," since I have not participated in the political life of France. It is true, however, that before my arrival in France, as well as during my stay here, I have published a number of articles in which I develop the idea that the Second and Third Internationals have exhausted their historic mission, have become a brake on the world workers' movement, and should give way to a Fourth International, equally independent of both reformism and the Soviet bureaucracy.

And how do you intend to accomplish this?

It is not at all a question of my personal efforts. In several dozen countries, including the United States, Canada, Cuba, and almost every country in Latin America, there are cohesive propaganda groups which could be called pioneers of the Fourth International. Some exist independently; others have entered parties with more of a mass character and function as factions within those parties. On the whole, these pioneer organizations are already far more homogeneous and influential than the founding groups of the Third International during the imperialist war years.

Then you consider the Soviet bureaucracy no longer capable of leading the international workers' movement? Why?

It has become a privileged layer that demands of the workers only their obedience. But revolutionary discipline has nothing in common with blind obedience. The Soviet bureaucracy has become a purely national and conservative force. The workers' movement has an international and revolutionary character. The Comintern, led by the Soviet bureaucracy, has brought about only defeats for the working class over the last decade.

Then you think the interests of the USSR conflict with the interests of the workers' movement in the other countries?

No, you didn't understand what I meant. The Soviet state as a new social system should not be identified with the Soviet bureaucracy, which is a social excrescence upon this system. The interests of the Soviet bureaucracy, in many respects, conflict with the interests of the Soviet state.

In what sense do you consider the policies of the Soviet bureaucracy to be conservative?

In the same sense that the leading French newspapers consider them conservative. Just read *Le Temps*! Soviet diplomacy defends the status quo, whereas the revolutionary movement strives to overthrow it.

But perhaps Soviet diplomacy is only temporarily forced

to adapt itself to the status quo?

That is how they [the Soviet bureaucrats] too viewed matters at first. But time has altered their psychology. We, as Marxists, believe that being determines consciousness. The conditions of their existence as an uncontrolled privileged layer, accustomed only to giving orders, inevitably cause them to grow conservative. Soviet diplomats, politicians, and journalists can be seen at every turn issuing statements of a kind that would be absolutely impossible if the authors gave any thought to the fact that the working masses of the whole world would also be listening to them.

Would you consider the rapprochement between the USSR and France to be a workable arrangement?

Yes, for the reasons I have just mentioned, it could turn out to be quite workable.

Do you think the assassination of the Serbian king [Alexander I] *was the handiwork of the Hungarian and Italian governments, as* Le Populaire *and* L'Humanite *maintain?*

I would readily concede that these governments were involved through one agency or another behind the scenes. But it is completely absurd to imagine that the Croatian and Macedonian terrorists are simply the agents of a fascist government. The terrorists' aim is their own national liberation, in pursuit of which they are seeking some base of support in the antagonisms between states. This is an old tradition, especially in the Balkans. In their struggle against the Turks, the Balkan revolutionists more than once kept their bombs in czarist consulates, but this did not prevent these terrorists from showing themselves, when the time came, as irreconcilable enemies of czarism.

What sort of repercussions, in your opinion, will the terrorist act have?

That is hard to predict. Individual terrorism is an adventurist tactic, the results of which can almost never be foreseen.

Do you think a war is possible in Europe within the next two years?

I would not exclude it.

What are you personally occupied with at the present time?

I am writing a book on Lenin, the story of his life and a description of his theory and strategy. The book takes up all of my time. ∎

A proposal to co-opt Dubois into the plenum[125]

January 31, 1935

To the Members of the Plenum

Dear Comrades:

By this letter I make a formal proposal to co-opt Comrade Dubois into the plenum. These are my reasons:

Comrade Dubois is a very experienced comrade with a past of struggle and of experience. He adhered to us in a difficult situation, which is a mark of revolutionary sincerity. The cadres of experienced comrades that we possess are not numerous. It is necessary to know how to utilize them. It is necessary to reinforce the plenum by a comrade who will surely be able to contribute an individual note to our discussions and an effective collaboration. Comrade Dubois knows the movement in different countries and commands three

A PROPOSAL TO CO-OPT DUBOIS INTO THE PLENUM / 179

languages. His knowledge of the Anglo-Saxon movement and of the English language will be of great use to us.

What objections can be made? Comrade Dubois "does not collaborate systematically in any of our sections." That is correct. But I believe that the fault lies much more with the sections than with Comrade Dubois. The German leadership did not want to have either Parabellum [Arkadi Maslow] or Dubois. Bauer accused them of having wrong ideas on the permanent revolution, etc. The German leadership supported Bauer in this affair. We saw later on the firmness in principle of Bauer himself. It is quite possible that there are different nuances in our conceptions. But do we want an absolute monolithism? Certain doctrinal divergences may prevent collaboration when they translate themselves in an irreconcilable manner in political activity. It is the common experience that will finally judge. But on the condition that this experience be made.

We cannot impose collaboration with Comrades Parabellum and Dubois upon our German section. But we cannot, as an international organization, tolerate being deprived of a collaboration that we deem useful and necessary.

Comrade Dubois has been and remains against the entry of the League into the SFIO. This is regrettable. But in this question too it is experience that will have the last word. Because of this political difference, Dubois did not separate himself from us like Bauer and did not declare war upon us by basing himself against us upon the sterile opportunists of the SAP.

Nobody proposes to hand over the leadership to Comrades Parabellum and Dubois. It is only a question of introducing one of them, notably Dubois, into the plenum. Let us suppose for a minute that the collaboration proves to be a failure. We shall be enriched by one more experience and we shall pass over to the next point on the agenda. How else can one make the selection of leading comrades without putting qualified comrades to the test?

In this domain as in all others, more initiative and flexibility are necessary, even a little audacity. We are already too much threatened by routine and the spirit of the closed circle.

I beg you, dear comrades, to reflect on this question and to express your vote as soon as possible.

Crux [Leon Trotsky]

Disturbing signs[126]

January 31, 1935

Dear Comrades:

Along with Felix and Marie we have carefully studied the minutes of the Central Committee and want to offer you some criticisms and suggestions resulting from this study. Please communicate them at least to all who have the privilege of receiving the Central Committee minutes.

Comrade Craipeau's attitude seems very disturbing to us because of his deviations on the most important questions, deviations which are becoming deeper but no better defined. Here are some examples:

The Fourth International. Comrade Craipeau says: "We left the Third to go toward the Fourth . . . then we abandoned this perspective to enter the SP, which belongs to the Second." It is very surprising to hear such a statement not from a Stalinist or an SAP leader but from a leading member of our own movement. Have we abandoned the slogan and perspective of the Fourth International? Those who have done so should be expelled from our movement instantly. But on the other hand those who reproach us for having quit the road of the Fourth should be called to order. We never expected a line that leads without any turns to the Fourth International. Let Craipeau reread all our documents of the last two years. They always left the door open to all possible developments. It is enough to recall that it was a year and a half ago when we achieved our British section's entry into the ILP.

What we should above all demand of young intellectuals, especially of Young Socialists who are unfamiliar with the history of our movement, is to study our documents in order to establish the necessary connections between our activity and our ideological education. How can Craipeau do this educational work successfully if he belittles or ignores our history?

We are well acquainted with Craipeau's positive personal qualities and his important role. That obliges us all the more to cry out: "Stop, you are on a dangerous bridge!"

The USSR. No less dangerous is the position on the question of the USSR taken by Craipeau and supported by Rigaudias.[127] Many times we have asked these comrades to present their ideas, their criticisms, and their doubts in writing—that is, to make them explicit—in order to open a discussion which otherwise seems to us superfluous. Instead, these comrades are satisfied with creating doubts about our fundamental positions without coming out against them openly. They only sow skepticism, to say nothing of ideological demoralization. At the same time Comrade Rigaudias takes a stand against the "systematic distortion" of his point of view. There can be no distortion where there is no form. And there can be no form where there is no content. All you have are doubts, Comrade Rigaudias, and since they are doubts of a sentimental and not a theoretical or political character, you can't take the risk of "giving them form."

With unforgivable impressionism you adapt your sentimental doubts to every new situation and every new event, and since nobody, including you, can grasp the trend of your thinking, it seems to you that everybody only distorts your point of view.

The crimes of Stalin and his clique, especially to the Soviet youth, are terrible. The Stalinist regime creates an atmosphere favorable to individual terrorism and pushes disoriented, unbalanced and desperate Young Communists onto the road to terrorism. And on the basis of that, the Stalinist clique physically exterminates the youth, thus making its regime more heinous. This makes us feel indignant. That's natural. But it is not sufficient. It is necessary to be strong enough to change the situation. We are weak. And weakness always drives people to seek artificial satisfactions. Thus they pick a quarrel with our theoretical concept of the Soviet state. They think that downgrading the USSR theoretically will give us moral revenge against Stalin. . . . ■

After the Belgian conference[128]

March 24, 1935

Dear Comrade Lesoil:

It has been called to my attention that our Belgian friends were dissatisfied at the time of their last conference over the fact that I did not say anything in my letter about possible entry into the POB. I deliberately did not want to do this. The general line was determined by the last [ICL] plenum. In this case it was only a question of the concrete appreciation of the prevailing situation in the POB and the possibilities that flow from it. Unfortunately I am not sufficiently acquainted with Belgian affairs to form a definite opinion on the above.

I was inclined to believe that the Belgian comrades should await the positive results and experiences from the entry of the youth and of the French League in order to be able to effect the entry with a minimum of losses.

The necessity of giving up *La Voix* [*Communiste*] in order to enter appears to be a dangerous symptom. A column in *L'Action* [*Socialiste*]?[129] Do you find that adequate? And what are the guarantees for this column?

The latest issue of *Le Temps* reports that the leadership of the POB was unanimously in favor of Spaak's[130] proposal authorizing the leaders to enter a cabinet of national unity. If this is true, it would be an act of consummate betrayal. In this case we should unleash a relentless campaign against Spaak. Unfortunately Spaak's general attitude does not allow me to speak in advance: the information in *Temps* might be false. Spaak's position remains ambiguous and we cannot identify ourselves with him even if the dispatch in *Temps* is false.

La Voix frequently writes: "The leaders of the POB do not understand, do not see, etc." This is not correct. They understand and they see everything but for the most part they are beneficiaries of the bourgeois regime. Our mission is not to educate Vandervelde, Anseele[131] and Company but to denounce them. We can do this in a reserved manner if conditions require it, but never on a false note.

It is shocking to read in *La Voix* that the general strike is a "legal" method, etc. The general strike has always been emasculated in Belgium by restricting it into the bed of legality. The very essence of the general strike is that in paralyzing the governmental apparatus, it thereby paralyzes conditions of legality and obliterates the dividing line between legal and illegal actions. It is precisely by this procedure that the general strike poses the question of power.

These are a few observations which I want to make to you.

My best greetings,
Crux [Leon Trotsky]

On the Teachers' Federation[132]

March 24, 1935

Dear Comrade Dommanget:[133]

I want to thank you warmly for your *Pages Choisies* of Babeuf.[134] As of this moment, I have not read more than a third. But I have leafed through the rest and do not want to put off any longer expressing my totally sincere admiration for your work, which is marked by historic insight, scientific honesty, and a remarkable erudition.

Unfortunately, I cannot congratulate you at all on the activity of the Teachers' Federation, its leaders or its paper. On the contrary, all of that gives me the impression of something doomed. A petty bureaucracy is sometimes worse than a big one. Impelled by the need for self-preservation, it identifies itself with Monmousseau at a time when the

Stalinists are proving themselves a rotten and worm-eaten clique. We must simply cross out this generation of teachers who came over to communism in order to retire among themselves, to cultivate their little garden and their little federation, and to wake up . . . in their little concentration camp. Hopeless!

But if one is going to stand aside from the kind of activity required by our epoch, then the best thing one could do would be scientific investigations such as you have made.

My best regards to your companion and you. ∎

Notes on the SAP and the London-Amsterdam Bureau[135]

Mid-April 1935

N: The last German conference revealed that within the IKD there still exist serious differences of opinion and lack of clarity on the tactical approach to the SAP and the London-Amsterdam Bureau. The conference's resolution on the SAP and the guidelines for plenum members concerning their conduct with respect to the Paris conference of the London-Amsterdam Bureau are both imbued with a conciliatory spirit.

TROTSKY: It is absolutely necessary to maintain a consistent line on the SAP. The SAP expresses the feelings of numerous confused elements and is representative of an entire international frame of mind. It is the chosen leader for people with all kinds of shortcomings, and all of its efforts are directed toward maintaining these shortcomings and sowing new confusion. In the process, it leans both on the sectarian Bauer and the unprincipled apostle of unity Doriot. The SAP is very skillful in disguising its confusion with our arguments. Let us not forget that the leaders of the SAP have had a thorough schooling—in the Comintern, with the Brandlerites, and they have even learned something from us. This "skillfulness" makes the SAP one of the most dangerous centrist currents we now face. Although they don't represent much themselves, the SAP tries to intervene everywhere with its emigre groups scattered all over in different countries and to put a brake on the revolutionary movement. We have to teach the SAP, which seems to be the group closest to us, a very thorough lesson. We have to stop toadying to them and carry out a determined fight against them.

Our conduct toward the IAG must proceed from the same considerations. We do not pursue a policy of hollow fetishism on organizational questions. *Theoretically*, there is indeed a possibility of entering the Bureau, provided that a clear leftward tendency exists within the organization. At present, however, our concern in the fight against the Bureau is rather the SAP leadership in the Bureau, since it is primarily responsible for the rightward course. The precondition for the theoretical possibility of entering the IAG is a relentless struggle against the SAP, which at the present time represents conservatism and reaction within the workers' movement.

In the International Youth Bureau the SAP plays the same role. *The SAP has hoisted itself up on our shoulders; now we are supposed to bend so the SAP can scrape before Tranmael and Kilbom.* While Comrade Schmidt of the OSP was in prison, de Kadt and Walcher seized control of the leadership of the Youth Bureau in order to fight against our line. Now that de Kadt has flown the OSP *because of his betrayal during the July struggle in Amsterdam,* Walcher is trying to continue the same policy with the Swede Kilbom. The latter denied our Comrade Held residence in Stockholm in order to pass the leadership over to Brandt of the SAP.

The political intervention of our comrades at the Lille [youth] conference was inadequate. They remained mute about everything the SAP did and allowed the SAP to exercise a virtual dictatorship at this conference. We have to take energetic measures to put a stop to the SAP's machinations.

N: Many of the SAP groups inside Germany (but, of course, far from all of them) are much further to the left than the SAP leadership abroad. They express themselves openly in favor of the Fourth International and often respond positively to our efforts to establish comradely collaboration and discussion. However, they still follow their leadership abroad, which tries to block us at every turn, as for example in the unity negotiations in X, where the SAP regional committee was advised to set senseless conditions like forbidding "recruitment of the other organization's members," etc. I am of the opinion that we should issue a statement about the senselessness of such demands, but that we should not allow ourselves to be taken in by such tricks and not allow the negotiations to collapse *in cases where local unity negotiations have a progressive political and organizational character.*

TROTSKY: I won't render an opinion on this special case in X since I am not acquainted with the details. In general, errors committed by comrades inside Germany can be viewed with forbearance. As a result of the conditions of extreme illegality, there is a lack of the necessary general picture of international affairs among the comrades working there. But on all international questions the leadership abroad must be unyielding and initiate a determined struggle against the SAP. Despite forbearance in internal German matters, the leadership abroad must maintain elbow room on all international questions. A split in the SAP is by no means out of the question. We must continually point out that it is only the SAP that sees *political* obstacles in the way of a fusion. Under no circumstances should we play hide-and-seek with the Fourth International, and we must act with great self-assurance in all instances.

N: There are no important differences within our ranks with respect to *evaluation* of the London-Amsterdam Bureau. Instead, the question is often raised as to whether we should let the Bureau disintegrate on its own, or whether we should, on the contrary, try to actively transform it in a revolutionary direction through our entry, or, if necessary, work to break it up from within.

TROTSKY: If we were to enter the London-Amsterdam Bureau in the present situation, we would group everyone there against us. We would become the centrists' only target. The struggle against us would be the *only* raison d'etre of the London-Amsterdam Bureau. If, however, we remain outside, criticize them sharply, and leave them to their own devices, all the latent contradictions will manifest themselves, since, practically speaking, there are three tendencies in the London-Amsterdam Bureau: one favoring the Second International (Sweden), one favoring the Third (the ILP in England), and one favoring the Fourth (RSAP).[136]

We have already gained a certain amount of experience through the participation of the Dutch, and our views have only been confirmed. Doriot himself declared that the only positive aspect of this conference [in February 1935] was the condemnation of Trotskyist ideas. Indeed, everything was aimed at condemning the Fourth International. That was the only glue holding together the groups represented there (with the exception of the Dutch).

N: The spokesmen for the conciliatory line toward the London-Amsterdam Bureau always raise the comparison with Lenin's attitude toward Zimmerwald and Kienthal.

TROTSKY: The big difference between then and now is that

at the beginning of the war there did not exist any real communist group anywhere. In France, for example, those furthest to the left were Merrheim and Bourderon,[137] and they were moderate centrists who were of the opinion that the Second International should be rebuilt after the war. Even Liebknecht changed his mind; at first he was still in the same organization with the Independents. In Sweden it was Hoeglund and in Norway [ ], a very moderate leftist.[138] In those days the first channels had to be opened. Yes, if Lenin had only had groups of ten workers, or even five (he always said that three good workers were more important to him than all the centrists put together) ... For this reason it was necessary to participate in those conferences then. Lenin, however, was the first one ready to break with Zimmerwald.

(This position was not, however, a hindrance to working within the Social Democratic organizations. During the war for example, Inessa Armand[139] and others worked together with Trotsky in France and took part in [Social Democratic] meetings. Lenin himself worked in the Swiss organization. Trotsky, along with Fritz Platten,[140] was a delegate to a Swiss party convention and was kept from speaking there by right-wingers. At the following party convention, Lenin also took part.)

Everything depends on whether or not you have some forces in the country, on whether you can develop independent international action. In any case, the point is not whether one takes part in the conference or not (we are not expelling Comrade Schmidt); instead, what is decisive is to perceive and struggle against the ruinous implications of this political line. *It is having illusions and not any possible participation which is dangerous.* These illusions in our own ranks correspond to illusions about the SAP leadership.

All centrist currents are now undergoing their most important test on the international questions. In Germany the SAP can hide pretty well. But on the international questions every trained Marxist can see where they are headed. To be sure, the SAP is against Hitler, but on the international questions it supports Tranmael and Kilbom and *thus is preparing the way for the Norwegian and the Swedish Hitler.* They do this in an underhanded way, using radical phrases, but in the final analysis they say this: *We work with Tranmael, but not with the Trotskyists.* This is the most miserable sort of treachery. They steal our arguments against Tranmael, dull the cutting edge of these arguments a bit, and then use them to impress our people ("watered-down Trotskyism"), *but in practice they work with Tranmael against us.*

A second example: de Kadt. We were the first to recognize him for what he is, and we criticized him in an extremely sharp manner. (See *Unser Wort.*) Shortly thereafter, de Kadt exposed himself as a scoundrel and was expelled from the Dutch party. He never represented himself as a Marxist, and is in fact a reactionary philistine. But the leaders of the SAP allied themselves with him in the struggle against us.

There is also the example of France. The rightist Frossard represents nothing in the SFIO. Nevertheless, Blum continually bows to him, while he treats Marceau Pivert, who represents broad revolutionary layers, like dirt. That is the time-honored method of the centrists. They bow to the right and treat the left like a doormat. *That* is decisive, and not the theoretical formulations the centrists use. The SAP adorns itself with purloined revolutionary phrases, but marches with Tranmael, Kilbom, and Zyromsky against the revolutionary wing. *This discrepancy between word and deed must be exposed now.* Therein lies the essence of centrism. Of course, the words of the centrists are inadequate too. But we will accomplish little with complicated theoretical debates in front of an unschooled audience (even when such debates are necessary).

In France we face tasks of historic proportions. What is decisive for a correct political line is an accurate analysis of the political situation. (See the French pamphlet *Whither France?*) What exists in France today is a situation similar to the one in Germany in 1923 and then later in the years 1929–33. Here again we find ourselves in a *prerevolutionary situation which must lead to revolution or counterrevolution.* What characterizes all centrists is that they are afraid to see and understand this. The centrist is afraid to act. That is why he hedges in his analysis of the situation. The SAP people give this fear theoretical expression. We must take this as our point of departure.

In 1923 Brandler and Walcher missed the revolutionary situation. Later they failed to understand this. From this—the greatest experience of their lives—they learned nothing. Since they were obliged to defend themselves for quite some time, they collected all the arguments for turning a revolutionary situation into a nonrevolutionary situation. It is necessary to fight out the battle in the light of the 1923 experience. Because now the SAP is beginning to exercise its restraining influence on all revolutionary elements; in France on Marceau Pivert. This is dangerous. By leading the battle against us along with Zyromsky, Pivert, and Doriot, they are repeating their bad experience of 1923.

We characterize the present situation in France as prerevolutionary and that determines our attitude toward Blum, etc. On the other hand, we have repeatedly explained to Walcher that he is repeating the political orientation of the Anglo-Russian Committee.

Marceau Pivert says to himself: "The political situation seems to demand a decisive revolutionary approach." Blum, however, does not want a revolutionary approach, and fundamentally neither does Zyromsky, since he doesn't want to break with Blum. We say to Marceau Pivert: "The political situation is more important than Blum's frame of mind. One must take the political situation as the basic point of departure and determine one's attitude toward Blum and Zyromsky on this basis." Then Walcher jumps in and says: "Yes, the

Trotskyists have a very good analysis of the political situation, but they are sectarians, and they want to isolate you, Marceau Pivert, and condemn you to impotence. They demand that you break with Zyromsky." In this way they reinforce the centrist side of Marceau Pivert against the Marxist side.

The SAP will hardly venture to take up the discussion of the character of the political situation with us. They would much rather concentrate on their specialty: struggling against our "sectarianism." Their attitude toward the centrist leaders (Zyromsky and Blum, etc.) is derived from a totally different evaluation of the political situation in France, one which is dictated by their fear of revolutionary action. They accept our analysis in words, but ". . . we shouldn't be sectarian and under no circumstances should we break with Zyromsky." That means that they should not draw the practical conclusions of their own analysis of the situation.

Just as the SAP *in practice* supported Tranmael and de Kadt against us in the past, now they are supporting Zyromsky against us, but on a much more important question, in a situation of far-reaching significance, not just for the French proletariat, but for the entire European working class. ■

News about the family[141]

April 25, 1935

We have a new family "complication." Alexandra Lvovna [Sokolovskaya],[142] the mother of my two late daughters, has been exiled to Siberia. Three grandsons who were living with her have been left hanging in midair. Seryozha, my younger son, who is not political, "disappeared" at the same time. Undoubtedly, they've arrested him; it would be good if they just exiled him . . . without the slightest political reason, just for revenge. Nothing has been heard of him for a long time. You can imagine our anxiety. ■

Laval and the French CP[143]
May 1935

During the municipal election campaign in France at the end of April, minister of foreign affairs Laval had a peculiar run-in with the Communist Party in the electoral district of Aubervilliers, the municipality where Laval is the mayor. The Communists accused Laval of not wanting to sign the pact with the Soviet Union, of not wanting to help assure peace in that way. In a special poster, Laval reproached "the representatives, authorized or not, of the Third International" for violently attacking him just at the time of his negotiations with the Soviets; and at the same time he denied that his opponents had the right to speak in the name of the Soviet government. This electoral squabble interests us only insofar as it brought into the open for a moment a delicate question that by all appearances has occupied and continues to occupy no small place in the diplomatic negotiations of the West European states with Moscow: the question of the relationship between the Soviet government and the Third International.

For the past sixteen years, i.e., from the day the Comintern was founded, in Europe and America it has become firm tradition to identify the Comintern with the Soviet government. This identification—of course not accidental—had two versions: the White Russian emigres have declared the "anti-national" Kremlin government to be simply an agent of the International; on the other hand, foreign governments and especially the press have declared that the International is simply an agent of Soviet national diplomacy. No matter how logical the purely juridical arguments used by the Kremlin to refute both versions might have been, the opponents did not feel the least convinced. They knew that the founder and inspirer of the International was Lenin, the head of the Soviet government; and that the Bolshevik Party—through its Central Committee, which formed not only the Council of People's Commissars but also the presidium of the Comintern—had played a decisive role in the life of the International as well as of the Soviet state. By comparison with those facts, the question of monetary subsidies from the Bolshevik Party to foreign sections was only secondary.

How sensitive and irritating this question is to the government of Great Britain is well known. A careful reading of the official communique on the results of Eden's[144] visit to Moscow makes it possible, even without the aid of the British press, to suppose that the question of the subsequent fate of the Comintern, persistently raised by the lord privy seal [Eden], prompted a reassuring enough explanation from the Soviet government. The French foreign minister's election poster, denying that the French Communists have the right to speak in the name of the Soviet government, seems to mark a new stage of development in an area that has also troubled French official opinion more than a little. The fair share of irony that can be seen in the poster by the mayor of Aubervilliers does not lessen the fact that the French minister of foreign affairs, in the midst of the process of negotiating with Moscow, is making a political declaration whose meaning can be expressed roughly as follows: there is no reason to fear that French Communists can in any way influence future relations between Paris and Moscow.

We will say it straight out: we believe that the French minister of foreign affairs is absolutely right in his statement. We have in mind, in this regard, not the juridical side of the matter, which has remained, if you will, unchanged; but the *political* side, which for the past ten to twelve years has changed radically. ∎

Toward the new youth international[145]

Spring 1935

The current dispute in the Stockholm Bureau is of the greatest importance for the development of our youth organization. Given the fact that the SAP representative feels constrained to sign our delegate's statement, the situation seems very favorable. In order to make it yield all the desired results, it is necessary to follow through to the very end without the slightest concession. All of our youth sections would have to declare that they categorically refuse to collaborate at all with Mot Dag—which, by the way, refused to allow our delegate to attend its meetings and to participate in the life of its organization.

If the Swedes agree to withdraw their mandate from Mot Dag and be directly represented, we will be able to do nothing for the moment except renew our proposition to reorganize the Stockholm Bureau more equitably—that is to say, organize it in keeping with the actual relationship of forces, with a bureau made up of five delegates (IS, France, Holland, SAP, Sweden).

That solution, even if it succeeds, which is not at all certain, could only be a stage, since the future of the international youth organization is completely bound up with the development of the Fourth International.

The Open Letter for the Fourth International, once it has been signed, will naturally be sent to the Stockholm Bureau—or, more precisely, to the one that will be created tomorrow.

After the creation of the Bureau for the Fourth International, the youth will naturally regroup according to their political positions: for or against the Fourth International.

Comrade Held's proposal to create a provisional secretariat in Paris and to call an emergency international youth conference must be made subordinate to the progress of work specified above. If calling a conference for the Fourth International proves feasible within a relatively short period of time, it would be entirely appropriate to call a youth conference at the same time and place, for reasons that need no elaboration. If not, it is of course possible to contemplate calling a youth conference independently, in accordance with material resources, technical feasibility, etc.

In any case, if the Stockholm Bureau is definitely broken up, which is quite possible, the IS, in agreement with the youth, will have to guarantee a provisional secretariat in Paris. ■

Why are we Bolshevik-Leninists?[146]

A friendly explanation to party comrades
Spring 1935

The French people are approaching great dangers, but also enormous opportunities. The Socialist Party finds itself faced with grave responsibilities. The first condition for carrying them out is theoretical and political clarity. But political clarity does not fall from the sky. It must be acquired by conscious and collective efforts. For a large party this inevitably means by discussion.

The worst kind of pusillanimity is to be afraid of an open and loyal clash of opinions in the party. The greater the problems to be solved are, the more passionate is the confrontation of ideas and tendencies. Let no one say that factions are a harmful thing. No one has yet invented the means for avoiding and eliminating them. When there are serious differences, the party's adherents inevitably group into different tendencies. *True discipline in action can only come out of a loyal and frank confrontation of tendencies*, each of which tries to persuade the rest of the party of the correctness of its program.

We Bolshevik-Leninists are a tendency: that of the extreme left of the Socialist Party. In order to better explain the place we occupy and the aim we pursue it is necessary to take a clear look at the overall political picture of the party. It is no secret to anyone that our party is not homogeneous, that it contains three principal tendencies: reformist, centrist, and Marxist.

Reformism, in our party as elsewhere, represents the past. It is the inheritance of a bygone era when capitalism was vigorous and on the rise, when parliamentary democracy seemed to be full of promise. In the past, despite its insufficiency and myopia, reformism was able to render the proletariat certain material services. Now, in the era of capitalism in decay, reformism is condemned to total impotence. That is why the reformist tendency, which is very strong in the leading apparatus of our party, among the parliamentary deputies, the mayors, the general and municipal council members, the union leaders, etc., is embarrassed to openly acknowledge its true program.

It is not easy to carry the reformist banner when the reforms go bankrupt. It is not easy to be a mouthpiece for parliamentary democracy when democracy decomposes in front of everyone's eyes, rots, fouls the atmosphere and finds itself forced to abdicate more and more in favor of the supraparliamentary, Bonapartist government.

It is also not easy to acknowledge one's *patriotism* when the country condemns its best sons and daughters to permanent poverty, at the same time preparing a new carnage which would mean the extermination of several generations and the fall of our civilization.

Reformism is caught in a dead end. The most consistent reformists are quitting the camp of the working class and openly passing over lock, stock and barrel to the besieged camp of capital. The best example is that of the Neo-Socialists. Not all of them left us. Frossard stayed in the party up until recently in order to use it as a springboard at the favorable moment. There are others of the same type. The party of the working class cannot afford to include elements representing the enemy class which we need to fight. We must not wait until the Frossardists follow Frossard. They must be unmasked in good time and they must not be allowed to keep their comfortable timeserving posts living on the back of the proletariat.

We Bolshevik-Leninists believe that we exactly reflect

the thinking of the revolutionary workers when we refuse to "understand" this indulgence and courtesy, very close to complicity with the renegades, toward traitors and candidates for treason. When we are talked to about unity in general, totalitarian unity, we answer: *we are against unity with the traitors. We are for class-struggle unity.*

But there are many camouflaged and even half-repentant reformists—the centrists. At the moment this is the broadest as well as the most diverse faction. The collapse of democratic and patriotic reformism forces many representatives of the workers' movement to seek temporary refuge in the centrist tendency. *The fundamental characteristic of this tendency is that it has lost its naive faith in democratic reforms, but still has all its fear of the proletarian revolution.*

The centrist tendency lives by equivocation; it borrows revolutionary formulas from the Marxist vocabulary, but it removes from them all their practical consequences. It is ready to talk about revolution but not to prepare for it. The *Bataille Socialiste* tendency, headed by Zyromsky, is the incarnation of centrism in our party. The representatives of this tendency never reply to either our criticism or our proposals. They very often form a common front with the reformists against us. We accuse the centrists of becoming the right wing's self-defense organization against the left wing.

We Bolshevik-Leninists are absolutely certain that many comrades, especially workers who are now passing through the centrist stage, will soon find their place in the revolutionary camp, but to help them go through this healthy evolution we intransigently refuse to make the slightest concession of principle to centrism, that is, to confusion and prostration.

Our intransigence is neither gratuitous nor arbitrary. It only reflects the intransigence of the class struggle. The proletariat has no other choice than to take the power in its hands through revolution or to rot along with the rotting capitalist system. Our motion simply gives clear expression to this fundamental fact. The march of events, which does not depend on our will, tells us: "You will win or you will die. But you will only win when you want to and know how to."

We call ourselves Bolshevik-*Leninists* not because we want to blindly imitate the Russian Bolsheviks in a different situation and in different conditions; even less do we do so because we are capable of bowing to the commands of the Soviet bureaucracy. Not a bit! The tyranny of the top bureaucrats in Moscow over the Comintern was what broke its spine and now makes the Stalinist leaders play the truly reactionary role they do in the workers' movement. The reason we call ourselves Bolsheviks is that the great party of Lenin has given us two imperishable lessons: the defeatist attitude during the war and the revolutionary conquest of power.

We call ourselves Leninists because, after Marx and Engels, their continuator, Lenin, is the greatest theoretician of the working class. It was he who masterfully applied Marxist theory to analyze our era, not only for Russia but for the entire capitalist world. Today there is no other road to Marx than Lenin's. Every new event in any capitalist country demonstrates the correctness of the Leninist conception.

The Stalinist bureaucracy distorts Lenin's thought as the Social Democracy distorted that of Marx. But the great events taking place in our country, the sharpening of the class struggle, the social war and the imperialist war methodically prepared by big business, this whole terrible chain of events forces every conscious worker to turn toward the source of Leninism.

Against reformist capitulation, against centrist softness, for the proletarian revolution—that is the slogan of the Bolshevik-Leninists. ■

Three telegrams to Norway[147]
June 7–12, 1935

JUNE 7, 1935

[To Minister of Justice Trygve Lie][148]

I have the honor of applying for permission to reside in Kristiansand or environs for my wife and myself for rest and medical treatment. I most respectfully request that you telegraph acceptance to the consulate in Paris.

JUNE 11, 1935

[To Minister of Justice Trygve Lie]

In the event that the Norwegian government grants me a residence visa, I promise not to take part in the public life of the country. The Norwegian authorities can in no way be more responsible for my personal safety than they can for any other foreigner. I respectfully request speedy action.

JUNE 12, 1935

[To Minister of State Johan Nygaardsvold][149]

Trusting in the promises of the Norwegian party leaders, I have given up my lodgings and obtained my Belgian transit visa. The French government believes that I deceived it and demands that I leave France within twenty-four hours. I am ill and my wife is ill. Situation is desperate. I solicit immediate favorable decision. ∎

Underground work in Nazi Germany[150]

June 1935

TROTSKY: What do you consider to be the task of the inner leadership?

K: P. should among other things take responsibility for education in the groups. Sch. should work the region. F. should be agitprop leader (what this entails is, to be sure, not clear from O.'s remarks).

TROTSKY: It is impermissible for a comrade of the inner leadership to go down to the groups and do educational work. This sacrifices the security of the organization. There is some question whether exceptions might be allowed in the case of Group X because of the excessively close acquaintance of the members. The first prerequisite of underground work is that the leadership achieve clarity about its nature, that is, about questions of security of the organization and leadership, making new arrangements if necessary.

Hence the leadership has responsibility for maintaining security in *every respect,* precisely because it takes responsibility for very concrete tasks of a secret nature which exclude *open* functioning in the groups. Such tasks are, for example, (1) transport and courier service, (2) arranging for distribution and transmission of materials, (3) external political, agitational, and propaganda activities. No one should act on his own initiative in all these areas; instead, the leadership must come to formal decisions and strictly observe them. This is the only way to achieve regularized activity.

As for the further work of the leadership, it must (a) distribute the materials to the individual groups, already arranged and in ready-to-use form, (b) occupy itself with a review of the political questions on a continuing basis, (c) work out political instructions for the inner circle, i.e., consulting with it about political work, for example, in important discussions, in propaganda, etc. In the case of a discussion, say, it is always necessary to determine how the material should be distributed, the discussion carried out, and the report given to the leadership. (Also, of course, transmitting reports on discussions to the leadership abroad in proper form with the conclusions well summarized.)

Furthermore, *regular* reporting must be organized. The leadership must, of course, test to see which comrade can carry out this task or that, but it must always take into account that you cannot force anyone to do anything and that you must be patient. (NB: If you just think how unspeakably bad your organizational work has been up till now, then it goes without further saying that the members had to have as much patience with the leaders at the time as the leaders with the members. I am convinced that at your leadership meetings no fixed agenda is worked out and no attempt is made to summarize the decisions—even in the most abbreviated form. But such things are indispensable and an important tool for self-control and self-education. You must get used to orderly decision making and strict carrying out of decisions. At every meeting the decisions reached at the previous meeting must be reviewed on the basis of minutes, and things overlooked placed on the agenda again. Organizational things are difficult to learn, so no one needs to feel "belittled" or "exalted" by such reviews. But in general a leadership must have ten times as much patience with the members as the members with the leadership.)

Making reports is of course one of the most important tasks. The leading comrades themselves must pick out an area to report on. They can do this much more easily because many threads run together in their hands and because they have more of an overview.

The best form for reports: Investigation of what happens politically. Study the question (you study it by collecting the facts), as concretely as possible, making continual reports. You have to get together and ask yourselves what can be done in this area or that (the outstanding example: the church question).[151] Communication of the leadership with the inner circle and through them with the groups provides political discussion in the course of which you should continually demand new concrete facts. If you proceed in this way, you will, moreover, have your hands full with things to do and little time for idle talk and squabbling. On the contrary, on the basis of real work you will find more and more real satisfaction.

Further tasks of the leadership are preparing the correspondence for abroad and circulating the complete correspondence. In the regions it must deal only with the trusted people. Again the general rule in all conspiratorial work: it concerns only the leadership and the leadership may utilize only specially suitable and trustworthy comrades.

Now then: "F. should be agitprop leader." What is this supposed to mean? As far as cultivating *individual relationships* is concerned, *everyone* is a propagandist. Evaluating the question of how far we can go with external propaganda is a task for the *entire* leadership (after careful investigation of all the details based on the work of the *entire* organization) and not an area for specialization. We must be extremely cautious about working with the old CP concepts and divisions of labor, which are nothing but covers for political ineptitude. Those who understand nothing about politics usually invent "posts." You must never imagine that one person can carry out a task alone—careful and collaborative consultation is required. Classification here is idiocy. Every one of the tasks mentioned is a collective task for the leadership (and in a broader sense for the organization as a whole) which cannot be "divided up" as such. The inner leadership must evaluate, for example, whether and to what extent external propaganda is possible. Let's take the church conflict for example. Can we perhaps put out a leaflet with protests and demands concerning this? And in what form? It is clear, of course, that we must make an effort to sharpen the conflict wherever a real opportunity arises. In the church conflict it isn't absolutely necessary to act in the name of the IKD. (We have no experience in such things and must first become accustomed to the kinds of work and underground methods involved.) Let us assume that something happens, and we have to take a position on it. Perhaps we put out a leaflet which says: At such and such a place the Nazis perpetrated this despicable act without any provocation (analyze the grounds in the most political way possible). It is clear that National Socialism lives by the brutal suppression of *every sort* of criticism, and that it cannot grant the smallest freedoms (not in religion, not in professional associations, and of course no political freedom). And then you sign the leaflet *as a beginning* with let us say, "A Group of Freedom-loving Citizens and Workers." If the church raises demands perhaps we can put out another seemingly neutral leaflet in which we call for general freedoms, the right of association, the press, etc. Use all of the Nazi atrocities to write a propaganda article to stir up general indignation. Political exposes and support to every form of opposition—we must develop along these lines and appear as the pacesetter of liberation.

What opportunities are there for us to come forward as

the IKD? What kind of work are we doing with the SP, the CP, etc.? We have Trotsky's letter to the French workers[152] now—an extraordinary opportunity for propaganda. Isn't it possible to put out something like that? (NB: Newspapers should be sold and not given away. The leadership must determine when to begin sales and external propaganda, but we cannot refrain from all propaganda for years on end.)

Furthermore you should strive to put political questions down on paper and to write articles. We need contributors to our press.

And finally, there must be periodic reports on the organizational and political activity of the group and the region. Here it is of extraordinary importance to summarize the experiences, decisions of the leadership, results of the work, political events and their analysis, etc., etc., to forward this to the national leadership (and with their help to the whole national organization) and abroad in order to establish a real national organization, consistent exchange of experiences, and unified work on a national scale.

The inner circle is made up of the most reliable and most active comrades and should in particular regulate liaison and communication with the groups. You should avoid things like considering someone as a member of the inner circle because he gives special reports. No! What is essential is whether he is reliable and dependable enough to maintain contacts with the groups and carry out political assignments. The inner circle is especially concerned with regulating meetings, transmission of materials, collection of reports. Before I forget: I don't believe that it is your practice to circulate reports and letters in the groups—and this is not the case only with you.

K: That's right. This is something that has already been a subject of concern. We've suffered from it.

TROTSKY: And rightly so! This is one of the greatest shortcomings. Organizational secrets, written documents relating to this, and letters with addresses are of course no concern of the membership, but the reports and the political letters from both the leadership and individual members must be brought to *everyone's* attention. Without this there is neither control nor sufficient information. And without both of these there is neither an overview nor organizational-political education and development. It must never be forgotten: all education is based on reciprocity and control. He who can learn nothing from the dumbest and simplest person will carry away nothing but the mere words of the most clever. I could give you amazing examples. Thus, under all conditions every report and all nonconspiratorial material must be given to the groups so that the comrades (a) will have an example of how reports are in fact written (many comrades shy away from writing a report or a letter because they always think it has to be something "profound"; but any random example will convince them that it is not a feat of acrobatics), (b) can make additions and add new facts, (c) will have an overview of what has already happened and what has not happened.

K: The inner circle also takes control of how the comrades work and makes a criticism of their work.

TROTSKY: How do the comrades work? Do they work in groups or as individuals?

K: L., for instance, is a specialist on the economy. We observe and see what our individual friends can do and then assign them their particular tasks. We ask ourselves: Are the comrades in a position to do a particular kind of work, and do they do it? We have established a set plan for the work of the groups again, which fundamentally includes the following points:

(1) Street supervision; (2) factory supervision; (3) making a criticism of all legal and illegal newspapers and materials; (4) political and newspaper reports; (5) reading a daily newspaper, reports and taking positions on day-to-day questions;

(6) study of our Marxist literature; (7) participation in a legal organization (trade union, labor front, air raid wardens, church organization, etc.); (8) educational work in the groups; (9) contacts with other people, receiving reports about them, recruitment of new people.

TROTSKY: Starting with contacts: How far can a new contact go? I have been observing for some time and I find that we are very rigid. The sympathizer question has to be reviewed. We can try to get sympathizers to (1) provide material assistance, (2) become readers of the newspaper, (3) provide a cover address for some purpose or other.

Naturally, with some we will achieve little, with others everything. It seems to me that we are not geared to turning sympathizers into members and instead are demanding 100 percent certainty, which is not possible. A lot depends on orientation: development into long-term sympathizers or into revolutionaries. In many cases a tested sympathizer can be made into a useful member.

And what do you consider a sympathizer? Is the "sympathy" directed more toward a person or the cause? Both forms have to be utilized to overcome certain technical difficulties. A devoted personal friend who is sufficiently isolated from the movement could, for example, keep the files. You have such friends (for addresses too) and should make an effort to decentralize the files by area of work.

On factory and street supervision and newspaper criticism: In carrying out these tasks the leadership and the inner circle must show the way. You must supervise the inner circle yourselves. The leadership and the inner circle must take the lead in commenting on *Unser Wort* and the other materials. Many issues of *Unser Wort* and documents were in X, but I don't know of any thorough criticism by the leadership. And this throws significant light on the absurdity of O.'s complaint that there is too much "unprocessed" material in X. Perhaps there really isn't that much to "criticize"; they are in general satisfied, only miss this or that, wish they had more of it, and are, moreover, in agreement. I myself am not of this opinion. There is a great deal to criticize. But the "criticism" exercised so far runs absolutely along these lines. We have comrades in high positions who confuse nitpicking with criticism, but carelessly pass over obvious absurdities and contradictions and even sing hymns of praise to bad work. There are comrades like this in X too. Of course we are not "angry" with these comrades, but as long as they themselves do not find out where the real deficiencies lie, they should not feel superior to others and they should not demand anything of them that they themselves are not yet capable of. This makes the "argument" over materials which "others" have not "processed" even more stupid.

On reports: We have had reports from X. For a time X was the leader in this respect; more than half of all reports came from its region. Unfortunately things have not developed further along these lines but regressed significantly. It is to be hoped that there will be a reawakening here too in connection with the new tasks. And of course, the leadership must once again give an example, start things off, and not use what others have "not" done as excuses for itself.

On education: If possible, classes and workshops should be held. Special practice is necessary here and a great deal of experience has to be gathered—the circles are today one of the major forms of activity and are far too insufficiently developed.

As for the classes held up till now in X, many mistakes have been made, and the comrades have been antagonized. Under all circumstances you must be honest, not make a class into a secret or something for the "chosen few," make it known through the stewards when a class will be given. It is wrong to divide up the classes in the way you have done. You sat down *beforehand* and said: This one or that is no good for this class. Openness toward the comrades is necessary.

If you're going to have a class, tell everyone. The number of participants must be left open and the class can be repeated accordingly. Then you discuss the composition and say: Come to an agreement among yourselves about who will take the class first. You should also consult, look for suitable topics in the groups, ask the comrades what they are interested in, and perhaps let them choose the topic themselves.

The study of Marxist literature: There is a prevailing tendency to measure comrades by what they have or have not read. This was unequivocally clear from O.'s organizational plan for last year. There it said, in essence, more or less, that only those who have read a certain number of Marxist works can be counted "fully" [as members]. Under certain circumstances you will have to reconcile yourselves to the fact that there are comrades who are not going to read *Anti-Duehring* and will also not participate in classes. In these things as in others one must be very flexible! Everyone must be taken as he is—a set "program" whose requirements everyone must fulfill is of no use here. As individuals, all the comrades act differently but the common minimum has to be (1) get the paper and be responsible for it, (2) make a financial contribution, (3) carry out specific and sometimes very modest work of a technical or other nature.

But I must say again, always give our friends an example, and don't hold them in contempt because they haven't read *Anti-Duehring*. In making judgments about comrades, orient toward what is most important: the *movement*. That is, if the political movement in a country starts to grow, then suddenly comrades who were not of much use become necessary, because now, all of a sudden, a field of activity has opened up for them in which they can move. You must wait for this time and look at comrades from the angle of their potentialities. Anyhow, before we reach the point where everyone is "up to par" we will have to wait a long time. In the future we will need very experienced and dedicated people for every post. Real relationships of trust on the basis of solid work, confidence in the leadership—one is unthinkable without the other.

So, no rigidity in questions of work. At first, demand work only from the leadership and the inner circle and in this way set an example for the comrades. Above all, it is necessary to overcome arrogance *in one's own consciousness*. For comrades who today are "not very good" can be in important posts tomorrow, for example, commanders in the Red Army, who are at least as important as Commissar for People's Enlightenment O.

If you wish to make yourself hard, it is indispensable to be elastic. Otherwise you are only obstinate. In general, intellectuals have a much more difficult time in this area than workers. They are more difficult to discipline than workers because usually they have broader knowledge to start with, a formal education which makes them arrogant. Intellectuals have big plans in their heads and comprehend everything in the bourgeois realm very easily; but not Marxism. They don't understand how, for instance, the masses go into motion. The schoolmasters used to do all their thinking for them.

Intellectuals must give much more attention to self-discipline. They usually learn strict compliance only slowly and through a series of serious crises. At a certain stage even the best intentions are no longer enough. One must be able to relinquish one's ego; then one becomes far more tolerant towards others. Intolerance is always a sign of inward imbalance. In X almost the entire group suffers from this malady. Marxism develops a certain attitude towards life because one can observe its correctness in daily life on the street. It must be a vital concern for our lives and cannot be treated as an academic question. This, then, must be learned: how to let the basic intellectual (or theoretical) precepts of Marxism color everyday life. It is not a question of a good suit or a shabby one or of manners—you may remember how mercilessly I ridiculed Bauer and others who confused the essence of Bolshevism with a tasteless provincial and philistine spirit.

Moreover, one makes the revolution with relatively few Marxists, even within the party. Here the collective substitutes for what the individual cannot achieve. The individual can hardly master each separate area—it is necessary to have experts who supplement one another. Such experts are often quite passable "Marxists" without being complete Marxists, because they work under the control of genuine Marxists. The whole Bolshevik Party is a marvelous example of this. Under Lenin's and Trotsky's supervision, Bukharin, Molotov, Tomsky, and a hundred others were good Marxists, capable of great accomplishments. As soon as this supervision was gone, even they collapsed disgracefully. This was not because Marxism is a secret science, it is just very difficult to escape the colossal pressures of the bourgeois environment with all of its influences.

The X Group as a whole: It does not seem to me that the group is hopeless at all, and particularly because there are *political* proofs to this effect. I could not follow in more detail the course of its discussion about the turn in the French League [in 1934], but it is clear that the X Group revealed the greatest amount of political life precisely at the time of the turn. That is certainly no accident. I base my opinion, rather, on letters that I received (which I always read very carefully and compare with one another), and I think that this discussion, which brought on a crisis in all the other groups, shows that your group is fairly well developed *politically*, and that all of the attendant circumstances testify to the conclusion that it can be made into a normal group again on the basis of political questions. At that time there was not less substance for personal conflicts and frictions than today. "Normally" in the other groups, these conflicts broke out on the occasion of the turn. In your group, they receded and the political danger welded you together. There was no crisis and the political and organizational life remained intact. We must base ourselves on this and take it as a proof of political maturity. For the X Group this was, in fact, a marvelous opportunity to test and apply certain organizational and political ideas which it had been concerned with much earlier and more thoroughly than was the case with other groups. One can say without reservation that consciously or unconsciously at that time the whole group put its theoretical understanding to the test. The experiment was entirely successful. I never hesitated for an instant to use you as an example. For don't think that your position was not important. Nationally and internationally it made our victory easier and strengthened our position from the outset. That is not a small matter—it is everything. Now we must apply ourselves to systematic work on the questions at hand in order to be able to return to political work with the experience of two years. I maintain that in times when one must attend to political matters, when political news is coming in, and the interest of the group should be concentrated on political questions, the real character of a group comes to the fore. And in this respect I am optimistic about you. Ninety percent of your difficulties can be traced back to technical shortcomings. One could even go so far as to say that in fact your political and theoretical reserves have created a certain perplexity and a certain lack of political friction. In contrast to all others you understood the French turn so well that you did not apply it to the SAP in a more or less mechanistic way. On the church question, say, our comrades are pacesetters. That is: we have a certain uniform tradition—from what we learned in a few years of common work [before 1933], to the French turn, to the SAP question, and to present-day tasks, there is a straight line. The problem now is, after all the organizational and methodological mistakes, to find the road to regular, organized practical work, which is all the more necessary as more and more political tasks present themselves. I am sure that with something like a general "amnesty" and with generosity we will be moving forward quickly again. And in a while, today's "tragedies" will excite only mild laughter (to be sure: without forgetting the lessons of the tragedies). As I said, I have less doubts about all this because there will soon be political work to do. The first rule: the leadership should not worry itself about gossip and neither should all good comrades.

On the feeling occurring now and then that we have been marking time and have wasted two years: In reality, no work actually performed is in vain, however negative it may seem. Seen concretely, it is through work that we educate and develop ourselves. And if after two years there were no other result but that we made an accounting of a chapter in our lives and gained recognition of this or that mistake, then even that is a result that cannot be highly enough valued for personal and collective development. We are always looking for examples of the dialectic. Well, here is one! What good master tailor has not thoroughly ruined a dozen suits in his apprentice and journeyman's years? No, we should try with all our power to fish out the positive elements among the negative (insofar as there is any correctness in the judgment that the last two years of work have been in vain) and direct all our efforts toward decisively overcoming the weaknesses and shortcomings that have come to light during the last two years on the basis of our experience. In general, people learn only from their mistakes—especially in the proletarian movement. All the comrades who went through the old movement could, I suppose, from a certain viewpoint, regard this as "wasted" time. In reality, this activity, seemingly in vain, made us what we are today: halfway Marxists, at least.

It will appear that we are marking time as long as we do not now go over to actually carrying out the real necessary work on the basis of the experience we have gained. Anyone drawing a balance sheet today would have to say: had the work suggested here been carried out by the leadership and in the leadership, significantly more progress would already have been made and there would be organizational advances to record.

Moreover (and much more important) a certain marking of time in the political sense is unavoidable as long as political life is so narrowly limited and hemmed in that only circles, small groups and the like can exist. This fact—that fascism leaves little room for political life (for the time being we have no workers' movement, only a life in circles)—will exhaust many comrades under conditions of illegality, will make the situation seem hopeless to them, and heighten their dissatisfaction with the organization. On the other hand, this process has a good side: under no other conditions can such stable, well-trained, and disciplined cadres be formed through determined work as under the conditions of illegality. ■

Norway (1935–36)

Please pay attention to the youth question[153]

June 21, 1935

To the International Secretariat and all youth sections

Dear Comrades:

It is only now that I have understood how the Stockholm Bureau, so called even though it resides in another country, functions. What is the cause of this? The most important of the organizations, the Swedish [Socialist Youth League], refused from the beginning to extend hospitality to the international youth secretariat in order to preserve themselves from the criminal nucleus of Leninists. This single fact is completely sufficient to assess the Swedish youth leadership at its real worth. I think we made a serious error right from the start in accepting this unworthy and humiliating condition. A revolutionary organization can never be based on equivocation and bureaucratic maneuvering, even when the bureaucrats are very young.

After "expelling" the secretariat from its country, this organization found it necessary to transmit its mandate to Mot Dag, that is, to a numerically very weak organization without the least revolutionary merit. This arrangement sufficiently demonstrates how much importance the young

Swedish bureaucrats accord to the international organization. Everything is based on fictions and manipulations. Can anyone truly believe that with such a "base" the working class youth can be won on a world scale?

The political attitude of Mot Dag is pernicious from all points of view. Not only did the representative of our youth, Comrade Held, have to protest with vehemence and demand that the Swedes withdraw their mandate from Mot Dag, but even the representative of the SAP, Brandt, found it necessary this time to sign Comrade Held's protest.

The Swedes have not yet officially responded. Held supposes that they would rather not disown those to whom they have entrusted their mandate, who are besides no more opportunistic than the Swedes themselves. It can be supposed that negotiations are right now being held between the Swedes, Mot Dag and Brandt—unbeknownst to our Comrade Held—to settle the affair amicably, that is, to the detriment of revolutionary principles and of our organization.

It would be absolutely criminal on our part to adapt to the SAP representative, who himself wants to adapt to the Swedes, even though they are inclined to adapt to the Mot Dag group. Held has proposed that we set up for the interim period a provisional youth secretariat in Paris (one representative of the IS, one representative of the Bolshevik-Leninist youth of France, one representative of the SAP) to convene as soon as possible an international youth conference, which should on its part set up a new international bureau. It seems to me that we have to decide as soon as possible for the proposal of Held or for an analogous combination to get us out of this untenable compromising situation. I beg you, comrades, to give your attention to this very important question, which is inextricably tied to the renewal of our campaign for the Fourth International.

Crux [Leon Trotsky]

Chen Tu-hsiu and the General Council[154]

August 10, 1935

Dear Comrade:

With the help of Comrades H. and V. [Harold Isaacs and Viola Robinson] I have plunged once more into the Chinese question. I am only at the beginning. I must in the next several days study the more important documents and you will understand that I cannot now give my opinion on the differences within the Chinese section. But I am exceedingly anxious to write you at once on the more immediate and burning question of Comrade CTH [Chen Tu-hsiu].

He is an international figure. He is in prison. He remains faithful not only to the revolution but to our tendency in particular. We are now creating the Fourth International and the General Council as its guiding theoretical and consultative body. In principle, the GC will be composed of two kinds of members: (1) direct representatives of the sections of the ICL and other adhering organizations and (2) individuals who by their past and present are fit to contribute to the elaboration of our program, strategic principles, etc. It is my conviction that Comrade CTH undoubtedly belongs on the GC, despite his important differences with the Chinese section, whose direct representative, in my opinion, should be Comrade NS [Niel Shih].

You must take into consideration the fact that the composition of the GC must be impeccable, in the sense that it will guarantee us against unfortunate crises, capitulations, treasons, etc. That is why it is necessary to recommend for the GC only comrades who are known, proved and absolutely dependable.

It may be replied—and some Chinese comrades will certainly reply—that on a number of important questions CTH has opinions which appear to them to be absolutely false. For the time being I express no opinion on differences whose content I have not yet sufficiently studied. But the Chinese comrades, like all others, must clearly understand that the creation of groupings for the Fourth International has changed the situation, in that we, the Bolshevik-Leninists, represent only one faction among these groupings. Thus the GC must reflect not only the Bolshevik-Leninist sections, but *all* the revolutionary forces moving in the direction of the Fourth International. I will give you an example: The well-known German comrades, Maslow and Ruth Fischer, who led the German party in 1923–25, adhere to the organization of forces for the Fourth International without adhering to the German section of the ICL, with which they have serious differences. Nevertheless, the IS has unanimously proposed Maslow as a member of the GC. There is an analogous case in Czechoslovakia, etc. Thus you see that it is not a question of making an exception for China.

I draw your attention to another aspect of the same matter. Because of its extremely difficult situation, the Chinese section remains quite weak. Arrests and persecution deprive it of organizational stability. We are all absolutely sure that the Chinese section, which has devoted and courageous comrades, will grow in the nearest future. But for the moment, to introduce into the GC a young, entirely new comrade, unknown internationally, would be imprudent. This is my personal opinion only, but I believe that the arguments I have advanced here are dictated by the whole situation. I have no need to tell you that the Chinese section has the full right to propose other candidates, just as all other sections have, but I am sure that the candidacy of Comrade CTH will be supported by all our sections, because it would be a serious blow to the authority of the Fourth International to renounce the collaboration of CTH while the possibility still remains of settling the existing differences through international organizational procedure.

The Chinese section has not formally broken with CTH and for that I sincerely rejoice. At the same time the Chinese section has formed its own Central Committee entirely independently of CTH and his partisans. This is naturally the full right of the Chinese section. The introduction of CTH into the GC need not in any way, of itself, change the situation in China, the composition of the Chinese Central Committee, its political leadership, etc. On the other hand, the GC will be able to intervene in an amicable fashion, to clarify the differences, soften the conflict and improve relations.

With the creation of groupings for the Fourth International, I again emphasize, we dispose of larger organizational cadres and of new possibilities of action. I will give you a recent example: In Belgium our section, as you know, has become a faction of Vandervelde's opportunist party, the POB (wherein, incidentally, they have made great progress). The Vereecken group in Brussels separated from our section and thus remains outside our international organization. But after the launching of the Open Letter for the Fourth International, Vereecken declared solidarity with it, and it is quite possible that he will be admitted as a sympathizing organization. The adherence of his group to the Fourth International will give us the possibility of drawing him once more into our section and in any event to impose upon him a loyal and friendly attitude towards our section. You see by this example that we are far from considering the Fourth International as a simple reproduction of the International Communist League and this fact alone can serve to demonstrate to the Chinese comrades that CTH can and must have his place in the cadres of the Fourth International.

I do not mean by this that every group which will proclaim itself in favor of the Fourth International will be automatically admitted. I named Vereecken because his attitude toward the Bolshevik-Leninists after the split provoked by him remains loyal. He sees, besides, the great success of our section and in the last number of his journal he advocated support for the *Action Socialiste* faction in the POB. There is thus a vast difference between the attitude of Vereecken and that of a Weisbord or a Field, who attack our international organization and the WPUS in a venomous and disloyal fashion and who attack in the same manner our French section which today marches at the head of our whole international organization.

I regret very much that you did not come with Comrades H. and V. and that I have not had a chance to meet you. I regret it the more since I should have liked to discuss with you not only the Chinese questions but also and especially the South African question. I will ask our IS to send you all the documents thereon and we will await with interest your assessments, comments, and advice.

I ask you to transmit my most fraternal greetings to all the Chinese comrades.

Yours fraternally,
Leon Trotsky

For a bloc against Oehler[155]

August 13, 1935

Dear Comrades Weber, Abern and Glotzer:

I have attentively studied all the documents, theses, and minutes of the [Workers Party's June 1935] plenum and all your letters. My supposition has now become an absolute conviction. All Marxists, all true revolutionaries, must join in an implacable struggle against Oehlerism.

It is really an unbearable scandal at a time when our French section is fighting on all fronts with admirable courage and is making remarkable progress, which opens before us a whole new perspective, that a part of the WP should be defaming our French comrades with ignoble accusations and calumnies. We have the right to demand reparation, i.e., a pitiless condemnation of the Oehler group by a majority of the party.

I believe that in the name of our common principles you must, despite all past conflicts and secondary differences, effect a rapprochement with the Cannon-Shachtman-Swabeck group. To improve the regime in the party it is necessary that the party as a whole intervene and for this to be successful it must be freed of unscrupulous sectarianism. I beg of you to conquer yourselves and to take the necessary steps toward rapprochement.

I retain the most sincere and faithful sentiments for all three of you.

Fraternally yours,
Leon Trotsky

Dear Comrade Swabeck:

I have received your letter of August 1 and the statement of Cannon-Shachtman-Swabeck on the situation in the Workers Party. I have just sent two letters dealing with the questions that form the main content of your statement. Without involving myself in secondary questions on which, naturally, I am not in a position to hold definite opinions, I am entirely in agreement with you on the primordial issue—the harmful role of sectarianism, represented in an especially harmful manner by the Oehler group.

I believe that you must win over Comrades Weber, Glotzer and Abern for common action by means of frank and friendly mutual explanations. I have written in the same sense to those comrades. Since you are stronger and are in the leadership you can—permit me to say—take the first step towards a reconciliation in the name of common principles. If there were some mistakes in procedure on your part (it is quite possible and even inevitable that there were), it is necessary for you to recognize them openly in order to knock the props from under the accusations now being leveled at the "regime." Such a declaration on your part can only strengthen the authority of the leadership. I assure you that Lenin always acted thus. You are right as to policy. You can make concessions, even considerable concessions, as to form.

I am not in a position to give you any advice concerning Comrade Muste, since, unfortunately, I do not know him. But I believe that we all have the utmost interest in not prejudicing his authority, which is the common property of the party and of our international movement. I am sure that you are of the same opinion and that you have acted in accordance therewith.

I attach hereto a brief supplement to my preceding letters meant for the attention of all the comrades.

Fraternally yours,
L. *Trotsky*

The Cannon-Shachtman group should make concessions[156]

September 4, 1935

Comrades Cannon and Shachtman

Worthy Comrades:

In response to your letter of August 15 to the IS: It is understood that Oehlerism must be politically liquidated. On that we are in complete agreement. Does this inevitably have to mean a split-off of Oehler and of the core of his group? That I am not able to judge. If this could be avoided, then of course we should avoid it.

Oehler is not a political thinker. Such people can only pose as political leaders in periods when the movement is still in swaddling clothes. This does not necessarily mean that they are useless for the movement. Ryazanov, for example, wanted to be a political, and especially a trade union, leader, at any price. But he didn't have the qualities to be one. After some more experience, he finally concentrated on Marxist scholarship, and in this he secured imperishable gains for the party and the International. It is possible that Oehler will, in the future, also find his place in the movement. We should, if possible, not close the door to him. As an independent political figure, however, he can only compromise himself and harm the movement.

The question would arise, however, *in what way and at what tempo* should we liquidate Oehlerism? To form an opinion from here is not easy. But I have the impression, from all the facts and the documents, that you gave Oehlerism a free hand for a long time, and then moved so harshly all at once, that the organization was taken by surprise and a division was created in the leadership.

The sharp disagreement with Muste is most lamentable, not only in its international aspects, although Muste is an international figure; from a purely *national* standpoint also, your break with Muste will signify, for a long time to come, a blow at the authority of the leadership and at the whole organization. We don't conduct unification negotiations for half a year and longer in order then to come to a split half a year later. Such a result would strengthen the talk about the "impossible methods" of the Bolshevik-Leninists in the highest degree. The SAP is already informing its sections that the WPUS is on the brink of a split.

What do I mean by that? I mean that, even if we can make no principled concessions to Oehlerism—if it doesn't work otherwise—we can and should make concessions to the Muste and Weber groups, *in regard to the forms and methods of the struggle against Oehlerism*. You still can't hide from the fact that even if you win a majority, it will be a very narrow one, and in this case your group will face an organizational combination of the three other groups. You can call this combination unprincipled, "harmful," etc. This designation will not remove it from the face of the earth. I don't want to, and I hardly could, go into the question, to what extent much too severe and overly subtle methods (without adequate political and psychological preparation) bear responsibility for the organizational combination of the three groups coming into being. But you are duty-bound to take the hard facts into account.

In any case, in your communication that Muste suddenly, without any prior political difference, broke off relations with you, I can't help but see an irrefutable proof that you undertook extremely important steps without consulting Muste on them day in and day out and without giving him the necessary time to consult with his close friends. The fact that the position of Muste, the party secretary, appeared to you as something "sudden" and unexpected tells me that not everything in your procedure was all right.

I ask myself: How would Lenin act in an analogous situation? I believe I can say with assurance that he would go before the party with roughly the following explanation: The Oehler tendency endangers the development and the future of the party. To struggle against this tendency is the absolute duty of every Marxist. However, the *way* in which *we* have fought it has aroused dissatisfaction in two other groups, of which the Muste group is of great importance. *We are therefore completely prepared to make far-reaching concessions to the Muste and Weber groups in regard to the methods of fighting sectarianism.* Such an explanation would undoubtedly make the best impression on the wavering elements, would only heighten your authority, and would knock the weapon out of the hands of your opponents.

You can answer me: This would signify a "rotten peace," would strengthen the Oehler group, cripple the party, etc. I don't think so, for this perspective can be compared not to some ideal state of affairs, but to the state of affairs of an impending split under an extremely unfavorable relationship of forces. New *events* will only compromise and weaken Oehlerism. Muste and Weber will have to turn their backs on him more and more; your authority will only grow. This is how Lenin operated, for example, in the struggle against the Ultimatists, and, as the result showed, with success.

The Muste group is, of course, politically more important than the Weber group. Both are, however, more or less bound up with each other, and *you have absolutely no stake in keeping the Weber group in permanent opposition.* It is extremely likely that certain memories of old conflicts, personal ties, etc., play a significant role in the attitude of this group. Of course, this isn't correct. Still less correct, however, is to view the group as hopeless. It is in political agreement with us. If, by meeting them halfway—which in this situation will be a sign of strength and not of weakness—you are able to eliminate the old animosity, you will pull the rug out from under the independent existence of this group and you will only strengthen your own position. This is all the more important since the leader of the youth, Gould, who seems to be a capable and active comrade, adheres to this faction.

That is the general impression that I have gained after careful examination of the material available to me.

With the friendliest greetings.

Yours,
L. *Trotsky*

P.S. Have you received the materials that I sent you on the struggle in the French section? (A handwritten French and a German report on the demonstration of July 14, an issue of the confiscated *Revolution*, the leaflet of July 14, excerpts from letters, etc.) In *The New Militant* I have, unfortunately, seen none of this. Maybe I haven't got all the issues of your paper. The best means of struggle against Oehlerism is accurate information on what is really happening.

L.T.

The policy of the Abern-Weber group[157]

September 4, 1935

Dear Comrades Abern and Weber:

In reply to your letter of August 18, I have studied very carefully all letters and documents and the entire material on the June plenum. My opinion may be wrong but it is certainly not based on "one-sided" information.

Always when I speak in my letters of the leadership, I mean in no way only Cannon-Shachtman-Swabeck, but naturally also the group of Comrade Muste. The differences in the leadership among the two most important groups became clear to me only from the minutes of the June plenum. This changes the situation in the negative sense, but does not change the evaluation of the position of your group.

In your previous letters you sharply reproached Cannon and Shachtman for being insufficiently critical with regard to the Muste group, for tolerating much too much its weaknesses, and for trying to exclude discussion for half a year for the sake of peace. Now you make the opposite reproach to Cannon and Shachtman: They have treated the Muste group with insufficient consideration, as if they were alone in the leadership. This highly persuasive argument alone shows what a sharp turn you yourselves have made in the last weeks without noticing it. This shows that subjective moments, reminiscences and old ties determine in a great measure the policy of your group: *the slogans and reproaches change, but the opposition remains permanent.*

That I consider Comrade Muste and his group as most

important factors not only in the WPUS but also in the international movement, I need not say just now. I follow with great interest everything that he writes, because, as I have personally written him, I hope that the common signature on the manifesto [Open Letter] for the Fourth International means a fraternization in struggle, so to say, for a lifetime.

I cannot consider it a crime that Cannon and Shachtman tried to avoid discussion in the first period after the fusion. Discussion is not the only and not the primary element of party life. When discussion is fed not by action but by itself, the party is lost. The new party should have been given the possibility to participate in mass actions, to gather experience, to make mistakes, so that the discussion could develop on a higher level and be fruitful. The party remained, as you underscore, without a position on the French turn. This also is no misfortune in and of itself. At one time, for instance, I advised the Dutch comrades, in view of the sharp differences of opinion on the question of the SFIO, not to take a position immediately, but to await critically what the experiences would show. That your group has defended the French turn is naturally to your credit. But that from this question also you tried to forge a weapon against the leadership I consider a mistake. With joy I take cognizance of the fact that you have contributed to winning Comrade Muste to the French turn. But I consider it indisputable that the *experience itself* was decisive in this question. Therefore it would have been false through untimely discussion to call forth a split or a paralysis of the party instead of letting events speak for themselves for a certain period of time.

With regard to the question of the American SP I consider your criticism of the Cannon-Shachtman theses as highly exaggerated. Comparing the Abern-Muste-Weber theses I can find only nuances which, however, are developed in a purely speculative manner into infinity. We are not empiricists, that is true. But we are also not transcendentalists. We should keep closer to reality, gather experiences with regard to the SP, test them critically and, after a certain interval, discuss. It is wrong in a tactical-practical question to commit ourselves for eternity. But fanciful variants of possible development should not be made a hindrance to the next step.

My conclusions? An alliance, direct or indirect, open or concealed, of the Muste and Weber groups *with the Oehler group* against Cannon-Shachtman would be *a crime* against the party and against the Fourth International. The next plenum and the discussion must, in essence, mean the alliance of Cannon-Muste-Weber against the Oehler group. Only in this case would the discussion have a principled character, the Oehler group would shrink together and its most stubborn elements would think ten times before they split to disappear into nothingness.

It is possible that Cannon and other comrades wanted to proceed against the Oehler group too rashly, too sharply, too "bureaucratically," as you say. But today the situation is altogether different. The discussion is in full swing. Party democracy can no longer be reproached. Now one should not speak of "bureaucratic" mistakes of yesterday, but take a correct and clear position in the discussion which will be understood nationally and internationally.

Dear friends, do not take this letter in bad part. "Hier stehe ich, ich kann nicht anders." [Here I stand, I cannot do otherwise.]

With best greetings to you both, also to Glotzer.

Yours,
L. *Trotsky*

Nothing in common with the decadent Comintern[158]

September 18, 1935

Dear Comrade Muste:

The decisions of the [Workers Party's] Political Bureau communicated in your letter of September 6 correspond completely to my own understanding of the situation. It is clear that my letters cannot in the least be considered as official or semiofficial documents. I have given expression to my views not only because various American friends asked my opinion. Formerly too, when it was a question of the [Communist] League, which was an official section of our international organization, I have always considered my letters as private advice intended for those comrades who were interested in this advice. This is especially so with regard to the WPUS, which is not organizationally connected with our Secretariat. A party which would accept pronouncements of individual comrades and not decisions of its bodies as "directives" would not be worth being regarded as a revolutionary party. I hope that the Fourth International in its whole structure as well as in its internal life will have nothing in common with the disgusting mores and customs of the decadent Comintern.

I am sending you a detailed treatise on the ILP. Recently I received a friendly letter from Fenner Brockway: he speaks with satisfaction of the meeting with Isaacs, sends me the *New Leader*, etc. I am taking this opportunity to get into regular correspondence with him. The Seventh World Congress [of the Comintern] will push the ILP or its greatest portion away from the Comintern. My article pursues the aim of hastening the development of the ILP toward the Fourth International. In publishing this article *The New International* could possibly prepare separate copies for our English comrades. In any case, please send Fenner Brockway the proper issue of *The New International* with an accompanying letter. Possibly in this way your leadership will get into relations with the ILP. This could be of great service.

Yesterday I received news from Spain. Our section there has fused with the Catalonian Federation and is now about to proclaim a new party for Spain. Our comrades assure us that the leadership of the Federation has come closer to us and they hope to be able to bring this organization on the path of the Fourth International.

With warmest revolutionary greetings.

Yours,
L. Trotsky

P.S. It is possible that my criticism of the Oehler group seemed to some comrades to be much too sharp. If this is the case, I am naturally ready to make my sincere apologies for the form of the criticism. It must be taken into consideration, however, that it is not an American but a French and an international question; that our direct enemies, like Bauer, and the leading clique of the SAPites have been spreading rumors for months that the WPUS, under the influence of the Oehler group, considers our French comrades as capitulators and condemns them sharply. That this situation created and creates utmost difficulties for us precisely because of the authority of the WPUS, I need not go into at length here.

The article on the ILP will follow tomorrow.

L.T.

An appeal to A.J. Muste[159]

September 24–25, 1935

Dear Comrade Muste:

Your letter did not reach me until recently as I am at present not in Honefoss but under a doctor's care in Oslo. I regret very much, therefore, that these lines will not reach you before October 4. This, however, is not the result of elements under my control. Since yesterday I have gone over the documents you sent me with all the care which they deserve.

Cordial thanks for the confidence your letter reposes in me. I feel that I can repay it in no better fashion than to state my candid opinion of the state of things in the American party.

The basic point for me remains the political position of the Oehler group and the approach to it of the various groups in the party. Why? Because the Oehler tendency is a form of a disease, because it has international implications (and international connections), and because, if we are serious about building the Fourth International, it must be internationally defeated.

I do not know whether Oehler and his close associates have changed their position. If so, I will be very happy. The fact remains, however, that the Oehler group in the past year, a period so important to us, has stood in close connection with our enemies, combated our movement and our best elements. That is what is politically decisive.

Every ideological and factional fight raises dust. Groups accuse one another of disloyalty, of unreliability and even of dishonesty. In the Bolshevik parties, even in their best periods, this was not entirely avoided. (We should not raise any illusions in retrospect.) If, however, we wish to separate the realities from the forms and the incidental aspect, one must always try—so I at least try to proceed—to understand the issue from an international point of view as well. Tell me with whom you go internationally and I will tell you who you are. Let us estimate the situation somewhat. The Oehler group rested itself on Bauer and his supporter Eiffel.[160] Bauer is now in the SAP, that is, in a thoroughly opportunist organization which fights us to the hilt. The Oehler group supported Vereecken who broke with us. The Oehler group combated our French group upon whose position we pride ourselves. In this connection we come to a most important point, one which cannot be disputed.

Nobody was bound to accept the "French turn" in advance. Everyone had the chance to express his opinion and his criticism freely. One year, however, has passed. Facts have spoken. He who closes his eyes to facts is incurable. Let us assume that the turn had proved to be a mistake (that we found no support in the SP, were expelled, etc.). This was a possibility that had to be reckoned with. But the failure of a tactical turn is far from being a capitulation. Oehler has accused the French section and our international organization of capitulation, of betrayal. In this question the French section and the international organization have the right to expect of the comrades of the Workers Party some political satisfaction. That is, if the actions of the Oehler group are not formally judged, none of us will know how to understand it.

The Oehler group has made propaganda for the periodical *Que Faire?*[161] This publication is the enterprise of five or six individuals who have either split from us or have been expelled and who represent at least seven tendencies.

The Oehler group declared that the Stockholm Bureau was the only central youth organization for the new International. In reality the thoroughly opportunistic majority of this bureau stands in inflexible opposition to the Fourth International and has "shut out" the representative of the ICL, Comrade Held.

The Oehler group defended the SAP against us. The SAP, however, takes a much worse position toward us than the American Lovestoneites, to whom, by the way, the Walcher group has a spiritual tie through their past history and training.

The Oehler group denied the right of our French youth section to be represented in the miserable Stockholm Bureau, and demanded this right for the Spanish youth without even knowing anything about them.

On the basis of this information, which Bauer received from his American friends, the SAP is now spreading the information in their bulletins that the WPUS stands on the verge of collapse.

In a word, the Oehler group stood in the course of this all-important year on the other side of the barricades, in closest association with people who fought our sections, slandered and lied about them. That is a fact. It cannot be disposed of. To this fact I believe all tendencies in the WP are bound to take an exact and unequivocal position.

The Oehlerites claimed that Cannon and Shachtman were in secret contact with the Social Democratic leaders. That was proven to be false. The Oehlerites, however, are really in contact with betrayers and renegades of the Bauer stripe. This fact is internationally known, is used by our enemies and brings our friends under a cloud. The WPUS must, in all its groups, take a position on this fact.

I will assume for a moment that C-S [Cannon and Shachtman] are really taking an opportunist approach to the question of the SP. First, however, it lies with the future to make the transfer to a higher political stage where this tendency of which C-S are accused will be brought to light and will be vigorously fought by us. But these tendencies, which really belong to the future, do not today constitute the main hindrance in our way. That is the sectarianism which finds its worst expression in the Oehlerites.

The whole method of thought of Oehler is un-Marxian and undialectical. He has a certain conception of every question and bothers little about the realities of any situation. Thus he works without trouble on the conception of the excellent Stockholm Bureau; with the conception of the Spanish youth who only wait for his friendly gesture; with the conception of the SAP as friendly to the Fourth International; with the concept of the mighty and revolutionary *Que Faire?* etc., etc. I have not considered a single political tenet of Oehler which was correct. He lives in an out-and-out perverted world. He has only a sovereign contempt for reality. He has no political mind and the tragedy of it is that he presents himself as a political leader, thus causing confusion. The anti-Marxist pattern of thought which he uses and which is completely divorced from all reality must, in my opinion, be examined in the most decisive manner by the WP, for one must learn from such events in order to be able to go forward.

With all this I do not mean to say that Oehler can find no place in the ranks of the Fourth International. The problem of leadership is to estimate such persons correctly and find the right place for them to function. Ryazanov[162] thought for years that he was a political and trade union leader and only caused confusion. As a Marxist historian, however, he did exceedingly valuable work for the labor movement. Similarly the members of the WPUS must be warned against the political ideas and actions of Oehler.

Out of these last documents, I have gained the impression that the bloc of Muste-Weber-Oehler seeks to assert itself against C-S. I cannot, my dear and esteemed Comrade Muste, align myself with this bloc, either directly or indirectly. In the light of the national and international situation only one bloc seems to me to be progressive; Muste-C-S-Weber against

Oehler. That is also the only way to bring the temporarily misled Oehlerites to their senses and to keep the damages of the party convulsion down to a minimum.

You may answer me: and what about the "methods" of C-S, the question of the regime, etc.? In your document you say quite correctly that the methods depend on the political line. I might answer to this that this affects not only the "leadership" or the majority of the leadership but the opposition as well. A second consequence seems to me, however, even more important: the connection between organizational forms and methods does not flow automatically and directly from the political position. Many other factors also play a part. If one seeks to correct the leadership and its position in a small organization which has no great mass basis, one may explode the entire organization. Far be it from me to attempt to take the responsibility for the manner in which C-S conduct themselves. I can very well understand that one or another group in the party should protest against specific methods. Even here, however, we must preserve a sense of proportion. Genuine democratic centralism you will establish when you have more "democracy," that is, more masses in your ranks. That, however, you can only accomplish when you have cleansed your party of sectarianism.

Two examples: I cannot judge whether Cannon purposely provoked Zack[163] in order to in turn provoke the Oehler faction. The question in itself is not without significance, but it must be judged in connection with concrete surrounding circumstances. The political position of Zack is basically false and Oehler did not pass up the chance to take up his defense. That is clear, unequivocal and significant.

Your documents reproach *The New International* for publishing an article against the SAP at the moment when the central committee was establishing fraternal relations with the SAP. It is quite possible that the method of the editor of *The New International* was not correct in this case. But this question fades into the background compared to the position of the central committee to the SAP, and to whether or not it is correct. To me, for example, it is impossible to understand how *The New Militant* and why *The New Militant* can give publicity to the miserable, opportunist, thoroughly antagonistic *Neue Front*. The Dutch comrade Schmidt, who was allied and worked with the SAP for many years, has found it necessary to declare the most uncompromising war against it. In *De Nieuwe Fakkel* he recognizes that the "Alchemy" article's insistent stand that the Fourth International will be built without and against the SAP has been proved correct by the actions of the SAP.[164] That alone is significant and about this matter your theses say nothing.

In order not to allow any room for misunderstanding, I must again repeat: I am ready to assume, a priori, that Comrades C-S sought to resort to hasty and thereby oversevere organizational methods. I have noticed this tendency in other sections as well. The last twelve years of the history of the Comintern and the general turmoil in the movement have not been without their effect on us. In the fight against the soulless apparatus, one was oneself more or less bureaucratized; the oppositions hasten to resort to the weapons of breaking discipline and of split, the leadership hastens to mechanical suppression or expulsion. One depends far too little on discussion, on ideological struggle, on the testing of ideas through joint political experience. Here we must all unlearn and relearn to build the Fourth International on a sound basis. To this sound basis, however, it is necessary to come by rejecting combinations that divide political tendencies on purely organizational grounds.

I am glad that the Political Committee, by official action, has characterized my letters as private documents, as personal advice. I never had any other conception. The explanation gives me the possibility of bringing my views to the fore with full freedom. I need not tell you that—as far as I am able to evaluate them—my evaluation of the situation does not rest on any personalities or sympathies. I view this crisis as a testing period, which the party will survive with great gains for itself, and I hope to stand in the closest political and if possible personal relationship to the representatives of all the various groups.

I also need not tell you, Comrade Muste, that for you I have the warmest personal regard and affection.

The letter is not signed by me for I have dictated it to my friend Jan Frankel, who is here in the hospital to visit me and who will get off the letter to you with all possible speed.

SEPTEMBER 25, 1935

Dear Comrade Muste:

I was forced to break off my letter yesterday as the visiting hour had run out. Today I have as visitor the same Comrade Held whom the "brother" party, the SAP, put out of the Stockholm Bureau, not because he is against but because he is for the Fourth International. I use the opportunity of his visit to round out my letter of yesterday. I want, at all costs, to avoid giving the impression that I passed over your documents' section on the C-S attitude to the SP. No, I have studied it very faithfully. I have the impression that you have succeeded in proving that the position of C-S to the SP and to its left wing has undergone very considerable changes. I have not, however, gained the impression at all that C-S can be accused of capitulation. The question in *America* seems to me to be artificially built up as a reflex of the important tactical changes in Europe. In France and Belgium the question stood very plainly: should one or should one not enter the reformist party? In America no one proposes such a solution. What possibilities there may be for you within the SP can be found not by speculation as much as by action. I do not, of course, quarrel with the importance of a perspective to evaluate the possibilities and the dangers. In purely tactical questions, however, one should not be prepared to lay a line for eternity. The Workers Party feels it incumbent upon itself to function as an independent party. It does not really have to repeat every third day that it will not dissolve itself in a reformist organization. The need for such reiteration sounds more like a confession of weakness than a declaration of strength.

The question from this side of the ocean, I repeat, seems to us to have been artificially raised by the Oehler group. They, moreover, keep it no secret; they look for small unimportant symptoms to prove the plans drawn up in Paris mean a betrayal in America. Now we in Europe do not consider ourselves as betrayers. The fears and denunciations of Comrades Oehler, Stamm, etc., seem to us to be sectarian childish babble, their main question, and in this question we await a clear answer from the Workers Party.

Today I studied the documents which you sent to all sections of the party on August 14. I find there, for example, the statement by Stamm on August 5, "the capitulators of Charleroi." What gives Comrade Stamm the right to characterize—or rather to abuse—the Belgian comrades in this way? The Charleroi group consists almost entirely of mine workers; there is not a single intellectual in the leadership. They are all over forty years of age, every one has been victimized by the employers for strike action, mass action, etc. All belonged to the CP from the beginning, and to the Left Opposition from 1923 on, without having weakened a moment. By their own efforts they have established a weekly paper which has appeared regularly for years. They joined the reformist party based on the trade unions, just as in England, not to capitulate but to fight the bitter struggle for the leadership of the vanguard. One can be of the opinion that their work will bring no results (although they have already considerable work to their credit). But how can one call them capitulators? They have capitulated to nothing and no one and do not intend to. It is correct that they must observe certain care in how they express themselves. In the unions revolutionists do the same thing. As I understand it, however, Comrades Oehler and Stamm think the combination of "legal" with illegal work goes only for the Workers Party. When, however, these combined methods are applied in the reformist party, it is betrayal. Comrade Muste, these comrades stand in crying contradiction to the most elementary conceptions of Marxism and Bolshevism.

And they complain about the "regime," naturally not only about the regime of C-S, but especially about the regime of the ICL: all and everything is tainted with bureaucracy; everywhere we hound the genuine revolutionists who want to save us from the swamp if not from direct betrayal. When one reads such stuff, one either laughs or scorns, according to one's temperament.

I do not at all want to idealize our methods or ways, but the sectarians (Bauer, Vereecken, Oehler, etc.) are really the last ones to give us lectures on the subject, for on the plane of organizational methods, as on the theoretical level, they are only a concentrated expression of our weaknesses. I will deal with this later in a longer theoretical article.

Two more observations. Our Belgian friends, the "capitulators," speak in their paper *Action Socialiste Revolutionnaire* not of everything (they also have allies who have not thought matters through to the end as yet), but on the most important and burning issues—national defense, the turn of the Comintern—they take an open, excellent and Leninist position. And to speak the revolutionary message in Belgium today requires ten or a hundred or a thousand times more revolutionary courage than to do it in the United States which is not menaced by a Hitler.

The second observation is of a personal character. I do

not believe that I can be accused of impatience toward these individuals. I could prove that by American examples: Field and Weisbord. I was in communication with both of them for a long time. They were both of them in my house for considerable periods. After the [first] expulsion of Field, I did everything I could to see that he was again accepted for membership. I also attempted to lay the tracks between Weisbord and the CLA. Not all the American comrades were enthusiastic about my efforts and perhaps rightly so. This same position I took in regard to Vereecken, Bauer, etc., but one does not go forward without a few splinters left on the way. Oehler's claims against the leadership of the WP, I am firmly convinced, are entirely without basis, at least as far as the present period is concerned. The more strongly he is made to feel that, the more we will be able to hope that he will not be lost to us.

This letter also is not signed by me because it was typed only in the city and then sent off. ∎

The open letter and the ILP[165]

Autumn 1935

Our group in the ILP feels uneasy about publicly signing the Open Letter. Perhaps they could resort to something like this: draw up a letter to the leadership of the ILP about the question of international affiliation. This document should point out the treachery of the Third International on the war question, the most burning of all, and call attention to the miserable position of the SAP (on disarmament), of the Swedish [Socialist] Party (you will soon receive material on this), and above all of Doriot—and it should conclude that the struggle against war and against sanctions is possible only under the banner of the Fourth International. Such a document signed by our sympathizers would have the same weight as signing the Open Letter, but it could not incriminate our comrades for a violation of discipline. ■

Foreword, Mitt Liv[166]

October 1, 1935

I am writing these lines in Norway, or, to be more precise, in the Municipal Hospital in Oslo. An unexpected development! One can often foresee great historical events, but it is difficult to anticipate one's own fate. I remember a particular situation: After the French government had deported me to Spain [in 1916] because of my insufficient enthusiasm for the czar and the Entente, I was arrested by the government of Alfonso XIII[167] on some convenient pretext or other. I lay on a cot in Madrid's "model" prison and asked myself: How and why am I here? An unexpected development! The gist of my answer was this: No matter how capriciously my personal life might turn out, it nevertheless developed under the influence of important historical factors such as war, revolution, and counterrevolution. One must know how to accept one's fate as it is hammered out on the forge of history. And it is no exaggeration when I say that I felt just as comfortable with a book in my hand in the Madrid prison as I did a year or a year and a half later in Smolny or the Kremlin.

That was almost twenty years ago—a rather long period of time in the life of a single individual, especially considering that these two decades have been filled with great events, affecting the whole of humanity. But through all the vicissitudes and tremors, I have nonetheless maintained my inclination to laugh at the annoyances of my personal life. And the fact that now, as the eighteenth anniversary of the October Revolution draws near, I am lying sick in the capital of Norway can least of all inspire me with the feeling that I have been "mistreated" by the historical process or lead me to rue my personal fate. It is true that the transition from the present, totally bankrupt social system to a new, more harmonious system is taking place much more slowly than one could have expected or desired. The conservatism and gullibility of the masses, the stupidity and treachery of their leaders, throw humanity back and demand untold and extreme sacrifices—but the victory of the new society is certain, and that is what counts. Fais ce que doit, advienne que pourra. [Do what you must, come what may.]

My first exile was of such short duration (October 1903–February 1905) that it can hardly be called an exile. Between two periods of underground work, between two periods of imprisonment and two escapes in czarist Russia, a young Russian revolutionary simply spent a year and a half in Western Europe,[168] where he studied Marxism and revolutionary politics in the midst of two generations of experienced emigrants (Plekhanov and Axelrod,[169] Lenin and Martov).

My second exile lasted ten years, corresponding to the deep, dark period of reaction between the two Russian revolutions (1905 and 1917). The last portion of this exile stretched through the war years, with their chauvinist poison dividing the world proletariat and setting it far back.

My third exile began in January 1929 after a year's deportation in Central Asia, and has now lasted about seven years. This period has been characterized by a tremendous deepening of capitalist contradictions throughout the world, by the growth and advance of fascism, and by terrible defeats for the world proletariat (Germany, Austria, Spain). There is nothing accidental about the correspondence between the periods of my personal life and periods of historical development. The fate of many revolutionary generations, not just in Russia but in all countries that have undergone deep social upheavals, has followed the same curve: from prison and exile to power, and from power to prison and exile.

But here we have to raise an objection: the counterrevolution did not triumph in Soviet society. Even now social development continues on the basis laid by the October Revolution. But it is from that very same Soviet society, which the author of this book had a hand in creating, that he was forced to depart into his third exile. How can we explain this contradiction?

There is no riddle involved here. The capitalist counterrevolution did not triumph in the Soviet Union, that is quite true. But only the most shortsighted persons, or those directly implicated, can overlook the deepgoing degeneration during the last ten or twelve years of the party that carried out the October Revolution, and of the state that the victorious working class created. A *bureaucracy* now rules over the Soviet state. This bureaucracy has consolidated unlimited power and countless material privileges in its hands. It may be said in passing that it would be very instructive to make an accounting of just how much of the national income this ruling caste consumes, but such statistics are among the most closely guarded state secrets. The bureaucracy, by definitively freeing itself from the control of the masses and hoisting itself up above the mass of disenfranchised workers, was inevitably obliged to select from its midst an all-high commissar-arbiter, a man of destiny, an absolute and infallible "Leader." In him, refracted through Byzantine ideology, the bureaucracy's desire to play a role as the eternal, unremovable, and well-paid representatives of the people finds its highest (or rather, its lowest) form of expression. But this enlightened absolutism has and can have nothing in common with administration of a workers' state, let alone a "classless socialist society."

The Soviet state's technical, economic, and cultural accomplishments are far-reaching. This is an indisputable fact. These results have been obtained through nationalization of the means of production and through the heroic efforts of the working masses. But only the so-called "friends of the Soviet Union" (in reality, friends of the Soviet bureaucratic leadership) can claim that the development of socialism is predicated on a personal dictatorship, on the unaccountability of a bureaucratic regime, and on the merciless suppression of the thinking and criticism of the advanced workers. In reality, Bonapartist arbitrariness, which is a result of the bureaucracy's struggle to maintain its position, comes into increasingly deep and sharp contradiction with the prerequisites for building the new society. Sensing the untenability of their own position in the face of the growing economic and cultural strength of the popular masses, the bureaucracy introduces a system of mutual assurances and passes merciless judgment on anyone who dares to doubt that their usurped privileges are of anything less than divine . . . nay, "revolutionary" origin. This is the reason for the vicious suppression of the ten thousand older and younger revolutionaries who have remained faithful to the banner of the October Revolution. In this sense, I can say that my third exile coincides with the period of deep bureaucratic reaction in Soviet society.

Just a few days ago, *Le Temps,* the leading paper of the French bourgeoisie, commented as follows on the reinstitution of symbols of rank in the Red Army: "This alteration of outward appearances is one of the signs of the deep changes that have been taking place in all of Soviet society for some time. The regime, now at last firmly established, is gradually beginning to take definite form. Revolutionary habits and customs, both in the family and Soviet society, are giving way to the feelings and customs which still prevail in the so-called capitalist countries. The Soviets are becoming more and more bourgeois" ("Les sovjets s'embourgeoisent," *Le Temps,* September 25, 1935).

These sentiments from an important, cautious, and thoroughly conservative bourgeois newspaper require no comment. We encounter such statements by the thousand. They incontrovertibly demonstrate that the process of bourgeois degeneration among the *leaders* of Soviet society has gone a long way. At the same time they show that the further development of Soviet society is unthinkable without freeing that society's socialist base from its bourgeois-bureaucratic and Bonapartist superstructure. This in a word is the explanation for my third exile.

For four and a half years I lived with my wife, my staunch comrade and companion on my journeys, in Turkey, on the island of Prinkipo; for two years in France; and finally the last few months in Norway.

In completing this foreword I cannot fail to mention that my stay in the Ullevaal Hospital has given me a rare and unexpected opportunity to come into contact with certain categories of Norwegians: doctors, nurses, male and female orderlies. Among all these people I have encountered nothing but attentiveness, sympathy, direct and honest humaneness. I will always have warm memories of my stay in the Ullevaal Hospital.

On the table where I am writing these lines there is one of the hospital's New Testaments in Norwegian. Thirty-seven years ago, in my solitary-confinement cell in the Odessa prison—I was not yet twenty years old—I had the same book in various European languages. By comparing similar passages in the various texts, I practiced languages: the New Testament, because of its style and the precision of the translation, lends itself excellently to the task of learning languages. Unfortunately, I cannot promise anyone that my new encounter with this old and familiar book will contribute to the peace of my soul. But reading the Norwegian New Testament can all the same help me to acquire the language of the country which has offered me hospitality and whose literature I learned to love and admire in my youth. ■

For or against?[170]

October 16, 1935

Dear Comrade Theo van Driesten:

Through you, I am addressing these lines to all our young Dutch friends who are assembled, during this crisis of the youth organization, around the truly revolutionary, Marxist banner. The bitter character of the struggle and the fact of the split carried out by the opportunists of the SAP testify to the enormous importance of these questions, which are placed on the historical agenda.

To be *against* the Fourth International means: consciously or unconsciously to adapt to and spread illusions about the Second and Third Internationals. That is the road that leads to once again turning the proletarian vanguard into cannon fodder for capitalist patriotism.

To be *for* the Fourth International means: a clearly determined program; revolutionary class struggles; intransigent internationalism; no illusions in the bankrupts or their agents; educating and forging the youth in the spirit of the proletarian revolution.

Yours,
Leon Trotsky

Youth secretary nominations[171]

October 21, 1935

To the IS of the ICL

Dear Comrades:

I am in complete agreement with the enclosed proposal for the first steps in the direction of a new youth international. It would be best to propose, as provisional secretaries, Theo van Driesten and Held. In the event that you are in agreement with the proposal, as I presume in advance, please set it in motion as soon as possible.

Crux [Leon Trotsky]

Support of the Dutch fight against SAPism[172]

November 5, 1935

Dear Friend:

Just a few lines. At the moment I do not want to go into which of the [Dutch] executive committee's mistakes and omissions in the past have now made it necessary to take much harsher steps. All of us (including our friend Schmidt) will have time to think it over... It is enough for me that the struggle the executive committee is leading is a struggle *for the revolutionary future of the party,* in order for me *to support this struggle with all forces and with no restraint on an international scale.*

I enclose a circular letter of Comrade Muste's. Things still seem to be going pretty well on the outside with respect to the controversial questions (SAP, IAG, Fourth International). You can make very good use of this letter in the internal struggle (maybe read it to the congress). I don't need to tell you that you have my warmest greetings and wishes. I am absolutely sure that this crisis will weld the party together in a revolutionary manner and will assure it a great future.

With warmest revolutionary greetings.
L. Trotsky

P.S. You can send the Muste letter back to me at your convenience. Fred Zeller is now here on a visit. Will stay here ten days. (Seine youth federation membership now 3,000; *Revolution* circulation 12,000.) The successes in France are heartening. Zeller is writing a longer article about them, which I will send you right away.

L.T.

P.P.S. As far as Luteran is concerned, I suppose that he is quoting from my article on Pivert, where I take up the permissibility (inevitability) of temporary factions inside the Fourth International. But there is a distinct *limit* to the formation of these factions: today it is the recognition of the Fourth International and the sharp struggle against SAPism.

L.T.

Conversations with Earle Birney[173]
November 1935

American problems

QUESTION: Was the Cannon-Shachtman slogan of "No discussion for six months" [in the Workers Party] correct?

TROTSKY: Mainly. Compare the Dutch fusion. There any focusing upon "discussion" immediately after the merger would only have split the party again. It was necessary there, and in America, to concentrate on practical mass work and on discussion of the problems arising directly from that work. It was the sectarian Oehlerites who always wanted more *discussion*. A sectarian is always like a drinker of salt water; the more he swallows the thirstier he is. Because the sectarian proceeds from the conviction that he cannot be wrong, that he has nothing to learn from action, that everyone will agree with him if only he can just talk to them long enough.

QUESTION: Is there a danger of political "gangster" psychology affecting our American movement?

TROTSKY: There seems to be. In general, although America had the privilege of preceding Europe economically, she has inclined to tail behind Europe politically and in the most exaggerated manner to repeat the worst mistakes and splits. All the sects generated in Europe eventually end up in the United States.

Also, our own movement still has a large proportion of intellectuals. Disputes among intellectuals assume a sharpness out of proportion to the seriousness of the differences. Organizations not deeply entrenched in the masses are therefore not disciplined by the masses. The latter move slower than ideas. The worker is more patient in dealing with questions which become sharp and bitter with intellectuals; the worker is used to dealing with materials which do not yield quickly, with wood, iron, steel.

Our comrades in America and everywhere should not think that "gangsterism" is confined to the American movement. Stalinism has introduced police tactics and bureaucratic centralism into the whole international radical movement. Even the fights between the Bolsheviks and the anarchists and Narodniks were on an entirely different plane from this. Even in the vacuum of emigre politics—in the Bolshevik past—there has never been such corruption as Stalinism has brought to the workers' struggles. It is natural that our comrades should react sharply to any evidence that this is creeping into our own movement, and it is better at the present time to exaggerate "democracy" than to tolerate tendencies to Stalinist methods. Headlong split action must be avoided; it is easy to break an arm—it takes only a second—but the bone may take months to knit together again.

TROTSKY: Eastman talks about the revolutionary who sets about to create a revolution as an engineer conceives a plan and builds a bridge according to it. Engineers! Bridges! Revolution! Eastman knows nothing about them. He knows nothing about bridge-building. Does an engineer build a bridge out of his head or does he receive a command from the capitalists whose economic needs require the bridge? Does he form the plan out of his head or is it the product of the accumulated knowledge of years of bridge-building, incorporated in textbooks?

Is the engineer of value as an individual or because of his creative power when, in accepting that command, he coordinates in the best interests of those who command him the elements of nature and science, which exist independently of him?

If Eastman meant "engineer" in this sense, we could accept his definition. But he thinks of the revolutionary genius as a man who conceives a plan a priori and then gives orders. No, there are many "engineers" and many "plans." The mass does its own selecting among them and chooses the engineer and the plan that answers its historic needs. It was this that Marx explained and that Eastman never understood.

International lineups

QUESTION: Will the Italo-Ethiopian War[174] lead directly to world war?

TROTSKY: That is not at all certain. The great powers are not yet clearly drawn up in opposing lines, but the Ethiopian invasion is serving that purpose. It is realigning the states and preparing the minds of people for war much in the manner that the Balkan War served as the overture to the opera of 1914.

QUESTION: Which of the European powers really dominates the situation at present?

TROTSKY: None of them. Yesterday France was too economically dependent, its geographical basis too small. It was only a center of equilibrium for the moment. Then Germany reached a point in the restoration of its productive forces where it could openly rearm. From that moment France became a secondary figure. Hitler spoke openly of colonies, of expansion. This in turn gave Italy its opportunity. Mussolini[175] was able to force panicky France into a common front against Hitler's threat to the west and south, and to utilize the alliance for an African attack. But then Britain mounts the stand and begins to referee, to hold the balance of power as in the old days. It was for this advantage that it had allowed Hitler to rearm. Britain moves to protect its own interests in Africa and to upset the Franco-Italian bloc. Hoare[176] threatens military sanctions. Italy can win all Africa, and Mussolini become its negus[177]—but he will not be able to come home, for Britain will have his metropolis. This is the problem for Italy; but French capital is too desperate from internal crisis either to oppose Britain or to accede *completely.* France can do nothing but delay, and seek to appease Mussolini with the evidence that it sabotages. "Look, we postponed the Geneva performances and gave you time to attack. Now we save you from Britain's military sanctions." But Mussolini replies: "Your 'financial' and 'economic' sanctions can lead only to war. What are you going to do?"

But neither France nor Britain can supply the answer. Baldwin[178] can only say: "Yes, we will blockade," and "Italy must then capitulate or fight—*but first we must ask Uncle Sam.*" This is the real hierarchy now. Italy asks France, France asks England—and Baldwin whispers to America. Uncle Sam, knowing he is on top, sticks his hands in his pockets and says to Mr. Baldwin what Mr. Baldwin used to say to Europe: "Wait and see." The USA has no immediate interest in sanctions; *it* does not need to keep the Mediterranean open for the passage to India. It has its own garden to tend, in the Pacific. So Britain, having allowed Germany to rearm to secure the balance of power from France, now finds that it must itself spend many pounds sterling on further battleships not only to keep Germany on its side (for that matter Germany has much need of Britain for its proposals regarding Russia), but also to meet the threat of combined action by Italian and French battleships. In the meantime, the war does not end in Ethiopia; the restlessness of all exploited African natives increases, there are serious reactions in Egypt—and Uncle Sam continues to do nothing. Whether the workers are to have another breathing space or whether they are to proceed from this to a world war will be decided—so far as it can be by any one power—by American capitalism.

QUESTION: Do you think that the USA will eventually line up with Britain in a world war?

TROTSKY: No. This was the view of Lovestone, who argued that the U.S. and Britain would unite to avoid the destruction of our planet. Lenin and I argued against him that these two powers, despite their diplomatic amenities, represent the most fundamental antagonisms existing between capitalist states in the world today.[179]

War, the USSR, and the Red Army

QUESTION: In *War and the Fourth International* (sections 44–5), we read: "It would be absurd and criminal in case of war between the USSR and Japan for the American proletariat to sabotage the sending of American munitions to the USSR."

May not this formulation provide the entering wedge for social patriotism?

Actually, in such a situation, American workers would have no means of knowing *where* arms shipments went to, once they left America. And we would have to remind the less class-conscious that American arms manufacturers were undoubtedly shipping supplies to both sides, and—much more important—that the American bourgeois government could never be trusted to aid the war against Japan if at any moment American capitalism stood to gain more by not doing so. If, for example, the San Francisco dockers had reached the high stage of militancy necessary, under such conditions, for them to be on the point of declaring for a strike against the export of *all* war supplies—and we persuaded them not to, because the shells were labeled "Russia"—it might happen that before the ship crossed the Pacific, the USA (whether still neutral, or an ally of the USSR) made a deal with Japan, in order to prevent a proletarian revolution in Japan, or because of threatened war with Britain, or etc. Then those munitions would be diverted to the killing of Japanese revolutionaries or British workers.

The brochure states that "the policy of a proletarian party in an 'allied' as well as an enemy imperialist country should ... be directed towards the revolutionary overthrow" of its own bourgeoisie. But the concessions made immediately preceding, by the same brochure, are precisely those which would deflect and perhaps even betray that policy.

TROTSKY: It is not a question of subordinating strikes or the revolutionary movement in countries allied to the Soviet Union in the interests of the effectiveness of that alliance for the Soviet Union. They must be encouraged and developed if they are part of the revolutionary uprising. The question is one of military aid on the part of the most advanced section of the American working class to its ally, the Soviet Union. Naturally, the American proletariat must do everything possible to fight against its own boss class, but in an organized fashion, by a general development of strikes—not in an anarchistic fashion.

However, suppose that in the event of a Japanese-Soviet war, an American factory is sending an important war machine to Japan and we know it. It is not a question of the American revolution but of military strategy. We would, through a central committee, send a group of courageous comrades to destroy that machine. It is true that such action might prejudice the American movement to some extent, but it is an act of military importance on the part of an ally of the Soviet Union.

If on the other hand goods are destined for the Soviet Union, and you know it, you must do everything in your power to ship that material. It is a question of special measures, of sacrifice, if necessary, to help the Soviet Union or hinder its enemy. In the long run, the victory of the Red Army, whatever it meant to Russia, would be an aid to us in our own revolution.

Suppose we do not know where goods are going. We must rely upon the Soviet agents in America, who should have information, since the Soviet Union would have buying agents for war materiel in the USA. We would need a united front with the Soviet bureaucracy on this. If we agitated against the loading of war goods bought by the Soviet Union in America, we would be having a united front not with the Soviet agents but with Japanese agents, who would no doubt be represented in the working class movement.

If there was no way of knowing where goods were going to, we would have to take a chance. Risk cannot be avoided; danger, as Clausewitz said, is the main element of war. But in our actions we would find it much easier to organize the American workers, among whom there would be considerable general sympathy for Russia—and among the petty bourgeois too.

QUESTION: In the same brochure (*War and the Fourth International*, section 46), there is some emphasis laid upon the strength of the Red Army. In view of recent analyses by military and economic observers (especially even from those friendly to Russia) is it not possible that there is here a dangerous overestimate of Russia's strength to resist attack—and by implication an underestimate of the need for building a new International?

TROTSKY: It is true that, until two years ago, conditions in the Soviet Union were unfavorable to the growth of morale in the Red Army. But in the last two years a very important economic improvement has taken place, both in agriculture and industry. As a result, not only have the privileged sections secured more privileges and the bureaucracy added new top layers, but also the lower strata are better off than before. Moreover, the situation of the poor peasants and workers had been so bad that a slight improvement (comparatively) made for a large improvement in their minds.

This in turn was reflected in both the technology and the psychology of the Red Army. Greatly improved technical equipment in the army has engendered a confidence in its personnel somewhat comparable to the change that advanced mechanization introduced into the Prussian army before 1914. Even the development of mass parachuting, though it has been utilized by the bureaucracy to divert attention from politics, is a new and important step in popular military education.

The general increase of confidence which arises from these things is aided by the knowledge that the two main immediate enemies of the Soviet Union, Japan and Germany, are the most hated countries in the world today. It is impossible to think that the Russian peasant, however disaffected he may still be, would be willing to see his own bureaucracy replaced by Hitler or the Mikado.

This does not mean, unfortunately, that the future of the workers' state is secure because the Red Army is strong. On the contrary, a victory for the Red Army would mean another step backwards toward state capitalism and the increase of private capitalism.[180] After a successful war, the military leadership would no doubt replace the old bureaucracy with one much more capitalistic in its policies.

All this could happen without a civil war, for the latter would depend upon the Marxist understanding and the courage and capabilities of the workers. It was, if you like, an omission from my article "[The Workers' State,] Thermidor and

Bonapartism" that I did not suggest that a military coup d'etat, following or during a successfully prosecuted war of defense, could lead, equally as well as a counterrevolutionary victory in a civil war, to the overthrow of the workers' state. Of course, a proletarian revolution in the country defeated by the USSR would have tremendous repercussions upon the Soviet Union itself. But without such an event, all the centrifugal forces at present working in the Soviet Union would be irresistible. Feudal powers defeated Napoleon, but the result was the introduction of capitalism into the victorious feudal countries. The victory for socialism in the USSR is not, as Stalin says, "assured," "accomplished," etc., and cannot be assured until the productive forces in the Soviet Union are higher than in any capitalist country, until the proletarian state can, in a sense, "undersell," when its own level of living is higher. In the meantime, war approaches steadily, and in that war the Red Army, although it will be a very powerful war instrument, will not and cannot save the *workers' state*. ∎

Greetings to 'Robitnichi Vysti'[181]

November 26, 1935

To the editors of *Robitnichi Vysti*

Dear Friends:

Two Canadian comrades paid me a visit and familiarized me with the situation in your struggle for the banner of Marx and Lenin. I have just received your anniversary issue, which made me rejoice for the breadth of its coverage and the richness of its content.

I send warm greetings to the editorial board, co-workers, distributors, and readers of *Robitnichi Vysti*.

With revolutionary Bolshevik greetings,
L. Trotsky

Letters about Anton Ciliga[182]
December 1935–January 1936

LETTER TO JAN FRANKEL[183]
DECEMBER 15, 1935

Dear Friend:

Thank you for the letters and the information (concerning the theoretical discussion in the [Soviet] isolation prison).

The man's letter makes a strong impression. But for the same reasons as with Tarov,[184] I have to ask the same questions: How did the man get out of the country? Who helped him escape? Whom is he in contact with here? What does he mean when he says that he intends to liberate his comrades "by any means necessary"? There is nothing in the letters about this. These are, however, questions of the greatest importance. They must be cleared up. I do not disregard the person, who makes the best possible impression. But one cannot rely on personal impressions alone. Theoretically, it is possible that the GPU scoundrels, who are willing to use any means necessary to get the best of us, are sending us one of their people to wheedle his way into our confidence in order to give his employers an opportunity to create a criminal, i.e., real Stalinist, amalgam. You write that Comrade R. is personally acquainted with him. Naturally this is not without importance, but it is in no way decisive, since the GPU must of course recruit agents for their provocations from the ranks of former revolutionaries. Who knows how many former Oppositionists have sunk to the level of agents under pressure, through exhaustion or corruption?

There is nothing in these lines that should insult your confidant. If he is an honest revolutionary, as I assume, he himself must understand our caution with respect to Stalinist scoundrels. Please discuss this with R. I am sending a copy of this letter to Durand [Leon Sedov].

Your Old Man [Leon Trotsky]

LETTER TO JAN FRANKEL
DECEMBER 24, 1935

Dear Friend:

As I have already written to the new arrival [Ciliga], it is absolutely necessary to build a broad-based organization to help revolutionaries imprisoned in the USSR. Couldn't we interest Willi Schlamm[185] in chairing such a committee *in Prague*? Perhaps there are also other candidates? For the Bolshevik-Leninists, perhaps Weiss,[186] as a former provincial deputy, could participate. It is a matter of winning over a few "representative" figures who have connections with the democratic press. At the same time, similar work should be carried out in Paris. It goes without saying that the initiative should be transmitted to all other countries immediately. It is of the highest importance to make a correct start, so that the thing does not appear as a factional maneuver.

Comradely greetings,
L. Trotsky

LETTER TO WILLI SCHLAMM
DECEMBER 24, 1935

Mr. Willi Schlamm
Prague

Dear Comrade:

The bearer of this letter [Ciliga] spent several years in Stalin's prisons. It is the greatest disgrace of our time that the workers' organizations remain silent about the crimes of the Stalinist bureaucracy. This is only the other side of the tendency to capitulate to fascism. However, it is time that those who are not deceived, corrupted, or simply bribed by the Soviet bureaucracy raise their voices in support of the heroic, revolutionary victims of the Bonapartist caste. Don't you think that yours should be among them? In my opinion, it is a question of a determined and systematic struggle, which could also open up important perspectives for Europe.

Best regards,
Leon Trotsky

LETTER TO OLAV SCHEFLO[187]
DECEMBER 24, 1935

Dear Comrade Scheflo:

I have read your rejoinder to the local Stalinists with great pleasure. I think it necessary to tell you about the following facts:

The French and Norwegian Stalinists—I know from reliable sources—did not want to deal with this shady affair, although these people are not in general very choosy. But they have been forced to do it. So for instance the Norwegian [CP's] executive committee was told from Moscow that in case "something" happens, they, the poor fellows, will have to bear full responsibility. Finally the poor devils decided to make the whole silly matter public. What is the aim of Moscow? To slander me, to make a scandal, to frighten the bourgeois parties and to make my stay in Norway difficult.

But this is not the most important lesson in the matter with the postcard. Everybody who can think must ask himself: If these people attempt to represent a childish postcard as a terroristic instrument, what do they do in this field in the Soviet Union where nobody can control them? If Zeller[188] would have been arrested in Russia he would have been shot within twenty-four hours as a member of a terrorist organization.

The Zeller story throws light on the Kirov case, where dozens were shot who had nothing to do with it. Zinoviev and Kamenev were condemned to ten years' imprisonment, only because in 1932 they made derogatory statements about the collectivization policy and because the young terrorist Nikolaev came from the Leningrad Opposition in 1926, an opposition which had tens of thousands of members. You know perhaps that I have no personal sympathy for Zinoviev or Kamenev. But I think it is an unbearable shame that the workers' organizations of the whole world are silent about this affair for reasons of convenience. This inertia is only the other side of the tendency to capitulate in the face of fascism.

Yugoslavian Comrade Ciliga, after being in Stalin's prisons for five years, has arrived on the Continent. He has written his first letter about the crimes of Stalin's bureaucracy.

As soon as I get his letter in German I will send it to you. The significance therefore of the campaign with the postcard is that it illustrates how Stalinism leads bacteriological warfare against the consciousness of the world proletariat. Metallurgists have explained how harmful the phosphorus found in metal is for the quality of iron. They say, "Phosphorus is the syphilis of iron." With the same right one might say: Stalinism is the syphilis of the international workers' movement.

LETTER TO JAN FRANKEL
DECEMBER 31, 1935

Dear Friend:

I hope that Comrade C[iliga] has received my second, long letter written in Russian. Here I want to draw Comrade C.'s attention, through you, to the necessity of the utmost caution on his part.

There is no doubt that C. is already under the closest surveillance of the GPU's foreign bureau, and that those scoundrels, with the help of their hirelings in the so-called Communist Party, will risk everything to compromise C., to involve him in the most miserable scandals, to denounce him to the enemy, etc., etc. You probably already know what an international campaign these scoundrels have whipped up over a humorous postcard written by F. Zeller. C. *is much more important* for them now: first of all, they have to try to justify their hangman's work and attempt to compromise all of us through him. *Therefore, the utmost caution,* in correspondence as well as in personal contact.

Yours,
L.T.

LETTER TO ANTON CILIGA
JANUARY 2, 1936

Dear Comrade Ciliga:

I learned a little lesson today which seems to me to be of great importance for our campaign and which I hasten to communicate to you.

In a private letter, I wrote to a serious and honest member of the Norwegian Labor Party [Olav Scheflo] about the persecution of revolutionaries by the Stalinist bureaucracy. I will quote the following interesting passage from his answer: "The matter forces, so to speak, every honest person into opposition against the people who now have power in the Soviet Union. The difficulties will lie in not destroying anything else than what deserves to be destroyed. Here in Norway we have a saying: One should not throw out the baby with the bathwater. . . . I want to mention one of my plans here: A letter should be sent to the Soviet government. This letter must be written in such a way that every individual will understand that it comes from real friends of the Soviet Union and that the intention is to strengthen the workers' state. The entire project must be directed by a committee formed in such a way that it is completely above suspicion."

What is the lesson for us? I took a sharper tone in my letter ("Stalinism is the syphilis of the workers' movement," etc.). The comrade concerned here is critical of the Soviet bureaucracy. The idea of a committee and a mass petition to the Soviet government was completely his own. (There was nothing about this in my letter.) Nevertheless, he considers it necessary, even in addressing me, to emphasize that one should not throw out the baby with the bathwater. The lesson lies in this observation.

The open enemies of the Soviet Union will not support us. They will use the crimes of the Soviet bureaucracy to compromise the Soviet Union *and us too*. In our campaign we can rely only on *honest* friends of the Soviet Union. These honest friends are often very naive politically. They have many illusions not only about conditions in the Soviet Union but also about the character of the bureaucracy. They are very much inclined to close their eyes to the dark side. On the whole, this state of mind is the reflection of a much more important factor, namely, the state of mind of the broad working masses, who, in the face of the crisis and the fascist threat, are inclined to idealize not just the Soviet Union but also the bureaucracy. A critical Marxist attitude remains for the time the privilege of a small minority, which is gathered more or less around the banner of the Fourth International. These elements are of the highest importance as the *motive force* of the campaign, but in no case as its *base*.

Hence it is of the highest importance to find sympathy and support among the *honest* friends of the Soviet Union (it is not worth discussing those scoundrels who are bought and have a personal stake, although they account for a high percentage of the official "friends"), since these honest elements, whose best representative is the comrade mentioned above, will find the necessary tone to provide the campaign with a much broader base. The necessary practical consequences following from this are perfectly clear.

It goes without saying that younger and more determined elements—including Bolshevik-Leninists—must be represented in all committees as practical motive forces. Politically, however, they should let others do more of the talking.

With best greetings.

Yours,
L. Trotsky

LETTER TO JAN FRANKEL
JANUARY 24, 1935

Dear Friend:

We've heard that you've "stirred things up" a bit there, which makes Erwin [Wolf] and me very happy.

Of course, I completely agree with you that a committee should be established immediately, even if it is an unofficial one, so that an official committee can be carefully built, taking advantage of all favorable circumstances.

Comrade Ciliga interpreted my last letter as if, so to speak, I "gave him the right" to negotiate individually with Mensheviks and Left SRs about support for the prisoners (in any case, on his own responsibility!). The sentence in question in my letter only meant that if Ciliga persisted in his illusions, he would find out through his own experience, which could not involve us in any way. In his last letter, he comes forward more or less as the political defender of the Mensheviks and Left SRs. From my latest article, you must have noticed that there was no mention at all of Mensheviks and SRs during the last party purge, while at least ten thousand Bolshevik-Leninists were expelled, arrested, etc.[189] Under *these* conditions, from a purely *practical* point of view, it would be nonsense for Ciliga to ally himself with the Mensheviks merely because they have a few dozen old comrades in the USSR in exile. (Not to mention the principled side of the question!) It is very possible that some Menshevik or SR will attach himself to Ciliga in order to rise from his own position of insignificance. All the more reason not to give these people an inch.

In enduring friendship,
L. *Trotsky*

The Lenin-Trotsky papers[190]

December 28, 1935

The correspondence from the time of the civil war and the following years up until 1923 is arranged in such a way that commentary is almost superfluous. As long as no complete and objective history of the civil war has been written, it will, in any case, be necessary to consult Trotsky's collection *Kak Vooruzhalas Revolutsiya* (How the Revolution Armed Itself), 5 vols., (Vishy Voyenni Redaktsionni Sovet: 1923–25) to find the necessary documentation for the various military episodes.

The correspondence begins with Trotsky's departure for Brest-Litovsk in January 1918.

The correspondence, almost in its entirety, has a "telegraphic" character; even the letters were in the majority of cases transmitted by wire.

The direct correspondence between Lenin and Trotsky makes up only a fraction of the collection. For what happened in most cases was that when Lenin issued an order or a recommendation to a military or party body while Trotsky was absent from Moscow (which was the rule) he always had a copy sent to Trotsky in order not to upset coordination of the work. Trotsky did the same thing insofar as central bodies and Moscow authorities in general were concerned.

The large number of purely military orders signed with Lenin's name can create the impression (and this is now also the interpretation of the official historiography) that Lenin personally intervened in the leadership of military operations over the heads of the military authorities. This interpretation is completely false. Lenin had a high regard for system and order. His signature under many purely military orders is explained by the fact that in Trotsky's absence from Moscow, his deputy Sklyansky called upon Lenin to strengthen the decisions of the Moscow-based headquarters with the authority of his signature in all important questions.

The collection in no way covers the collaboration between Lenin and Trotsky in its entirety. It only partially reflects the workings of the leadership in the civil war. The most important questions were usually handled in Moscow after Trotsky's return to the capital, in meetings of the Politburo, or often in personal or telephone conversations. Many details about this can be found in Trotsky's autobiography *My Life*.

The photocopies which are included also cover only part of the correspondence. Their origin is as follows: In the year 1924, at the time when the great falsification of party and revolutionary history was systematically introduced, the Politburo (Stalin, Zinoviev, and Kamenev were allied then) passed a resolution obliging every party member, every state official, every citizen in general to turn over every letter, telegram, etc., from Lenin in his possession to the Lenin Institute. In return he would receive a photocopy of the document in question. This last obligation was, however, only *partially* fulfilled and in a *tendentious* fashion.

In any case, the machine copies were very carefully made.

On many documents there will be found notations and markings in red or blue pencil. These have nothing to do with the collection. They indicate excerpts, etc., that Trotsky used in composing his autobiography and other writings during his residence abroad. ■

Results of the Open Letter[191]

January 18, 1936

Dear Friend:

I am in your debt, since I have let your letter of November 10 of last year go unanswered. There were, to be sure, mitigating circumstances. Now I am on "vacation," which I can use to resume my correspondence with you.

In any case, I have concerned myself recently very little with German affairs. But I have taken note of the Parabellum [Arkady Maslow]-Johre polemic and I agree, as you may know, with Johre on the disputed questions. I have read nothing of what the latest discussion has to say regarding the Jewish question. It is only the disproportions in the articles of the latest issues that have made a somewhat odd impression. I was also somewhat amazed—I must confess—by the title of the article by Jan Bur, since what he charges is not that Comrade Johre committed an error on the Jewish question but that his entire mode of thought was scholastic. That seemed a bit too sharp to me, in a discussion between two editors of the same tendency. But this is based on external appearances. I am not yet in a position to form an opinion on the essence of the question.

The major part of your letter was devoted to the Fourth International. The main task is to create a workable secretariat in Amsterdam. In recent days I have received letters from Comrades Sneevliet and Schmidt, which *for the first time* give assurances that the Dutch comrades will do everything necessary. In addition, we have no reason to be ashamed of the results of the Open Letter [for the Fourth International].

Holland and America—those are two important and for now secure addresses. The French section wanted for a time to distance itself a little from the banner of the Fourth International, in order to be "more free." The results are well known. Now the youth is beginning to declare itself for the Fourth International. On the other hand, the adventurists from the *Commune*, who lost out on the deals with their centrist friends, are also making a jerky turn toward the Fourth International. In Belgium the expulsion of *Action Socialiste Revolutionnaire* and the merger with *Spartacus* under the banner of the Fourth International are getting closer. The most important event in recent times, however, is the manifestation of the great strength of our movement in the Soviet Union. In an article which you may already be familiar with, I was able to establish, on the basis of the official figures in the Moscow *Pravda*, that in just the last four or five months of 1935 at least 10,000 Bolshevik-Leninists were expelled from the Stalinist party of the Soviet Union; there were certainly more. The significance of this fact can't be ignored. All our press should alert its readers to this important fact. And in letters as well, we should not fail to bring the strength of the Russian section to the attention of all comrades. The moral influence of the indomitability of our tendency in the Soviet Union will be encouraging for all sections, just as—I'm sure—the public declaration for the Fourth International was extremely stimulating and encouraging for the Russian comrades, especially after the Seventh Congress of the Comintern.

In no way do I fail to appreciate the importance of a regularly functioning secretariat of the Fourth International, of the preparation of the conference, of the publication of manifestos, resolutions, etc. But material facts speak louder than documents; as, for example, everything that the Serbian comrade Ciliga communicates. This can and must be used for the greatest effect in the interest of the Fourth International.

It is most lamentable that *UW* [*Unser Wort*] has until now published nothing on this. Perhaps a special German bulletin could be put out with the three or four documents of Ciliga, my article on them (it was sent to Paris), and maybe with an introduction from the editors of *UW*. Such a bulletin would be of greatest importance for many countries: Scandinavia, Holland, Czechoslovakia, Switzerland, etc. It would greatly facilitate the construction there of committees for support to the imprisoned Bolshevik-Leninists.

It is also to be lamented that the Czech document (the war theses) has up to now not been published, for it could render the Fourth International a great service in Czechoslovakia. ■

Schmidt's trip to England[192]

January 19, 1936

Dear Comrade Robertson:

Our Comrade Schmidt is going for some time to England where he wants to meet not only with the leading elements of the ILP but also with the comrades of our tendency. He has the necessary addresses.

You know that Comrade Schmidt is a leading comrade of the Dutch party, but now, with Comrade Sneevliet, he should be playing the role of secretary for the Fourth International. It is above all in this capacity that he will be making his investigations in England. You also certainly know about the excellent struggle that he has waged in his own party against the SAPists. At the same time I would like to underline the fact that Schmidt is tied by long friendship to the head of the ILP and that he has perhaps a certain uneasiness, not to say mistrust, towards our friends as "sectarians." He would perhaps rather be inclined to insist on the necessity of our comrades continuing their work in the ILP. I am bringing up all these circumstances in order *to make mutual understanding easier.*

Comrade Schmidt will also be seeking to contact the comrades of the former "majority" who are now working in the ILP. I hope very much that our friends will aid him in his task of gathering information and getting contacts. I would like very much to have your impressions of his visit later.

Who is Ethel Mannin? Her article on Soviet Russia revealed several theoretical faults, but at the same time, as far as the substance is concerned, she has better understood what is going on in the USSR than all the others. What a shame that her theoretical conceptions are not clear! She appears to have courage, sincerity, intelligence and the power of observation.

I thank you very much for the *Times*. I am only uneasy because of the work and the expense that this causes you. You could just as well send me the *Times* once a week, omitting everything that is not necessary. I practically read only *the inside pages,* above all because I receive *The Economist*. My sincere thanks to all the friends.

Warmest regards,
Leon Trotsky

Educating against centrism [193]

January 24, 1936

Worthy Comrades:

I suggest that a brief circular with the following contents be sent to all sections and sympathizing organizations:

The question of the independent centrist organizations and their international alliance (IAG) always retains a very large principled significance for us.

In France a part of our section wanted to erase the dividing line between us and centrism and wrought considerable damage thereby; at any rate it reduced itself politically to nought for a time.

In Spain, our section, which at first harshly condemned the entry into the SFIO, has fused with a centrist organization on an unprincipled basis, and the result of this is complete political betrayal.

Clear understanding of the specific role of the independent conservative formations in our epoch is the most important condition for a successful struggle for the Fourth International. This explains why we must subject every one of the organizations that adheres to the London Bureau to a thoroughgoing Marxist critique. After the article by Comrade Trotsky on the ILP we have sent our sections and sympathizing organizations the following materials:

"The End of the 'Red Front' (Austria)," by Werner Keller [Jan Frankel].

"The Program of the Swedish Socialist Party," by W.H. [Walter Held].

"The Betrayal of the Spanish POUM," by L. Trotsky.

Since our press and our bulletins have already brought

out sufficient material on the SAP, we can assume that each of the organizations of the Fourth International has been thoroughly educated on the true physiognomy of the IAG and the parties that adhere to it. It is of utmost importance to publish articles on this question in every organization, and even to institute special classes, for we cannot arm our propagandists for the Fourth International better than through Marxist criticism on the inadequacy of the hybrid organizations that are in this period springing up out of the ground like mushrooms.

Those organizations that possess the appropriate technical capacity could put out a collection of all the above-named articles, printed or at least mimeographed, as a reference material for propaganda work. ■

The heyday of the People's Front[194]

January 24, 1936

Dear Comrade:

If you could conclude from my letter that I am inclined toward discontinuing our correspondence, then I expressed myself very badly. Your letters are still quite valuable to me, because they give me not only your opinions and suggestions but also firsthand information.

The People's Front is going through another period of quite relative "success" and optimism. The war danger creates a favorable atmosphere for the bacilli of pacifism, centrism, adventurism, etc. The petty bourgeoisie is going through its own extremely acute social crisis, which makes it very susceptible to the charlatanry of the "left" and right. This wave, powerful in its powerlessness, forces us into isolation again. The blissful, merry and stupid optimism now reigning in the People's Front reminds me of the atmosphere after the February revolution [in Russia in 1917]: one was smothered by rose-tinted stupidities; one felt a thousand times superior to the People's Front leaders of that time. At the same time one remained isolated, persecuted, and even ridiculed. Comparison is not proof; but the analogy is all the same interesting, instructive and promising.

We must find some young workers and pay serious attention to them, even individually.

This is the point that still worries me. Can it be that our comrades, including the young ones, are too concerned with "high politics"? And not enough about the revolutionary education of the young workers!

Can you tell me what *La Commune* represents today as a group (its press run, the number of adherents, the character of their work, etc.)? The same for the Bolshevik-Leninists and the youth. Precision in political matters is unfortunately not a French quality. For that reason it is quite difficult to get an exact picture of the forces of an organization and its day-to-day work.

What happened to the Legue and Margne group?

You must already have heard that during the last four or five months of 1935, the Communist Party of the USSR expelled *at least* 10,000 "Trotskyists" (perhaps even many more). This is a fact of great political importance! ■

Two statements on Hearst[195]

January 28, 1936

A CABLEGRAM

Publication of Tarov article by Hearst common press gangsterism. But impudence of Hearst no excuse for crimes of Stalin clique. Gave statement to the Associated Press.

A LETTER

Dear Comrade:

I am sending you a copy of our telegram and our statement for the Associated Press. I am not at all sure that the letter will be forwarded by the AP representative here.

I should remind you that the agents of the GPU cooked up a similar affair a few years ago in Poland (the publication of an article in the reactionary press attributed to me) and that two days later Yaroslavsky published a facsimile of my alleged article [see "Scoundrels and Their Assistants" in *Writings 30–31*]. It is very possible that the business in America was also instigated by the GPU. Of course I cannot judge that for certain from this vantage point.

I believe that according to American laws I have the right to sue Hearst for infringing upon my rights as an author and for the great political and moral harm he has caused me with this infringement. It would be well to confer with Mr. Lieber (Maxim Lieber, 545 Fifth Avenue, New York, Tel MUrray 2-3135–3136) or with a friendly attorney on this. It would be good if we could use the judicial process to extract a tidy sum from Mr. Hearst for the benefit of the Fourth International.

With best greetings.

Yours,
L. Trotsky

A conversation with Maurice Spector[196]
February 1936

SPECTOR: I think we can finish today, we can summarize. When we return we want to be able to report clearly the grounds on which you favor the entry. You appear to put it on two grounds: (1) the present situation in the party is hopeless; (2) you conceive that positive gains will accrue from entry.

TROTSKY: To say hopeless is a little exaggerated. In the immediate future I don't see important possibilities for the independent organization, and in that situation the inner crisis can become fatal. On the other hand, I see no other possibility (for activity or development) which can be compromised if you enter. And even if the positive results of entrance will be modest (I think they will be important), even then the great advantage will be that the experience will have been accomplished: and all can look forward for a new road. The entry, too, will have advantages for yourselves. The illusions [about work in the SP], if they are that, will be smashed.

The centrists are measured by fighting, not by theses. Our experience will at the same time be a very vital experience for the Socialists. It will be fatal for the centrists. Your road will be different after that, but on a higher level. Discussion will then be not on the miserable SP, but on the objective situation rather than the subjective. All the good things we have done in mass action will and must continue, pursued as before. If this is impossible, it is clear that the entrance would be prejudicial. Both sides say in their reports that it is possible to continue such work in the SP.

SPECTOR: It goes without saying that in the event of entry, we put forward our maximum demands regarding the right of our press, *The New Militant*, etc., etc. But if we can't secure these concessions, do you still believe in entry?

TROTSKY: In the beginning the juridical conditions are important only so far as they reflect objective conditions. If the latter are favorable, the juridical conditions play a secondary role. To insist in the negotiations on juridical conditions might be unwise. One can't show all his cards to the adversary. After all, it is possible to so elaborate the juridical conditions as to make entrance impossible. The position of Norman Thomas must be thought of. We must not give the SP rank and file [Old Guard, right centrists, etc.] arguments against him [opposing our entry]. I am sure if you decide to enter you will find objective conditions which will permit you, with your strength and unity, to develop your work in a growing spiral.

SPECTOR: This matter has a bearing on the Canadian situation, which I am not charged to discuss officially. . . . The other day I indicated that the WP was not condemned to be merely a propaganda group. We can hope to repeat the successes in Minneapolis and Toledo.

TROTSKY: What recruits have you had as a result of your successes?

SPECTOR: In Minneapolis perhaps fifty recruits. We also

had some in California as a result of Sacramento. I don't know about Toledo.[197] But do you not think that these experiences indicate that the WP can function as an independent organization?

TROTSKY: I believe that the workers followed our comrades not because they were members of the WP. You can only personally, by small groups, win recruits personally for the party. The loss of the name WP (the firm-name) will not be decisive. I even believe that the cover of the Socialist name will be more winning because it is more known. Our duty in the SP will be not discussion with centrists, but mass work, teaching the youth to do it. I cannot say that independent participation cannot lead to the growth of the independent revolutionary party, but this way [entry] is the shortest way.

The past of America is full of strikes and heroic leadership, but without political crystallization. There is a change in the objective situation now. It must produce a change in the minds of the workers. Maybe it is a change that will take six months or six years—we cannot know that.

SPECTOR: What perspective do you see in our possible entry—long or short range?

TROTSKY: Rather short—because the Militants without the Old Guard and with their inconsistent leadership, between pressure from you on the one hand and the Stalinists on the other, cannot last for long. Part [of their following] will go to you and part to the Stalinists. Yes, it will be rather short. Of course, depending on the objective situation, on strikes, etc.

SPECTOR: What do you think of the thesis of the possible reform of the SP? Or of the probability?

TROTSKY: It is improbable that the reform of the SP will be possible. We have not two policies—(a) reform of the SP, (b) to split it. No, our policy is the same in both cases. It is to search for the youth, to create groups, personal relations, lead to mass action, compromise the centrists in the process by pointing out that it is the centrists who oppose such mass action. We must compromise, in the course of practical action, a certain part of the party [the centrists] in the eyes of the other. A split is inevitable. The initiative will probably be taken by the apparatus. It is very important for us to grasp just that moment when the apparatus realizes that moment because adaptation to the apparatus at that time is very dangerous. [Cites Molinier, Belgian situation, etc.]

SPECTOR: The Oehlerites and the Bauerites claimed that the French turn was not specifically limited to the French situation. They claimed that the ICL had in view an extension of the turn to all countries, i.e., entry into the Socialist parties. And apparently that is the way things are working out.

TROTSKY: But that has been forced on us by the objective situation. Originally the French turn was suggested by me. If the experience in France would have been negative we would have learned something. But the experience was positive. And the other way, of independence, in other countries did not give positive results, in any country. It [the extension of the entry] was also caused by conjunctural factors.

SPECTOR: In view of what you said about the Comintern assuming the functions of the Social Democracy, should we be in favor of the unity of the Second and Third Internationals?

TROTSKY: Unity will be managed by the two bureaucracies. Unity is a good thing. We fight on the question of the manner and content of unity. We cannot fight unity itself. If we could enter the CP we should do so, of course, but it is impossible. In the unity negotiations, the first request of the Stalinists will be the exclusion of the Bolshevik-Leninists. [Cites French experience; Stalinists demanded exclusion of B-Ls as condition of unity; now, B-Ls are out, Stalinists stalling on unity.]

SPECTOR: In the old days the KAPD[198] predicted liquidation of the Comintern, visualizing it as some formal and dramatic act. Actually, there has occurred a liquidation of principles, a filling up of the old forms with neo-Social Democratic content. Does the Comintern really require unity with the Social Democracy?

TROTSKY: They drag out the affair because they have on very important questions trump cards in their hands. They will more or less destroy the SP. Fusion is, however, not excluded.

SPECTOR: Do you conceive a left zigzag on the part of the Comintern to be possible?

TROTSKY: That is not excluded. Naturally, such a zigzag would be very important from the point of view of our possibilities, because the CP contains many different strata of people, unemployed, declassed intellectuals, functionaries, petty bourgeois, etc. Many of these think the People's Front is a good thing and the CP is the best part of it. Many workers think the People's Front is a maneuver. There is a difference between what the CP sometimes says at its own meetings and what it says in public, and thereby it accumulates contradictions, social and political.

There can be an episodic turn to the left, but for many people such a turn would be a disintegration. For the workers it would appear as a maneuver perhaps, but for the others it would be a disintegration. A turn to the left would be catastrophic to the petty bourgeois, philistines and opportunists in the CP.

SPECTOR: Do you think a realignment in the relations of the powers would lead to a change in USSR foreign policy, a return to Lenin's formula of revolutionary defeatism, on the part of the Comintern?

TROTSKY: Certainly, if the USSR were attacked by Japan, Germany, etc., the bureaucracy would threaten the world with social revolution. Even the diplomacy of the Entente and Wilson (and the Germans) aimed to create revolutionary situations in the enemy countries. But [the bureaucracy is no longer Bolshevik] ... and becomes itself the most privileged stratum. It becomes a new social stratum in itself, defending itself against the proletariat with all its power. It is interesting to note that this did not take place during the early lean years. Then there was no fat of privilege to be had. Now that the country has become more or less prosperous, acquired a stock to satisfy not all, but many of its needs, the inequality which arises becomes a very important political fact. I am sure that if this process continues, not smashed by a war or counterrevolution, there will be another political revolution. [Cites struggles of bourgeoisie among itself in France after French Revolution.]

Marx and Engels could not foresee this eventuality because of the complications [of the concrete process of the proletarian revolution]. We can be sure that the Russian proletariat will accomplish the social revolution by a new political revolution when the conditions become more favorable. The new numbers of the Bolshevik-Leninists in Russia are a prelude to that development.

The change in army ranks, the new military titles, is of great significance. Stalin is marshal of the marshals. His political base is not the party but the new nobility, the new orders. These new orders express great privileges in pay, lodging, education, automobiles, special rooms in public libraries even ("znat," from the word "to know," is the symbol of the nobility, a man known by the country). This symbol is now reestablished for the new nobility. The new nobility rests on the contradictions between the forms of socialist property, socialist production, and the bourgeois norms of distribution.

[Spector here recalls that the Stalinists claim these inequalities are not subject to the above interpretation so long as the means of production remain in the hands of the Soviet state—there being no basis in the private ownership of land, etc., to establish a new ruling class.]

TROTSKY: It is a bourgeois regime as regards distribution. The Soviet bureaucracy lives the same kind of life as Morgan.[199] The question now is whether the social basis which remains from the October Revolution will overthrow the superstructure or whether the superstructure will alter the social basis. The basis can overthrow the bureaucracy only by a political revolution. It will require more than police measures. Two years ago, the latter would have been enough. But these two years witnessed the stabilization of privileges in the ruling strata, especially in the army and police. It is stupid not to recognize that this is a social fact of the greatest social and political importance. The contradictions can become so acute that the bureaucracy, in order to protect itself, may have to revert to [private] property relations. It may have to strike at the roots of the present social system.

SPECTOR: Besides the Bolshevik-Leninists, are there not Mensheviks in Stalin's jails? Should we not also call for their release?

TROTSKY: At the present time in the USSR there is absolutely no mention of Mensheviks. The press attacks only five categories: White Guards, fakers, spies, Trotskyists and Zinovievists. But never Mensheviks. Occasionally it mentions Right Oppositionists, meaning those opposed to the Stakhanovite movement[200] for technical and other reasons. But Mensheviks are totally discredited in the minds of the people. There are only forty or fifty old men of their number left—the great bulk of their number are supporters of Stalin. All the Opposition goes under our flag—or that of the White Guard.

The bureaucrats are afraid of this fact. They sometimes refuse to recognize it. Then suddenly an astonishing article calling the attention of the people to it comes from *Pravda*. In Leningrad 9,900 were expelled as Oppositionists. No less than 200,000, 10 percent, have been expelled recently from the party, and this does not include all. The minimum expelled is 7 percent, the maximum is 16 percent; in Siberia, 13 percent; and 7,000–8,000 Zinovievists to be found only in Leningrad, all others Trotskyists. The writer in *Pravda* says one-third of those expelled in Siberia are former White Guards and kulaks. The remainder are divided into four categories of which the first is Trotskyists. Which means that at least one thousand are Trotskyists. In Kharkov, 2,300 expelled. More than 5 percent for Trotskyism. If we apply even this figure of 5 percent to the whole 200,000, there must be more than 10,000 Trotskyists. [The purge referred to dates from the summer of 1935 to the present; the report of the commission in charge is not published.]

❋

TROTSKY: Ah-ha. A private letter from Cannon a short time ago was bad.[201] But now it must be good because your trip is good, and if the letter is good, my telegram is good. But perhaps I should receive no delegations and receive no telegrams.

It was the aim of my telegram to overthrow a nearly equal balance in the party to the side of Cannon. It is the only solution of the crisis in the party.

SPECTOR: Your telegram has apparently influenced Weber toward submission to the possible majority on the question of independence.

TROTSKY: And that signifies that the others are against submission?

SPECTOR: Yes, that is correct. Cannon has opened an attack, a vicious attack on us, on my trip. The convention will be like an old CLA convention.

TROTSKY: I shall be glad to write a letter on the subject of your trip, if you will take dictation.

(Dictates letter to Spector, declaring our delegation never presumed to speak in name of whole party, but loyally presented standpoint of Muste-Weber group. Views of Trotsky on one hand and Spector-White on other remain same as before. Suggests sending cablegram on this if considered useful.)

(End of session. Conversation resumed after supper.)

SPECTOR: How do you conceive the main stages in the development of the Fourth International?

TROTSKY: The movement for the Fourth International is growing stronger. In Belgium it is possible to have an important party. It will adhere to the Fourth International. The French youth will adhere; everybody will know that an important fraction of the SP is for the Fourth. Nothing has changed. As I wrote to Muste and Cannon at the time of the Open Letter, I looked on it [the collaboration with Muste] as a lifelong alliance. I do not know at what stage the Fourth will arrive. Nobody knows. It is possible that we will have to enter again into a unified International with the Second and Third. It is impossible to consider the fate of the Fourth International apart from the fate of the national sections and vice versa. Maybe the American section will have to make only formal restrictions in its adherence to the Fourth. Capitalist legality begins first with illegality to bourgeois democracy and the Stalinists and Social Democrats are now the representatives of bourgeois democracy. All their attacks are directed against us. In this case, we must foresee situations without precedent in history.

At the Second Congress, Lenin was for the independence of revolutionary parties. That party, created under the hand of Lenin, has become the greatest barrier to the new revolutionary movement. It is a new situation now. We discussed in our own midst the necessities of proper action. We are convinced of the necessity of an independent party. But how to build it? Public opinion, starting with Roosevelt and ending with Browder,[202] is against us. In the next period the pressure of that opinion will be heavy. When we climb up a cliff we must search for crevices, for footholds. That little foothold now is the SP. Tomorrow we will see.

If we consider the Fourth International only as an international "firm" which compels us to remain independent propagandist societies under any conditions, we are lost. No, the Fourth International is a program, a strategy, an international leadership nucleus. Its value must consist in a not too juridical attitude. It is not the immediate fact that our best comrades must go under the yoke of the centrists. It is disagreeable. We must aim far. We must be patient, wiry, like Muste. [Trotsky smiles good-humoredly.]

SPECTOR: We have already spoken about the possibility that if our group at the convention found the relation of forces such that we could not continue independently, then in order that the entry be as concerted and effective as possible it would be necessary to have recognition of the rights of the minority.

TROTSKY: It is my conviction that such an understanding is absolutely necessary and I will write to that effect to Cannon-Shachtman and their caucus.

I believe now that you will have about a third of the convention. In that third you will have a part absolutely against a split. The worst thing in such a situation are illusions. The individual fluctuations toward Cannon or to the direction and discipline of the majority are symptomatic of an important current. There are not four, there is only one perspective. You will have a third for the *idea* of a split. *Concretely* you will have possibly only the Cohenites.[203] If your policy is oriented now towards split, you will worsen your situation. If you say you will fight to the end, and then say, "Good, you have the majority, your policy is false. But we must go through the experience; we will accompany you in it. But the question is so important that we want the means to defend our point of view in our united caucus within the SP. We want this right, not as the vanquished, but as party members, equals," I believe it will be in the interests of the party as a whole. The situation from the point of view of discipline will change in the new milieu. Discipline can be supported in the new conditions only with the necessary moral authority of the Central Committee. It is not sufficient to depend on the formal arithmetic of numbers. The constitution, the guiding organs of the whole group must be so studied as to give the necessary assurance to the majority of the party that it, the central organ, will be guided only by the unanimous wish for the good of the party. It is a matter now for the victors not to abuse the victory. ■

How to avert a split[204]
February 8, 1936

Dear Comrades:

We have discussed in detail with comrades Spector and White. My general impression is the following:

1. In the opposition there must be a strong tendency which is moving towards a breach with the majority. This tendency can be explained only in part by the opposition to the entry into the SP. The second, very important reason is the fear of being violated by the leaders of the majority and of remaining disfranchised inside the Socialist Party.

2. A split would be highly injurious, nationally as well as internationally. I believe it can be averted (with the exception, perhaps, of an insignificant splinter). How? By your intelligent

conduct! Politically, you have been victorious in the disputed question. So far as I am informed, you will have about a two-thirds majority for the entry. In order to make it possible for the minority to bow to the adopted decision, you must *meet it halfway* on the *organizational* field. *The greatest danger for the victorious faction consists in this, to abuse its victory.* I adjure you, do not make this mistake! The great art of Lenin lay in carrying on the sharpest political struggle against the opposition (without, however, employing threats or insults) and then, when the political victory was assured, to make the greatest organizational concessions to the opponent, in order to preserve the unity of the party and to convert it into a tradition and also in order to make the vanquished of today the friend and collaborator of tomorrow.

3. This policy is also imperatively prescribed for you by the new milieu of your activity. Inside the SP, you will be able to preserve purely formal discipline to an even lesser extent than inside the independent party. Many comrades, on the occasion of any conflict, will fall into the attempt to declare: "Very well, then I shall do the same work without submitting to the discipline of the faction." Should the central committee proceed too rigorously, it will be exposed before the party leadership of the SP or before the membership at their meetings. That is why your central committee must possess, inside the SP, a very great, a so to speak uncontested moral authority. On the organizational field it is therefore absolutely necessary to make the most extensive concessions to the opposition (for example, in the composition of the central committee, in appointments for functions connected with the press, etc.).

4. The political struggle must and will naturally be fought out to the end. Your victory—as has been stated—is assured. A great deal, however, depends upon *what tone* you carry through the party conference with. The opposition must see clearly from your words and deeds that you are not pursu-

ing any vengeful policy; on the contrary: it must see that you, once the political aim has been attained, are prepared for the most peaceful and friendly negotiations about the future composition of the party leadership. Since you have the majority, you must, in my opinion, *take the initiative*. This would only enhance your authority—both nationally and internationally.

5. In the question of the entry, I am supporting you politically to the fullest (also on the international field). But—and I don't conceal this from you—I am disturbed about your tactical and organizational measures. I consider, for example, the condemnation of the trip of Spector and White as erroneous. Where there are two caucuses and where the whole question stands on the edge of the knife, such incidentals should not be formalized. Moreover, the attitude of both comrades was absolutely loyal and I definitely hope that they will influence their faction in an entirely good, that is, in a conciliatory spirit (assuming, naturally, that you pursue the corresponding policy).

6. I believe I may assume that Comrade Weber is against a split. It is absolutely necessary to strengthen his position in this respect. But this cannot be done if one declares: we are ready to go along with Muste, but not with Weber. Without saying anything about the fact that Weber, Spector, and all the others will be of the greatest value for our cause inside the SP, the split cannot be averted now otherwise than by overcoming personal antipathies with regard to certain leaders of the opposition.

7. I have communicated to you my opinion without the slightest reserve. This letter of course bears a private character. But if you deem it expedient to read this letter to your caucus, in whole or in part, then I have no objection.

With best greetings.

Yours,
L. *Trotsky*

Remarks for an English comrade[205]

April 8, 1936

1. That the centrists make use of our ideas in order to fight against us is a classic trait of centrism, but it in no way proves that these gentlemen are *really* coming closer to us. Among the young, honest elements this is sometimes the case. Among the routinists, however, this is only the expression of their deep-rooted lack of principles and their bureaucratic "dexterity."

2. The forty-three (!) splits: If we survey the history of the ILP since it left the Labour Party, it is nothing but a history of splits, splinterings, resignations, desertions, etc. If we were to tally them, they would certainly come to more than forty-three. The only difference is that with us splits are always the expression of programmatic or political struggle, so that one can easily tally and number them according to the documents. Unlike the ILP where, as in the SAP, everything happens behind a veil of confusion, carelessness, and concealment. Thus it *appears* to these stout gentlemen that they have shrunk from 25,000 members to 3,000 without any "splits." Our method has at least two advantages: (a) the membership learns something from it; (b) we grow from it as a result. The SAP-ILP method of concealing what is doesn't teach anybody anything and will not save these parties from ruin.

3. The idea of turning the ILP into a revolutionary party, I believe, *must now be described as utopian*. We must construct an independent perspective for the revolutionary party.

L.D. Trotsky

The center must stay in Europe[206]

April 8, 1936

Dear Comrade Martin:

1. You are certainly correct to point out the need for a reorganization of the work of Theodor. But I don't at all think that this work could be transferred to New York. Europe exists all the same. It would be excellent if the Americans could create a special body for America and the Pacific Ocean countries. Their entry into the SP might create difficulties for them in this area. At any rate they should be sounded out on it. But the center must stay in Europe. Anyway, the candidates that you yourself propose for the plenum are almost all located in Europe.

In principle, I would be in complete agreement on the need to create a secretariat with purely administrative functions consisting of three young comrades familiar with international questions. In that case the plenum ought to meet regularly once every two or three months. But I propose to put this question off for a few more weeks so that the situation in the French and Belgian sections can be clarified more or less definitively. Perhaps the secretariat could even be set up in Brussels. In any case it is necessary for the Belgian section to participate actively in the nomination of the leading bodies.

2. On the question of the People's Front, I say something in the preface for the French edition of *Terrorism and Communism*. That part of this preface certainly could be reproduced by our press. The French translation is already done, I assume.

3. As for Maurin, it is necessary to pay attention to

him a little more consistently. His principal slogan is the "democratic-socialist" revolution; this is nothing but a permutation of the "social-democratic" revolution. Marx wrote in 1876 about the falseness of the term "social-democratic": socialism cannot be put under the control of democracy. Socialism (or communism) suffices for us. "Democracy" has nothing to do with it. Since then, the October Revolution showed conclusively that the socialist revolution cannot be effected within the framework of democracy. The "democratic" revolution and the socialist revolution are on opposite sides of the barricade. The Third International codified this experience in theory. The "democratic" revolution in Spain has already occurred. It is renewed by the People's Front. The personification of the "democratic" revolution in Spain is Azana, with or without Caballero. The socialist revolution must be carried through in implacable struggle against the "democratic" revolution along with its People's Front. What then does this "synthesis" of a "democratic-socialist" revolution signify? Nothing whatsoever. It is nothing but eclectic gibberish.

As for the "turn" of *La Batalla* toward the Popular Front, it cannot inspire us with confidence. One cannot say on Monday that the League of Nations is a band of thieves, on Tuesday urge the electors to vote for the program of the League of Nations, and on Wednesday explain that yesterday it was only an electoral activity and that now the real program comes out. The serious worker would have to wonder: what are these people going to say Thursday or Friday? Maurin seems to be the very incarnation of an agile, superficial and versatile petty-bourgeois revolutionary. He studies nothing, understands little and spreads confusion all around himself.

My best wishes,

Orient to the Spanish youth[207]

April 14, 1936

Dear Comrades:

Thank you for your friendly letter. I do not have the slightest reason to doubt the sincerity of your feelings. But politics is not influenced by personal feelings. It demands correct principles, courage, and perseverance. Unfortunately, these three elements were and still are missing in the leadership of the [Spanish] Communist Left, not to mention that of the POUM.

The situation in Spain was exceptionally favorable for a revolutionary Marxist group. By the appropriate policies, such a group would have been able, in the last five years, to become a leading force in the Spanish revolution. Unfortunately, Andres Nin, Andrade, and the others did everything they could to compromise this situation. They treated principles lightly. They dodged all serious discussion about the duties of revolutionaries and they always sought the line of least resistance. They declared their solidarity with any dissent that was prejudicial to the international policy of the Bolshevik-Leninists.

They were in league, against the Fourth International, with that unprincipled petty bourgeois who calls himself Maurin. Andres Nin and Andrade will be remembered historically as men who betrayed their banner.

As for you, dear comrades, you will never win the POUM over to Marxism, because it is not a mass organization but a small sect around Maurin, Nin, etc. The experience of the last five years has demonstrated that there is nothing more to be done in that quarter. You must turn toward the youth and toward the mass organizations. A year ago, you had every opportunity to win over the Socialist youth. A policy of passivity and conservatism on the part of Nin and Maurin prevented you. This work must be begun, despite the Stalinists' success. It is necessary to penetrate the youth [milieu] and turn our backs on Maurin, Nin, and the others. Otherwise, all your beautiful plans will remain empty phrases. I am speaking to you in all frankness because you have no time to lose.

I am sending you a letter to a Spanish comrade. It is written in German. Please translate it into Spanish and circulate it to every comrade who might possibly be interested in my ideas.

P.S. I have just received *La Batalla*, the April 10, 1936, issue, bearing in a headline this formula borrowed from the bourgeois journal *El Liberal:* "The People's Front is the only conservative guarantee in Spain."

That is completely true. But why did the POUM help to construct this conservative guarantee? Haven't Nin and Andrade grasped what it was? However, the international literature of the Bolshevik-Leninists long ago analyzed and made known the mechanism of the People's Front's betrayal. But your leaders have chosen, here as in all other important problems, the line of least resistance and greatest detriment to the revolution. ■

Eleven letters to Victor Serge[208]
April–August 1936

APRIL 24, 1936

Dear Victor Lvovich:

I have just received your letter. I have sent you a telegram. How happy it made N. I. [Natalia Sedova] and me, and how pleased we are that you are finally abroad, that you are in good spirits, and have retained your friendly feelings towards us. The news of the death of Solntsev[209] distressed me greatly; I remember him well and have always had a great affection for him. My closest collaborators are tragically disappearing one after the other—Glazman, Butov,[210] Blumkin, and now Solntsev.

Do you know what would make us happy? For you to come and spend a few days here so that we might discuss everything at leisure, in depth, and *at whatever length we wish,* for I hope that our relations with you have only just begun. If your traveling here is not immediately possible, would it perhaps be so at a later time? It would make us very happy!

In any case, we await your letters; give us as many details as possible. For our part, we promise to write to you conscientiously. Could you write for the next issue of the Russian *Biulleten* a few lines about Solntsev and about the basic things we do not know about yourselves and the general situation? I well understand that it can't be easy for you to write when you have only just arrived, but it would only have to be a *brief report.*

How have you settled in at Brussels? What are your plans

for the future? Do you hope to find a paid writing job right away? I am sure you will write a book on the USSR that will be read throughout the world. I am now finishing a political work of a theoretical nature on the USSR (two hundred printed pages).[211] I would like to have your opinion of it. But do you feel up to it right now? If you should agree, I will send you the manuscript immediately.

Have you met our Belgian friends? What are your impressions? I highly recommend Lesoil to you: he is a serious and very trustworthy comrade. I do not know Dauge personally; he has come much closer to us in the course of the past year. Do you ever see Godefroid, the youth secretary? I do not know him personally, but I have *no* confidence in him. I will be very pleased to know your opinion.

But above all, tell us about yourself and your family in particular, especially your material situation. How good it is that you are abroad!

I know that you have ties with Ch. Plisnier;[212] he has sent me his poem, which, *contrary to all my expectations*, is dedicated to me (nowadays poets of the "left" generally dedicate their works . . . to Gosizdat [Soviet government publishing house] and its masters). I have written a few words to Plisnier, but I am afraid I expressed myself badly, and that he thought I wanted to play the role of mentor (which was the farthest thing from my mind!). That annoys me a lot. If I am mistaken, reassure me when you get the chance.

Have you heard any news about our son Sergei? Anyway, I am certain you will share with us everything that you know.

I hope that in the meantime you will be able to acquaint yourself with the press of the Fourth International, and that we will be able to exchange our views on the subject. Right now in Belgium there are *many things* that can be done on the condition that Dauge and his group align themselves with Lesoil rather than with Godefroid.

Insofar as it is possible to entrust your "secrets" to the mails, you can write to the address that you have with complete "candor."

N. I. sends you and your family her most cordial good wishes. My warm fraternal greetings.

Yours,
L. Trotsky

APRIL 29, 1936

Dear Victor Lvovich:

I am a little sorry I wrote in my telegram, "letter follows," which could have caused you to wait for my letter and postpone sending your letter. Need we say that we await your news with feverish impatience?

I am writing you this time to give you some information and to share with you my thoughts on some of our mutual acquaintances and former comrades. I am thinking especially of Souvarine and the Paz couple.

When I arrived in Turkey, I did everything I could to reach an agreement with Souvarine, whose professional and journalistic qualities I always appreciated, but for whom I have never had much regard as a *revolutionary*. The letters that we exchanged revealed to me very quickly that we had nothing in common. Souvarine is a purely analytical soul and, moreover, a formal and negative thinker. When people like him belong to a serious group and remain faithful to a great tradition, they can render important services to the movement. But Souvarine's character prevents him from belonging to a group. He is absolutely incapable of independent political work. In his search for an independent line running directly from Marx to himself, bypassing Lenin and Bolshevism, Souvarine has accidentally discovered . . . *Menshevism*. I have found nothing else in him. His book on Stalin, which I have only skimmed, is valuable for its conscientious selection of facts, but from a theoretical and political point of view it is, alas, worthless.

As far as I can tell, Souvarine attaches very great importance to the fate of the Mensheviks in the USSR. Must we defend them or not? He has launched numerous attacks against us because we have not made and do not make any commitment on this question.

At this time repression against the Mensheviks is not a topical problem, even for the bureaucracy; the overwhelming majority of Mensheviks find Stalin's regime suits them just fine, and they help in persecuting our friends. The Menshevik movement is not experiencing any influx of new forces; that is the conclusion that emerges from all the information that we have from their own statements. There remains the problem of the ten or twenty "scapegoats" that Stalin needs to prove that he is not persecuting only the Bolsheviks.

Politically, the problem of the Mensheviks can be posed in a correct manner only in an international perspective. Everywhere in the world the Social Democracy is joining hands with the Stalinists, the proof of which is the tenacious persecutions directed against us internationalists, partisans of the Fourth International. The preparation of the sacred union in anticipation of an impending war is beginning with the "sacred union" of the Second and Third Internationals against the real revolutionary vanguard. You can see this better than anyone in Belgium at the present time. Throughout the world the Mensheviks are expelling our comrades from the party, and where possible, from the unions, in order to be able at the time of mobilization [for the war] to deliver them more safely into the hands of the imperialist police. There is no possible doubt that the GPU is drawing up lists of internationalists in every country and agrees to provide information to the police of "friendly countries." As such, Dan[213] is of little interest to me. But he belongs to the same international army as Vandervelde, Leon Blum, etc. Politically, the problem for us is not so much to know how to defend the dozen scapegoats who are suffering, in effect, for nothing—that is, for the purpose of strengthening the Stalinists' prestige—but rather to know *how to protect ourselves from the treacherous blows of international Menshevism and Stalinism*, while waging a pitiless campaign to expose them. That is the only important problem, but Souvarine does not see it at all. That is why he would be prepared to divide his justice equally between the Mensheviks and us. Given his position, we do not have and cannot have anything in common with him.

I draw your attention in passing to the fact that the Yugoslav oppositionist Ciliga has departed from his ultraleft positions and he, too, has been derailed into the road to friendship with the Mensheviks. His reasoning is approximately as follows: The USSR is not a workers' state but a Bonapartist state of the capitalist type; democracy would be a step forward for the USSR; the Mensheviks are in favor of democracy; hence the Mensheviks are our allies. It is no use to try to make sense out of this pile of nonsense since in any case, as I pointed out above, we cannot carry out a worthwhile policy towards the Mensheviks in "a single country."

The task of the proletarian vanguard in the USSR is not to be concerned with the Mensheviks, out of altruism, but to prepare the revolutionary overthrow of the Bonapartist bureaucracy. One might ask what would be the policy of the party of the Fourth International towards the Mensheviks if it came to power. We cannot make any commitment on this subject. It would all depend on the international situation, the relationship of forces, the policy of the Mensheviks themselves, etc. If Dan's allies of the Second International imprison and assassinate another Liebknecht, we will obviously have no smiles for the Mensheviks. But all this is in the future.

There is no need for me to dwell on the subject of the Paz couple. Magdeleine Paz[214] has fought for your freedom; it is the only praiseworthy thing she has done in her life. About him [Maurice Paz] I can't even say that much. He is a bourgeois conservative, tough, narrow-minded, and profoundly repulsive. If he joined the Left Opposition at one time it was only because that gave him, absolutely free of charge (which for him is the decisive factor), a certain halo, while not involving him in any obligation at all. Because my point of view on the Bolshevik-Leninist movement is somewhat different from his, my arrival abroad prevented Paz from continuing the pretense that he shared my ideas. The break was inevitable, and I blame myself only for having been too patient and having wasted my time corresponding with the Paz couple.

No doubt you are aware of my differences with *Rosmer*. That affair is already a thing of the past, and it is unnecessary to explain it in detail. In any case, Rosmer is a person of an entirely different caliber. Despite his great discretion and tact, when at a certain point he found himself in disagreement with me over a secondary issue, he became overexcited and refused not only to reach some agreement with me but even to explain his conduct. Because of this we did not meet during my stay in France; but our respect and sympathy for both of them, Alfred and Marguerite,[215] are as great as ever, and I think they feel the same toward us. Rosmer wrote a very fine book on the workers' movement during the war [*Le Mouvement Ouvrier Pendant la Guerre. De l'Union Sacree a Zimmerwald* (Librairie du Travail, Paris, 1936)]. He is one of the people who can always be counted on in these difficult times. There is no doubt that our personal relations will be restored and will become firmer than ever.

To change the subject: It seems to me that you have arrived in Belgium at the most opportune time to understand the nature of the work we have done there, our methods, and our internal organization. At this time Belgium is a very precious field of experience. *Lesoil, Vereecken,* and *Dauge* represent three currents in our *international* movement. The present minister Spaak came to see me in Paris for a "consultation" (a few months before his betrayal), and he told me he considered Lesoil and Vereecken to be the two best workers in Belgium. I hope you have already met them as well as Dauge, and that you will share with me your detailed observations and impressions.

My greatest fear in regard to Belgian matters is the conciliatory and temporizing attitude of Dauge and, in part, the others as well, towards Godefroid, who pretends to be a friend of the people expelled [from the POB], and who will change sides at the last minute and help Vandervelde to isolate us. It is a shameful role, similar to that played by Marceau Pivert in France, with the help of our people.

Enough for this time. Hearty greetings from N. I. and myself to you and your family. Best personal wishes.

Yours,
L.T.

P.S. Have you heard news about Alexandra Lvovna [Sokolovskaya], [her sister] Marie Lvovna, and their children?

I have an opportunity to send the largest American press agency a communication of any kind at all about the USSR (apparently in any tone I wish). Could you perhaps write a statement on the political prisoners and exiles? It could be presented as a letter from you to me. But there is the question of your name. I do not think that you will be able to stay "in the shadows"; that would remove nine-tenths of the value of your revelations, and in any case the French and Belgian Stalinists would "find you out." It seems to me that it would be better to act openly. But it is possible that I am not up to date on all your thoughts and all your projects.

MAY 8, 1936

Dear Victor Lvovich:

I have received your two letters, the last dated May 6. Write in the language that suits you best, either Russian or French. Your Russian is impeccable.

First problem: do the exiles receive money and parcels from abroad? We have sent several things, with no reply. Do you know anything about this? It is one of the most important points of our propaganda: the exiles are given no jobs, and at the same time are not permitted to receive money. We must get the opportunity to send them money.

Your "political" situation: I too undertook, when I received my visa for Norway, not to involve myself in the political life of this country and not to cause any concern among "friendly governments." But that only means not committing any "illegal" act, such as "conspiracy," preparation of "terrorist actions," etc. Any other interpretation makes no sense. I do not involve myself at all in Norwegian life. But I collaborate openly with publications that appear legally in many other countries. I think that you ought to accord yourself the same status by taking direct action. It would certainly be possible for you to go and establish yourself in France now, but it could also bring many kinds of reprisals. It would be better for you to collaborate with French publications while you remain in Belgium. That is my first impression.

In October there will be elections here. The Labor Party hopes to win an absolute majority. It is not excluded that you might come and settle here. But that would be a last resort, given that Belgium presents some enormous advantages—the language, the big city, the low cost of living.

Marie Lvovna was in Kirov, near Odessa, with her children. If she has been deported (which is certainly the case), what happened to her children? They were probably placed in an orphanage, unless they have gone to swell the numbers of abandoned children. No family will dare to take them in.

When you decide to write again, could you perhaps send a few words for our press on Alexandra Lvovna? It would be easier for you than for me. I have told the essentials of my relationship with her (if that is of any use to you) in my autobiography.

You know that Stalin and his GPU scoundrels have tried many times to blame the Opposition for "terrorist" acts. These attempts continue. There will be such accusations against you as well, when you come out into the open. That is why it is so important to unmask in advance this aspect of the GPU's work, with an article or an interview. We must cut the ground out from under the practitioners of the amalgam.

Once again, it is necessary to present the authorities with a fait accompli. Given the participation of the Socialists in the government, they will not expel you. Besides, where would they send you? After all, you are not doing anything illegal. The Belgian constitution does not oblige you to eulogize Stalin, especially in the foreign press.

What do the doctors think about your wife's health? Is there any hope of recovery? What would it take? Tell us everything; perhaps we can help you. We have some friends who are doctors, and it is possible to raise some money. *Give us some details!*

Some years ago, we were "rich" (*The History of the Russian Revolution*)! Now we live in a period of severe crisis. But I hope that in a month or two, our situation will be better. In any case we have friends to whom we can have recourse. So write to us in complete frankness.

Has anything of yours been published yet in America? Only in America do they pay for literary work. But for that, you will have to *make some noise* around your name! Give some consideration to an interview for the American press. When your book on the USSR comes out, it will be possible, at least I hope so, to penetrate the American market with your previous books as well.

I have an idea! Right now, I am working on a long introduction to the second edition (cheap) of *The History of the Russian Revolution*. This introduction is a description of the USSR, around two hundred printed pages long. *I must quote you once, twice, or even more often in the introduction,* even if only personal letters (on the bureaucracy, the disagreements between it and the population, the violence against the Opposition, etc.). I could say straightforwardly (in a footnote) that you are preparing a book. Think about it and give me as soon as possible something that would be suitable. *That would have great practical importance* (since my publisher is doing a great deal of publicity).

I would be very grateful to your son if he could send me the portrait of B. Mikh. [Boris Mikhailovich Eltsin][216]

And is it not possible to have a photo of you? For us personally and for our press. Warmest personal greetings.

Yours,
L. *Trotsky*

P.S. We are going to investigate the matter of the lost telegram. It was of no importance: "Fraternal greetings. Letter follows."

MAY 19, 1936

Dear Victor Lvovich:

I am awaiting your reply to my last letter, in which I made a certain number of practical propositions to you. To be sure, *you should not think you are bound in any way by these proposals.* If for any reason they do not seem suitable to you, tell me frankly: from here I can only imperfectly judge your situation and still less your state of mind on personal and political matters.

I would like to return to that very subject, politics. In the May 16 issue of *L'Action Socialiste Revolutionnaire* I found your letter to the editors of *La Revolution proletarienne*[217] dated April 21. I will not conceal from you the fact that it bothered me. Not so much because you wrote to a syndicalist group as because you wrote *exclusively* to them. If that means that you feel you are politically closer to syndicalism than Marxism, then it remains only for me to take note of this profound difference between us. But I dare hope that there is nothing to it, and I account for your letter by the fact that according to the information you have, it was this group, above all others, that fought for your release.

On this latter point also I fear that you do not have a completely correct view of the real mechanics of the struggle as it has been carried out these last few years. By giving a speech or writing an article when the circumstances lent themselves, or even getting influential people to intervene, the people of *La Revolution proletarienne,* Paz and the rest, acted as *liberals*. For me as well, Magdeleine Paz took the necessary steps to request a visa for England [in 1929]. It is a role that she can play naturally. But the *Revolution proletarienne* people do not go one inch beyond this kind of action. Our comrades, on the other hand, went to Stalinist meetings, launched appeals, provoked "scandals" during the most solemn meetings, were beaten up dozens of times—in short, they made big trouble for the Stalinists and their friends like Barbusse, Romain Rolland, and others. Again, in recent days, during Bukharin's stay in Paris, the Bolshevik-Leninists burst into his meeting and made an appeal on behalf of the prisoners in the USSR. Of course they were thrown out of the hall. It is only because of this kind of revolutionary action that the liberals could score a certain victory: "reforms" (such as your release) are always a *by-product* of revolutionary struggle.

Ciliga, who is doing his best to rally everyone behind the

defense of the Soviet prisoners and to whom we are obviously not opposed on this point, although we do not share his illusions, also appealed to *La Revolution proletarienne*. They promised him that at the trade union congress their representatives would take the floor to speak especially on this subject. Ciliga wrote me an enthusiastic letter. But his enthusiasm was premature: nobody spoke on the subject. The *Revolution proletarienne* group at the present time is on excellent terms with the reformist faction of the trade union bureaucracy, which is allied with the Stalinists and doesn't want the question of the Soviet regime to cause it problems. To write an article for some magazine is one thing, but to take the floor to speak at a hostile meeting is another. The *Revolution proletarienne* group is an altogether conservative sect, not at all combative, and lacking any political significance. They have their circle of readers whose number decreases little by little, and for whom they publish their type of magazine. The revolutionary spirit left them a long time ago.

I understand perfectly well that having arrived abroad after years of incredibly harsh tribulations you are in no hurry to define your position and do not want to give anyone the right to "classify" you according to your past allegiances or other considerations. The situation in the international workers' movement at this time is extremely complex, and it is not easy to see clearly. *The sole aim of my letters is to provide you with information, nothing more.* I am prepared to wait patiently for the time when you feel it possible to locate yourself clearly in relation to the different political groupings.

P.S. May 20, 1936—After writing this first page, I received your lengthy letter in which you describe life in exile at Orenburg. Thank you very much for this work. I have already extracted from it everything that can be published;

in fact, with the exception of a few deletions, almost the entire text has been reproduced in several copies, and we are in the process of sending it to different countries (without your signature, of course, in order not to cause you any problems with the police).

As for the American press agency, I am going to draft a statement, in my own name, based on the documents you have sent me, and will send it to them quickly, again without mentioning your name. From London the dispatch will be sent to hundreds if not thousands of American papers; moreover, there is no necessity to limit the length of the text. When I get a chance, I shall also send you a copy of this statement.[218]

Once again, I ask you not to consider the first part of this letter as a sermon or a "rebuke." I simply want to eliminate any artificial character from our relationship right away; even supposing that serious differences exist between us (and I hope not), the best way to get to the bottom of them is complete *franchise* [frankness], if I may use that French word in Russian letters.

Best personal wishes. Greetings to your family from us both. I will be happy to know how you found Alfred [Rosmer] is getting along.

Yours,
L. *Trotsky*

JUNE 3, 1936

Dear Victor Lvovich:

I have received two letters from you; one in Russian dated May 23, and one in French dated the 27th. Let me speak first of all about your personal matters. I read in an article by the late Pavlov that they had begun to treat schizophrenia effectively by means of long, drug-induced sleep, and have had great success. Do the Belgian doctors know of this? In any case this treatment is possible only, so far as I know, in a clinic. Natalia and I were very elated at the general improvement of your wife's condition. It is not hard for us to imagine the extraordinary difficulties of your situation.

As far as working for money is concerned, it is America that offers the greatest hope. First of all, you will have to publish the big book that you are preparing or are going to prepare. I am quite sure you will succeed. I also think that you could clear the way for yourself in the large American press by means of a series of articles on Soviet literature and art in general. In this connection, there appeared a year and a half or two years ago a book by Eastman [*Artists in Uniform: A Study of Literature and Bureaucratism* (Alfred A. Knopf, New York, 1934)]. Do you know it? Do you read English?

I would be very happy if you would agree to translate my new book into French. By so doing, you would not be "taking work away from anyone else," and obviously I cannot dream of a more qualified translator than you. I am impatiently awaiting your book *Defense of the USSR in 1936*.[219]

I fear you may have written me in Russian for my own convenience. It doesn't matter: choose whatever suits you best. I understand your French almost as well as your Russian—at least, without difficulty.

Let us turn now to political questions.

1. On *La Revolution proletarienne*. You know my former ties with this group, ties that go back to the war. I came to Constantinople with the firm intention of working with them. I made many efforts to establish personal and political contact, particularly through the mediation of Rosmer, who was more skeptical about it from the start than I. He was right. You speak of the necessity of being friends with the "revolutionary syndicalists." That is altogether true, but

where are they? The *Revolution proletarienne* people are neither syndicalists nor revolutionaries. They are quite simply a small group that is cut off from living reality. Monatte has grown old and stepped aside. Louzon is an extravagant petty bourgeois, an outdated caricature of Proudhon.[220] He has various acquaintances, but they do harm to him and his readers rather than helping them. Those among them who are syndicalists grovel before Jouhaux and Company and have nothing but hatred for our movement. This group is dead. That is the conclusion that I have come to, not lightly, not at first impression, but on the basis of my experience, my patient experience over several years. I should add that a year ago, at my urging, the French comrades tried once again to carry on a common struggle with *La Revolution proletarienne* against social chauvinism. This attempt was fruitless, because those people are incapable of struggle and do not know what struggle is. Obviously that does not preclude "personal relations." But you will soon realize yourself that there is absolutely no reason to view the members of *La Revolution proletarienne* as "revolutionary syndicalists."

2. If I have understood your letter from Paris, you are dissatisfied with our behavior toward Andres Nin, behavior that you find "sectarian." You do not and cannot know the political and personal history of our relations. You can easily imagine how happy I was when Nin arrived abroad. For several years, I corresponded with him quite regularly. Some of my letters were veritable "treatises" on the subject of the living revolution, in which Nin could and should have played an active role. I think that my letters to Nin over a period of two or three years would make up a volume of several hundred pages: that should indicate how important I regarded Nin and friendly relations with him. In his answers, Nin affirmed over and over again his agreement in theory, but he always avoided discussing

practical problems. He asked me abstract questions about soviets, about democracy, etc., but he never said one word about the general strikes that were occurring in Catalonia. Of course, no one is obligated to be a revolutionary. But Nin was the head of the Spanish Bolshevik-Leninists, and by that fact alone, he had a serious responsibility, which he failed to carry out in practice, all the while throwing dust in my eyes. Believe me, dear friend, I have a certain gift for these things: if I am guilty of anything with regard to Nin, it is of having nourished illusions for too long on his account, and thereby of having given him the opportunity of maintaining under the banner of Bolshevism-Leninism the passivity and confusionism of which there is already a surfeit in the Spanish workers' movement—and I mean in its highest echelons. If in Spain there had been, instead of Nin, a serious revolutionary worker like Lesoil or Vereecken, it would have been possible, during those years of revolution, to accomplish significant work there. Pushed by the ambiguity of his position, Nin systematically supported in all countries those who, for one reason or another, launched a struggle against us and generally ended up as pure and simple renegades. How did the rupture come about? Nin announced that he was absolutely opposed to the tactical entry of our comrades into the French Socialist Party. Then, after long hesitation, he declared that in France it was a correct tactic and that he should act in the same way in Spain. But instead of that, he joined with the provincial organization of Maurin, which had no perspective at all, but which allowed him to lead a peaceful existence. Our International Secretariat wrote him a critical letter. Nin responded by breaking off relations and publishing something on the subject in a special bulletin. If I were not afraid of wasting your time, I would send you the file of my correspondence with Nin; I have kept copies of all my letters. I am sure that you, like other comrades who have become familiar with this correspondence, would accuse me of excessive patience, a "conciliatory spirit," and not of sectarianism.

3. I can understand perfectly well that *La Revolution proletarienne* or the Pazes have maintained much better relations with you than *La Verite*; they have many more opportunities, leisure time, material means, and facilities for that purpose. Do not forget that our youth are inexperienced and are struggling with innumerable difficulties. You speak of provocateurs. I am sure there have been some, and there still are. Provocateurs obviously have nothing to gain from Louzon or Magdeleine Paz. On the contrary, they are penetrating all their forces into the Bolshevik-Leninists, who preach a general strike, organize a militia, and wage a fierce antipatriotic propaganda campaign. How could there not be provocateurs? I am far from approving of negligence or inexperience on the part of our young friends, with whom I am in continual struggle on this question. But I cannot help seeing many of their faults as being the other side of the coin from their priceless qualities: they are *revolutionaries*, while the Louzons and Pazes are peaceful, conservative philistines.

4. Let us look at the case of Belgium. We have been accused of being too intolerant of Vereecken. Without the entry of the Lesoil group into the Belgian party we would not have enjoyed the modest yet definite successes that we now have. But Vereecken was opposed to entry at any cost. Should we then have capitulated before him and given up the chance to make a great step forward? (Our success could have been much more important if we had had a firmer and clearer policy towards Godefroid from the outset.) Under these circumstances the split with Vereecken was inevitable. But I have always thought, as I said to the comrades and put in writing, that we would find Vereecken again at the next stage. Now I hope that we will ally with him, despite

his sectarianism (which is, after all, the reverse side of his good qualities).

5. On the subject of our campaign in behalf of Stalin's political prisoners, I am sending you my statement which has already been sent by cable through the Associated Press to the USA, where it will be published, in whole or in extracts, in hundreds of newspapers. Unfortunately, I wrote this document in German, since I don't know English very well. You will see that I have no qualms about using an agency of the bourgeois press. Does that constitute "sectarianism" on my part? I am prepared to say, and will say, given the chance by the press, that to carry out a People's Front policy abroad and to prepare for the fusion of the two Internationals while keeping the Mensheviks in prison is utterly disgraceful, because repression against the Mensheviks is due not to the exigencies of the revolution but to the needs of an internal cover-up; so that they can say that they are arresting not only Bolshevik-Leninists, but also the Mensheviks who remain loyal to their tradition, etc. It is nevertheless hard to imagine a more stupid act than Ciliga's having his article published by the Mensheviks. I mentioned in a separate document that I agreed with your position on Ciliga; immediately after his letters, I decided he was no more than a hot-headed Menshevik.

6. To be sure, your observations on the exiles and your comments have an inestimable value, especially for me. However, I cannot bring myself to agree with your negative assessment of the tens of thousands of Trotskyists, Zinovievists, etc., who were recently expelled. I am quite willing to believe that their petty-bourgeois characteristics are very strong, but the petty-bourgeois type is the triumphant type of Thermidor. Capitulations are most often due to petty-bourgeois causes, and reflect the period and the milieu. Nevertheless, the bureaucracy would not have set out to expel tens of thousands of people without very

serious political reasons. The American worker, Smith, who changed from an idealistic Stalinist (before he left for the USSR he gave all his savings to the CP) into a fierce enemy of the USSR, relates in his book[221] how in the factories the strongest supporters of the "line" and the most violent denunciators of the Opposition were clandestine oppositionists. Most of those people continue to play a double role both in prison and in deportation (your letter contains some allusions to this as well). We cannot wait in the meantime for a mass opposition that is as clear in theory and as courageous in individual action as were the first two generations, who participated in discussions, read, etc. And besides it is no accident that the GPU labels some of the expelled as Trotskyists, others as Zinovievists, others as rightists, etc.

7. The Fourth International: I confess I do not understand what "founding" the Fourth International means. There exist in different countries organizations and groups that struggle under this banner. They try to determine together their position on all the world events. They are preparing a common program based on practical and theoretical concepts rooted in history. Some Ryazanov of the future may try at his leisure to resolve in retrospect the question of when exactly the Fourth International was founded. But as for us, we have simply to continue to develop our work.

I think that is everything. You will not find it easy, in your circumstances, to digest this letter, especially since it includes enclosures.

I find the portrait of B.M. Eltsin very well done, and I recognize in it one of his expressions. Since I have no other way of giving my regards to your son, I am sending him my photo.

I would be very very happy if you and I could come to an agreement on *essentials*. I have no intention of involving you in little day-to-day disputes. If you write a book with the talent that is yours and that I discovered only while abroad, you will be more useful to the movement than in any other way.

Warmest personal greetings.

Yours,
L. *Trotsky*

JUNE 5, 1936

Dear Victor Lvovich:

In my last letter, there were some omissions. Let us start with Nin. If you think that there is some possibility of his returning to us, why don't you try to get him back? I personally cherish no hope of seeing Nin become a revolutionary, but I could be wrong. Find out for yourself, if you think it necessary. I could only approve of that step.

Of course, we could not be satisfied with verbal assurances from Nin (at which he is quite prolific), but with actual deeds. At this moment, Nin is allied with the sworn enemies of the Fourth International, who hide their petty-bourgeois hatred of revolutionary Marxism behind hollow phrases on the subject of "organizational" differences, as if serious people could break with revolutionaries and ally themselves with opportunists because of secondary differences. If Nin wants to return to us, then he must openly raise the banner of the Fourth International in Spain. The pretexts that he invokes for refusing to do so are in the same class as those that Blum invokes with regard to the class struggle, which, according to him, while being a good thing in general, is, however, not appropriate for our epoch. Blum's politics consist of class collaboration, although "in theory" he recognizes the class struggle. Nin recognizes the Fourth International in words, but in deeds he helps Maurin, Walcher, Maxton, and his other allies wage a bitter struggle against the Fourth

International, exactly like the struggle that the pacifists like Longuet and Ledebour[222] waged against the revolutionary internationalist partisans of the Third International during the last war.

On the subject of the Pazes, I have nothing to add to what I have told you already. But in all conscience, I have to forewarn you that in no case should you use them as your literary agents. I give you this little bit of advice because I have learned the hard way that it can be very costly to ignore it. In any case, if they were to make any proposals in this regard, I would like you to let me know before making a definite decision, so that we can unite our efforts to assure the greatest possible success for your new book.

Sincerely yours,
L. Trotsky

Supplementary comments on Comrade Ciliga's letter: The letter is so contradictory to the Marxist method of politics that it is really difficult to find the most important points to refute. Ciliga says: if you can ally yourself with Blum against the fascists, why can't you do the same with Dan against the Stalinist "reaction"? I have already dealt briefly with one aspect of this "argument," and here is another. In comparison with the fascists, Blum represents a lesser evil. But can it be said that the Mensheviks represent a lesser evil in comparison with the Stalinists? In no way. If, in the USSR, we had only a choice between the Stalinists and the Mensheviks, we would obviously have to pick the Stalinists, since the Mensheviks can serve only as stepladders for the bourgeoisie, which would destroy the planned economy and institute in the country a regime that would be a mixture of typically Russian fascism and economic chaos on the Chinese model. The *economy* of the country would be set back fifty years. The planned economy is the only way to preserve the independence of the USSR and its future. The

Stalinists themselves are preparing the destruction of the planned economy, but not on such short notice: we can hope that the proletariat will succeed in doing away with the bureaucracy before it destroys collective property.

You could, if you wanted to, call the Soviet economy "state capitalism," but if you consider the other parts of the globe, you have to say that it is the only regime that is capable of further developing the forces of production. Not to see that, because of the ignominy of the bureaucracy, is to be a liberal and not a revolutionary Marxist.

JUNE 9, 1936

Dear Victor Lvovich:

I have just received your little note of June 6 in which you tell me of your concern at not having received my letter. I hope it was simply a day late, since I sent it by registered mail. In any case I am sending you a copy. I had enclosed with the letter a photo for your son in thanks for the portrait of B.M. Eltsin (the portrait was very good and gave me great pleasure).

To this long letter I had added in handwriting approximately the following:

I have no selfish intention of involving you in day-to-day practical work. Although we have in recent years made great progress in the formation of cadres (which is the most difficult work and the least externally visible), we have not yet left the period of "infantile disorders." With your literary talent and your artistic gifts, which I was only able to appreciate from abroad, I would think it altogether unreasonable for you to waste your energy in *day-to-day* political life. All things considered, your books will be of much more benefit to the Fourth International than would your participation in daily work. That is my general impression.

Of course, that does not rule out your participation as an elder and authoritative comrade at some important meeting or in some organization. But these, to be sure, are only hypotheses. You yourself must decide, based on your later understanding of what has happened and what is happening in the world arena.

In *Spartacus* and in the latest *Action Socialiste Revolutionnaire* I found extracts from your letters to Paz and Gide.[223] It is too bad I don't have the complete text. These letters would give me the opportunity to make some indispensable quotations in my book on the USSR. Do you have a complete copy? (After I have used it, I shall return it to you.) Or have these letters perhaps been published already somewhere in the press at full length?

You are going to Paris. I envy you a little. Two or three times a day I hear on the radio about the birth pains of the French revolution.[224] This massive strike is undoubtedly the beginning of the revolution. All these leaders (Blum, Jouhaux, Salengro,[225] Cachin, etc.) tremble before the advancing revolution, they run for cover, they tell lies, and in their gestures and their speeches they imitate Kerensky, Tsereteli,[226] and Dan, in spite of the much higher standards of the French school of rhetoric! French politics in the coming months could determine the fate of France and of Europe for many years. I will be very pleased to know your impressions from Paris.

A sympathetic German publisher wants to publish a monthly Marxist theoretical journal under my direction, giving me a free hand while knowing in advance that this periodical will be the theoretical organ of the Fourth International. I am thinking of starting in the autumn, and I hope that we will succeed in carrying out the same thing in France.[227] I am firmly counting on your participation on the staff of this future publication. It goes without saying that I would like to invite Alfred [Rosmer] also, but I wouldn't want to run into a refusal (I hope there would be none), and that is why I would prefer to make the first contact *through you.* If Alfred is in agreement on this principle, then I will write to him as soon as possible.

Warm personal greetings.

Yours,
L. *Trotsky*

P.S. I have just received your card telling me you have received my long letter, and the proofs of your letters to Paz and Gide.

Thank you. Everything is fine.

L.T.

JULY 3, 1936

Dear Victor Lvovich:

Up to now I have not yet really replied to your last two letters, of June 16 and 24; I have contented myself with a brief note, for reasons which I have already explained. Now I would like to make up for lost time. I do not know where you are right now, whether in Brussels or Paris, so I am sending this letter to both your addresses at the same time.

You write of the necessity of profiting from major events and mobilizing all those who have "as much as a revolutionary vein" in their bodies. I agree with you absolutely, and I consider it a great advantage to our cause that you, who have just arrived from abroad, without any preconceived ideas and without having developed any personal bitterness, can go and find a whole group of people and verify whether this revolutionary vein is there or not. Of course, I am thinking above all of Rosmer. Personally, I do not doubt that he has all the "revolutionary veins" he needs. But is he therefore ready to *come toward* our movement? That would please me very much. Obviously, I am not speaking of involving him in minor, day-to-day work. But he could be a very useful collaborator, even indispensable for our publications, especially the monthly I have projected. For this publication I would like to have not only Rosmer's name but also Martinet's.[228] Would you please try to find out if they agree in principle, and if so, I shall write to them in greater detail. We are going to begin a German monthly and at the same time we are going to launch a French publication of the same kind. If you have other candidates for collaboration in this project, please tell me without delay.

We obviously have no differences on the subject of the tremendous importance of the June upsurge [in France]. You expressed the supposition that the European proletariat will require several years to "recover." This "recovery" coincides in practice with the formation of a new revolutionary vanguard. It would of course be wonderful if history allowed us still "several years" for the task, even say, two or three years. Unfortunately, I don't think that is so. Events in France could develop much more quickly than in Spain. In Spain, the toiling masses had to in fact begin the revolution all over again, after their leaders had killed the first revolution [in 1931]. In France, the bourgeoisie is infinitely stronger and more intelligent, and will not so easily give the proletariat a chance to correct the bankruptcy of their leaders. That is why the formation of a party is a task of prime importance in France as well as in Belgium. I would not be opposed to the Belgian comrades' forming a party, even if it has to be numerically weak. Of course, a small party does not necessarily become a large one; but without a party the revolution is inevitably doomed, whether it be in Spain, France, or Belgium.

Let us turn now to Ciliga. I would be very happy if you or someone else could bring him back to the revolutionary road. But for the moment, the facts remain: he is collaborating with the Mensheviks and writes shameless criticisms of us in their paper, while the French Mensheviks, who share the ideas of their friend Dan, seize our French paper and turn our friends over to the police. To take up a position on the wrong side of the barricades is no small crime.

You ask whether I have not judged your two letters too harshly. I found your letter to Gide remarkable. The element of "diplomacy" (as you call it—it would be better called decorum) is absolutely inevitable in this case, and takes nothing away from your letter. I would like to put this letter in its entirety in an appendix to my book, if you are agreeable. In the letter to Mr. Paz, there are some excellent passages, but I have such an aversion to his rhetoric, his duplicity, his stubbornness, etc., that he casts a shadow even over your letter. I am impatiently awaiting your book *In Defense of the USSR*.

The French translation of my autobiography is not just "careless," but outrageous from beginning to end. It is more a joke than a translation—not a single sentence is my own. I even thought of suing, but the French courts always decide in favor of the proprietor, in this case the publisher. I finally made Parijanine come to Prinkipo; he spent a month with me, and every day we worked together on the translation of my *History*, which was written and translated into French infinitely better than my autobiography.

You have suggested to me a collection or anthology of my works, and you say you are ready to take on this task yourself. I obviously can't help being delighted by your intention, though we would have to find a publisher willing to pay sufficiently for your work. Several years ago the Nouvelle Revue Francaise publishing house proposed something of this nature, but I was then absorbed in writing my *History*. Perhaps they would still be interested. Needless to say, you have complete freedom to dispose of my "author's rights."

(I will answer your questions in the order you have put

them.) We have no news from Sergei, absolutely none. You can easily understand the effect this has on N.I.

So that you may better understand my position on the events of June and on the new perspectives, I am sending you my draft theses[229] for *your own information* and eventual criticism. These theses must still be discussed collectively before being published.

A few words on Belgian matters. I do not know Hennaut personally, but in the past I have done everything I could to reach an agreement with him. He seems to be a charlatan, unworthy of any trust. People like him will join when they have no other choice; he will not be convinced by words. As for Vereecken (you referred to Lesoil by mistake), he is an inveterate sectarian despite his many valuable qualities. I am in correspondence with him, and I am using all my efforts to bring him back towards us. Lesoil is not a sectarian at all, but he is, alas, very sick and extremely depressed; he needs a long rest. Young Dauge shows a great deal of energy, but he has a stomach ulcer which now and again paralyzes him completely. What a shame!

Here is what I know of the Italian, Ambroggi. He openly declared himself a Bordigist at the time of Bordiga's last visit to Moscow; it was as a Bordigist that he then came to see me. I have, moreover, never understood the real reasons for his visit, and the fact that nobody bothered him astonished me somewhat. At least one of these scoundrels would have to be shown in his true light.

Hearty greetings.

Yours,
L. Trotsky

P.S. In about eight days you will receive a visit from the American comrade, Muste, who is a very serious comrade and of great value. He spent about a week here with us, during which we discussed and worked together. I will be very happy if you get along with him. He is a former Calvinist minister. Now he is a revolutionary Marxist. He is traveling with his wife.

Yours,
L. T.

JULY 6, 1936

Dear V. L.:

I am sending you a draft appeal on the subject of the prisoners and exiles of the USSR. Could you try to collect signatures in favor of this draft (if need be, you may change or adapt it as you wish)? I find the quotation from *Pravda* very important: it is a bad omen. In addition it is new proof of the fact that it is essentially *our* comrades who are the object of the purges.

You will obviously do what you can. I am sending this draft to a whole list of other addresses.

Yours,
L. *Trotsky*

JULY 30, 1936

Dear Victor Lvovich:

I received your letter of July 27, written after a conversation with our American friend [A. J. Muste]. Unfortunately, I cannot agree with you. I am afraid that your approach to problems is too artistic, too psychological—that is, not political enough. Moreover, a number of your reactions are based on a misunderstanding of the history of our activities here during the last seven and a half years. Basically, you accuse me of sectarianism. I cannot accept your reproach. I think that your own brief personal experience, if correctly understood, completely refutes the accusation. It is much easier to unite people in order to aid deportees and prisoners than it is to unite them for the social revolution. You have a name and authority on two counts: as a revolutionary, and as a man who has just escaped from Stalin's clutches. It would seem that it should be easier for you than for anyone else to unite broad circles—without sectarianism—for an international campaign against the Stalinist assassins. And yet in one of your recent letters you complain that your efforts remain fruitless. Yours is not the first such experience. Is it an accident? No, it is no accident. Our allegedly sectarian organizations are also conducting a struggle to defend the deportees. They are even the only ones to be doing so. But the efforts to broaden the struggle—efforts which I fully agreed with and which I aided in every way that I could—have not to this day produced the slightest result. Do you think that the philistines who cannot be moved even over a problem as acute as that of the Stalinist repressions can find a place in a revolutionary proletarian party? I do not think so. Today our task is not only to issue general condemnations against sectarianism. *It is necessary to demonstrate through experience that another road is possible.* To this day, all those who have sought another road have simply left us and passed into the other camp. Those are the facts, dear Victor Lvovich; and I am in the habit of judging according to the facts, not according to general considerations.

A little while ago you were reproaching us for having an incorrect attitude toward the "revolutionary syndicalists." I replied that I do not know the address of those people and that *La Revolution proletarienne* is only a boardinghouse for the disabled. After which, you left for Paris. Did you find any revolutionary syndicalists there? Please let me know their address. Did you find any revolutionary fire burning in Louzon's hearth? If so, I am ready to immediately do everything necessary to bring us closer to them. Let me know concretely what must be done. Unfortunately, after your trip to Paris you did not say a word about the "revolutionary syndicalists."

Now you speak to me of the Teachers' Federation, where there are several hundred sympathizers who could be attracted to us if only we could "win their confidence." Here your reproach is completely unjustified and incorrect. I lived for a whole year in France among those people of the Teachers' Federation.[230] I had interminable conversations with them; we corresponded; and we even organized a veritable little conference with all the leaders of the federation. Obviously neither I nor my closest friends could become more intelligent, more refined, or more handsome, just for their benefit. But we did do everything we could to attract them to work with us. They came to see us and then found a thousand excuses to slip away. Their secret in fact is quite simple: *they are petty-bourgeois right to the marrow;* their homes, their gardens, and their automobiles are a thousand times closer to their hearts than the destiny of the proletariat, even if they still retain terribly radical ideas in their heads. I have visited some of their homes, I have seen the way they live—and I have not only seen it, I have also smelled it. Pardon me, Victor Lvovich, that smell does not deceive me. To count on those people is like building on sand. There are revolutionary elements among the young teachers who are looking for the correct road. But the leadership plays a reactionary role by preventing the youth from making their way toward us. That is the reason why I flogged these gentlemen in one of my latest articles, and I will grab hold of the next opportunity to whip them even harder.

You mention Martinet. I had already mentioned him in my letter to you. If you succeed in convincing him, that will be very good. You also speak of Dommanget. I know him personally. He joined us, then quit. He is a good enough historian; if he can give our magazine a little article on Babeuf once a year, that would be excellent. I doubt that he is capable of anything more. You also speak of Simone Weil.[231] I know her very well; I had long conversations with her. For a while she more or less sympathized with us, then she lost faith in the proletariat and in Marxism; she wrote some foolish idealistic articles in defense of "individuality"; in a word; she evolved toward Radicalism. It is possible that she will swing left again. But is that worth dwelling on? In any case, there is not a single new name in your proposals. We have already had a lot of experience—negative experience—with all those people. Each one of them has a thousand reasons that prevent him from joining us and devoting himself to revolutionary work: our style is poor, our translations are bad, our polemics are very sharp, etc. These people speak of everything except what is essential: *the program, the strategy, the struggle to win the masses.* Must we adapt our political line to this gang of good-for-nothings? No, that would be a fundamentally wrong orientation. We must find the means of reaching the *workers* while avoiding the former revolutionaries and even elbowing them out of our way.

Here is a fresh example. A few months ago, our comrades tried to establish a syndicalist monthly with the people of the Teachers Federation. Well, nothing came of it. These mediocre petty bourgeois—really, I can find no other word for them—have no taste for struggle. Meeting in order to gossip about revolutionary topics, setting up a kind of talk-shop for tired radicals, that they are ready to do. But that's not what *we* want to do.

I have heard many times what you write me about my "meddling" and about the necessity of "collective" actions. And do you know from whom, Victor Lvovich? From those who requested my intervention but did not obtain it because I disagreed with them. There are many people like that. The echo of their complaints has reached you. You speak to me of Rosmer. You know how highly I regard him. But why has he left us? He got into a conflict with Molinier. The conflict became bitter. I had nothing at all to do with the affair; I did not even know anything about it. Rosmer and Naville tried to have Molinier expelled, but only won the support of a small minority within the organization. Rosmer then asked me for my help. I answered approximately as follows: "Even if it appeared obvious to me that it was necessary to expel Molinier, I could do nothing from here; *it is up to you to convince the majority of your organization.*" After that, Rosmer broke off all political relations with us and left the organization. I am ready to do everything necessary to reestablish cooperation with him. I do not think, however, that he is suited for membership in the revolutionary movement at the present time. As a contributor to a magazine he is very valuable. Let him write his second volume on the war; that will be an enormous gift to the working class. But Rosmer is not a political fighter, and sharp differences would quickly develop between him and the revolutionary youth. You judge a priori while I speak from seven and a half years of uninterrupted experience.

You speak to me again about Treint. Do you know that I asked him to come to Prinkipo, that he spent nearly a month with us, and that I had to wage a stiff battle with the Pazes, Rosmers, Navilles, and many others, so that he could work with us, as he did at one time? But alas, he was a madman—not in the figurative but the literal sense of the word. He broke with us, not because we prevented him from expressing his obsessions, but because we did not agree with them. So what was to be done? A nonsectarian policy consists among other things in freeing ourselves in time from sectarians who prevent us from finding the road to the workers. Thus, at a certain point we freed ourselves from the sectarian Vereecken in Belgium; without him and against him we have won over an important number of workers, and now he is joining them. Perhaps Treint too will return to us some day, when we are stronger. But adapting our political line now to Treint, to madmen and sectarians, would mean cutting ourselves off from the road to the workers.

Let's go on now to the question of Nin. Some people (for example, Rosmer) consider my very sharp criticism of his policies to be sectarian. If it is sectarian, then Marxism is sectarian, since it is the doctrine of class struggle and not of class collaboration. The present events in Spain in particular show how criminal was Nin's alliance with Azana:[232] the Spanish workers will now pay with thousands of lives for the reactionary and shameful conduct of the People's Front, which has continued to support with the people's money an army commanded by the executioners of the proletariat. Here it is a question, dear Victor Lvovich, not of minor details but of the very essence of revolutionary socialism. If Nin today were to pull himself together and realize how discredited he is in the eyes of the workers, if he should draw all the necessary conclusions, then we would welcome him as a comrade; but we cannot permit the spirit of cronyism in politics.

From your amendments to my theses on the revolutionary upsurge, I got the idea that some important groups will be breaking away on the left of the Socialist and Communist parties (I have already alluded to that but too succinctly). I unfortunately cannot accept your other amendments, because I don't consider them correct. A marvelous historian of the Russian revolution, you refuse, I do not know why, to apply its essential lessons to other countries. Everything you say about the People's Front applies to the bloc of the Mensheviks and Social Revolutionaries with the Cadets (the Russian "Radicals"). And yet we led a merciless struggle against that People's Front, a struggle which alone made our victory possible.

Your practical propositions concerning Spain are excellent and correspond completely to *our* line. But try to find a dozen people outside of our "sectarian" organization who will accept your propositions, not in words but in deeds. The fact that you make these magnificent *practical* propositions bears witness in my opinion to the fact that we stand on common ground, and I am patiently waiting for you to compare your a priori conceptions with the living political experience, and to draw the necessary conclusions. I do not doubt for a single moment that your conclusions will correspond with ours, which we have formulated *collectively*, in *different* countries, basing ourselves on the experience of *great* events. Despite our so-called sectarianism, we are steadily growing and expanding, while those who criticize us have been able to build nothing.

That's enough for today. I have answered your frankness completely frankly. I think that we will follow that path in the future, to our mutual advantage.

Cordial wishes.

Yours,
L. *Trotsky*

P.S. A word about your translation.

I will supply the corrections to the chapter on the *family* [in *The Revolution Betrayed*], so it would be better not to translate it for the time being. I will send you the last part of the book Tuesday, in five days.

AUGUST 18, 1936

Dear V.L.:

N.I. and I have just returned from a short trip to the seaside, as we wanted a "rest" from politics, but politics (and what politics!) joined us on our trip. We learned during our trip of the attack on our apartment. Two and then four fascists (including their chief of propaganda) followed us closely in a car for three or four hundred kilometers. We lived beside the sea in a [illegible] situation. The chief of the Norwegian secret police paid us a visit to ask some polite questions. Then the Tass news agency burst out with the odious declaration that shocked the world.[233] I am preparing to write something on the subject of this amalgam.

What you write me about the Spanish Anarchists, or more exactly the Catalan Anarchists, is completely correct, and I am delighted to the extent that this expresses our unity of opinions on that *essential* question at this time. Unfortunately, you and I are only spectators. At this time, the most important thing would be to find organic forms of collaboration between the POUM and the trade unions in Catalonia (juntas, councils, soviets, action committees?), even at the price of big organizational concessions. But one can only solve those problems on the spot.

Your comments about the translation of my book prove that you are extremely conscientious about this task. You are such a good stylist that there is no need at all for you to check with me on the "freeness" of your translation; I fully endorse your formulations in advance. If anything I have written is unclear as to *meaning*, that is another matter.

I received your timely letter in which you told me that your Soviet citizenship had been revoked, but to tell you the truth, I hadn't thought that could prevent you from going to Blum's kingdom, where, moreover, Blum reigns least of all.

"Sectarianism," in the general meaning that you give to the word, is quite simply a psychological reaction because of age and an extremely *difficult* development (fascism, Comintern, Soviet bureaucracy, People's Front, etc.). It is necessary to pass through all these difficulties and all these stupidities with patience (which of course does not mean passivity).

I am in a hurry. This is my first letter after a two-week interruption.

Warmest greetings.

Yours,
L. *Trotsky*

P.S. I am very happy with your comments on the theory of the state. I myself had the impression that I had succeeded in clarifying certain points. ■

Our kind of optimism[234]

April 27, 1936

Dear Comrade van Riel:

I apologize for not having answered your previous letters: sudden illnesses, frequent changes in my general condition, and overwork got in the way.

I share completely your opinion that we should drive the work of the Fourth International ahead with all our might, and that we have the best possibilities to do so. It is not correct that the situation in America is "very unclear and confused." Our American friends have been, and remain, one of the most loyal points of support of the Fourth International. They have never failed to prove it: first, by ardently following all the disputed questions in the European sections and learning a great deal from them, and second, by giving, and continuing to give, material and moral support to different sections.

As you can see from my enclosed letter to Comrade Spanjer, we can hope that the banner of the Fourth International will be quite triumphant, precisely in America. You are probably aware that we are now taking an important step forward in Belgium. From several private reports, it is evident that our Polish comrades, who have also entered the Social Democratic party, have in the meantime not been idle, and the events now unfolding in Poland give us cause for great hopes. In a word, I too do not see the slightest reason for pessimism. Quite the contrary. Our optimism, however, cannot be purely formal, that is, bureaucratic, but must be dynamic and dialectical. We have to know how to take developments and use them just as they arise in the nature of things, and not as we would like to have them in our own conception and especially for our own convenience. In order to avoid any misunderstanding, I would like to emphasize here that *I do not at all mean to say that our Dutch party should imitate the American method.* But it is necessary to learn from the American experience, without prior assumptions. And there will be plenty to learn! Of that we can be sure. There is also a great deal to be learned from the experience of the ILP in England. This party wanted to turn its back not only on the Labour Party but also on the trade unions and the Co-op Party. In doing so, they had no program of their own. The last conference proved, however, that you can't get very far with pure *negativism* and *conservatism*. The ILP finds itself in continual retreat and in internal disarray.

I'm sorry that I have to restrict myself to these brief observations. A job that can't be put off is making a claim on my time. ■

Walter Held's thesis on the evolution of the Comintern[235]

May 26 and June 18, 1936

MAY 26, 1936

Dear Friend:

To supplement yesterday's conversation:

1. I think it would be more advisable to set aside all further statements concerning the Soviet Union since they will have to be presented as self-contained theses anyway, and we have to avoid duplication of effort. It would suffice if you incorporated these things in short sentences as taken for granted.

2. A rather wide-ranging concluding section should certainly be appended, however—an overview of the current situations of the Comintern parties and the undeniable growth, plus their electoral successes. The correct assessment of these successes: in view of the crisis and the fear of the threatening war, the masses swing to the left and find there the only gateway known to them, that of the Comintern. But while the masses hope that the Comintern will rescue them from the dangers of war, the Comintern sets about becoming the main political instrument of the imperialist war. The Comintern thereby supersedes the Second International in the service of bourgeois democracy, and with it, imperialism; but this also brings big contradictions with it.

3. Our perspectives and tasks should at the same time also be more clearly depicted. Several of our sections have entered the Socialist parties. This is proving to be but a brief stage.

The workers are now gathering around the Comintern. The most important struggle against social imperialism will be the struggle against the Comintern. Since the Comintern is now drawing the workers to itself with indisputable success, we will have the task of freeing these workers from the Comintern leadership. The ways and means of this work will be very differentiated and diverse, according to each country's whole development and peculiarities. The most important precondition for future successes in this area is to observe developments with open eyes, assemble material, and study all of the conflicting tendencies in order to be able to intervene energetically and in good time.

Without this last part the theses would have a purely academic character, i.e., would be better suited to a Marxist university than to a political gathering.

With best wishes for both of you.

Yours,
L. Trotsky

JUNE 18, 1936

Dear Comrades:

Comrade Held has worked out a draft thesis on the Third International. I find his effort sufficiently thorough and serious to recommend it as the basis for discussion and possible inclusion in an international conference. Of course, it still must be painstakingly gone over by each section and appropriate suggestions for changes sent as soon as possible to the IS as well as to the author. Especially important in my eyes are those suggestions *related to the particular situation of the Communist Party in a given country.* Even if all these ideas cannot be incorporated into the text of the resolution, they will still not fail to influence the final draft of the text. ∎

Let's end this nonsense[236]

May 28, 1936

Dear Friend:

I want to expand on my proposal for important and timely extracts from the resolutions of the first four congresses [of the Communist International]. We must give thought to the program of the Fourth International and at least begin with a respectable, i.e., a precisely worked out, platform. Perhaps as soon as the next conference we could, if not definitively finalize, at least approve such a platform as the basis of international discussion. To achieve this end means painstakingly collecting and arranging everything of importance concerning imperialism, democracy, fascism, war, revolution, parliamentarism, the trade union question, the role of the party, etc., etc. Later on, this work could be finished in a commission.

If you accept the proposal (and this would be indicated by your immediately setting to work on the relevant material), it would be necessary to take into account the American and Dutch platforms, our [1933] eleven points, the [1934] theses on war, etc., in order to select the best formulations. I have already noticed many times that we (I by no means exempt myself from this) frequently give new formulations to a question every time it comes up, ignoring what we had written previously in a better and more precise fashion. It is now time to put an end to this nonsense once and for all. This work should be much more important than something on the People's Front and fascism.

Yours,
L. Trotsky

'State capitalism' data sought[237]

June 7, 1936

To the AK of the IKD

Dear Comrades:

1. Is it true that there is a lively discussion going on in the SAP on the question of affiliation to the Comintern? The significance of this question is far greater than the significance of the SAP itself. The collapse of the SAP would mean the automatic ruination of the London International and would increase considerably and directly the opportunities for the Fourth International. We thus have the greatest interest in intervening in the current discussion within the SAP *in our own way*. The first thing would of course be to bring the discussion into the open. Fifty sensational lines in *Unser Wort* and in all the other newspapers of the Fourth International would do for a start. But the announcement must be sharply, clearly, and bitingly written and meant not just for the Germans, but for all the sections, so that the English, for instance, can make good use of it.

2. In the closing chapter of my book on the USSR I am now tackling the question of "state capitalism." I would like to have the most detailed and recent data on the German economy under the Nazis. Which of the comrades follows the details about this? I cannot put the matter off, and so I would need to go through as little material as is necessary. I would be thankful for any help in this regard.

The crux of the matter for me is as follows: people say "state capitalism" without making clear just what they mean by that. State railroads are state capitalism. On the basis of state subsidies, certain industries are state capitalism. Industrial associations under the control of the state are state capitalism. And the entirely nationalized and plan-directed Soviet economy is supposedly also state capitalism. But I will show that what is unfolding economically in the USSR could only have come about as the result of a revolution. For there the state is not the head commissioner, not the *go-between*, etc., but instead the *owner*. ∎

The international conference and the Dutch section[238]

June 16, 1936

Dear Comrades:

I have received a letter from Comrade Sneevliet on your behalf, which, I admit, troubles me greatly. It concerns the participation of representatives of your party in the next editorial commission in Berne. According to this letter, your party declines to send delegates because of the travel expenses, and withholds its opinion about the decisions that will be taken at this meeting.

In this dark hour, I do not need to underline the extreme importance of this meeting. Furthermore, the expenses are not at all excessive. In any case, other organizations, which are certainly no richer than you, have considered it their duty to participate. I could also mention the American section, which has been accused, even though wrongly, of violating the agreement it gave to the Open Letter, and which has nonetheless, designated its delegates after the first invitation, and now only awaits a telegram to send them to Europe.

I must also add this: the Dutch party took charge of the secretariat of the Fourth International. This secretariat, unfortunately, has not functioned at all, something which has produced a certain astonishment on the part of numerous sections. I will not say anything more about this now, however, even though my repeated letters to the secretaries have generally remained without response. You cannot ignore the fact that the absence of any Dutch delegate at a meeting where there will be a responsible American delegate, at a higher cost of money and time, would produce a painful impression.

There is another circumstance which tends to add to our concern. In effect, Comrade Sneevliet informs me that you have decided to participate in the deliberations of the organizations of the London Bureau which will take place a few weeks from now(!), as well as to propose that the IS take an identical position. How can this be explained? The representatives of the Dutch party have neither the time nor the money to participate in the meeting of their own international organization. You do not reply to our proposal to prepare the international conference. And yet now you decide to participate in an eventual conference of a different organization which is deeply hostile to us. The simple listing of these elements can only poison the atmosphere around the Dutch party and, I fear, in that party itself, by nourishing dangerous theories, suppositions, etc. It must be said openly that no one who thinks politically would explain this conduct by invoking financial and technical reasons, which are in general secondary. Rather, one will seek, and with good reason, for deeper political causes.

I am certain that in all of our international organization, one could find not one section, not one group, perhaps not even a single comrade inclined to take part in the deliberations of the London Bureau. As for me, I cannot understand how, after all that has happened, one can still conceive of this idea. In any case, I hope that a discussion can be organized at Berne and that a common decision will be arrived at.

This is why I permit myself to ask you earnestly, once more, to reconsider your decision about the Berne conference, and to send at least one representative there. As far as I am concerned, this is the only possibility of avoiding an international discussion on this extremely urgent question. For, once this discussion is started—and for some time now voices have been raised from many sides asking that it be started—it could not but have consequences for the internal life of the Dutch section. And in any case, I do not want to believe that the differences have become so sharp that they cannot be resolved within the frame-work of an international discussion.

As for the delay, everyone is ready to take your wishes into account as much as possible. In case you do not send more than one representative to Berne, a larger meeting with two or more of your representatives could be held closer to you with the aim of arriving at definitive decisions. The method is of no importance. The question, however, is to know if we have a "general council," if we value it at all, and if we recognize the importance of its decisions, especially now, on the eve of major events in a whole series of European countries. ■

Congratulations on a good publishing job[239]

June 18, 1936

Dear Comrade Shachtman:

The book sent to me, *The Third International After Lenin*, really gave me *great* pleasure. An extraordinarily good edition, in every respect: your introduction, so important and informative, and the irreplaceable explanatory notes only cause me to regret that eight years ago I had to write the book in haste, and thus could not be as comprehensive and exact as I would have liked. Unfortunately that can't be helped now. The typographical quality is really splendid and does Pioneer Publishers the greatest honor. Please transmit my best and most heartfelt thanks to all the collaborators, from the typesetters to the general editor and back again.

I am reminded that six years ago I looked a bit skeptically upon your plans to establish a publishing house in order to publish my books. Now I have to concede that my unjustly arrived at skepticism has been "harshly" punished, in a way that makes me very optimistic.

For the book *The Stalin School of Falsification* I will have to make a few, very short, additions; at least one is very important. Am I right in thinking that I still have time to do this?

You are, of course, following the events in France and Belgium with the necessary attentiveness. Our friends will now have to pass a very hard test. They are already standing in the center of the persecutions and baiting anyway, and that is not a bad start. How the Belgians are getting on I don't know yet, but I believe that they are doing their bit and will emerge from this strike movement with a significant gain. Just this little bit for now.

Yours,
L. *Trotsky*

N.I. [Natalia Sedova] sends very cordial greetings. ■

The London Bureau and the Fourth International[240]

July 1936

The rearmament of Germany and the Italian invasion of Ethiopia mark the end of the postwar epoch and the official beginning of a new prewar epoch. With the strike movement in France and Belgium in June 1936, a new revolutionary wave set in. All opportunist, social patriotic, and centrist-pacifist parties and groups are now caught in a wedge between the approaching war and the approaching revolution. The first result will be the crushing of the splinter groups which are federated in the so-called London Bureau.

The events of the past two years have fully established the Marxian evaluation of the parties and groups of the London Bureau as conservative-centrist organizations which are utterly incapable of resisting the pressure of reaction and chauvinism. The mere enumeration of the facts removes every shadow of doubt on this point.

The SAP, the driving force of the London federation, incited a split in the Dutch RSAP for the sole purpose of dragging this party onto the road of centrism; it entered into the People's Front of the German emigration, the most lifeless, miserable, and deceptive of all the People's Fronts; it undertook the hypocritical defense of the Stalinist bureaucracy against the Bolshevik-Leninists and in reality waged a struggle exclusively against the Fourth International.

The Independent Labour Party attempted in the Italo-Ethiopian conflict to take a correct principled position. However, the pacifist-parliamentary clique of Maxton and Company, which regards the party merely as a handy tool, forced it by means of a rude and brutal ultimatum back into a pacifist prostration; and at the same time the party adopted special measures against "factions," i.e., in effect against the revolutionary Marxian wing. In connection with the problem of the USSR, the ILP fails to distinguish between the October Revolution and the Bonapartist bureaucracy, keeps silent about the crimes of the bureaucracy, and in particular heralds the servile compilation of the Webbs, which is calculated solely to lead the workers astray as to the real ways and methods of the proletarian revolution.

The Spanish Workers Party of "Marxist Unification" (POUM) put in the forefront of its platform the "democratic-socialist revolution" and thereby utterly abandoned the theory of Marx and Lenin and the lessons of the October Revolution, both of which demonstrate that the proletarian revolution cannot develop within the framework of bourgeois democracy, that the "synthesis" of bourgeois democracy and socialism is nothing else than Social Democracy, that is to say, the organized betrayal of the historic interests of the proletariat. In full accord with its own platform, the party of "Marxist Unification" found its place in the Spanish People's Front, as a tail to the kite of the left bourgeois parties, which include the present president of the Republic, Azana. The subsequent criticism of the People's Front by the leaders of the party does not in the least degree mitigate their crimes, for revolutionary parties are judged by the way in which they act in moments of crisis and not by what they say about themselves once the crisis is past. During the fateful years of the Spanish revolution, the party of Maurin-Nin showed itself absolutely incapable of passing from petty-bourgeois talk to proletarian deeds.

In France the bloc between Doriot—who has just founded the "French People's Party," now that the fascist leagues are dissolved—and Marceau Pivert against the Fourth International quickly manifested its reactionary character. The mayor of Saint-Denis, Doriot, under whose protection the latest conference of the London Bureau took place, very soon thereafter passed over, with his organization, into the camp of reaction. Marceau Pivert today functions as the special agent of Leon Blum in matters relating to the left—Leon Blum who through the bourgeois police confiscates the only revolutionary paper in France and countenances the prosecution of the followers of the Fourth International by bourgeois judges.

It is unnecessary to make any special observation with regard to the Swedish party, which does not pass beyond the framework of provincial pacifism, not to mention the Italian Maximalists or the groups in Poland, Rumania, and Bulgaria, which do not possess the slightest qualitative or quantitative significance.

The Stockholm Youth Bureau, affiliated with the London Bureau, carries on the politics of the SAP, i.e., of equivocation and falsehood, which has an especially demoralizing and pernicious effect on the new generation of revolutionaries. The real character of the Stockholm Bureau may be best indicated by the fact that in order to pursue unmolested its friendly politics toward the worst opportunist and patriotic groupings, it took it upon itself to expel from its own ranks the representative of the Bolshevik-Leninists, who was in the minority in the Bureau and sought for himself only the right of free criticism. By this act the leaders of the London and Stockholm Bureaus have shown even the politically blind that there neither is, nor can be, a place in these organizations for revolutionaries.

The international conferences of both these bureaus represents half diplomatic, half parliamentary institutions and assemblages, after the image of the Second International but on a much smaller scale, which serve no other purpose than to furnish right-centrist organizations with a decorative international cover, behind which they may pursue their national opportunist politics. The declarations and the so-called decisions of these international conferences, which are in themselves thoroughly eclectic, exercise no influence on the actual course of the affiliated national organizations.

What the "international Marxian basis" and the "revolutionary homogeneity" propagated by these conferences really amounts to is shown in the fact that no agreement exists in this midget International on a single question of principle or of current politics. In the Italo-Ethiopian conflict, for example, the ILP of England is an opponent of sanctions by the League of Nations and condemns any collaboration of the labor movement with the League of Nations. The Italian Maximalists, on the other hand, implore the League of Nations, whose driving force is England, to sharpen the sanctions against Italy. The Spanish section of the London Bureau, for its part, signs the bourgeois program of the Spanish "People's Front," which calls for a foreign policy in conformity with the principles and methods of the League of Nations. The same confusion prevails in the position of the London Bureau toward the treacherous policy of the People's Front of the Stalinists. While the last session of the Bureau greets the People's Front, while the Spanish section has participated in the Spanish People's Front, and while the German and Italian sections participate in the People's Front comedies among the German and Italian emigration, the ILP and obviously also the Socialist Party of Sweden reject the policy of the People's Front (which they recognize internationally!) for their own countries. The ILP even goes so far as to refuse candidates of the Labour Party its support against bourgeois candidates. But the London Bureau becomes enthusiastic over the French People's Front, which elects bourgeois a la Herriot to parliament with the votes of Socialists and Communists.

It is enough to say that in May 1935, at the last congress of the NAP, the only mass organization affiliated to the London Bureau, not a single voice of protest was raised against breaking off relations of this party with the London Bureau. This eloquent fact proves beyond controversy that the connection with the London Bureau bears a purely nominal character, which imposes not the slightest obligation on anyone, does not manifest itself in the inner life of the section and consequently cannot promote the formation even of a trace of a left wing.

The parties of the London Bureau have neither a distinctive theory, nor distinctive politics. They eke out an existence between the left wing of the Second International and the Third International in its newest phase, a phase which represents fraternization with their own bourgeoisie in the ostensible interest of the workers' state, defense of the democratic "fatherland," the antifascist People's Front, etc. Thus they constitute a new edition, in miniature, of the Two-and-a-Half International. During the past two years the London Bureau did not take a clear revolutionary position on a single question, had no fructifying influence on the labor movement by any of its activity, and not only did not attract the hostile attention of the Second and Third Internationals but on the contrary grew closer to them in their baiting of the Fourth International. Today, when the two old Internationals have drawn so near each other, the existence of an intermediate International becomes pure nonsense.

The interests of the Fourth International, i.e., of the proletarian revolution, exclude any compromise in principle, and compliance or toleration for parties, groups, and individual politicians who constantly misuse the names of Marx, Engels, Lenin, Luxemburg, and Liebknecht for the purposes which are in direct contradiction to the ideas and actions of these teachers and warriors.

As the specter of the new war began to take on flesh and blood, the London Bureau under the leadership of the SAP advanced the meaningless slogan of a "new Zimmerwald" in place of a Marxist program, a Bolshevik policy, and the selection of revolutionary cadres. All those who are frightened by revolutionary difficulties hasten to seize upon this apparently Leninist slogan. A few months have passed and even the initiators have forgotten their own discovery. The task of building the new international on the granite foundation of principle remains in all its magnitude. Not so lightly shall we find our way through this historic situation.

The leaders of the most important organizations of the London Bureau are not adolescents or novices. All have a long history of opportunism, pacifism, and centrist shifting behind them. Neither the war, nor the October Revolution, nor the destruction of the German and Austrian proletariat, nor the treacherous turn of the Comintern, nor the approach of a new war, have taught them; rather, they have served to demoralize them. There is not the slightest reason to expect their revolutionary reeducation. The direct duty of proletarian revolutionists is, therefore, the systematic and uncompromising exposure of the hesitations, equivocations, and hypocrisies of the London Bureau as the nearest and most immediate obstacle in the way of the further building of the Fourth International. ■

Deep differences with the Dutch comrades[241]

July 7, 1936

Dear Comrade Shachtman:

I have just received your letter of July 5. Muste left Oslo yesterday, and by now you have certainly met him in Amsterdam.

In order for Muste to be able to participate in the conference, it would have to take place toward the end of this month. I do not see when you could find the time to come here before the conference. Wouldn't it be better for you to return to Geneva and not come here until after the conference?

(Muste's *statement* has a completely objective character and cannot possibly raise difficulties or differences. In any case, you will still have the possibility of consulting with Muste in this regard.)

The most important problem seems to me to be the attitude of the Dutch comrades. No one is going to understand or explain it as anything but preparation for their going over to the London Bureau. I agree with Sneevliet that it is a matter of deep and perhaps decisive differences. Otherwise, the two Dutch comrades could not have completely neglected the work that they had agreed to undertake, failed to reply to letters, and now, boycott the conference and, in the bargain, want to reserve the right to take a public stand against the positions already adopted: all this constitutes an explicit indication of their desire to exclude themselves from the Fourth International.

A discussion has become inevitable. I had hoped that, through a collective meeting, we could give the eventual discussion the form of an internal debate. But, in so far as it appears that the Dutch comrades are looking to prepare their own party, slowly and imperceptibly, for a rupture with the Fourth International, the conference must take up the Dutch question in all its aspects. I reserve the right to present a detailed letter to the conference. We take this affair too seriously to imitate the methods of the London Bureau, where the Norwegian party [the NAP] was a member for a long time without really belonging. Belonging to an international organization does not only mean using its name, but also fulfilling all obligations.

I am certain that Muste and you have done all that was necessary to urge the Dutch comrades to change their unfortunate decision and participate in the conference. If you have not succeeded in this, I must give up all hope in this case and say simply: the Dutch party is now doing exactly the same thing that the OSP in de Kadt's time did when faced with the Declaration of Four. We want neither illusions nor fictions. We must know, yes or no, on whom we can count during the coming months and years. Of course, personal visits cannot take the place of regular ties. Besides which, I shall have to take a period of complete rest after the tiring work of the month of August.

There no longer is any question of a trip by Rous: it comes too late! For now, all our efforts must be concentrated on using the last week of July as efficiently as possible. All the necessary texts have been prepared and will be assembled at Geneva. If you return immediately, you will be able to do some important work with the English translations.

I hope that, in any case, dear friend, you will come to spend several days with me after the conference, so that we can discuss all that needs to be discussed. I rejoice in advance at your visit.

It goes without saying that I await an immediate response from you. ■

How the conference was and wasn't prepared[242]

July 17, 1936

Dear Comrade Muste:

I received your letters of July 11 and 12 at the same time and with great joy. Best thanks for the detailed nature of the letter on Holland and especially for the frankness and sharpness with which you criticize my stand in this question. Like you, I consider necessary a frank and sometimes even brutal language when it is a question of important and decisive matters and where diplomatic nuances can only call forth misunderstandings. Yet I believe that several misunderstandings have occurred in your judgment of my way of acting in the Dutch question.

1. You record a contradiction between my treatment of the Dutch question during my discussion with you and in my letter to Sha[chtman]. Everything necessary on this score is said in my letter to the Central Committee of the RSAP, copy of which is enclosed. During your stay here I hoped hourly that we would receive a reassuring letter from Holland which would remove all my doubts and misgivings in this vitally important question. This also explains why I employed such reserved language which expressed only part of my apprehensions. I could not, after all, explain the failure of the Dutch comrades to answer my letters exclusively by negligence. In the last letter, dated July 11, Sneevliet writes at the very beginning: "It is a fact that we have not yet got around to answering the letter of June 16 which arrived on June 19." All due respect to the fishermen's strike and to all other circumstances. But

that various sections must wait weeks on end because an urgent letter, containing the news of the arrival of the Americans, is left unanswered, and this for the n'th time, seems to me to be truly fatal. If it is negligence, then it does mean something that comes pretty close to indifference towards international affairs. The letter of Sha., which bore an informational and objective character, was the final occasion for an energetic intervention. What remains to be said on this point you can read in my letter to the Dutch CC.

2. It is also incorrect that there are no political differences. I reported to you on this point pretty much in detail and you will find concisely enumerated the points of difference, all of which seem to me fairly symptomatic, in the enclosed letter. I haven't the slightest inclination to exaggerate these differences. I firmly hope to overcome them by means of friendly discussions with the aid of experience. But I consider it impossible simply to close one's eyes to the disputed questions, for the facts are mightier than our pious wishes and if we do not now start to work on the points of difference, then under the pressure of events they may take on an explosive character.

3. In the letter to the Dutch I state what is necessary—in brief—on the French question. To attempt to explain the lack of interest in the most important revolutionary problems of our time by the fishermen's strike, is to me . . . inexplicable, at the very least. The conference, let us hope, will treat the French question as the main question. I believe the conference should make public a short appeal to the proletarian vanguard of the entire world, calling upon it to follow the events in France, and to come to the material and moral aid of the revolutionary vanguard, that is, the new party. Belgium should also be mentioned in this connection, for its fate is closely intertwined with that of France.

4. Every one of us will be very happy if we succeed in putting more order and system into the work of the International Secretariat. But in this point too I must remove, with all the necessary emphasis, the false notions about the past and illusions about the future:

a. All of us unanimously charged Comrades Schmidt and Sneevliet with the work of the secretariat. Why? Because they were experienced comrades with international authority and because they based themselves upon a substantial organization and could thus also more easily take hold of the technical work. On our part, that is, the IS (myself included) decided to put all our forces at the disposal of Comrades Sneevliet and Schmidt. We came to an understanding with our American friends permitting the publication of appeals on a series of questions by the Amsterdam Bureau in agreement with the Geneva Secretariat, where no new, unknown or disputed questions were involved. When we sought to come to an understanding with Amsterdam, nothing came of it. Why? Is somebody's "individualism" at fault? Systematic, not individualistic, not anarchistic work consists—does it not—in the assigned organ producing the necessary initiative or in taking over the initiative of others and in putting things on the right track. But as a rule we did not receive any reply to the most important letters. Do you perhaps think, Comrade Muste, that we are less occupied than the comrades in Amsterdam? No, just as much! The latter, however, forced us to write two, three and four letters instead of one, thereby engendering wearisome discussions about why things were not effected, instead of answering us in time in a few lines.

At the time of the acutest crisis in France, when the *Commune* arbitrarily proclaimed itself a section of the Fourth International, we endeavored to obtain from the Amsterdam Bureau a suitable intervention. I wrote letter after letter. In order to facilitate the work of the Amsterdam secretaries, I even wrote a draft for the letter that they were to send to Paris. But to this day I have not received a reply. I do not know if this method can be called "individualistic" but in any case it is certainly inadmissible.

In all questions I have stood and continue to stand in closest touch with the IS. I wrote letters fairly often and I always send a copy to Sneevliet who is, moreover, a member of the IS. He never reacted to these letters, except for the American question and even here very belatedly, that is, when the matter had already been decided de facto over there.

Can you kindly advise me how one should have acted in such a situation? Or should one quit acting altogether because Comrades Sneevliet and Schmidt did not fulfill the obligations they had taken over? The reasons for this nonfunctioning of the Amsterdam Bureau may be as important as one wishes; but after all, great events and disputed questions cannot be brought to a standstill. We must react to them if we bear a certain responsibility. In what manner? By stating one's opinion. I know no other way.

In the American question, the discussion lasted from one and a half to two years, the Franco-Belgian prediscussion included. Schmidt was *for* the French turn, Sneevliet *against*, the IS for (with the exception of Dubois, who was "against," moreover, in all questions and who then gave up the work altogether). There were certain shadings of opinion on the American question in the IS, and among a few comrades there were vacillations. Not all of them read English and follow American developments. To have taken a formal decision under these conditions would not have been of great value. In any case, the supporters of entry in the IS were in the majority. We could easily have outvoted Sneevliet and sent a formal decision to America. But it is precisely in this extraordinarily important question that such a decision did not seem suitable to us. So we gave Comrade Sneevliet, the representative of the minority, the full liberty of expressing his opinion. Nor did he fail to make ample use of this freedom. Against the Belgians he even took a position publicly in his paper, despite the fact that he is aware that he is entirely alone in the IS in this question (with the exception of Dubois who, de facto, has long ago ceased to work there). On what side, then, is the "individualism"?

You yourself, Comrade Muste, bring up as an example of the defective organizational work the inadequate preparation of the conference, and you adduce the fact that you found no letter at hand in London, etc. I gladly take up this question too, for it proves the *opposite* of what you presuppose. Since April 11 (!!) we have been hard at work on this matter with Braun and Held. Dozens upon dozens of letters were sent off without counting the work on the theses, documents, etc. The Parisian members of the IS also did everything in their power. We exerted ourselves to foresee all the details and to combine them in advance in order to remove unnecessary friction. *But from April on, we were unable to fix the date because the Amsterdam comrades simply left the letters unanswered, in spite of having promised to reply, then raised new objections again and again and left the whole question of the conference in constant obscurity.* Therefore we had to do three, four and five times as much work and still we could not get to any precision.

Braun wrote to America that he would cable the required date of arrival in Europe. The affair, however, dragged on interminably and we were unable to send a cable. You can easily imagine the disquietude that reigned among us here. You and Sha. then decided to depart without a cable (and I salute your decision with all my heart), but your arrival without a previous cable from us was a surprise and we were unable to provide you with an itinerary in London for we ourselves did not know where and when and even *if* the conference would take place. That the Dutch comrades charge us on this point with inadequate preparation is not only unjustified in my opinion, but I consider it quite unheard of, and I raise my voice in most decided protest!

We took everything into the bargain, calmly and patiently, for the cause itself stands, with us, above all the lost time and effort, but *if the Amsterdamers do throw the question of the inadequacies of the international work on the floor of the conference, then I shall demand that this letter be read to the conference.*

b. I said above: nobody should have any illusions about the future. The leadership of a revolutionary International in such a stormy historical period cannot function in the same way as the leadership—let us say—of a national trade union or cooperative. We are separated territorially; every one of us has his opinion and will continue to want to express it. Events do not wait; at least, not always. Good collective work can be demanded only when every member of the leading bodies attentively follows the international events and replies as soon as possible to letters and proposals. Everything else can only have secondary importance. An automatism of leadership will not be attainable by us even at this conference.

The most important *psychological* precondition for profitable work of the leadership is that one really feels himself a part of the leadership, does not stand outside and does not, from time to time, proclaim his indignation.

5. What you report about the NAS, dear Comrade Muste, appears to me to be in no way satisfactory or reassuring. Quite the contrary. Two and a half years ago I also heard from my friend Sneevliet that nobody any longer had any "illusions" about the NAS, that we must only wait for the suitable time, etc. So much the worse—say I. Illusions could

explain much. Illusions are tested by experience. Illusions can be got rid of. But to get rid of conservative, trade unionist inertia is much harder. Proof: The hopeless NAS now exists for almost half a century.

It is said: The reformists expel the elements sympathizing with NAS *without protest* from the membership. This argument turns absolutely *against* the NAS, for it proves that the NAS, despite its decades of existence, is incapable of arousing the slightest sympathy among the membership of the reformist trade unions. For I cannot assume that the whole Dutch working class has been swamped beyond redemption and that the revolution is dependent exclusively upon NAS. Naturally the fakers have it easy to throw out embarrassing left-wing elements, for they are able to present them to the workers as the agents of a competing shop. The workers hang on to their organizations and want no competition. The *NAS should open up an open political unity campaign* with all forces and emphasis. The French trade union example; the revolutionary events in France and Belgium; the probable strike wave in Holland; the threatening fascist danger; the approaching war—all these should be adduced by the NAS *in order to strike the sharpest tone for trade union unity.* Under such conditions, the trade unions of the reformists would find it hard indeed to expel the revolutionary elements and to reject the offer for unity. If they do (as Jouhaux did ten times) then the NAS gains sympathy within the ranks of the reformist trade unions and at the next stage it will surely get the possibility of forcing the unity. This dynamic I utterly fail to find. One is content with the fact that one entertains no illusions and one waits for the positive solution by means of developments, that is, the police. These purely passive illusions are much more dangerous than the active ones and they may cost our Dutch party its life.

6. You are of the opinion that it would be better not

to dig up the organizational *past* at the conference. I am entirely of the same opinion. In the interests of the conference! I am also of the view that the discussion on the world situation, especially on the French and Belgian situations, is much more important. If the Dutch comrades agree that the organizational questions should be dealt with in a normal and objective manner at the end of the conference, I would heartily welcome it. Yet I do not see a catastrophe in having the "organizational questions" pushed to the foreground. And if we are attacked, we shall defend ourselves, and that's something we are able to do.

7. We are very happy here that you carried off good impressions from Belgium and that the conference, as it appears, went through satisfactorily.

I do not need to tell you, dear Comrade Muste, that I promise myself the best results from your participation in the conference, not only from the general political standpoint but also from the standpoint of the elimination of superfluous friction. This is the spirit in which I understand your whole letter, too. I have answered your frank criticism with just as frank a counter-criticism. Our newly established friendship can only gain thereby.

Yours fraternally,

P.S. I am not sure that this letter will reach you on the road and I am at the same time very anxious to have you receive the above-outlined considerations as soon as possible. This letter is destined only for yourself. You may, naturally, if you find it necessary, communicate it to the Dutch delegates to the conference. Of course, I must reserve to myself the right to communicate copies of this letter to all the delegates to the conference in the event that the Dutch comrades (which I cannot believe) come to the conference with bellicose intentions. ■

Molinier's expulsion[243]

July 1936

LETTER TO ERWIN WOLF
JULY 27, 1936

Dear Friend:

Can't you let me know, in confidence, how R[aymond] M[olinier]'s expulsion came about in the Central Committee? I am inclined to suppose that Naville and the others said to themselves: "R.M. is leaving for Oslo, and the Old Man is going to want to play around with the conciliators again and mess up all our work. We had better speed things up and expel him immediately." That is the only way I can explain this haste, which could cost us dearly. Since, on the other hand, I do not want to give the slightest bit of encouragement to the people around R.M., please conduct this little inquiry as discreetly as possible (but don't forget the lineup of votes in the Central Committee on the expulsion). Naturally, we must insist with all our might that the published decision be confirmed unanimously, thus making it impossible for R.M. to start a new party.

With warm greetings,
Crux [Leon Trotsky]

LETTER TO ERWIN WOLF
JULY 29, 1936

Dear Friend:

I have just learned that R.M. is proposing once again to leave for America, so as not to have to come into conflict with the Fourth. I don't have the slightest confidence in this proposal. Our man is always very conciliatory when he is cooking up his rotten schemes. It must also be remembered that his supporters—judging by Desnots,[244] who is a member of the Political Bureau(!)—are totally alien to us, and that R.M. is a captive of his own supporters. They—I mean the "leaders"—won't have any scruples about coming into conflict with the Fourth, and R.M. will have to follow suit, even if he doesn't want to. But he does want to, and his proposal is an attempt to lull his opponents to sleep. On that score I have no illusions. That is why *the expulsion absolutely must be confirmed as unanimously as possible*. Afterwards, it would be possible to *enter into brief negotiations* with R.M. and his friends. What could be proposed to these people? If R.M. really does go to America—and we should set a specific timetable—he will certainly not be admitted into our section, but he could be asked perhaps to join the Socialist Party as an individual, in order to demonstrate his loyalty to the Fourth inside it.

As for the others, the gangsters who infest this adventure, perhaps they would not have to be expelled, on the condition that they commit themselves, before an international commission, to behave in the future with total loyalty. In any case, every one of them, in my opinion, should be cleared out of the Central Committee. The new IS could be charged with carrying out these decisions.

If the clique accepts and carries out all these obligations, and I consider that to be 95 percent excluded, the advantages will be quite clear. But if R.M. tries to trick us, or if the others will not agree, the Central Committee can show R.M.'s followers that we have again taken steps toward conciliation, but that we failed because of the Molinier clique's bad faith. We could perhaps even go so far as to promise R.M. that if his clique is peaceful for six months he could return to France, and by and by the question of his readmission would be reopened.

In any case, it seems to me that *after the expulsion is confirmed* such negotiations would be permissible and even useful. What strengthens the Central Committee's hand is the threat of an international commission: if R.M. doesn't accept the proposal, the control commission's decision will be published in all the journals of the Fourth.

With warm greetings,
Crux [Leon Trotsky]

LETTER TO OTTO SCHUESSLER[245]
JULY 1936

Dear Friend:

I would like to briefly recapitulate my position on the French question. It is possible that the Central Committee, for its part, has not been blameless in its tactical proceedings, thus making the work more difficult. To let our attitude be determined by tactical considerations of this sort would be completely wrong, even fatal. That we have to get R.M. and his clique off our back as quickly as possible—this is indisputable to everyone who possesses a tiny kernel of political understanding. R.M.'s expulsion is already public. His return (even in a purely tactical sense) is no longer possible.... The International has to make good on the tactical mistakes announced by our national section, that is, it has to ratify the expulsion as unanimously as possible, and declare any political connection [with R.M.] to be incompatible with membership in our organization.

This is the only way to reduce the crisis to a minimum and to assure our French section the necessary freedom.

With warm greetings,
L.D.

P.S. As regards the list of comrades worked out for the new IS, I suggest, in accord with Erik [A.J. Muste]'s suggestions, that Abern be included in the list. ■

When the conference selects the leadership[246]

July 24, 1936

Dear Friends:

After you left, I received the enclosed proposals (on the conference agenda and on the organization of the leading bodies of the Fourth International) and I ask you to be so good as to translate, reproduce and distribute them to all concerned.

1. Regarding the conference agenda, I think that we can accept the proposal, with certain changes. The organizational commission, for which we here proposed Erik as chairman, should in any case consist not of three, but of five or even seven members.

2. Comrade M. suggests naming the leading body Political Bureau. This name is now much too much in disfavor. I would rather insist on the name General Council. Anyway, it's not a question of principle.

3. The composition of the General Council (Political Bureau) corresponds roughly to our proposal, except that Comrade Erik doesn't mention the USSR, but names Crux personally.

4. The Secretariat ought to be elected by the gathering

itself, since it more or less overlaps with the future General Council.

5. Of greatest importance is the proposal that the General Council (Political Bureau) meet every month, and that the presence of the representatives from France, Holland, and Belgium constitutes a quorum. In the event that the meetings are held in Belgium, there will always be two Belgians present, but more often only one person from France and one from Holland. In practice that means entrusting the entire leadership to *one* country. The same applies to France, in case the meetings are held in Paris. A Political Bureau of only three countries, with changing composition, could offer less assurance of political continuity than the Secretariat. If, however, the Political Bureau is for practical purposes limited to three countries, which has no advantages, then I would be for *three members of the Secretariat participating in the discussions with decisive vote.* That would mean that the Political Bureau would consist of at least seven members, which promises a significantly greater degree of assurance of continuity.

6. I also do not think that we can give the sections the right to recall or replace their representatives to the General Council at will. At most, this should happen only with the approval of a two-thirds majority of the General Council.

7. It's hard to be enthusiastic about Paragraph 9 of the proposal. It won't work to have the decision of two "resident" General Council members be binding on the Secretariat, because: a) The Secretariat has a much broader international overview than the two Political Bureau members of the country in question; b) These members may not agree, which would make a decision impossible. It is entirely sufficient for the Secretariat (in the event that it consists of only three members) to be expanded for important or disputed questions, by adding two "resident" General Council members, and for the decision to then be taken by a simple majority. (In general, I fear that Muste's proposal understates a bit the importance

of the Secretariat as a permanent working institution.)

8. The proposal of a poll of all members of the General Council (referendum) can in no way be opposed in principle. When there are differences, however, the business can degenerate into a form of obstruction and make all activity impossible. It must therefore be made a rule that in case the majority declares a question to be unpostponably urgent, the referendum procedure, although it must be carried out to satisfy the minority, must not restrict the execution of the decision.

Those are the fleeting and insufficient observations that I am in a position to communicate to you quite hurriedly, for I must send this letter by air mail tomorrow, so that it will arrive in good time.

With best greetings.

Yours,
Crux [Leon Trotsky]

P.S. Please share this letter immediately with Comrade Erik. ■

Advice for the conference[247]

July 25, 1936

Dear Sha[chtman]:

1. Is it necessary to *vote* on the two resolutions on America? You would have against your resolution the two from Hol-

land, Vereecken, *Muste,* perhaps still others. Is it necessary to create a factional division as long as the resolution was *in fact* adopted a long time ago? Think it over!

2. Comrade Erik [Muste] proposes for the IS Comrade Abern as a good organizer. His candidacy could have serious advantages. Perhaps a provisional decision can be made: *Sha*[chtman], and if the [American] central committee does not agree with that, then *Abern.* This formula would give the central committee a greater voice in the decision!

3. Thank Erik in my name for his two letters which I received after your departure; unfortunately, I cannot answer him directly.

My best greetings,
Crux [Leon Trotsky]

GPU and Gestapo[248]

August 27, 1936

The Moscow trial certainly finds its culmination in the allegation of a link between the supposed terrorist leaders and the German Gestapo. My name is also mentioned in this amalgam. I haven't the slightest reason to be upset. The monstrousness of the accusation is negated by its stupidity. I can freely speak of it quite calmly. The GPU's accusation is no more than a copy of the one which was once leveled by the Provisional Government of Kerensky against the entire Bolshevik leadership, Lenin and myself included.

Anyone who lived through the Great War well remembers that whoever opposed the war or even simply the excesses of chauvinism was immediately labeled an enemy agent. It was in that capacity that I was deported from France in 1916 by the minister Malvy. But only a few months passed before Malvy himself, just like Caillaux, was condemned by Clemenceau as an enemy agent.

In Russia, where the tremors of revolution created a whirlpool of people and ideas, this accusation took on a much more frequent, brutal, and cynical character. After July 1917 the newspapers were filled with testimony on the disappearance of Lenin on a German plane, on German gold in my possession and that of Zinoviev, Kamenev, Lunacharsky, Kollontai. If Stalin was not named on this list it was because his role in the revolution was too modest to attract public attention. Stalin, with Sokolnikov—the one more moderate, the other more radical—together edited *Pravda*, which did its best to refute these monstrous accusations. It would have been quite difficult at that time to predict that Stalin would repeat those same accusations, not only against Sokolnikov, but against the entire Old Bolshevik leadership.

To measure the depth of the Thermidorean reaction the reader must recall the composition of the Political Bureau during the period of the rise of the revolution: Lenin, Trotsky, Zinoviev, Kamenev, Rykov, Tomsky, Stalin, with Bukharin as a candidate member. Among the other members of the Central Committee, Sokolnikov and Smilga were the most prominent and closest to the central leadership. Today Stalin accuses all the members of Lenin's Politburo except Lenin himself, who is protected by his mausoleum, of being terrorist enemies of the state and agents of the Gestapo. This fact is catastrophic enough in itself. But there is worse still: the accused, especially the most important among them, like Zinoviev and Kamenev, have acknowledged the justice of the charge of a terrorist plot. The revolution has passed over an entire generation, made up of militants who were once full of ardor and courage but are now tired, worn out, and demoralized from the weight of events. The old Politburo of Lenin tried to fight against the new conservative, narrow nationalist ruling caste, which found in Stalin its chief and its personification, but one after another they capitulated. From capitulation to capitulation they became second-class citizens, third-class citizens, prisoners of the GPU, who had to abandon their reason to save their lives. The GPU used them at each new stage for new confessions, that is, to launch new trials with their aid against the adversaries of the bureaucracy and of Stalin personally. The last trial, predicted many times by me in the press since 1927 and especially since 1929, had as its supreme goal—the prosecutor Vyshinsky acknowledged it openly—to compromise and annihilate, at least politically and morally, the author of this article. The defendants confessed everything. They always sought to anticipate the official charges. There was a point, however, at which even Zinoviev and Kamenev stopped: that is, the trumped-up link with the Gestapo. Terrorists? Yes. Opponents of the regime? Conspirators? Agents of Trotsky, that is, of world imperialism? Yes. But as for the Gestapo, they were not in direct league with it. The lash of the prosecutor could not force them to make that confession. In their terrible and heart-sickening degradation they kept a grain of dignity. ■

A possible hunger strike[249]

End of August 1936

Dear Friend:

The day before yesterday I made the following statement to the chief of police: I cannot make a political concession and thereby take upon myself responsibility for the government's measures—*that is excluded*. My wife and I, however, *will not create any practical difficulties in complying with the new conditions,* provided that the authorities will honor our most elementary interests and rights. But on the basis of some symptoms already evident we can assume that the government not only intends strict enforcement but is also contemplating purely material repression as well (for example, cutting off correspondence—not just supervising it, a harsh climate that my wife could not bear, poor living conditions, etc.). We would not submit quietly to any of that. In such a case we would employ *passive resistance,* and the police would have to physically carry my wife and me through Norway. If it becomes necessary, we will both resort to a *hunger strike.* I will make this completely clear to the chief of police. But it would be good if this could be taken into account beforehand in party circles.

L.T. [Leon Trotsky]

Our friends should not wait[250]

End of August 1936

Dear Friend:

Lund is hereby removed from political life for an indefinite period. In any case, our friends should send him all materials pertaining to the Moscow trial: I hope that the postal blockade can be breached at least in *this* case. Lund told me at our last consultation that he is sure that his temporary inactivity, far from hampering our friends' energies, will on the contrary double them. Our friends should in no case wait for the pamphlet [on the Moscow trial previously promised]—how, when, why? Nobody knows [when such a pamphlet can be sent]!—instead, they should do everything possible independently. In this field practical agreements are permissible, not only with Social Democrats but also with bourgeois democrats and "respectable" elements in general, for the Cesare Borgia of Tiflis [Stalin] and his methods rank much lower than capitalist democracy. Exposing the frame-up will bring unforeseeable consequences. One should not forget that Borgia-Stalin, armed with the most modern technology, still has many poisonous "surprises" in his bag: he has not spoken his last word by a long shot, and he will stop at nothing on this road since this is a political life-and-death struggle for him. Therefore we must not grow tired or dissipate our energies, but proceed in an organized way, not losing a single day. A special central commission ought to be created to handle this matter, with V.S. [Victor Serge] at its head, and many assistants ought to be made available.

Lund and Mrs. Lund feel composed and confident and expect the same from all their friends.

The annihilation of all opposition in the Soviet Union could elicit new terrorist moods among the youth. Hence it is once again necessary to warn against such fatal "methods" as energetically and loudly as possible. *Individual terrorism can benefit only the Bonapartist rabble.* We have always said that! We are the only ones who can authoritatively restrain the despairing youth from terrorism and lead them onto the path of Marxism.

Best greetings and wishes.

Yours,

Translator troubles, publisher problems[251]

September 10, 1936

... I write in *German* so as to expedite the censorship. Your letter of August 28 was received three days ago. ...

I feel compelled—despite an inner reluctance—to give the following information on Eastman's role as translator.

1. My agreement with the publishers of the *History* freed me of any expenses with regard to the translation. Eastman entered into an independent agreement with the publishers as translator. Then he turned to me with the request that I cede him *voluntarily* 10 percent of my earnings.

In this way his work would be paid from two to three times better than mine (I worked almost three years). But I did not find the courage to say *NO* (in such matters it is always very hard for me to get up the courage). Thus up to date I have paid Eastman voluntarily about $4,000; in addition he received a very high fee as translator.

2. Unmindful of this he viewed the translation as something incidental. Only the first volume is translated *well*. The second and especially the third are full of errors—I demanded that he correct these for the new edition, but have received no reply up to this very day. And nevertheless from this second edition Eastman will again receive 10 percent of my earnings. It is necessary to know these things to understand what followed.

3. At the time of entering into the *Lenin* agreement I declared in writing that unfortunately I could pay nothing to the translator (you, dear Sara, know the reasons well enough). After the agreement was signed I again received a letter from Eastman: in truth, he knows my decision with regard to the translation, etc., but nevertheless he requests again that I cede him part of my earnings. I answered this time in very friendly fashion—that the whole situation makes it *impossible* for me to agree to his proposal; that therefore I will have to be satisfied with a less qualified translator, etc. A new letter from Eastman; I should at least cede 4 percent of my earnings. Why? I answered nothing.

4. Meanwhile, during my illness, the publishers Simon & Schuster urged that I prepare an ample introduction for the second edition of the *History*. I struggled against this inwardly in the highest degree: I was in the hospital, did not know when I would come out, and had especially on my conscience the Lenin book. Then I received a letter from Eastman. I have this letter in my files. The letter reads: *You have written so much during the recent years on the USSR, you need only to bring this in order—and this work (introduction) will enhance enormously the sale of the* History. And he added: I will translate the introduction and it will appear in serial form in a magazine

(please keep in mind that Eastman received always from the *History* 10 percent of my earnings). I gave in to these arguments.

5. I said to myself: so long as I am ill and cannot work regularly, I will finish the introduction on the basis of old preliminary work in two or three months maximum and this will give me financial security for my Lenin work. I miscalculated greatly. The illness proved more persistent and the work more difficult than I had thought. I became the prisoner of the subject. I could not produce a superficial work on the USSR. I became more and more engrossed in the theme—with frenzy and desperation. Nights I saw Doubleday Doran. But I said to myself: But then I will write with complete freedom a *good* book—the best of my books—on Lenin. For this I need time. And the second edition of the *History* will make me financially secure.

6. The introduction grew into a book, which precisely now, after the infamous Moscow trial, assumes for me—and not only for me—tremendous importance. Doubleday Doran really have full right to be dissatisfied, I admit this. But that Eastman should write them, "Give up hope on the Lenin book," is an unheard-of piece of cynicism! Does he want in this fashion to appease his ill feeling toward me? Unheard of!

7. I am ready to give Doubleday Doran the book on the USSR *without any advance.* The English publisher pays [ ], The American publisher, I believe, should pay at least [ ]. Doubleday Doran can simply subtract this sum from the advance on the Lenin book. At the same time the Lenin agreement retains its full force, that is, I remain obligated to deliver the book to D.D.

8. In actuality I have not given up or interrupted the Lenin work for a single day; my study is full of folders with excerpts, clippings, manuscripts, semifinished work, etc. *I have an obligation to D.D. I have an even greater obliga-*

tion to Lenin and to myself. I will write the book and it will be a good book.

9. If Doubleday does not want the new book (on the USSR) let it appear by some other publisher. I am ready to turn over the advance which I would receive to D.D. without thereby disengaging myself from the Lenin agreement. I am ready in any manner to give satisfaction to D.D. But on their side they must understand that my life does not run as smoothly as that of an American publisher and that very often I am subject to force majeure . . .

Now in addition: from the very beginning my condition was that the translation be made parallel with the receipt of the manuscript; in this fashion many chapters would have been serialized in time. But Eastman did not consider the interests of the author at all: therefore this frightful delay in the serialization as with the book itself. . . .

The book must appear as soon as possible: it is the best answer to Stalin's infamy. The last chapters are best suited for serialization; they are translated, I hope? . . . ■

Still imprisoned[252]

October 4, 1936

My Dear Nicolle:

Enclosed is the picture for Plisnier; it is the only one I have. I read that Plisnier wrote a novel. Natalia and I would be pleased to be able to read it here.

I am receiving *ASR* and *Spartacus*. I also received the issue of *Soir* and the issue of *Peuple* that you sent.

The situation here is the same: we are still imprisoned, in the strictest sense of the word. Literary work is impossible. Preparations for the trial here are moving very slowly. But I do not doubt at all that the Moscow trial will become a great historic landmark—with important immediate repercussions.

My book on the USSR should appear soon. Several copies should be sent to our Belgian friends (one for Plisnier).

Warmest greetings from Natalia and from me. ∎

Still gagged[253]

October 12, 1936

Excuse me for not being able to send you the article about the trial that I promised you for the coming number of the *Biulleten:* it obviously was not because I lacked the desire to send it . . . but I am sure that you yourselves will say what is indispensable about this rotten frame-up. ∎

The trip to Copenhagen[254]

October 12, 1936

Dear Lyova:

Regarding Copenhagen, the following questions need to be cleared up, facts established, and depositions of witnesses taken.

1. The Comintern press explained the significance of my trip to Copenhagen (and later my entry into France) by saying that I wanted to prepare military intervention (by France!!) against the Soviet Union—with the aid of the Second International. The appropriate statements in the press should be carefully collected, in particular those of the Danish and Norwegian Stalinists, and the set of quotations should be sent to me.

2. In my Copenhagen file (1932) I found a letter by the Swede *Peter Carlsson*. He could not come to Copenhagen as Molinier had suggested to him, and moreover he had no address (for me). He wrote to you in Berlin from Legnaes Persnaes on November 20, 1932 (when might the letter have arrived in Berlin?), and you forwarded this letter from Berlin to us in Copenhagen during our stay there. At the end of this letter, in your own handwriting, it says [in French]: "This letter arrived today. I gave Carlsson the same address, i.e., Denise Naville, P.R., Copenhagen." The difficulty, however, is the following: In Carlsson's letter your name is carefully crossed out. The letter begins: "Dear XXXX." That is because Germany stood in the shadow of the Papen-Schleicher government, and you had every reason to delete your name upon forwarding the letter. For the same reason, the closing preceding the signature at the end is crossed out. It looks

like this: "With xxxxxxx, Peter Carlsson." (It probably said "With Communist greetings," or something like that....)

This letter is one of ten or twenty pieces of evidence that you were in Berlin at the time and not in Copenhagen. However, we need to have all of the necessary explanations concerning the letter from Carlsson himself. The most important thing is whether and how he knew that you were in Berlin and not in Copenhagen. Perhaps he has a letter from you from those days?

3. I have found two letters of recommendation from Erwin [Bauer]'s father to Martin Andersen Nexoe and G.L. Skjoldbo. In both of them the addressee is asked to recommend a good doctor to me in Copenhagen. The text mentions that the letter will be turned over by Mr. Grylewicz (who is referred to as my "secretary"). The author mentions also that he is writing the letter at the wish of his son, who is a friend of Trotsky's son. Had you yourself traveled to Berlin, he would of course have presented the letter to you, that is quite obvious. The difficulty consists of the question, why the father did not send the letter via his own son. But this too is easily answered: Erwin did not know until the last minute whether he would be able to travel to Copenhagen, and in fact arrived only a few hours before our departure. (As we had to leave Copenhagen in a hurry I could make no use of the letters; therefore, they remained in my archives.)

4. In Copenhagen I had a lengthy discussion with a student group. In the same file I find a list of their names, which are: Mogberg Petersen, Jorgen Neergaard, Harold Petersen, Pluet (?) Mein (of the student newspaper); Bredsdorff (chairman of the students in Copenhagen), Cris (?) Toersleff (chairman of all the students in Denmark)—both Communists—Vibelse Jensen, Forge, Crindgoord (Lindgoord?), Moellman (?) Tinggaard, Willadssen, Tore Rasmussen (leaders of the Socialist students). Then follows a note in Jan [Frankel]'s handwriting [in French]: "Names of the students who visited L.D."

This list could be very useful if the individuals were looked up and asked:

a. What were the circumstances and where could they have met with me (a series of intermediaries, strict controls—I was never alone, and so on, and so forth)?

b. Whether any one of them heard anything about my son in Copenhagen?

c. In what manner did I speak with them on the topic of the Soviet Union: as a "friend" or as an enemy?

d. Whether they recall the news of Zinoviev's death and what it was that they heard?

e. It would be well to check the student newspaper to see how the conversation was presented in interview form.

5. In Copenhagen I had a meeting with the elite of the left-oriented intellectuals in the home of the late Boeggild. So that I could better orient myself he seated the guests in a specific order and gave me a penciled outline that I now have before me: Frisch, a Social Democrat, was a lecturer; Mueller, a friend of Munch, a lecturer; Rindung, philosopher, friend of Munch, master of arts; Anton Hansen, artist, Communist; Birsch, national economist (since deceased, I believe); Sindballe, professor of law; Brande, professor of philosophy; Jorgen Jorgenson, professor of philosophy; Boeggild, the host; Frankel, who came with me.

We discussed the USSR the whole evening ("socialism in one country," etc.). It would be interesting to ask the participants about my positions on the USSR.

6. We (my wife and I) found ourselves among friends with the Boeggild family. Boeggild himself is no longer among the living. But Mrs. Boeggild and her two children could certainly answer the question whether our son was in Copenhagen with us.

7. The Danish press reported many details about me, my wife, our traveling companions, etc. In no paper, however, will anyone find anything about our son (verify it!).

8. On the return journey by auto through all of Denmark we were guests of a brother of Boeggild, a schoolteacher, and got to know his daughter and two sons (unfortunately in my archives I cannot find the *place*). Along with our companions we spent several hours with the family of the teacher and had a friendly conversation. Was our son present there? The members of this family will of course answer *no*. (The family can easily be located through Mrs. Boeggild in Copenhagen.)

9. We lived in Copenhagen in a small house (villa) belonging to a Danish ballerina, who, I believe, was away in Argentina. The house was occupied solely by ourselves and our traveling companions—the address was kept a strict secret. For that reason I do not find it among my papers. However, anyone can verify this with the police: *two policemen were constantly posted on the ground floor*. If possible, the house should be visited, the entry should be photographed from the street, etc. The ground floor was occupied only by our traveling companions (the "guard"). Natalia and I lived on the second floor. It has (had?) one bedroom, one bathroom, a small adjoining room with a bed which Jeanne [Martin des Pallieres] and Lucienne [Tedeschi] occupied, and a *small office* where I worked and received all visitors. In order to be admitted to see me, one had first of all to learn the address: only a very limited number of friends (I believe only two) had the right to give out the address, after consulting with me. Then it was necessary to present credentials on the ground floor in order to come up the stairs to me. Any improvisation was therefore excluded. That can and must be attested to by thirty or forty statements of witnesses.

10. A very important witness is Mr. E. Falk from Mot Dag, who came from Oslo to Copenhagen to visit me. The questions which should be asked him are: In what manner did he obtain my address in Copenhagen? To whom did he

write? How did he find the house, and how did he get upstairs to me then? Did he have to wait for a while? Were there people on the ground floor? How many? What did the room look like in which I received him—Large? Small? Did I pace about in the room? Was it even possible to walk around in this room? (It was very small and filled with furniture.) Mr. Falk is politically hostile toward me and friendly to the Stalinists (if I am not mistaken). Therefore I attach especially great value to his statement. It would not be without interest if he would also convey the content of our conversations. What, for example, was my attitude toward the USSR? What was the purpose of his visit? What was his political relationship to me at the time? But these questions have less importance.

11. The defendants, who allegedly visited me in Copenhagen, had me walking about in the room (the only "living" part of the scenario!). Therefore, my room should be *measured!* At the time it contained a desk, an armchair and a large sofa. Visitors had to be seated on the sofa as there was no additional space for chairs. (I didn't even pace back and forth during serious discussions; moreover, since 1924 that has been forbidden by my doctors; even when dictating I sit or lie down. This detail, too, is not without interest.)

12. On November 23, 1932, we arrived in Esbjerg (Denmark). The same day we were in Copenhagen, where we remained for nine days. On the next to last day our address became known to the journalists (or so it seemed to our friends). I was immediately moved to a very proper inn located outside the city. Our traveling companions: Oskar Fischer and M. Shachtman (no—perhaps more likely P. Frank?); Molinier, I believe, was the chauffeur. All of that should be established through those involved and duly recorded! (Shachtman was not in Copenhagen at all.) Unfortunately I do not have the complete list of visitors. We stayed there less than twenty-four hours. During the

course of the day my wife paid a visit to me there. Despite the "conservative" character of the house (surrounded by a magnificent park) the owner was exceptionally considerate and friendly to me and my attendants. It suffices to say that she did not want to accept any payment!! This woman will certainly confirm that I received no visitors in her house (she will scarcely have forgotten it as my stay with her was an "event" for her). In addition, I was even less accessible there than in the home of the ballerina. If Goltsman, Berman-Yurin, and David had really visited me in Copenhagen, they would certainly have said a few words to the court about the ballerina's very unusual dwelling or about the even more interesting inn in the huge park. On the concrete circumstances of our alleged meeting they maintained a careful silence! Thus, it is imperative to look up the inn, and to take photographs of it, or find some, and to obtain a detailed statement from the owner (to whom I later sent my book with an inscription). Naturally, she saw no "son" either. The above-listed points by no means exhaust the "Copenhagen" question. *Nor* are they the most important. They are, however, the ones that must be investigated in *Denmark,* and to some extent in *Norway* (E. Falk) and *Sweden* (P. Carlsson)—in other words in Scandinavia. It is thus necessary to find a *lawyer in Copenhagen* who will carefully check all details with the help of active friends and the workers' press.

At the same time someone in France should locate the telegram from Natalia Sedova-Trotsky in the archives of the foreign minister or of the prime minister, in which the mother requests a visa for her son [Leon Sedov] from Mr. Herriot: that was *the beginning of December 1932.* Herriot arranged immediately by telegraph for the visa to be issued to you from Berlin for France. These documents are irrefutable and definitive. They prove that your meeting with us took place only during our return trip in France.

Thus the miserable defendants are supposed to have seen you in Copenhagen at a time when you were in Berlin. They claim to have met you in the Hotel Bristol which has not existed since 1917. Concerning myself, however, my house, my surroundings (the secretaries, the guards, etc.), they could not utter a single dying word in court!

I have *many more* interesting documents pertaining to Copenhagen. It was a really unfortunate idea for Stalin-Yagoda to set the conspiracy in Copenhagen: the lie thereby acquires an extremely concentrated character and cannot fail to be strikingly obvious even to a philistine. In the next letter I will discuss still more facts and documents on this chapter on Copenhagen. But I have to admit that an uneasiness frequently comes over me when I have to deal with filth like this. For the most stupid, most unlikely, and most ignorant thing is the *political* content of the charge. That I should concern myself with murder plots—in collusion with the Gestapo—against bureaucratic mediocrities, who in my eyes are only unconscious tools of a gigantic historic reaction. . . . And this aspect—the most important—is what I will have to clarify. But I will do it in *Russian* in order to give my thoughts the necessary precision. In order for the work to be complete, however, I must have in my hands the results of all the investigations that I indicated earlier in this letter—and the sooner the better. This letter must be corrected by a German, then duplicated for Mr. Puntervold, G. Rosenthal (Paris), for Bill (Prague), for the lawyer who will conduct the investigation in Copenhagen, etc. The division of labor should be strictly observed throughout.

In a week, perhaps earlier, I will draw up a list of additional questions—still on the Copenhagen chapter.

I will formulate some of them now:

13. I was "filmed" in Copenhagen. A very well-to-do merchant made his apartment available for the purpose. My secretaries visited him several times to arrange the matter.

Had my son been in Copenhagen, this hospitable and charming man would certainly have met him. To get his name and everything else connected with this will be child's play!

14. The representatives of the film company dealt with and associated with my secretaries to a considerable extent. Did they notice my son?

15. Then there are the journalists. I have in my file a mass of telegrams, letters, and calling cards from those days. The journalists surrounded my secretaries in swarms. Did any of them ever see or hear about my son?

I will mention here several names from my collection, without being certain whether all were actually in Copenhagen: Mrs. E.A. Koefoed *(Christian Science Monitor)*; John Ahl-Nielsen *(Chicago Tribune)*; Chv. Stampe (?) *(Politiken)*; William Parker (Hearst Press); Lasse Lemkow *(Berlingske Tidende)*; William H. Stohneman *(Chicago Daily News)*; Hans Tholstrup (on his visiting card: Central 2266); Mordechai Danzis *(The Day*, New York); a representative of the Columbia Broadcasting Corporation (Saerchinger?); several representatives of Fox-Movietone News; etc., etc.

All of these people will surely confirm that: (a) nobody knew my address; (b) they always had to negotiate via the intermediary of my secretaries; (c) I always came to the filming accompanied by several friends; (d) none of the journalists, film people, etc., ever heard anything about my son, and all of them, quite understandably, had a professional interest in my personal life.

16. Above I said that I do not have a list of visitors. By that I mean those who had access to our house, i.e., political friends and like-minded comrades. They numbered about twenty-five. I recall *all* of them, but confusion is always possible; e.g., Shachtman came with us from Prinkipo to France (1933), not to Copenhagen (1932). The list of *all* the comrades is, however, easily established, and that should be done as quickly as possible. In any case there was among

them *only one* who could speak Russian, i.e., Senin, who arrived shortly before our departure from Berlin. Senin however is not identical with any of the three alleged "terrorists."

To be continued.
Leon Trotsky

Reading Ibsen again[255]

October 1936

OCTOBER 17, 1936

Dear Comrade:

Since you are a bibliophile, I have sent you a copy of the new American edition of my *History [of the Russian Revolution]*. I hope you have received it. Fortunately, I completed this work while I was still in backward Turkey. In a modern democratic country, let alone one ruled by a Socialist party, this task would have been virtually impossible.

Natalia wished on several occasions to inquire about Karin's health, but that is not so easy from here. Please let us know how she is.

Of course, we would be very glad to see you again. But . . . in the good old days in prison I used to receive visits once, twice a week or more. But then that was also in the most backward countries (czarist Russia, Spain under Alfonso XIII, etc.). But, as we have said, we live under the sign of modern democracy, which is too delicate to allow internees to have visitors.

You wouldn't happen to have a *German* translation of Ibsen in your library, would you? In my youth, Ibsen was one of my greatest literary loves. But, as is quite understandable, I paid more attention to the Brands, Doctor Stockmann, Rosmer, etc., than to the . . . *others,* who often made life miserable for the author himself. Thus I would like to read Ibsen again now in order to have a little closer look at the "others." This might actually be of some use, perhaps for a possible new edition of the autobiography.

Warmest greetings from both of us to your wife and your daughters.

Yours,
L. Trotsky

P.S.—And Mr. Scharffenberg? Has he completely calmed down since the time when he delivered the incomparable, heroic "directive" to me? Oh well.

L.T.

OCTOBER 22, 1936

Dear Comrade:

Many thanks for the Ibsen. *Pillars of Society* was the first play to strike my attention. A fortunate occurrence! We should study and study again the best way to shore up society.

I am not at all acquainted with your article in *Kampf und Kultur*. Why will I find "to my distress" that the article is written in the spirit of the attorney Krapp? I can't believe that of you. Please send it to me. In any case, I am making some efforts in the area of the Norwegian language—it's still hopeless.

We were *very* glad to hear that Karin is well. Bravo! We hope that little Elly (?) is also well?

With best greetings,
L. Trotsky

Pyatakov and the trial in Novosibirsk[256]

November 26, 1936

Dear Mr. Puntervold:

I am hurrying to transmit a very important piece of evidence to you. It deals with the trial in Novosibirsk. In this case the internment actually serves my son and me. In a moment you will see how. So far I know about the trial only what is contained in the dispatch in *Arbeiderbladet* (Monday, November 23). It reads that, according to the testimony of the "witness" Drobnis, a conference between Pyatakov, Smirnov, and Sedov (my son) took place in Berlin. Pyatakov himself is said to have told Drobnis about this conference.

In order to be able to describe the testimony more vividly, I must tell you the following:

From 1923 to 1927 Pyatakov played a fairly important role in the Opposition, but he had already lost his taste for fighting by 1926-27, and stayed in the Opposition merely out of inertia. I sometimes said in his presence: "If the reaction wins, Pyatakov will peacefully go to the office every morning with his briefcase—even under a Russian Bonaparte."

Pyatakov was also the first among the Trotskyists to capitulate (in the beginning of 1928). In the correspondence of the Left Opposition as well as later in articles in the Russian *Biulleten,* Pyatakov was always treated with ironic contempt because of the fact that this young man (at the time of his capitulation he was no more than forty years old) ran out of steam so soon. After the capitulation, Pyatakov was completely integrated into the bureaucracy, and they always treated him as one of their own, in contrast to most of the capitulators, who always lived more or less like pariahs. This explains how we (I, my wife, and our son, who lived with us in Central Asia and in Turkey) acted toward him in general.

Now for the small but very important episode. My wife remembers it better than I do, i.e., she remembers all the details. (She has a very retentive memory for the purely *human* experiences and events, while my memory is of a more abstract nature.)

At the time when we were living in Kadikoy, near Constantinople, i.e., after the fire in Prinkipo, we received a letter from our son, who at that time was already studying in Berlin, in which he informed us among other things: "Guess whom I met on Unter den Linden? The Redhead.* I looked him straight in the eye but he turned his face away, as if he did not recognize me. What a miserable fellow!" This, approximately, is the text of the letter, according to my wife's recollection, which has also refreshed my memory about this incident (which was completely unimportant at the time). I do not know whether the letter can be found. Perhaps it is by chance among the papers stolen in Paris. All this has to be checked.

The following is important. This testimony of my wife was written down by me at a time when *we did not and could not receive a single line* from our son *about the trial*

---

* Pyatakov was often called this among the young people because of the color of his hair.

in Novosibirsk. The [Norwegian] Central Passport Bureau should be well aware of this. I will also get a receipt from the captain of the guard about the time (date, hour) I hand this letter over to him. You will then be able to get a statement from our son about his "meeting" with Pyatakov, before he had written us anything about it or received anything from us. Then the two versions can be compared, for I hope that my son is not yet prohibited from defending himself against outrageous charges. In this case the internment serves to establish the truth! "There are more things in heaven and earth, Horatio."

I do not have to point out what an extraordinary significance this incident has for the "Trotskyist" part of the amalgam. As for the fascist part of the trial in Novosibirsk, I cannot say, of course. I consider it is beyond question that the Nazis maintain a big, powerful apparatus in the USSR and that they are expanding it in preparation for the eventuality of a military attack on the USSR. It has to do with "Trotskyism" as little as it has to do with the Milky Way—even less, because the Milky Way is neutral while "Trotskyism" enthusiastically stands on the side of the USSR against Hitler and Japan. I do not want to further expand on this, in order to remain within the framework of strict, *"factual"* information.

P.S. Yesterday you suggested calling a doctor in a very friendly manner. Thank you very much! Under the given circumstances the visit of a doctor cannot do very much. Dr. Karl Mueller has observed my illness for the last few weeks. I am now going through an acute phase. The conditions necessary for a recovery unfortunately lie outside the realm of medicine. In case Dr. Mueller considers it necessary, I can always come to him, in order to take up less of his time.

With best regards,
Leon Trotsky

Posthumus and the archives[257]

December 2, 1936

Dear Leon:

I have received the second part of copies of my letters to you, without any letter from you. Yesterday Mama directed that you be sent 270 kroner. I am writing at the same time to G. Ros[enthal] about my depositions concerning the theft of my archives. I sent Naville a letter yesterday. I have received two documents by Pero. Bravo and thanks! I am very pleased. *Le Matin* seemed to state that Posthumus did not attribute any great importance to my archives. I do not want to analyze the sources of this report. But Posthumus visited me in Norway at his own initiative. For two hours he tried to win me over (that is, to win over my archives) for his institute. I refused. He asked me to think about it further. That's the background of this affair. One can be "prudent," but it is necessary to be truthful.

Your silence about the Russian [language] edition of my book [*The Revolution Betrayed*] astonishes and upsets me. Do you have a contract? Has a publication date been set?

Mama has made a deposition (for Puntervold) on your "encounter" with Pyatakov in Berlin (she remembers it better than I do). You have to give Puntervold your version, so that he can compare them.

Love from Mama and me,
Papa

Mexico (1937–40)

Answers to a Mexican press service[258]

January 23, 1937

Of all the questions you've asked, one strikes me in particular: you ask whether—in the event of a war between the USSR and Germany and Japan—I would side with the USSR or remain neutral. The very existence of such a question can only be explained by the hold that systematic slanders have on public opinion. I fought for the October Revolution; I participated in establishing new property relations in the Soviet state. This marked a tremendously important historic step. How could I not defend these social acquisitions against imperialist attacks? I am certain that my cothinkers in the USSR will be in the front ranks of the Red Army, which I helped to create in order to fight imperialist aggression.

Where does this question originate? The explanation is perfectly clear. The Soviet state is no longer what it was at its birth. Due to the play of historical circumstance, which I have analyzed in my recent book *The Revolution Betrayed*, a powerful privileged caste has formed—to the detriment of socialist progress. This new bureaucracy, which exploits the gains of the revolution for its own benefit, identifies itself with the Soviet state and with socialism. It looks upon the slightest criticism of its privileges and arbitrariness as an attack against the state. It considers itself infallible. In order to compromise the Opposition, which is motivated by the interests of the working masses and not by those of the new privileged caste, the bureaucracy accuses the Opposition of being allied with fascism. The latest trial, which begins in Moscow today, January 23, is solely inspired by the new bureaucratic caste's spirit of domination. The Opposition is fighting this caste. It will fight despite all of the persecution, despite all of the judicial machinations. But the Opposition is fighting the bureaucracy precisely in order to preserve and develop the social foundation of the new regime—to prevent it from degenerating. And I ask you: if indeed my friends are selflessly defending the October Revolution against the bureaucratic stranglehold, how could they not defend the Soviet state against the Germany of Hitler or the Japan of militarist aggression?

I cannot answer your questions regarding Latin America. I have already explained why to the metropolitan press. I know too little about Latin America to allow myself to publicly pass judgment on the questions concerning it.

I will devote myself in the near future to a study of Mexico and of Latin America in general. I ask that you allow me enough time to form an opinion. Besides, you must know that I have decided not to mingle in any way at all in the political affairs of the country which has so generously accorded me its hospitality and which has many difficulties to overcome.

You ask whether I plan to visit the different Mexican states. Absolutely. I would very much like to finish my study of this country, which is so diverse and rich in contrasts, by making a first-hand tour. Besides, both books and friends inform me that a trip through Mexico provides unequalled aesthetic and intellectual gratification. I would like to be able to visit the Yucatan Peninsula, which you have recommended for its social history and its archaeological treasures. ■

Two crooked lawyers[259]

February 1, 1937

Despite his high and mighty titles (King's Counselor, Member of Parliament), the British attorney D.N. Pritt is a "juridical" agent of the GPU. Moscow concealed its plans for the Zinoviev-Kamenev trial from the whole world until the last moment. On the other hand, Pritt was invited well in advance. Before the opening of this disgraceful judicial comedy the GPU already held no doubts, one must conclude, of the future favorable "expert opinion" of the impartial king's counselor. The GPU was not mistaken. The echoes of the shots the GPU fired into the backs of the heads of its sixteen falsely condemned victims had not even died away before Pritt published the pamphlet *The Zinoviev Trial*, in which self-satisfaction is unable to conceal a guilty conscience. The pamphlet serves as the GPU's chief means of defense abroad and is sold in various countries at a very low price. Just how cheaply Moscow bought it is another question.

Still worse, if possible, is the role of the French attorney Rosenmark, who, no one knows why, has appointed himself the highest authority in questions of "revolutionary" jurisprudence and political morality. Pritt, at least, operates in his own name and takes upon himself personally the risk of his unseemly mission. Rosenmark lacks even this much "courage": he operates under cover of the French League for the Rights of Man (!). On November 15, 1936, while I was in confinement in Norway, a "report" of unparalleled cynicism by Rosenmark was printed in the pages of its paper, using pitiful sophisms to justify the Moscow amalgam in its entirety and announcing that in any other country, Trotsky would be sentenced to be shot. I declare: public opinion should and does sentence Mr. Rosenmark to eternal infamy!

I am prepared to bear responsibility for my grave accusations against Pritt and Rosenmark before any independent court, or before an authoritative international commission of inquiry. Let the international agents and "friends" of the GPU, whatever weapons they use, be more cautious. Their trial has opened and will be carried through to the end! ■

Postponing the Swiss trial[260]

February 19, 1937

Dear Friends:

Enclosed is a copy of my letter to Dr. Jan Adler, Prague. All the arguments developed therein are concerned in somewhat attenuated form, with the coming legal proceedings in Switzerland. *In the present extremely favorable situation we have no right to voluntarily expose ourselves to even the slightest danger of a setback.* We are holding the best cards. We don't have to be as impatient as at the time of my internment in Norway. Each new week strengthens our positions (of course, on the condition that each of us exerts all our powers). The Stalinist scoundrels in Switzerland and elsewhere will get theirs. Just a little patience, please. We want first to expose the great "leaders" in all their depravity. Then the lackeys will have their turn. To go at it the other way round would be politically, tactically, juridically mistaken. I am certain that our Swiss lawyer, Dr. Strobel, will agree with me in the assessment of the newly created situation. I am writing directly to him as well.

Dear friends, I have a good picture of all the efforts that have been made so far to get the trial under way. It is always difficult to bring the momentum of one's own work to a standstill. But we must orient ourselves by the big perspectives of the collective situation and not by secondary aspects and impressions. *Through the American commission of inquiry we will win the case with absolute certainty.* Then we will be able, with calm and persistence, to go further, until we have discredited the last slanderer in the last corner of this planet. For now, however, this means putting the brakes on the trial in Europe, directing all attention to New York and Mexico City, sending all documents and affidavits, notarized, to me and the New York committee. One can say with assurance that in the next period we will achieve the greatest political victory on American soil. We need only persistence, patience, and promptness in our work! Of course this does not mean forsaking all activity in Europe. Quite the contrary. It is of the greatest importance to prepare public opinion for the future trials in Czechoslovakia, Switzerland, etc. In the first place, this means making the most important documents available in the appropriate languages. For example, I would be very happy if my ungiven, or half-given, New York speech could appear in the near future in French, German, and Czechoslovakian.

With warmest greetings.

Yours,
L. *Trotsky*

Answers to the 'Chicago Daily News'[261]

March 3, 1937

Q: Briefly, what do you wish the American people to know about the present situation in Russia, and particularly your connection with it?

A: Above all, it would be the greatest error, from the economic, diplomatic, and military point of view, to identify the Soviet Union with the present leading group. Stalin's clique, as the Moscow trials demonstrate, has entered into the stage of its death agony. The Soviet Union will live and will develop. On the new social bases created by the October Revolution, it will produce a regime of true democracy and will become the greatest factor for peace and for the social emancipation of humanity.

Q: How dependable is Walter Duranty?

A: Mr. Duranty's dispatches, like his book on the USSR, do not merit any confidence whatsoever. Duranty arrived in Moscow when the liquidation of the revolution had begun. As against such American journalists as John Reed and others, who had exhibited a great devotion to the revolution and to the people of the Soviet Union, Duranty and those like him are connected only with the bureaucracy—more exactly, with the ruling clique, for which they are nothing more than loudspeakers. In defending Stalin these gentlemen defend themselves.

Q: Is the present Russian regime turning away from Marxian socialism and toward state capitalism?

A: The answer to this third question is given in my book *The Revolution Betrayed*. The problem is so complicated that it is difficult to summarize it in a few lines.

Q: What is the attitude of the Mexican government toward your residence here?

A: I have found only goodwill and hospitality on the part of the Mexican government. I am proud to find myself under the protection of a country which has undertaken the defense of the Spanish revolution with great courage and resolution.

Q: Do you consider that you are personally in danger, and if so, from whom?

A: That the Soviet bureaucracy first deprived me of my citizenship and then declared me outlawed is known to all. What "practical" measures it will take only the future can tell.

Q: To whom are you indebted for your transport and maintenance here?

A: The initiative for my transfer to Mexico came from my great friend Diego Rivera.[262] His initiative from the very first met with an extremely friendly attitude on the part of President Cardenas[263] and the members of his government. The statements which came from Europe, to the effect that I would have preferred to remain interned in Norway, are completely absurd. I accepted the visa which was offered to me with deep gratitude, in the hope that I would be able to devote myself entirely to literary work in the kindly climate of this country. The last Moscow trial destroyed my plans, forcing me to appear before world public opinion with revelations. But I hope that the series of bloody frame-ups will end before long and that I will be able to return completely to systematic scientific literary work.

Q: Do you consider that Mexico is communist in the sense that Russia is?

A: I believe that it is a very great distortion to identify the Mexican regime with the regime of the USSR. Mexico has her own history, her own particular national and social structure, and her own particular program. There is no greater crime than schematization in the domain of politics! ■

A correction and requests[264]
March 26, 1937

My dear Shachtman:

I am very, very glad that the internal relations are once more good and that you regard the future with an assurance of success.

We here are busily preparing ourselves for the forthcoming session of the inquiry commission. I hope that everything will be satisfactory.

Some questions and information. First, your affirmation that the Hotel Bristol was reestablished during the Moscow trial happens to be a mistake: a Danish paper said in a purely ironic sense that the Hotel was "reestablished" during the trial. Actually, it doesn't exist today any more than in 1932. This information is from Europe. It would be well if you made a correction in the Bulletin. Second, you told me that you have in your possession the explanation of Stalin, Rykov and Kuibyshev to the effect that Trotsky, Zinoviev and Kamenev must be fought not as Jews but as bad fellows. Wouldn't it be possible to find this document?

After I had written my article on anti-Semitism, I found two very interesting documents in my archives. I will complete my article for the Jewish paper and publish it in an American or English magazine, as well as include it in my book. The above-mentioned document is necessary for this purpose.

Pyatakov "confessed" that in 1931 he obtained funds for my counterrevolutionary activities through certain German firms. I have the full possibility to establish that in this period I furnished, for revolutionary and not counterrevolutionary enterprises, a sum of about $13,000–15,000 from my royalties. The most important depositions will come from Rosmer, his wife Marguerite, and Naville, who disposed of the special treasury created by my contributions. But I suppose that you are also acquainted with the matter. On the other hand, at that time or a bit later I furnished the American League a certain sum, apart from the Paris "treasury." Testimony on this matter from you and Swabeck would be very necessary for the inquiry. Please take care of this as quickly and as exactly as possible.

My best greetings,
Leon Trotsky

Stalin's latest threat[265]

March 29, 1937

STATEMENT TO THE ASSOCIATED PRESS

Stalin's last speech announces a new campaign of extermination against the Opposition. The medieval accusations of the last trials are used as a basis for the campaign. Let us imagine for a moment something quite impossible, that after the misfortune in the Texas school which has stirred the whole world, the administration of the United States had opened a campaign against the Third International, accusing it of the premeditated extermination of children. Then we would have a picture of the political and moral character of

Stalin's campaign inside the USSR.

One of the tasks which Stalin sets for himself is to sharpen the internal struggle in the working class of the world, transporting the methods of the GPU to the international arena.

Stalin's policy does irreparable damage to the international prestige of the USSR. In Berlin and in Tokyo, in any case, it is known by the ruling circles better than anywhere else that the accusation of high treason against the Trotskyists is a complete invention. From this they may conclude: the USSR is weak if Stalin has recourse to such useless methods. However, the conclusion is profoundly in error. Stalin's policy indicates not the weakness of the USSR, but the growing weakness of Stalin's clique within the USSR.

STATEMENT TO THE UNITED PRESS

The purpose of Stalin's last speech is evident: to turn the growing discontent of the Soviet masses with the arbitrariness of the bureaucracy against "Trotskyism" and to detract the attention of the working class of the world from the fatal consequences of the Comintern's policies in Spain through badgering the Fourth International.

The proclamation of Trotskyism as the "chief enemy of the USSR" is founded on the principle: "L'etat, c'est moi." In fact devotion to the historic interests of the USSR is now inconceivable without opposition to the demoralized oligarchy.

During the last twelve years Stalin has proclaimed at least a dozen times that Trotskyism was dead. The new declaration of war testifies to the failure of the previous struggle. It will go no better this time.

The characterization of the Fourth International as a band of spies, agents of reaction, etc., repeats word for word the characterization which the reaction of the entire world, beginning with the czarist police, accorded the Bolsheviks, in particular Lenin and myself. Stalin's gross insults against his political adversaries is the infallible sign of the confusion and alarm resulting from the general distrust of the Moscow trials. ■

Opinions and information[266]

May 12, 1937

1. The attitude of the Belgian leadership during the by-election is a severe blow to the prestige of the Fourth International and especially to its Belgian section. On this question we are fully in agreement with the IS and the Paris *Lutte ouvriere*. Comrade Give [Vereecken] seems to want to separate the Belgian question from the Spanish question. This is a purely mechanical conception. The opportunism in the attitude toward the POUM is more obvious and more profound because it concerns a revolutionary situation. In the question of the by-election the same opportunism only takes on a more trivial form, more flat, more traditional. But basically it is only a matter of two manifestations of the same tendency. We see again how formal intransigence serves to cover basic opportunism. Our Belgian friends have to examine their consciences seriously.

2. I regret very much that the English comrades were unable to publish my reply to the miserable maneuver of Fenner Brockway. Under pressure from below he changed

his method, but his objective remains the same. The Pritt method failed. He wants now to follow the Beals method, i.e., to have his hand in the investigation in order to compromise it and thus win the favor of the Stalinists. To adapt one's attitude to the new technique of Fenner Brockway and his similars means only to aid them. Naturally the publication or nonpublication of an article is not decisive, but the symptom is extremely disquieting.

3. Schwab [Jacob Walcher] refused to give his deposition [to the commission of inquiry into the Moscow trials]. I read Braun's [Erwin Wolf's] letter, which seemed excellent to me. I regret only that Schwab is addressed as comrade. No, we can have no comradeship with this miserable fellow! Mr. Schwab is mistaken, besides, in believing that one can refuse or agree to give testimony at one's will. No, it is a matter of public duty. I have transmitted to the commission a report and several letters from Schwab concerning his [1933] visit to me at Royan. I have emphasized that these documents come from a man who has since become our most envenomed adversary. As for measures of prudence [to protect people submitting or mentioned in depositions to the commission], they will be the same for all German emigres, Italian emigres, etc. (In the same way a document concerning the visit of [Fritz] Sternberg was transmitted. Like Schwab, he will be cited before the commission of inquiry.)

4. Kingsley Martin of the *New Statesman* visited me in a state of inebriation. He scarcely understood what I said to him and I was furious over losing my time with this drunkard. Several times during the hour he stole from me I was tempted to kick him out. [Bernard] Wolfe, Van [Heijenoort], and I think Jan [Frankel] are aware of this lamentable episode. I had the impression that Martin, although drunk, understands that I saw his drunkenness and is angry at me because of his own lamentable state. He

takes his revenge by saying I was not stable in my statements. The fact was, the world was turning around in this drunkard's eyes. ■

Obstacles in Britain[267]
May 21, 1937

Dear Comrade Sumner:

I am sincerely grateful to you for your friendly and very informative letter. I can very well understand the obstacles you have to overcome, but it is beyond doubt that every new month will see the situation change in your favor. The only difficulty was to *begin* the investigation; now the truth will reveal itself almost as automatically as a natural force. All these ladies and gentlemen, including such political old wives as Brailsford and Fenner Brockway, will soon notice that the ground is becoming hot under them and they will try to join the camp of the truth to avoid being definitely compromised. We can, openly and with full assurance, predict our victory over the masters of frame-up and their agents of the first and second degrees. The shift which is now occurring in the United States will undoubtedly influence your situation in England favorably.

Please transmit my respectful greetings to your mother and my best wishes to all our friends in England.

Fraternally yours,
Leon Trotsky

No reason to complain[268]

August 10, 1937

Dear Comrade Meyer:

Many thanks for your book. It is really quite remarkable—I lived in Norway so quietly and unnoticed that I might as well have been in Mexico, and the government through its actions succeeded in making me something of a factor in domestic politics, even though I had been sent off to Mexico. This dialectic is the result of the not thoroughly dialectical mind of Trygve Lie and his cohorts.

In Mexico we live quite undisturbed. The government does everything possible to make our stay easier. We are enduring the climate fairly well. I can carry on the struggle against the Moscow trials quite openly. As you can see, I have no reason to complain.

From time to time, I receive information on Norwegian life, in which I still retain a warm interest. I keep the Ibsen you sent me always at hand, and frequently read it with great pleasure, again and again bringing Konstad, Trygve Lie, etc., to mind.

With greetings of friendship from Natalia and me to you and your wife.

Leon Trotsky

P.S.—Perhaps you have heard that in Czechoslovakia a German emigre, Grylewicz, has been arrested and charged with espionage. I know Grylewicz quite well—ever since my last exile began. He is a real proletarian, an unyielding fighter, a man of unblemished character. It is absolutely certain that the whole business has been manufactured by the GPU. These scoundrels are trying to apply Moscow methods in the countries dependent on them [for military aid]—Spain, Czechoslovakia—in order thus to contaminate the workers' movement of Europe and the whole world. ■

Literary theft[269]

August 21, 1937

Dear Comrade:

In the Russian newspaper *Novoe Russkoe Slovo*, published in New York, two articles are reprinted from *Biulleten Oppozitsii*, number 56–57. In the *Novoe Russkoe Slovo* of August 9 there is reprinted under the title "The Beginning of the End of Stalin's Dictatorship" my article "The Decapitation of the Red Army." At the end of the article in the *Biulleten* it is decreed in English that all rights remain with the author. The arbitrary reprinting of the article by *Novoe Russkoe Slovo* inflicts serious material damage on me, because the article was intended by me for the American press.

The August 16 *Novoe Russkoe Slovo* reprints from the same issue of the *Biulleten* N. Markin's [Leon Sedov's] article "The Mdivani-Okudzhava Case." The article in the *Biulleten* is written under the name of the author, N. Markin. In *Novoe Russkoe Slovo* the article is reprinted so as to appear to be by Trotsky. "N. Markin" is not my pseudonym. The article was written by another individual and first read by me in the *Biulleten.*

I don't know whether the laws of the United States provide the right to call a newspaper to account for literary theft, complicated by literary forgery. (Unfortunately, the second article lacked a note reserving literary rights.) I earnestly ask you to either immediately present the appropriate material demands to *Novoe Russkoe Slovo* in the name of the *Biulleten Oppozitsii* and for its benefit, or to enter into an agreement with a lawyer for the purpose of obtaining a judicial opinion.

I ask you to regard the present letter as formally conferring full powers of attorney.

L. Trotsky

A pamphlet on Spain[270]

September 17, 1937

Dear Comrade Walker:

I collected and studied for a long time materials, documents, concerning the Spanish revolution. I could now easily write a small book, better to say a pamphlet, on Spain. Besides the general analysis of the character of the revolution, it would contain polemics against the different, especially American, newspaper correspondents, interpreters, and falsifiers of the Spanish revolution, such as Louis Fischer, *The Nation* and *The New Republic.* Work on such a book of 100–150 pages would require no more than six weeks on my part. I could send the manuscripts in parts so that the translation could be ready almost as soon as the Russian manuscript.

It seems to me that such a pamphlet is indispensable now for large circles of public opinion. Even from the commercial point of view, it could be a worthwhile enterprise. It would be excellent if Doubleday Doran would accept such a manuscript. I am sure that the company would make a lot of money from such a publication. The handicap is only that the pamphlet would be written in an open revolutionary spirit, that is, in the spirit of the Fourth International. Wouldn't Doubleday Doran be afraid of such a book of "propaganda"? If yes, it would be very difficult for me to give the pamphlet to another publisher because it would be a misuse of their patience in waiting so long for the Lenin book.

At the same time I must confess that I am very anxious to write this pamphlet on Spain. The facts and the documents are of tremendous importance. The new generation of Marxists cannot find a better school of political education than the Spanish events. It would be excellent if Doubleday Doran accepted the proposition. My financial demands can be reduced to the minimum: for example, no advance at all, if that is necessary to bring to a successful conclusion the conversations with Doubleday Doran. The work on the autobiography could proceed simultaneously because the greatest part of the latter work is of a purely technical nature (reproduction from the diary, copying, etc.). I will await with the greatest interest an answer to this proposition.

With best wishes and greetings,
Leon Trotsky

The international conference must be postponed[271]

September 25, 1937

Dear Comrade Adolphe:

Received your letter of September 10. I gave the North American and Mexican press an interview on the circumstances of Erwin [Wolf]'s arrest. On the basis of Held's letter I concluded that Tioli is an agent of the GPU. Your letter leaves the matter in doubt. This disturbs me greatly and I am impatiently awaiting your further clarification. I also informed the New York Commission of Inquiry to this effect. I am going to write exhaustively about this to the New York Defense Committee. And I will also write to Hjoerdis [Wolf] right away.

Now that the struggle with Sneevliet has come to a public settlement, it would be completely wrong to agree to any fundamental concessions. Of course it was proper to invite his organization to the conference. Of course we have to continue our criticism as objectively and as calm in tone as possible. To give up the "faction work" in the meantime would be disastrous. We don't deny Sneevliet the right to conduct his faction work as he has up to now (Muste, Ver[eecken], Gorkin, Maslow-Fischer). What's right for the minority must also be fair for the majority.

Sneevliet's current flirting with Thalheimer, the Vyshinsky-philosopher, is really droll. Sneevliet is obviously seeking to exhaust every means of compromising himself. It would be timely to put a short notice in our press about the vile Brandler-Thalheimer circular letter concerning the Moscow trials. Since the Lovestoneites have meanwhile quite altered their attitude to Stalin and Moscow, it would be fitting to ask the Brandler-Thalheimer people if they are still as happy about the GPU as they used to be.

I could have used the last two or three weeks to occupy myself with the draft program. Unfortunately I lost my Russian coworker [stenographer] and therefore I am completely disarmed in the face of more important work.

I think you should demand regular financial contributions for Theodor from the American central committee. In the past weeks I have finally studied the press service and the bulletins that I hadn't seen since my internment. Theodor did a very good job. The national bulletins—the German, French, Spanish—are also very interesting; most of the articles on Spain, including the ones by Rous, are very, very good. In the German bulletin from Barcelona I found an article that seemed really excellent to me. Isn't it from Johre's pen?

The background to the German split is completely unknown to me. In principle I haven't the slightest hesitation, if I have to choose between Johre-[Oskar] Fischer-Held on the one hand and Bur-Maslow-[Ruth] Fischer on the other. We have to support the first group with all our might. I'm sure this is also your opinion.

The consultation must be postponed until February. Not just because of the situation in the United States but also because of the French crisis, which absolutely must be settled by then. I also believe that we have every reason to await the results of the London Bureau and of the IVKO, so that we will have the last word.

In America things seem to be going pretty well, as you can see from Cannon's letter as well. After the verdict of the Commission of Inquiry, which should be made public in the near future, the political atmosphere for the American section will become much more favorable. ∎

The U.S. recession and a new political orientation[272]

October 2, 1937

Dear Comrade Cannon:

1. Possibly I will write, in the near future, an article concerning the probable consequences of the new approaching crisis. As to the crisis itself I wrote very briefly about it in my article concerning the coming war. The obvious symptoms of the approach of a new crisis are given by the convulsions of stock exchanges, especially in New York but also abroad. The question is intimately connected with the rearmament programs. A general slump is inevitable, if not during the next year, then at least in 1939. We haven't until today sufficiently considered that the flourishing of the Stalinist parties on the basis of a new turn is determined 90 percent by a semireal, semifictitious prosperity. The People's Fronts in different countries were possible only thanks to the fact that the situation of large masses even of the middle classes became better or, at least, the process of worsening was arrested, and to the new big illusions aroused by the reformists on one side and the middle-class parties on the other. The new crisis, which promises to be more terrible than the last one, will deliver a terrible blow to all these illusions (People's Front, democracy vs. fascism, social reforms, New Deal, etc.). Even if the crisis should not provoke a new war (and I hold that a war as a result of the end of "prosperity" is almost inevitable), the crash of the People's Fronts, the pacifist masquerades, and the flourishing of the Stalinist parties and their auxiliaries would be as tremendous as

the crash of the prosperity itself.

If the great slump occurs, as it is supposed, during the Roosevelt administration, it will compromise the Democratic Party even as the slump of 1929 under Hoover compromised the Republicans. But if nine years ago the Republican administration was compromised in favor of the Democrats, this time the Republicans can have only a partial profit from a new crisis. The masses of the workers and possibly of the farmers will, so it seems to me, under the successive blows, look for a *new political orientation*. I don't believe that fascism can become an important factor in the States before the creation and the political experience of a third or farmer-labor party. The crisis will undoubtedly reinforce all the tendencies towards an independent labor party. The attitude of John Lewis is very symptomatic in this respect. We do not, of course, have to change our principled position concerning a labor party. But this general attitude many times expressed and defended in our papers can become insufficient. A current for a labor party can for a period of time absorb all the progressive and semirevolutionary tendencies in the proletariat. The crash of the Stalinist party can, under these conditions, signify its dissolution into the labor party. We cannot and will not naturally remain aside. This does not signify that we will necessarily enter a labor party or that we shall prepare for such a possibility or begin to fight for it: it would be pure Don Quixotism. A labor party would be based naturally upon the trade unions, especially the CIO. *Our* preparation for the perspective can and must now consist in systematic efforts to penetrate into the trade unions and to participate in mass work.

It seems to me that is our general perspective for the next period. I would be glad to hear the opinion of you and the other comrades upon my *hypothetical* considerations. The perspective should be developed in a series of articles from an economic, political, national and international point of view in the *Socialist Appeal* and in the *New International*. The earlier we orient our cadres to the new perspective, the greater will be our political success.

2. Comrade Rae [Spiegel] sent you yesterday a list of articles and letters concerning internal discussions in different sections. I merely wish to know whether they reached you. You will make whatever use you think advisable. I hope you will reestablish an internal bulletin, for which most of them are more or less destined.

3. We had yesterday a discussion of a general character, with the participation of Comrades Sterling, Hansen and Granger. Comrade Granger was here yesterday for the first time in our house. He will remain here [in Mexico City] for some months. I would like to have some information about him from people who know him well.

4. With Comrade Selander we didn't have luck. He was here for about four weeks but he never communicated his address and we never could get in touch with him. Only this morning I learned from Rae that he wished to see me today because he was leaving tomorrow morning. I must admit I was a bit astonished by this attitude. He had the possibility to write at least a postal card and to ask for the meeting. My time today is taken up and I confess I am not inclined to change my program in order to protect the negligence of a comrade who considered himself, as I understand, too much as a tourist and too little as a party man. The general situation is now of such a kind that we should ask from every comrade a greater degree of responsibility.

5. I wrote to different comrades about the question of Erwin Wolf. I hope that the question will not be neglected in spite of the manifold activities of the party.

6. I received from the publisher, Harcourt, Brace & Co., a book of Eugene Lyons, *Assignment in Utopia*. It

seems to me that from all the books written by the disillusioned bourgeois-democratic and Communist persons about Russia, this is the best one (though, it is true, I read only a small part of the book). Do you believe that the man is worthy of attention? The publisher wrote me a letter, asking me to write something about the book. I would do it—naturally, in a cautious manner—if the comrades believe that my conditional approval would not be compromising.

7. Suzanne La Follette wrote me that the liberal and radical press continues to observe a conspiracy of silence concerning all the Stalinist crimes and particularly in Spain. I believe that the real means to break this conspiracy is by publishing a *correspondence bulletin for the bourgeois press* with news articles, etc. Possibly Hearst will grab at it. I don't see any disadvantage in this. On the contrary, if the liberal rascals cover up by their silence the assassination of Nin, the arrests of Grylewicz and Erwin Wolf, etc., etc., we are obliged to use every means in order to inform public opinion directly or indirectly. It would be absolutely naive, not to say stupid, to stop before the accusation from the Stalinists, who murder our comrades and reproach us with unmasking these crimes in the reactionary press.

8. We are very pleased with the arrival of Comrade Hansen and our general impression is that the collaboration will be all right in every respect.

9. The car he brought is excellent and even too imposing for our courtyard door, which must now be adapted to the domination of the vehicle. I am, I confess, a bit embarrassed by the untiring attention and generosity of the American friends. I cannot express to each of them Natalia's and my thanks but possibly you will find the opportunity to assure them that the gratitude is very real.

Very comradely yours,

An article on Kronstadt[273]

November 14, 1937

Dear Comrade Wasserman:

1. It is not necessary for me to tell you how highly I appreciate the activity of Pioneer Publishers. It would not be an exaggeration to say that it is now the only publishing house of revolutionary Marxist literature in the entire world. Pioneer Publishers has international importance. The enterprise must be developed at any cost if we are willing to educate new Marxist cadres and to build up a new International. No sacrifices are too great in supporting and developing Pioneer Publishers.

2. I understand very well your insistence upon the Kronstadt matter, but if I come back to this question for the second time it should be done in an absolutely exhaustive manner. I do not have at the moment either the necessary materials or the time for such an article. I advised my son to prepare a pamphlet on the question including all the necessary facts, documents, and so on. On the basis of this material I would willingly write an article for the *Socialist Appeal*[274] or for *The New International*.

My best greetings,
L. Trotsky

Suggestions for a pamphlet on Kronstadt[275]

November 19, 1937

Dear Friend:

It is absolutely necessary to write a short pamphlet on Kronstadt. I hope that the anarchist material has been sent to you. Anyway, I will find out about that. Here are the key points that could be made:

1. Kronstadt had been completely emptied of proletarian elements: All the sailors belonging to the ship's crew had become commissars, commanders, chairmen of local soviets. When I wired a request at the end of 1919, or in 1920, to "send a group of Kronstadt sailors to this or that point," they answered, "No one left to send." Even the different armies were beginning to refuse reinforcements from Kronstadt (also those from Petrograd, in part). I do not know if there are many documents on that, but this point must be heavily emphasized.

2. As far as I understand, Victor Serge says: "But Kronstadt wanted free trade, and the Bolsheviks had to introduce the New Economic Policy during the insurrection itself. Therefore, Kronstadt was in the right. So why was it crushed?" This argument is false on two and even three counts.

   a. Kronstadt represented the tendencies of the landowning peasant, the small speculator, the kulak. We were obliged to make some concessions to these bourgeois tendencies. This in no way meant that our program—in which the workers made concessions to petty-bourgeois tendencies—was identical with the petty-bourgeois program. There is a wide gulf between the two.

b. Precisely because it made these economic concessions, the proletariat had to hold political power in its hands with redoubled energy. That is why it did not have the least right to surrender the fortress to the rebellious petty bourgeois.

c. The peasant sailors, led by the most antiproletarian elements, could not have wielded power even if we had surrendered it to them. In their hands, power would have been only a bridge—and a short one at that—to a bourgeois regime.

3. Victor Serge, it seems, says that if the party had agreed to my [economic] proposal a year earlier, the Kronstadt uprising might not have taken place. Let's grant that. But we could not surrender the fortress to the sailors as punishment for a mistake made by the leading party.

4. The uprising was preceded by discussions, negotiations, etc. They did not begin by firing shots. But dissatisfaction was very great. The anarchist and Menshevik elements, the counterrevolutionaries in disguise (there were quite a few of them), did their best to lead things to an uprising. They succeeded. So nothing remained but armed struggle.

5. The workers who marched over the ice against the fortress represented the proletarian revolution, in spite of all the mistakes made by the party. The sailors in revolt represented the peasant Thermidor.

6. At the party congress itself, we discussed what to do about the fortress. Stalin suggested—but not very strongly—that the rebels be abandoned to their fate; in two or three weeks, half-starved, they would yield. I argued against this proposal. Some sleds had already arrived from Finland with provisions. A few weeks later, the ice would have melted, and ships could easily have come from Europe. We would then have had a new intervention, extremely dangerous because of the fortress and the battleships. It was decided to attack

the fortress immediately.

7. Dan comes to Kronstadt's defense too, as does Kuskova, the old gossip. This is very instructive. It is enough to recall the Mensheviks' attitude toward Kronstadt in 1917, when, led by the working masses, it was really at the head of the revolution.

There you have the comments I can make from memory. But what is most important is to marshal the facts so they can speak for themselves.

I would be very glad if you could send me the manuscript, and even major citations, as your work progresses. I might even make a short article out of it for our press, and it could serve as an introduction to your pamphlet.

P.S. I hope that Comrade Wasserman is sending you all the anarchist documents. ■

An article on the Soviet state[276]

November 30, 1937

Dear Comrade Cannon:

I am sending you herewith an article, on the Soviet state. Though written against the thesis of Burnham-Carter,[277] the article has a more general character. Together with Rae [Spiegel] and Joe [Hansen] we put some time and work into it in order to give it a more precise and clear form. That is the reason why we believe here that the article should be published not only in the [internal] bulletin—or not in the bulletin at all—but in the *Socialist Appeal* or in *The New International*. The difficulty now is that Burnham, Carter, and Craipeau are specified in the article. But you can eliminate the names either by replacing them with initials, or by an expression such as "some comrades," "certain comrades," and so on. I hope that this article will deliver me for some time from the necessity to go back to this question.

I read with the greatest pleasure your letters to the people on the West Coast. Excellent in every respect.

My best greetings,
Hansen [Leon Trotsky]

Sale of the archives[278]

December 21, 1937

Dear Friend:

I have an idea which I will submit to you and other nearest comrades. In a couple of weeks all the documents presented by us to the commission[279] will become free. They have an indisputable historical value. They include for example a copy of my correspondence with Lenin during the civil war (only a very small part of it was published). I believe that we could sell this whole documentation to an American scientific institute. The advantage would be double: (a) full security; (b) money. The sale should of course be arranged on some conditions. For example: (a) that I can use the documents for my work without any limitation; (b) the institute can use them for publication only with my consent; (c) certain documents should be guarded with all the necessary guarantees especially against the Stalinists and their agents and so on.

I could even add to the evidences other parts of my archives concerning the history of the Left Opposition. It would be good to have in this state in some institute a collection of all the accessible materials concerning the history of the Russian Opposition. Leon [Sedov] could furnish important matter from Paris. But that is a secondary part of the matter. The first one is the sale of my documents now in the possession of the commission. I believe that you could consult about this with Comrade Goldman.[280] If there are not some unexpected objections on his part, he could possibly consult Dr. Dewey.[281] I send the copy of this letter simultaneously to Comrade Goldman. In order to avoid misunderstandings I remind you that one copy of my correspondence with Lenin during the civil war was sold to the Dutch historical institute under the condition that they cannot use it without my authorization.[282] They paid $1,000 for it. This institute is very small and poor and the payment was in accordance with that. The Dutch institute has also a photostatic copy of part of the copies. I have the right to make from these photostats new copies if the American institute should care to have them.

It would be absolutely unreasonable to preserve these documents here in our home. To place them in a safe would signify permanent expense. It is from every point of view preferable to sell them immediately under the above indicated conditions.

I shall wait with impatience your first communication about the matter.

My best greetings and wishes,
Leon Trotsky

Kronstadt and the commission's function[283]

January 17, 1938

Dear Mr. Wendelin Thomas:[284]

1. I fail to see the advantage of a private correspondence upon Kronstadt. It is a matter of facts and of points of view. Only public opinion can judge the differences. In the second issue of *The New International* an article by J.G. Wright[285] has been scheduled to appear concerning the factual aspect of the reactionary mutiny at Kronstadt. In the next few days I shall publish an article on the same question from a more general point of view. I cannot admit any other way of elucidating a historical and theoretical problem than through a literary discussion.

2. The Inquiry Commission had a totally concrete task: to verify the Moscow verdict. The task of the commission was defined by its chairman at the beginning of the sessions. As a witness I participated in the investigation of this *concrete* question. The commission never pretended as a commission to express its point of view upon historical, theoretical, or political questions. Such a pretension would be in contradiction not only to the aim of the commission but to elementary common sense. Every member of the commission can upon his personal responsibility draw from the investigation all the philosophical, historical, and political conclusions he wishes. But the commission as a whole is not more competent to reach a verdict upon political questions than the Supreme Court of the States upon astronomy or esthetics. If a crime results from a fight between two literary schools, the court must know all the pertinent facts including the

characteristics of the two fighting tendencies, but its verdict can concern only the crime and not the value of literary or esthetical schools.

3. I leave without answer those assertions and expressions which I am not inclined to tolerate in a private correspondence. You have the full right to characterize Lenin and me as you please in your public articles. I shall not assail you about this in private letters.

Yours sincerely,
Leon Trotsky

Thomas's letter and Dewey's speech[286]

January 26, 1938

Dear Friend:

I sent you a copy of my letter to Wendelin Thomas. His letter to me is very stupid and arrogant. Even now he continues to affirm that the [Dewey] commission cannot avoid expressing its opinion that the Stalinist policy is the result of Bolshevism. How can he make such assertions after the decision has been arrived at?

I am a bit disquieted about this, especially in connection with the speech of Dewey.[287] Contrary to the opinion of some comrades, I must say that it was not very loyal on the part of the "old man" to vociferate his own political views in the name of the commission. It was doubly disloyal because I trusted to him the reading of my cable which sorrily abstained from any political enunciations. What Dewey said did not represent the decision of the commission and was contrary to the opinion of some members of the commission: Rosmer, Zamora, to a large extent Ruehle and, I believe, also Tresca.[288] Not all the members are liberals. Not all of them believe that the decay and degeneration of the Soviet bureaucracy disqualifies communism and that the decay of democracy proves the vitality of liberalism.

I will explain this in an article written against Dewey but I am a bit concerned with the supposition that Wendelin Thomas may have been successful in introducing some such "naivetes" in the text of the commission. It is *absolutely necessary* to verify the text from this point of view. If the text includes tendentious political appreciations from the liberal point of view, it is necessary to warn the editors that we will consider it as an abuse of confidence and that we will appeal to Rosmer, Zamora, Ruehle for reconsideration of the corresponding part of the text. I hope my disquietude is without foundation; all the better! But the most attentive verification is absolutely necessary.

It is superfluous to say that all this is very *confidential* and that I would be unhappy to disturb my friendly relations with the commission members by some incautious step. Please speak also with Comrade Cannon on this matter.

In enduring friendship,
Your Old Man [Leon Trotsky]

Eastman and 'The Young Lenin'[289]

February 3, 1938

Dear Friend:

Regarding Walker's efforts to arrange publication of the book on Lenin in an expedient way, I must draw your attention to a fundamental question, that of the translation. I could easily get out of the affair by "serializing" the first part of the book, *The Young Lenin,* and we could then put out other chapters as they are written. But here's the problem: Eastman neither wants to let go, that is, give up the translation, nor work along with me. He has, naturally, his own concerns. But from the very beginning I asked the publisher not to involve Eastman precisely because he is too high and mighty to accommodate himself to my most basic concerns. That was how he completely blocked the "serialization" of *The Revolution Betrayed.* Now it's the same thing with *Lenin.* We could make other arrangements for the translation. This would give some very well-paying work to our own comrades. (Perhaps even [Eleanor] Clark would be disposed to take it on?) From every point of view the question of the translation is fundamental, [Eastman's translation of] *The History of the Russian Revolution,* in spite of the magnificent style, is full of errors. And why? Because I had no opportunity of controlling the translation. At the last minute Eastman would dictate the translation in fits and starts, depriving me of the possibility of revising the translation as well as serializing it. I wrote to Doubleday Doran that I was ready to give up "serialization" rights (10 percent of royalties), but I made it conditional on a change in how the translation was being done. I got no results and the question has been left hanging. I very much regret not having written all this to you before. Having thought it through, I see that getting free of Eastman is the only way to succeed.

Explain this in a firm way to Walker. Perhaps someone could approach Eastman himself and explain to him that my sole desire is to separate my work from his. He must therefore understand that I cannot subordinate my literary work and my basic interests to the habits and convenience of the translator. Take this matter in hand.

Best wishes,
L.T.

Explanation of a complaint[290]

February 5, 1938

My Dear Comrade Wright:

Permit me to say with all the sincere and warm friendship which I feel for you that in the "Joe" case of the translation you are not just. The factual responsibility falls totally upon me. I was from the beginning very vividly interested in the absolute correctness of *this* translation for many reasons:

a. It is a preface to the *Communist Manifesto* and I have a great respect for this document.

b. The English translation is to be translated into Afrikaans which opens a possibility for multiplication of every mistake.

c. I hoped that our English-speaking sections will publish the *Manifesto* with this preface, and so on.

That is why I asked you to send me a copy of your translation. I was the first to read it over and to find five or six factual errors, two or three of which were of importance. Unfortunately I can find errors but I am incapable of correcting them with good English. For this reason I asked the assistance of Joe. He corrected not only the factual errors annotated by me but several stylistic unevennesses, or what seemed to him to be unevennesses. These are the facts of the matter. If you had rejected some of Joe's stylistic changes, neither I nor I am sure Joe would have reproached you. You are the author of the translation and the corrections had the character of advice or proposals and not of "command." If in *The New International* I had found your translation without any stylistic changes but with the important factual corrections, we here would have been entirely satisfied. What seemed to me absolutely incomprehensible was the fact that nobody even read the corrected text: otherwise it would have been absolutely impossible to have left the evident errors unchanged. (And that the editors had our text in time was clear from the changed title.) Under these conditions the appearance of the old text without any corrections (even "cosmopolitan" was not replaced by "metropolitan") seemed to me a manifestation of lack of good will. And this explains the sharp form of my protest. Joe had absolutely nothing to do with it.

We haven't as yet received the second issue of *The New International*. I wait for it with great interest. I sent an article to the *Socialist Appeal* about Kronstadt supplementing your own. I wrote it without materials but I hope not to have committed mistakes. If it is not too late it would be very good if you would attentively read the manuscript as you have all the facts fresh in your mind.

I am sure that we will find the necessary forms of col-

laboration, eliminating nervousness on both sides.
With my friendliest greetings.

> Yours as ever,
> Leon Trotsky

Why I can't pay now[291]

February 7, 1938

Dear Sir:

Naturally in view of the fact that I agreed to arbitrate the case before Den Norske Sakforerforening, Oslo Krets, I shall pay the sum which I have been asked to pay as soon as possible.

But your request finds me in a very difficult financial situation. You know, I am sure, that your government under orders from the GPU held me in prison for four months, depriving me of the possibility of working and made me pay for the imprisonment at least two times more than I would have expended normally.

Your government confiscated my bank deposit which represented the earnings from more than a year's work. Concurring with the government, the "Socialist" municipality imposed a monstrous tax upon me in absolute discrepancy with my means and my kind of life.

After my liberation from the "Socialist" prison in Norway the new Moscow trials obliged me to devote almost a year in refuting the infamous accusations.

That is precisely why I am now in the greatest financial difficulty. I shall not repeat again that I didn't receive any real help from Mr. Michael Puntervold. But in spite of all, I hope that I can send the necessary money during the month of March.

Yours faithfully,
Leon Trotsky

Jules Romains on Lenin[292]

February 7, 1938

My Dear Friend:

I am now sending you the official notification from the Norwegian lawyer. I cannot help but pay it. If you succeed in making money from the last article and from the operation with the Lenin book please send the sum of Kr. 1094.14 immediately to the address indicated in the letter.

Did you receive my letter about the serializing of the Lenin book and Eastman's translation? *That is the most important question* and it should be resolved by the transfer of the book to a new publisher. Somebody should visit Eastman and explain to him that his elementary duty is to let me free. Don't forget that Simon and Schuster are his friends and that the transfer can enslave me still more to the translator than I am now. I never could clear up the matter with the manuscript of *The Revolution Betrayed* when it was supposed to be a "preface" to *The History of the Russian Revolution* because Eastman covered Simon and Schuster and Simon and Schuster covered Eastman. In every collision with my publishers Eastman was every time against me. I am a bit tired of this "collaboration." If he will not abandon my book on Lenin he must take upon himself the obligation to translate immediately the first part of the manuscript and to deliver it to me for revision and serialization.

In the last volume of his epopee, Jules Romains pictures the figure of Lenin at the beginning of the war in 1914. I am ready to write an article on Jules Romains and Lenin with a general characterization of the epopee and especially of Lenin. I believe that the article could be marketed.

You never write about your own life and particularly about your health. Is it better than it was the last period here? Do you have good medical care?

My heartiest greetings.

Yours as ever,
L.D.

Marx's living thoughts[293]

February 10, 1938

Dear Friends:

For the second time I have received a proposition from Mr. Alfred O. Mendel, representative of Longmans, Green & Company, publishers, to give in 108 pages the condensation of Marx's thought in his own words together with a preface of 20 pages of my own. As payment he proposes $500 for all rights. The idea of making such a work is very attractive in itself but it is a tremendous task. Marx's style is condensed to the limit. To reduce his thought as an economist, sociologist, historian, philosopher, journalist, leader of the First International,[294] to 108 pages of 340 words to the page requires a great deal of time, if in general the work is feasible. It is a bit astonishing that in this collection of books "The Living Thoughts of Marx" has the same allotment as Machiavelli, Montaigne, Loyola, and Napoleon. Condensing the works of Napoleon to 100 pages is a matter of a week's work and Napoleon's thought would not suffer very much. But with Marx the question is very different.

I believe also that in the next period Marx will be more widely read in the States than Montaigne or Loyola, even Nietzsche and Spinoza. During the next ten years, thanks to the educational work of crises, Marx will be one of the most widely read authors in the United States. Such a condensation can become, and, if it is well done, must become, a book with 100,000 readers. But the book must be readable and I cannot imagine, I repeat, the possibility to expound the dialectical materialism, the historical materialism, the economic theories, and the revolutionary strategy *in Marx's own words* in 108 pages, and to summarize them in 20 pages. It seems to me that the publisher should give two volumes for Marx. The first volume could be devoted to the general philosophical, historical, and revolutionary conceptions of Marx with only a short reference to his most important work, *Capital*. The second volume could be devoted to *Capital* itself. The first volume would be more readable than the second and would sell like ice cream.

In any case the proposed payment seems to me absolutely inadequate, in view of the great difficulties of the work itself and of the perspectives for the book. The $500 is not even sufficient as an advance, and royalties must be based upon a permanent percentage.

With the best greetings.

Yours,
Leon Trotsky

Leon Sedov's papers[295]

February 28, 1938

Mr. Ambassador of France
Mexico

Mr. Ambassador:

Our son died in a Paris clinic on February 16. Given the suspicions surrounding the causes of his death, the French police undertook an investigation which was, moreover, along the exact lines of a telegram we sent from here. Leon Sedov's papers were seized during the inquiry of the authorities. The will signed by Leon Sedov leaves all that was in his possession, including documents, to his companion, Jeanne Molinier, nee Martin des Pallieres.[296] We believe the testament raises some difficulty given the fact that the marriage of our son with Jeanne Molinier nee Martin des Pallieres was never legalized.

Under these circumstances we ask you, Mr. Ambassador, to communicate to the French government our most ardent wish that Leon Sedov's papers do not fall into the hands or under the eyes of Soviet representatives. Neither we nor our son had or have anything to hide from French authorities. If they submit the seized papers to careful examination, they will have one more occasion to convince themselves of the ignominious character of the accusations made by the GPU against Leon Sedov. But if our son's papers come to be known by Soviet authorities either directly or indirectly, some third persons could suffer terribly, as in the case, for example, of Ignace Reiss[297] and, perhaps, of our son himself. ∎

Questions about Sedov's death[298]

March 1, 1938

Henri Molinier
Paris

Dear Friend:

We have received your letter that brought us the first precise information about what happened. One thing stands out most of all in the report signed by Jeanne. The patient's situation is favorable for four hours after the operation; then an abrupt change. He staggers deliriously down the halls of the hospital! The surgeon [Talheimer], seeing this sudden change, went so far as to wonder whether the patient had intended to commit suicide. This fact seems fundamental to me. Suicide in this case could only involve poison, in any case not a revolver. Why couldn't this poison have come from someone else? But immediately afterwards, the doctors rejected the hypothesis of a murder by poisoning. How can this contradiction be explained? I admit I don't grasp it. Until such time as Talheimer's question about an attempted suicide is clearly explained, the enigma will remain.

The figure of the Russian nurse remains fairly sinister in this context. The report signed by Jeanne says that this nurse not only interested herself in what the delirious patient was saying in Russian, but that she tried to obtain some confidential information by questioning him. Did she make a report or any communication about the content of the delirium to Jeanne or any other friends of Leon? If not, she must have made her report elsewhere. This question also remains unclarified. Perhaps at a distance things seem out of place. But I can only base myself on the text of the report.

Now the question of the [Sedov] archives. The importance of this question is clear to you, but now it takes on exceptional sharpness because of the new trial.[299] We must at least put those documents and letters that can help refute the new calumnies to use as soon as possible. Here is what I propose, in agreement with Natalia. We give, for our part, a mandate to a commission comprised of Alfred Rosmer, Paulsen, and Gerard Rosenthal or Alexis Bardin[300] (they should decide among themselves). This commission of three, or even of all four if they think it more convenient, should establish relations with Jeanne, with you as a go-between, because you seem to us, dear friend, to be the man most suited to resolve the question in the most satisfying manner. The task of this commission is two-fold: (a) assembling the documents immediately utilizable, making photostats; (b) arranging, in agreement with you, the shipment of these documents under conditions of absolute security to the United States.

Natalia and I would like, as well, to have as soon as possible all our letters written to Lyova [Leon Sedov] as well as his old letters to us stored in the Paris archives.

As for Sieva,³⁰¹ we would be embarrassed to make proposals from here. We leave all possibilities open for the moment. Natalia is waiting for proposals from Jeanne. For my part, I believe that the boy himself must at least have a consultative voice in this question.

The "practical" character of this letter explains its tone. Our gratitude to you is very deep. You will know how, as a solid friend, to do what there is to do.

Our warmest greetings,
L.D.

I am sending you a copy of a letter that Van personally delivered to the French ambassador here. ■

Krestinsky's repudiation³⁰²

March 2, 1938

In the first session of the [current Moscow] trial, Krestinsky, Stalin's predecessor as secretary of the party, then commissar of finances, and later ambassador to Berlin for five years, repudiated the preposterous confessions he had made during his secret examination by the GPU. What does this signify? It is possible that this reawakening of dignity and courage might induce other defendants to do the same. That would represent the most disgraceful fiasco of the whole judicial machinery. It would be the political end of Stalin. That is why it is necessary to be cautious with predictions. During the night Krestinsky, like all the other defendants, has to return to his cell. During that time the GPU is the master of the situation. What will Krestinsky say tomorrow if he discovers during the night that his wife and daughter can become the first victims of his boldness? Let us therefore await the further development of the trial. To compensate, let us keep this moral denunciation in mind, even if it is short-lived. It demonstrates, even to the blind, how this trial was prepared.

Poor old Rakovsky confessed that he had hatched a conspiracy with the Japanese when he was in Tokyo on an official mission representing the Soviet Red Cross in 1934, all this after his political capitulation to Stalin.

For his part, Bukharin confessed that during his visit to Paris in 1936 he had received instructions for terrorist acts from Leon Sedov, my recently deceased son. For the moment I do not want to stop to examine the intrinsic absurdity of this testimony, but I permit myself to reproduce below a brief dialogue taken from the stenographic transcript of Dr. Dewey's commission of inquiry at Coyoacan. This is what can be read on pages 472–74 [of *The Case of Leon Trotsky*, 2010 printing]:

"GOLDMAN: Do you care to give us any opinion about any future trial involving Bukharin and others? . . . Do you expect that Bukharin and Rykov also will be connected with you?

"TROTSKY: Everything is possible. . . . I know only that Bukharin was sent abroad in 1936, the beginning of 1936. . . . He was in Prague, a tourist. Now, I ask myself if it was not with the purpose of preparing with him a new combination. He gave a lecture in Prague, totally in the official spirit. But it is possible they sent him in order to have the possibility to affirm that abroad he entered into communications with Trotskyites and German agents. I don't know, but it is quite possible. The same with Rakovsky. Immediately [after his capitulation], he was sent to Japan. I was a bit astonished. What was the meaning of it? It was at the end of 1934, and the British friends of the Soviet Union . . . declared: 'You see, the repentance of Rakovsky is totally sincere. The government sent him abroad.' . . . Now, I ask myself if it did not have a second purpose, to frame him afterwards—that he was connected with the Japanese military chiefs in the government, and so forth."

This prediction, made in April 1937, has been confirmed. It was easy to do: when one knows the coefficients of a geometric progression, one can easily calculate the terms n, n+1, etc. When one knows the coefficients of a frame-up, one can, after the earlier trials, foresee the outcome of a new trial. ∎

The third Moscow trial[303]

March 4, 1938

The present trial is built around a method that consists of increasing the sensational character of the preceding trials. This crude method of functioning carries the accusations to complete absurdity in all directions. It asserts that the Bolshevik Old Guard was entirely at the service of foreign governments. The heads of the government (Rykov) and of the Communist International (Zinoviev, Bukharin) were fascists. In 1921, I, a member of the Political Bureau and head of the Red Army, had become an agent of Germany, which at the time was on the road to complete collapse. Who will believe it?

On the subject of the anti-Soviet declarations of Butenko[304] in Rome in the middle of last January, Litvinov stated: Either it is a fraud, or these declarations were extorted from Butenko through torture. With infinitely more truth one can say: On the defendants' bench are the wretched shadows of Old Bolsheviks. All of their confessions were dragged from them by the methods of the Inquisition.

The alleged international combinations of alleged conspirators are adapted retroactively to the present international conjuncture. I and my alleged agents would have to have been conspiring as far back as 1921 with Germany, Japan, Poland, and England. France, which until 1934 was considered the principal enemy of the USSR, is not on this list; nor is the United States. The Kremlin spares its "friends." One can say with certainty that England was added at the last moment, in accord with Chamberlain's new orientation.[305] The grossness of the falsification, so characteristic of a totalitarian regime, leaps to the eye!

One of the most important tasks of this trial is to justify, after the fact, the execution of nine generals, which shocked world public opinion last June. The absolutely false testimony of Krestinsky, Rosengolts, and others about my liaisons with Marshal Tukhachevsky[306] only reveal in the clearest way the criminal character of the decapitation of the Red Army.

The French Surete Nationale know perfectly well that I could not have met with Krestinsky in Italy in October 1933. On October 9, with the knowledge of the French police, and in ill health, I left Saint-Palais, near Royan, where I had been since July 25. My destination was Bagnieres-de-Bigorre, where I stayed until November 1, the date that I moved to Barbizon. Irrefutable proof of these facts can be found in New York, in the possession of Dr. John Dewey's commission.

The choice of such an unfortunate date can most probably be explained by this fact: in October 1933, Krestinsky was actually at Merano, and since the movements of an ambassador are watched closely by the police of the countries involved, the GPU had to adapt my calendar to Krestinsky's.

It is exactly the same problem as Pyatakov's famous flight from Berlin to Oslo in December 1935.[307]

The staging of endlessly repeated judicial falsifications reveals the extent of the resistance that the totalitarian dictatorship faces even in the ranks of the bureaucracy itself. Stalin's regime has become the principal threat to the USSR, in the economic, moral, and military domains. ∎

Answers to Mrs. Celarie[308]
March 6, 1938

It is very difficult, Madam, to express in one brief formula the irreconcilable differences that exist between Stalin's politics and mine. Besides, I have already amply dealt with this subject in my book *The Revolution Betrayed* (Grasset, 1936). If I may use a concise formula, I will say that my politics represents the interests of the laboring masses, those who made the October Revolution. Stalin's politics represents the interests of the bureaucracy, this new caste of parvenus who dominate and oppress the people.

Hatred of the bureaucracy on the part of the popular masses is the sentiment that generally prevails in the USSR. A terrible fear of the people on the part of the bureaucracy is its result. Trembling for its unlimited power and its growing privileges, this bureaucracy tries to crush in the egg all opposition, all criticism, all expression of discontent. But since it is not possible to say to the people that the sin of the Opposition consists of demanding more freedom, more well-being for the workers of city and countryside, they must attribute to the Oppositionists crimes that appear to the people to deserve repression. That is the origin of the sensational Moscow trials. They did not fall from the sky. Their history is already a long one. Since 1923–24, the leading layer began defaming and slandering the Opposition, attributing objectives to it that were different from its actual aims. This systematic falsification was possible thanks to the totalitarian regime, which permits control of the press to be concentrated in the hands of the leading clique. Increasing the slanders and falsifications from year to year, from month to month, Stalin managed to poison public opinion and impute to the Opposition vices and methods that are unimaginably abominable, cruel, and absurd. After this preparation, which took at least six years, the staging of these trials, prepared in the dungeons of the GPU, began.

To these trials, Madam, I devoted another book, *Les Crimes de Staline,* which was published several months ago in French by Bernard Grasset. It seems to me that this book provides a sufficient explanation, political as well as psychological, of the mockeries of justice, simultaneously theatrical, treacherous, and frightful, which are taking place in Moscow, especially since the end of 1934.

The unanimity with which the accused admit their guilt? The general explanation is quite simple. The witches all admitted their guilt in the hands of the Holy Inquisition. They even indicated with scrupulous precision the time and place of their nocturnal commerce with the devil. Human nerves have not changed much since the Middle Ages. They cannot withstand pressure beyond certain limits.

Is it a question of physical torture? Not in the usual sense of the word. The technique of the Inquisition has been modernized, but it rests on the same foundation. The arrested persons are subjected to complete isolation. They are given only the official press, which rails against them and daily calls for their death. They are subjected to interrogation lasting twenty-four hours and more, almost without interruption, under powerful and hypnotic lights. Their wives, their mothers, their children are arrested, and a confession is demanded as ransom for the hostages. During the preliminary investigation the most recalcitrant prisoners are shot, to teach the others a lesson. Thus it was that during the preparation for the last trial, they shot, without any trial, the former Soviet ambassador, Karakhan, and the former secretary of the Central Executive Committee of the Soviets, Yenukidze, for refusing to admit their guilt for crimes they had never committed.

In a totalitarian regime, where the judges, the defense attorneys, and the press are controlled by the same person, the processes that come to be used are the ones that prove the most useful for staging the most outrageous mockeries of justice.

Your final question, Madam, concerning the future of the USSR, is as difficult to answer briefly as your first question on the politics of Stalin and the Opposition. Furthermore, these two questions are closely related to each other.

I will permit myself again to refer to the two books I mentioned above, in which I tried to give French public opinion as complete an account as possible of the actual situation in the USSR, of my program, and of the way I view the future. I can say here only that the Stalin regime cannot last. It is in a historic impasse. The Moscow trials are only the convulsions of this dying regime. What will replace them?

There are only two possibilities. Either Stalin will be overthrown by the forces of capitalism (domestic, international, or a combination of the two)—in this case, nationalized property and the planned economy would give way to capitalism; the political regime would be the most brutal fascism, to subdue the masses trained in the school of revolution—or, and this is the second alternative, the masses themselves will overthrow the demoralized bureaucracy and will establish a true democracy based on nationalized property and a planned economy. This development would be toward socialism. It is not necessary to say, Madam, that all my efforts are directed to this end. ∎

Roosevelt and a visa[309]

March 30, 1938

Dear Friend:

We received the clipping concerning the speech only yesterday. Your telegram was not comprehensible before the clipping arrived. The statement is extremely important, especially from the standpoint of general policy. I hope it can also be used from the personal standpoint. In any case, everything possible must now be done.

You are of course well acquainted with the situation. Natalia has required serious medical treatment for a long time. This need is all the greater since the recent tragic events. Permission to stay six months would be truly salutary. A return visa can certainly be assured in advance. It is not necessary to add that while there I shall remain completely outside politics, apart from occasional statements refuting insults and slanders.

How should the question be posed? I could pose it directly and officially from here. But to incur an official rejection would be very disagreeable. What means have you there?

The lawyer Ernst[310] has been suggested to me, but perhaps there are others. What must happen is that the authorities understand the situation, that is, that I do not have the slightest political ulterior motive. I am quite able to write articles for the press of the Fourth International here. What we need is a change of climate for several months and good medical treatment.

As to the practical questions that you have raised with Van, we will reply to you in the next few days. The overriding question at the moment is that of the visa.

My warmest greetings,
Your Old Man
[Leon Trotsky]

Carlo Tresca is a target[311]

March 31, 1938

Margaret De Silver
Brooklyn, New York

My Dear Friend:

I have learned that you contributed again so generously toward the new conditions of security which are being created here through the solicitude of friends from the United States and Mexico. Until recently I tried to avoid these new efforts and expenses which cannot be effected without injury to the movement. But the sudden death of our son, the very precise revelations of the French and Swiss police concerning terroristic attempts against Leon Sedov and myself, the trip of Abbiatte, a professional assassin of the GPU, to Mexico and finally an attempt to introduce a package allegedly from General Mujica[312] vanquished my resistance. I will not be accused that I offered a too easy victory to the GPU.

In this terrible time of triumphant reaction and approaching war every revolutionary represents an element of the future. Self-preservation becomes to a certain degree a revolutionary duty. The Kremlin beast is wounded but not dead. Its last convulsions can be terrible. I believe, for example, that Comrade Tresca is now one of the targets for the hatred and revenge of the GPU: He should be very cautious in his movements and meetings.

I thank you heartily and I transmit best greetings from Natalia and myself.

Yours sincerely,
Leon Trotsky

Finishing the transitional program[313]

April 5, 1938

Dear Comrade Cannon:

I am enclosing the English translation of my letter addressed to the League of Nations.[314] The original text in French, dated March 31, has already been sent. It would be very very desirable to publish this document integrally in the bourgeois press. But if we give it here to the press they would send it by cable only in short excerpts. That is why I am sending it to you. You can transmit it directly to the American papers or to one of them. If it is necessary, you can give it exclusively to the *New York Times* or to the *Herald Tribune* under the condition that it be published as it is. Otherwise it would be better to give it freely to the whole press.

Please cable us when the letter will appear in the American press so that we can give it simultaneously to the Mexican press where it will surely be published integrally.

Our work on the transitional program goes on with success. In two days I hope to send you the first half and in five or six days the end. I would be very glad to have your criticism and suggestions from the American comrades. Your plenum could adopt it, if in general only in principle, and leave to the Political Committee the right to introduce necessary amendments.

My best greetings to Rose [Karsner],[315] to you, and to all friends.

L. Trotsky

A Russian encyclopedia[316]

April 26, 1938

Dear Friend:

I am now working on the Stalin book[317] and parallel with it the Lenin, but I see with absolute clarity that it will be impossible to proceed without a Russian encyclopedia. At every page I am faced with research upon geographical, historical, chronological, biographical, etc., data. Would it not be possible to find an old prerevolutionary encyclopedia in New York? What is the price of a new Soviet encyclopedia? I began in France and in Norway to buy it and I have the first three volumes of the *small* encyclopedia. How many volumes have appeared up until today? What is the price?

The ideal would be to have an old encyclopedia and the small new one. The minimum program is to have one of them.

Walker sold my war article to *The Yale Review*[318] and the necessary money to buy the encyclopedia could be extracted from these royalties. It would be very good if Sara or another comrade could take the encyclopedia with them, because its sending by railway would signify two or three months' delay.

The question is very important to me because otherwise my work would be handicapped at every step.

With best greetings,

Political personality and the milieu[319]

May 10, 1938

Dear Comrades:

In my two books on Lenin and Stalin, on which I am working simultaneously, I find it necessary to clarify a theoretical question which is also of great political importance. Basically, it concerns the relationship between the political or historical personality and the "milieu." In order to go directly to the heart of the problem, I shall refer to Souvarine's book on Stalin, in which the author accuses the leaders of the Left Opposition, myself included, of various mistakes, omissions, blunders, etc., from 1923 on. By no means do I wish to deny that there were many mistakes, blunders, and even stupidities. What is important, however, from the theoretical as well as the political point of view, is the relation or rather the disproportion between these "mistakes" and their consequences. It was precisely in this disproportion that the reactionary character of the new historic stage was expressed.

We committed no few mistakes in 1917 and in the years that followed. But the revolutionary momentum filled in the gaps and repaired the errors, sometimes with our assistance and sometimes even without our direct participation. But for this period the historians, including Souvarine, are indulgent because the struggle ended in victory. During the second half of 1917 and the years following, it was the turn of the liberals and the Mensheviks to commit mistakes, omissions, stupidities, etc.

I want to illustrate this historic "law" again with the example of the Great French Revolution in which, viewed in retrospect, the relationship between the actors and their milieu appear much more clearly defined and crystallized.

At a certain juncture in the revolution the Girondist[320] leaders completely lost their bearings. In spite of their popularity and their intelligence, they committed nothing but mistakes and blunders. They seemed to participate actively in their own downfall. Later it was the turn of Danton[321] and his friends. Historians and biographers have never ceased to wonder at the confused, passive, and puerile attitude of Danton in the last months of his life. The same for Robespierre[322] and his friends: disorientation, passivity, and incoherence at the most critical moment. The explanation is obvious. At a given moment each of these groups had exhausted its political opportunities and could advance no further against the reality of internal economic conditions, international pressure, the resultant new currents among the masses, etc. Under those conditions each step produced results contrary to what they hoped for. But political abstention was scarcely more favorable. The stages of the revolution and the counterrevolution succeeded one another at an accelerated pace; the contradiction between the protagonists of a particular program and the changed situation assumed an unexpected and extremely acute character. This gives the historian the possibility of displaying his retrospective wisdom by enumerating and cataloguing the mistakes, omissions, and blunders. But unfortunately these historians have refrained from indicating the correct path which could have led a moderate to victory in a period of revolutionary upsurge, or on the other hand from indicating a revolutionary policy which would be both reasonable and victorious in a Thermidorean period.

It is unfortunate that we do not possess a library here, which compels me to ask the assistance of our French friends. It is necessary to search through the histories of the French Revolution and the biographies of its heroes to find the most typical references on this subject. It is necessary to present a full array of references from the historians and the biographers, beginning with the first historiographers of the French Revolution and ending with Mathiez[323] and his pupils. The more varied the political viewpoints of the historians and biographers (ranging from royalist to socialist), the more clarified the question will be.

How is this work to be organized? It could, perhaps, be divided up among several friends sufficiently competent and interested in the subject. The basis of the division of labor should be neither the historical personages, nor the events, but only the books. In other words, each participant would assume the task of searching through a certain number of historical and biographical works and of extracting from them everything which directly or indirectly concerns the question before us. It is better to show too much than too little. All the references must be absolutely exact, indicating the work, the edition, and the page. It is unnecessary to say that this assistance would be most valuable to me. ∎

Muenzenberg's expulsion[324]

June 5, 1938

Dear Friend:

You should write to Adolphe [Rudolf Klement] so that our press might publish a note on Muenzenberg as soon as possible, along more or less the following lines:

The prudent and clever Muenzenberg has been expelled from the Central Committee of the German Communist Party. Naturally, this measure is simply the preparation for expelling Muenzenberg from the party. The bureaucrats move cautiously because Muenzenberg knows too much. But, devoid of political courage, Muenzenberg lets things proceed, that is, he permits his expulsion by successive installments. Perhaps he hopes in this manner to gain favor with the GPU. We have often seen artful and cunning diplomats and maneuvering bureaucrats prove themselves stupid and blundering when faced with a decisive crisis. The only course for Muenzenberg, as shown by the examples of W. Krivitsky and A. Barmine,[325] is to openly break with the GPU, openly denounce its crimes, and depend on the protection of public opinion. But there is reason to believe that Muenzenberg will not do this. In the end he will pay dearly for his lack of courage and political steadfastness. But that's his affair.

                         Best regards,
                         L.T.

Molinier and the international conference[326]

June 9, 1938

Dear Comrade:

I am writing you this letter after much hesitation, for experience has shown me that it is very difficult to convince the French comrades of the necessity of careful and energetic maneuvers toward this or that opponent. They let themselves be carried away by their feelings, by a purely psychological "intransigence," and in the end it comes to nothing.

The problem is always the Molinier organization [the PCI].[327] It is the greatest obstacle for the development of our section. This impostor throws an extremely unfavorable light on the Fourth International and repels the workers. They tell themselves: Yes, these are good ideas, but these people are capable of nothing.

We must know how to use the next [international] conference to settle this troublesome question. I suppose that Molinier will make an attempt to participate in the conference. Our section will naturally be opposed. But that is not sufficient. A purely negative attitude would leave everything as it is now, that is, in very bad shape. Moreover, the international conference could not respond with an outright rejection to any organization whatsoever that proposes to join. That is why I think that the conference should name if need be a special commission to analyze the character of the PCI (its composition, its policy, its financial sources, etc.). The same commission should of course also pose the personal question of Molinier. If the commission's investigation shows that the majority of the PCI is seeking nothing but to demur to the Fourth International, we could very well formulate some conditions. For example, that Molinier leave France and go to the United States, and remain there for two years without being accepted by the American section. For two years he would demonstrate through his attitude his right to be reinstated. The new members of the PCI can enter the POI[328] as full members. The former members, those who left the POI, must pass through a provisional period, let us say six months. All this is just an example. I do not believe we can settle the whole question definitively, but we certainly could shake up the obstacle posed by the PCI, and if Molinier and his friends refuse to accept the decision of the conference, the latter could adopt a motion based on full knowledge of the situation and thereby strike a decisive blow against the Molinier group. In passing, we can disarm Vereecken and others like him who have begun to flirt with the PCI. The advantage of such a procedure is enormous. But it requires a calm, firm, and intelligent attitude on the part of the leadership of the POI, which must not oppose setting up the commission, not rush through the investigation, not compromise the plan through careless articles or even conversations before or during the conference. In the event that Molinier and his friends do refuse, you would hold all the cards; the decision forbidding Molinier from engaging in political activity retains full force and his disloyalty is obvious.

This letter is strictly confidential. I would consider its disclosure directly or indirectly by any comrade as a disloyal act.

My sincerest greetings,

An introduction worthy of Rosa Luxemburg[329]

June 14, 1938

Dear Comrade Wasserman:

It is absolutely impossible for me to write an introduction to the letters of Rosa Luxemburg. I am now totally absorbed by my books and an introduction should be worthy of Rosa.

It would be very good to publish *I Confess*[330] under the condition of a very good translation, which is not so easy. Diego Rivera promised to illustrate this book if the parts of the translation are sent to him in time.

I hope to receive the final report of the Dewey Commission [*Not Guilty*] in a sufficient number of copies in order to impress public opinion here. At least fifteen copies would be necessary.

Don't occupy yourself further about Breton's books. We obtained them here. I am very glad to hear from you that Mr. Meyer Schapiro[331] is not antagonistic to us but sympathetic. I am writing him today.

Yours comradely,
Leon Trotsky

Fusion with the Lovestoneites?[332]

July 29, 1938

WEBER: The Lovestoneites have been discussing in their organ the question of unity with us. My impression is that Lovestone is absolutely opposed, but the rank and file have a sentiment for unity. Shouldn't we have interfered? Do you think we should have taken this question up in our press, intervened at that point, and have said something about it?

TROTSKY: I believe we must approach this question in a very calm, serious, and even friendly manner. One thing is we must continue our polemical articles against Lovestone, but if we have an objective reason for affirming that some part of the Lovestoneites are willing to merge with us, we will say, of course we should be glad to realize such a fusion. The question is only on what basis.

It is indisputable that in some very important questions the divergences are diminishing. In the very acute question of the Moscow trials, the question is whether we are revolutionary communists or fascists. The question, I believe, is a very important one, especially for a merger. Yesterday they were of the opinion that we were fascists and now, God be thanked, they understand that we are not fascists. Good. In the whole appreciation of the Stalinist regime (the appreciation of the Moscow trials is only a small part of the appreciation of the Soviet state)—yes, we see here some rapprochement to our point of view, but a very important question remains.

If we diverge only five or ten degrees, the international divergence is tremendous. Now what is our international point of view—the London Bureau or the Fourth International? That is the question. In Spain it is the POUM and a revolutionary party. That is the question. We cannot merge with the POUM and we cannot merge with the London Bureau. You must check your national orientation by its international projectives. That is for you the question and we will discuss with you frankly the questions which we have discussed with you in the past, on the basis of our existence as an independent organization. There was the Russian Revolution. Here is a test. Then it was the Chinese Revolution—we began with this. The Anglo-Russian Committee, the attitude towards the labor party and the trade unions.

Now we have had new experiences of tremendous size and it seems this time we have organized into a new International. We have a program of transitional demands. What do you say about this? Our appreciation of the centrists? Our appreciation of the POUM? The labor party? I believe most important now is the POUM because of the defeat of the Spanish revolution. I thank you very much, Mr. Bertram Wolfe,[333] that I am not an agent of Hitler, but what do you think of the POUM?

WEBER: In case of a concrete proposal for fusion, could we admit into our party such men as Lovestone, Wolfe?

TROTSKY: I believe that it is excluded that we can work with these men. It is my sincere conviction that the old generation is completely consumed, used up. We see that even in our own ranks. It is difficult to work with the old people—Sneevliet, Serge, and even Rosmer. Vereecken too belongs to the old generation. Because of the catastrophes, a series of defeats, they have been ground down and now their dissatisfaction with the march of history makes them very critical and distrustful; they have no patience, and patience is a very necessary quality in a revolutionary. Every time they see the cause in our own movement, because it is not strong. That is why we must base ourselves on the youth, our only elements who are sufficiently persistent and strong to go forward after all defeats.

Now Lovestone and similar people showed fifteen years ago that they are only bureaucrats who adapt themselves to everyone in power. First Lenin and Trotsky, then Zinoviev, Kamenev, and then Stalin, and as Stalin was the last hope, they remained with him until the last moment. Now they are with Martin[334] in the automobile union in the sense that in their trade union work they support Martin. They are absolutely incapable of going with the masses against the leaders. Their whole mentality is to adopt some leader. It is possible that they can even adapt themselves to us for a time.

That is why we must proceed in a quiet and free manner towards the rank and file and check the leaders by concrete questions in the discussion. We saw with the Musteites that the less prominent leaders were eliminated in the discussion [in 1934]. Then Muste remained a short time. Also it is possible that Wolfe and Lovestone will split. We cannot see these details, but if it is a necessary conjunctural episode we can accept even that only with the condition that he begins with our present divergences—the question of Spain.

WEBER: On the question of defense groups, this question arose also in France. It arose at that time through Craipeau, and here it also has a practical significance in our attempt to build our defense group in Newark, although I think our own forces are so small that they are discouraged at the idea of forming a defense group; there are so few who would fit into that kind of work. Still we would form such a group, but would it be possible to take workers from the Workers Alliance[335] and from unions to try to form a larger body and thus give encouragement to ours?

TROTSKY: I believe it is the only one road if you have the slightest possibility to do it. Of course we can begin only with the selection of some militant elements as future organizers, not in the name of our party but in the trade unions, Workers Alliance, etc., for it is clear that they will be the first victims of fascist gangsters. Then it is only the question of forming such groups and connecting these groups together. Our comrades should try to be the link between different groups.

But this work should be put on the base of existing mass organizations. In Germany it was the question whether these organizations should fight. It was the united front. The Social Democrats had their Iron Front with Catholics, etc., with bourgeois parties. Our problem was that the Social Democratic organization should separate from the bourgeois and unite with the Red Front. Here it is the question only to inculcate the necessity of the party. There it was the question of which party to join. Here the problem is that we must inculcate into existing organizations the necessity of defending themselves. In order to overthrow society we must have these defense groups. We must for a long time give them the character of a defense organization. We must defend our rights and existence. ■

Answers to Gladys Lloyd Robinson[336]

August 18, 1938

QUESTION: What do you think of President Roosevelt as a man?

ANSWER: Even his most bitter opponents do not venture to deny his exceptional personality. Without doubt he possesses more outstanding personal qualities than the modern dictators, Mussolini, Hitler, not to speak of Stalin. I admit it the more readily since an abyss separates my program from the program of Mr. Roosevelt.

QUESTION: What is your opinion of Mr. Roosevelt's measures to alleviate the social and economic ills in the United States? How would you handle the self-same situation?

ANSWER: These measures have a purely palliative nature. Private property paralyzes further economic development of the United States. Under these conditions social reforms are but the expenditure of accumulations for the amelioration of the most glaring social ills. It is clear that this method does not open up wide perspectives. A program which wishes to maintain the foundations of capitalism untouched cannot offer a way out of the crisis.

You ask me how I should have acted in the place of Mr. Roosevelt. But I could not be in his place—we express opposing historical interests. Mr. Roosevelt desires to ameliorate the situation of the toilers insofar as it is necessary to *save* the capitalist system. I see the only way out through *liquidating* it once and for all.

QUESTION: What do you believe will be the final outcome of Mr. Hitler and Mussolini?

ANSWER: In the next great war the fascist regimes will

be the first to collapse. Hypothetically we can lay down the following order in the catastrophes: Japan, Italy, Germany. Fascism is a temporary historic means for suppressing irreconcilable internal contradictions. In wartime they will, however, burst to the surface with such force as perhaps the history of humanity has not yet known. In place of fascism will come the socialist revolution.

QUESTION: What will be England's fate in the next war?

ANSWER: The economic power of England long ago ceased to correspond to the gigantic magnitude of her empire. The interests of the metropolis and the colonies and the dominions are deeply contradictory in all parts of the world. During the first period of the war the different parts of the Empire might temporarily be brought closer together through the instinct of self-preservation; but at the end of the war Great Britain will inevitably fall apart and this in turn will lead to social convulsions in England.

QUESTION: Will the final result of the present conflict in Spain give us the answer to the immediate political system of Europe?

ANSWER: The second collapse of Spanish democracy within the last six years shows with unusual force that the framework of democracy is much too narrow for the solution of the social problem. Capitalism in the future can maintain its existence only with the help of open military violence. Since Caballero, Garcia Oliver, Negrin, and Stalin prevented the Spanish proletariat from conquering power for the socialist revolution, the state inevitably fell into the hands of Franco.[337] Only political blindness could not foresee this outcome.

QUESTION: Do you believe that democracy has failed in America?

ANSWER: The blossoming of American democracy was based on the blossoming of American capitalism. Naturally therefore the incurable crisis of capitalism is transformed into a grave crisis of democracy.

QUESTION: Is Mayor Hague[338] a symbol of menace to American democracy—how strong a menace in your opinion?

ANSWER: Yes, I think that Mayor Hague has very great political significance which far exceeds his own very trivial and limited personality. Through his actions Hague says that the capitalist regime can no longer be upheld by democratic means. It is true that Hague himself denies the fascist characteristics of his policy. But long ago he had a forerunner who spoke in prose without suspecting it. The number of imitators of Hague will inevitably grow. It is impossible to overcome fascism by constitutional means since fascism operates on a different level.

QUESTION: When do you think that the present chaotic condition of the world will reach a crisis?

ANSWER: I do not undertake predictions as to dates. Nevertheless the present tense situation cannot last years. The denouement must begin in a very short space of time. It can take the form of either war or revolution. At the present moment war seems closer than revolution. But war will undoubtedly carry revolution in its wake.

QUESTION: How do you think the youth of the world will meet these problems?

ANSWER: The new generation of toilers and intellectuals enters conscious mental life under absolutely exceptional historic conditions—crisis of the world economic system, collapse of democracy, disintegration of the Socialist and Communist Internationals, increasing rottenness of the Soviet bureaucracy, the deepening danger of war. Under these conditions civilization can be saved only by exceptionally daring revolutionary means. In order to find these means it is necessary to review the old heritage critically. That is why I think that the new generation will distinguish itself by great daring of thought and will. It will reject the philosophy of half-measures. It will demand complete answers to the problems of our epoch and it will lend its forces to transform these answers into life. Only under these conditions can humanity move forward. ■

Isaacs's book about China[339]

October 23, 1938

The Tragedy of the Chinese Revolution. Last month [Harold R.] Isaacs's book (502 pages) appeared under this title in English. The book, which presents the history of the Chinese revolution, offers an exceptional example of contemporary Marxist literature. The author is exceptionally well acquainted with the subject. He spent several years in China as an active and serious observer and in part as a participant in events. The body of international literature that served as the basis of his work is truly enormous. The author has a facile command of the method of historical materialism and writes in clear, precise, and convincing language. The book should be a handbook for everyone who is really interested in the future of China and the Chinese revolution. The aim of this note is to direct all the comrades' attention to Comrade Isaacs's book. I want to express also the hope that the book will appear soon in other languages. Above all it must be translated into Chinese. ■

Latin American problems: A transcript[340]

November 4, 1938

TROTSKY: Some of our comrades have proposed a general discussion upon the political situation in Mexico and Latin America in view of the return of Comrade Curtiss.[341] The discussion will be of a general character with the sole view of informing our comrades of the situation.

CURTISS: The last few days have been very busy for me in trying to get some clarity and unity into my notes. . . . I am more acquainted with the local situation in Mexico than I am with the rest of Latin America.

It appears to me that comrades in Mexico, in Puerto Rico, in Cuba, and in other regions, as much as I have been able to observe, have an extremely mechanical approach to the problems of permanent revolution. They take an idea, tear it out of its context, and I think that this in part gives rise to some of the difficulties you have heard about in the Mexican situation.

Mainly it is a misunderstanding of the question of skipping over stages. The literature of the revolutionary movement is posed mainly from the point of view of the industrially advanced countries and only understood in the light of the industrially advanced countries. For example, this question of skipping over stages is posed like this for the Mexican comrades: Why can't we in Mexico skip over intervening stages and arrive directly at the stage of proletarian revolution?

No attempt is made to look upon the movement from the point of view of accomplishing the democratic tasks. They are not used to thinking in that fashion, and this I believe gives rise to many misunderstandings.

One question, for example, is the relationship in Mexico between the liberal bourgeoisie and our movement, the Fourth International. When an attempt is made to correct the Mexican comrades, they pose the abstraction of the permanent revolution and then come back with the claim: "Comrade Trotsky is reneging on his principles in regard to Mexico because of his desire to safeguard his exile." This is not always expressed openly but it lurks in the back of the minds of the comrades.

It is not very difficult to argue against this, utilizing the case of China, as it is somewhat similar. In the case of the other countries with semicolonial problems, our attitude is generally the same. The comrades there are not particularly well-read or interested in these problems. What they are interested in is what strikes them immediately.

An explanation is necessary about the relationship between our movement and the general democratic movement. Emphasis should be placed upon the study of each concrete case, not upon abstractions only but upon each concrete case. For example, if socialism were achieved in the United States, it would be possible for all countries to skip these intermediate stages. Each special circumstance will have to be taken into consideration and an attempt made to telescope them into a shorter space of time.

TROTSKY: On the question of permanent revolution in colonial countries—

CURTISS: Just a minute if I may—I would like to emphasize one more question. The misunderstanding on the part of leading comrades on this concrete question gives rise to difficulties and obstacles that make it practically impossible to approach the mass movement in Mexico, to approach the movement of the people generally.

TROTSKY: Yes, I believe that Comrade Curtiss is right. The question is of tremendous importance; and schematicism of the formula of permanent revolution can become and does become from time to time extremely dangerous to our movement in Latin America.

That history can skip stages is absolutely clear. For example, if a railroad is built through the Yucatan jungles, it is a skipping of stages. It is on the level of American development of roads.

And when Toledano[342] swears by Marx, that is also a skipping of stages, because the Toledanos of Europe in the time of Marx swore by other prophets.

Russia skipped the stage of democracy, not totally, but compressed the stage. The fact is well known. The proletariat can skip the stage of democracy, but we cannot skip the stages of the development of the proletariat.

I believe our comrades in Mexico and other countries attempt abstractly in respect to the proletariat, even in respect to history generally, to skip—not with the masses over certain stages, but over history generally—especially over the development of the proletariat.

The working class of Mexico participates, cannot help but participate, in the movement, in the struggle for the independence of the country, for the democratization of the agrarian relations, and so on. In this way the proletariat can come to power before the independence of Mexico is assured and the agrarian relations are reorganized. Then the workers' government can become an instrument in order to resolve these questions.

It can occur; possibly it will occur. But it is necessary to lead, to guide the workers—issuing from the democratic tasks to the taking of power. Not to pose an abstract socialist dictatorship to the real needs and desires of the masses, but starting from these daily struggles to oppose the national bourgeoisie on the basis of the workers' needs, winning the leadership of the workers and gaining the power.

Latin American society, like every society—developed or backward—is composed of three classes: the bourgeoisie, the petty bourgeoisie, and the proletariat. Insofar as the tasks are democratic in a large historical sense, they are bourgeois-democratic tasks, but the bourgeoisie here is incapable of resolving these democratic tasks, as the bourgeoisie was incapable in Russia or in China.

In that sense, during the struggle for the democratic tasks, we oppose the proletariat to the bourgeoisie. The independence of the proletariat even in the beginning of this movement is absolutely necessary, and we especially oppose the proletariat to the bourgeoisie in the agrarian question, for that class will rule in Mexico as in every Latin American country which has the peasants. If the peasants remain in support of the bourgeois class, as is now the fact, then it will be such a semidemocratic, semi-Bonapartistic state as now exists in every country of Latin America, with inclinations toward the masses.

This is the period in which the national bourgeoisie searches for a bit more independence from the foreign imperialists. The national bourgeoisie is obliged to flirt with the workers, with the peasants, and then we have the strong man of the country orientated to the left as now in Mexico.

If the national bourgeoisie is obliged to give up the struggle against the foreign capitalists and to work under the direct tutelage of the foreign capitalists, then we have a semifascist regime, as in Brazil for example. But the bourgeoisie there is absolutely incapable of creating democratic rule, because on one side stands imperialist capital, on the other side they are afraid of the proletariat because history there skipped a stage and the proletariat became an important factor before the democratic organization of the whole society.

Even in these semi-Bonapartistic-democratic governments the state needs the support of the peasants and through the weight of the peasants disciplines the workers. That is more or less the situation in Mexico.

Now the Fourth International recognizes all the democratic

tasks of the state in the fight for national independence, but the Mexican section of the Fourth International is in competition with the national bourgeoisie before the workers, before the peasants. We are in permanent competition with the national bourgeoisie as the only one leadership which is capable of assuring the victory of the masses in the fight against the foreign imperialists.

In the agrarian question we support the expropriations. That does not signify, of course, that we support the national bourgeoisie. In every case where it is a direct fight against the foreign imperialists or their reactionary fascist agents, we give revolutionary support, preserving the full political independence of our organization, of our program, of our party, and the full freedom of our criticism. The Kuomintang in China, the PRM in Mexico, and the APRA[343] in Peru are very similar organizations. It is the People's Front in the form of a party.

Of course, the People's Front in Latin America does not have so reactionary a character as in France or in Spain. It is two-sided. It can have a reactionary attitude insofar as it is directed against the workers; it can have an aggressive attitude insofar as it is directed against imperialism.

But in our appreciation of the People's Front in Latin America in the form of a national political party, we make a distinction from France and from Spain. But this historical difference of appreciation and difference of attitude can be permitted only under the condition that our organization doesn't participate in the APRA, Kuomintang, or PRM, that it preserves absolute freedom of action and criticism.

The questions of the conquest of power and of socialism should also be concretized. The first question is the conquest of power by the workers' party in Mexico and the other advanced Latin American countries. The second question is that of building socialism. Of course, it would be more difficult for Mexico to build socialism than for Russia. Yet it is not at all excluded that the Mexican workers may conquer power before the workers of the United States if the workers of the United States continue to be as slow as they are now. I will say that it is especially possible if the imperialist movement in the United States pushes the bourgeoisie to domination over Latin America [presses the bourgeoisie in its drive for domination over Latin America]. Latin America is for the United States what Austria and the Sudeten[344] were for Hitler.

As the first step of the new stage of American imperialism, Roosevelt or his successor will show the fist to Latin America in order to assure their economic-military tutelage over Latin America, and that will provoke a more decisive revolutionary movement, as in China—we believe with more success. Under these conditions the workers of Mexico can come to power before the workers of the United States. We must encourage them in this direction.

But that does not signify that they will build their own socialism. They will resolve to fight against American imperialism and they will, of course, reorganize the agrarian conditions of the country and abolish the perfidious and parasitic society which plays a tremendous role in these countries, giving the power to the workers' and peasants' soviets and fighting against the imperialists. The future will depend upon events in the United States and the whole world.

CURTISS: As Comrade Trotsky was speaking, many questions that comrades ask one another over all Latin America and many parts of the world arose in my mind.

Let us discuss the case of Mexico. There are two problems that are connected. At the start of the labor movement here, I believe when Morones[345] was the most important figure, the argument of Morones was that it would be possible to conquer power in Mexico but that the workers could not dare do so because of the inevitable military intervention of the United States.

No matter what his own opinion was about the necessity of socialism, Morones took care of himself first of all.

Now we find theoretically posed in *El Popular*, Lombardo Toledano's paper, the reverse of the same problem. And there was one article in *El Machete*, the Stalinist organ, which I did not study extremely carefully, similarly posing the question as to whether or not it would be possible to achieve socialism in Mexico or achieve the conquest of power peacefully. I am conscious that the workers give quite a bit of thought to this question. It is posed in many articles. The new socialists are all intrigued with this idea.

The actual path toward the conquest of power seems to take the form of union control. The union struggles for control. The butchers, for example, have threatened to go out on strike in order to gain control of the slaughterhouses. The railroads are under workers' administration.

I don't know exactly what the situation is in the petroleum industry, but here are some of the reports. That in the mansion formerly owned by a representative of the oil company, the representative no longer lives there. Instead a trade union bureaucrat occupies his place.

The question of democracy, it appears to me, not only is a question of state form, but a burning question within the labor movement. A concrete problem that our comrades in Mexico face is how to meet the bureaucracy. I thought the trade union bureaucracy in the United States was pretty bad, but I think they are just taking lessons from the Mexican bureaucracy. An iron hand is wielded. If the members do not obey, they are excluded. The advance of our movement hinges on that particular question.

There is a bureaucracy of the state and also a bureaucracy of the unions, and in many respects they are not so very far apart in Mexico. That is a problem in both spheres that is becoming very acute.

I think the concrete application of the transitional program to Mexico will have to take into account these laws and these backgrounds. Attempts at workers' control, attempts to democratize the trade union movement. I think it is necessary to issue a slogan of armed workers' militia, not only against the bourgeoisie, but to defend the conquests they themselves have already made from the trade union bureaucrats.

On the question of winning over peasants. Here we find that the schoolteachers seem to play a key role. . . . The schoolteachers, along with the railroad workers, are the connecting link between the peasantry and city workers.

Two questions I would like Comrade Trotsky to comment on: One, our attitude toward the petroleum expropriation and arising bureaucracy and the attempt of the bureaucracy to place part of the burden on the workers; and, two, the exact reason for the swing leftward on the part of Cardenas—why the swing is so decisive, and why so deep, because of all the presidents, Cardenas seems to have gone further in facing the land problem than any other.

A note on the APRA. It is an important organization but subsidized at the present time by the Mexican government. One of the chief arguments of the APRA and of the leaders of the APRA, and I think this is a question not only for the comrades of Latin America but also for us in the United States, is this: They claim there is no chance or no use in attempting to have anything to do with the workers of the industrially developed countries because they are not interested in colonial problems.

I think the attempt by comrades of the Fourth International in industrially advanced countries to face the problems of the colonial and semicolonial countries would be a strong blow against the argument of the APRA.

LANKIN:[346] I would like a little more information about the Mexican organization. How many members it has and what the composition of the party is. What publications, etc.

CURTISS: It is difficult to determine the exact number. It

is in a stage of reorganization.

Social composition: Composed of two levels, schoolteachers and workers. The workers are in the main of the building trades, not industrial workers but building-trades workers.

The official publication is a newspaper, *Cuarta Internacional*. It has a very good circulation. The group has done a great deal of publishing but very little of it is sold, most of it is distributed.

Of course, *Clave*,[347] a new theoretical magazine, is very sympathetic to our point of view.

From the point of view of theory there is a big gap in the organization. The schoolteachers are well read in Marxism. Most of the other comrades know very little about Marxism from a theoretical standpoint. Some attempts have been made at education with some success in the cities, but it was not carried out on a national scale.

LANKIN: You said before when you spoke about the unions that if you disagree with union leaders you can be taken off the job. Would a leader in the Mexican unions have full power in the sense of a government official over that particular group of workers, or do they have the same democracy they are supposed to have in the United States?

CURTISS: In all Latin American countries, the constitutions of the trade unions are perfect models of democracy, but the leaders carry on dictatorial practices. All unions have all sorts of guarantees, but these guarantees don't mean a thing.

A leader can expel anyone from the union, and the expelled member finds himself in a very, very disagreeable position. No attempt can be made at appealing the expulsion. The only real appeal would be the appeal of fists.

John L. Lewis, Green, and all our American trade union leaders like them have nothing on the Mexican trade union bureaucracy.

ROBINSON: I would like to ask how the Mexican section of the Fourth International is taking the decision of the conference[348] which was printed in the *Appeal*. How is the Communist Party growing recently? Is it having success? Is it growing stronger? How do we stand in relation to the CP?

CURTISS: The Communist Party is a powerful organization in Mexico. It controls many public offices. When our comrades deliver literature to the post office, if it falls into the hands of the CP, it will never get to its destination.

The Stalinists of Mexico are making a drive for a total of 75,000 members. In the United States they are making a drive for 100,000 members. From this you can get an idea of the organizational strength of the CP. From the point of view of members, it is a powerful organization. However, it is wrong to look upon them as an unbreakable mass. . . .

The decision of the International congress was taken very, very poorly by the comrades in Mexico City, especially the Galicia group. It has given rise to many tendencies, and we may be left with a much smaller organization than we figure now. The decision was taken very badly by these comrades. They agreed to submit to the decision but only under protest. The motion to accept under protest was passed with only a few comrades voting against. . . .

TROTSKY: Regarding the estimate of membership of the Communist Party in connection with its campaign for 75,000, I am very doubtful. Political statistics in Mexico are not the most exact in the world. For example, the CTM[349] gives out as its membership, a million. When I asked a former official of the CTM if this were true, he replied:

"No, it is exaggerated."

"How many, a half million?"

"No, I believe forty or fifty thousand, and especially insofar as it concerns workers."

The figures of the Communist Party, however, are very, very confused.

Diego Rivera believes, and he knows the situation, that the party is strong in Mexico City. It had, I believe he said,

12,000 and not more than 14,000 members, some 11,600 or 11,700 bureaucrats, and 2,000 or 3,000 workers.

In regard to the bureaucrats, they cannot be politically recognized as genuine members of the party. The official leader of the trade union is a Communist. He obliges everyone under him to be a Communist. If they don't attend a meeting, they must forfeit their salary for five days.

The trade unions in Mexico are constitutionally statified. One cannot obtain a job if he is not a member of a trade union, and the bureaucratic trade unions receive dues through the state. With a teacher, for example, the leaders decided that every teacher pay 1.5 percent of his salary. The secretary of finances ordered that from their salaries 1.5 percent should be deducted for the trade union.

In the general context of Mexican politics, the trade unions are now at a very interesting stage. We now see a general tendency to statify the trade unions. In the fascist countries we find the extreme expression of this tendency.

In democratic countries, they transform the former independent unions into instruments of the state. The trade unions in France are being transformed into an official bureaucracy of the state. Jouhaux came to Mexico as a representative of his government in order to safeguard the interests of France in Mexican oil, and so on.

The reason for this statifying tendency is that declining capitalism cannot tolerate independent unions. If trade unions are too independent then the capitalists push the fascists in order to destroy them or to frighten the leaders with a fascist alternative in order to discipline them.

Jouhaux has been disciplined in this manner. He is sure that if he is a better republican, then the French will not establish a fascist regime. We saw in Spain that in the most anarchistic trade unions the leaders became bourgeois ministers during the war.

In Germany and Italy this is assured in a totalitarian

manner, the unions being incorporated directly into the state, together with the owner-capitalists. It is only a difference in degree, not a difference in essence.

We see in Mexico and the other Latin American countries that they skipped over most stages of the development. It began in Mexico directly by incorporating the trade unions in the state. In Mexico we have a double domination. That is, foreign capital and the national bourgeoisie, or, as Diego Rivera formulated it, a "sub-bourgeoisie"—a stratum which is controlled by foreign capital and at the same time opposed to the workers; in Mexico a semi-Bonapartist regime between foreign capital and national capital, foreign capital and the workers.

Every government can create in a case like this a position of oscillation, of inclination [tilting or leaning] one time to the national bourgeoisie or workers and another time to foreign capital. In order to have the workers in their hands, they incorporated the trade unions in the state.

They skip over economic relations also, stages of development in the sense that they expropriated oil, for example, from foreign capital and yet didn't give it to the national capitalists. They don't distribute it or sell it to the Mexican bourgeoisie, especially because they are afraid of the class struggle of the workers, and they give the oil fields to the state.

They create a state capitalism which has nothing to do with socialism. It is the purest form of state capitalism.

At the same time they incorporate the workers, the trade unions, which are already statified. They incorporate them in the management of the railroad, the oil industry, and so on, in order to transform the trade union leadership into government representatives. The foreman is at the same time the representative of the workers, of their interests nominally, yet really the representative of the state over the workers. And he has the right—better to say the possibility—of ruining for the workers their chance to work, because in the name of discipline of the trade unions he can do it in the interest of production.

In that sense, of course, when we say the control of production by the workers it cannot mean control of production by the statified bureaucrats of the trade unions, but control by the workers of their own bureaucracy and to fight for the independence of the trade unions from the state.

In Mexico that is the most important task—the liberation of the trade unions from the tutelage of the bourgeois state and the liberation of the workers from the dictatorship of the bureaucrats in the trade unions. That is workers' democracy.

We must underline the fact that now the trade unions cannot be democratic trade unions in the old sense of the word. The imperialists cannot tolerate them. In the old countries as well as in Mexico, they can be instruments of the imperialist bourgeoisie or revolutionary organizations against the imperialist bourgeoisie.

That is why, of course, we begin in Mexico with slogans—liberation from the state, workers' democracy, free discussion, and so on. But they are only transitional slogans, leading to the more important slogans of the workers' state. It is only a stage which can give us the possibility of replacing the present directors of the trade unions with a revolutionary direction [leadership].

They cannot be independent as in the good old times, tolerated by the bourgeoisie because it was possible to allow this much freedom to the trade unions. It is no longer possible now to establish the old democracy in the trade unions just as it is no longer possible to establish democracy in the state. It is an absolutely parallel development.

In Mexico, Toledano utilizes this condition only to assure his domination of the workers as every Latin American state uses it in order to assure its own dominance. It is a semi-Bonapartistic rule, inclined now to the left, now to the right. It depends upon the concrete historical stage in every country. But here we cannot skip the stages. We cannot say to the workers, Give us the leadership and we will show you what to do.

It is absolutely certain that the Fourth International is capable of assuring revolutionary direction to trade unions during the transitory stages in Mexico. The Fourth International will defend this Mexican stage against imperialist intervention. It is not as in France, as in the United States. We fight in order to prevent its being transformed into a colony, into slavery.

But as the Mexican section of the Fourth International, it is not our state and we must be independent from this state. In this sense we are not opposed to state capitalism in Mexico; but the first thing we demand is our own representation of workers before this state. We cannot permit the leaders of the trade unions to become functionaries of the state. To attempt to conquer the state in this way is absolute idiocy. It is not possible in this manner peacefully to conquer power. It is a petty-bourgeois dream.

That was Stalin's plan with the Kuomintang, and it was because of this idiocy of Stalin that the Kuomintang now rules China. We will enter the Kuomintang, said Stalin, then we will politely eliminate the right wing, then the center, and then the left. Thus we will conquer power without any trouble.

We of the Left Opposition pointed out that the right wing of the Kuomintang is imperialist. They have in their hands the army. We cannot conquer power without opposing this machinery. Insofar as we are in the hands of the Kuomintang, we are in the hands of the genuine bosses of the country. Absolutely.

The APRA now affirms that they are the most revolutionary party in Peru. This is only because they are in opposition; but even in opposition they are more cautious than is the administration of Cardenas. Insofar as I can judge the last programmatic letter[350] of the leader of the APRAists, the party is controlled by leaders who are connected with foreign capital. They are interested, like all the reactionary generals in Mexico, in building a dominating clique as an instrument of foreign capital, in working if possible for the increase of the national capital.

Of course, the interests of foreign capital and national capital are not always identical, and they come from time to time into sharp clashes. Thus it is possible in favorable conditions for the national capital to oppose the exigencies of foreign capital.

During the time of Roosevelt's "good neighbor policy," Cardenas tested the possibility of military intervention and he succeeded to a certain degree in conquering certain positions, beginning with English capital, then American, and so on. Now it seems that he is beginning to make concessions again. He tested the limits of the possibilities.

The national bourgeoisie needs an inner [domestic] market and the inner market is more or less a satisfied peasantry. That is why the agrarian revolution, especially at the expense of foreign owners, is a direct gain to the national bourgeoisie. The peasants will buy more goods and so on. This policy is of a political character. It is not clear at the beginning how far the limits are. The administration cannot say how long the bourgeoisie will tolerate, or how long the American bourgeoisie will tolerate, or how far it can go without intervention from Great Britain, and so on. That is why it is of an adventuristic character. From one side probing and from the other jumping, and then a retreat.

I believe that we must fight with the greatest energy this idea that the state can be seized by stealing bits of the power. It is the history of the Kuomintang. In Mexico the power is in the hands of the national bourgeoisie, and we can conquer power only by conquering the majority of the workers and a great part of the peasantry, and then overthrowing the bourgeoisie. There is no other possibility.

The APRA says that there is no use going hand in hand with the workers of the United States because they are not interested in colonial questions, the same with the European proletariat, and so on. The real reason for that attitude is the need for political protection from the White House. It is not an ideological mistake or error. It is a political calculation of the national bourgeoisie of Peru.

They know that they need the confidence of the White House, especially of Wall Street. If they win in Peru, they will need the protection of Wall Street as do all the governments now in Latin America, and if they enter into connection with the workers, to win them for the struggle, that signifies they must break all relations with the White House.

For some time it was difficult for me to get a clear picture of the program of the APRA. But the last letter of the head of the party is absolutely clear. He says that the United States is the guardian of Latin America's liberty; and if a foreign power threatens this liberty, the APRA will immediately call upon the United States, and so on—not a word about the workers.

It is a People's Front party. A People's Front is included in the party, as in every combination of such nature. Direction is in the hands of the bourgeoisie, and the bourgeoisie fears its own workers. That is why this party, although so strong that it could gain power by revolution, is afraid to enter that road. They do not have the courage or the class interest to mobilize the peasants and the workers, and they will replace them by military maneuvers or by direct intervention from the United States.

Of course, we cannot enter such a party; but we can create a nucleus in it in order to win the workers and separate them from the bourgeoisie. But under no circumstances can we repeat the Stalinist idiocy with the Kuomintang in China.

CURTISS: On the question of the statification of the trade unions, I think an important aspect of that is the National Labor Relations Board set up in the United States, which has played havoc with the fighting spirit of the workers.

I think that if we were to characterize the tendency in Mexico—the attempt to achieve a theoretical peace, a peaceful transition to socialism—it could be called a bureaucratic dream of the trade union leaders, who come into a soft and easy job through this process. That seems to them the acme of development toward socialism.

TROTSKY: It would be well to ask our comrades in Mexico to verify the statistics of the Communist Party. Diego Rivera estimates 12,000 were in the central drive for 75,000. He is not exaggerating. The Communist Party itself credits itself with not more than a total membership of 24,000. ■

Lombardo Toledano's lies[351]
November 8, 1938

During the twenty months I have enjoyed the hospitality of this country, Mr. Toledano and his advisers and assistants have publicly made a whole series of incredible assertions:

That I collaborated with the fascists in this country and others;

That I was preparing a general strike to overthrow the government of General Cardenas;

That I entered into a plot with Cedillo;
That I had secret contacts with Dr. Atl;
That I inspired the article by General Abelardo Rodriguez in connection with the coming election campaign.
Etc., etc.

After the first assertion of this type, I wrote the government, asking it to officially investigate. But the government felt there was no reason to make such an inquiry.

Over and over again, in the press, I characterized the statements of Toledano and his advisers (Laborde, etc.) as willful slander and false testimony. The object of these slander campaigns is to deprive me of the right of asylum and to give the GPU a chance to get hold of me.

Recently—in the November 5 issue of *Hoy*—I once again publicly proposed to Mr. Toledano to present proof for his assertions to an impartial commission which could be designated by the Mexican government or, for example, the International Federation of Trade Unions at Amsterdam. Instead of replying clearly and precisely to my challenge, Mr. Toledano, in the November 8 public meeting at Bellas Artes, offered a torrent of gross insults and added new slanders on top of the old ones.

I will not enter here into a political polemic with Mr. Toledano. I would simply say that if types like Kerensky-Toledano are considered "revolutionaries," then obviously I must be a "counterrevolutionary." But that is not the question; not at all. The question is whether I prepared a strike against the government of General Cardenas, whether I entered into a plot with the fascists, whether I had liaisons with Cedillo, whether I secretly met Dr. Atl, etc. Yes or no?

If I really did all that, I have no right to the hospitality of this country. If I didn't do any of that, Toledano is a perfidious slanderer who systematically deceives public opinion in this country on behalf of the GPU.

In that way, and only in that way, is the question posed.

The public insults only testify to the shamelessness of those who utter them. They cannot take the place of evidence.

I say once again to the workers, peasants, and all citizens of this magnificent country:

What Toledano is telling you about me is a deliberate lie. Don't believe it! ■

Can the 'Daily News' be sued?[352]
November 11, 1938

Dear Friend:

I am writing you to ask for your help in the complicated intrigue which the Stalinist agency is now creating around me. You know that the New York paper the *Daily News* has published editorials—for the third time, I think—saying that the expropriation policy of General Cardenas's government is . . . the result of my advice. There is no need to say how absurd such an assertion is. But in case this assertion might be brought into court, I am communicating the following to you: I have had no interviews with General Cardenas, I have not had any conversations with either him or the members of his government, either directly or by intermediaries, and my correspondence with the authorities has been limited to formal questions related to my residence in Mexico. The instigators of the insinuations printed in the *Daily News* and other publications know perfectly well the resolute and independent character of General Cardenas, who has no need of my "advice" to conduct his own policy. Furthermore, there is no need to say that the program I advocate is far from the program of the Mexican government. Anyone who is not illiterate knows this. No honest person would dare to question it. But we are in the presence of people who, while they are not illiterate, are manifestly without honor.

My first idea was that this intrigue was started by property-owners whose interests were harmed [by the recent nationalizations], who were using this means to try to somehow compromise the Mexican government. I still think today that this thread is definitely part of the intrigue. But there is another thread, the main one, which leads to the Stalinists. These gentlemen simultaneously work their game in two directions. The local agents of the GPU started by accusing me, in public speeches and articles (by Toledano and Laborde), of preparing an uprising against General Cardenas in alliance with fascist generals, etc. Such inventions were too obviously absurd to everyone, and the intrigue that had been launched in this direction quickly proved its sterility. (In a moment of lucidity or imprudence, Toledano himself acknowledged that such accusations could be launched only for ... insane people.) Of course, people who have nothing much to lose have continued to repeat this insanity. But the main attention of the GPU has turned in another direction. It seems today, if we are to believe Toledano, that I myself am trying to give the impression that I am the ... intimate adviser of the government of General Cardenas. Baseness and stupidity, as you can see, know no limits. There is no need to explain how much I appreciate the refuge the Mexican government has offered me and the degree of my concern that the government should not for a minute doubt my total loyalty. For what reason would I begin to claim to be what I am not and what I have no wish to become? Obviously for reasons ... of pride. Here the slanderers reveal their full intellectual and moral stature.

CAN THE 'DAILY NEWS' BE SUED? / 481

I have received from a well-informed source the information that the inspirer of the *Daily News* articles was a certain X . . . , a member of the Stalinist party in the United States and a collaborator of Federated Press. As an appendix to the present letter, I am sending you a written account on this individual which has not been published up to now. The mechanism of the provocation is perfectly clear: on one hand, the Stalinist agencies give the *Daily News* manifestly false information, thus utilizing the bad faith of a reactionary publication belonging to big capital; on the other hand, the publication of these articles is used (through the intermediary of Toledano and Company) to give the impression that I myself was the inspirer. Finally a supplementary "profit" accrues to these gentlemen in that they can immediately interpret my replies and refutations as an intervention on my part in Mexico's internal affairs. Baseness has no limits. The whole mechanism of this provocation carries a quite specific trademark consisting of three letters: GPU. It is easy to see this trademark on the faces of these eminent slanderers.

The purpose of this letter is to pose to you, dear friend, the juridical question: do the laws of the United States give me the opportunity of filing suit against the *Daily News* and in so doing to expose the provocateurs? I am hoping there are provisions against journalists who knowingly spread false information in order to cause a particular person material and moral harm. And here it is a matter of a not unimportant harm: this whole plot is aimed at depriving us, my wife and me, of the hospitality of Mexico and delivering us into the hands of the GPU's executioners. I would like to add that, in the latest article in the *Daily News,* October 29, 1938, it is stated that Mexican oil is being sold to Japan and Italy on my recommendation and furthermore that my objective is military damage to the Soviet Union. This statement is clearly aimed at dishonoring me politically, and, I presume, falls under the normal legal provisions in North America safeguarding the moral and material interests of individuals and citizens. ∎

A conversation with William R. Mathews[353]

Published December 13, 1938

America faces a "terrible revolution" whose course will depend much on what the Rockefellers, as a symbol of the American ruling class, tell Mayor Frank Hague of Jersey City, as a symbol of American political reaction, to do. Within two years there will be a terrible worldwide war, and "you will be in it." American capitalism has reached its natural zenith in the capitalist era, and is now decaying. The democracy of the capitalist system is doomed. In France it is giving dying gasps, while in Britain it is rapidly disintegrating. The New Deal is merely a program of palliatives and is certain to fail. The Stalin regime in the Soviet Union is doomed to an early fall. The recent trials in Moscow symbolize the decay of the Stalin "aristocracy" and the mounting unrest and discontent of the Russian masses. The Communist leaders in Mexico are Stalinists and his personal mortal enemies. Trotsky is in Mexico because it was the only country in the world that offered him a refuge. He is still a Marxian socialist believing in the ultimate triumph of the working class.

Such is the gist of a one hour private interview I had with the first military master of the Russian Revolution; the first commissar of war of the Soviet Union; the associate and executor of Lenin in overthrowing the old regime in Russia and establishing the first dictatorship of the proletariat; and today a political exile in Mexico: Leon Trotsky. I found him living with his wife and a few devoted followers in the modest villa donated to him by Diego Rivera, the Mexican muralist, in the small and ancient village of Coyoacan where nearly 400 years ago Cortez once made his headquarters. At the conclusion of the interview he explicitly gave me permission to quote him "to the best of your memory, Mr. Mathews."

By a mere coincidence I happened to meet a man who has the confidence of Mr. Trotsky. Yesterday noon when I met him I told him of my desire to meet the Russian revolutionary, that I had been in Russia the year previous, and had read several of Trotsky's books. He offered to take me out and see if I could get in. When I suggested that we telephone ahead for an appointment, he said he thought it would be better to go out and take our chances. At four o'clock yesterday afternoon we motored out to the little village of Coyoacan. As we turned off the main road into one of the narrow bumpy streets of the village my companion said, pointing ahead, "That's the place where those policemen are standing guard."

We drove up to the side of one of those Mexican houses built flush with the street. The police knew my friend from previous visits. Standing with the police was a brawny, tall, blond young man with a cartridge belt and pistol slung about his waist. He was Jean van Heijenoort, a Hollander born in France who joined Trotsky at his first exile on the island of Prinkipo. I was introduced to him, told who I was and what I sought, how I had been in Moscow a year previously. He replied he would see what he could do. He walked to a gate where on ringing a bell, he was admitted.

A few minutes later van Heijenoort came out and waved for us to come on. We entered the patio and walked up the steps of the veranda. Across, on the opposite veranda, was an elderly, small, faded blond woman sitting in a chair reading a book, one arm resting on the iron rail of the veranda. She was Mrs. Trotsky. We entered a room where another man, also wearing a pistol, took out a book and in good English asked my name and address, which he wrote down.

Led by van Heijenoort, we walked around the veranda of the patio towards the little faded blond woman, but stopped short before an open door. Van Heijenoort motioned for me to enter. I entered. From a corner behind a desk and large table piled with books and reams of scattered typewritten manuscript, a moderate sized grey-haired man wearing familiar pince-nez eyeglasses and a short goatee, arose alertly, came forward and in perfect English greeted me cordially. He ushered us to our chairs and took up his seat behind his work desk. At his side was a dictaphone. In his shirt sleeves and his shirt unbuttoned at the collar, his forehead bald at the temples, his grey hair brushed back over his head, he appeared more as a working newspaperman than the former military master of one-sixth of the area of the world.

He started talking familiar shop immediately. He explained how he talked with Senator Henry J. Allen[354] of Kansas a few weeks ago, and that Senator Allen had written articles in which he, Trotsky, was charged with promoting Communism in Mexico and implying that the Mexican Communists were taking advice from him.

"I do not think that Senator Allen is quite an honorable man, because I told him that one of the conditions of my stay in Mexico was that I was not to participate either directly or indirectly in any kind of political activity. That

I would work with Laborde and Toledano is ridiculously false. They are agents of Stalin and mortal enemies of mine. Why should I risk my life and the only refuge open to me in the world?"

He threw back his head and with a smile and a sigh said humorously:

"It reminds me of that play of Shakespeare, what is the name of it? One man accuses another of being dishonorable, and the other replies, 'You are a senator.'"

He then spoke to my friend about a New York newspaperman who had endeavored to see him, and remarked that he would not see that man unless he would give bond to print answers to questions exactly as answered in writing.

"I know what they are trying to do," he remarked with incisiveness.

Turning to me he said, "And you have been to Russia recently?"

I explained that I had and that during my stay I had seen the name Trotsky used time after time in the Moscow newspapers.

"I believe that you are the one man in the world whom Stalin fears most?" I continued.

Trotsky raised up his chin, a dreamy look came into his eyes, and then softly he said:

"Stalin does not fear me, no, he does not fear me. He fears the Russian masses, and his fear is a reaction to the insecurity he feels."

"How long do you think that the Stalin regime can last?" I queried.

"It cannot last long. The recent trials are a symbol of the increasing discontent of the Russian masses. They show how weak the Stalin 'aristocracy' is, and how it is failing to meet the demands of the masses. Stalin has only two alternatives. He must either give in to those who want private property back, or he must establish a democracy. If he establishes either, he and his privileged class³⁵⁵ will fall.

"Nothing that I can say or do will have any effect," he continued as he leaned forward to emphasize words. "He has established a privileged class, and that class is not meeting the needs of the Russian masses. You must give the people food and clothing if you are to continue in power."

"Will such a possible change take the form of a palace revolution or of forcible revolt?"

"That I cannot say. A palace revolution is possible, but what form the change takes is beyond the power of any man to say. I simply know this, that the Russian masses will find a way of expressing their desires."

"Would you say that the New Deal is a step in the direction of creating a revolutionary situation in the United States?" I asked.

"No, no, the New Deal is not revolutionary. It is a program of mere palliative seeking to cure a badly diseased body. It will of course fail, because it is doing nothing to cure the causes of the disease. It represents the culmination of the final contradictions in the decay and fall of capitalism."

"Then you think that the United States will have a revolution?" I asked with interest.

"Yes, Mr. Mathews, you will have a revolution, a terrible revolution," he replied, shaking his head slowly and speaking in a sad voice. "What course it takes will depend much on what Mr. Rockefeller tells Mr. Hague to do. Mr. Rockefeller is a symbol of the American ruling class, and Mr. Hague is a symbol of its political tools."

Again leaning forward and measuring his words slowly, he exclaimed, "Mr. Hague is more powerful than Mr. Roosevelt."

"When will this revolution come?"

"Oh, I cannot say just when. I may be gone, but I hope to live to see it. But it is certain to come because capitalism has reached its zenith in America, and has exhausted itself.

It is now living on its savings, consuming its own fat. Your society in the United States is decaying, because capitalism has served its purpose. Look at your unemployed. No form of society can continue long that permits such conditions to exist. Oh, you can feed them for a while, but you are consuming your savings. You are doing nothing to increase wealth.

"Another depression will come, and it will be much more severe than the Hoover crisis. Then is when you will have exhausted all the resources capitalism has. What the ruling class in America tells Frank Hague to do, what support it gives him, will determine the course of American destiny.

"If the American masses will rise and adopt socialism, America could bring the world to its feet. Your great monopolies have developed the technique of administration of large units. You could plan your production for increased wealth. You have a continent, you do not need colonies. You have everything to make socialism a success."

"Then you believe that there is enough intelligence available to make the intricate planning of socialism a success?"

"Yes, yes."

"Will it not be possible to win the support of the directing personnel of these successful large units?"

"You will have to use some of them, but not all, but the best will be with true revolution."

"In such a scheme would it be necessary for the government to use only the instruments of production and leave distribution to private enterprise?"

"That is merely incidental. You could produce so much, everybody could have so much of everything they want, that the form of distribution would take care of itself."

"Marxian socialism requires a dictatorship of the proletariat, does it not?"

"Yes, yes, it does. That would be part of the revolution, but in America it might be accomplished peacefully if the people could be taught how 90 percent of them would be better off. Only 10 percent would be less well off."

"Will you explain what you mean about the capitalistic decay in America?"

"Capitalism has fulfilled its function and reached the point where its manifest contradictions defeat its progress. Capitalism has served its purpose. You see in the first life of man, the barbarians would, after conquering their enemies, eat them. Then man became more civilized, and merely killed them. Then he put them in chains. After that he progressed to the point where he put them to work as slaves. Then he made them serfs, and then he found that he could better himself by making them free. Now another period is coming to an end, and in the future everybody will under socialism have everything they want. All men will have their wants satisfied. Capitalism has thus served its purpose, and fulfilled its mission."

"Then with a possible dictatorship of the proletariat we cannot look forward to democracy?"

"The democracy of capitalism is finished. Look at France where it is making dying gasps. Do you note how Daladier is asking for full powers? That means dictatorship. England, and France too, with their colonies face the rise of Germany. You notice how both Germany and Italy are now asking for colonies. Yes, your democracy of capitalism is finished, but in America you could, of all places in the world, work out a socialist democracy."

"Do you believe that Germany and Italy constitute a menace to the Western Hemisphere?"

Before answering he leaned back in his chair and looked out of the window. Then turning slowly in measured words he answered:

"There will be a great world war, and you in the United

States will be in it, everybody will be in it."

"Do you expect it soon?"

"Yes, very soon."

"Eighteen months or two years?"

"Yes," he replied quietly, and then in an animated voice, for one of the few times he had to stop to think of the proper English word for the French word for "vanguard," he continued:

"The vanguard of it is already in sight. Look at Munich. We are told we were to have peace. That conference is only a few weeks past, and Italy is now demanding Tunis and Corsica of France. Germany will next be making similar demands of England."

By this time I saw the master revolutionary was tiring, so I arose to take my leave. He arose with me, but I could not resist getting in a few more questions. So, standing with him in the center of the room, I asked:

"How do you expect this war will be precipitated?"

"That I cannot say; no man can say, but the antagonistic forces exist and, because they are contradictory, will clash."

"Will Germany attack Russia?"

"Who knows? I cannot say as to details. What I recognize are the conflicting forces."

"Can an independent Poland survive?"

"That will be decided at the peace conference."

Then, looking intently in my eyes, he declared with feeling and incisiveness:

"When Germany attacks Russia, you will have to take sides against her. Everybody will have to take sides. You cannot afford to allow Germany to become master of all that area and gain all those resources to use against you later. There will be a terrible war, and we will all be much poorer. You will be in it; everybody will be in it."

"You are still a Marxian socialist?"

A smile split his face from side to side; his eyes kindled in a kindly twinkle.

"Ah, yes," he said softly, "and I believe that socialism will eventually triumph."

As we again shook hands, I told him I would be willing to write out the interview and send my manuscript to him for correction.

"No, Mr. Matthews, that will not be necessary. You are free to quote me to the extent of your memory."

We walked out through the gate of the patio and out to the car where my friend's wife awaited. We greeted her cordially. Again all of us shook hands. As we drove away, the wooden gate of the patio swung shut behind our host. The Mexican policemen walked their posts, while van Heijenoort, wearing his cartridge belt and pistol, waved us a good-bye. We had been inside for a little more than an hour.

Trotsky appeared to be in good health. He speaks perfect English with a slight Slavic accent. He radiates good nature. He has a quick, alert manner and mentality. He uses simple words and expresses his thoughts with a clarity and confidence which cannot be misunderstood. The only time he dodged or seemed reluctant to answer categorically was when I asked him about the program of the Mexican government. All he would say was that the situation in Mexico was entirely different than in the United States, where capitalism had reached what he called its zenith. He saw the Mexican situation as a mass movement of people struggling up from a feudal poverty.

When I asked him about his Fourth International and what he was doing to promote it, he said that all he could do was done by his writing for publication. "I have had articles printed even in China, and I have had my writing translated into various languages throughout the world," he explained.

He told of the recent meeting of the Fourth International, in Switzerland; of the hounding of its members by Stalinist agents of the OGPU. He accused Toledano of Mexico of meeting with Stalin OGPU agents during his recent trip to Europe. He explained that directions for the Mexican Communists came from New York and Washington, and that those places in turn took their orders from Moscow. In defending himself against the charge that he was assisting Mexican Communists, he spoke bitterly of the recent meeting in Mexico City of Stalinists of the Western Hemisphere and how the Stalinists had excluded from the meeting and refused to pay the expenses of a few delegates who had had the temerity to criticize.

"Laborde wants me driven from Mexico because he says I am a German fascist agent; your Senator Allen says that I am giving advice to Laborde and other Mexican Communists. Now what am I?"

Throughout the talk the master revolutionary seemed to be more concerned with actual mass movements and technical situations than in personalities. He never mentioned Mussolini or Hitler, but seemed much concerned with the dynamic energy that was being developed in Germany. He seems to have absolute confidence in his diagnosis of these mass movements and their ultimate course. In speaking of Rockefeller, Hague, and Roosevelt, he spoke of them as symbols of the great movements under way in America.

During my drive back, my friend who had arranged the interview said that Trotsky had unburdened himself more to me than to any other man he had taken out. He said that usually the interviews were of a formal nature and arranged for a period of ten or twenty minutes, or that questions would be submitted in advance and answered in writing.

Thus ended the most fascinating meeting I have ever had,

and an interview with one of the makers of history who, at one time, was the military master of one-sixth of the area of the world; with one who, as an expert in the technique of revolution, upset the rule of the once all-powerful czar, and who now, as a political refugee, spends his time writing his memoirs in a small old villa in an ancient Mexican village guarded by a few faithful disciples and a detachment of Mexican police. The mighty do fall. ∎

Investigate the U.S. fascists[356]

December 12, 1938

Dear Friends:

It would be well to begin the biweekly *Socialist Appeal* with a detailed investigation throughout the country of the fascist, semifascist, and reactionary organizations in general. Possibly the Stalinists have already tried to do something of the kind. However, the situation changes, the old organizations disappear and new ones arise. In any case, it would be an excellent job for our local organizations, particularly the youth.

Of course, it would be good to involve not only our party branches but also the local trade unions, sympathetic organizations and so on. We must instil in the vanguard of the proletariat an understanding of the growing threat of fascism. It is the best weapon with which to demolish the prejudices of Americanism: "democracy," "legality," etc.

With a biweekly the question of a systematic political campaign will become even more important than now.

Comradely,
Hansen [Leon Trotsky]

The French question[357]

December 13, 1938

Dear Friend:

I highly appreciate and support with all my heart the initiative you and the [SWP] National Committee take in the French question. As you say in your letter to Vincent Dunne,[358] it will signify a step forward for the American party itself. Within the next few days I may possibly send you some more on the French question; but now I shall speak a little about the Mexican question—more concretely, about Charlie and Lillian [Curtiss].[359]

I discovered yesterday in my discussion with Charlie, the situation has become critical. The modest bit of money they brought here is exhausted. Even more, I learned with stupefaction that Charlie spent some money of his own on the review [*Clave*]. What is to be done now? The agreement you made about the sojourn of these comrades in Mexico was not very clear to me. I believe that you discussed the practical question with Diego in my absence.

Now Diego stands aside from the Mexican organization and participates only in the magazine. I do not know his present financial situation and I am by no means sure that it is good. After a long period of bad health and passivity Diego returned to painting. It seems that he favors painting and avoids political questions and discussions. It would not be easy for me to approach him on this delicate question now. I believe that it would be best for you to write Diego immediately, explaining the whole situation to him and asking for his advice or help. It is absolutely necessary to settle the matter before your departure for Europe.

Comradely,
Hansen [Leon Trotsky]

Letters about Sieva Volkov[360]

September 1938–April 1939

TO SIEVA VOLKOV
SEPTEMBER 19, 1938

My dear little Sieva:

I am writing to you for the first time. Our poor little Leon always kept us informed, Natalia and me, about your life, your development and your health. Now Uncle Leon is no more. It is necessary for us to establish direct communications, my little grandson.

There are some things I am very concerned about, first of all about language. You have completely forgotten Russian. It is not your fault, my little Sieva, but it is a sad fact. I do not know where your father is now, or if he is alive. But in the last letter he wrote me, now more than four years ago, he very insistently asked me whether you had forgotten Russian. Although your father is a very intelligent and educated man, he does not speak any foreign languages. It would be a terrible blow for him if, on being reunited with you, he found himself unable to communicate with you. The same goes for your sister. I hope that she is in good health and will be reunited with you some day. You can well imagine how sad this reunion would be if you were not able to converse with your little sister in your native language. For me and for Natalia, who loves you very much, the language question is very important.

But it is not just this. We want to talk to you about things concerning your Uncle Leon, your life now that he is dead, and your future.

I proposed to Jeanne immediately after Uncle Leon's death that she come here with you. Jeanne replied that she could not do this. Of course, she may have reasons of her own. But my decision is firm: you must come here for a while—with Jeanne if she is willing, without Jeanne if she cannot. Here, we can easily discuss with you and with Jeanne (if she comes) questions concerning your future and take care of this matter with the Russian language.

You are a big boy now. I must talk to you about a very important matter, about the ideas which were and are still common to your mother, to your father, to Uncle Leon, and to me and Natalia. I am very anxious to explain to you face to face the great value of the ideas and objectives which have brought about so much suffering for our family, which is your family.

I have complete responsibility for you, my grandson, in my own eyes, in your father's eyes, if he is alive, and in yours. That is why my decision on your journey is irrevocable.

I hug you warmly, my little Sieva, and Natalia does too. Let us say: A bientot.

TO GERARD ROSENTHAL
DECEMBER 8, 1938

My Dear Counselor and Friend:

This letter is a power of attorney for you to represent me in the matter concerning my grandson Vsievolod (Sieva) who is now living with Mrs. Jeanne Martin des Pallieres. I would like to briefly review the history of this matter with you.

After the death of my daughter Zinaida, Sieva's mother, in Berlin in January 1933, Sieva was taken in by my late son Leon Sedov (died February 16, 1938), who was then living as man and wife with Mrs. Jeanne Martin des Pallieres in Berlin. After a number of difficulties associated with the coming to power of the Nazi regime in Germany, during which Sieva was separated from my son for a short time, he was reunited with him in Paris in 1934. Since the death of my son, the question of where Sieva will live has naturally been posed.

Mrs. Martin wrote to me concerning Sieva on March 17:

"I have no legal right to him, but many moral rights, perhaps. Nevertheless, if you ask for him, I will give him to you. But be aware of this, although I can be hard when it is necessary, you should understand that I have a heart and that it cannot be idly played upon or played with. If you take Sieva from me, it will be for good. . . ."

She was very insistent that my reply be immediate and decisive.

In reply, I invited Mrs. Martin des Pallieres to come to Mexico to discuss with my wife and me all the undecided questions and perhaps to live with us together with Sieva. I could see no other way of resolving the question. She wrote back with brusk haughtiness, a bit put out as is her nature: "Either give him to me or take him from me, but right away, and once and for all." I do not know Mrs. Martin des Pallieres very well and the little I do know does not inspire the unlimited confidence she demands of me. At issue here is a child whose father, missing for almost five years, perhaps still alive in one of Stalin's prisons, may still one day demand his rights. In his absence, all formal rights rest with me. Mrs. Martin recognizes this herself. I am very much inclined to recognize the moral claims to which she is entitled as, among other things, my son's companion, but I can in no way consider my grandson, the sole remaining member of my family, as an object I can give as a present, "right away and once and for all," to Mrs. Martin, who from the time she wrote her letter has done everything possible to inspire in me the greatest mistrust of her character and attitude.

On September 19 I sent Sieva a letter by way of Mrs. Martin. She told my friends Alfred and Marguerite Rosmer that she never received it. This is not true. The registered letter was never returned. Moreover, the copy sent to Mrs. Martin through Mrs. Marguerite Rosmer suffered the same fate. I never received any reply.

While our son was alive we always received regular news about Sieva and letters from him. Now we face what in effect amounts to a sequestering of the child by Mrs. Martin who, as she herself put it, has "no legal rights." All of my attempts to settle the question on an amiable basis, my repeated proposals about coming to Mexico, my firmest insistence that she come here with the boy or send him with my friends, all of this has produced not the slightest result.

Despite all of this, I am still prepared, even now, to do everything I can to satisfy Mrs. Martin's moral claims, along with my legal and moral rights. But I will not "give her" the boy, now less than ever. If Mrs. Martin comes here with the boy, she will have the rights of a member of our family as concerns him, no more and no less. Otherwise, Sieva must come here as soon as possible, that is, as soon as you have taken care of the legal formalities.

With my warmest regards.

TO GERARD ROSENTHAL
APRIL 10, 1939

Dear Counselor and Friend:

1. It seems that Mrs. Jeanne Molinier is claiming that my first marriage, to the mother of my daughter Zinaida, was not legal. This is a worthless allegation like so many others. In the first volume of my autobiography, I said of my partnership with Alexandra Lvovna: "To avoid being separated [in deportation], we had been married in the transfer prison in Moscow" [page 196, *My Life*, 2009 printing]. And I had not the slightest reason to invent this passing assertion, the truth of which is, besides, well known to all my friends. As was mandatory under czarism, we not only had a civil marriage but a religious one as well. Alexandra Lvovna from that time on used my legal name, Bronstein, and this name was published in the Moscow press at the time of Alexandra Lvovna's deportation to Siberia in 1935. If necessary, one could easily verify this in the Moscow edition of *Pravda* of that time.

2. No less worthless is the allegation by Mrs. Molinier that my late daughter Zinaida was not legally married to Professor Volkov. Mrs. Jeanne Molinier's allegation is all the more contemptible because she herself is well acquainted with the facts. Zinaida came to join me in Turkey with a legal Soviet passport in the name of her husband, Volkov, which would hardly have been possible if they were not legally married. Moreover, her son, my grandson, was included in the same passport under the name Vsievolod Volkov. That signifies that the marriage was recognized as legal by the Soviet authorities.

3. My grandson Vsievolod Volkov traveled from Turkey to Paris and from Paris to Germany with a legal passport issued by the Turkish authorities on the basis of Soviet documents issued by the Soviet consulate in Constantinople. This legal passport was kept by my late son and is today in the possession of Mrs. Jeanne Molinier. She must produce this

passport. Her refusal is tantamount to a confession of fraud. Besides, as I have already stated in my letter to the Minister of Justice, one may easily find in the records of the French police official documents on the two entries into France of the young Vsievolod Volkov, grandson of Trotsky.

4. On January 5, 1933, my daughter Zinaida Volkov committed suicide in Berlin. The matter had major repercussions in the world press, and especially the German press. Enclosed is a small part of the press clippings I possess: twenty German clippings, one Russian clipping, and one French clipping. All or almost all of these clippings refer to the press release of the Berlin Prefecture of Police, which was based on the most legitimate documents, and spoke of my daughter as Mrs. Volkov, nee Bronstein. These clippings also explain how the Soviet consulate in Berlin had used trickery to rescind my daughter's Soviet passport. This is why the only document identifying Vsievolod is a Turkish passport, which is, I repeat, in Mrs. Jeanne Molinier's possession. The aforementioned press release of the Berlin Prefecture of Police proves the legality not only of my daughter's marriage to Volkov, but of my marriage to Alexandra Lvovna, for it explicitly speaks of Zinaida Volkov, nee Bronstein. Besides, if it would not be inconvenient to refer to the Prefecture of Police in Berlin, the facts could be confirmed without the least difficulty.

5. I enclose in addition three letters written by the German lawyer Oscar Cohn to my daughter Zinaida. They had to do with the extension of my daughter's German visa, and Dr. Oscar Cohn, who knew what a legal name was and was familiar with the documents, spoke of Zinaida as Mrs. Volkov.

6. I enclose a letter from my son-in-law Platon Volkov to me during my exile in central Asia (1928). Naturally, the letter does not contain any formal information on the legality of the marriage, but by its content it shows that the relationships in their family were close and affectionate.

7. I enclose photostatic copies of three postcards writ-

ten by my daughter Zinaida a short time before her death. Their importance lies in the fact that they are signed Zinaida Volkov, my daughter's legal name.

8. There was, besides, never the least doubt on the part of Mrs. Jeanne Molinier about my legal rights with respect to my grandson Vsievolod Volkov, and she proved it beyond all misunderstanding a few months ago in a letter to me of March 17, 1938, in which she acknowledged with no prompting that she had no legal rights to custody of my grandson, and in which she asked with insistence that I "give" him to her, a request which would have made little sense had she herself not recognized that henceforth I was to be the only one in the world who could "give" him or not.

9. I never entrusted my grandson to Mrs. Molinier, but to my son Leon and, as she was my son's companion, to Mrs. Molinier. I should establish here that Mrs. Molinier had four years previously broken all relations with my wife and me. The reason for that was that we had not come to the defense of her former husband, Mr. Raymond Molinier, who was under heavy moral and political criticism. From long experience I had come to the conclusion that this criticism was completely justified and that Mr. Raymond Molinier is not worthy of trust. The sole fact that I had not come to his defense (which I could not do in good conscience) sufficed for Mrs. Jeanne Molinier to break off all correspondence with us, to communicate nothing to us about my grandson, even when I was interned in Norway or when I had to leave Europe for Mexico. During the past three years it has been my son who had kept us informed about Vsievolod Volkov's growth. Under these conditions there can be no possibility of my giving custody of the little boy to Mrs. Jeanne Molinier personally.

10. After our son's death I tried with all my might to establish friendly relations with the woman who had been his companion. I even suggested to Mrs. Jeanne Molinier that she come into our home and live with us as our daughter. I

in no way overlooked the moral authority she had acquired with my grandson, who had spent several years in her company. But in order to come to an agreement there must be goodwill on both sides. Unfortunately, I received nothing from Mrs. Molinier but ambiguous answers, laced with false allegations and full of poorly concealed hostility.

11. You know, dear friend, the history of my archives, which Mrs. Molinier has attempted to seize, against my will, for purposes which remain obscure, to say the least. She tried in an unspeakable fashion to abuse the wishes of my son for ends absolutely opposed to those wishes. My son, who, as she herself wrote in her deposition before the judge, "venerated his father," wished that, given the difficulties of my situation, Mrs. Molinier help me in recovering my own papers. In her letters to me Mrs. Molinier acknowledged that these papers were mine and were no concern of hers. At the same time she tried to extort from me a power of attorney which would have allowed her to transfer my papers to Mr. Vereecken, a man in the confidence of Mr. Raymond Molinier, an open enemy of my son and myself, a man who heaped hateful slanders on my son during his last illness.

12. Since in this affair Mrs. Jeanne Molinier has acted as nothing but Mr. Raymond Molinier's agent, I quote here from two letters from my son to me which show clearly how my son himself, after long resistance, came to assess the character of Mr. Raymond Molinier. For me it involved having the testimony of Mr. Raymond Molinier and his brother Mr. Henri Molinier concerning my stay in France, in relation to the well-known Moscow trials. My son, who, like myself, had tried for a long time to defend Mr. Raymond Molinier against his opponents and had been forced to realize that the accusations were justified, strongly advised me against approaching Mr. Raymond Molinier and his group *(La Commune)*. On my insistence he finally approached Mr. Henri Molinier, refusing, however, to take any responsibility by this statement: "It is up

to you to decide whether we can make public use of the testimony of an individual like Raymond Molinier." He informed me later that he had received from the Raymond Molinier group an "arrogant, stupid, and at the same time dishonest" response. He warned me again that these people were going to try to make of their testimony "a political scandal of the most demoralizing kind" (letter of February 22, 1937).

I shared and still share this evaluation of Mr. R. Molinier. Even if I were willing to call him as a witness in a political inquiry, I have at the same time always wanted to keep him from having the slightest influence on my grandson's life and education. While my son was alive there could never be any question of anything like that. But everything is changed since my son's death. Mrs. Jeanne Molinier's words as well as her deeds have shown at each step that she has become merely an agent of a man who is extremely untrustworthy and violently hostile towards me and all my friends. Could I have my grandson in this poisoned atmosphere? I continued to urge Mrs. Jeanne Molinier to come here with the boy. She equivocated. She was evasive. Each of her letters was nothing but boldfaced lies, whether about my grandson or my archives. In this situation nothing remains for me but to resort to legal channels.

Mrs. Jeanne Molinier is making her last attempt, profiting from my difficult situation as an exile deprived of documents and without freedom of movement. She denies the most obvious facts. She invents others. She distorts my life history. She is attempting to induce a miscarriage of justice. She even dares to invoke French law on mistreated and morally abandoned children.

You are aware, my dear friend, that this matter involves nothing but hateful slander. I neither materially nor morally abandoned my grandson for an instant. During the first three or four years of Jeanne Molinier's life together with my son the material support of the couple and of my grandson Vsievolod Volkov was guaranteed completely by me. During the last three years, while my material situation worsened, Mrs. Jeanne Molinier took responsibility for a certain part of the family's expenses. But my son's and my grandson's expenses were in any case covered by my contributions.

The situation changed only after my son's death. I then wired several thousand francs and I intended to continue these dispatches every month. Mrs. Jeanne Molinier hurried to reply that she was setting this money aside for her lawyer (the one, I suppose, who is conducting this case against me) and not for Vsievolod. Given the previously described circumstances I decided to cease financial support and demand custody of my grandson.

I am writing these lines in a hurry so that the letter will arrive in time. But I could confirm each of my allegations with irrefutable letters and documents. I could as well present at least an approximate record of the money I sent and also show that at no time was Vsievolod Volkov "abandoned" to the exclusive care of Mrs. Molinier. Compiling this list would take several weeks of research.

In closing this letter I reaffirm once more in the most solemn manner my absolute faith in the integrity, honesty, and devotion of my dear friends Alfred and Marguerite Griot [Rosmer], to whom the French authorities have given custody of my grandson. I thank you, dear friend, for your unflagging and nobly disinterested devotion, and I sign affectionately.

Your devoted,

P.S. I am adding an appendix, which is a good summary concerning the money that I sent.

APPENDIX

The enclosed letter from Leon Sedov of April 8, 1937, shows that during my stay in Norway I sent monthly the sum of 270 Norwegian crowns (roughly equivalent to 1,400 francs at that time). These contributions were much more modest than the contributions of the preceding period, due to my own financial difficulties.

During the first year of our stay in Mexico my son received from the European publishers of my works about the same amount. During that year he also earned some money from his own literary work.

After his death one hundred and fifty dollars and one thousand francs were sent by wire to cover various expenses.

In April 1938 forty-five dollars was sent for Sieva, then twenty or twenty-five dollars per month. The last contribution of twenty dollars was made in January 1939.

All of that can be substantiated by documents, affidavits, etc. ∎

No doubts about Rudolf Klement's fate[361]

November 1938–August 1939

NOVEMBER 29, 1938

Dear Mrs. Ruthe:

I have just received your letter of November 16. Unfortunately, I cannot send you anything to relieve or reassure you. What my friends in Paris write me leaves no room for any hope. Rudolf was my collaborator for a certain time (in Turkey and in France). After that I was in friendly correspondence with him. Rudolf was always faithful to his cause, and that is why his enemies killed him. In the last two years my wife and I have lost our two sons in a similar way. We share Rudolf's mother's sorrow all the more.

No, dear Mrs. Ruthe, Rudolf is unfortunately not at my home. I would consider myself lucky if I could lodge him with us. Unfortunately, I do not have the slightest hope as to his fate. I have no doubt that the criminals killed him.

Rudolf was very talented. From a scientific point of view he had developed a lot during the last eight years. He wrote excellent articles and knew nearly all the languages of the civilized world. He was unselfish and courageous. I was sure that he would play an important role in the future. The terrible blow struck me and all his friends all the more heavily. That is unfortunately all that I can tell you for the moment, dear Mrs. Ruthe.

If you want any additional information, I am of course completely at your service.

With my sincere condolences for Rudolf's mother and for you, I am

Yours respectfully,
Leon Trotsky

AUGUST 2, 1939

Dear Mrs. Ruthe:

I never received your second letter. The third arrived while I was sick. That is the reason for the very regrettable delay in my answer. The judge in Paris has the letter that Rudolf's mother asked about. So I can only send you a photocopy of the letter as well as a copy of my analysis of the letter that I sent to the judge.

As for me, I am absolutely certain that the letter was a forgery. It has absolutely false and worthless statements, made by someone whose knowledge of Rudolf's situation and previous activity was extremely general and incomplete.

The resemblance of the handwriting [to Rudolf's], which is undeniable, in no way proves that the letter was authentic. First, it is only a similarity; second, Rudolf's enemies have the best specialists in the world in this field, who have already made similar performances many times.

This completely contradicts the opposing theory according to which Rudolf joined the camp of his enemies of his own free will. Besides, in this case he would not have had the least reason to hide himself. On the contrary, he would then have openly opposed his comrades of yesterday; otherwise, his joining would have made no sense. It is also certain that in this case he would have given his mother an indication that he was alive.

For me the situation is absolutely clear and I have not the least doubt that Rudolf has been killed by his enemies. If I had the least doubt, dear Mrs. Ruthe, I would not take away a last hope from his mother. Unfortunately, the language of facts is blunt and unambiguous.

With my best greetings and wishes to you and your family and to that of your sister.

Yours faithfully,
Leon Trotsky

A GPU stool pigeon in Paris[362]

January 1, 1939

Extremely confidential, extremely important, and extremely urgent.—I have received extremely important information from a source that is unidentified but claims to be in contact with senior GPU agents, to the effect that a long-standing collaborator of the *Biulleten Oppozitsii* is allegedly a stool pigeon: Mark.[363] This stool pigeon was working until 1938 and perhaps is still working in Nikolaevsky's[364] institute. He is the one who allegedly stole the archives in this institute [in 1936]. His age: 32 to 35. Nationality: Jewish, from the Russian part of Poland. Writes well in Russian. Wears glasses. Has a wife and a very small child. This stool pigeon has no revolutionary past. That is why the confidence placed in him is astonishing. Moreover, nearly four years ago he was a member in Paris of the Society for the Repatriation of Russian Emigres. He was a stool pigeon even in this organization. This stool pigeon meets regularly with representatives of the Soviet embassy in Paris. The informant is sure that it would be very easy by shadowing this stool pigeon to confirm his relations with the embassy. That is the communication. As for its source, two versions are equally possible: (1) it's a timid friend; (2) it's the GPU, wanting to spread demoralization in our ranks. Both hypotheses should be examined and checked out. It is absolutely necessary to organize the shadowing in a discreet and effective manner. It seems to me that Nikolaevsky has to be brought into it. A commission of three should be created: Rosmer, Gerard, Nikolaevsky, plus two or three young people separately and in absolute secrecy, for the task of shadowing. If the information is confirmed, the opportunity must be arranged to denounce him to the French police as the robber of the archives under conditions that won't permit his escape. Communicate this information to Rosmer immediately. The best way would be through Cannon if he has not already left [for Europe] or Shachtman if he should be leaving. Find a way [to get it there] yourselves. Acknowledge receipt immediately. Greetings Van [Leon Trotsky].[365] ∎

The Hearst press changes its mind[366]

January 6, 1939

Dear Mr. Knickerbocker:

I should be very glad to meet you, one of the most remarkable journalists of our time, not only to answer all the questions you wish to ask me, but also to gain from you your impressions of world affairs; but . . . it is a question of the Hearst agency which you represent. The attitude of Mr. Hearst and his press during my ten years of exile has been very hostile toward me which is natural because we occupy opposite political poles. But his press has lacked elementary loyalty.[367] I publicly refused to give any statements to the Hearst press. Mr. Hearst for his part bought my statements from others and published them as if they were articles written directly for the Hearst press. Many of my unscrupulous adversaries in the opposite camp have affirmed over this period of years that I am in a bloc with Mr. Hearst who is in a bloc with Hitler.

You explained to my friend, Joe Hansen, as he has informed me, that the management of the Hearst agency and press has changed. It has become more loyal. Good. I am ready to open a new "era" in my relations with the Hearst press. That is, to treat it on the same basis as all other capitalist newspapers. But at the threshold of the new "era" I must have a small proof of loyalty. I will give my first statements to the reorganized Hearst press under two conditions: (1) the new management should telegraph confirmation that my statement, which naturally will be far from the position of the Hearst press, will be published integrally without any alterations; (2) I ask that for all my previous statements which have been printed illegally by the Hearst press, the new management pay, we will say, $1,000 toward the aid of German revolutionary exiles persecuted by Hitler (American Fund for Political Prisoners and Refugees,[368] Room 1609, 100 Fifth Avenue, New York City, N.Y.). This modest payment would have a symbolic character and I hope would successfully inaugurate a new chapter in our mutual relations.

With best regards,
Leon Trotsky[369]

The plight of our refugee comrades[370]

January 9, 1939

Dear Comrade Rose:

I have received a letter from Comrade Walter Held concerning the fate of our German comrades in Europe. I am sending you a copy of the respective part of the letter. Unfortunately it is in German, but I hope that some of the comrades can translate it into English. The question is very important and I would be happy to know that Held's plan is feasible.

About two weeks ago I received a request for visas from fifteen Czechoslovakian comrades. I did all I could, but I am not very hopeful. The difficulties here are growing parallel with the pressure from all sides. We procured visas easily for Otto [Schuessler] and Julik only as my collaborators who were to live in my house; but during our negotiations concerning Julik we were compelled to declare that he would be the last collaborator for whom we would ask a visa. Unfortunately, our general request does not look very promising.

Held is in correspondence with Comrade Novack[371] on his own case and that of the other German comrades. I hope that you will consult him and will do everything possible in order to save the precious cadres of our German section.

I would be glad to hear if the plan is feasible, what is done and what will be done.

Comradely yours,
L. Trotsky

What the youth do to our principles[372]

January 9, 1939

Dear Comrade Held:

I now reply briefly to your letter of December 19. Simultaneously I am writing to the comrades in the States about your case. I hope that they will do everything they can.

Here the situation in connection with the visas becomes more and more difficult. I was able to obtain visas for Otto [Schuessler] and Julik only as my personal collaborators who will live in my house and for whom I am responsible in every respect. Our attempts to procure visas for the

Czechoslovakian comrades, beginning with Solze, are not very hopeful.

The door is too small and the pressure from all parts of Europe is too great.

I cannot agree with you on the youth question. To dissolve the youth into the adult organization signifies the repulse and loss of the youth. That the youth "dilutes" our principles (or more often transforms them into sharp quintessence) is the most important reason for the necessity for a youth organization and not against it. It is the only nonbureaucratic conception of the question.

Also, I can't follow you on the question of the March 1921 crisis in Germany. Our position on this question was absolutely clear and uncompromising; but we did not forget that we had not only to do with principles and ideas, but with a living, mass organization which needs time for a transition from one attitude to another. Paul Levi was a qualified "Literat" and no more. That in his writings you can find some happy formulations which you can interpret now as prophetic, cannot change my appreciation of his personality and his role one iota. I am a bit afraid that you are considering the question too much from a literary point of view and not enough from a political one.

I hope by the time this letter reaches you that you will have become a father and so have left the "youth" officially. Natalia and I warmly embrace Synnove and yourself.

With best comradely greetings.

Yours,
Leon Trotsky

Letters to the POI Central Committee[373]

February–July 1939

FEBRUARY 14, 1939

Dear Comrades:

We are very worried here about the situation in France. During the international conference [in September 1938] it was decided, as I understood it, that the POI would assign a significant part of its membership to work within the PSOP.[374] There was talk of a third or a quarter. Unfortunately, nothing was done. Why? Here we do not know. We were prevented from being able to go through an important experience during recent months, and perhaps from heading off the split.

The split is now a fact. I don't regard this as a tragedy. While it is an important question, it remains despite everything a purely tactical one. Our comrades have enough character not to get lost in the PSOP. It seems there was a certain danger from the other side. The split was determined by the long stagnation (for which there are good reasons) and by the recent error noted above. We must politically adjust to this fact.

It seems however that some comrades among you are inclined to consider the entry into the PSOP as a betrayal. That would be a very great error, which could isolate you in France and in the International. You have the newspaper, a powerful tool; you can influence the activities of the faction in the PSOP provided that you set yourselves the task of aiding them, not compromising them.

Do not forget, dear comrades, that everyone is wondering how and why this stagnation and even decline came about in such favorable conditions. Everyone is inclined in advance to approve and uphold the faction that is seeking new, practical ways to act. If you were to appear to the International as simple conservatives and especially as "saboteurs" of the initiative of the other part of the section, the results would be fatal for the POI.

Nothing is lost or compromised if our friends of the POI do not let themselves be carried away by a purely formal intransigence or a sectarian spirit.

The Americans have made a magnificent effort to help you. They have demonstrated their ability to maneuver in very complicated conditions. They have not experienced any stagnation. On the contrary, they have grown. In passing, they have practically liquidated the Socialist Party. They are moving forward. In these conditions the French section can indeed profit not only from their money, but also from their experience. Cannon has an excellent political flair. I am sure he can be very useful to the French section during the period of this delicate turn.

We would be very happy here to learn your current thinking on the situation, and your plans for the future.

L.T.

MAY 9, 1939

Dear Comrades:

In a situation as critical as the present one, and by that I mean the objective situation as well as the situation within your organization, half-measures are fatal. One must decide one path or another and not remain in the middle. You may remember that in September I was on the whole against the entry into the PSOP. What were my reasons? (1) I imagined that the social composition of the PSOP was much worse than it was; (2) I had no idea, being far away, that the state of the POI was as bad as it was; (3) France was passing through one of its most critical periods, and it could be feared that our organization would be paralyzed at the outbreak of the war.

This evaluation of the situation has been proven incomplete, one-sided, and even false. Your activity since the last congress and the split does not allow you the glimmer of a perspective for the future. You wish simply to continue publishing *La Lutte,* that is, to present the appearance of continuing the party's activity. You wish, it is true, to have your "essential forces" enter the PSOP, inviting Rous and his comrades to "coordinate" their activity with yours. Until today the difference seemed to be limited to the entry question. Now that you have decided for the entry of your "essential forces," you speak of "coordination," that is, you would maintain the split within the PSOP. What are your political reasons? You do not indicate them at all.

At the same time you want to maintain a nucleus outside the PSOP with *La Lutte* and *Quatrieme Internationale.* In other words, what you want is that side-by-side with the faction of Bolshevik-Leninists in the PSOP under the direct influence of the IS, there will be another faction, under the influence of the nucleus "which is going to publish *La Lutte* and *Quatrieme Internationale.*" Thus you want to maintain not only the split between the two Bolshevik-Leninist groups inside the PSOP but also your quarrel with the IS. What are your political reasons? The conflict had the entry question as its origin; the majority of the IS was against you. So what are your differences with the IS now? You say nothing of them.

When the POI was a united and independent organization it proved incapable of regularly publishing a newspaper and a magazine. How do you suppose you will accomplish publishing them after the split and after the entry of your "essential forces" into the PSOP? Do you think you can get financial support from the members of the PSOP for your publications? But this is impossible from all points of view. On the other hand, you naturally cannot imagine that the American comrades are going to subsidize an isolated little nucleus, independent in fact of every organization, including the IS. The American comrades wished and still do wish to help you get out of your stagnation. They have made an exceptional effort in this regard. But I very much doubt if they are ready to subsidize the existence of a problematical nucleus which would have no other meaning but to maintain the name of the firm.

Comrades, you have lost too much time! The fact that the Molinier clique has gotten hold of the PSOP youth is the result of this delay. There can be no more beating around the bush. A radical decision is called for. The entire POI must enter the PSOP, with the exception of two or three comrades who are necessary for the work of the IS and who, I fear, would have difficulty being accepted into PSOP membership.

But then, one may object, the Fourth International will be left at this critical moment with no publication in the French language. You know that our American section was in fact left for a certain period without its own paper and it nevertheless came out of this difficult situation strengthened and seasoned. But I don't think we need to be left without any French-language publication. The Bolshevik-Leninist faction within the PSOP has undertaken to publish a magazine. Why can this not be the tribune of the united faction of the Bolshevik-Leninists? This is the only possibility of having an organ which is a true expression of the experience of the Bolshevik-Leninists in the PSOP, that is, an instrument of political action and not the expression of the individual ideas of some little nucleus, cut loose, in reality, from all national and international control. What remains is only to assure an adequate composition of the editorial staff of this internal magazine.

For their part, our American comrades envisage the

publication of a monthly or bimonthly magazine under the sponsorship of the IS to serve the needs of all the French-speaking countries, in the first place, of course, France. The editorial board of this magazine would be made up of one or two POI comrades who would not enter the PSOP for the reasons mentioned above, a representative of the Belgian Central Committee, maybe one or two representatives of other Latin countries who do not have their own organ. In short, we are talking about an organ of the Fourth International, one of whose tasks would be to aid the Bolshevik-Leninists inside the PSOP. The American comrades, as I see from letters from New York, would be completely prepared to guarantee the existence of such a magazine. In my opinion it should appear twice a month with a richer and much broader content than *Quatrieme Internationale*. The discussion among Bolshevik-Leninists, in particular among the different French tendencies or currents, would in no way be excluded, but would be within the framework of common work in the PSOP and under the IS's leadership.

These are the proposals adopted in the National Committee of our American section. For my part, I entirely support these proposals. I propose to the IS that it adopt them not as proposals (this procedure has outlived its usefulness) but as a firm and categorical decision. I am especially appealing to the Central Committee of our Belgian section to support our American comrades' initiative with all necessary energy. Besides, a theoretical organ with the direct participation of the Belgian section would have the greatest advantages for the section itself.

There is no need to seek those "responsible" for the stagnation of the POI. It is only necessary to emerge from it. All of the members of the POI need a new milieu. There is no more time to lose. The Fourth International, through its executive body, must direct its French section in a complete reorientation, and the French section should carry it out as an act of discipline. There is nothing humiliating about obeying the decision of one's international organization, and I am sure it will be obeyed.

My most fraternal greetings,
C. [Leon Trotsky]

JULY 19, 1939

Dear Comrades:

Thank you for your letter of June 30. I don't think it is necessary to discuss here your statement that I regard the PSOP as a "haven." For me it is a tactical step that could yield greater or lesser results depending on a whole series of circumstances. I consider it a patent crime, however, to break with the Fourth International on account of this tactical step.

You write that this break is a temporary one and that you have no intention whatsoever of harming the work of our comrades within the PSOP. I consider that declaration to be very important and of great value, and I would hope that it will not remain only on paper.

However, I know from long experience that when a political group, seized by animosity, factional conservatism, or ambition, carries out a split that has no principled justification, very often it finds itself obliged to seek such a justification and even to invent it. The only difficult part in the split is the first step; then the elements that have split begin to go downhill. That is the danger that is facing you. I hope from the bottom of my heart that you will avoid it. But how? *The creation of your own faction inside the PSOP would in my opinion be an unprincipled and criminal action.* The workers' movement has a broad arena. Since you think it is necessary to maintain an independent organizational existence in the present period, you must find a field of action for yourselves *outside* the PSOP and thereby establish a sort of division of labor. Only in that way can the negative consequences of the split be reduced to a minimum. For my part, I am prepared to apply all my influence in overcoming the split at the earliest possible opportunity.

One final remark. From an absolutely reliable source I have received new confirmation that the GPU has a great many special agents to provoke dissension and splits within the Fourth International. I would advise you to examine very carefully the identity of those "intransigents" who are trying with all their power to embitter our internal relations through false insinuations and accusations, and all kinds of gossip, etc. I don't doubt that vigorous inspection will reveal the GPU's tracks.

Bolshevik greetings,

A trap in Palestine[375]

February 14, 1939

Dear Comrade Glotzer:

Thank you for the information concerning Ruskin. Your letter arrived in time, that is, before his visit. The whole matter has not the slightest importance. Ruskin is interested in the Jewish question and I suppose he has some official function in connection with Palestine.

He questioned me as to what I thought about Palestine and the possible interference of the USSR in favor of the creation of a Jewish state and so on. There are 400,000 Jews in Palestine, but Ruskin and his associates hope to place 500,000 more there. (How? When?) I answered him that they were preparing a fine trap for the Jews in Palestine. Before you settle 500,000 people, you will have an inner Palestine question with the 2,500,000 United States Jews. With the decline of American capitalism, anti-Semitism will become more and more terrible in the United States—in any case, more important than in Germany. If the war comes, and it will come, a good many Jews will fall as the first victims of the war and will be practically exterminated.

"But," he answered, "it is necessary to do something."

Yes, but something effective. The French Revolution and then the October Revolution accomplished a bit more for the Jews than did Zionism and the other specific "solutions" to a question that has no solution under the regime of declining capitalism. Only the international revolution can save the Jews.

He found these arguments unacceptable. He is very far from sympathetic to our ideas . . . a conservative and limited petty bourgeois—possibly a despairing petty bourgeois, but no more.

My best thanks and greetings.

Comradely,
Leon Trotsky

Money-raising appeals[376]

February 20, 1939

Dear Comrade Rose:

We asked about the two small articles sent to the staff. One of them concerns the collection of money for the French party. Since the money was collected without articles it is possible that the editorial board found that it was not necessary to publish the appeal.

The other article was concerning the question of raising money from the liberal Jewish bourgeois. It is not the fate of the article which interests me, but the question itself. Did the comrades discuss the possibility of a revolutionary organization's getting money from Jewish liberals and radicals? I believe that it could be done. However it would be necessary to develop a systematic campaign on an individual scale with a "diplomatic" approach. It is in this connection that the appeal I, or anyone else, proposes could be of use, but not simply as an article.

Comradely yours,
L. Trotsky

Utilize the opportunities in the Communist Party[377]

March 8, 1939

Dear Joe:

I see again from your letter, as from my discussion with two women comrades who came here from New York, that there exists a very poor state of affairs as regards the work of our party inside the Communist Party. There are no connections at all and there is a certain fatalism in this respect. "We are too weak. We do not have enough manpower to begin a systematic action. Etc."

I find it absolutely false, dangerous, almost to say, criminal. It is my opinion that we must register all the comrades who came from the Communist Party within the last two or three years, those who have personal connections with the Stalinists, and so on. Organize small discussions with them, not of a general, but of a practical, even an individual character. Elaborate some very concrete plans and rediscuss the matter after a week or so. On the basis of such a preparatory work a commission can be crystallized for this purpose.

The end of the Spanish tragedy, the truth about the activities of the Stalinists in Spain, and such articles as the excellent correspondence from Terence Phelan[378] in Paris, will inevitably create some disintegration in the Stalinist ranks. We must be present to observe these processes and to utilize the opportunities presented. It is the most important task of the party in this period.

As you can imagine, it is with the greatest impatience that I await your ultimate information about the manuscript.[379] Your procedure is not clear to me, but I am inclined to suppose that it is good. We will see the results.

We are glad to hear that your and Reba's[380] personal situation is more or less OK and that you have the full possibility of devoting yourself entirely to the *Socialist Appeal*.

We learn from the *Socialist Appeal* that our friend Andrews has been arrested. We saw the photos in which he was participating in the "bull fight," not of the Mexican but of the Yankee "breed."[381] We should be very glad to have some personal lines from Chris himself.

Friendliest greetings from Natalia and myself to you both.

Comradely,
L.T.

P.S. I see no reason for writing to Malamuth.³⁸² He happened to be a poor translator. I did everything in my power to smooth the matter over and not to offend him. He sent me a very appreciative letter. Then, against all my warnings, he permitted himself a condemnable indiscretion with my manuscript. I protested. His elementary duty should have been to apologize for his mistake and everything would have been in order again. I also find that Comrades Burnham and Shachtman committed an error in entering into a discussion with him about the quality of the manuscript without asking him whether or not he had my authorization to give them the manuscript. The best thing would be for Comrades Burnham and Shachtman, on their own initiative, to explain that they, together with Malamuth, committed something of an indiscretion and that it was best to recognize it as such and let it go at that.

Malamuth seems to have at least three qualities: he does not know Russian; he does not know English; and he is tremendously pretentious. I doubt that he is the best of translators. . . .

L.T.

James's trip to Mexico³⁸³

March 29, 1939

Dear Comrade James:

I received your documents and have read part of them. I have not answered until now because I awaited your notification about your eventual trip to Mexico. From your letter I could not determine definitely whether you were coming now or postponing your trip. The saddest fact is your illness, which is bad in itself, and also as it hinders you in the big plans for your work.

It is my opinion insofar as I am informed, that you should devote the next months exclusively to the care of your health, if necessary, even postponing the projected book on the Negro question. As I understand it, you suffer from a stomach ulcer. In this condition, your trip to Mexico represents—I say it with the deepest regret—a direct danger. Mexico City, by its specific conditions, is a genuine infection center for the stomach and the digestive organs generally. Everyone, even those who have sound stomachs, suffer from stomach trouble here; and those who have it abroad suffer doubly and triply in Mexico City. I know it from my own experience and from the experience of several friends. That is why, if you have the choice, you should cure your stomach before making the trip here, and even in this case it would be advisable not to live in Mexico City.

Your ideas for the Negro organization and the Negro paper are very interesting and important, but the first condition is the reestablishment of your health.

With sincerest greetings.

Yours comradely,
Leon Trotsky

Diego Rivera's defection[384]

March–April 1939

MARCH 31, 1939

Dear Friend:

I received your letter with the enclosure. Many thanks. It came on time.

I also received a letter from Comrade Goldman concerning the propositions he made to the library and to some universities. That is all that can be done. If we succeed in this it will be excellent. If not, we will arrange something else.

Your proposition of sending an American doctor here is not advisable. Nothing is new other than an aggravation of the chronic things. The general name of my illness is "the sixties" and I do not believe that in New York you have a specialist for this malady.

I sent you the documents concerning the painter. I hope that they are in your possession. I believe it would be best that a special commission, established in New York, send the painter concrete questions either directly or through Comrade C[urtiss]. If Dobbs comes to Mexico, as seems likely, then you seem to have a very good investigator who can work here in the name of the Pan-American Committee.[385] The same is true for [C.L.R.] James, if he comes in the next period. I do not know whether or not Jim [Cannon] is planning to come here for a week or so in order to discuss the French question. On the whole, you have enough possibilities for the investigation. But it must be done as promptly as possible in order to prevent the painter from expanding and aggrandizing his fantasies.

It is also necessary to prepare an explanation for our press, because I am sure that within the next days the "sensation" will appear in the Lovestoneite press, for he has communicated the news to them. And it will also appear in the bourgeois press.

Warmest greetings.

Comradely,
L.D.

APRIL 12, 1939

Dear Friend:

This morning *Excelsior* published a sensational note under the heading, "Trotsky Breaks His Relations With the Painter, Diego Rivera." The note is very vicious and contains various slanders, as is natural in such cases. One thing is clear from the note: the whole thing came from Rivera himself, from his babbling to different painters, artists and so on. The question of the house is largely and falsely presented. Now journalists will surely try to ask me or my collaborators about the matter. We will use the formula that we have nothing to communicate that could be of interest to the public. But further than that it is necessary to have in reserve a clear and short statement from the Pan-American Committee.

In previous letters I have insisted upon the refutation of three false assertions of Rivera's. It continues to be necessary, but I believe that these concrete refutations of concrete assertions should have a preamble, which *if absolutely necessary* could be given to the press. This preamble or short statement could be in approximately the following form:

"The Pan-American Committee (directly or through a commission) has investigated a series of assertions made by Diego Rivera against LT and has found them absolutely devoid of any basis. On the contrary LT had done everything in his power on every occasion to defend Rivera against animus [hostile] critics. The Committee regrets that Rivera found it possible to spread false assertions without the slightest reason or foundation."

Something of this kind. It could also be used, not as a preamble, but as a conclusion for the longer statement; but I insist that it should be categorical in its essence and mild toward Rivera in its form. That is why I propose the word "regrets" and not "condemns."

Please do not delay the investigation too long.

My best greetings,

APRIL 20, 1939

Dear Friend:

I received your letter concerning your propositions to the universities and the second enclosure. I also received a corresponding letter from Comrade Goldman. Everything is done that can be done and now we must wait.

Have you received all the documents concerning the painter? What are your plans in respect to this matter? His political "evolution" is very rapid. A few days ago he declared, in the society of a heterogeneous group, that Lenin was no more than a bourgeois. His new friend, O'Gorman,[386] confirmed this profound opinion and proclaimed that for the genuine revolutionary, the only way remaining was toward anarchism. The sooner we openly separate ourselves from him politically, the better.

On the personal plane, I wish simply a serious warning to him as quickly as possible, without publicity. It can be done only by the Pan-American Committee. James is here and can make the necessary investigation upon your commission. I hope that Dobbs will also come here and you can use him for the same purpose. You have here your official representative, C[urtiss]. What more can be done? You are completely informed.

My warmest greetings,
L.D.

P.S. I have just received the two statements of the PAC concerning the painter and his Partido. Very well. Now the political question is almost liquidated, but the personal one remains. ■

Where Munis should go[387]

May 1, 1939

Dear Friend:

It is my opinion that we must bring Munis here as quickly as possible. Curtiss has done everything that could be done under the conditions; and I do not see any reason for keeping him here now when his work could be used to better advantage in the States. Also, the climate here is very unfavorable for Lillian, and in spite of the fact that she was a very precious collaborator for me, I must insist on the necessity for her to return as quickly as possible.

Curtiss makes his return dependent upon Munis's arrival. I do not know Munis's plans or inclinations: when he is leaving France or whether or not he is going to the States. Curtiss fears that efforts may be made in New York to retain him for the Pan-American Committee. It would be false. Munis should come here where he would be ten times more useful. Please do everything possible in this direction.

Comradely,
V.T. O'Brien [Leon Trotsky]

Pan-American Committee personnel[388]

May 1, 1939

My Dear Friend:

I understand very well the difficulties the work of the Pan-American Committee encounters. Nobody wishes serious work, especially when the work is of a technical and anonymous character. The only solution I can see to the difficulties is the creation of a technical bureau of the PAC. The bureau should consist of young and devoted people. If you can find them, one or two Germans among the exiles would be of great value. That is, of course, if they are not lazy, which also happens among Germans from time to time.

Before I received your last letter I communicated my propositions concerning France as well as the Pan-American Committee. In spite of the expense we must send two comrades in order to bring the matter to a real solution, otherwise the new trip can turn out to be useless and deepen the crisis in France as well as provoke a crisis in the States.

Warmest greetings.

Yours,
L.T.

Victor Serge's crisis[389]

May 6, 1939

Dear Comrade:

Your letter, while very friendly in a personal sense, demonstrates to me anew that you are passing through a protracted ideological crisis and that you are turning your dissatisfaction with yourself into dissatisfaction with others. You write about intrigues, false information, etc. I don't know about any of that. I know only your writings and your actions. Against the Fourth International you support everybody "supportable." This demonstrates that politically your solidarity with us is much weaker than your antagonism. After the inevitable setbacks to your politics, which for my own usage I call individualistic and even, permit me the word, adventuristic, you ought to change your way of doing things. I do not lose the hope of seeing you return to the road of the Fourth International. But at present you are an adversary, and a hostile one at that, who demands nonetheless to be treated as a political friend.

My best regards,

Another anonymous letter[390]

May 10, 1939

Dear Friend:

I am sending you an anonymous letter received from San Francisco some days ago. Two or three days before we received a phone call from San Francisco from someone asking for Natalia or for a secretary who spoke Russian. We could not answer the call because it was not on our telephone system and it would have been necessary to go outside the house, it was night, and we were doubtful about the whole story. Then in two days came this letter in two copies, one addressed to me and the other to Natalia.

The importance of the letter is clear from the letter itself. I believe the author is the same who previously sent us a letter from New York asking for an answer in the *Socialist Appeal*. I considered the first letter as seventy-five percent a provocation for the purpose of making us suspicious of a certain comrade. Also the allusion to Lushkov[391] was too improbable. The enclosed letter seems incomparably more trustworthy. I cannot see what interest the Three-Letters [GPU] would have in sending us such a message. I suppose that the author is the same, namely, W.[392] In that case, if both letters came from the same source, the first letter merits more attention (I have never received any communication about the results of the investigation).

What interest can W. have in acting in such an enigmatic manner? I believe that he does not trust us. He knows some agents in our milieu. On the other hand, he is more or less inspired by some animosity toward us. He told our common, deceased friend [Leon Sedov] about some attempts prepared against his father. He even communicated some details. I do not know them because at that time it was planned that W. would meet me and tell me everything he knew. But then, under some mysterious influence, he changed his attitude. Possibly he simply noticed that we were absolutely foreign to him. On his own initiative he broke off almost all relations with our young friend. After the death of our friend, he sent me a cable of condolence. That was all.

The reason for his going to the States and the people who helped him are absolutely unknown to me. I am sure that he knows *incomparably more* than he says or writes. Many things that he knows are surely compromising for himself; he was not an *observer* in these affairs. . . .

Is he really the author of the enclosed letter? It would be necessary to find out whether he visited the San Francisco Exposition, but first it is necessary to find him. The question is of the greatest importance. Even if he is not the author of this letter, he knows of the preparations for different attempts, as of many other things. *He must speak.* We are interested in averting every difficulty for him and *we can even help him in this respect.* You recall, of course, that his first presentation to public opinion was made in accordance with a plan proposed by us after the catastrophe of Ignace [Reiss]. We can be very useful to him in this respect in the future. But he must speak. His letters (if they are really his) show that he feels himself where his duty lies. However, we must *underline* it. If necessary, I could send you our young friend's letters in which W.'s knowledge of the attempts were mentioned. These letters are documents. We are not interested in using them publicly, but he must speak. It is necessary to find him at any price. The enclosed letter might possibly serve you as a "credential."

I wrote about the matter to Joe [Hansen] (before I received this letter), but I fear that I was not explanatory enough. Please discuss the matter with him and elaborate a plan of action.

Explain to W. that, in spite of divergences, we can have a very close united front in the fight against the Three-Letters. I am, of course, ready to meet him under conditions that will assure him of full safety. I believe that our discussions could also be of some value in his literary activity. For example, it is very important that he go back to the Moscow trials in the press, and many other questions.

I shall await your communications on the matter with the greatest interest.

Comradely,
L.D.

Problems of the 'Socialist Appeal'[393]

May 27, 1939

Dear Friend:

I am a bit astonished by the absence of any information from the States and personally from you.

From the minutes I see that you are having difficulty with the *Socialist Appeal*. The paper is very well done from a journalistic point of view; but it is a paper for workers and not a workers' paper. I hope that the administrative change in the editorial board will be salutary not only from the financial but from the political standpoint.

As it is, the paper is divided among various writers, each

of whom is very good, but collectively they do not permit the workers to penetrate to the pages of the *Appeal*. Each of them speaks for the workers (and speaks very well), but nobody will hear the workers. In spite of its literary brilliance, to a certain degree the paper becomes a victim of journalistic routine. You do not hear at all how the workers live, fight, clash with the police or drink whiskey. It is very dangerous for the paper as a revolutionary instrument of the party. The task is not to make a paper through the joint forces of a skilled editorial board, but to encourage the workers to speak for themselves.

I am in entire agreement with the PC that a twice-weekly can be put out by two, even by one, editors under the condition that the whole party participates in the paper not only financially but politically and journalistically. The paper must have correspondents, researchers and reporters everywhere. Three lines from a shop or a meeting can often give more than a well-written article by the staff. Only such a paper can penetrate into the masses and receive great support from them.

A radical and courageous change is necessary as a condition of success. The paper is too wise, too scholarly, too aristocratic for the American workers and tends to reflect the party more as it is than to prepare it for its future.

Of course it is not only a question of the paper, but of the whole course of policy. I continue to be of the opinion that you have *too many petty-bourgeois boys and girls* who are very good and devoted to the party, but who do not fully realize that their duty is not to discuss among themselves, but to penetrate into the fresh milieu of workers. I repeat my proposition: Every petty-bourgeois member of the party who, during a certain time, let us say three or six months, does not win a worker for the party, should be demoted to the rank of candidate and after another three months expelled from the party. In some cases it might be unjust, but the party as a whole would receive a salutary shock which it needs very much. A very radical change is necessary.

I sent Comrade Goldman a letter, but have not yet received his acknowledgement. I hope that he is now in France.

Comradely,
V.T. O'Brien [Leon Trotsky]

A visa for Elsa Reiss[394]

June 5, 1939

Dear Comrade Rose:

I am writing you in re Elsa Reiss. You know that she wishes to come to the States with her son at any price. There are three or four plans. One is that we obtain a visa to Mexico for her as my secretary. I am, of course, ready to do everything possible, but the plan is very inconvenient. I cannot abuse my privileges in the matter of secretaries. When she comes to Mexico as a secretary she and her son should live in our house, which is already overcrowded. This creates the greatest difficulties for Natalia especially. If she comes here and lives outside the house, the authorities would interpret it as an abuse of confidence, and I wish to avoid such suspicions at any price. Then too, it is Elsa's aim to go to the States and it would not be easy to go to the States from here.

The second plan is that she marry a Mexican and become

a Mexican citizen. It is feasible, but the difficulty of entering the States remains.

The third plan is that she marry a citizen of the United States. It seems that such a plan was accepted with Jim, but to date nothing has been heard about its realization. I should be very thankful if you would let me know what has been done and what will be done.

I wrote a letter to Jim about the social composition of the party. I am afraid that the coming convention will pass over this question with a general resolution, but without energetic, practical measures. Every social milieu has its conservatism and especially the milieu of the Jewish petty bourgeoisie. Without heroic and if necessary surgical measures, a turn in the party's policy toward a totally different social milieu is impossible.

Comradely,
L. Trotsky

A party census[395]

June 23, 1939

Dear Friend:

Do you not think it would be feasible to make a general census of the party and establish who are all the comrades not bound by their jobs to a certain locality, especially New York? The comrades on relief could then be distributed throughout the provinces in provincial industrial centers.

The best thing, it seems to me, would be to create from these comrades two or three, or so, special brigades and to send them out for the "conquest" of a certain town or of a certain branch of industry in this town.

Fraternally,
V.T. O'Brien [Leon Trotsky]

For the Ukrainian pamphlet[396]

September 1939

Dear Comrade:

Although I do not allow myself any great illusions in regard to Vinnichenko, I fully support your proposal to delete the words "of the type of Vinnichenko and Company" from my article. You may immediately remove these words from the text you have. I am simultaneously writing to New York with the same correction.

You are right that my information on the Ukrainian question, especially in the sphere of individual and group moods, is far from being adequate. If my evaluation of Vinnichenko's line is mistaken, I am fully prepared to acknowledge this publicly (in particular if the article has already been printed in the Russian *Biulleten* with Vinnichenko's name in it).

Of course I am willing to write him not one but a dozen letters, since a rapprochement with him would of course have great significance. But I hesitate to write him now in France because of the war, as my letter might compromise him. It would be good if you or some other comrade who has contact with Vinnichenko were to inquire what his attitude is toward the positions I have developed [on the Ukraine] in my recent articles.

I am submitting a short piece on Kerensky and Company for your pamphlet; in my opinion it would go well there. In addition I am submitting a short preface for the pamphlet.

I would be grateful to you if you would inform me of developments from time to time in the future.

Warm greetings and wishes for success. ■

A disagreeable incident[397]

September 7, 1939

Dear Mr. Ross:

Of course I remember very well our meeting in November 1917. (You were more or less in favor of the Social Revolutionaries!) But I remember incomparably better that you were a prominent member of the Dewey Commission, which demanded moral courage, alas, not very common in our days.

I have never accepted tourists but, of course, I agreed immediately to meet Mrs. Harris with your letter of introduction. I must, however, confess that I had a great disappointment. She came, not alone, but with three gentlemen. While the gentlemen showed some understanding of my position, Mrs. Harris occurred to be a passionate Stalinist.

It is her right, of course. But she began to defend the Moscow trials. Totally astonished, I asked her: "But Mr. Ross pronounced himself about the Moscow trials as frame-ups." She answered: "Mr. Ross is an old man and makes mistakes." "So?" I answered. "The one mistake of Mr. Ross I know of is that he gave you, too generously, a letter of introduction to me." All three gentlemen with her were indignant with her attitude and expressed it openly in her presence. When she left I refused to shake hands with her.

I find it necessary for me to communicate to you this disagreeable incident.

With warmest wishes and greetings, I remain

Yours sincerely,
Leon Trotsky

The first article in the Russian discussion[398]

September 28, 1939

Dear Comrade Rose:

I didn't answer your last letter because we had here a very hot time with the *Life* article and other things.

I will write as often for the *Appeal* as I can. The American friends do so much for our household that I don't see any reason why they should pay for my articles. The best thing would be *to sell the archives* which could give me the possibility to devote all my time to the party press. Can you speak about this again with Goldman and Glenner [Jan Frankel]?

I send simultaneously the Russian text of the USSR article to Vanzler for translation. I don't see, I must confess, any reason to hinder discussion on this matter. Better to take the initiative and to show that the events did not take us unaware.

It would be good if you communicate to me the reactions of comrades of both camps to the last article on the USSR.

With warmest comradely greeting,

L. Trotsky

Accepting the invitation of the Dies Committee[399]

October 12, 1939

Dear Friends:

I enclose a copy of the invitation sent me by J.B. Matthews to appear before the Dies Committee and a copy of my reply. All of us here believe that I cannot refuse such an exceptional tribune. My concrete proposals are as follows:

1. I should be glad to have, if possible, Comrade Goldman as my attorney before the Committee. If the statutes of the Committee permit, and if Goldman agrees, I will notify Matthews so that Goldman can use his credentials for all the steps he finds necessary.

2. It would be necessary also to arrange the trip of Comrade Glenner, if it is possible and if he thinks it advisable, with all the books, materials, etc., at his disposition.

3. It would be of course good if other comrades, especially Comrade Shachtman and Comrade Vanzler, could come with materials from their archives.

4. In a telephonic conversation with Joe Hansen, Matthews said that the Committee will cover the expenses. The cable says nothing about this. If the covering of the expenses of witnesses is a general rule, I don't see any reason for refusing payment. The question is practically very important for me as you understand.

But you will decide this for yourselves and undertake eventually through Comrade Goldman the necessary steps.

5. I believe that you could very discreetly contact newsreel, broadcasting companies, and so on, with the proposal to utilize the trip from this point of view.

According to the Matthews cable I should be in Austin about the tenth of November. It would be best if Comrade Goldman came a day or so before this in order to arrange with the authorities all the practical questions.

In accordance with the request of the Committee the matter should be kept discreet at present.

Leon Trotsky

J.B. Matthews, Chief Investigator
Special Committee on Un-American Activities
Washington, D.C.

I accept your invitation as a political duty. I will undertake necessary measures in order to overcome practical difficulties. Please arrange under the same conditions entry for my wife. She is indispensable for the purpose of locating the necessary documents, quotations, dates, in my files. Necessary to have your questions as soon as possible in order to select the necessary documents. Also desire exact quotations from depositions of Foster and Browder concerning me personally.

Leon Trotsky

Outline of a magazine article[400]
November 15, 1939

Twin stars are either of purely optical or of physical character. The question is, do Hitler and Stalin represent a physical or an optical twin star? Hitler insists upon the first, Stalin tries to impose the second. Hitler is right—for the next period we will have a real twin star with Hitler as the main star and Stalin as the satellite.

The fundamental characteristic of the European and thus of the world situation at the present time is that all the bridges to peace have been burned. A long and pitiless war is ahead of us. Just at the moment when the inevitability of such a war became obvious, the Comintern sharply veered in its policies from sugared phrases about the defense of democracy and peace to the slogan, abandoned five years ago, of the world revolution (Molotov, Dimitrov, Browder, etc.). The impression is given that the Kremlin is prepared to use the war, and the upheavals which it will inevitably provoke, for the "Sovietization" of Europe—and not Europe alone. It is precisely this impression which Stalin wishes to spread. It is for this purpose that Dimitrov, Browder, and the others are ordered to don frowning masks. The entire world press echoes the turn. In reality Stalin wishes to sell to the highest bidder the revolutionary thunderbolts which he dug out of the cellar and which he now brandishes in his fist, just as he sold the "defense of democracy" to Hitler for part of Poland and trusteeship over the Baltic states. The thunderbolts are a bluff. Whoever believes in them will find himself deceived as London and Paris were deceived during the negotiations with Moscow.

Before war produces a revolution it produces speculation

on revolution. Even the conservative Chamberlain bases his plans on a kind of monarcho-democratic revolution in Germany. Instead of bombs he drops leaflets. It is striking how little the statesmen learned from the experience of the last war and how blind they are to the greatest events of history—wars and revolutions. To believe that a "moderate," a "reasonable," a "conservative" revolution against Hitler is possible in Germany is as absurd as the belief that it was possible to satisfy Hitler with the Sudeten mountains. In Germany only a socialist revolution is possible. Unlike Chamberlain, Stalin understands and fears this.

A totalitarian regime is by its very essence an iron hoop around a barrel of explosives. A totalitarian regime is necessary where the internal contradictions have reached the point of unbearable tension. That is why we can foresee that in the series of revolutions which the war cannot help but provoke, the totalitarian countries will be the first on the list. It is fantastic to imagine that Germany could be Sovietized from Moscow as was small and backward Galicia. For the bursting of the hoop of National Socialism tremendous explosions will be necessary. Millions of people will be set in motion. And revolutions are contagious. In the chain of political regimes the Stalin dictatorship is one of the weakest links.

But before revolution there is the war. During the next period Stalin will remain Hitler's satellite. During the coming winter he will in all probability make no moves. With Finland he will conclude a compromise. He will seek another more important compromise with Japan against the United States. So long as the military position of Hitler remains favorable (and it will be so in any case during the first year of the war) Stalin will satisfy himself with what has already been attained. If and when Germany finds herself in a difficult situation, and that is inevitable but not so near, Stalin will try to cut loose from Hitler. He will, for example, Sovietize the Baltic countries and possibly ask for the independence of Hitler's Poland in order to

Sovietize it too, and he may become active in the Balkans.

However, all this is but the final convulsions of two totalitarian regimes. The military crash of Hitler will inevitably provoke a revolution in Germany and the consequences of this will be the overthrow of Stalin's oligarchy in the USSR. Already at this early date these two occurrences loom as the most certain to materialize from the bloody chaos.

This sketch of course will be filled in with positive dates, concrete illustrations, some personal characterizations, and so on. The article will be from 3,000 to 3,500 words. ■

A false report[401]

December 26, 1939

Editor, *Excelsior*
Mexico City

Dear Sir:

On the front page of *Excelsior*, December 25, in a note entitled "Alliance Against Communism," it is stated that General [Emilio N.] Acosta had approached me to obtain materials for the struggle against the communist "doctrine." Permit me to make the following statement in the columns of your newspaper:

1. I do not have the honor of knowing General Acosta and have never had any relations with him.

2. In general, no one has approached me to obtain mate-

rials either against the communist doctrine or against that caricature of communism which covers up the attitude of the international agents of the new Soviet aristocracy.

Someone or other appears to be interested in mixing up my name in enterprises with which I do not and could not have anything in common.

L. Trotsky

Dialectics and the answer to Burnham[402]
January 9, 1940

Dear Friend:

Yesterday I sent the Russian text of my new article written in the form of a letter to Burnham. Not all comrades possibly are content with the fact that I give the predominant place in the discussion to the matter of dialectics. But I am sure it is now the only way to begin the theoretical education of the party, especially of the youth and to inject a reversion [revulsion] to empiricism and eclectics. (I believe Van [Heijenoort] could be very useful in discussion on this matter.)

If the comrades of your faction find that something in my article is not adequate please make concrete propositions for changes during the time of translation. I will answer by airmail and even by cable if necessary.

I received yesterday some materials concerning the Negro question with a not signed carbon copy of a letter addressed to me and dated December 13. There is also a copy of a letter to Comrade Johnson [C.L.R. James] and other materials. I don't know who sent me all this material and why they arrived with such a delay. In any case I am very thankful for the communications and I agree completely with the proposition insofar as I am able to judge them from here.

W. Rork [Leon Trotsky]

Farrell Dobbs's arrival[403]

January 16, 1940

Dear Friend:

Smith arrived yesterday. The first contact is made, the impression is very favorable. We wait now for a telegraphic answer from you about the date on the convention in order to settle our one-week or two-weeks plan.

They brought us the Webster dictionary and candy. The beautiful dictionary is now the sensation of the household, especially of our grandson. The candies bear a very friendly trademark. Long live Salem! Please transmit our best thanks to the comrades who sent the Webster dictionary. Our warmest greetings to you both.

Yours,
L. Trotsky

P.S. What miserable writing is Shachtman's open letter. Its only merit is that it obliged me to tell him the full truth about his politics. My answer is already dictated, I have only to polish it. Unfortunately it will not be shorter than my letter to Burnham.

L.T.

A discussion with Carleton Smith[404]

Published February 2, 1940

The United States will join the Allied forces, win the present European war, become the greatest capitalistic nation in the world, and then America's sixty families will hire British diplomats and statesmen as their bellboys, Leon Trotsky, exiled Russian Communist leader, told Carleton Smith, music critic who once served as commentator with the St. Louis Symphony Orchestra, Smith said yesterday as he alighted from a plane which brought him here from Fort Worth. He saw Trotsky two days ago.

Smith, a native of Bement, Illinois, a graduate of the University of Illinois, Chicago University, and the London School of Economics, despite his mere thirty years of age, has made a worldwide reputation as a music critic. Back from a four-and-a-half month tour by air of South America, where he visited the president of every South American republic, and such figures as Trotsky and Diego Rivera, the eminent artist in Mexico City, Smith is enthusiastic over the possibilities of perfecting a real good-neighbor policy through the medium of art and music.

But of Trotsky and his interpretation of world events, the youthful critic, attired in a soft light brown fur coat, made from the pelts of the vicuna, an almost extinct animal found in the highlands of Bolivia, had much to say.

A virtual prisoner in Mexico City, where he lives in a house behind thick twelve-foot-high walls with electrically charged wires and machine guns as protection, Trotsky told Smith, "The first real Communist nation in the world will be the United States. The reason Russia has never been a real socialist state is because in order to have such a state you must first of all have something to divide up. The United States has much to divide, while Russia had practically nothing.

"The United States will join the war in order to defeat Hitler and when he is whipped Stalin will sell him out in order to make a better deal with the victorious Allies. The strongest firm always wins in those cases and the United States will be that firm. It will rule over the miserable and destroyed nations with usual American benevolence and will be considered a nation of great guys." ∎

Factionalism and the IEC[405]

February–April 1940

TO THE IEC OF THE FOURTH INTERNATIONAL[406]
FEBRUARY 1, 1940

Dear Comrades:

We received two days ago an article of Comrade Lebrun,[407] "The Defense of the USSR in the Present War." On the first page of the article we read: "Following the example of the American party, the International Executive Committee has decided to open the discussion in the International. This decision is in harmony with the wishes of our national sections and groups."

We the undersigned members of the International Executive Committee never before heard about this decision of the International Executive Committee: if the assertion of Comrade Lebrun is exact, it follows then that we were not only not asked about the matter, but that we never received the text of the mentioned decision.

What "national sections and groups" asked for the opening of the international discussion? We would be very glad to have copies of the respective decisions or letters and also of the mentioned decision of the International Executive Committee.

We are not at all opposed to an international discussion. But if the IEC actually made a decision to open such a discussion, we would like to know in what forms and by what proceedings this discussion is "opened."

Every section has, of course, the full right to discuss every question it finds necessary. To open an international discussion can have only one meaning, namely, to create a special international bulletin for the discussion articles. We don't see any other thinkable proceeding under the given conditions. However we have heard nothing about the creation of such a bulletin. The article of Comrade Lebrun gave us no indication as to who published it. Was it the IEC? Was it Comrade Lebrun himself?

We ask you comrades to inform us about the following matters:

First, who are the members of the IEC?

Second, who is the secretary?

Third, why did you not address us on the matter of an international discussion?

Fourth, did you receive other documents for the discussion?

Fifth, who published the article of Comrade Lebrun which has the subtitle, "Document for discussion in the International"?

The sense of our questions is, we are sure, completely clear to you: if an international discussion is officially opened, it should be conducted not in a free-lance manner, but under the direction of the leading body of the Fourth International.

With fraternal greetings,

TO THE EXECUTIVE COMMITTEE, FOURTH INTERNATIONAL[408]
FEBRUARY 20, 1940

Dear Comrades:

The coming minority convention in Cleveland, twenty-fourth and twenty-fifth of this month, can become decisive for the question of the unity of our North American section. We the undersigned believe that the Executive Committee has the duty to intervene immediately in the internal fight with the purpose of saving the unity of the party. This purpose must be absolutely clear to all the members of the Executive Committee independently of their individual sympathies or solidarity with the [SWP] majority or minority.

We propose an *immediate* meeting of the Executive Committee and we submit to this meeting the following propositions:

1. The Executive Committee delegates two of its members to the minority caucus in Cleveland with the mandate to act commonly in favor of unity of the party.

2. The minority, as the majority, should take the obligation to safeguard the unity of the party independently of the relationship of forces at the next convention.

3. The Executive Committee proposes to both parts its services in order to elaborate organizational measures which should dissipate the apprehensions of the minority of being treated as second-class party members, etc. (see the letter of Comrade Abern).

No minority can pretend to have in the party the same rights as the majority, but in view of the exceptional situation created by the sharp fight and profound divergences, the future minority can ask for certain reasonable guarantees for its ideological existence and we believe that the future majority should grant these reasonable guarantees in order to prevent a premature and not unavoidable split.

The delegates of the Executive Committee should act in this spirit. Not only in the Cleveland convention of the minority, but of course, also in the decisive meeting of the majority caucus, or at the majority convention if they convoke one.

It is necessary to act urgently and with full energy.

With comradely greetings,

DECLARATION[409]
MARCH 19, 1940

We, the undersigned, must establish the following facts.

The resident members of the International Executive Committee have not developed any activity for a long period. No international bulletin is published, no circular letters are sent to the sections, no letters are answered. The same concerns the Pan-American Committee.

On February 20 we the undersigned addressed the IEC with the proposition to intervene in the Socialist Workers Party discussion with the purpose of preserving unity. In spite of the extreme gravity and urgency of the matter we did not receive an answer. We must therewith conclude and openly establish that the IEC is nonexistent and that we cannot either directly or indirectly support the fiction of its existence.

From private sources we heard that Comrades Johnson [James] and Lebrun took part in the minority split convention and encouraged their pretension for an independent public organ, i.e., for a split under the camouflage of "unity." Is this true? We must confess that we cannot really believe such an enormity on the part of comrades appointed as members of the leading body of the Fourth International.

If, in spite of all, it is true, does Comrade Johnson act in agreement with our British section? Does Comrade Lebrun act in agreement with our Brazilian section?

All our information says that the overwhelming majority of the Fourth International remain true to the Marxist theory, to our program, to our political tradition and to the organizational principles of Bolshevism. The connections with Europe are very difficult. But we can and should immediately create a genuine Pan-American Committee based upon the active sections with the purpose of reestablishing as early as possible a new International Executive Committee really representing the Fourth International and capable of continuous revolutionary activity.

DECLARATION ON THE STATUS OF THE RESIDENT IEC[410]
APRIL 2, 1940

In view of the fact that the resident International Executive Committee has virtually ceased to exist as such, the undersigned must make known the following information.

1. The resident IEC was set up in New York immediately after the outbreak of the war, its composition being determined solely by presence in that city; an administrative secretary was assigned to work with the committee by the Political Committee of the SWP.

2. That committee was to serve as a secretariat with the fullest possible participation of other members of the IEC present on this continent.

3. Immediately following the opening of the discussion in the SWP, a majority of the members of the resident committee tended to align themselves factionally with the minority in that party, failing to utilize their function on the committee in order to mitigate the struggle and, in fact, ignoring the existence of the IEC for all practical purposes.

4. This nonfunctioning of the majority of the members of the resident committee was conclusively proven when IEC members Crux and Fischer and the representative of the Mexican and Spanish sections, Munis, addressed it on February 20 with the proposal to intervene in the Socialist Workers Party discussion for the purpose of preserving unity. The secretary of the committee forwarded this communication with Comrade Martel [Cannon]'s and his own endorsement. In spite of the extreme gravity and urgency of the situation, no reply was received from Comrades Trent [Shachtman], Anton,[411] Johnson, and Lebrun.

5. Comrades Trent and Anton participated in the Cleveland split conference of the minority as members of that faction in the SWP; Comrade Johnson—without any authorization from the British section and most certainly without any authority from the IEC. Comrade Lebrun endorsed the actions taken there, likewise without the approval of his own section and without consulting the IEC. The only communication received by the IEC from Brazil in the recent period informs us that the section there retains the position of "unconditional defense of the USSR," accepting the discipline of the Fourth International despite differences of opinion within its ranks. It also reprimands Lebrun for neglect of duty in relation to his own party. All these comrades have thus acted behind the back of the International Executive Committee and in utter disregard of their duties as members of that body.

6. All our information says that the overwhelming majority of the Fourth International remains true to Marxist theory, to our program, to our political tradition, and to the organizational principles of Bolshevism. The connections with Europe are very difficult. But we can and should immediately create a genuine Pan-American center based upon the active sections, with the purpose of reestablishing as early as possible a new International Executive Committee really representing the Fourth International and capable of continuous revolutionary activity.

7. To that end, and in view of the de facto nonexistence of the resident IEC, we fully endorse the initiative taken by the American, Canadian, and Mexican sections of the Fourth International in calling a Pan-American Conference. The conference, with the participation of all sections that can furnish mandates, can and must establish at once a representative body which will replace the defunct resident IEC. ■

Rivera's wild denunciation[412]

April 6, 1940

Dear Comrade Vanzler:

I send you an incredible document: an interview given by Diego Rivera to *La Prensa* about the Fourth International and me personally. The political content is as follows: Trotsky looks for a reconciliation with Stalin, he justifies the aggression on Finland, Stalin has given the order not to attack Trotsky anymore, etc. But not this is interesting. The center of the interview is the following sentence:

"Trotsky will support Stalin in his attitude toward Finland today in the congress of the Fourth International which is now taking place in New York and for the session of which Trotsky already sent his representative the Spanish-Mexican, M. Grandizo." I quote verbally and I enclose the Spanish text of the interview.

The statement is a wild denunciation and a false one. There is no congress of the Fourth International in New York (possibly Rivera with his confused mentality confounded the convention of your party with the congress of the Fourth International).

As far as I know, Grandizo is the real name of a Mexican Marxist whom I met several times under his political and literary name, Munis. He was never my "representative." He left as I learned yesterday during my absence from Mexico City. I was on a short vacation trip in the Vera Cruz region. The denunciation is thus, I repeat, completely false, but it remains nevertheless or even more a wild denunciation.

If a congress of the Fourth International were really being held in New York in secrecy (because our press didn't mention such a congress), then Rivera's statement could only signify an attempt to provoke a repressive action from the American police against this (nonexistent) congress.

More directly the statement is aimed at provoking police measures against Grandizo as my alleged representative.

Not necessary to say that the whole statement if taken seriously by the Mexican authorities could be prejudicial to my sojourn in the country.

I can't enter into polemics here with Diego Rivera because this is just what he wishes in order to throw into the press hundreds of similar affirmations, one more fantastic and absurd than the other. But I believe that the American section of the Fourth International from one side and Grandizo from the other should make a public statement in the most sharp and pitiless form on the denunciation and the denunciator. I believe even that it could be done in the name of the convention if it is still going on because Rivera is an important enough figure for such a kind of "attention" from one side and his statement concerns the convention under the name of the congress of the Fourth International from the other. If the convention is over, the statement could be made in the name of the National Committee and immediately communicated to the representatives of the Mexican press. You will agree, I hope, that a very energetic measure is necessary, otherwise Rivera, in the role of my ex-friend, will throw into circulation the most wild inventions and calumnies because he seems to be definitely demoralized by his own political treason.

Not necessary to add that I didn't give him the slightest pretext for his ignominious statement: since his desertion I never mention his name and neglected completely a series of less important falsehoods and provocations.

Leon Trotsky

A serious work on Russian revolutionary history[413]

May 2, 1940

Dear Comrade:

I read your manuscript attentively. My original impression was only reinforced: You are very well acquainted with the literature on the question and have composed a very serious work. I have no principled objections at all to make, only some isolated, partial observations. I am writing in Russian, because it is easier for me.

Your first chapter is called "Peculiarities of Russian Capitalist Development: An Historical Illustration of *Combined* and *Uneven* Development." I would put *uneven* before *combined*, because the second grows out of the first and completes it. Aside from that, in the text of this same chapter the concepts of *uneven* and *combined* development, although they are illustrated factually, are not defined by a single word. In my opinion, you ought to give a short theoretical definition of *uneven* and *combined* development.

On page 12, the tenth line from the bottom, it is said that the Narodniks[414] had no understanding *whatever* of the classes in society. This assertion is too categorical. Like any petty-bourgeois radical movement, they distinguished very well the class of the nobility, the big bourgeoisie, the bureaucracy, and even the kulaks. But they ignored the distinction between the proletariat and the peasantry, as also the stratification of the peasantry itself. In other words, they transformed all working people into one "class."

Page 13. At the end of the paragraph you ascribe to Lenin that which rightfully belongs to the Emancipation of Labor Group[415] (thirteenth line from the bottom).

Page 14. You write that Volkhovsky, Shishko, and Kravchinsky later remained with the *right* Socialist Revolutionaries. As far as I know, they all died before the Social Revolutionary Party split into lefts and rights. Kravchinsky died even before the founding of the Social Revolutionary Party.

On the same page it is said that around 1879 a section of the Narodniks lost faith in conspiratorial methods of organization. This could give cause for misunderstanding. The Narodniks lost faith in the possibility of illegal organization of the *masses*. But the organization of the Narodniks remained conspiratorial.

On the same page you say that the new organization was called "People and Freedom" [Narod i Volya]. This is a misunderstanding. The name was "People's Will" [Narodnaya Volya]; as is known, the word "volya" in Russian has two meanings: freedom and will, in the sense of the right to decide.

On the same page you say that Plekhanov organized a third group, which was called at first the "Black Redistribution." In reality "Land and Freedom" split into two organizations: "People's Will" and "Black Redistribution."

Page 16. You say at the beginning: "The Narodnik movement was anti-Marxist precisely because it ignored the workers." It would be better to say, it seems to me, that it ignored the independent class character of the proletariat, dissolving the workers into the laboring people in general.

On page 17 you say about the People's Will movement that it was quixotic and heroic. I would leave out the designation "quixotic." In quixotism there is a comical element that was altogether lacking in the People's Will.

Page 21. The thirteenth line from the bottom. Here you are talking about the adherents of People's Will; whereas you should, in my opinion, be speaking about the Narodniks in general.

Page 26. You speak of the fact that Plekhanov's view of the intelligentsia was a typical *Menshevik* view. This sounds like an anachronism, because the Mensheviks appeared significantly later.

At the end of the same page it is stated with condemnation that the Emancipation of Labor Group still adhered to terror. It would be necessary, it seems to me, to explain that it is a question of *individual* terror, which isolated the revolutionists from the workers' movement and concentrated all hopes on the activities of small circles of "heroes." We also stood for terror, but mass terror carried out by the revolutionary class.

Page 28. The opposition of Blagoyev and Plekhanov is true only to the extent that is well known. It is true that Blagoyev turned up in the Third International, which did him credit. But all the same he remained a fairly big opportunist in questions of revolutionary struggle.

These are all of my observations. As you see, they touch more the formulation than the essence of the thing. In general the work will be useful to the highest degree.

P.S. Has your interest been drawn to the so-called Tanaka Memorial[416] by the former Japanese minister of foreign affairs? The Japanese pretension to world supremacy is expounded in this memorial. Do you perhaps have, by any chance, any kind of materials or data related to this memorial? If not, it's not necessary to search for any.

Warmest greetings.

Yours,
L.T.

To Colonel Sanchez Salazar[417]

May 31, 1940

Sir:

Simultaneously with the protest I am sending to President Lazaro Cardenas, I find myself obliged to draw to your attention the following circumstances:

1. The [May 24] attack is not an unexpected accident which can be attributed to God, to Diego Rivera, etc. The incident is not the first of its kind; facing the prospect of an inevitable attack by the GPU, I had taken every precaution. Now that the attack is an accomplished fact, it is my friends and defenders who are apprehended, and suspicion lights on my former friends rather than on my true enemies, who are well known to all.

2. I know nothing of Mr. Rivera's chauffeur. But the attempt to ascribe a role in the conspiracy to the great artist himself is an utterly absurd fantasy.

3. That attempt accords surprisingly well with the effort of the attackers themselves by shouting "Viva Almazan!"[418] to give the impression that the attack was an incident of domestic politics. Rivera, as can be read in the press, was involved with the campaign of General Almazan. The classic rule of the GPU is to kill an enemy and throw the blame on someone else.

4. I have nothing in common with Diego Rivera's political activities. We broke off our personal relations fifteen months ago. For over a year I have had no dealings whatever with him, either directly or indirectly, that could provide so much as a superficial pretext for the monstrous fabrication making Rivera responsible for an act undoubtedly committed at the instigation of the GPU and covered up politically by the hateful campaign of Messrs. Toledano, Laborde, Encinas, Salgado, and others.

5. One of today's newspapers has printed the following: "There later arose personal differences between Trotsky and Diego Rivera. There was the further circumstance that the artist also had certain words with his wife, Mrs. Frida Kahlo,[419] which culminated in divorce. Trotsky moved out of his friend's house and into the villa where he now lives."

These disgraceful lines, which I am sure were written by some corrupt reporter, entirely disregard the official sources of information. My differences with Rivera were of a political, theoretical, and artistic character and were aggravated by his impulsive temperament. All the correspondence concerning the breach of relations between us is available for inquiry, if a serious inquiry is also made into this matter, which has nothing to do with the attack by the GPU.

My family left Rivera's home thirteen months ago. We learned of his divorce through the press only five or six months ago. It is with indignation and revulsion that I reject these insinuations, which have nothing to do with the attack by the GPU under the moral protection of Messrs. Lombardo Toledano, and others.

6. I am absolutely sure that the apprehension of my collaborators and friends is based on facts of the same kind as those concerning Diego Rivera. I am certain that the investigation is proceeding into a dead-end street. With each new day, with each new fact, with each serious new clue that arises, all of these artificial fabrications are fading and the true criminals are being unmasked, together with their instigators and intellectual protectors.

7. Until now I have been moved to absolute silence by the wish not to interfere with the investigation. But in view of the unexpectedly false turn it is taking, I reserve the absolute right to appeal to Mexican or international public opinion in this matter.

Yours truly,
Leon Trotsky

A letter to 'El Nacional'[420]

June 6, 1940

Editor, *El Nacional*
Mexico City

Dear Sir:
Carefully following the May 24 attack's reverberations in the capitalist press, I found in your worthy newspaper, in the issue dated May 27, a note under the heading "Trotsky Contradicts Himself." The note attributes to me differing versions concerning how I was saved from the gunfire and concerning the room in which I spent the night. This dispatch represents a poor fabrication from beginning to end. In my statements there was not, and there could not have been, the shadow of a contradiction. Your editorial staff was simply the victim of tendentious, not to say criminal, reporting, whose source should be sought very close to the source of the attack.

The note begins with the words, "The observers make various comments on the statements made by the former Soviet war commissar" (*El Nacional*, May 27, section 2, page 2). You could undoubtedly have done a very large service for the investigation and for public opinion by more accurately indicating who these "observers" are that gave you false information. These observers cannot be members of my household, nor can they be the investigators, nor can they be distant observers. Isn't this just some journalist who observed nothing, but rather carried out an order from the GPU? The ill-intentioned character of the information is dictated by two objectives: to mislead the investigation and to prepare the groundwork for the hypothesis of a self-assault.

No doubt you will understand the importance of these circumstances and will hasten to make the necessary clarification.

Very sincerely,
Leon Trotsky

The GPU and the Comintern[421]

July 17, 1940

Dear Friend:

The archives are leaving [for Harvard] this morning on the train. We are informing Mr. Metcalf likewise about the matter.

The deposition of Joseph Zack would be of tremendous importance. Please arrange it in the form of an affidavit. It is necessary that in the text of this document, Joseph Zack present himself as a former prominent member of the Comintern and so on.

My thesis is that all the most intimate functions of the Comintern have passed during the last period into the hands of the GPU. Can Joseph Zack say anything on this particular point from his own experiences?

Would it not be possible to obtain a similar affidavit from Benjamin Gitlow? from Krivitsky? from Eugene Lyons?[422]

During the years 1929–30–31 the Comintern published financial accounts in which subventions to the Comintern press played an important role. We have here this account for the three years mentioned above. Would it be possible to obtain copies of such accounts published for later years? Is there any information available about the financial beginning of the *New Masses*?[423]

Warmest greetings,

A bed and a plate waiting[424]
July 17, 1940

Dear Friend:

Natalia and I as well as the whole household were deeply disappointed that you could not come here. We hope that you will definitely settle your juridical situation and that your first trip will be to Mexico. You will find a bed and a plate waiting for you in our house.

We talked with Comrade Antoinette many times about you and Comrade Edith and Tyl[425] and we are now a little better acquainted with your family.

You know possibly that *El Popular, Futuro*, both Lombardo Toledano's, and *La Voz de Mexico* of the Communist Party have filed suit against me for "defamation" because I affirmed in the court that they are paid by the GPU. Juridically the accusation is without substance and they can never win the case, but I wish to be armed as well as possible. I am sending you a copy of my letter to Comrade Goldman—possibly you have in your inexhaustible archives some interesting information.

With warmest greetings
from Natalia and myself,
Your Old Man [Leon Trotsky]

UNFINISHED WRITINGS AND FRAGMENTS[426]

Petty-bourgeois democrats and moralizers[427]

1938 and 1939

A. Is it possible you are not frightened by the successes of fascism?

B. Fear is not a political response. In a state of fear, it is impossible to say or do anything intelligent. One must understand causes and deduce methods of action from them. In the advanced capitalist countries, which are now countries of *imperialism*, democracy has finally and totally exhausted itself, or to put it another way, imperialism has developed social contradictions of a kind that a democratic framework cannot make room for; this is why democracy, which seemed eternal, immutable, and the highest form of governmental administration, is collapsing now in country after country.

A. Does that mean, for your part, you want to help the fascists demolish democracy?

B. Here you fall into crude sophistry, seeking a scapegoat for your own politics. Don't forget that in Italy, Germany, and Austria, and so on, democracy's ascendance was total; all the possible variants of coalitions, blocs, People's Fronts, were thoroughly utilized; the current that I represent was a very insignificant minority and could not exert influence on the fate of these countries. The same is true of Spain as well; also now, of France and Czechoslovakia. Under these conditions to demand that critics from the left lay down their arms, seal their lips and allow you to continue the policy of blocs, People's Fronts, and so on and so on, means, in fact, to do a service for fascism.

※

A. But don't you recognize that workers have a duty to support bourgeois democracy when it is threatened by an imminent fascist overturn?

B. I recognize, of course, that workers must beat back and crush fascism when it threatens even imperialist bourgeois democracy. But workers must do this by their own means and with their own methods. In this connection, there is an old Marxist formula which says: "March separately, but strike together." In France, the Socialists and Communists for several years marched together with the Radicals. But when the time came to strike against reaction, they broke off relations and began to strike at one another. One might ask, What sense did it make to march together? The French proletariat would undoubtedly have been in the front ranks of the struggle against any threat from fascism or other forces of reaction; but for this to occur, there was no need to participate in the masquerade of the People's Front, hand in hand with their worst exploiters and oppressors, the Radical Socialists. For the working class, it would have been enough to remain in their own organizations and to carry on their own policy, for then the betrayal of the Radicals at least would not have caught the French workers off guard. I confess it is not without a feeling of awkwardness that I find myself obliged to explain such elementary truth to you.

※

A. But what about now, in China, during a war with Japan?

B. If you wish, we can have a separate discussion on China. But it is a bad Marxist who tries to fix common rules for imperialist France and colonial China. Not to distinguish oppressor countries from oppressed countries is the same as not to distinguish between the exploiting class and the exploited. Those who place imperialist and colonial countries on the same level, no matter what democratic phrases they may use to conceal this fact, are nothing but agents of imperialism.

※

A. But you contribute to *Liberty*?

B. Yes, I contribute to *Liberty*. That is, from time to time I use this magazine, as well as a number of others, to have the opportunity to make my ideas heard. But no thinking person lumps me with *Liberty* and makes me responsible for that magazine. Any thoughtful and honest person will understand and say that I use *Liberty* in the present exceptional conditions the same way I use a railway car, no more and no less.

But to take part in any joint action against the war and against fascism with Mr. Jouhaux and those like him, I would consider a betrayal. Jouhaux, an agent of imperialism, bears full responsibility for French imperialism's suppression of Algeria, Tunisia, Indochina, and the other colonies. Thousands of revolutionary students, workers, and intellectuals sit in the prisons of French imperialism and Jouhaux is one of their jailkeepers. To engage in one or another political activity hand in hand with him would mean to take responsibility for him in the eyes of the oppressed masses. This is treachery; this is betrayal.

※

A. What do you think about the fate of democracy?

B. The old democracy, that we know from the history of

Great Britain, France, and the United States, is doomed. The question of whether or not I believe in democracy is unimportant. What is important is that democracy does not believe in itself. I can't resist citing one small but clear illustration, despite its personal character. Isn't it astounding that the government of the most powerful democracy in the world does not dare allow one individual to spend several months in the United States to work in its libraries?

A. Who was that?

B. Me.

*

Yes, there are mistakes in Marxism and in Bolshevism. You, it must be said, have not pointed to them, but we will take your word. But are there not also defects in capitalism, and also in bourgeois democracy and in the entire system of reformism? Perhaps you could tell us, gentlemen, by what methods you propose to correct the small defects of capitalism and the small weaknesses of bourgeois democracy?

*

As regards the petty-bourgeois democrats—conservative and cowardly—they in general cannot imagine any possible role but that of toadying to the liberal bourgeoisie or the reaction. This is why to them it is absolutely indisputable that anyone who does not go with them tailing liberal imperialist democracy is ipso facto an accomplice of fascism. In other words, they start from a total denial of the possibility of an independent proletarian policy—in this lies the entire secret. This rejection of independent proletarian politics is now pressing upon the petty bourgeoisie with particular force as a result of the degeneration of the Soviet Union, the defeat of the workers in Italy, Germany and Austria, Spain, Czechoslovakia, and so on, and so on, and in view of the fact that the working class of the world has been thrown backward into a totally defensive position. But precisely in such a period, the revolutionary vanguard has the duty with special vigor and implacability to uphold the independent historical truth of the proletarian vanguard. Here opens the unbridgeable gulf between Marxists and the conservative petty-bourgeois democrats who once a week recall that they are socialists.

❋

These gentlemen, made of light-mindedness and ignorance, think that great historical questions are solved with the aid of tricky rhetorical formulas, cheap newspaper declarations, etc. They are capable of learning nothing. If tomorrow they learn nothing from the example of Czechoslovakia and France, repeating formulas which have experienced a total and ignominious bankruptcy; if tomorrow the system in the USSR collapses, they will shrug their shoulders and move to the next point on the agenda.

❋

Engels and Marx were always beset with charges that they were only the helpers of reaction. Engels wrote: "Marx and I were always in the minority and never minded it a bit." Lenin, in his turn, predicted his own fate, saying that revolutionaries who are persecuted in life, hounded, and shamelessly slandered, are usually declared to be virtual saints after their death in order to serve the cause of the oppressors against the oppressed.

❋

The attempt of the bourgeoisie during its internecine conflicts to oblige all humanity to divide up into only two camps is motivated by a desire to prohibit the proletariat from having its own independent ideas. This method is as old as bourgeois society, or more exactly, as class society in general. No one is obligated to become a Marxist; no one is obligated to swear by Lenin's name. But the whole of the politics of these two titans of revolutionary thought was directed toward this, that the fetishism of two camps would give way to a third, independent, sovereign camp of the proletariat, that camp upon which, in point of fact, the future of humanity depends.

*

The "betrayal" of the Social Democracy during the war was a malignant expression of its incompatibility with the new epoch. Amid the fire and smoke of imperialist war, a new International arose which counterposed to the reformist methods of adaptation to bourgeois society, the methods of revolutionary overthrow of bourgeois society. If the Second International was a political instrument of the proletariat in the epoch of industrial capitalism, the Third International was called upon to become the instrument of the proletariat in the epoch of the triumph of finance capital, the disintegration or downfall of democracy, the breakup of the old balance of power, and wars and revolutions. Social institutions do not, however, voluntarily leave the stage after they have exhausted their mission. This is true of private property, the nation state, and the regime of democracy and its political parties as well. The old political institutions and forms proved to have the most vitality in the most privileged bourgeois nations. The same is true of the reformist organizations of the proletariat. The conciliatory politics of the British or North American trade unionists was possible only because the Anglo-Saxon bourgeoisie was wealthy enough to keep feeding the millions of unemployed. Leon Blum got the opportunity to head a People's Front government twenty years after the war only because imperialist France came out of that war the victor and expanded its territory and its colonial domain. However, the difference in fate of the reformist parties of different countries is measured only by the term until their downfall. The old trade unions, like the old workers' parties, are now no less remnants of history than is private ownership of the means of production.

It is true that in the years after the war, the Social Democracy attained an extremely powerful outward image. The working masses, agitated and embittered by the war, raised on their shoulders to power the party which they were accustomed to seeing as their leader. But precisely this belated political ascent of the Social Democracy exposed its internal emptiness and rottenness.

*

Whereas the Social Democrats solidarize themselves in a totally open way with national imperialism, the Russian Mensheviks still try through force of habit to link work in the service of imperialism with general abstract slogans of internationalism. By the term "active internationalism," the Russian Mensheviks mean their bustling and clamorous adaptation to the official slogans of imperialist democracy. In other words, instead of exposing the real content of the policy of imperialism, democratic or fascist, they try to help one of the camps conceal its real interests under abstract slogans. This they call "active internationalism."

*

The light-minded babblers and phrasemongers who call themselves friends of the USSR make references to the fact that the capitalist reaction and the so-called Trotskyists alike attack the USSR. The capitalist reaction attacks the fact that in the USSR there exist public ownership of the means of production and a monopoly of foreign trade, i.e., the most important conquests of the October Revolution. We Marxists attack the fact that the bureaucracy is systematically undermining the conquests of the October Revolution and that its continued rule endangers the public ownership of the means of production and the monopoly of foreign trade. To lump together directly opposite ideological trends is the same as identifying criticism of liberalism by the feudal reaction with criticism of liberalism by the proletariat. Liberals always busy themselves with such identifications. Marxists are always merciless in denouncing this.

*

But if from our—that is a Marxist—standpoint, an agreement [of the USSR] with Hitler is not different in principle from an agreement with Leon Blum or Daladier as agents of French imperialism, then from the standpoint of the Second and Third Internationals, the difference is decisive. A bloc or even a semi-bloc between Stalin and Hitler signifies the collapse of the entire structure of lies, treachery and betrayal constructed since approximately 1934 and brought to an end by a series of catastrophes.

The fawning before France, England, and the United States pursues the particular interests of self-preservation: This in its way is practical politics. But the ideology built through the Comintern, as regards "People's Fronts" and the alliance of the democracies, represents a 100 percent reactionary falsification. The annihilation of the old generation of Bolsheviks, of all revolutionaries in general, necessary in order to strengthen the Bonapartist regime of oppression and exploitation, represented quite practical politics. But the trials, the accusatory combinations, the confessions which were put together in the Moscow courts, represented a total falsification. The ideology of "People's Fronts" and—from a juridical point of view—Vyshinsky's[428] indictment speeches, have the same political qualities. The collapse of all this grandiose falsehood is approaching with seven-league boots. This collapse is a necessary link, an initial link, for further revolutionary development. Revolutionary politics will not tolerate masks. Its principle is to say what is; the collapse of the lies of Stalinism will pave the way for the triumph of this principle.

*

The [Spanish] revolution subjected classes, parties, individuals, and doctrines to the test of experience. One must clearly understand what suffered defeat in the revolution and what, on the other hand, found its highest confirmation. All parties and organizations of the working class proved themselves bankrupt. From this, it is easy to conclude that not only anarchism but also Marxism was defeated. However, that is not quite the case. A mass Marxist party did not exist in Spain. The organization which called itself Marxist in fact functioned in a way that was totally at odds with every Marxist doctrine. Marxist analysis long ago showed that the epoch of democratic revolution for the capitalist countries had long since passed. Marxist doctrine showed that only by uncompromisingly advancing the class struggle could [the working class] succeed in time of revolution in uniting around itself all of the toiling and oppressed masses and insure victory. The parties calling themselves Marxist artificially and forcibly set bourgeois limits to the revolution and substituted class collaboration for class struggle. This policy meant a total break with Marxism, and precisely for that reason it suffered a bitter defeat. A defeat for a capitalist party, or even a Communist party, is not a defeat for Marxism; it is, on the contrary, the highest proof of Marxism's correctness. The matter is just the opposite with respect to anarchism. It proved in principle unable to provide answers to problems of the revolution. Marxism, as well as anarchism, wants to abolish the state. But, contrary to anarchism, Marxism understands that to abolish the state, you cannot turn your back on it. The state will remind you of its existence by striking a blow at your skull while your back is turned. Revolution is the highest concentration of power. In its essence, revolution signifies the struggle of a new class for state power. Because the anarchists do not understand the nature of the state, they end up being captives, in the servitude of the state power of the bourgeoisie. Their leaders are transformed into bourgeois state ministers. Anarchist doctrine has led to a dead end.

*

Victor Serge claims that his enunciations, statements, and corrections, always revolving around his own personality, must without exception be printed by the workers' publications. Why? On what basis? What does Victor Serge represent today in the workers' movement? An ulcer of his own doubts, of his own confusion, and nothing more. We have other tasks and concerns. Our paper is needed for other goals. We serve the revolution of the proletariat as it is and not the revolution which is being prepared by the moral confectioners. What do people of the Victor Serge type represent? Our conclusion is simple: these verbose, coquettish moralists, capable of bringing only trouble and decay, must be kept out of the revolutionary organization, even by cannonfire if necessary. ■

Fragments from the first seven months of the war[429]

1940

At the present time the books in fashion in the military sphere are those which say that defense is the best offense.

We see on the Western front the significant sight of all the big military powers intently defending themselves against a nonexistent enemy.

*

At sea, Germany is conducting a guerrilla war of the weak against the strong. On the land in general, there is no war. It is as though the countless masses armed to the teeth were intimidated and subdued by their own technology and the fortifications they have created. It might seem at first glance the realization of the old pacifist prophecy that the development of arms has reached such limits as to make the conduct of war impossible. But this is an optimistic fiction.

*

Mussolini does not have an international political strategy. He lives from day to day. Global plans are beyond his capacity. Hence the constant zigzags in his orientation and propaganda. He tried from the very beginning to spurn Hitler's advances, but in the end he yielded and began to follow Hitler's lead. At the beginning of the Soviet-Finnish war Mussolini sharply underscored his independence from Germany by attacking the Soviet Union and demonstratively aiding Finland. Now (March 16) Mussolini is again turning toward the Soviet Union.

Neither has Stalin any international political strategy. First and foremost he wants to keep out of the war. This determines his maneuvers.

Both belligerent democracies [England and France] are trying to defend themselves. That is what their world policies boil down to. Everything else is vague and empty talk, which no one believes.

Only Hitler has a global political plan. This plan will lead in the end to a catastrophe, not only for the National Socialist regime, but for German capitalism as well. But on the road to catastrophe, unity of strategy gives the whole policy of Germany exceptional strength. The only government leader who knows what he wants is Hitler.

*

The entire policy of Hitler is subordinated to the struggle for *Lebensraum*. This is dictated by the powerful development of German industry, for which the boundaries of the national state have long become unbearably restrictive. Many journalists excel at catching Hitler in contradictions, when statements in his book *Mein Kampf* differ from his current speeches. These contradictions are numerous and undeniable. But they are, all the same, superficial.

*

It is absolutely obvious, even to Hitler himself, that he overestimated the military power of France and underestimated the strength of resistance from the Soviet Union. His analysis [in *Mein Kampf*] was made more than ten years ago. Now it is necessary to reexamine a whole series of quantities. France's hegemony in Europe has been overthrown, without a war. Hitler did not expect this. The objective situation and the relationship of forces proved to be significantly more favorable for his plans than he calculated.

Regarding the Soviet Union, things have shaped up differently than Hitler imagined in 1926. The revolutionary strength of Moscow has not only receded but has been totally eliminated in the recent past. Hitler, better than anyone, is able to appreciate the significance of the [Moscow] trials where the leaders of Bolshevism and the civil war, mortally hostile to him, were depicted as his paid agents. The legend that Jews rule the Soviet republic has been shattered by the growth of anti-Semitism within the ruling caste and the removal of Jewish officials from all posts of any responsibility. (In his book, Hitler called Bolshevism the progeny of Hell and defined its historical meaning as follows: "In Russian

Bolshevism we must see an attempt undertaken by the Jews in the twentieth century to seize world power" [p. 751].)

*

Finally, in a technical sense, the Soviet Union has had great successes. Now numerous factories are producing motor vehicles; the arming of the military has reached significant heights; aviation has advanced; and war industry has developed into a powerful force.

It is possible that Hitler decided to make a turn in the direction of Moscow, i.e., radically change his strategy, abandon colonization of the East, and shift his attention to the colonies. To make a turn is not easy. Quite a long interval of silence is needed. It is precisely this interval that the Nazi government is now passing through. In all speeches and newspaper articles, there is virtually no mention of the Kremlin. Hitler made absolutely no mention of the East, or the Soviet government, in his programmatic speech on April 28 of this year [1940]. This could be interpreted as preparation for a radical change of the entire policy of Germany.

*

In a speech to the Reichstag on October 6, [1939,] Hitler raved that "the assertion that Germany has plans to expand into Ukraine and Rumania and so forth is a fabrication."

*

For Stalin, the alliance, or more precisely, the pact with Germany was necessary to safeguard his own position of neutrality. All that Stalin has agreed to and can offer Hitler is a free hand in foreign policy in the West and to the South, i.e., in the direction of the colonies. The Moscow protocols of September 29 [1939] are aimed at helping Hitler obtain the surrender of France and England but in no way tie Stalin's hands with a pledge of military aid to Hitler. And this is no accident. To Hitler, this is not enough. To rush into a struggle with England and France—and the United States at the first opportunity—with Italy as his only ally would be too light-minded. In the Mediterranean Sea, Italy could in a very short time be put out of action. Germany would be left alone. Behind her would be a neutral Russia. To what degree could this neutrality be relied on? Hitler cannot pursue such a combination now, expecting to obtain more later, as events put pressure upon Moscow. This transitional state of affairs explains Moscow's policy toward Berlin, a policy of flirting, biding time, delaying—and the policy of Berlin, which can be characterized as an interval of silence.

[It is suggested] that Hitler has by no means abandoned his idea of marching eastward, and is only observing silence now so as not to drive the Soviet Union into England's arms. This assumption would be more believable and convincing if [Hitler's anti-British campaign] had not taken on such a rabid and provocative character. The question of colonies has been advanced to the forefront. Maritime relations have been broken off; Hitler clearly indicates that he intends to test his strength against England's at sea; for that he needs to know his home front is secure. In criticizing Germany's prewar foreign policy, Hitler persistently repeated that its failing had been its inability to find the necessary allies. Germany suffered a defeat because it left them to the enemy camp. It should have found a common language with Great Britain or at least buttressed itself upon Russia. It did neither, and that was its fundamental crime. It cannot be supposed that Hitler forgot all these lessons and now intends to become an ally of Stalin and challenge the whole world.

※

The campaign against Great Britain is being conducted now in the German press in virtually the same tones as it always was during a war and never before a war. At the center of this campaign is what one might call a history of

English colonial plundering. In *Arbeitertum,* the official organ of the Labor Front, we find a series of articles which depict the cruelties committed by the English during the colonization of various parts of the world. It points up the contrasts between the lavishness of official buildings and the poverty of the Hindu masses, provides photos of Hindu poverty, and so on. In a word, the lowly race of Hindus has no better friends and the Anglo-Saxon aristocrats no sterner critics than the German National Socialists.

The British government has been so astounded by Germany's propaganda against Britain and against Britain's efforts to encircle and strangle Germany that it has fully revealed its own naivete—expecting gratitude from Hitler for services it had rendered him.

※

[But at the same time another note is being sounded.] Hitler commented in his April 28 speech to the Reichstag that his struggle, his persistent desire to bring friendship and collaboration between Germany and England, were dictated by his own personal feelings. . . . "Throughout all my political activity, I have never ceased defending the need for close friendship and collaboration between Germany and England."

※

In Poland, Hitler simply condemns millions of people to physical annihilation in order to clear the arena for Aryan settler colonies . . . thus preparing and expanding his base for a strike to the East.

※

In the German-Italian alliance, Italy represents the immeasurably weaker side as a result of its geographic position as well as the level of its economic development. Italy stands to suffer the hardest blows and even in the event of success, will be limited to receiving only crumbs. In Spain, the role of Italy was immeasurably more significant than the role of Germany; however, right now, in the economic benefits derived, Germany leaves Italy far behind.

For this reason, Spain resists joining the Axis in every way it can, since Spain's lot as a member would be to pull chestnuts out of the fire for its more powerful allies.

*

Of course, the USSR can cope with Finland, but the blow dealt to the Kremlin's prestige in the eyes of the world will to a certain extent be reproduced within the country.

*

The fate of this same country, Finland, shows that now it is not so easy to unite Europe under the fascist fist. Moreover, on this course, Germany will meet in its first steps the uncompromising opposition of the United States. A victory for Germany and its unification of Europe means only Germany's move toward an open struggle for domination of the world, including Latin America, with the support of Nazis inside the United States.

*

In which countries can one first of all expect a revolution? Obviously in those where a weaker economic foundation is subject to destruction by war earlier than in other countries. Such was czarist Russia during the last war, and after it followed Austria-Hungary. Then came Germany's turn: in spite of the high productivity of labor, its lack of raw materials undermined its lopsided economic foundation.

*

Sumner Welles[430] is going to Europe February 17 to hold talks on a future world that will rest "on a firm and stable basis." This is easier said than done.

Republican Senator Johnson[431] from California even thinks there is no reason to send Sumner Welles to Europe: "We should mind our own business." Unfortunately, Mr. Johnson does not indicate where the borderlines of "our own business" have been drawn. The borders of "our own business" include the same space that Hitler calls the Nazis' *Lebensraum*. Wars occur because different nations want to draw the borders of their own vital space in a different way.

❋

On February 16, the chairman of the Republican [National] Committee in the United States, John Hamilton,[432] said: "Today some nine million unemployed walk our streets. Another ten million are dependent upon government for their food and shelter, chained to made work which they must either take or starve. And why? Because the great masterminds of the New Deal said that our system of free American enterprise had reached the end of the road, that the law of supply and demand had been abrogated, that our only salvation lay in aping the European systems of planned economy and abandoning the American way which had led us to the heights we attained during a 150-year journey."

This same Hamilton said February 16: "What a pathetic spectacle it is to see those in high places preaching the necessity of saving democracy everywhere but in the United States."

It is impossible to possess with impunity the most powerful industry, more than two-thirds of the world's gold reserve, and ten millions of unemployed.[433]

Americans of varying political orientations visit me in my seclusion. I follow the press in the United States closely. My general impression of the ruling class of the great North American republic is its general disorientation. One can heap as many severe condemnations on foreigners as one wants. But that is not enough. What is necessary is a program for humanity to get out of the blind alley it is now in, moreover a blind alley that ends with an abyss. A program is necessary. I hold that neither the ruling class of Europe nor that of America has such a program. In this fact alone lies the strength of the extreme wings. One may, like [Herbert] Hoover, equate Bolshevism with the plague. However, strong words alone are not enough to resolve great historical problems.

❋

A totalitarian regime does not at all mean that the entire people has suddenly grown foolish. It means that the best part of the people has been suppressed and intimidated but has not stopped thinking. At the opposite pole, part of the population has an interest in maintaining the totalitarian regime. Between these two extremes is the disoriented mass of the people, which awaits further developments before joining one side or the other.

❋

Of course, the Soviet Union in its present form is in no way an indication of the road that the peoples of the world must take in the future. However, the experience of all other countries, the experience of the most civilized countries at least, since the war and the Versailles peace also clearly shows people what road not to take.

❋

The present world convulsions are the tragic confirmation of Marx's prognosis and at the same time an unmistakable sign that the denouement is drawing near. After terrible historical experiences, humanity will come out onto a new road, for which all of its previous development has laid the foundation. The seventeenth and eighteenth centuries opened the way for reason into technical areas and, in part, the governmental sphere. But the bourgeois revolution proved incapable of bringing reason into the realm of economic relations. In this area, the unlimited dominion of blind market forces has continued. In order to deliver humanity from chaos and insanity, it is necessary that the rule of reason not be restricted to science and technology but become firmly established in the realm of economic relations. Society will be constructed on a rational model, just as machines are now. State barriers will be knocked down. Natural resources will begin to be exploited in keeping with the interests of all humanity, as a socialist federation of peoples. ■

Fragments on the USSR[434]
1940

One conclusion flows inevitably from the Soviet-Finnish conflict. No one in the Kremlin foresaw anything, intoxicated as they were by their own bragging and by the successes which had fallen to Stalin as crumbs from Hitler's table. In the Kremlin, nothing was foreseen and no preparations were made. The initiative for the Kremlin's successes belonged totally and completely to Germany. Hitler nudged Stalin carefully and slowly at first against Poland and later against the Baltic. The resistance in Finland which may not have begun without direct assistance from Germany—by way of Italy—forced the Kremlin to make a decision on the spot.

Now we see the same characteristics and the same results in the diplomatic and military arena. Stalin was able to succeed in the Baltic because of a favorable military and diplomatic combination of forces. But where initiative and foresight were called for [in Finland], his policy brought the Soviet Union nothing but humiliation.

It was the same in Germany, where the key to the internal defeat was to a large degree in the hands of the Comintern, and the leadership of Stalin paved the way for Hitler's victory.

It was the same in Spain, where the Kremlin took into its hands the leadership of the civil war and doomed the Spanish people to the worst disasters. No one, neither Hitler nor Mussolini, rendered such service to General Franco as Stalin did.

*

The Kremlin's fear of an attack by Nazi Germany can be gauged by the colossal efforts and sacrifices expended on the defensive lines along the USSR's western borders.

*

The initial task of Bolshevism was the international socialist revolution. There could, of course, be no question of a backward and poor country, as Russia was and the Soviet Union still is, being able militarily to impose a socialist overturn on other peoples. It was a question of a revolution being made by the proletariat of the advanced countries. For the Soviet government, the task was, on the one hand, to help the development of these revolutions and, on the other, to hold its own ground until the victory of the proletariat in the other countries. The fundamental line of the international policy of the Soviet Union was to exploit the contradictions of the other countries in order to hold out. An aggressive military policy was unthinkable.

Bolshevism started from the understanding that within the borders of one country, and moreover a backward one, it was impossible to construct socialism, and that socialism, like capitalism before it, must encompass the whole world. The road to the world socialist revolution does not at all consist in the military expansion of the one state in which the revolution conquered earlier than in the others.

In the fall of 1924, Stalin first arrived at the conclusion that socialism could be built in a single country. This theory subsequently acquired enormous importance, in the internal as well as foreign policy of the Soviet Union. Over the people rose a powerful bureaucracy which concentrated in its hands all the power and the lion's share of the national income. Stalin advanced the slogan: We want no foreign soil, but we will give up none of our own. This purely conservative foreign-policy slogan fully corresponded to the material position of the ruling bureaucracy: it felt too weak for foreign war but strong enough for internal rule.

The only immediate danger was from Japan, and it was only dangerous to certain parts of the territory and not by any means a threat to the existence of the state. Moscow bought its way out of the Japanese danger with concessions. In the West, the USSR was shielded by a Poland which, although hostile, was weak and by a semifriendly weak Germany.

※

In 1924 in *Toward Socialism or Capitalism?*, five years before the appearance of the *Biulleten*, we tried to explain to the present masters of the Kremlin that the strength and vitality of a social order is determined by the productivity of labor. We demanded therefore the working out of various coefficients of labor productivity in the USSR and in capitalist countries as a fundamental criterion for clarifying whether the danger in the USSR from the capitalist direction was diminishing or growing, in economic as well as military respects; it is impossible to separate these two dangers. Stalin answered us by saying that socialist development does not depend on the tempo of development or consequently on the tempo of the growth of productivity of labor. Statistics operate exclusively by global figures and by themselves do not inspire great confidence. In the book *The Revolution Betrayed,* we again tried to explain the full significance of the relative productivity of labor and of the relative per capita income. All such calculations, exposing the low level of labor productivity in the USSR, are considered sabotage and suppressed in the harshest way. But economic nature, if you drive it out the door, will only come back through the window. Amid the convulsive fits and starts [of Stalinist economic policy], the popular masses cannot emerge from poverty. At the last congress [1939], Stalin was forced to make an attempt to explain this fact. He could think of nothing to say except that we are backward. We must catch up with the capitalist countries. More and more new sacrifices are necessary; in order to justify these sacrifices, Stalin was forced to give for the first time the ratios of the national per capita income. However, these bald ratios tell nothing. The dynamic is decisive. It is necessary to compare year by year the movement of labor productivity in the USSR and the capitalist countries in order to determine whether the present economic system in the USSR has justified itself or not. Only in this way can one decide the extent of the military viability of the state.

*

The most prominent military figure is now the head of the general staff, Shaposhnikov.[435] The revolution found him a ranking czarist general. His main feature is a characterless submissiveness. He adapted himself to all his bosses and survived them all. An exceptional case—a former czarist general who has become now a member of the Central Committee of the Bolshevik Party.

Budenny[436] was a daring leader of guerrilla cavalry on a big scale. He was awarded the rank of marshal and forced to betray all his associates. The cavalry general grew fat, but his military qualities remained the same. He needs to be led by a farsighted and well-educated military chief. He was absolutely incapable of providing such leadership himself. Thus, the entire course of things has been determined by Stalin. . . .

One could not, of course, have expected that Voroshilov[437] would correct Stalin.

It is generally impossible to speak seriously of Voroshilov either as a political figure or as a military chief. The qualities of a great administrator, the ability to thoughtfully combine in his head the diverse factors of a situation and foresee their future interaction, is totally alien to him. Now, having grown heavier with the years, lulled by official flattery, accustomed to his high post, the former daring guerrilla fighter is hardly distinguishable from the czarist war ministers of old.

It is still less possible to expect criticism and argument from the general staff: all of them remember too well the fate of Tukhachevsky and his colleagues.

※

It would be wrong to think that Litvinov obstructed Stalin's policies. He did not make policy but he undoubtedly embarrassed the present Politburo. He knew too well the better times and the specific weight of every member of the Politburo. He knew foreign life and foreign languages. At Politburo meetings, he could resort to arguments that the Politburo members could not answer and they did not always feel up to the mark facing him. Stalin more than once found himself in this position. Litvinov, like many others, fell victim to his own superiority over the Politburo members. His removal had no influence on the course of policy.

*

[In the Red Army] the problem of shifting to a militia system[438] played an enormous role in our work as well as in our military conceptions. We considered the question one of principle. We believed that only a socialist state could allow itself to shift over to a militia system. "If we are carrying out this shift gradually," I wrote in May 1923, "it is not out of political apprehensions but for reasons of an organizational and technical nature: it is a new undertaking—one of immeasurable importance—and we do not want to advance to a second stage without securing the first." All this great work came to nothing. The militia was abolished in favor of a standing army. The reasoning was purely political: The bureaucracy ceased to have any confidence in an army scattered among the people, merged with the people. It needed a purely barracks army, isolated from the people.

*

In the Red Army an order has been given to achieve success, at all costs, by February 23, the anniversary of the formation of the army. Such an order has been seen more than once in the past: "Make such and such a flight on the occasion of the new party congress. Regardless of climatic conditions, make a high-altitude flight on the leader's birthday," etc. Dozens of flight accidents have been caused by the fact that flights were made not in accordance with atmospheric conditions but according to the dictates of the official calendar.

*

Referring to a communique from its foreign office *Krasnaya Zvezda* (Red Star), the newspaper of the People's Commissariat of Defense, said February 18:

"The works of Trotsky occupy a very highly respected place in Italian libraries despite the fact that all books by Jewish authors have been removed from libraries. When asked by a visitor at the Milan public library, 'Isn't Trotsky a Jew?' the librarian answered:

"'Yes, but for his services he has been declared an honorary Aryan.'"

❋

In the Soviet Union, there are several million privileged families, privileged to varying degrees. This is quite enough for carrying out the official programs and assuring applause for double-dealing [i.e., the Stalin-Hitler pact].

❋

In Lenin's time, the presidents of all the Soviet republics entering the union had equal rights with the presidents of the top Soviet institutions. Now, Kalinin[439] alone is president of the Supreme Soviet. In this change the overall policy shifts with respect to the national republics is rather clearly symbolized. Of autonomy there remains not a trace. The Kremlin decides everything for everyone.

❋

A victory of the imperialist states over the Soviet Union would mean the collapse not only of the totalitarian bureaucracy, but also the collapse of the forms of property established by the October Revolution [and] could therefore have only a temporary character.

Just as after the Great French Revolution it was impossible to restore feudal relations in full measure for any extended period, so after the October Revolution full capitalist relations are impossible for any extended period. On the contrary, the new forms of property will spread more and more widely to other countries.

The case is somewhat different, to be sure, with geographic boundaries. They can and will be subject to change. One may suppose that in the process of war centrifugal and separatist national tendencies will develop, or more correctly, will come to light.

*

When Italy attacked Ethiopia [in 1935], I was fully on the side of the latter, despite the Ethiopian negus for whom I have no sympathy. What mattered was to oppose imperialism's seizure of this new territory. In the same way now I decisively oppose the imperialist camp and support independence for the USSR, despite the negus in the Kremlin. ■

Preface to a book on war and peace[440]

March–April 1940

To begin with, I am printing an article first published in May 1929, i.e., several weeks after my deportation to Turkey.[441] This article will, to a certain extent, serve as an introduction to several of the other articles, providing a perspective on the overall development. It has undergone eleven years of serious testing since that time. The article was printed in the American magazine *The New Republic*, before its editors had received their revelation of the "true word" from the Kremlin. The editors supplied my article with their own commentary, which now, eleven years later, acquires special interest. My principal misfortune, in the opinion of the editors, consisted in a "rigid Marxism," which prevented me from fathoming or grasping the "realistic view of history." The most glaring lack of a realistic view of history was shown in my evaluation of formal democracy, i.e., the parliamentary regime, which, I said in that article, had for the first time come into conflict with the development of society and would necessarily disappear from one country after another. *The New Republic* editors contended against me that democracy was subject to ruin only in those countries where it had established only "the feeblest beginnings" and in countries where "the industrial revolution has hardly more than started." The editors did not explain, or trouble themselves with the impossibility of explaining, why these feeble beginnings of democracy, if it is a viable form, did not undergo further maturation, as had happened with the older capitalist countries, but instead were swept away by various systems of dictatorship. The second reference, to the inadequacy of industrial development, or, more correctly, of capitalist development, holds relatively true for Russia, Italy, the countries of southeast Europe, the Balkans, and Spain. But one can hardly speak of the inadequacy of industrial development in Austria and Germany. Moreover, in these two countries democracy held out for about fifteen years before giving way to fascist dictatorships. *The New Republic* editors did not foresee this, although my own "rigid Marxism" and lack of "a realistic view of history" did not prevent me from forecasting such developments.

The third argument of the then editors of *The New Republic* is still more striking. Kerensky, with his weakness and indecisiveness, was, you see, "an historic accident, which Trotsky cannot admit, because there is no room in his mechanistic schema for any such thing." The weakness of Kerensky's character as an individual was, to be sure, an accident from the point of view of historical development. But the fact that a historically belated democracy, condemned from its very beginnings, could not find anyone but the weak and vacillating Kerensky to be its leader is no accident.

*

Democrats of various shadings ruled in Germany and Austria for a number of years. All allowed themselves to be removed from the political scene without resistance. One may say, of course, that the weakness of Scheidemann, Ebert,[442] Renner, and others was "an historic accident." But why were these people allowed to assume the leadership of the democracy? Are we not entitled to conclude that a historically belated democracy, torn by internal contradictions and condemned to historical death, cannot find anyone for its leadership other than people without clear ideas and strong wills? Or, if not, are we not justified in asserting that, independently of their personal character traits, the leaders of formal democracy in times of crisis lose their composure under the pressure of historical contradictions and give up their positions without a fight? If this kind of historical accident repeats itself time after time in states at various levels of development, then we have the right to conclude that before us are not isolated historical exceptions, but instances of a general historical law.

The most recent verification of this law was the fate of the Spanish republic.

One may say, to be sure, that the personal characters of Zamora,[443] Azana, Caballero, Negrin, and others are their unfortunate personal property and, in this sense, "an historic accident." But it was no accident that precisely these people assumed the leadership of the decadent, belated democracy and, although they put up a fight this time, they did surrender all their positions to a worthless clique of generals. I will therefore allow myself to think that a "mechanistic schema" is not so bad, if it allows one to foresee major events.

※

In the bourgeois press of the world it has now become the custom to depict the [present situation] as the product of the evil will of one man. The initiative for this concept belongs to France: "Isn't it really because of the will of one person, a single madman, that Europe and all humanity will again be plunged into the abyss of war?" This concept then crossed over to England and the United States. The story goes that the whole world is generally the flourishing site of peaceful and fraternal relations. But a dictator appeared from somewhere and this one person was able to plunge the whole world, with its millions of inhabitants, into war. This is the same concept *The New Republic* elaborated in regard to Kerensky and the October Revolution. There the trouble was that a weak person assumed the leadership of the democracy and did not know how to prevent strongmen from toppling the democracy and replacing it with a dictatorship. Here the misfortune is that in Germany a strongman in power has upset the peace that is favored by the more powerful democracies.

※

That which has happened is not, by far, what was foreseen in these articles. And what they foresaw is not, by far, what has happened. Such is the fate of every political prognosis. Reality is immeasurably richer in resources, variants, and combinations than any imagination. That the war would begin with the division of Poland between Germany and the USSR, we did not predict. A more attentive, detailed analysis might well have suggested that variant too. But when all is said and done, the division of Poland is only an episode.

A prognosis is valuable not insofar as it expresses or finds photographically exact confirmation in subsequent developments but rather in the extent to which, by projecting historical factors ahead, it helps us to orient ourselves in the actual development of events. From this point of view it seems to us that the articles collected in this volume have withstood the test. The author feels he has the right to add that even now, by illuminating the present in the light of the past, they [can still be of value].

*

Events work at such a pace that some predictions are realized or confirmed much earlier than one could suppose. Thus, when we spoke in an interview [with the *St. Louis Post-Dispatch*, February 14, 1940] of the inevitability of United States intervention in the war, it was seen as heresy which every party and every shading of party opinion in the United States rejected. That was only about a month ago, and today, as these lines are being written, the American press, commenting on the invasion of Scandinavia by the Germans, is saying that intervention by the United States is entirely possible in the year ahead.

*

On March 9, 1939, Mr. Chamberlain assured foreign correspondents that the international situation had improved, that Anglo-German relations had thawed, and that disarmament could be placed on the order of the day. Six days later the German army occupied Czechoslovakia.

In 1937 Mr. Roosevelt proclaimed neutrality, not foreseeing at all the incompatibility of that doctrine with the global position of the United States.

Such examples can be cited without end. One can almost state it as a law that the ruling posts in contemporary democracies are filled only by those who have demonstrated for a period of years that they cannot orient themselves in the present situation and can foresee nothing.

*

In June 1939 I had a chat with a group of American travelers on questions of world politics.[444] The talk touched upon the World's Fair in New York. This exhibit is undoubtedly a magnificent triumph of human genius. But when they call it "the world of tomorrow," they give it a one-sided name—one-sided at the very least. Tomorrow's world will appear differently. To give a true picture of tomorrow's world, they should have had bombers fly over and drop their loads for hundreds of miles around. The presence of human genius side by side with terrifying barbarism—that is the image of tomorrow's world. Here too our "rigid schema" has proved to be correct.

What is important in scientific thinking, especially in complicated questions of politics and history, is to distinguish the basic from the secondary, the essential from the incidental, to foresee the movement of the essential factors of development. To people whose thinking goes only from day to day, who seek comfort in all kinds of episodic occurrences without bringing them together into one overall picture, scientific thinking that proceeds from basic, fundamental factors seems dogmatic; in politics this paradox is met with at every turn.

*

If the author has foreseen some things correctly, the credit for this belongs not to him personally, but to the method which he applied. In any other field, people—or at least specially trained people—consider the application of a definite method to be essential. It's a different matter in politics. Here sorcery predominates. Highly educated people believe that, for a political operation, one's powers of observation, eye measurements, a certain stock of slyness, and common sense are sufficient. The illusion of free will is the source of this subjective arbitrariness. In America, the view of the politician as an "engineer," who takes the raw material and builds according to his own blueprints is especially widespread. Nothing is more naive and barren than this point of view. However, as in any philosophy, including the philosophy of history, there is a correct way of conceiving the interrelation of the subjective with the objective. In the final reckoning the objective factors always predominate over the subjective. Therefore correct politics begins with an analysis of the real world and an analysis of the trends at work within it. Only thus can one arrive at a correct scientific prediction and a correct intervention into a process on the basis of this prediction. Any other approach would be sorcery.

People of a vulgar turn of mind could now allude to the defeat of that political current to which the author of this book belonged and still belongs. How could it happen that the empiricist Stalin defeated the faction which followed the scientific method? Doesn't this mean that common sense has the advantage over doctrinairism? Every sorcerer has a certain percentage of patients who recover. And every doctor has a certain percentage of patients who die. From this, many primitive people are inclined to give preference to sorcery over medicine. But in fact, science can demonstrate that in the one case the patient recovered in spite of the intervention of the sorcerer, and in the other the patient died because medical science, at least at its present state, could not effectively overcome the destructive powers affecting the organism; in both cases one must correctly determine the relation between the objective and subjective.

In politics the scientific method cannot provide victories in all cases. Sorcery, on the other hand, in certain cases provides a victory when this victory is founded on the objective alignments and general tendencies of development.

※

There are people who consider themselves educated but who permit themselves such summary judgments as that "the October Revolution was a failure." And what about the French Revolution? It ended in the restoration, though episodic, of the Bourbons. And the Civil War in the United States? It led to the rule of the Sixty Families. And all of human history in general? So far it has led to the second imperialist war, which threatens our entire civilization. It is impossible not to say, then, that all of history has been a mistake and a failure. Finally, what of human beings themselves—no small factor in history? Isn't it necessary to say that this product of prolonged biological evolution is a failure? No one is forbidden of course to make such general observations. But they derive from the individual experience of the petty shopkeeper, or from theosophy, and [do not] apply to the historical process as a whole or to its overall stages, its main chapters, or its episodes. ■

Last words[445]

August 20, 1940

I am close to death from the blow of a political assassin . . . struck me down in my room. I struggled with him . . . we . . . entered . . . talked about French statistics . . . he struck me. . . . Please say to our friends . . . I am sure . . . of the victory . . . of the Fourth International. . . . Go forward. ■

Notes and acknowledgments

1. "An Offer to *Le Peuple*." By permission of the Harvard College Library. Translated from the French by Will Reissner. **Le Peuple** was the daily paper of the Belgian Labor Party, affiliated to the Second International.

2. Social Revolutionary **terrorists** charged with assaults on Soviet officials chose the Belgian Social Democrat, Emile Vandervelde, as one of their lawyers at the trial held in Moscow in June 1922 (although they withdrew this request after the Soviet government had granted it). The death sentences pronounced on the defendants were suspended on the condition that the SR leadership would pledge to stop conducting or encouraging terrorist attacks.

3. "The IS Reply to the British Majority." By permission of the Harvard College Library. Translated from the Russian by Ivan Licho. At the end of 1933 the British section suffered a split over the IS proposal that its members join the ILP. On December 17 the British National Committee adopted a statement, which it asked the IS to send to all sections. Trotsky wrote the document printed here as the draft of a resolution by the IS to accompany the National Committee statement. Three days later the IS incorporated Trotsky's text, slightly expanded, into a letter to the National Committee, signed by Bauer for the IS. The main difference between Trotsky's draft and the IS letter was that the latter explicitly withdrew the status of British section from both the majority and the minority, recognizing them only as sympathizing groups of the ICL.

4. "Differences with the British Minority." From the Cannon archives, Library of Social History. These two letters to the Brit-

ish minority were sent on the same day as the previous selection on the British majority. **Jack Weber** (b. 1896) joined the CLA in 1930 and was elected to the Workers Party National Committee in 1934. He supported the Abern faction until 1936. He was SWP educational director in the early years of World War II, and quit the SWP in 1944.

5. "The Jewish Question Has Been Internationalized." By permission of the Bund Archives of the Jewish Labor Movement, New York. Translated from the Russian by Marilyn Vogt. **Lazar Kling** (b. 1891) was a journalist who met Trotsky in New York in 1917 and in Moscow in the 1920s. After corresponding with Trotsky from New York in 1932, he became a member of the editorial board of *Unzer Kamf* (Our Struggle), the Yiddish-language paper of the CLA, 1932–33; he also belonged briefly to the CLA. Three other Trotsky letters deposited by Kling at the Bund Archives are in *Writings 32*.

6. The **Polish Jewish representative** then in Paris was Hersch Mendl Stockfisch (1893–1968), who used the names Victor (or V.) in 1934–35 and Karl in 1938. He later became a Zionist and his memoir *Zichrones fun a Yidishen Revolutsioner* by Hersch Mendl (Tel Aviv, 1959) includes his account of discussions with Trotsky in France.

7. **Birobidzhan** was a section of the Russian Republic on the border of China, set aside by the Soviet government in 1928 for colonization by Jews. It was made an autonomous region in 1934 and was dissolved in 1938–39 by Stalin, who claimed it had become a haven for opposition elements.

8. "Questions About Holland." From *Oeuvres*, volume 3 (Etudes et Documentation Internationales, Paris, 1978). Translated from the French by Mavis Parr. A letter to Walter Held, ICL representative in Amsterdam. The **Dutch conflict** was between the RSP (the ICL section) and the OSP over whether and how to merge. **De Kadt's article,** serialized in *De Nieuwe Weg,* expressed the views of the OSP right wing, increasingly hostile to the ICL. Trotsky's early drafts of **"War and the Fourth International"** were written at the end of 1933 but it was not adopted by the IS in its final form until June 1934 (see *Writings 33–34*).

9. "On the Workers' Militia." By permission of the Harvard College Library. Translated from the French by Michael Baumann. Unsigned. An attempted coup by right-wingers and fascists at the Chamber of Deputies on February 6, 1934, opened up a new period in French politics and serious discussion among the workers about how to stop fascism in France. A workers' militia and general arming of the workers were proposed by the French section of the ICL; Trotsky's major discussion of this question was in his essay "Whither France?" (reprinted in *Leon Trotsky on France*). His statement here, written for the French leadership and marked "Not for publication," expressed his views on the call for a "common militia" being raised by the Leninist Youth, the ICL's French youth group. Since he regarded this as an experiment "to make use of the illusions of a certain section of workers in order to prod them along a progressive path," he did not oppose it; instead, he suggested two conditions that should accompany the experiment.

10. "Things Are on the Move." By permission of Albert Glotzer. Translated from the German by Russell Block. This letter to Glotzer was written after his arrival in Paris as a U.S. delegate to the international youth conference that was to begin in Holland February 24. Another U.S. delegate to the conference was Fred Browner, representing the Weisbordite Communist League of Struggle.

11. "Against Centrism at the Youth Conference." By permission of Albert Glotzer. Translated from the German by Maria Roth. Signed "D.O." This letter to Glotzer, intended for the ICL's international youth commission and its delegates to the youth conference in Holland, was Trotsky's response to a resolution ("theses") submitted for the conference by the Socialist Youth League of Holland (SJV), which was affiliated to the OSP.

12. **Karl Kautsky** (1854–1938) was considered the outstanding Marxist theoretician after Engels until World War I, when he abandoned internationalism and opposed the October Revolution. During the war he took a pacifist position against both the prowar right wing and the antiwar left wing of the German Social Democracy.

13. **Angelica Balabanova** (1878–1965) had been a delegate to the Zimmerwald and Kienthal conferences and then a secretary of the Comintern. After being expelled from the CP in 1924, she was a member of the Maximalists, a wing of the Italian Socialist Party in exile. In the United States, her books were signed with the name Balabanoff.

14. **Leon Blum** (1872–1950) was the principal leader of the French Socialist Party in the 1930s and premier of the first People's Front government in 1936.

15. "Rakovsky's Statement of Submission." By permission of the Harvard College Library. Translated from the French by Jesse Smith. *L'Humanite* printed a dispatch from Moscow on February 19, 1934, reporting that Christian Rakovsky, next to Trotsky the best-known leader of the Left Opposition, had given up the fight against Stalinism. An abridged version of this letter to the IS, in another translation, was printed in 1934 and reprinted in *Writings 33–34*, where it had the date when it was published instead of the date when it was written. Two later statements, written when it became plain that Rakovsky had capitulated as well as submitted, are also in *Writings 33–34*. The **crushing of the Austrian proletariat** occurred in mid-February 1934 when the Austrian workers, heroically defending a general strike with arms in hand, were subdued by the artillery of the government headed by Engelbert Dollfuss. All their organizations, including the powerful Social Democratic Party, were outlawed.

16. "Ultraleft Tactics in Fighting the Fascists." By permission of the Harvard College Library. Translated from the French by Russell Block. Unsigned. This letter to the French Communist League leadership was written four days after a clash between the workers and police protecting a small group of fascists who tried to stage a provocative rally in Menilmontant, a working class district of Paris. References to the author's alleged residence in Switzerland and experience in Germany were intended to conceal his identity if the letter fell into the wrong hands. Actually Trotsky had been living incognito in Barbizon, near Paris, since the beginning of November 1933.

17. **Louis-Auguste Blanqui** (1805–1881) was a French revolutionary who spent almost half his life in prison for repeated participation in armed struggle against the government. Blanquism was the theory of revolution through insurrection by small conspiratorial groups, unlike the Marxist theory of revolution through mass action. A collection of Blanqui's writings, *La Critique Sociale*, was published in 1885.

18. **Gilded youth** were youth of wealthy background who sought excitement, including violence, in ultrareactionary movements like French Action, Patriotic Youth, and Croix de Feu, which were all involved in the Menilmontant provocation.

19. "After the Austrian Defeat." By permission of the Harvard College Library. Translated from the German by Russell Block. This was written as the foreword to a pamphlet by Maria Reese.

20. "Reproaching the Dutch Section." From *Oeuvres*, volume 3. Translated from the French by Mavis Parr. A letter to Sneevliet. The **article against de Kadt,** entitled "A Centrist Attack on Marxism," March 16, 1934, is in *Writings 33–34*. **Four German comrades** were among those arrested when the Dutch police raided the youth conference, and the Dutch government turned them over to the German Gestapo; as a deputy in the Dutch parliament, Sneevliet protested the government's complicity with the Nazis, as did the RSP and the NAS.

21. "Field's Expulsion." Karl Faber catalog, April 20–30, 1959. Translated from the German by Russell Block. The letter to B.J. Field from which this selection was excerpted was written shortly after Field was expelled from the CLA for violating its discipline during a hotel workers' strike in New York. Trotsky started the letter by expressing his disagreement with Field's course of action, although he said he did not know enough of the facts as yet, and ended by stating a willingness to continue correspondence with Field. But when he got more facts, he did not write Field again; this was the last of the thirteen Trotsky letters Field put up for sale in 1959. **Aristodimos Kaldis** (1899–1979) was a CLA member of Greek origin

active in the hotel strike. After a short period in Field's group, he left politics to become a painter.

22. "A Concert for Herriot." From *The GPU in the Trotskyist Movement*. According to Vereecken, Trotsky recounted this anecdote at a meal in Paris one evening after an IS meeting, a few weeks before the French government ordered him to leave the country.

23. "The Youth Conference's Unsatisfactory Resolution." By permission of Albert Glotzer. Translated from the German by Russell Block. Unsigned. The Dutch police raided the international youth conference in Laren shortly after it opened on February 24, 1934; four German delegates were turned over to the Nazis in Germany, and the other foreign delegates were deported to Belgium two days later. The conference reconvened on February 28 in Brussels, although for security reasons the site was referred to in contemporary literature as both Luxembourg and Lille. The ICL was represented in Brussels by delegates from its German, U.S., French, and Belgian youth groups; the SAP-OSP forces by delegates from its German, Dutch, and Norwegian youth groups; the delegate of the relatively large Socialist Youth League of Sweden had been denied entry by the Dutch authorities. Despite serious differences, the two main forces present adopted a resolution holding that the Second and Third Internationals had failed and that it was necessary to build a new youth International. The conference set up the International Bureau of Revolutionary Youth Organizations, which became known as the Stockholm Youth Bureau, with provisions for a secretariat of three: one member to be selected by the Swedish Socialist Youth League (Kurt Forslund), one by the German Socialist Youth League (Willy Brandt of the SAP), and one by the ICL youth (Walter Held of the IKD).

24. **Julius Martov** (1873–1923) was a coeditor of *Iskra* with Lenin and then the principal leader of the Menshevik faction of the Russian Social Democratic Labor Party. An opponent of the October Revolution, he emigrated to Germany in 1920.

25. **Louis Sellier** (1885–1978) was general secretary of the French CP in 1923 and was expelled in 1929 for criticizing its third-period

tactics. He was a founder of an opportunist group that evolved into the PUP, and became a People's Front deputy in 1936.

26. **Finn Moe** (1902–1969) represented the NAP at the youth conference; he left before it reached its decisions. He became foreign editor of *Arbeiderbladet* and a leader of the Second International.

27. "The Proposal to Fuse the CLA and the AWP." By permission of the Harvard College Library. Translated from the German by Russell Block. Unsigned. In March 1934 the CLA leadership sent the AWP leadership a proposal for the fusion of the two organizations. Copies of the proposal, together with a letter of motivation, were sent to the IS and Trotsky, soliciting their opinions. Trotsky sent these remarks to the IS before writing the CLA directly (see *Writings 33–34*).

28. "The Errors of Our Youth Delegates." By permission of Albert Glotzer. Translated from the German by Russell Block. This was a letter to Walter Held, who had lived in Holland for some months before the youth conference, and was soon to move to Norway as the ICL's representative in the Stockholm Youth Bureau.

29. Five days after this letter, the IS adopted a resolution expressing political agreement with the points Trotsky had made in his criticisms of the youth conference. But the IS did not insist on the changes Trotsky had demanded as a condition for participating in the Stockholm bureau, concluding only that the youth conference had been just the first step on the road to a revolutionary youth International, and that the ICL members had to remain representatives of Marxist clarity and revolutionary initiative in the new organization.

30. "Continuing the Struggle Through Unifications." By permission of Albert Glotzer. Translated from the German by Russell Block. This was a letter to Glotzer, who had returned to the U.S. after the youth conference.

31. The **antiwar theses,** written by Trotsky at the end of 1933 and adopted by the IS in June 1934, was *War and the Fourth International* (in *Writings 33–34*). It was translated into English by

Sara Weber (1900–1976), a CLA member who was a secretary of Trotsky in France, 1933–34, and in Mexico, 1938–39.

32. "My Interrogation by the Police." By permission of the Harvard College Library. Translated from the French by Russell Block. On his way from Paris to Trotsky's home in Barbizon, Rudolf Klement was arrested on April 12, 1934, for driving a motorcycle with a defective headlight. When searched, he was discovered to be carrying correspondence for Trotsky. The local police had not known where Trotsky was living, and the press was filled with sensational stories which led to a new clamor for his expulsion from France. This was Trotsky's account of his interrogation by the police on April 14 and the press distortions that followed.

33. "Why I Am Being Expelled from France." By permission of the Harvard College Library. Translated from the French by Jeff White. A Radical Socialist government had admitted Trotsky to France in 1933 and it was a Radical Socialist, Albert Sarraut, minister of internal affairs in the Doumergue government that was set up after the February 6 events, who issued a decree deporting Trotsky on April 17, 1934. The decree could not be put into effect until more than a year later because no other government would accept Trotsky in the meantime. But his status became more uncertain than before—the rumor was that he might be deported at any time to a prison camp in one of France's tropical colonies—and he was forced to leave Barbizon and find a place to live elsewhere.

34. "Suggestions for a French Program of Action." By permission of the Harvard College Library. Translated from the French by Russell Block. Unsigned. These suggestions were probably dictated between April 1934, when Trotsky left Barbizon, and July, when he reached Domene, an Alpine village near Grenoble, where he spent the last year of his stay in France. They were incorporated into the Communist League's manifesto, "A Program of Action for France," published in June 1934 and printed in *Writings 34–35*. This document was an early example of the method Trotsky used four years later when he wrote the principal programmatic resolution approved

by the founding conference of the Fourth International (see *The Transitional Program for Socialist Revolution*).

35. **Jean Chiappe** (1878–1940), police prefect in Paris, 1927–34, was a protector of the fascist gangs. His dismissal from this post in January 1934 was one of the reasons for their attempted coup on February 6. He later became an official in the Vichy regime.

36. **Serge-Alexandre Stavisky** (1886–1934) was a French financier whose sensational bankruptcy revealed that his long career as a swindler had been protected by friends in the cabinet, parliament, the police, and the judiciary. The police alleged that his death was a suicide, but it was widely believed he had been murdered to keep from further implicating his powerful friends, many of whom were compelled to resign, to the embarrassment of the Radical government.

37. **The Jacobins** were the strongest left-wing tendency in the Great French Revolution, dominating politics from the overthrow of the moderate Gironde wing in 1791 until their own defeat by a reactionary wing in 1794. Left-wing members of the French Convention were called the **Mountain**.

38. **Octobre Rouge** was the paper of the Leninist Youth, affiliated with the French section of the ICL, 1933–34.

39. "Proposals for the Next ICL Plenum." By permission of Tamara Deutscher. Translated from the French by J.R. Fidler. This was a letter to a member of the IS, Feroci (Leonetti).

40. **Dubois** was a pseudonym of Ruth Fischer (1895–1961). At Trotsky's suggestion she was placed on the IS in 1934 and was made a member of the ICL plenum in 1935. In letters and minutes, Dubois was referred to as a male for security reasons.

41. "Our Response to the French CP's New Turn." From the Cannon archives, Library of Social History. A 1934 translation. Signed "G." In June 1934 the French Stalinist leaders suddenly switched their line, abandoning their third-period policy of united fronts only "from below" and proposing a formal pact with the SFIO leaders for a united front against fascism and reaction. Negotiations were started in June and, despite some hitches, were successfully concluded at the

end of July. Trotsky's response was that the Communist League had to be inside the united front and his proposal, first broached in this letter, was that its members should join the SFIO. This tactic became known in the literature of the movement as the "French turn."

42. **Saint-Denis** was a working class suburb of Paris; the reference was to the CP there, which supported the mayor, Jacques Doriot, in his conflict with the national CP leaders, and was trying to follow an independent policy in the spring of 1934. The Communist League made attempts to influence its development, but with little success.

43. **Marcel Cachin** (1869–1958), a right-wing Socialist and supporter of World War I, became a leader of the French CP and one of its negotiators with the SFIO in 1934.

44. **Committees of Vigilance,** not controlled by any party, were created in March 1934 to work for united left-wing action against the fascist threat. Their influence declined after the SFIO-CP pact was signed in July 1934.

45. "Concentrate Inside the Socialist Party." By permission of the Harvard College Library. Translated from the French by Jeff White. As in other letters of this period, Trotsky tried to mislead unauthorized readers of his correspondence by pretending to write from places where the police knew he had not been.

46. "The State of the League and Its Tasks." *Internal Bulletin,* CLA, number 16, September 1934. Signed "Linier." That translation has been revised by Russell Block after an examination of the French original, by permission of the Harvard College Library. In preparation for a national conference at the end of August 1934, the Communist League held a discussion of the proposal to enter the SFIO. This document was included in the first internal bulletin of the discussion.

47. **Gabriel Cudenet** (1894–1948) led a split from the Radicals to create a party based on "genuine Radical principles." **Gaston Doumergue** (1863–1937), a former president of France, came out of retirement to replace Daladier as premier after the attempted coup of February 6, 1934. He promised a "strong" government and

restrictions on democratic liberties. He was replaced in November 1934 by Flandin.

48. **Leon Jouhaux** (1870–1954) was general secretary of the CGT, 1909–40 and 1945–47. He was a reformist, a supporter of both world wars, and an opponent of the Russian Revolution.

49. The SFIO's Seine Federation, the PUP, the Communist League, the Common Front, and other organizations were loosely grouped into an **alliance committee**, chiefly for purposes of liaison. The Seine Federation proposed a joint demonstration with the CP to commemorate the execution of the Communards at the **Pere-Lachaise** cemetery on May 27, 1934, but the CP rejected the offer because "counterrevolutionary Trotskyists" were in the alliance committee. In the end two separate marches were held, one by the CP and its allies, and then one by the SFIO and its allies, including the Communist League.

50. **Gaston Monmousseau** (1883–1960), a revolutionary syndicalist before World War I, was a Stalinist leader of the CGTU.

51. **Bataille Socialiste** was a public journal published by a leftist tendency in the SFIO, 1927–40. The same name was used by the group, led by Jean Zyromsky, that published it.

52. **Georget** was a pseudonym of David Rousset (1912–1997), a youth leader of the French section who helped direct fraction work in the SFIO and JS. After World War II he became a Gaullist deputy in parliament. **Leon Danno** (b. 1905) was a member of the SFIO since 1927, who had recently been won over to the Communist League and was doing work in its behalf in the SFIO. **Claude Just** (1888–1956) was a leader of an SFIO tendency called the Revolutionary Socialist Committee of Action (CASR), 1933–35, which published a journal *Action Socialiste*. After World War II he joined the French section of the Fourth International.

53. The **Seine Federation of the Young Socialists** was led by left-wingers among whom Fourth Internationalists had an important influence. Nationally, the JS claimed around 11,000 members, of whom around 1,000 were in the Paris region.

54. "The Catalan Conflict and the Tasks of the Proletariat." From the Cannon archives, Library of Social History. A 1934 translation,

which bore no date, described it as "a letter by Comrade T., collaborator with the IS." Editorial insertions in brackets have been added to clarify certain passages in the translation. In the spring of 1934 the right-wing Spanish government, in Madrid, annulled a progressive agrarian law enacted by the quasi-autonomous regional government in Catalonia (Generalidad), which was dominated by a nationalist party, the Esquerra, and other petty-bourgeois forces. On June 12 the Catalan parliament in Barcelona reenacted the law and withdrew the Catalan deputies from the central parliament in Madrid. This precipitated the crisis that Trotsky called **the Catalan conflict,** a period of ferment and uncertainty that lasted almost four months. On June 17, the Workers Alliance, a united-front coalition of several workers' organizations, held a regional conference in Barcelona and adopted a resolution that said: "If the counterrevolutionary Madrid government attacks Catalonia and if a Catalan republic is proclaimed as a result, the Workers Alliance will support the movement, striving to take its leadership so as to guide it to the victory of the federal socialist republic." One of the participants in this conference was the Communist Left of Spain (ICE), which was estranged from the IS and Trotsky but was still formally the Spanish section of the ICL. Trotsky probably wrote this letter to the IS after reading reports of the June 17 conference.

55. The **Spanish reaction** had ousted a Republican-Socialist coalition in the parliamentary elections of November 1933 and taken over the central government in Madrid, but it had not yet taken into the cabinet representatives of the profascist Spanish Federation of Autonomous Rightists (CEDA), the largest party in the parliament. The SP kept warning that the CEDA's admission to the cabinet would be regarded as a fascist coup and would be answered by a revolutionary insurrection. The **fascist danger** referred in part to the Falange, which had been organized in October 1933.

56. The **Workers Alliance** was a united front of workers' unions and parties created in November 1933. Included in it, beside the Spanish section of the ICL, were the SP, the UGT, some syndicalist groups, and the Workers and Peasants Bloc (BOC) led by Maurin (with which the Spanish section merged in 1935). But the powerful CNT refused to join, in line with its disgraceful abstentionist role in

1934, and the small CP did not join until September 1934. That was what Trotsky had in mind when he spoke, later in this letter, about the "extreme divisions among the Catalan proletariat."

57. Most of the Workers Alliance demands at its regional conference centered around working class interests: arming of the workers, freedom of organization and propaganda for all workers' organizations, the forty-four hour week in all branches of industry, etc.

58. The Catalan conflict was resolved, temporarily, early in October 1934 when the Madrid government took three CEDA representatives into the cabinet and the SP launched an armed uprising that was put down with great ferocity and many casualties. At the start of the insurrection the Generalidad in Barcelona proclaimed an independent Catalan republic, but even though it had its own armed forces and wide popular support, it capitulated without resistance at the first military show of strength by Madrid. As the showdown began, the Workers Alliance justified Trotsky's charges of "tail-ending" the petty-bourgeois forces by visiting the Generalidad to inform it that the Alliance was calling for a general strike against Madrid and to inquire what the Generalidad thought about the situation. The Spanish section did not advance any proposals or slogans different from those of the Workers Alliance.

59. "Alternatives for the Young Socialists." Internal bulletin, Communist League of France, number 2, August 1934. Translated from the French by J.R. Fidler. This was a letter to Yvan Craipeau, who was at first hesitant about the proposal to enter the SFIO and the JS. The entry proposal had been made in the name of the **"comrades in Bes.,"** a code name for the Bolshevik-Leninist unit to which Trotsky belonged while he was in France. It was also referred to as "the Besançon cell" and "the B. group."

60. **Paul Faure** (1878–1960) was a right-wing leader of the SFIO and its general secretary until 1940. He was expelled in 1944 for having supported the Vichy regime.

61. **Organic unity** was a movement term in the thirties for fusion of the SFIO and the CP and of the Second and Third Internationals. Trotsky's discussion of positive aspects of this question appears in "The Stalinists and Organic Unity" later in this volume; his analy-

sis of negative aspects will be found in his article "On the Theses 'Unity and the Youth,'" summer 1934, in *Writings 34–35.*

62. "Cross the Rubicon." By permission of the Harvard College Library. Translated from the French by Robert Cantrick. Unsigned. A letter to Raymond Molinier, a supporter of the entry proposal.

63. "The Stalinists and Organic Unity." By permission of the Harvard College Library. Translated from the French by Jesse Smith. A letter to the French leadership.

64. **Maurice Thorez** (1900–1964), who sympathized briefly with the Left Opposition in the mid-twenties, was general secretary of the French CP and a Stalinist from 1930 to his death. He served as a minister in de Gaulle's government after World War II.

65. **Jean-Baptiste Severac** (1879–1951) was Faure's chief aide as administrative secretary of the SFIO. He was on the committee negotiating the united action pact in 1934.

66. **Jacques Doriot** (1898–1945), mayor of Saint-Denis, was one of the French CP's most popular leaders until he began to advocate the united front in 1934 before the French leadership and Moscow had decided to switch to that policy. Expelled from the CP in June 1934, he fished around in various streams, including the London-Amsterdam Bureau, before moving to the ultraright and forming a fascist party in 1936.

67. "Supplementary Arguments and Suggestions for Articles." By permission of the Harvard College Library. Translated from the French by Robert Cantrick. Signed "Van."

68. **Jean Zyromsky** (1890–1975) was secretary of the SFIO's Seine federation and the principal leader of the Bataille Socialiste tendency. He advocated organic unity in the thirties and left the SFIO to join the CP in 1945.

69. **Albert Sarraut** (1872–1962) was Radical premier of France in 1933 and the first half of 1936. In 1934 he was minister of internal affairs in Doumergue's government. **Andre Tardieu** (1876–1941) had been a right-wing premier, 1929–30, and founder of the reactionary Republican Center in 1932. In 1934 he was Doumergue's

minister of state in charge of "constitutional reform" (restricting democratic liberties).

70. "Tasks of the ICL." By permission of the Harvard College Library. Translated from the German by Russell Block. This was probably a document for the IS. By this time opposition to the proposed French turn was being expressed not only inside the French section but also in the IS. The principal opponents there were Bauer of the German section and Vereecken of the Belgian section.

71. "Clouds in the Far East." *Esquire*, August 1934. Reprinted by permission of *Esquire* magazine © 1934 (renewed 1962) by Esquire Inc.

72. **Senjuro Hayashi** (1876–1943) was a Japanese general, minister of war, 1934–35, and premier, 1937.

73. **V.K. Bluecher** (1889–1938) was head of the Soviet partisan forces in Siberia during the civil war, the Red Army's military adviser to Chiang Kai-shek in the mid-twenties, and later commander of the Special Far Eastern Army. He was shot on Stalin's orders during the purges.

74. "Soviets in America?" *International Socialist Review*, April 1975. Translated from the Russian by John G. Wright in 1934, with revisions by George Saunders in 1975 after a checking of the Russian manuscript, by permission of the Harvard College Library. Trotsky wrote this prediction about a future soviet government in the United States for *Liberty* magazine but the editors of that weekly did not like the form he had chosen (a dialogue between an American and a Soviet engineer) and revised it drastically. Trotsky's American associates approved the revision because it did not distort Trotsky's political points, and it was ultimately printed under the title "If America Should Go Communist" in the March 23, 1935, *Liberty*. In that form it was reprinted in *Writings 34–35*.

75. The **NRA** (National Recovery Administration) was a New Deal agency set up in 1933 to prepare and enforce codes of practice for business and industry. While it established a minimum wage and maximum hours and recognized the right of workers to join

unions, it was primarily helpful to business interests that needed price floors and other measures to "prime the pump" as a way out of the depression. Roosevelt's right-wing critics called the NRA part of a conspiracy to "sovietize" America, and the U.S. Supreme Court ruled it unconstitutional in 1935. The NRA's symbol was a blue eagle, referred to later in this article.

76. **Soviet service** refers to a period of work under contract in the USSR. In its great need for technological skills in the twenties and thirties, the Soviet government hired many technicians from Europe and the United States. These skilled workers were not necessarily sympathizers of the Russian Revolution; many simply could not find as good a job in their country because of the economic crisis, while others took Soviet jobs out of a sense of adventure or curiosity.

77. **Technocracy** was a program and movement that arose in the United States in the early years of the depression, particularly in the middle classes. It proposed to overcome the depression and bring about full employment by rationalizing the economy under the control of engineers and technical experts—all without class struggle or revolution.

78. **Herbert Hoover** (1874–1964) was Roosevelt's Republican predecessor as president of the U.S. After his defeat in 1932, he headed various commissions on streamlining and rationalizing the government structure.

79. The **Monroe Doctrine** (1823) warned European monarchies against military and political intervention in the Western Hemisphere.

80. Roosevelt's advisers in the White House were called his **Brain Trust.**

81. **William Z. Foster** (1881–1961) was a leader of the American CP, its presidential candidate in 1924, 1928, and 1932, and later its national chairman.

82. This **Henry Ford** (1863–1947) was the founder of the Ford automobile company, noted for his antilabor and anti-Semitic activities.

83. The United States was formally **"dry"** from 1920 to 1933, when the sale of alcoholic liquor was prohibited by constitutional amendment. In 1933 this amendment was repealed, making the

country **"wet"** again.

84. **Georg Wilhelm Friedrich Hegel** (1770–1831) was the German philosopher whose writings on dialectics strongly influenced Marx. **Tennessee** and other states had laws that prohibited public schools from teaching theories of evolution developed by **Charles Darwin** (1809–1882). The 1925 Scopes trial in Tennessee was the most dramatic of the legal contests over these repressive laws.

85. This sarcastic reference to **Andrew Jackson** (1767–1845), a general and Democratic president of the U.S., may have been related to the ferociously anti-Indian policies and practices for which he was noted.

86. "The 'Belgian' Tradition in Discussion." Internal bulletin, GBL, number 2, October 1934. Translated from the French by Russell Block. The French section's national conference at the end of August 1934 voted decisively to enter the SFIO; by September most of its members had joined and were publishing *La Verite* as the paper of the Bolshevik-Leninist Group (GBL). A majority of the IS approved the French action, but Vereecken of Belgium was opposed and went to Paris to demand a formal IS meeting. He also went to Domene to discuss the question with Trotsky, who persuaded him that a formal meeting would not change the IS position and that he should let the French section proceed with the experiment it had started, restricting himself to a written statement. Vereecken wrote out a statement agreeing not to interfere with the French experiment and expressing his conviction as an opponent of the entry that it should not be extended to other sections. When an IS letter to the sections reported the first part of this statement but not the second, Vereecken wrote an angry letter of protest to the sections complaining about the "suppression" of the second part of his statement. Forty years later he was still complaining that his letter of protest was ignored and never answered by anyone. The present letter, printed in the French internal bulletin, shows that this claim was altogether unwarranted.

87. The **Neos** or Neo-Socialists were a right-wing group in the SFIO who were expelled in November 1933 for violating party discipline in parliament by voting with the Radicals to cut the salaries

of civil-service employees.

88. The **two French groups** mentioned here were the majority tendency at the August national conference, which had entered the SFIO as the GBL, and a minority tendency led by Naville, which refused for several weeks to enter and which constituted itself as a group separate from the GBL after it did enter.

89. "The Present Situation in the Labor Movement and the Tasks of the Bolshevik-Leninists." From *Documents of the Fourth International: The Formative Years (1933–40)*. The French turn produced serious differences inside the leadership and sections of the ICL, and an enlarged international plenum was called in Paris October 14–16, 1934, where the main discussion revolved around this resolution, written by Trotsky. Bauer of the German section, who was opposed to the French turn on principle, did not attend the plenum; soon after, he quit the ICL and joined the SAP. Present and voting against the resolution were Vereecken, Sneevliet, and Blasco (Tresso), a member of the Naville group. Molinier favored the main body of the resolution but was so opposed to the provision inviting the Naville group to return to the French section that he threatened to resign from the plenum. But the resolution, including this provision, was adopted by a vote of six to three.

90. The **Spanish SP** led an insurrectionary general strike that began on October 5 and was crushed by October 11, 1934.

91. **Rene Lhuillier** (1909–1968) was the leader of a small group in the French section opposed to entry. Eventually he entered the SFIO too, and remained there after the Fourth Internationalists were expelled in 1935.

92. "Cannon's Mission in Europe." From the Cannon archives, Library of Social History. Translated from the French by Mavis Parr. Unsigned, and dictated in French. Cannon was a member of the ICL plenum, representing the American section at its October 1934 meeting in Paris. At the plenum he accepted the assignment ("mission") of meeting with Naville, Bauer, and others in an effort to persuade them not to split. After the plenum, he visited Trotsky at Domene. The *Verite* manuscript mentioned by Trotsky was "Whither France?"

reprinted in *Leon Trotsky on France*.

93. "How to Answer the London-Amsterdam Bureau." Internal bulletin, GBL, number 3, November 1934, where it was entitled "The Reply of Comrade Vidal." The same bulletin printed a letter from the London-Amsterdam Bureau (formerly called the IAG) inviting the ICL to participate in an international conference scheduled for November 1934, a letter from the IS soliciting opinions of plenum members, and a letter from Molinier advocating participation. Trotsky's views on how to respond to this invitation, presented in this letter to the IS, were adopted by the IS, and the ICL did not send delegates to the conference, which was held in Paris in February 1935. It was attended, however, by two pro-Fourth International delegates from Holland and an ICL member from Poland. Trotsky's articles on the conference are in *Writings 34–35*.

94. "No Compromise on the Russian Question." Internal bulletin, GBL, number 3, November 1934. Translated from the French by Robert Cantrick. Signed "Vidal."

95. "We Should Join the Belgian Young Socialists." From the Cannon archives, Library of Social History. Translated from the French by Phil Courneyeur. The **JGS** (Socialist Youth Guard or Young Socialists) was affiliated to the Belgian Labor Party (POB); it claimed a membership of 25,000 in 1933.

96. **Walter Dauge** (1907–44) was a leader of the JGS left wing in 1934, an editor of *Action Socialiste Revolutionnaire*, 1935–36; and a leader of the Belgian section of the Fourth Internationalist movement, 1936–39. He defected after World War II began.

97. **Fernand Godefroid** (b. 1909), national secretary of the JGS, considered himself a left-winger in 1934 but participated in expelling Fourth Internationalists in 1936.

98. "Suggestions for the GBL." From the Cannon archives, Library of Social History. A 1935 translation from internal bulletin, GBL, number 4, January 1935. It was dictated in French to Alexis Bardin, a new GBL member in Grenoble, and addressed to Bardin's

brother in Paris, a GBL leader who used the name of J. Boitel. As Pierre Broué showed in his essay "Trotsky's Clandestine Activity at Domene" (appendix in *Writings 34–35*), Trotsky worked closely with Alexis Bardin and through him was able to intervene in the French labor movement despite the severe police restrictions on his activity.

99. **Eugene Varga** (1879–1960) was a cabinet member of the Hungarian Soviet Republic in 1919. After it was crushed, he moved to Moscow and became a leading economist of the Comintern and the USSR.

100. **Lucien Laurat** (1898–1973) was the pen name of Othon Maschl, a founding member of the Austrian CP and then an economist in Moscow. He moved to France in the late twenties where for a while he belonged to Souvarine's Marx and Lenin Circle and then joined the SFIO. Trotsky's criticism of his theories of the Soviet Union are in "The Class Nature of the Soviet State," October 1, 1933, in *Writings 33–34*.

101. **Helene and Rene** (1910–2001) **Modiano** were pacifist members of the SFIO, who joined the tendency led by Pivert in 1935 and with him became members of the PSOP in 1938.

102. "Remarks on the Kirov Assassination." From the Cannon archives, Library of Social History. A 1934 translation. Signed "Dur." in a confidential circular sent to the ICL sections by the IS; signed "Meunier" when it was published, slightly revised, in *La Verite*, December 15, 1934. On December 1, **Sergei Kirov** (1886–1934), Political Bureau member and party secretary in Leningrad, was assassinated at party headquarters in Leningrad by an obscure Soviet employee named **Leonid Nikolaev** (1904–1934). Stalin used this event to start the purges that culminated in the Moscow trials and the extermination of the entire remaining leadership of the October Revolution. Kirov's assassination apparently resulted from GPU bungling of an attempt to manufacture a plot that could be used to smear Trotsky as a terrorist, but at the time of Trotsky's circular the Stalinists had not yet publicly accused Zinoviev, Trotsky, and other Oppositionists of complicity in the assassination. When they did, Trotsky answered with a pamphlet

in his own name, "The Stalinist Bureaucracy and the Kirov Assassination," and a series of articles that exposed the frame-ups (in *Writings 34–35*).

103. **V. Volodarsky** (1890–1918), people's commissar for press, propaganda and agitation, and **Moisei Uritsky** (1873–1918), head of the Cheka in Petrograd, were assassinated by SRs. **Vatslav Vorovsky** (1871–1923), a Soviet ambassador, was assassinated by a White Russian while attending an international conference in Switzerland.

104. **Alexander I** (1888–1934), the monarch of Yugoslavia, was assassinated in Marseilles in October 1934 at the same time as the French minister of foreign affairs, **Jean-Louis Barthou** (1862–1934).

105. **Vyacheslav R. Menzhinsky** (1874–1934) was Dzerzhinsky's successor as chief of the GPU in 1926, but most of the power during his administration was held by his deputy, **Henrikh Yagoda** (1891–1938). After Yagoda assumed the top GPU post in 1934, he organized the first Moscow trials for Stalin; he later was made a scapegoat and was himself convicted in the third Moscow trial and executed.

106. **Nikolai B. Eismont** (1891–1935) was an economic administrator and Rykov's deputy in 1920, and later a member or sympathizer of the Right Opposition. He was expelled in January 1933, was arrested, and was not heard of again.

107. **Amalgam** was a term Trotsky frequently used to designate Stalin's practice of lumping together different or opposing political tendencies and accusing them of common crimes or sins. **Pyotr Wrangel** (1878–1928) was a czarist general who commanded the counterrevolutionary forces during the civil war. Stalin's **Wrangel officer** was a former White Guard named Stroilov who became a GPU agent and was ordered to join the Left Opposition in 1927 so that Stalin could accuse it of having "connections with imperialism."

108. "On the Draft Political Statutes." Internal bulletin, GBL (Youth), number 2, December 20, 1934. Translated from the French by Art Young. Trotsky's comments, dictated in French, concerned political statutes drafted for the GBL's youth group in the JS.

109. "A Few Remarks on *Revolution*." Internal bulletin, GBL (Youth), number 2, December 20, 1934. Translated from the French by Art Young. **Revolution** was a paper published by the Seine Alliance of the JS, reflecting the view of a bloc of left centrists and former members of the Leninist Youth. It became the paper of the Fourth Internationalist youth after they were expelled from the JS in 1935.

110. Trotsky had further thoughts on the question of **signed articles** in 1936, expressed in a pamphlet by his secretary, Erwin Wolf, which argued in favor of abandoning "the complete anonymity of the newspaper" *(La Verite)*; see footnote, *The Crisis of the French Section (1935–36)*, pp. 271–72 [2010 printing].

111. "Once More on Our Turn." Internal bulletin, GBL, number 4, January 1935. Translated from the French by Russell Block. The "Give" against whom Trotsky polemicized here was a pseudonym of Vereecken. By this time the Naville group had entered the SFIO, where they functioned separately from the GBL pending a formal conference to fuse the two groups.

112. On October 19, 1934, *La Verite* printed a headline that said, "Leon Blum bows down before the corpses of Barthou and Poincare. He still has not said one word for the heroic insurgent workers of Spain," and a box entitled "Condolences" that said, "The young Leninists of the JS communicate their heartfelt sympathy to Leon Blum for the double loss he has just suffered in the persons of Messrs. Barthou and Poincare." The top SFIO bureaucrats instructed administrative secretary Severac to meet with a *Verite* representative and make it clear that they were not challenging its right to express criticisms but that they had to find "a correct mode of expression so as not to injure party unity." At the meeting, according to *La Verite* on November 3, Severac told Raymond Molinier that he did not think the headline and box qualified as the correct mode, and Molinier told Severac that "Blum's articles about Barthou and Poincare had aroused righteous indignation, of which our headline was a reflection, but that in the future our editorial board would keep in mind the party secretary's comments as to the form of our criticism."

113. **Pierre-Etienne Flandin** (1889–1958), head of the Democratic Alliance in the French parliament, succeeded Doumergue as

premier in November 1934 and held the post until May 1935. In later cabinet posts he approved the Munich accords and served in the Vichy government in World War II.

114. "Notes on the GBL's Internal Problems." Internal bulletin, GBL, number 4, January 1935. Signed "Paul." Translated from the French by James P. Nolan.

115. **Lutte de classes,** edited by Naville, was the French section's theoretical magazine up to the August 1934 national conference. Naville began to publish it again, as the journal of his own group, after it entered the SFIO. Rosenthal, an associate of Naville for many years, remained with the French section and was a leader of the GBL, in favor of fusion with the Naville group and collaboration with its magazine.

116. The French section's Central Committee elected in August 1934 had established a four-member secretariat, of which Molinier was administrative secretary. In December a **reorganization** led to the secretariat being replaced with a seven-member Political Bureau, with Jean Rous becoming national secretary.

117. **Resignations** from the leadership as a way of lending emphasis to differences were a custom in the French section in the thirties. They were usually retracted in short order or ignored. In the recent period Molinier, Rigaudias, and Rousset had submitted their resignations over one matter or another, and the reorganized leadership's censure of this practice did not affect it seriously.

118. **Meche** was Jean Meichler (1896–1942), a founder of the French section and a member of the GBL Central Committee, who was executed as a hostage by the Nazis during the occupation of France.

119. **Jean Lasterade** (1910–1986) was secretary of the Communist Union, a sect that had split from the French section in 1933, and editor of its journal *L'Internationale*.

120. "Remarks on Our General Orientation." From the Cannon archives, Library of Social History. A 1935 translation from internal bulletin, GBL, number 4, January 1935. Signed "Etienne."

121. "The State and the USSR." From the Cannon archives, Library of Social History. A 1935 translation from internal bulletin, GBL, number 4, January 1935. Signed "Marcel."

122. The **Hohenzollerns** were the ruling family of Germany from 1871 until the revolution of November 1918, when Kaiser Wilhelm I abdicated.

123. "Against Desistance for the Radicals." From the Cannon archives, Library of Social History. A 1935 translation from internal bulletin, GBL, number 4, January 1935, where it was described as an excerpt from "a letter of I. to M." **Desistance** is a term used in French politics when a party decides to support candidates of another party by not running its own candidates against them. The idea of using this device to provide CP and SFIO support for candidates of the bourgeois Radical Party began to be discussed widely in France after the CP publicly proposed an electoral alliance of the three parties in October 1934; in fact, in some regions the CP and SFIO did desist in favor of Radicals in cantonal elections that month. In this letter Trotsky sought to arm his French comrades against People's Frontism, not by arguing against the Stalinists or Social Democrats but by polemicizing against the prodesistance arguments of some of his own comrades.

124. "Answer to Questions by Louise Bryant." By permission of the Harvard College Library. Translated from the Russian by Ivan Licho. **Louise Bryant** (1887–1936), American radical, journalist, and wife of John Reed, had known and interviewed Trotsky in Russia during the first years of the Soviet regime. This interview was conducted by mail shortly before or after she moved to France from New York.

125. "A Proposal to Co-opt Dubois into the Plenum." From the Cannon archives, Library of Social History. A 1935 translation. Dubois (Ruth Fischer) had been serving as a consultative member of the IS since 1934. She was co-opted by the plenum in March 1935. ICL plenum members who supported her co-optation were Leonetti, Lesoil, Sneevliet, and Trotsky. Opposed were Molinier and Vereecken. Craipeau's vote was judged "not clear" and Cannon's did not arrive on time.

126. "Disturbing Signs." By permission of Jean-Claude Orveillon, CERMTRI, Paris. Translated from the French by Mavis Parr. This was the first page of a letter to the French leadership; how it was signed is not known. The editors of the French *Oeuvres* speculate that in the opening sentence "Felix" may have referred to Alexis Bardin or Jean van Heijenoort, and "Marie" to Natalia Sedova.

127. **Louis Rigaudias** (1911–1999), also known as Rigal, was a member of the GBL's Central Committee and Political Bureau at this time, and a leader of its work in the JS. He was author of the youth political statutes Trotsky criticized in December 1934.

128. "After the Belgian Conference." From the Cannon archives, Library of Social History. A 1935 translation. A national conference of the Belgian section in March 1935 had authorized the leaders to effect an entry into the POB. This move was bitterly opposed by Vereecken, who threatened a split if it took place. In a letter for the conference Trotsky concentrated on criticism of Vereecken and did not discuss the specific entry tactic in Belgium ("The Belgian Dispute and the De Man Plan," March 2, 1935, in *Writings 34–35*). After the conference the Belgian leadership moved quickly to make the entry, at approximately the same time that the POB leaders, including Paul-Henri Spaak, entered into a coalition government of "national unity" with the capitalist politicians. Although Trotsky and the IS questioned the timing of the entry, they supported it once it was made. Vereecken and his group split away.

129. **L'Action Socialiste** (not to be confused with the French paper of the same name) was the journal of the POB left wing. It later changed its name to *L'Action Socialiste Revolutionnaire*.

130. **Paul-Henri Spaak** (1899–1972) was a leader of the POB left wing. He even visited Trotsky in France for advice on how to fight the right wing, but he did not follow the advice, becoming a cabinet minister in 1935 and, after World War II, secretary-general of the North Atlantic Treaty Organization (NATO).

131. **Edouard Anseele** (1856–1938) was a reformist leader of the Belgian Labor Party and a member of the Second International's executive committee.

132. "On the Teachers' Federation." From the Archives Dommanget, Institut d'histoire sociale, Paris, by whom Pierre Broue was given the right to copy and publish it in the French edition of Leon Trotsky's *Ouevres*. Translated from the French by Harvey McArthur. The **Teachers' Federation** was a small national union, affiliated to the CP-dominated CGTU, whose principal leaders had quit or been expelled from the CP because of their opposition to its third-period ultraleftism. In 1934 the Federation rejected an offer from the CGT teachers' union for a merger of the two unions; Monmousseau of the central CGTU committee had supported their rejection. Trotsky met with some of the Federation leaders at the time to try to persuade them, among other things, that they should reconsider their decision and work for the merger of the two unions as a step toward reunification of the CGT and the CGTU as a whole (see "The Tasks of Revolutionary Teachers," August 10, 1934, in *Writings 34–35*).

133. **Maurice Dommanget** (1886–1976) was one of the Federation leaders with whom Trotsky had met in 1934. He was a teacher and author of several books on French revolutionary and labor history, including *Babeuf et la conspiration des egaux* (Librairie de L'Humanite, Paris, 1922) and *Pages choisies* (Armand Colin, Paris, 1935). He resigned from the CP in 1930 and for a while belonged to the PUP. In a 1936 letter to Victor Serge, Trotsky wrongly recalled Dommanget as a former member of the Left Opposition; what Trotsky was actually thinking of was the Unitary Opposition, a left-wing caucus in the CGTU in which the Left Oppositionists worked, 1930–31. Together with Rosmer, Dommanget had been an organizer and leader of the Unitary Opposition.

134. **Francis Noel ("Gracchus") Babeuf** (1760–1797), a journalist and editor in the Great French Revolution, was one of the first theoreticians to advocate "communism." He organized a group that wanted to enforce the 1793 constitution and introduce community of property. He was tried and executed for conspiring to overthrow the government.

135. "Notes on the SAP and the London-Amsterdam Bureau." *Informations Dienst* (Information Service), number 6, July 1935;

this was the internal information and discussion bulletin of the IKD, the ICL's German section. Translated from the German by Russell Block. This transcript was subtitled "From a conversation with Comrade Crux." "N." may have been Nicolle Braun (Erwin Wolf), a member of the German section and of the IS. For **Erwin Wolf**, see note 271. The **German conference** cited at the start by N. was a meeting of the German section held in Dietikon, Switzerland, in December 1934. The Bauer group was not invited to this conference, which reflected the views of the section's leadership still active in Germany, where the section was still collaborating with the SAP, and not those of the section's exile leadership, which had for some time been fighting Walcher and other SAP leaders in exile.

136. The **RSAP** (Revolutionary Socialist Workers Party of Holland) was the name taken by the OSP and the RSP when they merged in March 1935. It was affiliated to both the ICL and the London-Amsterdam Bureau, and the latter's February 1935 conference in Paris was attended by both Schmidt and Sneevliet, who introduced pro–Fourth International resolutions.

137. **Alphonse Merrheim** (1871–1923) and **Albert Bourderon** (1859–1930) were French syndicalists in the right wing at Zimmerwald who later allied themselves with the reformists in the French CGT. Bourderon also belonged to the Socialist Party.

138. **Zeth Hoeglund** (1884–1956) was a founder of the Swedish Left Social Democratic Party in 1917, which joined the Comintern in 1920 and became the Swedish CP in 1921. He was expelled from the Comintern in 1924 and returned to the Social Democracy in 1926, which he represented as a member of parliament in the thirties. The unidentified **moderate leftist** at Zimmerwald may have been Ture Nerman (1886–1969), who was actually from Sweden, not Norway. A founder of the Swedish CP, he represented it in parliament after it was expelled from the Comintern in 1929. He joined the Social Democrats in 1939 and supported the U.S. war in Vietnam in his last years.

139. **Inessa Armand** (1875–1920), who was born in Paris and raised in Moscow, joined the Bolsheviks in 1904 and represented them at various international conferences. She was a personal friend of Lenin and active in the early Comintern.

140. **Friedrich (Fritz) Platten** (1883–1942) was secretary of the Swiss Social Democratic Party, 1912–18. He attended the first congress of the Comintern and was a founder of the Swiss CP.

141. "News About the Family." *Unser Tsait*, New York, December 1965, where it was quoted by I.S. Hertz in his article, "Leon Trotsky, on the Twenty-fifth Anniversary of His Assassination." Translated from the Yiddish by Russell Block. This was an excerpt from a letter to Sara Weber.

142. **Alexandra Lvovna Sokolovskaya** (1872–1938) helped recruit Trotsky to Marxism when he was nineteen; they were married and sent into exile together in 1900, and separated in 1902 when Trotsky escaped from Siberia to Western Europe. She was persecuted in the late twenties and thirties because she supported the Left Opposition. Her fate in the purges is unknown.

143. "Laval and the French CP." By permission of the Harvard College Library. Translated from the Russian handwritten fragment by Marilyn Vogt. Unsigned. **Pierre Laval** (1883–1945) was a Republican and minister of foreign affairs in May 1935 when he negotiated the Franco-Soviet pact which led the Stalinists to become supporters of French rearmament. He was premier, 1935–36 and again in 1942, when he collaborated with Germany. He was executed for treason after World War II.

144. **Anthony Eden** (1897–1977) was a British Tory politician holding the post of lord privy seal when he went on a diplomatic mission to Moscow in March 1935. Stalin told him during this visit that the British empire was "the greatest factor in the world for peace and stability." Later he became foreign minister and prime minister.

145. "Toward the New Youth International." By permission of the Harvard College Library. Translated from the French by Robert Cantrick. Unsigned. Trotsky had complained that the SAP-controlled Stockholm Youth Bureau did not fairly represent the forces affiliated and ought to be reorganized ("The Situation in the Stockholm Youth Bureau," March 23, 1935, in *Writings 34–35*). Here he suggested that a youth regroupment would probably be necessary even

if the bureau was reorganized. Held of the ICL was expelled from the bureau in August 1935 and it ceased to exist soon thereafter. The **Open Letter for the Fourth International,** written by Trotsky, was an updated continuation of the Declaration of Four, and was initially signed by representatives of the Dutch RSAP, the Workers Party of the United States, the ICL, the French GBL, and the Workers Party of Canada. Its text is in *Writings 35–36.*

146. "Why Are We Bolshevik-Leninists?" Information and discussion bulletin published by the GBL in the Isere Federation of the SFIO, number 1, July 8, 1935. Translated from the French by David Keil. Unsigned. The SFIO held a national conference at Mulhouse June 9–12, 1935. In the preceding weeks the local and regional groups of the party elected delegates to the conference, usually on the basis of brief platforms (called "motions") introduced by the different tendencies inside the party that sought representation at the conference. The GBL presented its own motion and sought to stimulate discussion and debate over its views inside the local groups. In the Isere department, the GBL members published their own discussion bulletin because, they claimed, they were being denied the right to publish preconference discussion articles in the local SFIO paper, *Le Droit du Peuple.* This article was probably written or dictated by Trotsky at Domene shortly before he left that area on his way to Norway through Paris.

147. "Three Telegrams to Norway." From *Oslo—Moskva—London* by Trygve Lie (Tiden Norsk Forlag, Oslo, 1968). Translated from the Norwegian by Russell Block. Signed "Leon Sedov." The first telegram, from Domene, was a formal application that the Norwegian authorities asked Trotsky to send after they decided that they would grant him a visa to live in their country. The other two, from Paris, were sent after the Norwegian authorities began to vacillate at the last moment about actually granting the visa (see *Trotsky's Diary in Exile, 1935*).

148. **Trygve Lie** (1896–1968), former legal adviser of the NAP, was Norwegian minister of justice, 1935–39, and was responsible for arresting Trotsky and holding him incommunicado after the

first Moscow trial in 1936. Later he was minister of foreign affairs, 1941–46, and secretary-general of the United Nations, 1946–53.

149. **Johan Nygaardsvold** (1879–1952) was minister of state in the 1935 Labor government, in effect prime minister of Norway.

150. "Underground Work in Nazi Germany." *Informations Dienst*, number 7/8, August 1935, where it had the title "On the Organizational Question." Translated from the German by Russell Block. This was the transcript of one or more conversations in Paris between Trotsky and "K.," an emigre leader of the IKD. The IKD editors sought to conceal Trotsky's identity by calling him "J." in the transcript, and by dating the transcript "July 1–18, 1935" (the only time Trotsky was in Paris in 1935 was June 10–13, when he was detained there because of the Norwegian government's last-minute vacillations on his visa; by July he was already in Norway). The Trotsky-K. discussion centered on the IKD's illegal work in a region of Germany identified only as "X" and some of the points made may seem elementary and obvious. But as the IKD editors wrote in an introduction to the transcript, "experience has shown that often the most obvious things in the world are the least recognized." The "inner leadership" referred to in the text probably corresponds to what would be called a regional executive committee under legal conditions; the "inner circle" to a party branch or cell; the "groups" to broader auxiliary organizations around the branch or cell; and the "stewards" to branch or cell secretaries or organizers.

151. The **church question** concerned the Nazi persecution of the Catholic and Protestant churches in Germany. The IKD strongly defended freedom of religion against the German government as part of its defense of democratic rights. Some leaders of the ICL opposed the IKD position and the IS set up a commission to study the question. After reading its minutes, Trotsky unambiguously supported the IKD policy ("Letter to the German Commission," August 19, 1935, in *Writings 35–36*).

152. Trotsky's **"Open Letter to the Workers of France,"** dated June 10, 1935, just as he was leaving the country, presented the Fourth International's program not only for France but for world revolution (see *Writings 34–35*).

153. "Please Pay Attention to the Youth Question." By permission of the Harvard College Library. Translated from the French by Tom Barrett.

154. "Chen Tu-hsiu and the General Council." From the Cannon archives, Library of Social History. Dictated in English. This was a letter to Li Fu-jen in China, written after Trotsky had received oral reports on the state of the Chinese section. The **General Council** was to be a new body created by the ICL at its next international conference, equivalent in its functions to an international executive committee and politically superior to the IS. Such a council, with Chen Tu-hsiu as a member, was elected at the First International Conference for the Fourth International in July 1936, but because of repression and defections it never met or functioned. **Harold R. Isaacs** (1910–1986), an American correspondent in China, where he had been won away from the Stalinists, and **Viola Robinson** visited Trotsky in Norway on their way home from China. Isaacs's report of their discussion is in *Leon Trotsky on China*. The first edition of his 1938 book, *The Tragedy of the Chinese Revolution*, included a preface by Trotsky, but Isaacs deleted it in subsequent editions, after he had rejected Marxism. **Niel Shih** was a pseudonym of Liu Jen-ching (1899–1987). A founding member of the Chinese CP, he became a Left Oppositionist in Moscow in the mid-twenties and met Trotsky in Turkey in 1929. After returning to China, he founded the October Society, which merged with other groups to form the Chinese section in 1931. He split from the movement in 1937 and became an anticommunist propagandist in the Kuomintang. He recanted his past after the CP came to power in 1949 and was given minor posts in the new regime.

155. "For a Bloc Against Oehler." By permission of Albert Glotzer. These translations were made in 1935. **Hugo Oehler** (1903–1983), a former CP organizer, joined the CLA in 1930 and became a member of its National Committee in 1931. In 1934 he opposed the French turn as a matter of principle, and launched a struggle against it that convulsed the new Workers Party in 1935. When Cannon and Shachtman sought to contain Oehlerism, politically, they were at first

resisted by Muste, Abern, and Weber. In this and subsequent letters Trotsky sought to convince the latter that they should subordinate their factional differences with Cannon and Shachtman and take joint action to repudiate Oehler's positions. This was finally done in October 1935 when Oehler violated party discipline by publishing his own journal and was expelled. He organized the Revolutionary Workers League, which survived into the 1950s.

156. "The Cannon-Shachtman Group Should Make Concessions." From the Cannon archives, Library of Social History. Translated from the German by Duncan Williams. This letter was marked "Personal!" For **David B. Ryazanov,** see note 162. The **Ultimatists** were an ultraleft faction of the Bolsheviks in 1908–09, whose leader Gregory Alexinsky, later became a monarchist and social patriot. For **Nathan Gould,** see note 411.

157. "The Policy of the Abern-Weber Group." By permission of Albert Glotzer. A 1935 translation.

158. "Nothing in Common with the Decadent Comintern." From the Cannon archives, Library of Social History. A 1935 translation. The **New Leader** was the weekly paper of the British ILP. Trotsky's **treatise,** "The ILP and the Fourth International," September 18, 1935, is in *Writings 35–36.*

159. "An Appeal to A.J. Muste." By permission of Albert Glotzer. A 1935 translation. This was dictated in two parts while Trotsky was in a hospital in Oslo.

160. **Paul Eiffel** was a pseudonym of Paul Kirchoff (1900–1972), a member of the IKD who joined Bauer in opposing the French turn and came to the United States where he joined forces with Oehler. In 1936 he split from Oehler to form his own short-lived sect.

161. **Que Faire?** (What Is To Be Done?) was a small French centrist group organized in 1934 that coalesced dissident CP members and former Left Oppositionists. Its chief leaders were expelled from the CP in 1936. It published a bulletin or magazine until 1939. Most of its members joined the SFIO in 1938 and advocated organic unity.

162. **David B. Ryazanov** (1870–1938) joined the Bolsheviks in 1917 and later became director of the Marx-Engels Institute. His scholarly and scrupulous attitude toward party history offended Stalin, who made him a defendant in the 1931 trial of a so-called Menshevik Center that was accused of plotting to restore capitalism in the USSR. He was dismissed from the Marx-Engels Institute and exiled.

163. **Joseph Zack** was the pseudonym of Joseph Kornfeder (1897–1963), an American CP specialist in trade union matters who joined the WPUS in 1934 and was expelled in 1935 for violating party discipline. He belonged to the Oehler group for a short time. Later he was a government witness against radicals in the witch-hunt.

164. The **New International,** edited by Shachtman, and **New Militant,** edited by Cannon, were periodicals of the Workers Party. **Die Neue Front** was the SAP's paper. In the spring of 1935 some former members of the AWP still hoped that the SAP would join with the Workers Party in signing the Open Letter for the Fourth International; while that hope remained, the Workers Party treated the SAP as a potential fraternal group. **De Nieuwe Fakkel** was the Dutch RSAP's paper. Trotsky's **"Centrist Alchemy or Marxism?"** dated April 24, 1935, is in *Writings 34–35*.

165. "The Open Letter and the ILP." From the Cannon archives, Library of Social History. Translated from the French by Mavis Parr. Signed "Crux." An extract from a letter to the IS.

166. "Foreword, *Mitt Liv.*" The Norwegian edition of *My Life* (Tiden Norsk Forlag, Oslo, 1935). Translated from the Norwegian by S. Siguneson.

167. The **Entente** was the World War I alliance against Germany. **Alfonso XIII** (1886–1941) became king of Spain at birth and abdicated in 1931, when the Second Republic was proclaimed.

168. Trotsky's memory misled him here. He reached London in his **first exile** in October 1902, not 1903, and he spent two and a half years in Western Europe, not one and a half.

169. **Georgi Plekhanov** (1856–1918) was the founder of Russian Marxism and, with Lenin, one of the editors of *Iskra* when

Trotsky first met him. He later became a Menshevik leader, a supporter of the czarist government in World War I, and an opponent of the October Revolution. **Pavel Axelrod** (1850–1928) was, with Plekhanov, a founder of the Emancipation of Labor Group in 1883, and later a Menshevik.

170. "For or Against?" *Bulletin*, ICL, number 6, December 1935. Translated from the French by Naomi Allen. This letter, written from the hospital, concerned a struggle against Dutch partisans of the SAP trying to split the RSAP and its youth group, and had been translated from the Dutch in *De Rood Gardist*, number 1. A letter to **Hendrik Theodoor ("Theo") van Driesten** (1911–1942), a member of the Dutch section and a founder of its youth group in 1935. He died in the Neuengamme concentration camp.

171. "Youth Secretary Nominations." From the Sneevliet archives, International Institute of Social History, Amsterdam, by whom Pierre Broue was given the right to copy and publish it in the French edition of Leon Trotsky's *Oeuvres*. Translated from the German by Duncan Williams. A letter to the IS after the expulsion of the Fourth Internationalists from the Stockholm Youth Bureau.

172. "Support of the Dutch Fight Against SAPism." From the Sneevliet archives, International Institute of Social History, Amsterdam, by whom Pierre Broue was given the right to copy and publish it in the French edition of Leon Trotsky's *Oeuvres*. Translated from the German by Duncan Williams. A handwritten letter to Henricus Sneevliet on the eve of a congress by the Dutch section that decisively defeated a disloyal SAPist faction. For **Fred Zeller**, see note 188. Trotsky's **article on Pivert**, "'Labels' and 'Numbers,'" August 7, 1935, is in *The Crisis of the French Section (1935–36)*.

173. "Conversations with Earle Birney." By permission of the Harvard College Library. **Earle Birney** (1904–1995), who used the pen name E. Robertson, was a member of the Canadian Workers Party who had also been active in the CLA and the Fourth Internationalist group in the British ILP. He and Ken Johnson traveled

from Britain to Norway to visit Trotsky in November 1935 and he prepared transcripts or condensations of some of their discussions that were published at the time (see "Once Again the ILP" and "Advice on Canadian Farmers" in *Writings 35–36*). He broke with the Fourth International in 1940 and later became a prominent Canadian poet. There are several reasons for doubting the accuracy of some of the statements attributed to Trotsky here. The present summaries, hitherto unpublished, contained the typed notice by Birney "Not for publication," to which he added in handwriting "or quotation." Birney sent Trotsky a copy, but Trotsky did not initial it, as he often did with summaries of discussions made by visitors to signify that he found them generally accurate. Certain passages conflicting with positions that Trotsky was stating repeatedly at the time may have resulted from Birney's flawed condensations of what was said. With these precautionary comments, we think the transcripts are worth printing. **Political "gangster" psychology** referred to an incident in Philadelphia in August 1935. The local Oehlerites had refused to recognize the authority of the Philadelphia city committee or to turn over to it documents belonging to the WPUS. Two members of the Cannon-Shachtman group, Leon Goodman and Herman Banks, went to the combined printshop and living quarters of the leading Oehlerite, Meyer Hirsch, in his absence and took the documents; on the way out, they were stopped by Hirsch's brother, Paul, and beat him up in the altercation that followed. The South Philadelphia branch, to which they belonged, acting on the recommendation of the city committee, condemned their conduct, suspending Goodman for a year, and Banks for three months. The Oehlerites complained that this punishment was inadequate. The WPUS Political Committee, acting on motions by Cannon, approved the action of the South Philadelphia branch and directed the party secretariat to send a letter to all the branches condemning the attack as "completely incompatible with the teachings and practices of our party." The letter to the branches by Muste, the secretary, also called attention to the fact that the WPUS, the AWP and the CLA had "a long record of the most determined struggle against the practice of individual violence or any form of hooliganism within the labor movement. Least of all should personal violence enter into discussions and controversies within the revolutionary party itself. The Political Committee calls upon all members to take this matter to heart and to carry out true revolutionary discipline by conducting the inner-party discussion on a political level. The branches should take advantage of this occasion to instruct especially younger comrades and new members in the Marxian position of opposition to individual terrorism, violence or hooliganism within the labor movement." No other incident of this type occurred in the WPUS or the SWP.

174. The **Italo-Ethiopian War** began with the Italian invasion of Ethiopia in October 1935, after long and public preparation by the fascists.

175. **Benito Mussolini** (1883–1945), a former member of the Socialist Party, founded the Italian fascist movement in 1919 and became dictator in 1922. He was overthrown in 1943 and was executed by partisans two years later.

176. **Samuel Hoare** (1880–1959), a Conservative, held several posts in the British cabinet. He was foreign secretary in 1935.

177. **Negus** was the title used by the absolute monarch of Ethiopia, Haile Selassie (1891–1975). Driven into exile by the Italian invasion, he was restored to his throne by Italy's defeat in World War II, and held power until an uprising deposed him in 1974.

178. **Stanley Baldwin** (1867–1947) was Conservative prime minister of Britain, 1923–24, 1924–29, and 1935–37.

179. It is hard to accept this passage in Birney's summary as accurate. It is true that Lenin, Trotsky, and other Comintern leaders in the early 1920s viewed the antagonism between American and British imperialism as "the most fundamental . . . existing between capitalist states in the world today," and that Trotsky retained this view throughout the decade. (As late as 1929, Washington admitted in 1975, the U.S. government was drafting a top-secret blueprint for war with Britain, aimed at driving the British out of North and South America and waters adjacent thereto, eliminating Britain as a strong competitor in foreign trade, an invasion of Canada with seizure of its key seaports, etc.; see *Intercontinental Press*, January 12, 1976.) But Trotsky abandoned that idea after Hitler took power in 1933, which changed the international picture and alignments drastically. From then on, he wrote frequently about the dynamics

of Nazi expansionism and how this altered diplomatic and strategic patterns. Would he have completely forgotten to add anything about this in 1935, or did Birney forget to write it down?

180. This is one of the examples in Birney's summary where Trotsky's meaning suffers from overcondensation. Why, how, and under what conditions would a Red Army victory mean "another step backward toward state capitalism and the increase of private capitalism"? Without explanation, this passage is unclear or misleading. Fortunately, the thought that Trotsky expressed at this point is available in print elsewhere, with all its nuances and conditional reservations intact (see "War and the Fourth International," section 47, in *Writings 33–34*); the term "state capitalism" is not used there at all.

181. "Greetings to *Robitnichi Vysti*." *Robitnichi Vysti* (Labor News), December 15, 1935. Translated from the Ukrainian by M. Gavrilovich. This was a Ukrainian-language journal in Canada sympathetic to the Fourth International.

182. "Letters About Anton Ciliga." From the Cannon archives, Library of Social History. Translated from the German by Maria Roth, except for the letter to Olav Scheflo, a "slightly condensed" translation made in 1936. **Anton Ciliga** (1898–1992) was a member of the Yugoslav CP's Political Bureau who moved to the Soviet Union in 1925 and became a member of the CP there. He belonged to the Left Opposition from 1929 to 1932, when he joined an ultraleft group. He was arrested and banished to Siberia in 1930, and was expelled from the USSR in 1935. After being convinced that Ciliga was not a GPU agent, Trotsky and the *Biulleten Oppozitsii* helped to publicize his revelations about Soviet conditions and repression in Stalin's prisons and concentration camps. When Ciliga began to collaborate politically with the Mensheviks, the *Biulleten* stopped printing his articles at the same time that it acknowledged the importance of their information (see "On Comrade Ciliga's Articles," June 3, 1936, in *Writings 35–36*). In 1938 Ciliga published a book in France that was translated into English as *The Russian Enigma* (Routledge and Kegan Paul, London, 1940).

183. Jan Frankel had recently returned from Norway to his native Czechoslovakia.

184. **Arben Tarov** (1898–1942) was another victim of Soviet repression who escaped and reached Western Europe earlier in 1935. Trotsky and the *Biulleten* printed several of his articles. Tarov was an Armenian worker in the Caucasus who became a Bolshevik in 1917 and fought in the civil war. He was expelled as an Oppositionist in 1927, arrested in 1928 and deported to Siberia, arrested again in 1931 and sentenced to three years in an isolation prison; after serving this term, he was banished again to Central Asia, from which he escaped to Iran, where he was twice imprisoned before getting to France. In World War II he fought as part of an Armenian Communist resistance group and was executed by the Nazis.

185. **Willi Schlamm** (1904–1978) was an Austrian CP leader and a founder of the Austrian Right Opposition in 1929. As editor of *Die Neue Weltbuehne* in Prague, he printed several important articles by Trotsky after Hitler came to power. Later he moved to the United States, where he became an editorial executive of the Henry Luce publications.

186. **Weiss** was a pseudonym of Oskar Seipold (1889–1966), a Communist member of the legislature in Prussia who joined the Left Opposition and defended its views in that body before Hitler's victory. He emigrated to Czechoslovakia, and was elected a member of the General Council of the Movement for the Fourth International in July 1936.

187. **Olav Scheflo** (1883–1959) was a leader of the Norwegian CP who broke with the Comintern in 1928 and rejoined the NAP, in which he had been a leader before it left the Comintern in 1923. When Trotsky came to Norway, Scheflo was editor of *Soerlandet*, a NAP newspaper in Kristiansand, in which he defended Trotsky against Stalinist slanders and, later, against the Norwegian government's repressive moves. In December 1935, the CP paper *Arbeideren* accused Trotsky of plotting terrorist action against the USSR and "the greatest leader of the world proletariat of our times, Stalin," and cited as proof for this charge an anti-Stalin postcard that a French visitor to Trotsky had mailed to France from Norway.

188. **Fred Zeller** (1912–2003) was the leader of the Seine Alliance of the JS, expelled with GBL members in July 1935 for their opposition to the right-wing leaders of the JS and SFIO. He visited Trotsky in Norway in the autumn of 1935, where he was won over to the GBL. He became international youth secretary of the ICL and a leader of the French section until 1937, when he was expelled for an indiscretion. He rejoined at the end of World War II but quit soon after. Later he became one of the leaders of French Freemasonry.

189. Trotsky's article, "On the Soviet Section of the Fourth International," January 11, 1936, reported a great deal of information, culled from the Soviet press, about the political sympathies of the victims of a vast purge then in progress (see *Writings 35–36*).

190. "The Lenin-Trotsky Papers." From *The Trotsky Papers, 1917–22*, vol. 1, where it was entitled "Remarks on the Collection of Leon Trotsky's Documents from the Years 1917–23" (Mouton, the Hague, 1964; distributed by Humanities Press, New York). Edited and annotated by Jan M. Meijer, with texts in both Russian and English. Translated from the German by Russell Block. Just as Stalin later regretted letting Trotsky leave the Soviet Union alive in 1929, he also regretted having let Trotsky take with him his "archives" containing thousands of documents, many unpublished, from the years 1917–29. Fearing that the GPU would steal or destroy these documents, Trotsky arranged in 1935 to sell the 1917–23 material to the International Institute of Social History in Amsterdam. Publication of the material took longer than anyone had expected: the first volume of *The Trotsky Papers*, as the Institute named it, was not published until 1964, the second not until 1971. In 1940, shortly before his death, Trotsky sold his archives as a whole to the Harvard College Library. **Brest-Litovsk** was a town on the Russo-Polish border where a treaty ending hostilities between Russia and Germany was signed in March 1918. Trotsky attended the negotiations as Soviet commissar of foreign affairs. The treaty's terms were exceedingly unfavorable to the new Soviet government, and there were sharp differences among its leaders about whether to accept them until Lenin's proposal to do so was adopted. **Efraim Sklyansky** (1892–1925) was Trotsky's deputy in the Council of Defense

during the civil war. He was killed in a boating accident during a visit to the United States.

191. "Results of the Open Letter." By permission of the Tamiment Library, New York University, New York. Translated from the German by Duncan Williams. A letter to Otto Schuessler, who had been active in the emigre leadership of the German section since completing a stint as Trotsky's secretary in 1933. For **S.L. Johre** and **Jan Bur,** see note 271; their polemics on the Jewish question were printed in *Unser Wort* in October 1935 and January 1936. *La Commune* was the paper published in December 1935 by the Molinier group in the French section; for publishing it in violation of party discipline the leaders of the Molinier group were expelled; now the expelled group had issued a statement supporting the Open Letter. For the Belgian **Spartacus,** see note 223.

192. "Schmidt's Trip to England." By permission of John Archer. Translated from the French by Nat London. This was a letter to Earle Birney in England. **Ethel Mannin** (1900–1984) was a prolific author of romantic novels, travel books, memoirs, and reflections on love, sexual relations, religion, and politics. She joined the ILP in 1932 and was associated with the circle around Fenner Brockway. The article referred to by Trotsky outlined her impressions of a 7,000 mile tour of the Soviet Union (*New Leader,* January 17, 1936); it reported the great progress made in housing, hospitals, and schools as well as the privileges of state and Red Army officials, and concluded the USSR was still far from having achieved a classless society.

193. "Educating Against Centrism." By permission of the Tamiment Library, New York University. Translated from the German by Duncan Williams. A letter to the IS. The Spanish **POUM** (Workers Party of Marxist Unification) was formed in September 1935 through a fusion of the Catalan Federation led by Maurin and the Communist Left led by Nin. Four months later it signed the People's Front pact, which Trotsky denounced in "The Betrayal of the Spanish POUM," January 23, 1936; reprinted in *The Spanish Revolution (1931–39)*. Maurin was elected to parliament in the February 1936 electoral

victory of the People's Front. Nin became minister of justice in the Catalan government in September 1936. The POUM was expelled from the Catalan government in December 1936 and was outlawed by the central government in June 1937.

194. "The Heyday of the People's Front." By permission of the Tamiment Library, New York University. Translated from the French by David Keil. A letter to **L. Biline,** the pseudonym of Robert Caby (1905–1992), a member of the French section and author of an anthem of the Fourth International. The **People's Front** was the name given to class-collaborationist coalitions between the traditional workers' parties and democratic capitalist parties in the mid-thirties, after the Comintern abandoned its third period policies. The Comintern's Seventh World Congress in August 1935 made this policy mandatory for all affiliates in capitalist and colonial countries. The French People's Front's program was published in January 1936. The People's Front came to power in both Spain and France later in 1936. Trotsky's analysis of both experiences will be found in *The Spanish Revolution (1931–39)* and *Leon Trotsky on France*. **Maurice Legue** (1912–1984) and **Charles Margne** (1911–1982) were members of the French section who tried to play a conciliatory role between the Molinier group and the French leadership.

195. "Two Statements on Hearst." The cablegram is from *New Militant*, February 1, 1936. The letter is from the Cannon archives, Library of Social History. Translated from the German by Russell Block. **William Randolph Hearst** (1863–1951) was the publisher of a chain of right-wing newspapers noted for their sensationalism. On January 19, 1936, Hearst's papers stole an article by A. Tarov that had appeared in the September 28 and October 19, 1935, *New Militant*. On the same day the Stalinist *Sunday Worker* printed a story calling Trotsky an agent of Hearst and promising to reveal the price Hearst had paid for the article. A later version of Trotsky's statement to the Associated Press is in *Writings 35–36*. Trotsky had not yet learned that his American literary agent at this time, **Maxim Lieber,** was a Stalinist who kept the GPU informed about Trotsky articles that passed through his hands and did not overexert himself

in trying to sell anti-Stalinist material to magazines.

196. "A Conversation with Maurice Spector." By permission of Albert Glotzer. A 1936 translation. This transcript was made by Spector and Lyman Paine ("White") at the end of a series of talks they had with Trotsky about a dispute in the Workers Party; in this transcript the clarifying words between brackets were added by Spector. In December 1935 the right wing of the American Socialist Party (the "Old Guard," which later became the Social Democratic Federation) split away, leaving the SP leadership in the hands of Norman Thomas and centrists who called themselves the Militants. A few weeks later the Cannon-Shachtman group proposed that the Workers Party dissolve so that its members could enter the SP; opponents of this proposal were Muste, Abern, and Weber (and Spector and Paine). A national convention was called for the end of February to decide the issue. On January 24, Trotsky wrote a telegram and letters to the WPUS leaders expressing his support for entry (see *Writings 35–36*). Weber announced that he would abide by the convention's decision and would enter the SP if it so decided; the other opponents refused to make such a statement, implying a possible split if they were a minority at the convention.

197. **Minneapolis** and **Toledo** were cities where the CLA and the AWP had led important labor struggles in 1934 and where the WPUS had significant workers' cadres. In **Sacramento** the WPUS was involved in organizing agricultural workers and a defense movement in behalf of workers arrested for their organizing activities.

198. The **KAPD** (Communist Workers Party of Germany) was founded in April 1920 after a serious ultraleft split from the German CP. Although it tended toward anarcho-syndicalism and opposed work in parliaments or reformist unions, it was recognized as a sympathizing party of the Comintern. But it soon lost most of its members and degenerated into an anti-Soviet sect.

199. **J. Pierpont Morgan** (1837–1913) and his son of the same name (1867–1943) were the outstanding finance capitalists of their time in the United States.

200. The **Stakhanovite movement** was a system of speedup in Soviet production named after a coal miner, Alexei Stakhanov

(1906–1977), who reportedly exceeded his quota sixteen-fold by sheer effort. This system was introduced in the Soviet Union in 1935 and led to great wage disparities and widespread discontent among the masses. Stakhanov was rewarded with special honors and privileges.

201. In 1935 Cannon and Shachtman sent the IS and Trotsky a **private letter** expressing their views about the factional line-ups in the WPUS. By mistake the IS printed it in an internal bulletin, leading to heated complaints by Cannon's opponents.

202. **Earl Browder** (1891–1973) was elected general secretary of the American CP at Stalin's directive in 1930 and was deposed and expelled at Stalin's directive in 1946.

203. The **Cohenites** were a small group, led by Larry Cohen, who were under Oehler's influence and opposed to entry on principle.

204. "How to Avert a Split." From the Cannon archives, Library of Social History. A 1936 translation. A letter to Cannon and Shachtman. The WPUS convention held February 29–March 1, 1936, voted by a heavy majority to enter the SP. Almost all the opponents of entry accepted the decision and entered with the others.

205. "Remarks for an English Comrade." From the Cannon archives, Library of Social History. Translated from the German by Duncan Williams.

206. "The Center Must Stay in Europe." By permission of the Tamiment Library, New York University. Translated from the German by Duncan Williams. A letter to Martin, a pseudonym of Alfonso Leonetti, a member of the IS in Paris. Trotsky's **preface** to a new French edition of his book *Terrorism and Communism* was entitled "France at the Turning Point," March 26, 1936; it is reprinted in *Leon Trotsky on France*. For **Manuel Azana,** see note 232. For **Largo Caballero,** see note 337. **La Batalla** was the central newspaper of the POUM.

207. "Orient to the Spanish Youth." From the Sneevliet archives, International Institute of Social History, Amsterdam, by whom

Pierre Broue was given the right to copy and publish it in the French edition of Leon Trotsky's *Oeuvres*. Translated from the French by Naomi Allen. A letter to members of the POUM in Spain who had written Trotsky. **Juan Andrade** (1897–1981) was a founder of the Spanish CP, from which he was expelled in 1927, and of the Spanish Left Opposition. Together with Nin, he led the Communist Left into a merger with Maurin's group, in which he supported the POUM's participation in the People's Front electoral bloc. Trotsky's **letter to a Spanish comrade** was entitled "Tasks of the Fourth International in Spain," April 12, 1936; reprinted in *The Spanish Revolution (1931–39)*.

208. "Eleven Letters to Victor Serge." By permission of Colette Chambelland, Musee sociale. From *La Lutte contre le stalinisme*, edited by Michel Dreyfus and translated from the Russian by Francoise Petit (Maspero, Paris, 1977). Retranslated from the French by Jeff White, except for the July 30, 1936, letter, which was retranslated by Art Young; excerpts retranslated earlier by Naomi Allen, for *The Spanish Revolution (1931–39)*, have been incorporated into the White and Young translations. In 1936 the Stalin regime, responding to a campaign by French intellectuals and the ICL, allowed Victor Serge and his family to leave the Soviet Union, where he had been banished to central Asia as a Left Oppositionist. In April, Serge arrived in his native Belgium, where he lived for some months before moving to France. Correspondence between him and Trotsky began quickly and continued through the summer until the start of the first Moscow trial; then it stopped partly because Trotsky concentrated on exposing the trial and was soon gagged by the Norwegian authorities, and partly because of political differences over the Spanish Civil War and the Fourth International. Serge was elected to the General Council of the Movement for the Fourth International at an international conference in July 1936, but he withdrew from and became an opponent of the movement in 1937.

209. **Eleazar B. Solntsev** (1899–1936), a Left Oppositionist, was arrested in 1929 and kept in an isolation prison for five years. Banished to Siberia, he was arrested again in 1935 and sentenced to another five years' imprisonment. After an 18-day hunger strike, he

was told he would be sent to exile in Siberia instead of prison, but on the way he became ill and died.

210. **Mikhail S. Glazman** was a stenographer and secretary of Trotsky during the civil war and later a member of his staff on the Military Revolutionary Council. He helped to edit some of Trotsky's collected works and was a supporter of the Left Opposition. He committed suicide after being expelled from the party in 1924. Trotsky's tribute is in *Portraits, Political and Personal*. **Georgi Butov,** another aide of Trotsky in the Military Revolutionary Council, was arrested for refusing to sign false charges against Trotsky, went on a hunger strike, and died in prison in 1928.

211. Trotsky's **work on the USSR** was to be named *The Revolution Betrayed: What Is the Soviet Union and Where Is It Going?* Originally, it was supposed to be a new introduction to *The History of the Russian Revolution*, but it grew into a separate book by the time it was completed in August 1936.

212. **Charles Plisnier** (1896–1952) was a writer and member of the Belgian CP who joined the Left Opposition in 1928 and soon became a sympathizer.

213. **Fyodor Dan** (1871–1947) was a leader of the Mensheviks and an opponent of the October Revolution. He was arrested in 1921, deported in 1922, edited Menshevik journals in exile, and was the Menshevik representative to the Second International.

214. **Magdeleine Marx Paz** (1889–1973) was a French civil libertarian and a supporter of the Left Opposition until 1929 when Trotsky broke with the Pazes and *Contre le Courant*.

215. **Marguerite Thevenet Rosmer** (1879–1962) was a revolutionary activist and friend of the Trotskys from the time she met them in Paris in World War I.

216. **Boris Mikhailovich Eltsin** (1879–1937) was an Old Bolshevik and Left Oppositionist who spent several years in prison before disappearing in the purges. His two sons suffered a similar fate.

217. **La Revolution proletarienne** was a syndicalist magazine started in 1925 by Pierre Monatte and his comrades after they left the French CP.

218. Trotsky's **statement,** "Political Persecution in the USSR," May 22, 1936, is in *Writings 35–36*.

219. **Serge's book,** when it was published in 1937, bore the French title *Destin d'une revolution: URSS, 1917–37* (Grasset, Paris) and the English title *Russia Twenty Years After* (Pioneer Publishers, New York). Before it appeared, he also published a pamphlet on the first Moscow trial and *From Lenin to Stalin* (reprinted by Pathfinder, 1973).

220. **Pierre-Joseph Proudhon** (1809–1865) was an early French theoretician of anarchism.

221. **Andrew Smith** was the author of *I Was a Soviet Worker* (Dutton, New York, 1936).

222. **Jean Longuet** (1876–1938), a grandson of Karl Marx, was a French Social Democrat and a pacifist who voted for government war credits in World War I and opposed the SFIO's affiliation to the Comintern. **Georg Ledebour** (1850–1937) was a German Social Democrat who broke with his party in World War I and helped to organize the USPD. He was against the USPD's affiliation to the Comintern or its return to the Second International, and maintained a small group of his own until the thirties, when he joined the SAP.

223. **Spartacus** was the name of Vereecken's paper in Brussels, 1935–36. **Andre Gide** (1869–1951), the eminent French writer, became a fellow-traveler of the Stalinists in the early thirties but broke with them in his book *Return from the USSR* at the end of 1936, after the first Moscow trial.

224. The French People's Front's decisive election victory in May 1936 was followed by a huge strike wave before the installation of Leon Blum's cabinet on June 4. For Trotsky's analysis of these events, see "The Decisive Stage," June 5, 1936, and "The French Revolution Has Begun," June 9, 1936, in *Leon Trotsky on France*.

225. **Roger Salengro** (1890–1936) was an SFIO leader and minister of the interior in the first People's Front government; in this post he denounced the sitdown strikers for occupying the factories and launched a witch-hunt against the press and leaders of the ICL's French section. He committed suicide when the ultraright press branded him a deserter from the army in 1915.

226. **Irakli Tsereteli** (1882–1959) was a Menshevik minister in the Russian Provisional Government, March–August 1917.

227. By the **autumn** of 1936 Trotsky was under internment in Norway and unable to get most of his letters mailed, let alone edit

a journal. The projected German monthly did not appear, but the French section began publishing *La Quatrieme Internationale* in October.

228. **Marcel Martinet** (1877–1944) was a French writer and playwright, sympathetic to the *Revolution proletarienne* group but inactive because of poor health. He wrote a pamphlet about Serge in 1933 and opposed the Moscow trials.

229. Trotsky's **draft theses** were published, after their adoption by the July 1936 international conference sponsored by the ICL, under the title "The New Revolutionary Upsurge and the Tasks of the Fourth International" (in *Writings 35–36*).

230. During Trotsky's **year** in Domene, he lived in the home of Laurent Beau, a teacher and member of the Teachers Federation, which was affiliated to the CGTU.

231. **Simone Weil** (1909–1943) was a French radical intellectual who was converted to mysticism and Catholicism before starving herself to death in England during World War II.

232. The **present events in Spain** refers to the outbreak of civil war thirteen days before this letter was written. **Nin's alliance with Azana** refers to the fact that the POUM had signed the Spanish People's Front program and pact with bourgeois politicians including **Manuel Azana** (1880–1940), prime minister, 1931–33, and president throughout the civil war until his resignation in Paris in 1939.

233. Trotsky was on vacation after completing *The Revolution Betrayed* when he heard about the **Tass** dispatch announcing the first Moscow trial and the charge that he had masterminded a pro-fascist conspiracy to overthrow the Soviet state.

234. "Our Kind of Optimism." By permission of the Tamiment Library, New York University. Translated from the German by Duncan Williams. A letter to **Rene van Riel,** the pseudonym of a Hungarian who emigrated to Holland after the Hungarian revolution was crushed in 1919. At first a partisan of the Right Opposition, he accepted the need of a new International in 1933 and joined the Dutch section. Trotsky's **letter to Bep Spanjer,** a leader of the Leninist Youth Guard in Holland, "How to Win the Socialist Youth," April 27, 1936, is in *Writings 35–36*.

235. "Walter Held's Thesis on the Evolution of the Comintern." From the Reichsarchiv, Oslo. Translated from the German by Warren Dean. The May 26, 1936, letter—to Held—and the June 18 letter—to the IS—were both about a study (thesis) on the rise and fall of the Comintern that Held had written for the international conference that was held in July. The **duplication of effort** that Trotsky wanted Held to avoid concerned a conference resolution that Trotsky was to write himself ("The Fourth International and the Soviet Union," July 8, 1936, in *Writings 35–36*). The international conference recommended Held's study among the documents that it urged its affiliates to use for educational and propaganda work. It is reprinted in *Documents of the Fourth International.*

236. "Let's End This Nonsense." From the Reichsarchiv, Oslo. Translated from the German by Warren Dean. A letter to Walter Held.

237. "'State Capitalism' Data Sought." From the Reichsarchiv, Oslo. Translated from the German by Warren Dean. A letter to the exiled leadership (AK) of the German section (IKD). Trotsky's discussion of **"state capitalism"** in his book *The Revolution Betrayed*, which was not completed until August 1936, actually takes place in the ninth chapter of that book, and not in the closing chapter.

238. "The International Conference and the Dutch Section." From the Sneevliet archives, International Institute of Social History, Amsterdam, by whom Pierre Broue was given the right to copy and publish it in the French edition of Leon Trotsky's *Oeuvres*. Translated from the French by Harvey McArthur. On April 11, 1936, the IS proposed that the sections of the ICL meet in what came to be called the First International Conference for the Fourth International. The conference, originally slated for June, was to be preceded by a meeting or preconference in Norway, referred to for security reasons as an "editorial commission in Berne." The preconference was never held, partly because the leadership of the Dutch section refused to participate, and the conference itself was not held until the end of July in Paris (publicly referred to as "Geneva"). This letter to the Central

Committee of the RSAP was an effort by Trotsky to pressure its leaders into participation. The leaders of the Dutch section considered the American section's entry into the American SP in 1936 a **violation** of the Open Letter for the Fourth International which both sections had signed in 1935. The Dutch leaders Sneevliet and Schmidt were in charge of the **Amsterdam secretariat** of the ICL, which was set up in 1935 to serve as the provisional contact committee for the groups that signed the Open Letter and which had been assigned the task of preparing the coming international conference. The **London Bureau conference** which Sneevliet said the Dutch section was going to attend was not held until the end of October 1936, in Brussels, that is, after the ICL's international conference in July.

239. "Congratulations on a Good Publishing Job." By permission of the Tamiment Library, New York University. Translated from the German by Duncan Williams. A letter to Max Shachtman shortly before he left New York for the international conference to be held at the end of July.

240. "The London Bureau and the Fourth International." From *Documents of the Fourth International: The Formative Years (1933–40)*. A 1936 translation. Trotsky's authorship of this resolution, adopted at the ICL's international conference in July 1936, was established through a copy of the Russian text found in the Cannon archives, Library of Social History. The **Webbs—Sidney** (1859–1947) and **Beatrice** (1858–1943)—were British Fabian Socialists who had been hostile to the October Revolution but were sympathetic to the Stalin regime in the thirties. What Trotsky called their "compilation" was the book *Soviet Communism: A New Civilization?*, 1935. The first issues of *La Lutte ouvriere*, the paper of the French section, 1936–39, were seized by the People's Front government in the spring of 1936 and indictments were handed down against some of the section's leaders. The **Maximalists** were a wing of the Italian Socialist Party in exile.

241. "Deep Differences with the Dutch Comrades." From the Sneevliet archives, International Institute of Social History, Amster-

dam, by whom Pierre Broue was given the right to copy and publish it in the French edition of Leon Trotsky's *Oeuvres*. Translated from the French by Harvey McArthur. This was a letter to Max Shachtman, then in Amsterdam; Trotsky also sent a copy to Sneevliet. The Central Committee of the RSAP answered it in a letter on July 11, to which Trotsky responded in a two-part letter on July 15–16 explaining that the sharp form of his letter to Shachtman represented a final effort to make the Dutch think through the meaning of not attending the international conference (see "The Dutch Section and the International" in *Writings 35–36*). After Trotsky's July 15–16 letter, the Dutch leaders reconsidered and decided to participate in the conference despite their differences with Trotsky and the IS. **Muste's statement** was probably "The Situation in the United States of America," reprinted in *Documents of the Fourth International*. Trotsky had welcomed **personal visits** promised by Schmidt on one occasion and by Sneevliet on another, but in both cases the visits were not made. Instead of **August** at the end of his sixth paragraph, Trotsky may have meant to write "July," a month when he was hard at work completing *The Revolution Betrayed*, writing resolutions for the international conference, etc. **Jean Rous** (1908–1995) was a former SFIO member who joined the French section in 1932 and later became one of its leaders and a member of the IS until World War II. He left the Fourth International early in the war and later rejoined the SFIO.

242. "How the Conference Was and Wasn't Prepared." By permission of the Tamiment Library, New York University. A 1936 translation. A letter to A.J. Muste, who had held discussions with Sneevliet and Schmidt in Amsterdam after having discussions with Trotsky in Norway, and who was now on his way to Paris for the international conference.

243. "Molinier's Expulsion." The two letters to Erwin Wolf, then in Paris, are from the Cannon archives, Library of Social History, translated from the French by Naomi Allen; the letter to Otto Schuessler in Paris is from the Nazi *Voelkischer Beobachter* (Berlin), August 12, 1936, translated from the German by Duncan

Williams. Raymond Molinier and his group were expelled from the French section in December 1935 for violating discipline by publishing their own paper, *La Commune*. The two groups were unified at the beginning of June 1936 but factional warfare was resumed almost immediately. In mid-July Molinier and another member of his group traveled to Norway to complain to Trotsky about the way they were being treated. While they were there, the Central Committee of the French section expelled him for having used financial blackmail against the section. This expulsion was confirmed by the international conference at the end of July, and the Molinierists withdrew from the French section several weeks later. The split continued for another seven years (see *The Crisis of the French Section [1935–36]*).

244. **Jacques Desnots** (b. 1867), also known as Le Ricard, was a former member of the CP in charge of peasant problems and then of the petty-bourgeois Social Front organized by Gustave Bergery. He led a small group of ex-Social Frontists into the Commune group, which chose him as a member of the Political Bureau when it reunited with the French section. He accompanied Molinier to Norway for the Trotsky interview in July 1936 and quit the French section in protest against Molinier's expulsion. During the German occupation of France in World War II he became a collaborator.

245. A group of Norwegian fascists broke into Trotsky's home on August 5, 1936, the day he left for a vacation after having completed *The Revolution Betrayed*. One of the documents they succeeded in taking was a copy of this letter to Otto Schuessler, which was published in *Vrit Volk* on August 10 as evidence supporting the fascist demand that Trotsky be deported from Norway because he was using that country to continue his revolutionary intervention in France. Hitler's *Voelkischer Beobachter* reprinted the letter to Schuessler two days later in a dispatch from Oslo that was entitled "How Trotsky Stirs Things Up" and that called for "serious attention" to an investigation of Trotsky by the Norwegian authorities. In this retranslation corrections have been made of names used in the Nazi paper, which, among other things, identified Molinier as general secretary of the Fourth International. But the most interesting aspect of the Nazi article is that it shows the German Nazis were

supporting the Norwegian fascist demand for Trotsky's deportation from Norway three days before the Stalinists announced the first Moscow "confession" trial, where Trotsky was accused of collaborating with the Nazis in a plot to restore capitalism in the Soviet Union. Ironically, it was Stalin who pressured the Norwegian government into granting the fascist demand for Trotsky's deportation.

246. "When the Conference Selects the Leadership." By permission of the Tamiment Library, New York University. Translated from the German by Duncan Williams. A letter to Shachtman and others in Paris preparing the international conference. The conference adopted "Rules Governing the Leading International Bodies," which named and defined the functions of the General Council, International Secretariat and International Bureau; reprinted in *Documents of the Fourth International*.

247. "Advice for the Conference." By permission of Albert Glotzer. Translated from the French by Mavis Parr. A letter to Max Shachtman, then in Paris on the eve of the international conference. Two resolutions on the United States were presented to the conference (both reprinted in *Documents of the Fourth International*). One of these was a general statement on the American situation, briefly noting the American section's decision to enter the Socialist Party; this was supported by Muste, who had been opposed to the entry decision, along with Martin Abern. The other, probably written by Shachtman, expressed the conference's approval of the entry decision. Both documents were adopted by the conference, without any dispute. Although Muste and Trotsky favored **Martin Abern's nomination for the IS,** Shachtman was strongly opposed and Muste in the end did not make the nomination at the conference. Shachtman himself was elected to the IS on the understanding that he would return to Europe shortly after the conference to devote himself to this work, but this promise was not kept.

248. "GPU and Gestapo." By permission of the Harvard College Library. Translated from the French by Tom Barrett. The fragment of an article for the British press, dictated in French shortly after the

execution of all the defendants in the first Moscow trial, a few days before the Norwegian government stopped Trotsky from talking to reporters. **Anatoly V. Lunacharsky** (1875–1933), an Old Bolshevik, was the first Soviet commissar of public education. **Alexandra Kollontai** (1872–1952), an Old Bolshevik and the first woman ambassador, was a leader of the Workers' Opposition in Lenin's time and a supporter of Stalin when his bureaucratic caste was consolidating its power. **Grigory Sokolnikov** (1888–1939), an Old Bolshevik who held many government posts, was sentenced to ten years in prison at the 1937 Moscow trial. **Ivan T. Smilga** (1892–1937), an Old Bolshevik, military leader in the civil war and economic official in the twenties, was expelled as a Left Oppositionist in 1927. He capitulated in 1929 but disappeared, without trial or confession, at the time of the Moscow trials. For **Andrei Vyshinsky,** see note 428.

249. "A Possible Hunger Strike." From the Cannon archives, Library of Social History. Translated from the German by Robert Cantrick. Shortly after the end of the first Moscow trial, the Norwegian government cracked down on Trotsky, denying him the right to meet reporters, to write about "political questions current in other countries," to send uncensored mail abroad, to live where he pleased, etc. As reported in this letter, Trotsky refused to sign a statement accepting these and other new restrictions; as a result, he was immediately placed under house arrest in the home of Konrad Knudsen, the Labor Party deputy with whose family he had been living in Weksal. When Trotsky continued to refuse to sign such a statement, the government on September 2 took him and Natalia Sedova away from Weksal and interned them at Sundby, where he lived until he was deported to Mexico in December. This and the subsequent letter probably were written between Trotsky's house arrest on August 28 and his internment at Sundby. The reference to **party circles** in the last sentence suggests that it was written to a friendly member of the Norwegian Labor Party, perhaps Knudsen.

250. "Our Friends Should Not Wait." From the Cannon archives, Library of Social History. Translated from the German by Robert Cantrick. Unlike the preceding letter after Trotsky was put under

house arrest, this one was a message for his comrades abroad. "Lund" was a name later used by Trotsky to sign some of his articles in Mexico. A note above the letter said: "H. might read this and send it to Lyova [Sedov] and Erwin [Wolf] and to others." H. was probably Hjoerdis Knudsen, the wife of Wolf, who as Trotsky's secretary was deported shortly after Trotsky's house arrest.

251. "Translator Troubles, Publisher Problems." From the Cannon archives, Library of Social History. A 1936 translation from the German. After Trotsky's internment, government censors read all of his mail and refused to let most of it be delivered. This letter to Sara Weber in New York, excerpted by her, was one of the exceptions.

252. "Still Imprisoned." From the Sneevliet archives, International Institute of Social History, Amsterdam, by whom Pierre Broue was given the right to copy and publish it in the French edition of Leon Trotsky's *Oeuvres*. Translated from the French by Naomi Allen. A letter to Erwin Wolf, who was deported from Norway at the time Trotsky was interned. The **trial here** referred to legal proceedings against the fascists who had burglarized Trotsky's home in August 1936. Spectators and reporters were barred when the case was finally heard on December 11, but Trotsky presented a written version of his testimony in "In Closed Court" (see *Writings 35–36*).

253. "Still Gagged." *Biulleten Oppozitsii,* number 52–53, October 1936. Translated by Mavis Parr. A letter to Leon Sedov, whose *Red Book on the Moscow Trial* was published in the same number. Trotsky had to write the letter in French because the Norwegian passport bureau was not willing or able to handle letters in Russian.

254. "The Trip to Copenhagen." By permission of the Harvard College Library. Translated from the German by Robert Cantrick. The Norwegian censors allowed this letter to Leon Sedov in Paris to be mailed. In it Trotsky detailed a course of investigation and action he wanted his comrades to follow in exposing specific lies connected with the first Moscow trial. Several of the defendants at that trial "confessed" they had met with Trotsky when he was in

Copenhagen in 1932; one, **E.S. Goltsman,** claimed he had met Sedov there, although Sedov had been unable to get out of Germany while Trotsky was in Copenhagen. **"News" of Zinoviev's death** referred to a false report circulated while Trotsky was in Copenhagen. For **Jeanne Martin des Pallieres,** see note 296. **Erling Falk** (1887–1940) was the founder of *Mot Dag* and the tendency around it that started inside the Norwegian Labor Party and then became an independent centrist grouping. **Adolph Senin** was the pseudonym of Abraham Sobolevicius (b. 1904), who visited Trotsky in Copenhagen in November 1932, shortly before he and his brother Ruvin, also known as Roman Well, split some members away from the German section and led them into the German CP. Many years later, when he was being tried as a Soviet spy in the United States, Senin-Sobolevicius testified that he and his brother had been operating as GPU agents since 1931.

255. "Reading Ibsen Again." From the Cannon archives, Library of Social History. Translated from the German by Russell Block. These were two letters to Haakon Meyer (1896–1989), director of the National Theater in Oslo and a NAP member since 1915, who had protested the government's treatment of Trotsky; his pacifism in World War II led him to collaboration with the Nazis and he fled to Sweden after being condemned to death by a Norwegian court. Trotsky's first article about the great Norwegian dramatist **Henrik Ibsen** (1828–1906) was printed during his first exile, in 1901. His interest in Ibsen was revived in 1936 when he detected similarities between Norwegian officials persecuting him and some of the despicable characters in Ibsen's plays. **Johan Scharffenberg** was a NAP official who had written in *Arbeiderbladet:* "Trotsky says he can prove the accusations made against him at the Moscow trials were false. If so, it is his moral duty immediately to go to a Moscow court." "An Answer to Mr. Scharffenberg," August 24, 1936, is in *Writings 35–36.*

256. "Pyatakov and the Trial in Novosibirsk." By permission of the Harvard College Library. Translated from the German by Russell Block. This was a letter to Michael Puntervold (1879–1937), a

Norwegian attorney who represented Trotsky's legal interests while he was interned. **Yuri Pyatakov** (1890–1937) was an Old Bolshevik; Lenin regarded him and Bukharin as the two ablest young men in the party. A Left Oppositionist, he was expelled in 1927, but recanted and was reinstated in 1928, and held high industrial posts until the purges of 1936. Charges against him were made by witnesses in the November 1936 **trial in Novosibirsk,** a tune-up for the second Moscow trial, in January 1937, where he was one of the principal defendants and was sentenced to death. The trial in Novosibirsk, allegedly of Ukrainian and Siberian Trotskyists, featured nine defendants accused of industrial sabotage at the orders of Pyatakov; six were executed after the trial. **Yakov Drobnis** (1890–1937) was an Old Bolshevik with a heroic record in the civil war. Through membership in the Democratic Centralism Group, he joined the United Opposition in 1926. Expelled in 1927, he recanted in 1929 and was reinstated in the party and assigned to work in Siberia. Arrested just before the first Moscow trial, he was a government witness at the Novosibirsk trial and a defendant at the second Moscow trial, where he was sentenced to death. **Ivan Smirnov** (1881–1936) was an Old Bolshevik with a long record of arrests and escapes under czarism and a leader of the Soviet victory over the counterrevolution in Siberia. He was people's commissar of communications, 1923–27, and then was expelled as a Left Oppositionist. He capitulated in 1929, was reinstated, and was put in charge of an automobile plant. Arrested in 1933, he was held in prison until the first Moscow trial, where he was sentenced to death.

257. "Posthumus and the Archives." By permission of the Harvard College Library. Translated from the French by Mavis Parr. This was a letter to Leon Sedov, written in French instead of Russian to expedite its handling by the Norwegian censors, who permitted it to be mailed. Trotsky listed the letters he had sent to and received from France in the hope of learning which ones had been seized by the censors, who refused to supply him with such information. **Nicolaas Wilhelmus Posthumus** (1880–1960) was a Dutch Social Democrat and professor. In 1935 he set out to create a place to preserve valuable documentary and archival material about the work-

ing class movement which had been dispersed throughout Europe by the fascist victories. That year he founded the International Institute of Social History in Amsterdam, with the financial help of the Central Workingmen's Institute and Deposit Bank. In 1939 he evacuated all of the institute's material to Oxford, England. During the war the German occupation authorities shut down the institute, which was not reopened in Amsterdam until 1951. Posthumus served as its director until he retired in 1952. Although Trotsky declined Posthumus's 1935 offer to store his complete archives at Amsterdam, he did turn over to the institute the material later published as *The Trotsky Papers*. **R. Pero** was the pseudonym of a refugee from Central Europe who joined the Left Opposition in France in 1932 while he was still a student and became a leader of the French section's youth group in 1936. A year later he was exposed as an agent of either the Nazis or the GPU and was expelled.

258. "Answers to a Mexican Press Service." By permission of the Harvard College Library. Translated from the French by Dan Rosenheim. Dictated in French after an interview by a provincial press service two weeks after Trotsky had arrived in Mexico.

259. "Two Crooked Lawyers." By permission of the Harvard College Library. Translated from the Russian by Donald Kennedy. This was written shortly after the end of the second Moscow trial (January 23–30, 1937), featuring Pyatakov and Radek as the best known of the seventeen defendants. All were convicted; thirteen were executed, four were imprisoned. Trotsky's analysis of this trial is in *Writings 36–37* and *The Case of Leon Trotsky*. **Denis N. Pritt** (1888–1972) was a British attorney and Labour MP, 1935–50. An uncritical admirer of Stalin, he called the first Moscow trial "an example for the world." Trotsky answered his pamphlet in "Shame!" December 18, 1936, in *Writings 35–36*. **Raymond Rosenmark** (1895–1950)**,** a French attorney, defended the Moscow trials through his position in the League for the Rights of Man, a civil liberties organization.

260. "Postponing the Swiss Trial." By permission of Pierre Broue. Translated from the German by Duncan Williams. When

Trotsky was interned and denied his right to sue his slanderers in the Norwegian courts, he decided to try to break the wall of silence around him through court action against his slanderers in other European countries. One such lawsuit was filed in his behalf in Basle, Switzerland, with a number of Swiss Stalinists and Comintern functionaries named as defendants. After his arrival in Mexico, Trotsky decided it would be better tactically for the Swiss trial to be postponed until after an American-based commission of inquiry had done its work, and that was the aim of this letter to European comrades who had worked to prepare the Swiss trial. According to an undated press release from the IS in the spring of 1937, the Swiss courts decided against the Stalinist defendants, awarding damages of 10,000 Swiss francs to the plaintiff, Trotsky. His **New York speech,** "I Stake My Life," February 9, 1937, is in *Leon Trotsky Speaks.*

261. "Answers to the *Chicago Daily News.*" By permission of the Harvard College Library. With the second question and answer deleted, this interview by Howard Vincent O'Brien, entitled "Stalin's Clique in Death Agony, Says Trotzky," was published in the *Chicago Daily News* on March 5, 1937. **Walter Duranty** (1884–1957), a *New York Times* correspondent in Moscow for many years, supported the Stalinists against the Opposition and defended the Moscow trials. His book was *Duranty Reports Russia* (Viking, 1934).

262. **Diego Rivera** (1886–1957) was the noted Mexican painter. A founder of the Mexican CP, he left it in 1927 over the expulsion of the Russian Left Opposition. He helped to get a Mexican visa for Trotsky and was his host until 1939, when political differences led him to break with the Fourth International. Trotsky's discussion of the break is documented in *Writings 38–39.*

263. General **Lazaro Cardenas** (1895–1970), president of Mexico, 1934–40, headed the only government in the world that would grant asylum to Trotsky in the last years of his life. His term in office was marked by agrarian reform, industrial development, clashes with the Roman Catholic Church, support of the Spanish republic in the civil war, and expropriation of foreign-owned oil properties.

264. "A Correction and Requests." By permission of Albert Glotzer. Dictated in English. A letter to **Max Shachtman,** who had reported an improvement in **relations** among the leaders of the American section after Trotsky had criticized their policy in the American Committee for the Defense of Leon Trotsky (see especially his letters of March 15, 1937, in *Writings 36–37*). For the **inquiry commission** headed by John Dewey, see note 279. At the first Moscow trial in 1936, the **Hotel Bristol** in Copenhagen was sworn to be the site of a meeting at which Leon Sedov gave terrorist instructions to coconspirators in 1932; Sedov was easily able to show he had not been in Denmark in 1932 and it turned out the Hotel Bristol had been torn down in 1917. **Valerian Kuibyshev** (1888–1935) was a Stalinist in many high posts before becoming chairman of the Supreme Council of National Economy in 1926. The **article on anti-Semitism** in the USSR, entitled "Thermidor and Anti-Semitism," February 22, 1937, will be found in *Leon Trotsky on the Jewish Question*.

265. "Stalin's Latest Threats." By permission of the Harvard College Library. Dictated in English. On March 28, 1937, two months after the second Moscow trial, Stalin made a speech in Moscow demanding "new methods for uprooting and dispersing these [Trotskyist] enemies," who "have degenerated into an unprincipled gang of wreckers, murderers and hired agents of foreign secret [services]."

266. "Opinions and Information." By permission of Albert Glotzer. Translated by Harold R. Isaacs in 1937. A letter to the IS; the first paragraph, in another translation, is in *Writings 36–37*. In March 1937 there was a **by-election** for a parliamentary seat from Brussels in which a fascist leader was opposed by Premier Paul van Zeeland of the Catholic Party. The Belgian Labor Party and the CP, seeking to help van Zeeland, did not run their own candidates. Neither did the Belgian section of the MFI, whose majority, led by Lesoil and Dauge, also wanted to help van Zeeland win. The minority of the section's leadership, headed by Vereecken, opposed this policy and wanted to run its own candidate. Trotsky and the IS condemned the majority position, but also dissociated themselves from Vereecken because of his opportunist attitude to the Spanish POUM. **Fenner**

Brockway's maneuvers around the commission of inquiry were discussed in "Fenner Brockway, Pritt No. 2," March 6, 1937, in *Writings 36–37*. **Carleton Beals** (1893–1979), an American journalist, served on the commission of inquiry in Mexico in April 1937, and then tried to discredit it by resigning in the middle of the hearings. **Kingsley Martin** (1897–1969) was an editor of the British *New Statesman and Nation*, 1930–60. According to Isaac Deutscher, Martin, when he met Trotsky, was concerned with "defending the honor" of his friend Pritt and insensitive about the honor of the defendants in the Moscow trials. Martin's version was in the *New Statesman*, April 10, 1937. **Bernard Wolfe** (1915–1985), a member of the American section, was Trotsky's English-language secretary for several months in 1937. Many years after leaving the movement he wrote a novel about Trotsky.

267. "Obstacles in Britain." From the Cannon archives, Library of Social History. Dictated in English. **Charles Sumner** and A. Boyd were pseudonyms of Hilary Sumner-Boyd (1911–1976), secretary of the British Revolutionary Socialist League and a delegate to the founding conference of the Fourth International in 1938. In 1937 he was secretary of the British Committee for the Defence of Leon Trotsky, which was finding it difficult to get much positive response in the labor movement or among intellectuals. **Henry N. Brailsford** (1873–1958) was a pacifist in World War I and editor of the ILP's paper in the twenties.

268. "No Reason to Complain." Arbetarrorelsens Arkiv, Stockholm. Translated from the German by Russell Block. A letter to Haakon Meyer, who had sent Trotsky a copy of a Norwegian book he had edited about the Moscow trials, *Bak Moskvaprozessene*. Trotsky's deportation made him **something of a factor** in Norwegian politics by contributing to the establishment of a Norwegian section of the MFI after he had left the country. **Leif Ragnvald Konstad** (1889–194?) was the head of the Norwegian central passport bureau, a sympathizer or secret member of Quisling's fascist movement, and the government functionary in charge of interning Trotsky before he was deported.

269. "Literary Theft." From the Cannon archives, Library of Social History. Translated from the Russian by George Saunders. A letter to Sara Weber. **Mikhail Okudzhava** had been a Left Oppositionist, like Mdivani; both were sentenced to death by the Georgia Supreme Court and shot in July 1937.

270. "A Pamphlet on Spain." From the Cannon archives, Library of Social History. Dictated in English. A letter to **Charles Rumford Walker** (1893–1974), the author of *American City* (about the Minneapolis teamster strikes), who was then acting as Trotsky's literary agent. Among other projects Walker was trying to market was a plan, which was never carried out, for Trotsky to prepare a continuation of his 1929 autobiography, utilizing already written material such as the *Diary in Exile, 1935*, later published posthumously. **The Nation** and **The New Republic** were liberal weeklies whose coverage of the Moscow trials and the Spanish civil war reflected the influences of Stalinist People's Frontism in 1937.

271. "The International Conference Must Be Postponed." By permission of Albert Glotzer. Translated from the German by Duncan Williams. Trotsky had hoped that another international conference could be held by the end of 1937, but in this letter he recognized that the **"consultation"** would not be possible before February 1938; in fact, it did not take place until September, when the Fourth International was formally founded. **Erwin Wolf** (1902–1937), who wrote under the name of Nicolle Braun, was a member of the IS who had served as Trotsky's secretary in Norway. In Spain on an IS mission in the summer of 1937, he was kidnapped by the GPU and murdered. Trotsky's statements on this case are in *Writings 36–37*. **Tioli,** whose address in Barcelona Wolf used to receive his mail, was suspected of helping the GPU to get its hands on Wolf. **Hjoerdis Wolf,** daughter of Konrad Knudsen, Trotsky's host in Norway, had married Wolf before he was deported from Norway during Trotsky's internment. Although **Sneevliet's struggle** against the MFI came to a head in 1937, a public break did not come until 1938. **Julian Gorkin** (1902–1987) was briefly a member of the Spanish Left Opposition in its early days; he became a leader of the POUM at its formation.

August Thalheimer (1884–1948) was Brandler's principal lieutenant in the German CP before their expulsion and in the Communist Right Opposition, whose international committee was called **IVKO**. The **draft program** that Trotsky was thinking about in September 1937 became known as the Transitional Program after it was completed in April 1938, and was the major document adopted by the founding conference of the Fourth International. **Theodor** was a code name for the IS. **S.L. Johre** was the pseudonym of Josef Weber (1901–1959), a leader of the German section in exile; during the war he was the principal author of the "three theses on democracy" that revised the basic program of the Fourth International. **Jan Bur** was the pseudonym of Walter Nettelbeck (1902–1976), a German CP member who joined the Left Opposition after Hitler came to power. He broke with the movement around the end of 1937 after organizing his own faction in the German section.

272. "The U.S. Recession and a New Political Orientation." By permission of Albert Glotzer. Dictated in English. A letter to James P. Cannon, one of several Trotsky wrote at this time as contributions to the American section's preconvention discussion before the founding of the Socialist Workers Party at the end of the year. Under Roosevelt's New Deal the American economy had been making a slow recovery from the low points of the Great Depression, but in 1937 it experienced a sharp recession. This letter indicates that Trotsky was the first to suggest that the American section should reconsider its position against advocating a **labor party,** which was done in 1938. Trotsky's **article concerning the coming war** was "On the Threshold of a New World War," August 9, 1937, in *Writings 36–37*. The **CIO** (Congress of Industrial Organizations) was created in 1935 as a committee in the American Federation of Labor seeking to organize industry-wide unions; the CIO unions were expelled from the AFL in 1938 and functioned as a separate federation until 1955, when the AFL and CIO were merged. **Rae Spiegel** was the name used by Raya Dunayevskaya (1910–1987), a member of the American section and Trotsky's Russian-language secretary, 1937–38; she quit the SWP in 1940 with the Shachtmanites, rejoined in 1947, and quit again in 1951. **Max Sterling** was a member of the American section, visiting his

wife, Rae Spiegel. **Joseph Hansen** (1910–1979) was a secretary of Trotsky, 1937–40. His accounts of Trotsky's life in Mexico, including his assassination, are in *Leon Trotsky, The Man and His Work* (Merit Publishers, 1969) and the introduction to Pathfinder's 1970 edition of *My Life*. After several years as an editor of *The Militant* and *International Socialist Review*, and as international representative of the SWP, he was editor of *Intercontinental Press*. **Peter Granger** was a name used for Peter Berlinrut, formerly a member of the American Workers Party in New Jersey. In a memoir forty years later ("A Talk with Trotsky," *Harper's*, February 1977) he said he had had little sympathy for Trotsky's ideas at the time. **Ted Selander** (1903–1996) was an AWP and SWP leader well known for leading unemployed and union struggles; he withdrew from political activity in the 1950s. Contrary to what Trotsky's secretary Rae Spiegel said, Selander was in Mexico City only four days, and he asked her by phone for an appointment with Trotsky on each of these days. **Suzanne La Follette** (1893–1983), a writer and editor, was secretary of the Dewey commission of inquiry, who met Trotsky during the hearings in April 1937. **Anton Grylewicz,** a leader of the German section living in Czechoslovakia, had been arrested and held in prison on false charges initiated by the GPU that he was a Gestapo agent.

273. "An Article on Kronstadt." From the Cannon archives, Library of Social History. Dictated in English. A letter to **Jac Wasserman** (b. 1908), director of Pioneer Publishers in New York. The **Kronstadt** naval base was the site of an uprising of sailors against the Bolshevik regime in 1921. The rebels demanded soviets without Communists and opposed many of the stern measures the Bolsheviks had taken during the civil war to safeguard the revolution. The uprising was suppressed by the Bolsheviks. It was raised as a political issue again in 1937 by anarchists and others arguing that Stalin's latest crimes were only a continuation of those committed by the Bolsheviks in the time of Lenin and Trotsky and that there was a basic identity between Leninism and Stalinism. Everything Lenin and Trotsky wrote on the subject is in *Kronstadt* (Pathfinder, 1979).

274. **Socialist Appeal** was the monthly journal of the Fourth Internationalist caucus in the American SP, 1936–37. When the

members of this group were expelled in the summer of 1937, they made it into a weekly, and it became the official paper of the Socialist Workers Party, 1938–41. Its name was then changed to *The Militant*.

275. "Suggestions for a Pamphlet on Kronstadt." By permission of Albert Glotzer. Translated from the French by Susan Wald. A letter to Leon Sedov in Paris. Sedov was Trotsky's first choice to write an article or pamphlet on Kronstadt, but he was too occupied with other work. In the end it was written by John G. Wright in New York. **Yekaterina D. Kuskova** (1869–1958), a journalist, wrote the **1899 manifesto** "Credo" which was a target of Lenin's polemics against economism. She clashed with the Soviet government over its policy on the 1921 famine, and later was deported from the USSR.

276. "An Article on the Soviet State." From the Cannon archives, Library of Social History. Dictated in English. The article was "Not a Workers' and Not a Bourgeois State?" November 25, 1937; it was published first in an internal bulletin containing articles written for the discussion that preceded the first SWP convention and is reprinted in *Writings 37–38*.

277. **James Burnham** (1905–1987) was a leader of the AWP, the WPUS and the SWP. In 1937 he and Joseph Carter introduced a resolution ("thesis") holding that the Soviet Union no longer was a workers' state but that it should be defended against imperialist attack so long as it maintained nationalized property. This characterization of the Soviet state was decisively rejected by the SWP's founding convention. After the Stalin-Hitler pact and the start of World War II, he rejected defense of the Soviet Union altogether, broke with Marxism, and split from the SWP with Shachtman. He later became an ultraright conservative.

278. "Sale of the Archives." From the Cannon archives, Library of Social History. Dictated in English. This letter to Jan Frankel initiated the efforts of Trotsky's comrades in the United States to sell his collection of correspondence and articles to a library. Trotsky expanded the list of things he would turn over to such an institu-

tion before negotiations were completed with the Harvard College Library in 1940.

279. Trotsky had given the **Commission of Inquiry Into the Charges Made Against Leon Trotsky in the Moscow Trials,** also known as the Dewey Commission, copies of a great many documents from his archives to support the testimony he presented orally at its hearings in Mexico in April 1937. After the Commission reached its verdict (see the 1938 book *Not Guilty,* reprinted by Pathfinder, 1972, 2008), it had no further use for these documents; they were ultimately deposited at the Harvard College Library.

280. **Albert Goldman** (1897–1960) left the American CP to join the CLA in 1933, left the CLA to join the SP in 1934, and was one of the left-wing leaders expelled from the SP in 1937. He was Trotsky's counsel at the Dewey Commission hearings and thereafter his U.S. legal representative. He was chief counsel as well as a defendant in the 1941 Minneapolis trial, and left the SWP in 1946 to join the Shachtmanite Workers Party. He later supported the U.S. government in the Korean War.

281. **John Dewey** (1859–1952) was the noted educator and philosopher who served at the age of seventy-eight as chairman of the commission investigating the Moscow trials. An exchange between him and Trotsky over means and ends in 1938 is in the collection *Their Morals and Ours* (Pathfinder, 1973).

282. Trotsky explained in a subsequent letter that his contract with the International Institute of Social History was somewhat more complicated than the way it was presented here.

283. "Kronstadt and the Commission's Function." From the Cannon archives, Library of Social History. Dictated in English.

284. **Wendelin Thomas** (1884–1947) was a leader of the German naval revolt that helped end World War I in November 1918, and a Communist deputy in the German Reichstag, 1920–24, who moved to the United States after Hitler came to power. He was a member of the Dewey Commission, which had reached its verdict in 1937 but had not yet released its full report *(Not Guilty)*. Trotsky's earlier reply to him, "The Questions of Wendelin Thomas," July 6, 1937, is in *Writings 36–37*.

285. **John G. Wright's article,** "The Truth About Kronstadt," was printed in *The New International,* February 1938, in abridged form. It appears in full as an appendix to *Kronstadt* by Lenin and Trotsky (Pathfinder, 1979).

286. "Thomas's Letter and Dewey's Speech." From the Cannon archives, Library of Social History. Dictated in English. A letter to Jan Frankel, who was assisting the Dewey Commission's staff in the preparation of its final report.

287. Dewey had made one **speech** on December 12, 1937, when he and other members of the commission discussed their verdict at a public meeting in New York, and another the next day in a program for the Columbia Broadcasting System's radio network.

288. **Francisco Zamora Padilla** (1890–1985) was born in Nicaragua and was granted Mexican citizenship because of his outstanding work as a journalist in defense of the Mexican revolution. He became a well-known economist and a Marxist, an editorial writer of *El Universal,* and a former executive committee member of the Mexican Confederation of Workers, before agreeing to serve on the Dewey Commission in 1937. He was not a member of the Fourth International although he collaborated on the *Clave* editorial board. **Otto Ruehle** (1874–1943) was a former Social Democratic member of the German Reichstag, a founder of the German CP and the ultraleft KAPD, and a biographer of Karl Marx; he lived in Mexico City. **Carlo Tresca** (1878–1943) was an Italian-American anarchist and editor of *Il Martello* (The Hammer); his murder on a New York street was never solved.

289. "Eastman and *The Young Lenin.*" From the Cannon archives, Library of Social History. Translated from the French by Phil Courneyeur. Trotsky's apprehensions about Eastman's translation of the first volume of the Lenin biography proved to be well founded. Although Eastman had the Russian manuscript in 1935, he still had not completed the translation at the time of Trotsky's death in 1940. Explaining that the Russian manuscript had disappeared in the 1930s and that he found it in his home thirty years later, he did not give the translation to a publisher until the late 1960s, shortly before his death. This was a letter to Jan Frankel.

290. "Explanation of a Complaint." From the Cannon archives, Library of Social History. Dictated in English. This was a letter to John G. Wright, who had been offended by Trotsky's complaint that his corrections to Wright's translation of "Ninety Years of the *Communist Manifesto*" had been ignored (see "Letter to the *New International*, December 15, 1937, in *Writings 37–38*).

291. "Why I Can't Pay Now." From the Cannon archives, Library of Social History. Dictated in English. This was a letter to Ragnar Christophersen, an attorney in Oslo representing the widow of Michael Puntervold, Trotsky's Norwegian lawyer in 1936. After Trotsky's departure for Mexico, Puntervold sent him a bill for lawyer's fees that Trotsky considered excessive. Before Puntervold's death they agreed to abide by the results of arbitration in the Norwegian courts, which eventually upheld Puntervold's claims.

292. "Jules Romains on Lenin." From the Cannon archives, Library of Social History. Dictated in English. A letter to Jan Frankel. **Jules Romains** (1885–1972) was a French novelist, poet, and dramatist, whose most famous work, an epic series of novels (epopee), was published in the United States in fourteen volumes under the title *Men of Good Will* (Knopf, 1933–46). Trotsky thought Romains was an "incomparable artist."

293. "Marx's Living Thoughts." From the Cannon archives, Library of Social History. Dictated in English. A letter to SWP leaders in New York. *The Living Thoughts of Karl Marx* was published by Longmans, Green in 1939, with an introduction by Trotsky and selections from *Capital* by Otto Ruehle. Trotsky's introduction as it was before the publisher abridged it is in *Marxism in Our Time* (Pathfinder, 1970).

294. The **First International,** or International Workingmen's Association, of which Marx was a leader, existed from 1864 to 1876.

295. "Leon Sedov's Papers." By permission of Tamara Deutscher. Translated from the French by Phil Courneyeur. Leon Sedov died under mysterious circumstances in a Paris hospital on February 16,

1938. In the subsequent investigation the police seized the papers in his home. This message to the French ambassador in Mexico, personally delivered by Jean van Heijenoort, sought to make sure that care would be taken to prevent the GPU from getting access to the papers. It was signed by Natalia Sedova as well as Trotsky.

296. **Jeanne Martin des Pallieres** (1897–1961) was a founder of the French section. Formerly married to Raymond Molinier, she became the companion of Leon Sedov and lived with him until his death, but she remained a member of the Molinier group that was expelled in 1935 and in bitter conflict with the French section until the war.

297. **Ignace Reiss** was the pseudonym of Ignace Poretsky (1899–1937), a GPU official who broke with Stalin in the summer of 1937 and joined the Fourth Internationalists. He was murdered by GPU agents in Switzerland in September 1937.

298. "Questions About Sedov's Death." By permission of Tamara Deutscher. Translated from the French by Phil Courneyeur. This letter to Henri Molinier was the first of several Trotsky wrote as it became increasingly clear that Sedov had been murdered; others are in *Writings 37–38*.

299. The **new trial,** which had just been announced, was the third Moscow trial, which opened on March 2 and lasted until March 13. The most famous of the twenty-one defendants were Bukharin and Rykov. All the defendants "confessed," all were convicted, and all were executed except three who were imprisoned.

300. **L. Paulsen** and L. Yakovlev were pseudonyms of Lilia (Lola) Estrine (1898–1981), who had joined the group in Paris helping Sedov to publish the *Biulletin Oppozitsii* in 1935. Later she married David Dallin (1889–1962) in the United States. **Alexis Bardin** (1905–1994) was the eldest of three brothers active in the French section; Trotsky had worked closely with him in Domene.

301. **Sieva** was the nickname of Vsievolod Volkov (1926–2023), the son of Trotsky's daughter Zinaida, who committed suicide in 1933, and Platon Volkov, who disappeared in Stalin's prisons during the thirties. After his mother's death, young Volkov lived with his uncle, Leon Sedov, and Jeanne Martin. After Sedov's death, the

custody of the child became a subject of bitter contention and legal action between Trotsky and Martin, who had Raymond Molinier's support. The courts decided in Trotsky's favor and in 1939 Sieva joined his grandparents in Mexico.

302. "Krestinsky's Repudiation." *Excelsior* (Mexico City), March 3, 1938, where it was entitled "Trotsky Predicts Krestinsky Will Plead Guilty to Save His Family." Retranslated from the French by Mavis Parr. **Nikolai Krestinsky** (1883–1938), an Old Bolshevik, broke with the Left Opposition in 1927 but was tried and executed after the third Moscow trial in 1938. He repudiated his "confession" on the first day of the trial, and then withdrew his repudiation at a later session. Trotsky said that both acts were part of the GPU's scenario for the trial ("To the Attention of Thinking People," March 3, 1938, in *Writings 37–38*).

303. "The Third Moscow Trial." By permission of the Harvard College Library. Translated from the French by Richard Lesnik. This was an exclusive statement for Havas, the French news agency.

304. **Fyodor Butenko** (b. 1905) was a Stalinist diplomat who defected to fascism early in 1938, announcing in Rome that he represented a widespread fascist sentiment in the USSR.

305. **Neville Chamberlain** (1869–1940) became Conservative prime minister of Britain in 1937. His new orientation in 1938 led him to try to appease Hitler through the Munich agreements on Czechoslovakia.

306. **Arkady Rosengolts** (1889–1938), a Soviet official who renounced previous connections with the Left Opposition in 1927 and became part of the Stalinist apparatus, was a defendant in the third Moscow trial. He was convicted and executed. **Mikhail Tukhchevsky** (1893–1937), a veteran commander of the civil war and a marshal of the USSR, was one of the first military figures charged with treason and executed in June 1937, at the start of Stalin's purge of the Soviet armed forces.

307. Pyatakov's testimony at the second Moscow trial about his alleged **flight to Oslo** to meet with Trotsky in December 1935 was disproved by Norwegian officials even before the trial had ended.

308. "Answers to Mrs. Celarie." By permission of Pierre Broue. Translated from the French by Richard Lesnik. **Lev Karakhan** (1889–1937) was deputy commissar for foreign affairs in 1918 and Soviet ambassador in China in the mid-twenties. He was executed without a public trial, like Old Bolshevik **Abel Yenukidze** (1877–1937), former secretary of the Soviet Central Executive Committee and former member of the Central Control Commission and Central Committee of the CPSU. It was widely believed that Yenukidze did not live to occupy the dock at the third Moscow trial because he refused to "confess."

309. "Roosevelt and a Visa." From the Cannon archives, Library of Social History. Translated from the French by J.R. Fidler. This letter to Jan Frankel concerned a statement by President Roosevelt at a press conference in Washington March 25, 1938, declaring that the United States would continue to be a land of refuge for victims of political or religious persecution, including "Catholics in Barcelona; antifascists in Italy; Trotskyists in Russia; Jews, Protestants and Catholics in Germany and Austria."

310. **Morris L. Ernst** (1888–1976) was for many years general counsel of the American Civil Liberties Union and a personal friend of Roosevelt. In 1934 he tried unsuccessfully to get Roosevelt to admit Trotsky to the United States after he was ordered to leave France.

311. "Carlo Tresca Is a Target." From the Cannon archives, Library of Social History. Dictated in English. This was a letter to Margaret De Silver (1890–1962), a member of the American Committee for the Defense of Leon Trotsky, whose companion was Carlo Tresca.

312. **Roland Abbiatte,** also known as Rossi, was the chief assassin in the GPU killing of Ignace Reiss. When he fled Switzerland in 1937, papers left behind showed that he had been planning to go to Mexico, undoubtedly to help prepare an attempt on Trotsky. **Francisco Mujica** (1884–1954) was minister of communications and public works in Cardenas's cabinet. In February 1938 a man claiming to have been sent by Mujica tried to deliver large packages at Trotsky's home. The guards refused to accept them and he took

them away, promising to return the next day with credentials from Mujica. But Mujica said the whole story was a lie.

313. "Finishing the Transitional Program." From the Cannon archives, Library of Social History. Dictated in English. A letter to Cannon, who had been part of a Socialist Workers Party delegation that visited Trotsky in March 1938 and discussed preparations for the founding conference of the Fourth International, including the writing of its chief programmatic document, popularly known as the **Transitional Program.** For transcripts of their discussions, see *The Transitional Program for Socialist Revolution* (Pathfinder, 1977).

314. Trotsky's **letter to the League of Nations,** March 31, 1938, renewed the request he had made in 1936 for an opportunity to testify before a projected League of Nations tribunal on terrorism so that he could indict the Stalin regime for its crimes. The letter is in *Writings 37–38*.

315. **Rose Karsner** (1889–1968) was a founder of both the CP and the Left Opposition in the U.S. She was Cannon's close political collaborator and companion from 1924. She was part of the SWP delegation to Mexico in March 1938.

316. "A Russian Encyclopedia." From the Cannon archives, Library of Social History. Dictated in English. A letter to Sara Weber.

317. In the spring of 1938 Trotsky began working on a biography of Stalin at the same time that he continued work on his biography of Lenin. The Stalin work, uncompleted at Trotsky's death, was published, with unauthorized interpolations by the editor, under the title *Stalin: An Appraisal of the Man and His Influence* (Harper & Brothers, New York, 1941).

318. Part of Trotsky's article, "On the Threshold of a New World War," August 9, 1937, was published in *The Yale Review,* June 1938, under the title "If a New World War Comes." The full article is in *Writings 36–37*.

319. "Political Personality and the Milieu." From the Cannon archives, Library of Social History. A 1938 translation from the French. The central part of this letter (without the date, the opening or the

final paragraphs) was included by Pierre Naville in his *Trotsky vivant* and, after Naville declined the *Writings* editors' request for the missing parts, was translated in that incomplete form in *Writings 38–39*, where it was entitled "The Individual in History."

320. The **Girondists** were a moderate bourgeois republican tendency in the French Convention (legislative assembly) in 1791. They wanted to overthrow the old regime but feared the city poor and peasant masses who were capable of doing it; they therefore wavered between the revolution and the counterrevolution, finally going over to the latter.

321. **Georges Danton** (1759–1795), a leader of the right wing of the Jacobins, was minister of justice from 1792, and was guillotined less than a year after the Girondists.

322. **Maximilien Robespierre** (1758–94) became the Jacobin leader and effective head of state in 1793. He was overthrown by the counterrevolution of the Ninth of Thermidor and was guillotined.

323. **Albert Mathiez** (1874–1932) was a French historian and author of *The French Revolution* (Knopf, 1928) and *After Robespierre* (Knopf, 1931).

324. "Muenzenberg's Expulsion." From the Cannon archives, Library of Social History. Translated from the French by David Segal. A letter to Jan Frankel.

325. **Walter Krivitsky** (1899–1941) was chief of Soviet military intelligence in Western Europe before his defection in December 1937. He revealed many Soviet intelligence secrets and wrote *In Stalin's Secret Service* (Harper and Brothers, 1939). He evolved to the right politically and later became associated with the Mensheviks. He died in Washington under mysterious circumstances six months after Trotsky was assassinated. **Alexander Barmine** (1899–1987), a veteran of the Russian civil war and a Soviet diplomat, most recently in Greece, broke with Moscow the same week as Krivitsky. He wrote *Memoirs of a Soviet Diplomat: Twenty Years in the Service of the USSR* (1938).

326. "Molinier and the International Conference." From the Cannon archives, Library of Social History. Translated from the

French by J.R. Fidler. This letter to Alexis Bardin (1905–1994) in France outlined the tactic Trotsky favored for handling the Molinier group's anticipated appeal for reinstatement at the founding conference of the Fourth International, which was then being prepared and was held in September 1938. Other letters on the subject are in *Writings 37–38*.

327. The **PCI** (Internationalist Communist Party) was the name of the Molinier group, 1936–39. Its paper was *La Commune*.

328. The **POI** (Internationalist Workers Party) was the name of the French section, 1936–39. Its paper was *La Lutte ouvriere*.

329. "An Introduction Worthy of Rosa Luxemburg." From the Cannon archives, Library of Social History. Dictated in English. A letter to Jac Wasserman in New York.

330. **I Confess** was a novel about the Moscow trials by Wolf Weiss, a young German refugee in the Soviet Union who was arrested during the purges but managed to escape.

331. **Andre Breton** (1896–1966) was the French poet, essayist, critic, and founder of the surrealist movement. He broke with the Stalinists in 1935, and visited Trotsky in Mexico in 1938, where they collaborated in producing a manifesto, "Towards a Free Revolutionary Art," reprinted in *Art and Revolution* (Pathfinder, 1972). **Meyer Schapiro** (1904–1996), art historian and professor in New York, was one of the anti-Stalinist intellectuals associated with *Partisan Review*.

332. "Fusion with the Lovestoneites?" From the Cannon archives, Library of Social History. After Trotsky and Jack Weber had a discussion about the slogan of a Workers' and Farmers' Government, reprinted in *The Transitional Program for Socialist Revolution*, they also discussed the possibility of a fusion between the Lovestoneites and the SWP. This part of the transcript, uncorrected by the participants, was not published anywhere at the time. The suggested fusion was not pursued by either party.

333. **Bertram D. Wolfe** (1896–1977) was a leader of the Lovestoneites until their dissolution in 1940. He later moved to the right, eventually supporting Nixon in the 1972 elections. His book about

Lenin, Trotsky, and Stalin is *Three Who Made a Revolution* (Dial Press, New York, 1948).

334. **Homer Martin** (1902–1968), a former preacher, became president of the United Auto Workers, CIO, in 1936. He later tried to lead the union back into the AFL, with the aid of the Lovestoneites. When the members prevented this move in 1939, he led a small split-off which degenerated into a racket run by gangsters.

335. In 1938–39 the SWP tried to get unions and other workers' organizations to form **defense guards** against vigilante and fascist assaults. In New Jersey, where a meeting for Norman Thomas was broken up by vigilantes in Newark and where the mayor of Jersey City ran CIO organizers out of town, the SWP made an attempt to form a broad defense guard that would include the **Workers Alliance,** the main unemployed movement of that period, but it did not succeed.

336. "Answers to Gladys Lloyd Robinson." By permission of the Harvard College Library. Trotsky's answers were dictated in English. **Gladys Lloyd Robinson** (1895–1971) and her husband, the actor Edward G. Robinson (1893–1973), met Trotsky, through Diego Rivera, in August 1938. Her account of the visit and the written interview Trotsky gave her were published in a Hollywood trade journal, *Rob Wagner's Script,* September 10, 1938. In his autobiography thirty-four years later her husband concocted a more fanciful version of the visit, which had Trotsky inquiring about parts of Brooklyn where he had spent "his childhood and early immigrant times"; expressing the opinion that "Lenin and Stalin were latter-day tyrants"; avowing his "deepest attachment" to the reactionary anti-Soviet forces in the U.S.; and referring to the Stalin-Hitler pact (which was not signed until a year later). Robinson also complained that his wife's account of the visit had wrongly given "the leading role" to herself (rather than to him?) (*All My Yesterdays,* Hawthorn Books, New York, 1973).

337. **Francisco Largo Caballero** (1869–1946) was the leader of a left tendency in the Spanish SP and premier from September 1936 to May 1937. **Juan Garcia Oliver** (1901–1980), Spanish minister of justice, 1936–39, was a right-wing anarchist who collaborated

with the Stalinists in crushing the revolutionary wing of the Loyalists. **Juan Negrin** (1889–1956), a right-wing Socialist, succeeded Caballero as premier of Spain and held the post until the end of the Civil War. **Francisco Franco** (1892–1975), the fascist general, organized the Spanish army based in Morocco and with military aid from Hitler and Mussolini overthrew the Spanish People's Front government.

338. **Frank Hague** (1876–1956), Democratic mayor of Jersey City, used governmental power, police violence, veterans groups, and company-hired thugs to prevent the CIO from organizing. Organizers and distributors of leaflets were arrested or run out of town. To charges that he was violating civil liberties guaranteed by the law, Hague replied, "I am the law." Trotsky considered him an incipient fascist.

339. "Isaacs's Book About China." By permission of the Harvard College Library. Translated from the Russian by Carol Lisker.

340. "Latin American Problems: A Transcript." *Intercontinental Press*, May 19, 1975. *Intercontinental Press* added some words in brackets for clarification of Trotsky's English, and shortened or omitted remarks by other participants in the discussion that was held at Trotsky's home two months after the founding conference of the Fourth International. Pseudonyms were used in the transcript for all the participants, with "Turner" for Trotsky. The identity of "Robinson" could not be established; he may have been a guard or a visitor.

341. **Charles Curtiss** (1908–1993) was a member of the SWP National Committee and the representative of the IS of the Fourth International assigned to work in Mexico, 1938–39. He left the SWP in 1951 and joined the Socialist Party.

342. **Vicente Lombardo Toledano** (1893–1968) was a Mexican Stalinist and trade union bureaucrat who played an active part in the slander campaign against Trotsky that was used to create the political climate for his assassination.

343. Mexico's ruling party, the PRI (Institutional Revolutionary Party), was founded in 1928 with the name PNR (Revolutionary

National Party) and was renamed the **PRM** (Party of the Mexican Revolution) from 1938 to 1946. The **APRA** (American Revolutionary Popular Alliance) was organized by Victor Raul Haya de la Torre (1895–1979) when he was residing in Mexico in 1924.

344. Hitler's troops occupied **Austria** in March 1938 and he won the **Sudeten** in Czechoslovakia through the Munich agreement of September 1938.

345. **Luis N. Morones** (1890–1964) was general secretary of the CROM (Mexican Workers Regional Confederation), a conservative union federation modeled after the American Federation of Labor.

346. **Sol Lankin** was a founder of the Left Opposition in the U.S. and a guard in Trotsky's household.

347. **Clave** (Key) was a theoretical review started in 1938 and distributed by the Spanish-speaking sections of the Fourth International. It was published in Mexico City and Trotsky was one of the actual editors, although not listed as such in the magazine.

348. The founding conference of the Fourth International adopted a resolution criticizing the sectarian policies and unprincipled factionalism of the leadership of the former Mexican section, which had voted to dissolve rather than meet with representatives of the Fourth International before the conference, and directing the IS to reorganize the section on the basis of the policies adopted by the conference. This resolution, originally published in the *Socialist Appeal*, is reprinted in *Documents of the Fourth International: The Formative Years (1933–40)*.

349. The **CTM** (Mexican Workers Confederation), the major union federation in the country, was organized in 1936 with government support. In the thirties it was dominated by the Stalinists, with Lombardo Toledano as its chief.

350. *Trade Unions in the Epoch of Imperialist Decay* expounds his views on **statification of unions** in both the colonial and imperialist countries. Trotsky's fuller evaluation of this programmatic **letter** will be found in "Haya de la Torre and Democracy," November 9, 1938, and "Ignorance Is Not a Revolutionary Instrument," January 30, 1939, in *Writings 38–39*.

351. "Lombardo Toledano's Lies." *Excelsior* (Mexico City), No-

vember 10, 1938. Translated from the French by David Keil. General **Saturnino Cedillo** was a right-wing army officer who led an uprising against the Mexican government in May 1938 and was killed by government troops in January 1939. **Dr. Atl** was a painter named Gerardo Murillo (1875–1963), a former revolutionary who had become a fascist sympathizer by the late thirties. **Hernan Laborde** (1896–1955), was the chief leader of the Mexican CP until 1940, when he was purged in a reorganization resulting from preparations of the Trotsky assassination.

352. "Can the *Daily News* Be Sued?" *Hoy* (Mexico City), November 12, 1938. Retranslated from the French by David Keil. A letter to Albert Goldman, who was able as Trotsky's attorney to get the *Daily News* to print Trotsky's refutation of its slanders (see "Answers to the Lies of the *New York Daily News*," December 28, 1938, in *Writings 38–39*).

353. "A Conversation with William R. Mathews." *Tucson Daily Star*, December 13, 1938. By permission of the *Daily Star* and Mr. Mathews.

354. **Henry J. Allen** (1868–1950) was a Republican U.S. Senator and former governor of Kansas. He launched a big red-baiting campaign against the Cardenas government after it began expropriating foreign oil properties. Trotsky's "Open Letter to Senator Allen," December 2, 1938, denounced Allen for displaying "the racist arrogance of an imperialist" *(Writings 38–39)*.

355. Here and later Mathews obviously misheard or misunderstood what Trotsky was saying. Neither at the time of this conversation, nor before, nor after, did Trotsky ever call the privileged Soviet bureaucracy a "class." The term he used consistently was "caste." His views on the distinction and its importance are in *The Revolution Betrayed* and *In Defense of Marxism*.

356. "Investigate the U.S. Fascists." From the Cannon archives, Library of Social History. Dictated in English. The *Socialist Appeal* became a twice-weekly paper at the start of 1939; it returned to a weekly schedule with the outbreak of World War II in September.

A few weeks after Trotsky dictated this letter to Joseph Hansen, the latter was in New York, starting a series of articles about American fascism for the *Appeal*.

357. "The French Question." From the Cannon archives, Library of Social History. Dictated in English. A letter to Cannon, who was getting ready to go to France to offer the SWP's political and organizational help to the factionally paralyzed French section.

358. **Vincent R. Dunne** (1890–1970), after many years of activity in the IWW and CP, was a founder of the Left Opposition and the SWP. He was a leader of the Minneapolis teamsters' strikes in the thirties and one of the eighteen SWP Teamster leaders prosecuted in 1941 and imprisoned for their antiwar activity.

359. **Lillian Curtiss** (1911–1985), a secretary of Trotsky in Mexico, 1938–39, and an activist in the SWP until 1983.

360. "Letters About Sieva Volkov." The two 1938 letters are from *Avocat de Trotsky*, translated from the French by Russell Block; the 1939 letter is from the Cannon archives, Library of Social History, translated from the French by Tom Barrett. **Oscar Cohn** (1869–1937), a Social Democratic member of the German Reichstag, joined the USPD in 1918 but later returned to the Social Democracy. He was the German lawyer of Leon Sedov and Zinaida Volkov in the early thirties. He took refuge in the USSR after Hitler came to power and disappeared in the purges.

361. "No Doubts About Rudolf Klement's Fate." From *Cahiers Leon Trotsky*, Paris, number 2, April–June 1979. Translated from the French by Nat London. These letters were given to Pierre Naville in 1966 by Hermann Klement, younger brother of Rudolf, who was murdered by the GPU in Paris on the eve of the founding conference of the Fourth International in 1938. Because his body was dismembered some people continued to hope that it had not been identified correctly and that he was still alive. The letters were addressed to Margarethe Ruthe, sister of Rudolf Klement's mother. In a public comment on the first letter he got from the aunt, Trotsky said she was a resident of Latin America ("On the Murder of Ru-

dolf Klement," December 1, 1938, in *Writings 38–39*). From the aunt Trotsky's letters were transmitted to the mother in Germany. Trotsky's **analysis of the letter** signed with Klement's name in July 1938 is in *Writings 37–38*.

362. "A GPU Stool Pigeon in Paris." From the Cannon archives, Library of Social History. Translated from the French by Mavis Parr. This confidential letter to the top SWP leaders in New York was prompted by an anonymous letter, dated December 27, 1938, that Trotsky had received from the U.S. The author, it was revealed many years later, was Alexander Orlov (1895–1973), an important GPU official in Spain, who had broken with the GPU in June 1938 when he was recalled to the USSR for probable liquidation and had escaped to the U.S.; he later wrote a book, *The Secret History of Stalin's Crimes* (Random House, 1953). In his letter to Trotsky, warning that the GPU had a dangerous spy inside the Fourth International in Paris and that it was preparing Trotsky's assassination, Orlov sought to conceal his own identity by pretending to be an American relative of another former GPU official who had escaped to Japan and was supposed to be the source of the information in the letter.

363. **Mark Zborowsky** (1908–1990), who used the pseudonym "Etienne," was a GPU agent who infiltrated the French section in 1934 and worked his way into the confidence of Leon Sedov and the editorial board of the *Biulleten Oppozitsii*. His information to the GPU made possible the murders of Sedov, Reiss, Klement, and others. Despite suspicions about his real role, it was not publicly exposed until 1955 during an investigation of a Soviet spy ring in the U.S., which led to his conviction for perjury and a five-year sentence in 1958.

364. **Boris Nikolaevsky** (1887–1966) was a Russian Menshevik who worked for the International Institute of Social History at its Paris office in the 1930s and later moved to the United States.

365. There was nothing else in the Cannon archives relating to the Orlov letter and its aftermath except another Trotsky letter dated May 10, 1939, stating that he had considered the Orlov letter "seventy-five percent a provocation for the purpose of making us suspicious of a certain comrade" and that he had never received a report

on the investigation he had requested on January 1 (see "Another Anonymous Letter," later in this volume). But from other sources the following can be added: Orlov's letter had asked Trotsky to acknowledge receipt by running a notice in the *Socialist Appeal* that the editorial office had received a letter from a Mr. Stein. Trotsky responded with an ad in the January 14 *Appeal* insisting that Mr. Stein visit the *Appeal* office immediately to talk to Comrade Martin. Orlov later testified in 1957 that he went to the office without disclosing his identity, "I took just a side look at that Martin, and he did not inspire too much confidence in me, so that was all" (*The Mind of an Assassin* by Isaac Don Levine, Farrar, Straus and Cudahy, 1959). Orlov said he tried to reach Trotsky by telephone but did not succeed, so Trotsky and his comrades were never able to discuss the Orlov letter with its author. According to Isaac Deutscher in *The Prophet Outcast* (1963), "The apparent lack of response on the correspondent's [Orlov's] part and the strange form of his warning made Trotsky doubt his trustworthiness. Nevertheless, a small commission was formed at Coyoacan to investigate the matter; but it found no substance in the charges against Etienne." Trotsky showed the Orlov letter to Lilia Dallin when she visited him in the summer of 1939 and, she testified in 1956, they both agreed after a discussion that it was a GPU hoax. Whether Cannon saw the letter before leaving New York for France in January is not known.

366. "The Hearst Press Changes Its Mind." From the Cannon archives, Library of Social History. Dictated in English. This letter was to H.R. Knickerbocker (1898–1949), an American correspondent working for the Hearst press and its International News Service, who had gone to Mexico to request an interview with Trotsky.

367. Here, as in many other places in Trotsky's writings and their translations, Trotsky really means "honesty" when he says "loyalty."

368. The **American Fund for Political Prisoners and Refugees,** headed by Rose Karsner, was established in 1938 in line with the decision by the founding conference of the Fourth International to create such groups wherever possible; see the conference resolution "On Organizing Defense and Relief for Persecuted Revolu-

tionists" in *Documents of the Fourth International: The Formative Years (1933–40)*.

369. Knickerbocker wired Trotsky's proposals to the INS in New York. On January 9 its manager, a Mr. Connolly, wired back an offer to pay Trotsky $1,000 for an interview, while stipulating that "This does not constitute recognition of any past claims about which Mr. Connolly knows nothing." But on January 10 Connolly came to the conclusion that "the American public is not interested in Mr. Trotsky's views" and withdrew the offer. Trotsky submitted the whole correspondence to the press with a final remark: "We can only congratulate Mr. Connolly on his conclusion and we hope that, in view of this state of the public opinion, the Hearst press will no longer purloin L.D. Trotsky's articles and statements."

370. "The Plight of Our Refugee Comrades." From the Cannon archives, Library of Social History. Dictated in English. A letter to Rose Karsner in New York. **Julik** was the pseudonym of Wenzel Kozlecki (1906–1995), a leader of the German section, who had emigrated to Czechoslovakia after Hitler came to power and to Mexico after the Munich pact dismembered Czechoslovakia.

371. **George Novack** (1905–1992), author of many books on Marxist philosophy and history, joined the CLA in 1933 and was elected to the SWP national committee in 1941. He was secretary of the American Committee for the Defense of Leon Trotsky, 1936–38, and secretary of the Civil Rights Defense Committee which was created in 1941 to help the SWP and Teamsters defendants in the Minneapolis trial.

372. "What the Youth Do to Our Principles." From the Cannon archives, Library of Social History. Dictated in English. A letter to Walter Held in Norway. Held had been active in Fourth Internationalist youth work for several years. In December 1938 he wrote Trotsky to complain that its current leaders were "watering down" its theories. He therefore opposed further attempts to build an independent youth movement, advocating that they be organized as part of the revolutionary party. The **March 1921 crisis in Germany** arose out of a defeat resulting from an inadequately prepared

insurrection against the government called by the German CP leadership. **"Our position" on this question** was the resolution adopted by the Third World Congress of the Comintern condemning the March action as a putsch. **Paul Levi** (1883–1930) was a leader of the German CP and an opponent of the March action; he was expelled for making his criticisms public instead of debating them inside the Comintern; he later joined the Social Democrats. **Synnove Rosendahl-Jensen** was the companion of Held in Norway; with him and their child she disappeared after being seized by the Soviet secret police in 1941.

373. "Letters to the POI Central Committee." From the Cannon archives, Library of Social History. Translated from the French by J.R. Fidler (first and third letters) and Tom Barrett (second letter). In the autumn of 1938 a factional struggle broke out in the Central Committee of the French section over a proposal to enter a new centrist party. A majority of the committee, including Boitel and Naville, who was the secretary of the IS, opposed entry; a minority, including Rous and Craipeau, favored it. A majority of the IS also favored entry, along with Trotsky after initial hesitation, and Cannon, who went to France on behalf of the SWP in January 1939 to try to help resolve the crisis. In February a split took place, and the members of the minority joined the centrist party. Trotsky's letters to the majority sought to bring about a reconciliation between the two factions or, if that was not possible, to ease the hostilities so that the majority would not hamper the work of the minority. In the end his efforts were unsuccessful and the IS withdrew its recognition of the POI as the French section. Other Trotsky letters of this period on "The Crisis in the French Section" will be found in *Writings 38–39*.

374. The **PSOP** (Workers and Peasants Socialist Party) was a short-lived centrist group, founded in June 1938 by Marceau Pivert and his followers after they left the SFIO. It was affiliated to the London Bureau. It rejected fusion with the POI but it was willing to accept POI members on an individual basis; it also let members of the PCI join but barred their leader, Raymond Molinier. POI members became part of a relatively large left wing soon after they joined.

NOTES FOR PAGES 518–521 / 681

The PSOP disintegrated after World War II began. Trotsky's articles on the PSOP will be found in *Leon Trotsky on France*.

375. "A Trap in Palestine." From the Cannon archives, Library of Social History. Dictated in English. A letter to Albert Glotzer in Chicago, about a liberal lawyer from that city, Harry Ruskin, who had obtained an interview with Trotsky.

376. "Money-Raising Appeals." From the Cannon archives, Library of Social History. Dictated in English. A letter to Rose Karsner. The second article mentioned by Trotsky was written December 22, 1938, and was circulated in letter form before being published eventually under the title "Appeal to American Jews Menaced by Fascism and Anti-Semitism" (see *Leon Trotsky on the Jewish Question*, Pathfinder, 1970).

377. "Utilize the Opportunities in the Communist Party." From "Healy Caught in the Logic of the Big Lie" by Joseph Hansen, in *Intercontinental Press*, August 9, 1976. This was a letter to Hansen, who had recently returned from Trotsky's staff to the U.S., where he was engaged, among other things, in a confidential assignment related to contacting a GPU agent in New York. Trotsky had been complaining for some time about the SWP's lack of attention to developments inside the American CP, whose ranks he thought could be influenced and won over through systematic, well-organized activity among them. Twelve days later, he participated in a discussion of this question with SWP members in his home; the transcript, "Our Work in the Communist Party," is in *Writings 38–39*.

378. **Terence Phelan** was the pseudonym of Sherry Mangan (1904–1961), an American writer and journalist who had joined the CLA in 1934. He went to France as a foreign correspondent in 1938 and was active there during the German occupation until he was expelled by the Petain government. He was technical secretary of the IS in 1939, a member of the European Secretariat, 1944–46, and thereafter a member of the IS.

379. The **manuscript** was a coded reference to Hansen's conversations with a GPU agent, under the direction of Trotsky, Cannon, and Shachtman. The conversations involved the manuscript of Stalin's

biography which Trotsky was writing.

380. **Reba Hansen** (1909–1990), who joined the CLA in 1934, was a member of Trotsky's secretariat in 1938 and was Cannon's secretary, 1946–52.

381. **Chris Andrews** (1911–1989), who had been a guard in Trotsky's home, participated in a widely publicized mass demonstration called by the SWP outside a fascist meeting in Madison Square Garden on February 20, 1939. His picture appeared in the press after this Yankee-type "bull fight," and he was arrested a week later for passing out leaflets at a CP meeting.

382. **Charles Malamuth** (1900–1965) was the translator of the Stalin biography. His **indiscretion** consisted of showing parts of the unfinished manuscript to certain people at a time when this could have interfered with Hansen's assignment. After Trotsky's death, Harper and Brothers appointed him editor of the Stalin biography, into which he inserted a number of anti-Leninist ideas.

383. "James's Trip to Mexico." From the Cannon archives, Library of Social History. Dictated in English. A letter to **C.L.R. James** (1901–1989), the West Indian author of *The Black Jacobins* and *World Revolution*. A leader of the British section, James had moved to the U.S. after the founding conference and became active in the SWP. Following a speaking tour of the U.S., he visited Trotsky in April 1939 to discuss the American Black struggle (transcripts in *Malcolm X, Black Liberation, and the Road to Workers Power*) and problems of the Fourth International (transcripts in *Writings 38–39*). He left the SWP with Shachtman in 1940, returned in 1947, and left again for good in 1951.

384. "Diego Rivera's Defection." From the Cannon archives, Library of Social History. Dictated in English. Three letters to Jan Frankel about Rivera's break with the Fourth International. Thirteen other letters and statements on the subject are collected in "The Diego Rivera Affair," in *Writings 38–39*.

385. **Farrell Dobbs** (1907–1983), a leader of the Minneapolis Teamsters' strikes, joined the CLA in 1934 and was elected to the Workers Party's national committee later that year. He became SWP labor secretary in 1939 and national secretary, 1953–72. He

was convicted in the Minneapolis Smith Act trial of 1941 and imprisoned with seventeen other defendants. He was the SWP's presidential candidate four times, 1948–60. He is the author of a four-volume history of the SWP's role in the Teamster movement. **The Pan-American Committee** was organized early in 1938 to help prepare the founding conference of the Fourth International, and was assigned the task of coordinating the International's work in Latin America and the Far East after the conference.

386. **Juan O'Gorman** (1905–1982) was a revolutionary Mexican artist and architect, and the subject of a difference between Trotsky and Rivera in November 1938 when his frescos at Mexico City's Central Airport were ordered destroyed by the Mexican government because they pictured Hitler and Mussolini in an uncomplimentary way (see *Writings 38–39*).

387. "Where Munis Should Go." From the Cannon archives, Library of Social History. Dictated in English. A letter to Cannon about **Grandizo Munis** (1912–1989) which was a pseudonym of Manuel Fernandez Grandizo, a member of a Mexican family who was born in Spain. He was a founder of the Spanish Left Opposition and opposed its fusion into the POUM. He returned to Mexico in 1935 but went back to Spain to fight in the civil war, where he helped to found a small section of the Fourth International. He was arrested on frame-up charges in 1938 but escaped to France in 1939. He returned to Mexico and became a leader of its section during World War II. Later he revised his position on the nature of the Soviet state and broke with the Fourth International.

388. "Pan-American Committee Personnel." From the Cannon archives, Library of Social History. Dictated in English. A letter to Jan Frankel.

389. "Victor Serge's Crisis." By permission of Pierre Broue. Translated from the French by Mavis Parr. A letter to Victor Serge.

390. "Another Anonymous Letter." From the Cannon archives, Library of Social History. Dictated in English. A letter to Jan Fran-

kel. Accompanying it was a copy of an anonymous, undated letter in Russian which sought to create the impression that it was written by a woman. The author asked Trotsky to keep the letter secret "since I have to return to the USSR." The author also expressed alarm over a radio report that Trotsky was awaiting the arrival of a thirteen-year-old grandson, presumably from the Soviet Union: "Remember, if your grandson is brought to you, that could not be done without a direct order by the GPU; that the GPU could send a different child in the guise of your grandson with the order to kill you; that even if your real grandson is brought to you, the GPU has had the time and has the means to convince him of the need to do a 'heroic' deed, i.e., an act of terrorism. Therefore, if your grandson arrives, you must search him and check whether he has any poison; don't let him have access to any weapons; don't let any friends and companions of your grandson's age into the house, since they might bring poison or a weapon or commit an act of terrorism directly themselves. Don't let anyone who brings your grandson come into your house, no matter how much confidence you might have had in them in the past." (At this time Trotsky was awaiting the arrival of his thirteen-year-old grandson, Sieva Volkov, not from the Soviet Union but from France. His companions on the trip, in August 1939, were the Rosmers, Trotsky's old friends.)

391. **G.S. Lushkov** (1900–1945) was a high GPU official who helped organize the first Moscow trial. When he saw that Stalin was purging the officials who knew the inside story about the trials, he escaped in the summer of 1938 to Japan, where he published his revelations. Orlov pretended in his December 1938 letter to Trotsky that he was an American relative of Lushkov, transmitting information from him.

392. Trotsky was wrong in his assumption that the December 1938 letter had been written by **W.** or Walter Krivitsky, who made contact with Leon Sedov in France after his break with the GPU at the end of 1937, and later moved to the U.S. Who wrote the May 1939 letter is still not known.

393. "Problems of the *Socialist Appeal*." From the Cannon archives, Library of Social History. Dictated in English. A letter to

Cannon. Trotsky quoted most of it in his article "From a Scratch to the Danger of Gangrene," January 24, 1940, in *In Defense of Marxism*.

394. "A Visa for Elsa Reiss." From the Cannon archives, Library of Social History. Dictated in English. A letter to Rose Karsner. **Elsa Reiss** (1900–1978) was the widow of Ignace Reiss, murdered by the GPU in Switzerland for adhering to the Fourth International. She later wrote a book about him, *Our Own People* by Elisabeth K. Poretsky (University of Michigan Press, Ann Arbor, 1970).

395. "A Party Census." From the Cannon archives, Library of Social History. Dictated in English. A letter to Cannon.

396. "For the Ukrainian Pamphlet." From the Cannon archives, Library of Social History. Translated from the Russian by Marilyn Vogt. A letter to T. Oleniuk in Canada, who was preparing a collection of Trotsky's recent articles on the Ukraine for publication as a pamphlet in Ukrainian. All of the articles, including the preface, are in *Writings 38–39* and *39–40*. Although the letter is undated, it was obviously written around a week after the start of World War II. **Vladimir K. Vinnichenko** (1880–1951), novelist and playwright, was a Ukrainian nationalist revolutionary leader, who served as secretary of the Central Ukrainian Rada in 1917 and a leader of the uprising against German occupation in 1918. He joined the Ukrainian CP in 1920 and held various posts after the Soviets took over in the Ukraine, but eventually emigrated to France.

397. "A Disagreeable Incident." From the Cannon archives, Library of Social History. Dictated in English. A letter to **Edward Alsworth Ross** (1866–1951), a professor emeritus of sociology at the University of Wisconsin who had served as a member of the Dewey Commission. He had interviewed Trotsky in Petrograd shortly after the October Revolution and had written two books about the Soviet Union.

398. "The First Article in the Russian Discussion." From the Cannon archives, Library of Social History. Dictated in English. A

letter to Rose Karsner. The *Life* article, dated September 22, 1939, was a biographical sketch of Stalin, reprinted in *Portraits, Political and Personal*. The USSR article, "The USSR in War," September 25, 1939, was Trotsky's first contribution to the bitter struggle over the class character of the Soviet Union that broke out in the SWP and the Fourth International after the signing of the Stalin-Hitler pact and the start of World War II. **Both camps** referred to the two factions in the SWP—one led by Cannon, reaffirming the SWP's previous position, another led by Shachtman and Burnham, that would deny SWP support to the workers' state in the war.

399. "Accepting the Invitation of the Dies Committee." From the Cannon archives, Library of Social History. Dictated in English. The letter was to the SWP leaders in New York; the telegram was to the **Dies Committee** of the U.S. House of Representatives in Washington, D.C., then called the Special Committee on Un-American Activities, which had invited Trotsky to testify at a hearing in Austin, Texas. "Your name has been mentioned frequently by such witnesses as [Earl] Browder and [William Z.] Foster," the invitation said. "This Committee will accord you opportunity to answer their charges." The Committee soon changed its mind and withdrew its invitation. Trotsky's statements on this subject are in *Writings 39–40*. **J.B. Matthews** (1894–1966), a former member of the SP and several CP front organizations, was "chief investigator" of the witch-hunting Dies Committee.

400. "Outline of a Magazine Article." From the Cannon archives, Library of Social History. Dictated in English. Trotsky submitted this proposal for an article on the war to *Liberty* magazine, which agreed to print it. The article, completed December 4, 1939, and entitled "The Twin-Stars: Hitler-Stalin," is in *Writings 39–40*.

401. "A False Report." By permission of the Harvard College Library. Translated from the Spanish by David Keil.

402. "Dialectics and the Answer to Burnham." From the Cannon archives, Library of Social History. Dictated in English. A letter to

Cannon, part of which Trotsky quoted in *In Defense of Marxism*. Also in that volume are Trotsky's "An Open Letter to Comrade Burnham," January 7, 1940, and Burnham's "Science and Style, A Reply to Comrade Trotsky," February 1, 1940.

403. "Farrell Dobbs's Arrival." From the Cannon archives, Library of Social History. Dictated in English. A letter to Cannon, the last paragraph of which was published in *In Defense of Marxism*. Dobbs had resigned his organizer's post with the International Brotherhood of Teamsters; before taking on his new assignment as the SWP's national labor secretary, he and Marvell Scholl visited Trotsky for extensive talks. Shachtman's "The Crisis in the American Party—An Open Letter in Reply to Comrade Leon Trotsky," January 1, 1940, was printed in the SWP *Internal Bulletin*, January 1940; Trotsky answered it in "From a Scratch—to the Danger of Gangrene," January 24, 1940 (see *In Defense of Marxism*).

404. "A Discussion with Carleton Smith." *St. Louis Daily Globe-Democrat*, February 2, 1940, where it had the title, "Trotsky Tells Writer That U.S. Will Join Allies and Win War."

405. "Factionalism and the IEC." The first three statements are from the Cannon archives, Library of Social History; the fourth is from *Documents of the Fourth International: The Formative Years (1933–40)*. When the war began in Europe in 1939, the Fourth International's center was transferred to New York where a resident International Executive Committee was established with those IEC members who happened to be available. When the factional struggle in the SWP became acute, it turned out that most of the resident IEC members supported the SWP minority faction led by Shachtman, Burnham, and Abern. This led to factional abuses by the resident IEC, loss in its authority, and ultimately in an inability to speak for the International.

406. Although most of the sections of the Fourth International, including those that were operating under wartime and illegal conditions, held their own discussions over the problems posed by the Stalin-Hitler pact and the outbreak of World War II, no formal "in-

ternational discussion" was initiated until January 1940 when the pro-Shachtman faction of the resident IEC announced one without consulting the other members of the IEC. This letter was signed by Trotsky (Crux) and Otto Schuessler (Oscar Fischer), two IEC members living in Mexico.

407. **A. Lebrun** was the pseudonym of Mario Pedrosa (1905–1982), a Brazilian in Paris who became a Left Oppositionist in the late 1920s. He helped to found a section in Brazil but repression forced him to leave the country. He was active in France until 1938, when he attended the founding conference and was elected as the only Latin American member of the IEC. He left the Fourth International with Shachtman in 1940.

408. In February 1940 the SWP minority faction held a national conference in Cleveland intended to harden its members around its demand that the SWP majority must recognize the minority's right to publish its own public paper. This demand increased the chances that there would be a split at the coming SWP national convention in April. At Trotsky's urging, the SWP majority promised to guarantee the minority all normal rights inside the party if its members would accept the convention decisions. In this letter Trotsky tried to get the IEC members to intervene at the Cleveland conference to avert a split. In addition to Trotsky and Schuessler, it was also signed by Grandizo Munis, representing the Mexican and Spanish sections.

409. Since the pro-Shachtman IEC members disregarded the February 20 letter and openly aligned themselves behind the Cleveland conference decisions, Trotsky took the position that the resident IEC was now a fiction and that a committee really representing the Fourth International needed to be created. Trotsky, Schuessler, and Munis signed this statement.

410. A split took place shortly after the April 1940 SWP convention in New York, and the pro-Shachtman members of the IEC adhered to the new Workers Party. Trotsky and the SWP leaders then decided to call an international conference, originally conceived as a Pan American conference, in order to adopt a manifesto and elect a leadership that would assure the political and organizational continuity of the International. The present statement was signed by

Trotsky, Cannon (Martel), Schuessler, Vincent R. Dunne (Jones), and Sam Gordon (Stuart), the IEC administrative secretary, and was endorsed by Munis and Richardson, representing the Canadian section. The emergency conference of the Fourth International was held in New York at the end of May 1940. Among other things it endorsed this declaration and adopted a "Supplementary Statement of the IEC" on the same subject (see *Documents of the Fourth International*); and it approved Trotsky's "Manifesto of the Fourth International on the Imperialist War and the Proletarian World Revolution" (see *Writings 39–40*).

411. **Anton** was a pseudonym of Nathan Gould (1913–1997), a youth leader of the SWP, a delegate to the founding conference, and a youth representative to the resident IEC. As a member of the Abern group, he left the SWP in 1940 to join the Workers Party.

412. "Rivera's Wild Denunciation." From the Cannon archives, Library of Social History. Dictated in English. A letter to John G. Wright, written during the SWP convention in New York. "SWP Answers Rivera Slander," written by Cannon, was printed in the *Socialist Appeal*, April 13, 1940.

413. "A Serious Work on Russian Revolutionary History." From the Cannon archives, Library of Social History. Translated from the Russian by Donald Kennedy. A letter to John G. Wright about the manuscript of his study, published, before this letter was received, under the title "Outline History of Russian Bolshevism, Book One: The Gestation Period of the Russian Proletariat" (Educational Department, Local New York, SWP, 1940).

414. The **Narodniks** (populists) were the major tendency of the Russian revolutionary movement in the nineteenth century.

415. The **Emancipation of Labor Group** was the first Russian Marxist organization. It was founded in 1883 by Plekhanov and his associates in Geneva and was dissolved in 1903 at the Second Congress of the RSDLP in London.

416. The **Tanaka Memorial** was a document submitted to the Japanese emperor in 1927 by Baron Gi-ichi Tanaka (1863–1929), prime minister at the time. It outlined the detailed steps of a pro-

gram of Japanese imperialist expansion, beginning with the establishment of Japanese control in Manchuria and leading eventually to domination of all China, Indonesia, the South Sea Islands, the Maritime Provinces of the USSR, and ultimately India, the whole Pacific basin, and Europe. Trotsky's May 1940 article telling how the Tanaka Memorial came into the hands of the Soviet government is in *Writings 39–40*.

417. "To Colonel Sanchez Salazar." By permission of the Harvard College Library. Translated from the Spanish by James P. Nolan. The GPU conducted an armed assault on Trotsky's home on May 24, 1940. By luck the Trotskys were not killed by the hundreds of shots fired into their bedroom, although a Trotsky guard, Robert Sheldon Harte, was taken away and found murdered weeks later. The chief of the Mexican secret police, Colonel **Leandro Sanchez Salazar,** decided that the whole thing was a "self-assault" staged by Trotsky to gain publicity, and arrested two of his guards, Otto Schuessler and Charles Cornell. A week after the assault, Trotsky protested to President Cardenas, who ordered Sanchez Salazar to release the guards and get to work on capturing the real criminals. On the same day Trotsky sent this letter to Sanchez Salazar, who later collaborated with Julian Gorkin in writing his account of the May 24 assassination attempt—and the final successful attempt three months later—in a book entitled *Murder in Mexico* (Secker and Warburg, London, 1950). Trotsky's other articles about the May 24 attempt are in *Writings 39–40*.

418. **Juan Andreu Almazan** (1891–1965), a general in the Mexican revolution, was the right-wing candidate for president of Mexico in the 1940 campaign.

419. **Frida Kahlo Rivera** (1910–1954) was an artist in her own right.

420. "A Letter to *El Nacional*." By permission of the Harvard College Library. Translated from the Spanish by David Keil.

421. "The GPU and the Comintern." From the Cannon archives, Library of Social History. Dictated in English. A letter to Albert

Goldman, who was helping Trotsky gather material for his document "The Comintern and the GPU," August 17, 1940 (in *Writings 39–40*).

422. **Eugene Lyons** (1898–1985) was an American journalist in the USSR in the 1930s, about which he wrote *Assignment in Utopia* (Harcourt Brace, 1937).

423. The **New Masses** was a Stalinist magazine in the U.S.

424. "A Bed and a Plate Waiting." From the Cannon archives, Library of Social History. Dictated in English. A letter to John G. Wright, whose citizenship problems forced him to cancel a long-anticipated visit to Trotsky in Mexico.

425. **Antoinette Konikow** (1869–1946) was born in Russia, became a member of Plekhanov's Emancipation of Labor group, and attended the founding congress of the Second International. After emigrating to Boston, she became a member of the Socialist Labor Party, a founding member of the SP, and a founding member of the CP. Expelled for "Trotskyism" in 1928, she became a Left Oppositionist, and was an honorary member of the SWP National Committee at the time she died. A physician, she was a pioneer fighter for women's rights. Her daughter, **Edith Konikow** (1904–1954), also an SWP member, was Wright's wife and the mother of their son **Tyl**.

426. "Unfinished Writings and Fragments." These four compilations are taken from three folders in the Cannon archives, Library of Social History. The folders contained sheets or scraps of typewritten passages spoken by Trotsky into a dictaphone or to his stenographer and transcribed by the stenographer or a secretary; very few of these passages had been corrected by Trotsky. Some were obviously sections of articles published by Trotsky himself, omitted from them for space or other reasons; others were notes for parts of articles Trotsky intended to write but did not complete for various reasons. Many were quotations from public figures without comment and others were dates of events Trotsky regarded as significant and which he would have discussed when he introduced them. The main problems in preparing this material were deciding the sequence in which to arrange the different parts and omitting

the more tangential, ephemeral passages. In a few places a word or phrase has been added in brackets to clarify meaning.

427. "Petty-Bourgeois Democrats and Moralizers." From the Cannon archives, Library of Social History. Translated from the Russian by Marilyn Vogt. This material appears to date from the end of 1938 to the summer of 1939, before the Stalin-Hitler pact and the start of World War II. Most of it is obviously related to "A Political Dialogue," December 20, 1938, a few months after the Munich crisis (see *Writings 38–39*). Trotsky began that article as follows: "This conversation takes place in Paris. It could for that matter also take place in Brussels. A is one of those 'socialists' who can only stand on their feet when they have some power to lean on. A is a 'friend of the Soviet Union' and is naturally a supporter of the People's Front. The author finds it rather difficult to characterize B, for B is his friend and co-thinker." The last two parts seem to be related to "The Class, the Party, and the Leadership," an article about why the Spanish proletariat was defeated that was still uncompleted at Trotsky's death (see *The Spanish Revolution [1931–39]*) and to "The Moralists and Sycophants Against Marxism" June 9, 1939 (see *Their Morals and Ours*).

428. **Andrei Vyshinsky** (1883–1954) was a Menshevik from 1903 until 1920, when he joined the CPSU. He received international notoriety as the prosecuting attorney in the Moscow trials and then was foreign minister, 1949–53.

429. "Fragments From the First Seven Months of the War." From the Cannon archives, Library of Social History. Translated from the Russian by Marilyn Vogt. Trotsky's articles, interviews, and letters on the first year of World War II are in *Writings 39–40* and *In Defense of Marxism*. This compilation of material in his folders consists chiefly of notes he was making for a magazine article up to and not later than April 1940, and may include passages he left out of articles that were published. At that time, much attention was being given to the "lull" on the front between Germany and France, so pronounced that the term "phony war" was applied to this period. In April Germany invaded Norway and Denmark,

and in May the lull on the Western front definitely ended with its invasion of the Low Countries and France. The military defeat of France led to Italy's declaration of war on Germany's side in June. The new situation probably explains why Trotsky did not complete this article.

430. **Benjamin Sumner Welles** (1892–1961) was U.S. undersecretary of state in the Roosevelt administration, 1933–43. He was sent to Europe in 1940 to discuss political and economic problems with European politicians in the lull before Germany's military breakthrough in the spring.

431. **Hiram W. Johnson** (1866–1945) was a Republican leader of the U.S. Senate from California.

432. **John D.M. Hamilton** (1892–1973) was chairman of the Republican National Committee, 1936–40.

433. Two days before Hamilton made his statement, Trotsky used this same sentence in an interview where he predicted that the Republican and ex-president Herbert Hoover would drop his advocacy of neutrality when the United States found itself impelled to intervene in the war because of its global position. See interview given to Julius Klyman of the *St. Louis Post-Dispatch*, printed under the title "The World Situation and Perspectives" in *Writings 39–40*.

434. "Fragments on the USSR." From the Cannon archives, Library of Social History. Translated from the Russian by Marilyn Vogt. All or almost all of these fragments were written after the Soviet-Finnish War, which began in November 1939 and was concluded by the signing of a treaty in Moscow in March 1940.

435. **Boris M. Shaposhnikov** (1882–1945), a general in the czarist army, joined the Red Army in May 1918. He held various high military posts and in 1940 was made a marshal of the USSR.

436. **Semyon M. Budenny** (1883–1973), who joined the Russian CP in 1919, won fame as a cavalry commander in the civil war. He was one of the few leading military figures to escape execution or imprisonment in the Stalinist purges.

437. **Kliment Voroshilov** (1881–1969), an early supporter of Stalin, became a member of the Political Bureau of the CPSU in

1926 and people's commissar of defense, 1925–40. He was president of the USSR, 1953–60.

438. Trotsky's proposal to gradually convert the Red Army into a popular **militia** was approved by the Ninth Congress of the CP (1920).

439. **Mikhail I. Kalinin** (1875–1946) was an Old Bolshevik who replaced Sverdlov as head of the Soviet state in 1919. He helped Stalin to expel the Left Opposition in 1927. He leaned to the Right Opposition in 1928 but helped Stalin to expel it too, in 1929.

440. "Preface to a Book on War and Peace." From the Cannon archives, Library of Social History. Translated from the Russian by Ron Allen. In March or April 1940 Trotsky got the idea of collecting several of his articles as a short book to be entitled *War and Peace*, if an American publisher could be found for it. While the search for a publisher was being made in the United States, he dictated these notes to be used in writing the preface for the book. He gave up the project a few months later, after the German victory over France. The proposed contents of the book were:

"Is Parliamentary Democracy Likely to Replace the Soviets?" February 25, 1929 (in *Writings 29*);

"Disarmament and the United States of Europe," October 4, 1929 (in *Writings 29*) (on second thought, Trotsky decided to omit this article);

"What Is National Socialism?" June 10, 1933 (in *The Struggle Against Fascism in Germany*);

"On the Threshold of a New World War," August 9, 1937 (in *Writings 36–37*);

"The Totalitarian Defeatist in the Kremlin," September 12, 1938 (in *Writings 37–38*);

"Only Revolution Can End War," March 18, 1939 (in *Writings 38–39*);

"The Riddle of the USSR," June 21, 1939 (in *Writings 38–39*);

"The Kremlin in World Politics," July 1, 1939 (in *Writings 38–39*);

"The U.S. Will Participate in the War," October 1, 1939 (in *Writings 39–40*);

"The Twin-Stars: Hitler-Stalin," December 4, 1939 (in *Writings 39–40*).

441. The article in *The New Republic*, May 22, 1929, which had the title "Which Way, Russia?" was the first translation of "Is Parliamentary Democracy Likely to Replace the Soviets?" Trotsky also discussed it in the unfinished article he was dictating the day he was assassinated, "Bonapartism, Fascism, and War" (in *Writings 39–40*).

442. **Philipp Scheidemann** (1865–1939) and **Friedrich Ebert** (1871–1925) were the right-wing leaders of the German Social Democracy principally responsible for derailing and crushing the German revolution of 1918. Scheidemann was the head of his party's fraction in the Reichstag until 1933, when he emigrated. Ebert was president of the Weimar republic, 1919–25.

443. **Niceto Alcala Zamora** (1877–1949), a large landowner and liberal Catholic, was head of the Progressive Party in Spain. He became the first prime minister of the republican government established in 1931, and was president of the republic, 1931–36.

444. Trotsky's **chat** with members of the Committee on Cultural Relations with Latin America, whose correct date was July 23, 1939, is printed under the title "On the Eve of World War II" in *Writings 39–40*.

445. "Last Words." From "With Trotsky to the End" by Joseph Hansen, reprinted in Leon Trotsky, the Man and His Work. Trotsky dictated these words in English from a hospital bed after being mortally wounded by a GPU assassin. Hansen reported that Trotsky tried to say more, but his words were incomprehensible and then he lost consciousness. He died the next day.

Works of Leon Trotsky published by Pathfinder

Art and Revolution
The Balkan Wars (1912–13)
The Case of Leon Trotsky:
Report of Hearings on the
Charges Made against Him in
the Moscow Trials
The Challenge of the Left
Opposition (1923–25)
The Challenge of the Left
Opposition (1926–27)
The Challenge of the Left
Opposition (1928–29)
The Crisis of the French Section
(1935–36)
Europe and America: Two
Speeches on Imperialism
Fascism: What It Is and
How to Fight It
The Fight Against Jew-Hatred
and Pogroms in the
Imperialist Epoch
The First Five Years of the
Communist International
(2 volumes)
The History of the Russian
Revolution
In Defense of Marxism:
Against the Petty-Bourgeois
Opposition in the Socialist
Workers Party
Kronstadt (with V.I. Lenin)
Leon Trotsky on China
Leon Trotsky on France

Leon Trotsky Speaks
Marxism and Terrorism
Military Writings
My Life: An Attempt at an
Autobiography
Not Guilty
Portraits, Political and Personal
Problems of Everyday Life:
Creating the Foundations
of a New Society in
Revolutionary Russia
The Revolution Betrayed:
What Is the Soviet Union
and Where Is It Going?
The Spanish Revolution
(1931–39)
The Stalin School of
Falsification
The Struggle Against Fascism
in Germany
Their Morals and Ours
The Third International after
Lenin
Trade Unions in the Epoch of
Imperialist Decay
The Transitional Program for
Socialist Revolution
Tribunes of the People and the
Trade Unions
Where Is Britain Going?
Women and the Family
Writings of Leon Trotsky
(14 volumes)

Index (1934–40)

Abbiatte, Roland ("Rossi"), 444, 668n
Abern, Martin, 225–26, 231–33, 363, 366, 550, 650n
Ackerknecht, Erwin ("Eugene Bauer," "Erwin"), 165, 186, 244, 245; and French turn, 138–39, 161–63, 237, 238
Action Socialiste (Revolutionnaire) L' (Belgium), 166, 183, 224, 244, 274, 309, 321, 623n
Adolphe. See Klement, Rudolph
Africa, 257, 258
Alcala Zamora, Niceto, 592, 695n
Alexander I, 150, 177, 619n
Alfonso XIII, 246, 631n
Allen, Henry J., 484, 491, 675n
American Fund for Political Prisoners and Refugees, 509, 678–79n
American Workers Party (AWP), 52–53, 59, 134, 141, 165, 640n
Amsterdam Bureau, 35, 56, 81, 354–55
Anarchists, 418, 526, 573–74
Andrade, Juan, 297–98, 642n
Andreu Almazan, Juan, 559, 690n
Andrews, Chris, 521, 682n
Anseele, Edouard, 183, 623n
Anti-Duehring (Engels), 210
Anti-Semitism, in USSR, 400, 576, 657n
Anton. See Gould, Nathan
APRA (American Revolutionary Popular Alliance, Peru, Mexico), 465, 468, 474–75, 476, 674n
Arbeiderbladet, 386
Arbeitertum, 579

Armand, Inessa, 189, 625n
Artists in Uniform, A Study of Literature and Bureaucratism (Eastman), 312
Assignment in Utopia (Lyons), 414–15
Associated Press, 280, 316, 401
Atl, Dr. See Murillo, Gerardo
Austria, 65, 591, 602n, 674n; Social Democracy in, 42–43, 51, 134
Austro-Marxism, 43, 51
Axelrod, Pavel, 247, 632n
Axis, 579–80
Azana y Diaz, Manuel, 296, 331, 345, 592, 645n

Babeuf, Francis Noel ("Gracchus"), 184, 328, 624n
Balabanova, Angelica, 29, 602n
Baldwin, Stanley, 257, 634n
Balkans, 177, 543, 591
Balkan War (1910–12), 256
Baltic countries, 541, 542
Barbusse, Henri, 309
Bardin, Alexis, 434, 666n
Barmine, Alexander, 450
Bataille Socialiste, 86, 149, 199, 609n
Batalla, La, 296, 298, 641n
Bauer, Eugene. See Ackerknecht, Erwin
Beals, Carleton, 404, 658n
Belgian Labor Party (POB), 15–16, 135, 144, 166–67, 182–84, 223–24
Belgium, 306, 358, 359
—Trotskyists in, 104, 129–32, 144–46, 160–61, 244, 274, 304–5, 335, 353;

697

election policy of, 403; and entry
tactic, 166–67, 182–84, 223, 224,
242–44, 315
Berlingske Tidende, 383
Berlinrut, Peter ("Peter Granger"),
414, 661n
"Betrayal of the Spanish POUM,
The," 277
Biline, L. *See* Caby, Robert
Birney, Earle ("E. Robertson"), 254–
62, 275–76, 632–33n
Birobidzhan, 22, 600n
Biulleten Oppozitsii, 45, 299, 375,
407–8, 507, 536, 585
Blanqui, Louis-Auguste, 39, 603n
Bloc of Four, 53, 103–4
Bluecher, V.K., 110, 613n
Blum, Leon, 30, 35, 75, 76–77, 105,
148, 151, 190, 191–92, 303, 333,
346, 570, 602n
Blumkin, Jakob, 299
Bolshevik-Leninists (USSR), 37, 270,
274, 275, 316. *See* also USSR, Left
Opposition in
Bolsheviks, 168, 174, 194, 212, 255,
584–85; slanders against, 366–
67, 402–3
Bonapartism: bourgeois, 78–79, 135,
145, 155, 164, 198, 472; Soviet,
152, 572
Bordiga, Amadeo, 325
Bordigists, 137, 139, 164, 166–67
Bourderon, Albert, 189, 625n
Bourgeois revolution, 31
Brailsford, Henry N., 405, 658n
Brandler, Heinrich, 191, 410–11
Brandlerites, 29, 186
Brandt, Willy, 54, 187, 220
Brazil, 464; Fourth International
section in, 552
Breton, Andre, 453, 671n
Britain, 73, 119–20, 194; Trotskyists in, 100, 181, 405; and World
War II, 257–58, 458, 575, 578–79.

See also ILP; Communist Party
(Britain)
Brockway, Fenner, 34, 234–35, 403–4,
405, 657–58n
Browder, Earl, 289, 540, 541, 641n
Bruening, Heinrich, 164
Bryant, Louise, 175–78, 622n
Budenny, Semyon M., 587, 693n
Budu. *See* Mdivani, P.K.
Bukharin, Nikolai, 212, 309, 367,
436, 437
Bur, Jan. *See* Nettelbeck, Walter
Bureaucracy: and a socialist America,
124; in trade unions, 467–68, 469;
and USSR, 124–25, 176–77
Burnham, James, 419–20, 522, 544,
546, 662n
Butenko, Fyodor, 437–38, 667n
Butov, Georgi V., 299, 643n

Caballero. *See* Largo Caballero, Francisco
Caby, Robert ("L. Biline"), 278,
639n
Cachin, Marcel, 75, 77, 105, 608n
Cahiers du bolchevisme, Les, 148
Canada, 120, 282
Cannon, James P. ("Martel"), 288,
289, 290, 411, 412, 552; and factions in American section, 225,
226, 227–30, 238, 240, 241, 242,
254; work with International,
140–41, 513, 524
Capital (Marx), 431
Capitalism, 197–98, 488
Cardenas, Lazaro, 399, 468, 475, 477,
478, 479, 480, 558, 656n
Carlsson, Petrus, 376–77, 381
Carter, Joseph, 419–20
Catalan Federation, 235
Catalan Workers Alliance. *See* Workers Alliance (Catalonia)
Catalonia, 88–92, 314, 333, 609–11n
Cedillo, Saturnino, 478, 675n

Central America, 120
Centrism, 199; crisis of, 189–91; need for educating against, 27–35, 48–49, 277–78, 294; need for organizational flexibility toward, 58–60
CGT (General Confederation of Labor, France), 25, 80, 82, 146–47
CGTU (Unitary General Confederation of Labor, France), 80, 82
Chamberlain, Neville, 438, 542, 594, 667n
Chen Tu-hsiu, 221–24
Chiappe, Jean, 67, 607n
Chicago Daily News, 383
Chicago Tribune, 383
Chile, Trotskyists in, 105
China, 114, 454, 474; Trotskyists in, 221–24
Christian Science Monitor, 383
Ciliga, Anton, 263–70, 274–75, 303, 309–10, 316, 319, 323–24, 635n
CIO (Congress of Industrial Organizations), 413, 660n
Civil war (Russia), 271–72
Clark, Eleanor, 425
Clausewitz, Karl von, 260
Clave, 469, 493, 674n
Cohen, Larry, 290, 641n
Cohn, Oscar, 499, 676n
Columbia Broadcasting Corporation, 383
Commission of Inquiry into the Charges Made Against Leon Trotsky in the Moscow Trials, 397, 400–401, 404, 410, 411, 420–21, 422–24, 436–37, 438–39, 537, 663–64n
Committees of Vigilance (France), 75, 608n
Commune, La, 274, 279, 354, 501–2
Communist International (Comintern, Third International), 43, 104, 105, 136, 234, 284–85, 558; betrayals by, 42, 245–46; character of, 29; decay of, 18, 84, 133–34, 176–77; and GPU, 562–63; led by Lenin, 194, 570; Left Opposition and, 96; policy in Spain, 402, 584; Seventh World Congress of, 234, 274; and Social Democracy, 134, 302, 336; and World War II, 336, 583–84. *See also* Communist parties of specific countries; Faction or party question
Communist League (France), 24–26, 38–41, 45, 64, 65, 66–67, 72, 80–83, 104, 168–69, 277, 609n, 621n; and CP, 74–75; and entry into SFIO, 76–77, 85–86, 96–97, 101–3, 109, 130–32, 138–40, 155, 183. *See also* France, Trotskyist factions in
Communist League of America (CLA), 21–22, 46–47, 640n; and fusion with AWP, 52–53, 141
Communist Left (Spain), 297
Communist Manifesto, The (Marx, Engels), 426–27
Communist Party (Austria), 43
Communist Party (Britain), 18
Communist Party (France), 74–76, 80, 84–85, 105, 193–95; in Saint-Denis, 75, 76, 608n; and SFIO, 93, 95–96, 98–100, 101–2, 105, 566
Communist Party (Germany), 449; and fascism, 43
Communist Party (Mexico), 470–71, 477
Communist Party (Soviet Union): expulsions from, 279, 287–88; 1939 congress of, 586; political character of, 176–77
Communist Party (Spain). *See* Catalan Federation; Maurin
Communist Party (U.S.): CLA and, 46–47
Conference of Revolutionary Socialist Youth Organizations (Laren, Holland), 26–35, 48–51, 54–58, 60

Craipeau, Yvan, 92, 180–81, 420, 456
Crimes de Staline, Les, 440
Critique Sociale, La (Blanqui), 39
Croatia, 177
Crux. *See* Trotsky, Leon
CTM (Mexican Workers Confederation), 470, 674n
Cuarta Internacional, 469
Cudenet, Gabriel, 79, 608n
Culture, 32
Curtiss, Charles, 461–77 passim, 493, 524, 527, 673n
Curtiss, Lillian, 493, 527, 676n
Czechoslovakia, 104, 222, 594

Daladier, Edouard, 79
Dan, Fyodor, 302–3, 321, 419, 643n
Danno, Leon, 87–88, 609n
Danton, Georges, 447, 670n
Darwin, Charles, 127, 615n
Dauge, Walter, 144–45, 146, 300, 305, 325, 617n
Day, The, 383
"Decapitation of the Red Army, The", 407
Declaration of Four, 33, 34, 53, 142–43, 169, 351
"Defense of the USSR in the Present War" (Lebrun), 547–49
Defense policy: against fascism, 155
De Kadt, Jaques, 23, 34, 44–45, 165, 186–87, 190, 192, 351, 600n, 603n
De Man, Hendrik, 15, 35, 145, 147, 166–67
Democracy, 154–56, 296; bourgeois, 482, 565–66, 567–68, 591–92
Democratic Party (U.S.), 413
Democratic centralism, 46
De Silver, Margaret, 443
Desnots, Jacques ("Le Ricard"), 361, 649n
Des Pallieres, Jeanne Martin, 379, 432, 433–35, 495–503 passim, 666n
Dewey, John, 421, 423–24, 663n, 664n
Dictatorship of the proletariat, 487–88
Dies Committee, 539–40, 686n
Dimitrov, Georgi, 541
Dobbs, Farrell ("Smith"), 524, 545, 682–83n
Dommanget, Maurice, 184, 328–29, 624n
Donzel, Maurice ("Parijanine"), 61, 324
Doriot, Jacques, 100, 101–2, 186, 188, 191, 246, 346, 612n
Doumergue, Gaston, 79, 102, 105, 164, 608–9n
Drobnis, Yakov, 386, 654n
Dubois. *See* Fischer, Ruth
Dunayevskaya, Raya ("Rae Spiegel"), 414, 419, 660–61n
Dunne, Vincent, 493, 676n
Durand. *See* Sedov, Leon
Duranty, Walter, 398, 656n

Eastman, Max, 255–56, 312; role as translator, 371–74, 425–26, 429–30
Ebert, Friedrich, 592, 695n
Economist, The, 276
Eden, Anthony, 194, 626n
Education of Marxists, 42–43, 56–58, 181, 209–10, 277–78, 544
Eiffel, Paul. *See* Kirchoff, Paul
Eismont, Nikolai B., 153–54, 619n
Eltsin, Boris M., 308, 317, 320, 643n
Emancipation of Labor Group (Russia), 556, 557–58, 689n
"End of the 'Red Front' (Austria), The" (Frankel), 277
Engels, Frederick, 200, 286, 569
Entente, 246, 631n
Entry tactic, 102–3, 109, 133–40, 160–

67, 179, 237, 277, 282–84, 355–56; in Belgium, 144–46, 182–84; in Britain, 180–81; in France, 75, 76–77, 86–87, 96–97, 512, 513–15; in U.S., 225–45, 281–84, 290–93, 513
Epe, Heinz ("Walter Held"), 23, 54–58, 60, 187, 196, 220, 238, 242, 252, 356, 410, 411, 646n; on Comintern, 336–37; and refugees, 509–10; and youth, 510–11
Erik. *See* Muste, A.J.
Ernst, Morris L., 443, 668n
"Erwin." *See* Ackerknecht, Erwin
Esquerra (Catalonia), 90, 91
Estrine, Lilia (Lola) ("L. Paulsen," "L. Yakovlev"), 434, 666n
Etienne. *See* Zborowsky, Mark
Ethiopia, 256, 258, 344, 345, 590, 634n
Excelsior, 525, 543–44

Faction or party question, 107–8, 133–34
Faction struggles. *See* International Secretariat; Left Opposition sections in specific countries
Falk, Erling, 379–80, 381, 653n
Fascism, 41–42, 145, 171, 248, 388, 457–59; and Catalonia, 88–89, 610n; cause of, 28; and France, 174–75; and popular frontism, 565–66; strategy to fight against, 38–41, 68, 102, 106, 155, 165, 566; and U.S., 413, 492; and USSR, 152, 388; victory of, in Germany, 133–34; workers' militias against, 24–26, 102. *See also* United front
Faure, Paul, 93, 611n
February revolution (Russia), 97, 279
Fernandez Grandizo, Manuel ("Munis"), 527–28, 552, 554–55, 683n
Feroci, A. *See* Leonetti, Alfonso
Field, B.J., 46–47, 224, 245

Finland, 542, 575, 580, 583–84
First International, 431, 665n
Fischer, Louis, 408
Fischer, Oskar. *See* Schuessler, Otto
Fischer, Ruth ("Dubois"), 27, 73–74, 178–80, 222, 355–56, 410, 411, 607n
Flandin, Pierre-Etienne, 164, 171, 620–21n
Ford, Henry, 125, 614n
Foster, William Z., 124, 540, 614n
Fourth International, 64–66, 96, 106, 175–76, 221, 289–90, 338, 339, 547–53; and colonial and semicolonial countries, 468; September 1938 conference of, 512–13; debate about need for, 34, 37, 44, 49–50, 142–43, 187, 188, 251–52; and entry tactic, 109; and IEC factionalism, 547–53; and Pan-American Committee, 524–27, 528, 550–51, 683n; plans to set up, 196, 223–24, 273–75, 277–78, 289–90; and refugees, 509–10; and Russian question, 552; Stalinist attempts to destroy, 491; structure of, 221, 222, 295, 363–65; and youth, 252, 274. *See also* Faction or party question; Entry tactic; ICL; Trotskyists
Fox-Movietone News, 383
France, 26, 64, 70, 78, 155, 171–72, 174–75, 190–92, 193–95, 566, 570; fascism and, 174–75; and imperialism, 567; June 1936 upsurge in, 321, 323, 344, 353, 358; organic-unity movement in, 95–96, 98–100, 170, 611–12n; popular frontism in, 79, 174–75, 570, 622n; Social Democracy in, 76, 98–100; trade unions in, 471; Trotskyist factions in, 131–32, 162–63, 329–30, 411, 450–52, 493, 512–18, 616n; and USSR,

176–77; and World War II, 256–58, 575–76. See also Communist League (France); Communist Party (France); Entry tactic; Faction or party question; French revolution; GBL; SFIO
Franco, Francisco, 458, 673n
Frank, Pierre, 169
Frankel, Jan ("Werner," "Keller," "Glenner"), 242, 263, 264, 270, 377, 378, 404, 429–30
French revolution, 69, 286, 447, 448, 589, 597
French turn. See Entry tactic
Frossard, Louis-Olivier, 190, 198
Futuro, 563

Galicia, 542
Gandhi, Mohandas, 32
Garcia Oliver, Jose, 458, 672–73n
GBL (Bolshevik-Leninist Group, France), 130–32, 139–40, 146–49, 163, 167–70, 197–200, 284. See also Communist League (France); France, Trotskyist factions in
General strike, 183–84
Georget. See Rousset, David
Gerard, Francis. See Rosenthal, Gerard
Germany, 31, 65, 80, 164, 591; Comintern and, 42; and fascism, 133, 173, 202–15, 541–43; international defense campaign for Trotskyists in, 509–10; International Left Opposition and, 222; March 1921 crisis in, 511, 679–80n; Social Democracy in, 43, 173; Trotskyists in, 104–5, 161, 162, 179, 185, 339, 411, 603n, 628n; and World War II, 115, 256–58, 261, 344, 575–76, 577–80, 593. See also Communist Party (Germany); Faction or party question; Unser Wort
Gestapo, 366–68, 382

Gide, Andre, 321, 322, 324, 644n
Girondists, 447, 670n
Gitlow, Benjamin, 562
Give. See Vereecken, Georges
Glazman, Mikhail S., 299, 643n
Glenner. See Frankel, Jan
Glotzer, Albert, 49, 58, 518; and international youth conference, 26, 35, 60; and Workers Party factions, 225–26
Godefroid, Fernand, 146, 300, 305, 617n
Goldman, Albert, 421, 524, 526, 534, 539, 540, 564, 663n
Goltsman, E.S., 381, 653n
Good Neighbor Policy, 475
Gorkin, Julian, 410, 659–60n
Gould, Nathan ("Anton"), 230, 552, 689n
Gourov, G. See Trotsky, Leon
Governmental slogans, 74
GPU, 150–51, 264, 317, 395, 506–7; frame-ups by, 406–7; infiltration by, 302–3, 410, 507, 518; physical attacks by, 559–60; slanders by, 280, 366–68
Gracchus. See Babeuf, Francis Noel
Granger, Peter. See Berlinrut, Peter
Greece: Trotskyists in, 45, 56, 74
Grylewicz, Anton, 377, 406, 415, 661n
Guernut, Henri, 61

Hague, Frank, 459, 482, 486–87, 673n
Hamilton, John D.M., 581, 693n
Hannibal, 111
Hansen, Joseph, 414, 415, 419–20, 508, 520–21, 531–32, 540, 661n, 681n
Hansen, Reba, 521, 682n
Hayashi, Senjuro, 110, 113, 613n
Hearst, William Randolph, 280, 508–9, 639n

INDEX (1934-40) / 703

Hegel, Georg Wilhelm Friedrich, 127, 615n
Held, Walter. *See* Epe, Heinz
Hennaut, Adhemar, 164, 325
Herriot, Edouard, 47-48, 348, 381
Het Fundament, 45
Hilferding, Rudolf, 35
Hindenburg, Paul von, 164
History of the Russian Revolution, The, 307-8, 324, 371-73, 384, 425
Hitler, Adolf, 173, 257, 541-42, 572; war policy of, 575-79
Hitler-Stalin pact, 589
Hoare, Samuel, 257, 634n
Hoeglund, Zeth, 189, 625n
Hohenzollerns, 173, 622n
Holland, 358, 600n; Social Democracy in, 135. *See also* OSP
—Trotskyists in. RSP (Revolutionary Socialist Party), 23, 44-45, 55-57, 59, 105, 131, 134, 165; RSAP (Revolutionary Socialist Workers Party), 165, 188, 232, 251, 253, 254, 340-42, 345, 350-51, 352, 625n
Hoover, Herbert, 413, 582, 614n
Hotel Bristol (Copenhagen), 400, 657n
Hoy, 478
Humanite, L', 39, 68, 77, 148, 177

IAG (International Labor Community). *See* London-Amsterdam Bureau
Ibsen, Henrik, 384-85, 406, 653n
ICL (International Communist League), 34, 104, 132, 133, 136, 154, 628n, 629n, 644n, 645n, 646-47n; and entry tactic, 102-3, 130-31, 182-83, 283-84; July 1936 conference of, 352-59, 363-65; and Kirov assassination, 154. *See also* Fourth International; International Secretariat; Trotskyists

I Confess (Weiss), 452, 671n
IKD (Internationalist Communists of Germany). *See* Germany, Trotskyists in
ILP (Independent Labour Party, Britain), 17, 19-21, 34, 100, 109, 134; disintegration of, 294; and formation of Fourth International, 245-46; and Labour Party, 335; and Stalinism, 345; Trotskyist entry into, 181, 275-76. *See also* Britain; Centrism
Imperialism, 565, 566, 567
Individual, role of, in history, 591-93
Intellectuals, 255
International Left Opposition. *See* Trotskyists
International Secretariat (IS) ("Theodor"), 49, 605n, 660n; and Britain, 16-19; factionalism and, 56-57; functioning of, 45, 341, 411
Isaacs, Harold, 221, 234, 460, 629n
Italo-Ethiopian War, 256, 345, 347, 634n
Italy, 257-58, 347, 589, 590, 591; and World War II, 579-80. *See also* Bordigists; Maximalists
IVKO, 411, 660n

Jackson, Andrew, 128, 615n
Jacobins, 69, 127, 607n
James, C.L.R. ("Johnson"), 522-23, 524, 526, 545, 551, 552, 682n
Japan, 110-15, 119-20, 258-59, 261, 285, 558, 585
Jewish question, 21-22, 273, 518-19. *See also* Anti-Semitism
JGS (Socialist Youth Guard, Belgium), 144-46, 167, 617n
Johnson. *See* James, C.L.R.
Johnson, Hiram W., 581, 693n
Johre, S.L. *See* Weber, Josef
Jouhaux, Leon, 80, 149, 313, 358, 471, 567, 609n

Julik. See Kozlecki, Wenzel
Just, Claude, 88, 149, 609n

Kahlo, Frida, 559, 690n
Kak Vooruzhalas Revolutsiya (How the Revolution Armed Itself), 271
Kaldis, Aristodimos, 47, 603–4n
Kalinin, Mikhail I., 589, 694n
Kamenev, Leon, 36, 266, 272, 367, 368, 400
Kampf und Kultur, 385
KAPD (Communist Workers Party of Germany), 284–85, 640n
Karakhan, Lev, 441, 668n
Karsner, Rose, 445, 534–35, 538–39, 669n
Kautsky, Karl, 28, 601n
Keller. See Frankel, Jan
Kerensky, Alexander, 174, 321, 366, 537, 591–92, 593
Kienthal, 97
Kilbom, Karl, 186–87, 190
Kirchoff, Paul ("Eiffel"), 237, 630n
Kirov assassination, 149–54, 266, 618–19n
Klement, Rudolf ("Adolphe"), 62, 449, 504–6, 676–77n
Kling, Lazar, 21–22, 600n
Knickerbocker, H.R., 508
Kollontai, Alexandra, 367, 651n
Konikow, Antoinette, 563, 691n
Konikow, Edith, 563, 691n
Konstad, Leif Ragnvald, 406, 658n
Korea, 114
Kornfeder, Joseph ("Joseph Zack"), 240, 562, 631n
Kornilov, Lavr, 174
Kozlecki, Wenzel ("Julik"), 509–10, 679n
Krasnaya Zvezda (Red Star), 588–89
Kravchinsky, 556
Krestinsky, Nikolai, 435–36, 438, 667n

Krivitsky, Walter, 450, 530–32, 562, 670n, 684n
Kronstadt revolt (1921), 417–19, 422–23, 427, 661n
Kuibyshev, Valerian, 400, 657n
Kuomintang, 465, 474, 475
Kuskova, Yekaterina D., 419, 662n

Labor Front (Germany), 579
Labor party, in U.S., 413–14, 660n
Laborde, Hernan, 478, 480, 485, 491, 675n
Labour Party (Britain), 73, 294, 335
La Follette, Suzanne, 415, 661n
Lankin, Sol, 468, 469, 674n
Largo Caballero, Francisco, 296, 458, 592, 672n
Lasterade, Jean, 169, 621n
Latin America, 120, 394, 461–77; agrarian reform in, 465; national bourgeoisie in, 463–65; trade unions in, 467–68, 469; Trotskyists in, 461–62, 468–69; and U.S. imperialism, 466
Laurat, Lucien, 148, 618n
Laval, Pierre, 193, 626n
Leadership question, 227, 239–40, 357
League for the Rights of Man (France), 395
League of Nations, 347, 444–45, 669n
Lebrun, A. See Pedrosa, Mario
Ledebour, Georg, 319, 644n
Left Opposition. See Trotskyists
Legue, Maurice, 279, 639n
Lenin, Vladimir I., 47, 200, 247, 258, 289, 292, 569–70; and fight against Stalin, 368; slanders against, 366–67, 402–3; tactical flexibility of, 97, 229; and Trotsky, 271–72, 420; Trotsky's book on, 178, 372–74, 429–30, 445, 446
Leninism, 200

INDEX (1934–40) / 705

"Lenin-Trotsky Papers," 271–72
Leonetti, Alfonso ("Feroci," "Souzo," "J.-P. Martin"), 75; and International Secretariat, 295
Lesoil, Leon, 300, 305, 314, 315, 325
Levi, Paul, 511, 680n
Lewis, John L., 413
Lhuillier, Rene, 139, 169, 616n
Liberal, El, 298
Liberty, 567
Lie, Trygve, 201, 406, 627–28n
Lieber, Maxim, 280, 639–40n
Liebknecht, Karl, 189
Life, 538
Litvinov, Maxim, 105, 437–38, 587–88
Liu Jen-ching ("Niel Shih"), 221, 629n
Lombardo Toledano, Vicente, 463, 467, 473, 485; and slanders against Trotsky, 480–81, 491, 673n
London-Amsterdam Bureau, 35, 51, 141–43, 169, 185, 186, 277, 339, 341–42, 647n; and Fourth International, 344–49, 350, 351, 411, 454
London Times, The, 276
Longuet, Jean, 319, 644n
Louis, Paul, 29
Louzon, Robert, 313, 327
Lovestone, Jay, 258, 454–55
Lovestoneites, 29, 46–47, 238, 410–11, 453–54, 525
Lunacharsky, Anatole V., 367, 651n
Lund. *See* Trotsky, Leon
Lushkov, G.S., 530, 684n
Luteran, Barend, 254
Lutte de classes, La, 168, 621n
Lutte ouvriere, 403, 514
Luxemburg, Rosa, 452
Lvovna, Marie, 305, 306–7
Lyons, Eugene, 562, 691n

Macedonia, 177
Machete, El, 467

Malamuth, Charles, 522, 682n
Malvy, Louis, 367
Manchuria, 110–11, 114
Mangan, Sherry ("Terence Phelan"), 521, 681n
Mannin, Ethel, 276, 638n
Manuilsky, Dimitri, 33
Margne, Charles, 279, 639n
Maritime Provinces (USSR), 111, 113–14
Markin. *See* Sedov, Leon
Martin, Homer, 455, 672n
Martin, Jeanne. *See* Des Pallieres, Jeanne Martin
Martin, J.P. *See* Leonetti, Alfonso
Martin, Kingsley, 404–5, 658n
Martinet, Marcel, 323, 645n
Martov, Julius, 48, 50, 247, 604n
Marx, Karl, 39, 127, 200, 286, 296, 431
Marxism, 211–12, 544, 568, 573
Maslow, Arkadi ("Parabellum"), 27, 179, 222, 273, 410, 411
Mathews, William R., 482–92
Mathiez, Albert, 448, 670n
Matin, Le, 389
Matthews, J.B., 539, 540, 686n
Maurin, Joaquin, 89, 295–96, 297–98, 314, 318–19
Maximalists (Italy), 346, 347, 647n
Maxton, James, 318, 345
Mdivani, P.K. ("Budu"), 407
Meche. *See* Meichler, Jean
Meichler, Jean ("Meche"), 169, 621n
Mein Kampf (Hitler), 576
Menilmontant demonstration (France), 38–40
Mensheviks, 301–2, 303, 316, 319, 418, 419, 571
Menzhinsky, Vyacheslav R., 151, 619n
Merrheim, Alphonse, 189, 625n
Mexico, 394, 399, 461–77, 523; trade

union bureaucracy, 467–68; Trotskyists in, 468–70
Meyer, Haakon, 384–85, 406–7
MFI (Movement for the Fourth International). See Trotskyists Militia. See Workers' militia
Modiano, Helene, 149, 618n
Modiano, Rene, 149, 618n
Moe, Finn, 50, 605n
Molinier, Henri, 433–35
Molinier, Raymond, 380, 500, 501–2; expulsion of, 360–62; and factions in French section, 330, 450–52, 515
Molotov, Vyacheslav M., 212, 541
Monatte, Pierre, 313
Monmousseau, Gaston, 85, 184–85, 609n
Monroe Doctrine, 120, 614n
Morgan, J. Pierpont, 287, 640n
Morones, Luis N., 466–67, 674n
Moscow trials, 333, 370, 375, 398, 404, 406, 410, 440–41, 453–54, 482, 485, 538, 572; and capitulators, 368, 386–87, 400–401; and Hitlerism, 576; Trotsky's defense against charges, 376–84, 428–29 (see also Commission of Inquiry)
—Zinoviev-Kamenev trial (August 1936), 395, 400
—Pyatakov-Radek trial (January 1937), 400
—Bukharin-Rykov trial (March 1938), 435–36, 437–39, 666n, 667n
Mot Dag group (Norway), 195–96, 219, 220, 379
Mountain, the (France), 69, 607n
Mouvement Ouvrier Pendant la Guerre, De l'Union Sacree a Zimmerwald, Le (Rosmer), 304
Muenzenberg, Willi, 449–50
Mujica, Francisco, 444, 668–69n
Munis, Grandizo. See Fernandez Grandizo, Manuel
Murillo, Gerardo ("Dr. Atl"), 478, 675n
Mussolini, Benito, 257, 575, 584, 634n
Muste, A.J. ("Erik"), 234, 293, 325–26, 350, 351, 364, 366, 410, 455; and entryism, 226, 228–30, 231–33, 234–35, 236–45, 289, 290; and fusion with CLA, 52, 53; and ICL conference, 352–59, 363, 364–65, 366, 648n
My Life, 272, 498

Nacional, El, 561
NAP (Norwegian Labor Party), 35, 56, 138, 142, 169, 348, 351, 651n
Narodniks (Russia), 556–57, 689n
NAS (National Labor Organization, Holland), 23, 45, 56–57, 131, 357–58
Nation, The, 408, 659n
Nationalization, 70
National Labor Relations Board (NLRB), 477
National question: in Ukraine, 536–37; in U.S., 523, 544–45
Naville, Pierre, 168, 169, 170; and entry tactic, 132, 139, 140, 161–63; and French section, 330, 360; and Moscow trials, 400–401
Negrin, Juan, 458, 592, 673n
Negro question, 523, 544–45
Neos (right-wing faction of SFIO, France), 130, 135, 198, 615–16n
NEP (New Economic Policy, USSR), 417
Nettelbeck, Walter ("Jan Bur"), 273, 638n, 660n
Neue Front, Die, 241, 631n
New Deal, 486, 581
New International, The, 235, 240, 414, 416, 420, 422, 427, 631n
New Leader, The, 234

New Masses, The, 563, 691n
New Militant, 230, 241, 282, 631n
New Republic, The, 408, 590–91, 593, 659n
New Statesman, 404
New Testament, 251
New York Daily News, 479, 481
Niel Shih. *See* Liu Jen-ching
Nieuwe Fakkel, De, 241, 631n
Nikolaev, Leonid, 150–52, 154, 266, 618n
Nikolaevsky, Boris, 507, 677n
Nin, Andres: assassination of, 415; politics of, 297–98, 313–14, 318–19, 331
Norway, 73; Social Democracy in, 43, 51, 268; Trotskyists in, 143; Trotsky's exile in, 406, 428–29
Not Guilty (Dewey Commission), 452
Novack, George, 510, 679n
Novoe Russkoe Slovo, 407–8
Novosibirsk trial (November 1936), 386–88, 653–54n
NRA (National Recovery Administration), 115, 120, 613–14n
Nygaardsvold, Johan, 201, 628n

October revolution (Russia), 31, 69, 97, 296, 393, 394, 571, 589, 597
Octobre Rouge, 71, 607n
Oehler, Hugo, 225, 227, 239, 243, 244, 629–30n
Oehlerism, 225–30, 233, 235–40, 243, 254, 284
O'Gorman, Juan, 526, 683n
Okudzhava, Mikhail, 407
Old Bolsheviks, 437–38
Open Letter for the Fourth International, 196, 223, 232, 245–46, 273–74, 289, 341, 627n
"Open the books" slogan, 67
Opportunism, 138
OSP (Independent Socialist Party, Holland), 31, 33, 34–35, 45, 52, 53, 55, 56–57, 131, 134, 138, 169, 351

Pages Choisies (Babeuf), 184
Paine, Lyman ("White"), 289, 291
Palestine, 518–19
Pan-American Committee (of Fourth International), 524, 525–26, 527, 528, 683n
Papen, Franz von, 164, 376
Parabellum. *See* Maslow, Arkadi
Parijanine, Maurice. *See* Donzel, Maurice
Paulsen, L. *See* Estrine, Lilia (Lola)
Pavlov, Ivan P., 311
Paz, Magdeleine Marx, 301, 304, 309, 315, 319, 643n
Paz, Maurice, 301, 304, 309, 315, 319, 321, 324
PCI (Internationalist Communist Party, France), 450, 451
Pedrosa, Mario ("A. Lebrun"), 547–49, 551, 688n
People's Front, 278–79, 285, 295–96, 298, 316, 412, 639n; and fascism, 565–66; in France, 570; in Latin America, 465; in Spain, 331, 345–46
People's Will (Russia), 557
Pere-Lachaise cemetery (Paris), 81, 609n
Permanent revolution, 179, 461–62
Pero, R., 389, 655n
Petty bourgeoisie, 173, 328
Peuple, Le, 15, 375, 599n
Phelan, Terence. *See* Mangan, Sherry
Pillars of Society (Ibsen), 385
Pioneer Publishers, 343, 416
Pivert, Marceau, 101, 170, 190, 191–92, 254, 305, 346, 632n
Planned economy, 69–71, 121–23, 319–20
Platten, Fritz, 189, 626n
Plekhanov, Georgi, 247, 557–58, 631–32n

Plisnier, Charles, 300, 374–75, 643n
POB. *See* Belgian Labor Party
POI (Internationalist Workers Party, France), 450–52, 512–18
Poland, 280, 541, 542–43, 579; Trotskyists in, 22, 74, 105, 165, 335, 600n; and World War II, 585, 593
Political revolution, 286–87
Politiken, 383
Populaire, Le, 25, 77, 148, 151, 177
Popular, El, 467, 563
Poretsky, Ignace ("Ignace Reiss"), 433, 531, 666n
Posthumus, Nicolaas Wilhelmus, 389, 654–55n
POUM (Workers Party of Marxist Unification, Spain), 297–98, 333, 345–46, 403; and Fourth International, 454, 638–39n, 645n
Pravda, 37, 274, 287–88, 326, 367, 498
Prensa, La, 553
Press: bourgeois, 61–62, 63, 64–65, 316, 415, 508–9
—revolutionary, 146–48; distribution of, 206; and entry tactic, 282, 514–16
—Stalinist, 376
—under socialism, 125–26
Pritt, Denis N., 395–96, 404, 655n
PRM (Party of the Mexican Revolution), 465, 673–74n
"Program of the Swedish Socialist Party, The" (Held), 277
Proletariat, 569–71
Proudhon, Pierre-Joseph, 313, 644n
PSOP (Workers and Peasants Socialist Party, France), 512, 513–16, 517, 680–81n
Puntervold, Michael, 382, 386, 389, 429
PUP (Party of Proletarian Unity, France), 93, 609n

Pyatakov, Yuri, 386–88, 389, 400, 439, 653–54n, 667n

Quatrieme Internationale, 514, 516
Que Faire?, 237, 239, 630n

Radical Party (France), 64, 174–75, 566, 622n
Rakovsky, Christian, 36–37, 436–37
Red Army, 113–14, 260–62, 588; decapitation of, 438; reintroduction of rank in, 250, 286
Reed, John, 398
Reese, Maria, 23, 27, 41–42, 44
Reformism, 197–99
Refugees: Trotskyist, 509–10
Reichstag, 577, 579
Reiss, Elsa, 534–35, 685n
Reiss, Ignace. *See* Poretsky, Ignace
Renner, Karl, 592
Republican Party (U.S.), 413, 581
Revolution, 157–60, 230, 253, 620n
Revolution Betrayed, The, 332, 389, 393, 398, 425, 439, 586, 643n
Revolution proletarienne, La, 309, 310, 312–13, 315, 327, 643n
Rigaudias, Louis ("Rigal"), 181–82, 623n
Right Opposition. *See* Brandlerites; Lovestoneites
Rimbert, Pierre, 169
Rivera, Diego, 399, 452, 470, 472, 477, 493–94, 524–27, 553–55, 559–60, 656n
Robertson. *See* Birney, Earle
Robespierre, Maximilien, 447–48, 670n
Robinson, Gladys Lloyd, 457–60, 672n
Robinson, Viola, 221, 629n
Robitnichi Vysty, 262–63
Rolland, Romain, 309
Romains, Jules, 429, 430, 665n

Roosevelt, Franklin D., 120, 289, 442, 457, 475, 594, 614n
Rosendahl-Jensen, Synnove, 511, 680n
Rosengolts, Arkady, 438, 667n
Rosenmark, Raymond, 395–96, 655n
Rosenthal, Gerard ("Francis Gerard"), 167–68, 382, 434, 496, 498, 507
Rosmer, Alfred, 304, 312, 321–22, 455, 497, 507; attitude toward Fourth International, 322–23, 329–30, 331; and Leon Sedov's archives, 434; and Moscow trials, 401, 424
Rosmer, Marguerite Thevenet, 304, 401, 497, 643n
Ross, Edward A., 537–38, 685n
Rossi. *See* Abbiatte, Roland
Rous, Jean, 351, 411, 648n
Rousset, David ("Georget"), 87–88, 609n
RSAP. *See* Holland
RSP. *See* Holland
Ruehle, Otto, 424, 664n
Ruskin, Harry, 518–19
Russia, 591; history of, 255, 271–72, 417–19, 555–58, 580. *See also* USSR
Russo-Japanese War (1904–05), 111
Ryazanov, David B., 227, 239, 317, 631n
Rykov, Alexei, 367, 400, 436, 437

St. Louis Post-Dispatch, 594
Salengro, Roger, 321, 644n
Sanchez Salazar, Leandro, 558–60, 690n
SAP (Socialist Workers Party, Germany), 35, 45, 55, 59, 134, 138, 161–62, 169–70, 179, 185–88, 228, 237, 238, 239, 240–41; and Comintern, 339; illusions of Trotskyists about, 189–90, 192, 251–52, 253–54, 294; on need for Fourth International, 50–51; and Stockholm Bureau, 195–96, 220; on war, 246
Sarraut, Albert, 102, 612n
Schapiro, Meyer, 453, 671n
Scharffenberg, Johan, 385, 653n
Scheflo, Olav, 265–67, 268–69, 636n
Scheidemann, Philipp, 592, 695n
Schlamm, Willi, 264, 265, 636n
Schleicher, Kurt von, 164, 376
Schmidt, Peter J., 186, 189, 241, 253, 273, 275–76, 354, 355
Schuessler, Otto ("Oskar Fischer"), 147–48, 362, 380, 509, 510
Schwarz. *See* Sedov, Leon
Science, 583, 595–96
Second International, 28–30, 43, 49–50, 84, 94, 96–97, 570. *See also* Social Democracy
Sectarianism, 138–39, 225–26, 326–27, 333
Sedov, Leon ("Markin," "Schwarz," "Durand"), 27, 264, 375, 376, 381, 389, 501–2, 503–4; archives of, 432–33, 434; death of, 432, 433–34, 443–44, 494–95; and Moscow trials, 386, 436; and Trotsky's archives, 421, 501
Sedova, Natalia I., 202, 325, 369, 381, 384, 387, 434–35, 442–43, 484
Seine Federation of the Young Socialists, 88, 253, 609n
Seipold, Oskar ("Weiss"), 264, 636n
Selander, Ted, 414, 661n
Sellier, Louis, 49, 604–5n
Senin, Adolph. *See* Sobolevicius, Abraham
Serge, Victor, 299–334, 370, 455, 529, 574, 644n; on Kronstadt revolt, 417–18; and sectarianism question, 326–27, 330–31; on Spain, 331–32, 333; syndicalism of, 309, 327–28
Severac, Jean-Baptiste, 98, 612n
SFIO (French Section of the Labor [Sec-

ond] International, the French Socialist Party), 76–77, 80, 81, 84–85, 190, 197–98, 232; and Communist Party, 93, 95–96, 98–100, 101–3, 105, 566; and Trotskyist entry, 76, 77, 85, 92–94, 96–97, 109, 130–31, 138–40, 155, 161–62, 164

Shachtman, Max ("Trent"), 58, 59, 238, 239–40, 241, 242, 522, 540, 657n; and CLA factions, 400; and July 1936 International conference, 356, 366; and Russian question, 545; and SWP factions, 552; and Workers Party factions, 225, 226, 254

Shaposhnikov, Boris M., 586–87, 693n

Shishko, 556

Simon and Schuster, 429–30

Sklyansky, Efraim, 272, 637–38n

Smilga, Ivan T., 367, 651

Smirnov, Ivan, 386, 654n

Smith, Andrew, 317, 644n

Smith, Carleton, 546–47

Sneevliet, Henricus, 23, 132, 273, 275, 340–41, 350, 455, 659n; attitude of, toward ICL, 352, 354, 355–56; and Dutch politics, 357; and entry tactic, 355–56; factional activity of, 410

Sobolevicius, Abraham ("Adolph Senin"), 384, 653n

Social Democracy, 134–36, 570–71; and Comintern, 134, 284–85, 302, 336–37. *See also* under specific countries

"Social fascism," 43–44

"Socialism in one country," theory of, 22, 83, 378, 585

Socialist Appeal, 414, 416, 420, 427, 492–93, 521, 532–34, 538, 661–62n

Socialist Party (France). *See* SFIO

Socialist Party (Spain), 134–35, 616n

Socialist Party (U.S.), 232–33, 242–43, 513

Socialist Workers Party (U.S.), 493–94, 532–34, 554–55, 671n, 672n; aid to French section, 516, 519–20; composition of, 535–36; expansion and turn to industry by, 535–36; and Lovestoneites, 453–56; and opponents work with CP, 520–21; results from SP entry, 513; and Russian question, 538–39, 544, 549–50, 551–52, 685–86n. *See also* Communist League of America; Workers Party

Socialist Youth League (SJV, Holland), 27–35

Social Revolutionaries (Russia), 150, 556, 599n

Soir, 375

Sokolnikov, Grigory, 367, 651n

Sokolovskaya, Alexandra Lvovna, 192–93, 305, 498, 626n

Solntsev, Eleazar B., 299, 642–43n

Solow, Herbert, 52

South Africa, 224

Souvarine, Boris, 161, 301–3, 447

Souzo. *See* Leonetti, Alfonso

Soviets, 33, 44; prospects for, in U.S., 115–19, 125

Spaak, Paul-Henri, 183, 305, 623n

Spain, 455, 458, 591, 645n; anarchists in, 333; and fascism, 88–89, 90–91, 610n; Social Democracy in, 134–35; Trotskyists in, 166, 235, 277, 297–98, 313–14, 411, 641–42n; and World War II, 580. *See also* POUM; Spanish Revolution

Spanish revolution, 323, 345–46, 402, 403, 408–9, 454, 573, 592; and Catalonia, 88–92, 333; and People's Front, 331, 347–48; and role of Stalinists, 415, 584. *See also* Spain

Spanjer, Bep, 335, 645n

Spartacus, 274, 321, 375, 644n

INDEX (1934-40) / 711

Spartacus League (Germany), 83
Spector, Maurice, 281–91, 293
Spiegel, Rae. *See* Dunayevskaya, Raya
Splits in Trotskyist groups: Britain, 16–21; France, 131–32, 512–16, 517–18; Germany, 411; Greece, 166. *See also* Fourth International
Stakhanovite movement, 287, 640–41n
Stalin, Joseph, 154, 182, 439, 440, 485, 596, 619n; China policy of, 474; economic policy of, 585–86; war policy of, 541, 542–43, 572, 575, 577–78; and Moscow trials, 382, 400, 401–3; role of, in Russian revolution, 367; Trotsky's book on, 445, 446–47
Stalinism, 49, 74–75, 104–5, 152–53, 255, 266–67, 479–81; and falsification of history, 272; and Menshevism, 319; origins of, 423–24; and World War II, 541–43
Stalin School of Falsification, The, 343
Stamm, Thomas, 243–44
State capitalism, 320, 339–40, 398, 472, 474, 646n
Stavisky, Serge-Alexandre, 67, 68, 607n
Sterling, Max, 414, 660–61n
Sternberg, Fritz, 404
Stockholm Bureau, 195–96, 219–20, 237–38, 242, 346; expulsion of Trotskyists from, 346–47
Strikes: in U.S., 282–83
Sumner, Charles, 405, 658n
Swabeck, Arne, 52, 225, 226, 401
Sweden, 51, 57–58
Switzerland, 104; trial in, 396–97
Syndicalism, 309, 312–13, 327–28

Tanaka Memorial, 558, 689–90n
Tardieu, Andre, 102, 612–13n
Tarov, Arben, 263, 636n
Tass, 333, 645n
Taxes, 70, 71
Teachers' Federation (France), 328, 624n
Temps, Le, 176, 183, 250
Terrorism, 150, 177, 182, 306, 307, 366–68, 371, 557–58
Terrorism and Communism, 295
Thalheimer, August, 410–11, 660n
Theo. *See* Van Driesten, Hendrik
Theodor. *See* International Secretariat
Thermidor, 448
Third International After Lenin, The, 343
Thomas, Norman, 282
Thomas, Wendelin, 422, 423–24, 663n
Thorez, Maurice, 98, 105, 612n
Tioli, 410, 659n
Tomsky, Mikhail, 212, 367
Totalitarianism, 582
Toward Socialism or Capitalism?, 585
Trade unions: in France, 471; in Germany, 471–72; in Holland, 357–58; in Italy, 471–72; in Mexico, 467–68, 471–74; in Spain, 471; statification of, 471–73, 477, 674n; in U.S., 413, 467, 469
Tragedy of the Chinese Revolution, The, (Isaacs), 460
Tranmael, Martin, 30, 34, 43, 49, 51, 186, 190
Trans-Baikal, 111
Transitional method, 67–71, 467–78
"Transitional Program, The", 444–45, 660n, 669n
Treint, Albert, 148–49, 330–31
Tresca, Carlo, 424, 443–44, 664n
Trotsky, Leon ("G. Gourov," "Vidal," "Lund," "Crux"), 246–51, 489–90,

553–54, 563–64, 631n, 644–45n, 646n, 655–56n; archives of, 389, 420–21, 501, 507, 538–39, 562; assassination of, 597; and Bolshevik Party, 212; collaboration of, with Fourth Internationalists, 234, 241–42; and custody battle for grandson, 494–504; defense against Stalinist slanders, 376–84, 437–39 (*see also* Commission of Inquiry); exile in Mexico, 399, 406, 477–79; exile in Norway, 406, 658n; expulsion from France, 60–66; finances of, 307, 371–73, 428–29; and Lenin, 271–72; on literature, 385; marriage of, to Alexandra Lvovna Sokolovskaya, 498; physical attacks on, 333, 444, 559–60, 561–62, 652n; and Diego Rivera, 559–60; Stalinist slanders of, 376, 400–401, 479–82, 588–89; threatens hunger strike, 369; visa for Norway, 201–2; visa application for U.S., 442–43; on World War II, 482, 488–89, 541–43, 546–47, 574–82, 660n

Trotskyists, 31, 96–97, 133–34, 421, 447; and capitulators, 36–37, 386–87, 400–401, 435–36; conferences, 73, 156; education of, 57, 277–78; fusions of, 52–53, 141, 165, 235, 254, 274; and other left groups, 50–51, 181, 245–46, 276; repression of, 36, 270, 275, 326; splits in, 131–32; Stalinist slanders of, 376, 393–94, 401–3, 440; war policy of, 246, 258–60, 285–86, 605–6n. *See also* Declaration of Four; Defense policy; Entry tactic; Faction or party question; ICL; Fourth International; names or countries of sections; Open Letter for the Fourth International; Splits

Tsereteli, Irakli, 321, 644n
Tukhachevsky, Mikhail, 438, 587, 667n
Turkey, 384
Two-and-a-Half International, 50, 96–97, 348

Ukrainian question, 536–37
Ullevaal Hospital (Oslo), 250
Ultimatists (Russia), 229, 630n
Ultraleftism, 38–40. *See also* Bordigists; Third period
Uneven and combined development, theory of, 556
United Front, 29–30, 81–83, 170; and fascism, 566; and France, 93, 104–5, 130, 155, 157; and Stalinists, 74–76, 104–7
United Press, 402
United States, 307, 412–13, 431, 597, 613–14n; anti-Semitism in, 519; and democracy, 458–59; and fascism, 413, 492; prospects for socialism in, 115–28, 486–88, 547; and Stalinism, 255; Trotskyists in, 334–35, 340–41, 405, 411, 454–55, 513, 633–34n, 657n; unemployment in, 581; and World War II, 257, 258–60, 482, 578, 580, 594. *See also* Communist League of America; Communist Party (U.S.); Socialist Party (U.S.); Socialist Workers Party; Strikes; Workers Party (U.S.)
Unser Wort, 190, 208, 275, 339
Unzer Kamf, 22
Uritsky, Moisei, 150, 619n
Usick. *See* Vanzler, Joseph
USSR, 136, 149–54, 248–50, 260–62, 319–20, 388, 401–2, 441, 582, 614n; attitude of workers in, toward bureaucracy, 153, 439–40, 485–86; bureaucracy, 268–69, 285–87, 303, 589; class character of state

in, 143–44, 172–73, 419–20, 539, 544; defense of, against attack, 33, 144, 148–49, 154–56, 258–60, 393–94, 398, 552, 571–72, 590; economy of, 31, 319–20, 339–40, 577, 585–86; and Finland, 542, 575, 583–84; foreign policy of, 193–95, 285–86, 518, 580; Jews in, 22, 400, 576–77, 657n; Left Opposition in, 37, 274 (*see also* Bolshevik-Leninists [USSR]); and national question, 536–37, 589; political prisoners in, 287–88, 305, 309–10, 316–17, 326–27; repression in, 152, 264–65, 270, 287–88, 299, 302, 645n; and Thermidor, 367–68; and World War II, 110–11, 112–15, 258–62, 285–86, 583–84, 586–87, 590, 593; youth, 182. *See also* Communist Party (Soviet Union); Moscow trials; Stalinism

Van. *See* Van Heijenoort, Jean
Vandervelde, Emile, 16, 183, 223, 303
Van Driesten, Hendrik ("Theo"), 251, 252, 632n
Van Heijenoort, Jean ("Van"), 404, 443, 483–84, 490, 544
Van Riel, Rene, 334, 645n
Vanzler, Joseph ("John G. Wright," "Usick"), 422, 426–28, 539, 540, 664n
Varga, Eugene, 147, 618n
Vereecken, Georges ("Give"), 45, 223–24, 237, 244, 245, 305, 314, 315, 410, 451, 455, 501; and entry tactic, 129–32, 161–63, 165, 166; position on Spain, 403; sectarianism of, 325, 330–31
Verite, La, 25, 64, 65, 71, 76, 81, 102, 147–48, 164, 170
Vidal. *See* Trotsky, Leon

Vinnichenko, Vladimir K., 536–37, 685n
Voix Communiste, La, 183
Volkhovsky, 556
Volkov, Platon, 498–99
Volkov, Vsievolod ("Sieva"), 435, 494–504, 666–67n
Volkova, Zinaida, 496
Volodarsky, V., 150, 619n
Voroshilov, Kliment, 587, 693–94n
Vorovsky, Vatslav, 150, 619n
Voz de Mexico, La, 563
Vyshinsky, Andrei, 368, 572, 692n

Walcher, Jacob ("Schwab"), 50, 186–87, 191–92, 238, 318, 404
Walker, Charles R., 408, 659n
War, 278–79, 541–42, 581; revolutionary policy on, 245–46, 259, 285–86
"War and the Fourth International", 23, 60, 142–43, 258, 260, 275, 600n, 605–6n
Wasserman, Jac, 416, 452–53, 661n
Webb, Beatrice, 345, 647n
Webb, Sidney, 345, 647n
Weber, Jack, 21, 225, 226, 228, 229–30, 231, 232–33, 288–89, 293, 600n
Weber, Josef ("S.L. Johre"), 273, 411, 638n, 660n
Weber, Sara, 60, 372, 606n
Weil, Simone, 329, 645n
Weisbord, Albert, 26–27, 224, 245
Weiss. *See* Seipold, Oskar
Well, Roman. *See* Sobolevicius, Abraham
Welles, Sumner, 580–81, 693n
Wels, Otto, 30, 33, 35
Werner. *See* Frankel, Jan
White. *See* Paine, Lyman
"Whither France?", 147, 191
Witte (Demetrious Giotopoulos), 45, 47, 166
Wolf, Erwin ("Nicolle Braun"), 270,

356, 360–61, 374–75, 404, 410, 414, 625n, 659n
Wolf, Hjoerdis, 410, 659n
Wolfe, Bernard, 404, 658n
Wolfe, Bertram D., 454–55, 671–72n
Workers Alliance (Catalonia), 89–90, 610–11n
Workers Alliance of America, 456, 672n
Workers' and peasants' government, 69–70
Workers' control, 67–68, 70–71
Workers' militia, 24–26, 68–69, 74, 102, 588
Workers Party (WPUS, U.S.), 224, 225, 226, 228, 232, 234, 235, 237, 238; and entry tactic, 242–43, 244, 291–92, 513; factions in, 291–93, 641n. *See also* American Workers Party (AWP); Communist League of America (CLA); United States, Trotskyists in
"Workers' State, Thermidor, and Bonapartism", 261–62
World's Fair (New York), 595
World War I, 319, 367, 570–71, 580
World War II, 155, 258, 457–58; causes of, 593; and Stalinism, 336, 541; Trotsky on, 482, 488–89, 541–43, 546–47, 574–83, 593, 594
Wrangel officer, 154, 619n
Wright, John G. *See* Vanzler, Joseph

Yagoda, Henrikh, 151, 382, 619n
Yakovlev, L. *See* Estrine, Lilia (Lola)
Yale Review, The, 446
Yaroslavsky, Emelyan, 280
Yenukidze, Abel, 441, 668n
Young Lenin, The, 425. *See also* Lenin, Vladimir I., Trotsky's book on
Young Socialists (JS, France), 88, 92–96, 129, 148, 156–57, 181; Seine Alliance of, 88, 156, 163
Youth, 25, 27–35, 109, 237–38, 459–60, 510–11; Belgium, 144–46; and class composition, 156–57; and Fourth International, 195–96, 219–20, 252, 274; France, 88, 92–96, 129, 156–57, 163, 181; international conference, Holland, 48–51, 54–58, 60; Spain, 297–98; and terrorism, 371; in USSR, 182

Zack, Joseph. *See* Kornfeder, Joseph
Zamora, Francisco, 424, 664n
Zborowsky, Mark ("Etienne"), 506–7, 677n
Zeller, Fred, 253, 266, 267, 632n, 637n
Zimmerwald, 48, 97
Zinoviev, Gregory, 36, 266, 272, 367, 368, 400, 437, 653n
Zinoviev Trial, The (Pritt), 395
Zionism, 519
Zyromsky, Jean, 101, 190–92, 199, 612n

OTHER WRITINGS BY LEON TROTSKY

The Revolution Betrayed
What Is the Soviet Union and Where Is It Going?

In 1917 workers and peasants of Russia were the motor force of one of the deepest revolutions in history. Yet within ten years a political counterrevolution by a privileged social layer, whose chief spokesperson was Joseph Stalin, was being consolidated. The classic study of the Soviet workers state and its degeneration. $17. Also in Spanish, Farsi, Greek.

The Third International After Lenin

Leon Trotsky's 1928 defense of the Marxist course that had guided the Communist International in its early years. Writing in the heat of political battle, Trotsky addresses the key challenge facing working people today: building communist parties throughout the world capable of leading workers and farmers to take power. $20. Also in Farsi.

The Challenge of the Left Opposition

Continuing the political fight V.I. Lenin began at the end of his life, Leon Trotsky explains that "our task is the rebirth of Bolshevik politics within the parties of the Communist International." Three volumes record the struggle Trotsky led in the 1920s to defend Lenin's proletarian internationalist course. $25 each

Writings of Leon Trotsky

Fourteen volumes covering the period of Trotsky's exile from the Soviet Union in 1929 until his assassination at Stalin's orders in 1940. $270 set

PATHFINDERPRESS.COM

BUILDING A PROLETARIAN PARTY

New!
The Fight Against Jew-Hatred and Pogroms in the Imperialist Epoch
Stakes for the International Working Class

V.I. LENIN, LEON TROTSKY
FARRELL DOBBS, JAMES P. CANNON
JACK BARNES, DAVE PRINCE

Jew-hatred and pogroms—such as Hamas carried out on October 7, 2023—are now part of the permanent social convulsions and wars of the imperialist epoch. The authors explain why fighting Jew-hatred is of decisive importance to the working class and oppressed nations of the world, and answer the question: *What is to be done to end it*—for all time. $10. Also in Spanish and French.

The Low Point of Labor Resistance Is Behind Us
The Socialist Workers Party Looks Forward

JACK BARNES, MARY-ALICE WATERS, STEVE CLARK

The global order imposed by Washington after its victory in World War II is shattering. A long retreat by the working class and unions has come to an end. The bosses and their government are stepping up attacks on our wages, conditions, and constitutional rights. This book highlights opportunities for building a mass proletarian party able to lead the struggle to end capitalist rule, opening a socialist future for humanity. $10. Also in Spanish, French, Greek.

Our Politics Start with the World
JACK BARNES

The huge economic and cultural inequalities between imperialist and semicolonial countries, and among classes within them, are perpetuated by the workings of capitalism. To build parties able to lead the revolutionary struggle for power in our own countries, vanguard workers must be guided by a strategy to close this gap. In *New International* no. 13. $14. Also in Spanish, French, Farsi, Greek.

$12 $20

$15

Three books to be read as one ...

about building a party that's working class in program, composition, and action. One that recognizes, in word and deed, the most revolutionary fact of our time ...

... that working people have the power to create a different world as we act together to defend our own class interests—not those of the privileged classes who exploit our labor, not of those who fear us as "deplorables," or just plain "trash."

As we advance along a revolutionary course toward workers power, we will transform ourselves and awaken to our own worth. Also in Spanish, French, Farsi, Greek.

Special Offer!
All three $30

The Turn to Industry and *Tribunes of the People and the Trade Unions* $20

Either book plus *Malcolm X, Black Liberation, and the Road to Workers Power* $25

PATHFINDERPRESS.COM

FROM THE DICTATORSHIP OF CAPITAL TO THE DICTATORSHIP OF THE PROLETARIAT

The Communist Manifesto
KARL MARX
AND FREDERICK ENGELS

Communism, say the founding leaders of the revolutionary workers movement, is not a set of ideas or preconceived "principles" but workers' line of march to power. It springs from a "movement going on under our very eyes." $5. Also in Spanish, French, Farsi, Arabic.

State and Revolution
V.I. LENIN

"The relation of the socialist proletarian revolution to the state is acquiring not only practical political importance," wrote V.I. Lenin just months before the October 1917 Russian Revolution. It also addresses the "most urgent problem of the day: explaining to the masses what they will have to do to free themselves from capitalist tyranny." $15

Their Trotsky and Ours
JACK BARNES

To lead the working class in a successful revolution, a mass proletarian party is needed whose cadres, well beforehand, have absorbed a world communist program, are proletarian in life and work, derive deep satisfaction from doing politics, and have forged a leadership with an acute sense of what to do next. This book is about building such a party. $12. Also in Spanish, French, Farsi.

Lenin's Final Fight
Speeches and Writings, 1922–23

V.I. LENIN

In 1922 and 1923, V.I. Lenin, central leader of the world's first socialist revolution, waged what was to be his last political battle—one that was lost after his death. At stake was whether that revolutionary government and the world communist movement it led would remain on the revolutionary proletarian course that brought workers and peasants to power in October 1917. $17. Also in Spanish, Farsi, Greek.

The History of the Russian Revolution

LEON TROTSKY

How, under Lenin's leadership, the Bolshevik Party led millions of workers and farmers to overthrow the state power of the landlords and capitalists in 1917 and bring to power a government that advanced their class interests at home and worldwide. Unabridged, 3 vols. in one. Written by one of the central leaders of that socialist revolution. $30. Also in French and Russian.

U.S. Imperialism Has Lost the Cold War

JACK BARNES

The collapse of regimes across Eastern Europe and the USSR claiming to be communist did not mean workers and farmers there had been crushed. In today's sharpening class conflicts and wars, these toilers are joining working people the world over in the class struggle against capitalist exploitation. In *New International* no. 11. $14. Also in Spanish, French, Farsi, Greek.

PATHFINDERPRESS.COM

THE FIGHT AGAINST FASCISM

Imperialism's March toward Fascism and War
JACK BARNES

"There will be new Hitlers, new Mussolinis. That is inevitable. What is not inevitable is that they will triumph. The working-class vanguard will organize our class to fight back against the devastating toll we are made to pay for the capitalist crisis. The future of humanity will be decided in the contest between these contending class forces." In *New International* no. 10. $14. Also in Spanish, French, Farsi, Greek.

Revolution and Counter-Revolution in Spain
FELIX MORROW

A contemporary account of the revolution and civil war in Spain in the 1930s in which workers and peasants, betrayed by Stalinist, social-democratic, and anarchist misleaderships, went down to defeat under the blows of an armed fascist movement. $17

Fascism and Big Business
DANIEL GUERIN

Examines the development of fascism in Germany and Italy and its relationship with the ruling capitalist families there. $20

Counter-Mobilization
A Strategy to Fight Racist and Fascist Attacks
FARRELL DOBBS

A discussion on strategy and tactics in the fight against fascist attacks on the labor movement, drawing on the experiences of the Minneapolis Teamsters movement of the 1930s. $5

The Jewish Question
A Marxist Interpretation
ABRAM LEON

The battle against reactionary forces aiming to exterminate the Jews remains central to world politics, as shown by the genocidal October 2023 pogrom in Israel. Why is Jew-hatred still raising its ugly head? What are its class roots? Why, as Abram Leon explains, is there no solution "independent of the world proletarian revolution"? Revised translation, new introduction, 40 pages of illustrations and maps. $17. Also in Spanish and French.

The Spanish Revolution (1931–39)
LEON TROTSKY

Trotsky recounts a decade of revolutionary struggles and the Stalinist betrayal in Spain that ensured a fascist victory in 1939, making World War II inevitable. $23

What Is American Fascism?
JAMES P. CANNON, JOSEPH HANSEN

Analyzes 20th century fascist currents in the US. "A fascist movement if it is to be successful must have a scapegoat on whom the petty-bourgeois masses can vent their rage in place of the capitalists who deserve it," wrote Hansen about Father Charles Coughlin's anti-Semitic "Social Justice" movement in the late 1930s. "Coughlin like Hitler and Mussolini has selected the Jew." $5

Leon Trotsky on France

An assessment of the social and economic crisis that shook France in the mid-1930s in the aftermath of Hitler's rise to power in Germany, and a program to unite the working class and exploited peasantry to confront it. $17

PATHFINDERPRESS.COM

CAPITALIST CRISIS AND THE FIGHT FOR WORKERS POWER

50 Years of Covert Operations in the US
Washington's Political Police and the American Working Class

LARRY SEIGLE, FARRELL DOBBS STEVE CLARK

How class-conscious workers have defended constitutional freedoms and fought the capitalists' drive to build the "national security" state essential to maintaining their rule. $10. Also in Spanish and Farsi.

In Defense of the US Working Class
MARY-ALICE WATERS

Drawing on the fighting traditions of the oppressed and exploited of all colors and national origins, in 2018 tens of thousands of teachers and other working people in West Virginia, Oklahoma, and other states waged victorious strikes. They fought for dignity and respect for themselves, their families, and for all working people. $7. Also in Spanish, French, Farsi, Greek.

Are They Rich Because They're Smart?
Class, Privilege, and Learning Under Capitalism

JACK BARNES

In battles forced on us by the capitalists, workers will begin to transform our attitudes toward life, work, and each other. We'll discover our worth, denied by the rulers and upper middle classes who insist they're rich because they're smart. We'll learn in struggle what we're capable of becoming. $10. Also in Spanish, French, Farsi, Arabic, Greek.

Opening Guns of World War III: Washington's Assault on Iraq

JACK BARNES

The murderous assault on Iraq in 1990–91 heralded increasingly sharp conflicts among imperialist powers, growing instability of capitalism, and more wars. Also includes:

1945: When US Troops Said 'No!'
by Mary-Alice Waters

Lessons from the Iran-Iraq War
by Samad Sharif

In *New International* no. 7. $14. Also in Spanish, French, Farsi.

The Teamster Series

FARRELL DOBBS

Four books on the strikes, organizing drives, and political campaigns that transformed the Teamsters across the Midwest in the 1930s into a militant industrial union movement. Written by Farrell Dobbs, the general organizer of these Teamster battles and leader of the Socialist Workers Party.

A tool for workers seeking to use union power in every workplace and advance the fight for an independent labor party. $16 each, series $50. Also in Spanish. *Teamster Rebellion* is also available in French, Farsi, Greek.

The Clintons' Anti-Working-Class Record

Why Washington Fears Working People

JACK BARNES

What working people need to know about the profit-driven course of Democrats and Republicans alike over the last three decades. And the political awakening of workers seeking to understand and resist the capitalist rulers' assaults. $10. Also in Spanish, French, Farsi, Greek.

PATHFINDERPRESS.COM

CUBA'S SOCIALIST REVOLUTION

Women in Cuba: The Making of a Revolution Within the Revolution
VILMA ESPÍN
ASELA DE LOS SANTOS
YOLANDA FERRER

The integration of women in the ranks and leadership of the Cuban Revolution was intertwined with the proletarian course led by Fidel Castro from the start. This is the story of that revolution and how it transformed the women and men who made it. $17. Also in Spanish, Farsi, Greek.

The First and Second Declarations of Havana

Nowhere are the questions of revolutionary strategy that today confront men and women on the front lines of struggles in the Americas addressed with greater truthfulness and clarity than in these uncompromising indictments of imperialist plunder and "the exploitation of man by man." Adopted by million-strong assemblies of the Cuban people in 1960 and 1962. $10. Also in Spanish, French, Farsi, Arabic, Greek.

Our History Is Still Being Written
The Story of Three Chinese Cuban Generals in the Cuban Revolution
ARMANDO CHOY, GUSTAVO CHUI, MOISÉS SÍO WONG
MARY-ALICE WATERS

"What was the key measure to uproot discrimination against Chinese and blacks in Cuba? It was the socialist revolution itself." New edition sheds light on Chinese Cubans' involvement in Cuba's internationalist course, including in Africa and Latin America. $15. Also in Spanish, French, Farsi, Greek, Chinese.

New Edition!
Che Guevara on Economics and Politics in the Transition to Socialism
CARLOS TABLADA

It's essential for working people to win state power, said Ernesto Che Guevara. "Then there's the second stage, maybe more difficult than the first"—the transition from dog-eat-dog capitalism to socialism. That includes moving from work as a condition for survival, to voluntary social labor through which we express our common humanity. Includes Fidel Castro's 1987 speech "Che's Ideas Are Absolutely Relevant Today." New edition with substantially expanded selections from Guevara's writings. $17. Also in Spanish.

Cuba and the Coming American Revolution
JACK BARNES

This is a book about the example set by the Cuban people that socialist revolution is not only necessary—it can be made. A book about the struggles of workers and other exploited producers in the imperialist heartland, and the youth attracted to them. About the class struggle in the US, where the revolutionary capacities of working people are as utterly discounted by the ruling powers as were those of the Cuban toilers. And just as wrongly. $10. Also in Spanish, French, Farsi.

Colombia: Fidel Castro on the Debate Around Revolutionary Strategy and Lessons of the Cuban Revolution
FROM THE PAGES OF THE *MILITANT*

Fidel Castro describes the Cuban leadership's efforts to end decades of war between the FARC guerrilla movement and Colombia's brutal regime. He explains why Cuban revolutionaries, unlike FARC leaders, rejected taking hostages and organized Cuba's working people to win state power, not pursue a "prolonged people's war." $5. Also in Spanish.

PATHFINDERPRESS.COM

EXPAND YOUR REVOLUTIONARY LIBRARY

Labor, Nature, and the Evolution of Humanity
The Long View of History
FREDERICK ENGELS, KARL MARX
GEORGE NOVACK
MARY-ALICE WATERS

Without understanding that social labor, transforming nature, has driven humanity's evolution for millions of years, working people are unable to see beyond the capitalist epoch of class exploitation that warps all human relations, ideas, and values. Only the revolutionary conquest of state power by the working class can open the door to a world free of capitalist exploitation, degradation of nature, subjugation of women, racism, and war. A world built on human solidarity. A socialist world. $12. Also in Spanish and French.

Thomas Sankara Speaks
The Burkina Faso Revolution, 1983–87

Under Sankara's guidance, Burkina Faso's revolutionary government led peasants, workers, women, and youth to expand literacy; to sink wells, plant trees, erect housing; to combat women's oppression; to carry out land reform; to join others worldwide to free themselves from the imperialist yoke. $20. Also in French.

The Transitional Program for Socialist Revolution
LEON TROTSKY

The Socialist Workers Party program, drafted by Bolshevik leader Trotsky in 1938, still guides communists the world over. The party "uncompromisingly gives battle to all political groupings tied to the apron strings of the bourgeoisie. Its task—the abolition of capitalism's domination. Its aim—socialism. Its method—the proletarian revolution." $17. Also in Farsi.

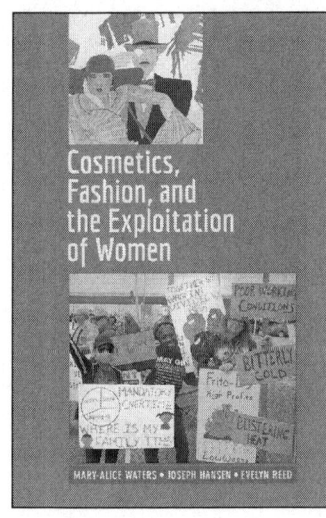

New Edition!
Cosmetics, Fashion, and the Exploitation of Women
MARY-ALICE WATERS
JOSEPH HANSEN, EVELYN REED

"Norms of beauty and fashion are inseparable from the class struggle" is the new opening chapter of this timely expanded edition of a lively 1950s debate in the *Militant*, a socialist newsweekly. How cosmetics and fashion monopolies rake in profits from social insecurities of women and adolescents. Why women's integration in the workforce and unions marks a major advance in the fight for their emancipation. A Marxist classic on the origins of women's oppression and the working-class road forward. $15. Also in Spanish, Farsi, Greek. Coming soon in French.

Malcolm X Speaks

"Being here in America doesn't make you an American. No, I'm not an American. I'm one of the 22 million Black people who are the victims of Americanism. One of the 22 million Black people who are the victims of democracy, nothing but disguised hypocrisy." $15. Also in Spanish.

Pathfinder Press **accessible e-books** for the blind, those with low vision, or other challenges reading print books

For a list of current accessible titles, go to: pathfinderpress.com/collections/books-for-the-blind.

Visit bookshare.org for information on how to sign up.

PATHFINDERPRESS.COM

PATHFINDER AROUND THE WORLD

UNITED STATES
(and Caribbean, Latin America, and East Asia)
Pathfinder Books, 306 W. 37th St., 13th Floor
New York, NY 10018

CANADA
Pathfinder Books, 7107 St. Denis, Suite 204
Montreal, QC H2S 2S5

UNITED KINGDOM
(and Europe, Africa, Middle East, and South Asia)
Pathfinder Books, 5 Norman Rd.
Seven Sisters, London N15 4ND

AUSTRALIA
(and New Zealand, Southeast Asia, and the Pacific)
Pathfinder Books, Suite 2, First floor, 275 George St.
Liverpool, Sydney, NSW 2170
Postal address: P.O. Box 73, Campsie, NSW 2194

BUILD YOUR LIBRARY!
JOIN THE PATHFINDER READERS CLUB

$10 / YEAR
25% DISCOUNT ON ALL PATHFINDER TITLES
30% OFF BOOKS OF THE MONTH
Valid at pathfinderpress.com and local Pathfinder book centers

Go to: pathfinderpress.com/products/pathfinder-readers-club